# CLYMER®

# SUZUKI

## GSX1300R HAYABUSA • 1999-2007

*The world's finest publisher of mechanical how-to manuals*

P.O. Box 12901, Overland Park, Kansas 66282-2901

Copyright ©2007 Penton Business Media, Inc.

FIRST EDITION
First Printing June, 2007
Second Printing May, 2011

Printed in U.S.A.

CLYMER and colophon are registered trademarks of Penton Business Media, Inc.

ISBN-10: 1-59969-148-5

ISBN-13: 978-1-59969-148-0

Library of Congress: 2007929293

AUTHOR: Clymer Staff.

TECHNICAL PHOTOGRAPHY: George Parise and Curt Jordan of Jordan Engineering, Carlsbad, CA.

TECHNICAL ILLUSTRATIONS: Mitzi McCarthy.

WIRING DIAGRAMS: Bob Meyer and Rick Arens.

EDITOR: Rick Arens and James Grooms.

PRODUCTION: Julie Jantzer-Ward and Justin Marciniak.

TOOLS AND EQUIPMENT: K & L Supply Co. at www.klsupply.com.

COVER: Mark Clifford Photography at www.markclifford.com. Motorcycle courtesy Bert's Mega Mall, Covina,CA.

**CLYMER**®

**Publisher** Ron Rogers

**EDITORIAL**

*Editorial Director*
James Grooms

*Editor*
Steven Thomas

*Associate Editor*
Rick Arens

*Authors*
Michael Morlan
George Parise
Ed Scott
Ron Wright

*Technical Illustrators*
Steve Amos
Errol McCarthy
Mitzi McCarthy
Bob Meyer

**SALES**

*Sales Manager–Marine*
Jay Lipton

*Sales Manager–Powersport/I&T*
Matt Tusken

**CUSTOMER SERVICE**

*Customer Service Manager*
Terri Cannon

*Customer Service Representatives*
Karen Barker
Dinah Bunnell
Suzanne Johnson
April LeBlond
Sherry Rudkin

**PRODUCTION**

*Director of Production*
Dylan Goodwin

*Production Manager*
Greg Araujo

*Senior Production Editor*
Darin Watson

*Production Editor*
Adriane Roberts

*Associate Production Editor*
Ashley Bally

**PENTON**

P.O. Box 12901, Overland Park, KS 66282-2901 • 800-262-1954 • 913-967-1719

**More information available at *clymer.com***

# CONTENTS

# QUICK REFERENCE DATA

## MOTORCYCLE DATA

MODEL:_____ YEAR:_____

VIN NUMBER:_____

ENGINE SERIAL NUMBER:_____

THROTTLE BODY NUMBER:_____

## TIRE SPECIFICATIONS

| Item | Front | Rear |
|---|---|---|
| Type | Tubeless | Tubeless |
| Size | 120/70 ZR17 (58W) | 190/50 ZR17 (73W) |
| Inflation pressure (cold)* | | |
|   Solo | 290 kPa (42 psi) | 290 kPa (42 psi) |
|   Rider and passenger | 290 kPa (42 psi) | 290 kPa (42 psi) |
| Minimum tread depth | 1.6 mm (0.06 in.) | 2.0 mm (0.08 in.) |

*Tire inflation pressure is for original equipment tires only. Aftermarket tires may require different inflation pressure.

## RECOMMENDED LUBRICANTS AND FLUIDS

| | |
|---|---|
| Brake fluid | DOT 4 |
| Coolant | |
|   Type | Antifreeze/coolant compatible with aluminum radiator |
|   Ratio | Mixed with distilled water @ 50:50 ratio |
|   Capacity | |
|     Engine | Approx. 2700 ml (2.9 U.S. qt. ) |
|     Reservoir | Approx. 250 ml (0.3 U.S. qt. ) |
| Engine oil | |
|   Classification | API SF or SG |
|   Viscosity | SAE 10W-40 |
|   Capacity | |
|     Oil change only | 3.3 liters (3.5 U.S. qt. ) |
|     Oil and filter change | 3.5 liters (3.7 U.S. qt. ) |
|     When engine completely dry | 4.2 liters (4.4 U.S. qt. ) |
| Fork oil | |
|   Viscosity | Suzuki L01 fork oil or equivalent |
|   Capacity per leg | 480 ml (16.2 U.S. oz. ) |
| Fuel | Unleaded |
|   U.S., California, and Canada models | |
|     Pump octane - (R +M)/2 method | 87 or higher |

(continued)

## RECOMMENDED LUBRICANTS AND FLUIDS (continued)

| | |
|---|---|
| Fuel | Unleaded |
| U.S., California, and Canada models | |
| Research octane | 91 or higher |
| All models except U.S., California and Canada | 91 or higher |
| Fuel tank capacity (total) | |
| 1999-2000 models | |
| California models | 20 liter (5.3 U.S. gal.) |
| All models except California | 22 liters (5.8 U.S. gal. ) |
| 2001-on models | |
| California models | 19 liter (5.0 U.S. gal.) |
| All models except California | 21 liters (5.5 U.S. gal. ) |

## MAINTENANCE AND TUNE-UP SPECIFICATIONS

| | |
|---|---|
| Battery | |
| Type | YT12A-BS Maintenance-free (sealed) |
| Capacity | 12 volt 36 kC (10 amp hour)/10 HR |
| Brake pedal height | 55-65 mm (2.2-2.6 in.) below the footpeg |
| Compression pressure (at sea level) | |
| Standard | 1200-1600 kPa (174-232 psi) |
| Service limit | 900 kPa (131 psi) |
| Maximum difference between cylinders | 200 kPa (29 psi) |
| Cooling system test pressure | 120 kPa (17 psi) |
| Drive chain 21-pin length | 319.4 mm (12.6 in.) |
| Drive chain free play | 20-30 mm (0.8-1.2 in.) |
| Engine oil pressure @ 140° F (60° C) | 200-500 kPa (29-73 psi) @ 3000 rpm |
| Fast idle speed | 3500 rpm (when engine is warm) |
| Front fork adjustments | |
| Spring preload | Fifth groove from top |
| Rebound damping | 3 clicks out |
| Compression damping | 9 clicks out |
| Idle speed | |
| 1999-2003 models | |
| Switzerland models | 1100-1200 rpm |
| All models except Switzerland | 1050-1250 rpm |
| 2004-on models | 1050-1250 rpm |
| Ignition timing* | |
| 1999 models | 4° BTDC @ 1150 rpm |
| 2000 models | |
| Cylinders Nos. 1 and 4 | 11° BTDC @ 1150 rpm |
| Cylinders Nos. 2 and 3 | 3° BTDC @ 1150 rpm |
| 2001-on models | |
| U.S., California and Canada models | 4° BTDC @ 1200 rpm |
| All models except U.S., California and Canada | |
| Cylinders Nos. 1 and 4 | 11° BTDC @ 1150 rpm |
| Cylinders Nos. 2 and 3 | 3° BTDC @ 1150 rpm |
| Radiator cap opening pressure | 95-125 kPa (14-18 psi) |
| Shift pedal height | 50-60 mm (2.0-2.4 in.) below the footpeg |
| Shock absorber | |
| Spring preload (spring set length) | |
| Standard setting | 183 mm (7.2 in.) |
| Softest setting | 180 mm (7.1 in.) |
| Stiffest setting | 190 mm (7.5 in.) |
| Rebound damping | 11 clicks out |
| Compression damping | 8 clicks out |
| (continued) | |

## MAINTENANCE AND TUNE-UP SPECIFICATIONS (continued)

| | |
|---|---|
| **Spark plug** | |
| Gap | 0.7-0.8 mm (0.028-0.031 in.) |
| Heat range | |
| Standard type | NGK: CR9E, Denso: U27ESR-N |
| Hotter | NGK: CR8E, Denso: U24ESR-N |
| Colder | NGK: CR10E, Denso:U31ESR-N |
| **Steering tension** | 200-500 grams (7.1-17.6 oz.) |
| **Throttle cable free play** | 2.0-4.0 mm (0.08-0.16 in.) |
| **Valve clearance (cold)** | |
| Intake | 0.10-0.20 mm (0.004-0.008 in.) |
| Exhaust | 0.20-0.30 mm (0.008-0.012 in.) |
| **Wheel runout limit** | |
| Axial | 2.0 mm (0.08 in.) |
| Radial | 2.0 mm (0.08 in.) |

*Not adjustable.

## MAINTENANCE AND TUNE-UP TORQUE SPECIFICATIONS

| Item | N•m | in.-lb. | ft.-lb. |
|---|---|---|---|
| Cylinder head cover bolt | 14 | – | 10 |
| Engine sprocket nut | 145 | – | 107 |
| Exhaust header bolt | 23 | – | 17 |
| Exhaust pipe hanger bolt | 23 | – | 17 |
| Front axle | 100 | – | 74 |
| Front axle clamp bolt | 23 | – | 17 |
| Handlebar clamp bolt | 10 | 89 | – |
| Handlebar holder nut | 35 | – | 26 |
| Lower fork bridge clamp bolt | 23 | – | 17 |
| Muffler connecting nut | 25 | – | 18 |
| Muffler hanger nut | 23 | – | 17 |
| Muffler pipe clamp bolt | 23 | – | 17 |
| Oil line banjo bolt | | – | |
| 6 mm | 10 | 89 | – |
| 14 mm | 28 | – | 21 |
| Oil drain bolt | 23 | – | 17 |
| Oil gallery plug | | | |
| 6 mm and 8 mm | 18 | – | 13 |
| 10 mm | 16 | – | 12 |
| 16 mm | 35 | – | 26 |
| Oil pan bolt | 10 | 89 | – |
| Rear axle nut | 100 | – | 74 |
| Rear brake master-cylinder-rod locknut | 18 | – | 13 |
| Rear sprocket nuts | 60 | – | 44 |
| Starter clutch bolt cap | 11 | 97 | – |
| Spark plug | 11 | 97 | – |
| Timing inspection cap | 23 | – | 17 |
| Torque arm nut | | | |
| Front | 28 | – | 21 |
| Rear | 35 | – | 26 |
| Upper fork bridge clamp bolt | 23 | – | 17 |

# CHAPTER ONE

# GENERAL INFORMATION

This detailed and comprehensive manual covers 1999-2007 Suzuki GSX1300R models.

The text provides complete information on maintenance, tune-up, repair and overhaul. Hundreds of photographs and illustrations created during the complete disassembly of the motorcycle guide the reader through every job. All procedures are in step-by-step format and designed for the reader who may be working on the motorcycle for the first time.

## MANUAL ORGANIZATION

A shop manual is a tool and, as in all Clymer manuals, the chapters are thumb-tabbed for easy reference. Main headings are listed in the table of contents and index. Frequently used specifications and capacities from the tables at the end of each individual chapter are listed in the *Quick Reference Data* section at the front of the manual. Specifications and capacities are provided in both metric and U.S. standard units of measure.

Some procedures refer to headings in other chapters or sections of the manual. When a specific heading is called out in a step it is italicized as it appears in the manual. If a sub-heading is indicated as being "in this section" it is located within the existing main

heading. For example, the sub-heading *Handling Gasoline Safely* is located within the main heading *Safety*.

This chapter provides general information on shop safety, tools and their usage, service fundamentals and shop supplies. **Tables 1-6**, at the end of this chapter, list motorcycle dimensions and general shop data.

Chapter Two provides methods for quick and accurate diagnosis of problems. Troubleshooting procedures present typical symptoms and logical methods to pinpoint and repair the problem.

Chapter Three explains all routine maintenance.

Subsequent chapters describe specific systems such as engine, transmission, clutch, fuel system, suspension, brakes and exhaust system.

## WARNINGS, CAUTIONS AND NOTES

The terms WARNING, CAUTION and NOTE have specific meanings in this manual.

A WARNING emphasizes areas where injury or even death could result from negligence. Mechanical damage may also occur. WARNINGS *are to be taken seriously*.

A CAUTION emphasizes areas where equipment damage could result. Disregarding a CAUTION could cause permanent mechanical damage, though injury is unlikely.

A NOTE provides additional information to make a step or procedure easier or clearer. Disregarding a NOTE could cause inconvenience, but would not cause equipment damage or injury.

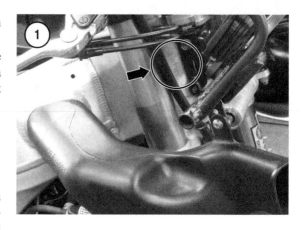

## SAFETY

1. Do not operate the motorcycle in an enclosed area. The exhaust gasses contain carbon monoxide, an odorless, colorless and tasteless poisonous gas. Carbon monoxide levels build quickly in small enclosed areas and can cause unconsciousness and death in a short time. Make sure to properly ventilate the work area or operate the motorcycle outside.

2. *Never* use gasoline or any extremely flammable liquid to clean parts. Refer to *Handling Gasoline Safely* and *Cleaning Parts* in this section.

3. *Never* smoke or use a torch in the vicinity of flammable liquids, such as gasoline or cleaning solvent.

4. If welding or brazing on the motorcycle, remove the fuel tank to a safe distance at least 15 m (50 ft.) away.

5. Do not remove the radiator cap or any cooling system hoses while the engine is hot. The cooling system is pressurized, and the high-temperature coolant can cause injury.

6. Dispose of coolant in a safe manner. Do not allow children or pets access to coolant.

7. Avoid contact with engine oil and other chemicals. Most are known carcinogens. Wash your hand thoroughly after coming in contact with chemicals. If possible, wear a pair of chemical-resistant gloves.

8. Use the correct type and size of tools to avoid damaging fasteners.

9. Keep tools clean and in good condition. Replace or repair worn or damaged equipment.

10. When loosening a tight fastener, be guided by what would happen if the tool slips.

11. When replacing fasteners, make sure the new fasteners are the same size and strength as the originals.

12. Keep the work area clean and organized.

13. Wear eye protection *any time* the safety of the eyes is in question. This includes procedures that involve drilling, grinding, hammering, compressed air and chemicals.

14. Wear the correct clothing for the job. Tie up or cover long hair so it does not get caught in moving equipment.

15. Do not carry sharp tools in clothing pockets.

16. Always have an approved fire extinguisher available. Make sure it is rated for gasoline (Class B) and electrical (Class C) fires.

17. Do not use compressed air to clean clothes, the motorcycle or the work area. Debris may be blown into eyes or skin. *Never* direct compressed air at anyone. Do not allow children to use or play with any compressed air equipment.

18. When using compressed air to dry rotating parts, hold the part so it does not rotate. Do not allow the force of the air to spin the part. The air jet is capable of rotating parts at extreme speed. The part may disintegrate or become damaged, causing serious injury.

19. Do not inhale the dust created by brake pad and clutch wear. These particles may contain asbestos. In addition, some types of insulating materials and gaskets may contain asbestos. Inhaling asbestos particles is hazardous to health.

20. Never work on the motorcycle while someone is working under it.

21. When supporting the motorcycle on a stand, make sure it is secure before walking away.

### Handling Gasoline Safely

Gasoline is a volatile flammable liquid and is one of the most dangerous items in the shop. Because gasoline is used so often, many people forget it is hazardous. Only use gasoline as fuel for gasoline internal combustion engines. Keep in mind when working on the machine, gasoline is always present in the fuel tank, fuel line and throttle body. To avoid an accident when working around the fuel system, carefully observe the following precautions:

1. *Never* use gasoline to clean parts. Refer to *Cleaning Parts* in this section.

2. When working on the fuel system, work outside or in a well-ventilated area. Wear fuel-resistant gloves if fuel might contact your skin.

3. Do not add fuel to the fuel tank or service the fuel system while the motorcycle is near open flames, sparks or where someone is smoking. Gasoline vapor is heavier than air; it collects in low areas and is more easily ignited than liquid gasoline.

4. Allow the engine to cool completely before working on any fuel system component.

5. Store gasoline in approved storage containers.

6. Immediately wipe up spilled gasoline with rags. Store the rags in a metal container with a lid until they can be properly disposed of, or place them outside in a safe place for the fuel to evaporate.

7. Do not pour water onto a gasoline fire. Water spreads the fire and makes it more difficult to put out. Use a class B, BC or ABC fire extinguisher to extinguish the fire.

8. Always turn off the engine before refueling. Do not spill fuel onto the engine or exhaust system. Do not overfill the fuel tank. Leave an air space at the top of the tank to allow room for the fuel to expand due to temperature fluctuations.

## Cleaning Parts

Cleaning parts is one of the more tedious and difficult service jobs performed in the home garage. Many types of chemical cleaners and solvents are available for shop use. Most are poisonous and extremely flammable. To prevent chemical exposure, vapor buildup, fire and serious injury, observe each product warning label and note the following:

1. Read and observe the entire product label before using any chemical. Always know what type of chemical is being used and whether it is poisonous and/or flammable.

2. Do not use more than one type of cleaning solvent at a time. If mixing chemicals is required, measure the proper amounts according to the manufacturer.

3. Work in a well-ventilated area.

4. Wear chemical-resistant gloves.

5. Wear safety glasses.

6. Wear a vapor respirator if the instructions call for it.

7. Wash hands and arms thoroughly after cleaning parts.

8. Keep chemical products away from children and pets.

9. Thoroughly clean all oil, grease and cleaner residue from any part that must be heated.

10. Use a nylon brush when cleaning parts. Metal brushes may cause a spark.

11. When using a parts washer, only use the solvent recommended by the manufacturer. Make sure the parts washer is equipped with a metal lid that lowers in case of fire.

## Warning Labels

Most manufacturers attach information and warning labels to the motorcycle. These labels contain important safety instructions for operating, servicing, transporting and storing the motorcycle. Refer to the owner's manual for the description and location of labels. Order replacement labels from the manufacturer if they are missing or damaged.

## SERIAL NUMBERS

Serial numbers are stamped on different locations on the frame and engine. Record these numbers in the *Quick Reference Data* section in the front of the manual. Have these numbers readily available when ordering parts.

The vehicle identification (VIN) number is stamped into the right side of the steering head (**Figure 1**).

The engine serial number (**Figure 2**) is stamped into the rear of the upper crankcase half engine.

## FASTENERS

*WARNING*
*Do not install fasteners with a strength classification lower than what was originally installed by the manufacturer. Doing so may cause equipment failure and/or damage.*

### Threaded Fasteners

*CAUTION*
*To ensure that the fastener threads are not mismatched or cross-threaded, start all fasteners by hand. If a fastener*

*is hard to start or turn, determine the cause before tightening with a wrench.*

Threaded fasteners secure most of the components on the motorcycle. Most are tightened by turning them clockwise (right-hand threads). If the normal rotation of the component being tightened would loosen the fastener, it may have left-hand threads. If a left-hand threaded fastener is used, it is noted in the text.

Two dimensions are required to match the thread size of the fastener: the number of threads in a given distance and the outside diameter of the threads.

The two systems currently used to specify threaded fastener dimensions are the metric system and the U.S. Standard system (**Figure 3**). Pay particular attention when working with unidentified fasteners; mismatching thread types can damage threads.

The length (L, **Figure 4**), diameter (D) and distance between thread crests (pitch [T]) classify metric screws and bolts. A typical bolt may be identified by the numbers, 8—1.25 × 130. This indicates the bolt has a diameter of 8 mm, the distance between thread crests is 1.25 mm and the bolt length is 130 mm. Always measure bolt length as shown in L, **Figure 4** to avoid installing replacements of the wrong length.

The numbers on the top of the fastener (**Figure 4**) indicate the strength of metric screws and bolts. The higher the number, the stronger the fastener. Typically, unnumbered fasteners are the weakest.

Many screws, bolts and studs are combined with nuts to secure particular components. To indicate the size of a nut, manufacturers specify the internal diameter and the thread pitch. The measurement across two flats on a nut or bolt indicates the wrench size.

## Torque Specifications

The materials used in the manufacturing of the motorcycle may be subjected to uneven stresses if the fasteners of the various subassemblies are not installed and tightened correctly. Improperly installed fasteners or ones that work loose can cause damage. It is essential to use an accurate torque wrench as described in this chapter.

Specifications for torque are provided in the appropriate chapters. Refer to **Table 6** for general torque recommendations. To determine the torque requirement, first determine the size of the fastener as described in *Threaded Fasteners* in this section. Torque wrenches are covered in *Tools* in this chapter.

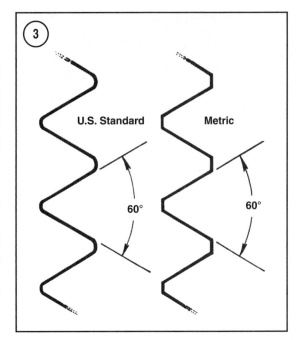

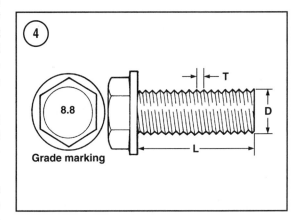

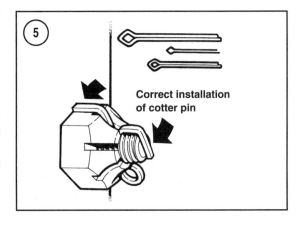

## Self-Locking Fasteners

Several types of bolts, screws and nuts incorporate a system that creates interference between the two fasteners. Interference is achieved in various ways. The

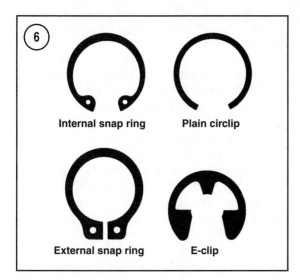

Internal snap ring — Plain circlip

External snap ring — E-clip

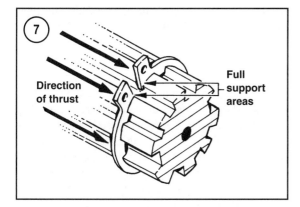

Direction of thrust

Full support areas

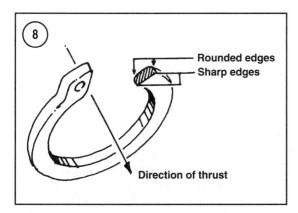

Rounded edges
Sharp edges

Direction of thrust

most common types are the nylon insert nut or a dry adhesive coating on the threads of a bolt.

Self-locking fasteners offer greater holding strength than standard fasteners, which improves their resistance to vibration. Self-locking fasteners cannot be reused. The materials used to form the lock become distorted after the initial installation and removal. Discard and replace self-locking fasteners after removing them. Do not replace self-locking fasteners with standard fasteners.

## Washers

The two basic types of washers are flat washers and lockwashers. Flat washers are simple discs with a hole to fit a screw or bolt. Lockwashers are used to prevent a fastener from working loose. Washers can be used as spacers and seals, or can help distribute fastener load and prevent the fastener from damaging the component.

As with fasteners, when replacing washers make sure the replacements are of the same design and quality as the originals.

## Cotter Pins

A cotter pin is a split metal pin inserted into a hole or slot to prevent a fastener from loosening. In certain applications, such as the rear axle on an ATV or motorcycle, the fastener must be secured in this way. For these applications, a cotter pin and castellated (slotted) nut is used.

To use a cotter pin, first make sure the pin's diameter is correct for the hole in the fastener. After correctly tightening the fastener and aligning the holes, insert the cotter pin through the hole and bend the ends over the fastener (**Figure 5**). Unless instructed, never loosen a tightened fastener to align the holes. If the holes do not align, tighten the fastener just enough to achieve alignment.

Cotter pins are available in various diameters and lengths. Measure the length from the bottom of the head to the tip of the shortest pin.

## Snap Rings and E-clips

Snap rings (**Figure 6**) are circular-shaped metal retaining clips. They secure parts and gears onto parts such as shafts, pins or rods. External type snap rings are used to retain items on shafts. Internal type snap rings secure parts within housing bores. In some applications, in addition to securing the component(s), snap rings of varying thicknesses also determine endplay. These are usually called selective snap rings.

The two basic types of snap rings are machined and stamped snap rings. Machined snap rings (**Figure 7**) can be installed in either direction because both faces have sharp edges. Stamped snap rings (**Figure 8**) are manufactured with a sharp and round edge. When installing a stamped snap ring in a thrust application, install the sharp edge facing away from the part producing the thrust.

E-clips are used when it is not practical to use a snap ring. Remove E-clips with a flat blade screwdriver by prying between the shaft and E-clip. To install an E-clip, center it over the shaft groove and push or tap it into place.

Observe the following when installing snap rings:

1. Remove and install snap rings with snap ring pliers. Refer to *Basic Tools* in this chapter.

2. In some applications, it may be necessary to replace snap rings after removing them.

3. Compress or expand snap rings only enough to install them. If overly expanded, they lose their retaining ability.

4. After installing a snap ring, make sure it seats fully.

5. Wear eye protection when removing and installing snap rings.

## SHOP SUPPLIES

The following section describes the types of supplies most often required. Make sure to follow the manufacturer's recommendations for lubricant types.

### Lubricants and Fluids

Periodic lubrication helps ensure a long service life for any type of equipment. Using the correct type of lubricant is important.

#### Engine oils

Engine oil for use in four-stroke motorcycle engines is classified by three standards: the American Petroleum Institute (API) service classification, the Society of Automotive Engineers (SAE) viscosity rating and the Japanese Automobile Standards Organization (JASO) T 903 Standard rating.

The API and SAE information appears on all oil container labels. The JASO information is found on oil containers sold by the oil manufacturer specifically for motorcycle use. Two letters (SF) indicate the API service classification. A number or sequence of numbers and letter (10W-40 for example) is the oil's viscosity rating. The API service classification and the SAE viscosity index are not indications of oil quality.

The API service classification indicates that the oil meets specific lubrication standards. The first letter in the classification *S* indicates the oil is for gasoline engines. The second letter indicates the standard the oil satisfies.

The JASO certification label identifies two separate oil classifications and a registration number to ensure the oil has passed all JASO certification standards for use in four-stroke motorcycle engines. The classifications are: MA (high friction applications) and MB (low friction applications). Only oil that has passed JASO standards can carry the JASO certification label.

Always use an oil with a classification recommended by the manufacturer. Using oil with a different classification can cause engine damage.

Viscosity is an indication of the oil's thickness. Thin oils have a lower number while thick oils have a higher number. Engine oils fall into the 5- to 50-weight range for single-grade oils.

Most manufacturers recommend multi-grade oil. These oils perform efficiently across a wide range of operating conditions. Multi-grade oils are identified by a *W* after the first number, which indicates the low-temperature viscosity.

Engine oils are most commonly mineral (petroleum) based, but synthetic and semi-synthetic types are used more frequently. When selecting engine oil, follow the manufacturer's recommendation for type, classification and viscosity.

#### Grease

Grease is lubricating oil with added thickening agents. The National Lubricating Grease Institute (NLGI) grades grease. Grades range from No. 000 to No. 6, with No. 6 being the thickest. Typical multi-purpose grease is NLGI No. 2. For specific applications, manufacturers may recommend water-resistant type grease or one with an additive such as molybdenum disulfide ($MoS_2$).

When grease is called for in this manual, use Suzuki Super Grease A (part No. 99000-25030) or an equivalent.

When moly oil is called for, use a 50-50 mixture of engine oil and Suzuki Moly Paste (part No. 909000-25140).

#### Brake fluid

> *WARNING*
> *Never put a mineral-based (petroleum) oil into the brake system. Mineral oil causes rubber parts in the system to swell and break apart, causing complete brake failure.*

Brake fluid transmits hydraulic pressure (force) to the brakes. Brake fluid is classified by the Department of Transportation (DOT). Current designations for brake fluid are DOT 3, DOT 4 and DOT 5. This classification appears on the fluid container.

Each type of brake fluid has its own definite characteristics. Do not mix different types of brake fluid because this may cause brake system failure. DOT 5 brake fluid is silicone based. DOT 5 is not compatible with other brake fluids or in systems for which it was not designed. Mixing DOT 5 fluid with other fluids may cause brake system failure. When adding brake fluid, only use the fluid recommended by the manufacturer.

Brake fluid damages any plastic, painted or plated surface it contacts. Use extreme care when working with brake fluid and wash any spills immediately with soap and water.

Hydraulic brake systems require clean and moisture-free brake fluid. Never reuse brake fluid. Keep containers and reservoirs properly sealed.

### Coolant

Coolant is a mixture of water and antifreeze used to dissipate engine heat. Ethylene glycol is the most common form of antifreeze. When selecting antifreeze, make sure it is specifically designed for use in aluminum engines. These types of antifreeze have additives that inhibit corrosion.

Only mix antifreeze with distilled water. Impurities in tap water may damage internal cooling system passages.

### Cleaners, Degreasers and Solvents

Many chemicals are available to remove oil, grease and other residue from the motorcycle. Before using cleaning solvents, consider how they will be used and disposed of, particularly if they are not water-soluble. Local ordinances may require special procedures for the disposal of many types of cleaning chemicals. Refer to *Safety* in this chapter.

Use brake parts cleaner to clean brake system components. Brake parts cleaner leaves no residue. Use electrical contact cleaner to clean electrical connections and components without leaving any residue. Carburetor cleaner is a powerful solvent used to remove fuel deposits and varnish from fuel system components. Use this cleaner carefully because it may damage finishes.

Generally, degreasers are strong cleaners used to remove heavy accumulations of grease from engine and frame components.

Most solvents are designed to be used with a parts washing cabinet for individual component cleaning. For safety, use only nonflammable or high flash point solvents.

### Gasket Sealant

Sealant is used in combination with a gasket or seal. In other applications, only a sealant is used. Fol-

low the manufacturer's recommendation when using a sealant. Use extreme care when choosing a different sealant. Choose sealant based on its resistance to heat, fluids and its sealing capabilities.

A common sealant is room temperature vulcanization sealant, or RTV. This sealant cures at room temperature over a specific time period. This allows the repositioning of components without damaging gaskets.

Moisture in the air causes the RTV sealant to cure. Always install the tube cap as soon as possible after applying RTV sealant. RTV sealant has a limited shelf life and does not cure properly if the shelf life has expired. Keep partial tubes sealed and discard them if they have surpassed the expiration date.

Suzuki recommends the use of the following sealants:

1. Suzuki Bond 1207B (part No. 99000-31140): a silicon-based sealant for vibration-prone, high-heat applications.

2. Suzuki Bond 1215 (part No. 99000-31110): UK, Australia and Europe models.

3. Suzuki Bond 1216 (part No. 99104-31160): a silicon-based sealant for high-crankcase pressure applications.

### Applying RTV sealant

Clean all old gasket residue from the mating surfaces. Remove all gasket material from blind threaded holes to avoid inaccurate bolt torque. Spray the mating surfaces with aerosol parts cleaner and wipe the surfaces with a lint-free cloth. The area must be clean for the sealant to adhere.

Apply RTV sealant in a continuous bead 2-3 mm (0.08-0.12 in.) thick. Circle all the fastener holes unless otherwise specified. Do not allow any sealant to enter these holes. Assemble and tighten the fasteners to the specified torque within the time frame recommended by the sealant manufacturer.

### Gasket remover

Aerosol gasket remover can help remove stubborn gaskets. This product can speed up the removal process and prevent damage to the mating surface that may be caused by using a scraping tool. Most gasket removers are very caustic. Follow the manufacturer's instructions for use.

## Threadlocking Compound

> *CAUTION*
> *Threadlocking compounds are anaero-*
> *bic and will stress, crack and attack*
> *most plastics. Use caution when using*
> *these products in areas where there are*
> *plastic components.*

Threadlocking compound is a fluid applied to the threads of fasteners. After tightening the fastener, the fluid dries and becomes a solid filler between the threads. This makes it difficult for the fastener to work loose from vibration or heat expansion and contraction. Some threadlocking compounds also provide a seal against fluid leaks.

Before applying a threadlocking compound, remove any old compound from both thread areas and clean them with aerosol parts cleaner. Use the compound sparingly. Excess fluid can run into adjoining parts.

Threadlocking compounds are available in a wide range of compounds for various strength, temperature and repair applications. Follow the manufacturer's recommendations regarding compound selection.

Suzuki recommends the use of the following compounds:
1. Suzuki Thread Lock Super 1303 (part No. 99000-321100): a high-strength, retaining compound.
2. Suzuki Thread Lock 1333B (part No. 99000-32020): a medium-strength, bearing and stud lock.
3. Suzuki Thread Lock Super 1322 (part No. 99000-32110): UK, Europe and Australia models.
4. Suzuki Thread Lock 1342 (part No. 99000-32050): a low-strength compound recommended for frequent repairs.
5. Suzuki Thread Lock Super 1360 (part No. 99000-32130): a medium-strength, high-temperature compound.

## TOOLS

Most of the procedures in this manual can be carried out with hand tools and test equipment familiar to the home mechanic. Always use the correct tools for the job at hand. Keep tools organized and clean. Store them in a tool chest with related tools organized together.

Quality tools are essential. The best are constructed of high-strength alloy steel. These tools are light, easy to use and resistant to wear. Their working surface is devoid of sharp edges and carefully polished.

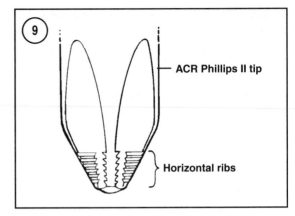

They have an easy-to-clean finish and are comfortable to use. Quality tools are a good investment.

Some of the procedures in this manual specify special tools. In many cases the tool is illustrated in use. Those with a large tool kit may be able to use a suitable substitute or fabricate a suitable replacement. However, in some cases, the specialized equipment or expertise may make it impractical for the home mechanic to attempt the procedure. When necessary, such operations come with the recommendation to have a dealership or specialist perform the task. It may be less expensive to have a professional perform these jobs, especially when considering the cost of equipment.

The manufacturer's part number is provided for many of the tools mentioned in this manual. These part numbers are correct at the time of first-edition publication. The publisher cannot guarantee the part numbers or tools listed in this manual will be available in the future.

When purchasing tools to perform the procedures covered in this manual, consider the tool's potential frequency of use. If a tool kit is just now being started, consider purchasing a basic tool set from a quality tool supplier. These sets are available in many tool combinations and offer substantial savings when compared to individually purchased tools. As work experience grows and tasks become more complicated, specialized tools can be added.

### Screwdrivers

Screwdrivers of various lengths and types are mandatory for the simplest tool kit. The two basic types are the slotted tip (flat blade) and the Phillips tip. These are available in sets that often include an assortment of tip sizes and shaft lengths.

As with all tools, use a screwdriver designed for the job. Make sure the size of the tip conforms to the size and shape of the fastener. Use them only for driv-

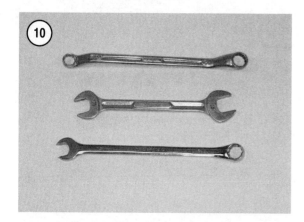

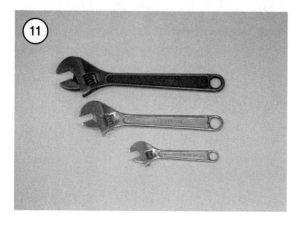

the screw, clean the screw recess to prevent possible contamination.

### Wrenches

Open-end, box-end and combination wrenches (**Figure 10**) are available in a variety of types and sizes.

The number stamped on the wrench refers to the distance between the work areas. This size must match the size of the fastener head.

A box-end wrench is an excellent tool because it grips the fastener on all sides. This reduces the chance of the tool slipping. A box-end wrench is designed with either a 6- or 12-point opening. For stubborn or damaged fasteners, the 6-point provides superior holding because it contacts the fastener across a wider area at all six edges. For general use, a 12-point works well. It allows the wrench to be removed and reinstalled without moving the handle over such a wide arc.

An open-end wrench is fast and works best in areas with limited access. It contacts the fastener at only two points and is subject to slipping if under heavy force or if the tool or fastener is worn. A box-end wrench is preferred in most instances, especially when breaking loose and applying the final tightness to a fastener.

The combination wrench has a box-end on one end and an open-end on the other. This combination makes it a convenient tool.

### Adjustable Wrenches

An adjustable wrench, or Crescent wrench, (**Figure 11**) can fit nearly any nut or bolt head that has clear access around its entire perimeter. An adjustable wrench is best used as a backup wrench to keep a large nut or bolt from turning while the other end is being loosened or tightened with a box-end or socket wrench.

Adjustable wrenches contact the fastener at only two points, which makes them more likely to slip off the fastener. Because one jaw is adjustable and may become loose, this shortcoming is aggravated. Make certain the solid jaw is the one transmitting the force.

### Socket Wrenches, Ratchets and Handles

*WARNING*
*Do not use standard sockets with air or impact tools because they may shatter and cause injury. Always wear eye protection when using impact or air tools.*

ing screws. Never use a screwdriver for prying or chiseling metal. Repair or replace worn or damaged screwdrivers. A worn tip may damage the fastener, making it difficult to remove.

Phillips-head screws are often damaged by incorrectly fitting screwdrivers. Quality Phillips screwdrivers are manufactured with their crosshead tip machined to Phillips Screw Company specifications. Poor quality or damaged Phillips screwdrivers can back out (camout) and round over the screw head. In addition, weak or soft screw materials can make removal difficult.

An effective screwdriver to use on Phillips screws is the ACR Phillips II screwdriver. Anti-camout ribs (ACR) on the driving faces or flutes of the screwdriver's tip (**Figure 9**) improve the driver-to-fastener grip. ACR Phillips II screwdrivers are designed for use with ACR Phillips II screws, but they work well on all common Phillips screws. ACR Phillips II screwdrivers are available in different tip sizes and interchangeable bits to fit screwdriver bit holders.

Another way to prevent camout and to increase the grip of a Phillips screwdriver is to apply valve grinding compound or Permatex Screw & Socket Gripper onto the screwdriver tip. After loosening/tightening

Sockets that attach to a ratchet handle (**Figure 12**) are available with 6-point (A, **Figure 13**) or 12-point openings (B) and different drive sizes. The drive size indicates the size of the square hole that accepts the ratchet handle. The number stamped on the socket is the size of the work area and must match the fastener head.

As with wrenches, a 6-point socket provides superior-holding ability, while a 12-point socket needs to be moved only half as far to reposition it on the fastener.

Sockets are designated for either hand or impact use. Impact sockets are made of thicker material for more durability. Compare the size and wall thickness of a 19-mm standard socket (A, **Figure 14**) and the 19-mm impact socket (B). Use impact sockets when using an impact driver or air tools. Use hand sockets with hand-driven attachments.

Various handles are available for sockets. Use a speed handle for fast operation. Flexible ratchet heads in varying lengths allow the socket to be turned with varying force and at odd angles. Extension bars allow the socket setup to reach difficult areas. The ratchet is the most versatile. It allows the user to install or remove the nut without removing the socket.

Sockets combined with any number of drivers make them undoubtedly the fastest, safest and most convenient tool for fastener removal and installation.

**Impact Drivers**

> *WARNING*
> *Do not use standard sockets with air or impact tools because they may shatter and cause injury. Always wear eye protection when using impact or air tools.*

An impact driver provides extra force for removing fasteners by converting the impact of a hammer into a turning motion. This makes it possible to remove stubborn fasteners without damaging them. Impact drivers and interchangeable bits (**Figure 15**) are available from most tool suppliers. When using a socket with an impact driver, make sure the socket is designed for impact use. Refer to *Socket Wrenches, Ratchets and Handles* in this section.

**Allen Wrenches**

Use Allen, or setscrew wrenches, (**Figure 16**) on fasteners with hexagonal recesses in the fastener head. These wrenches are available in L-shaped bar, socket and T-handle types. A metric set is required

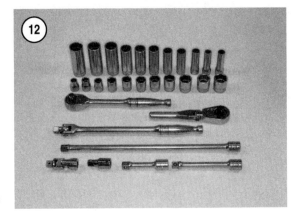

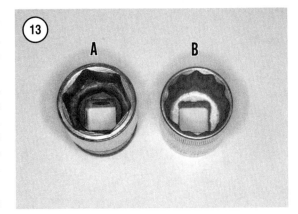

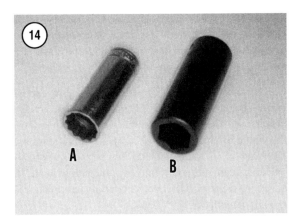

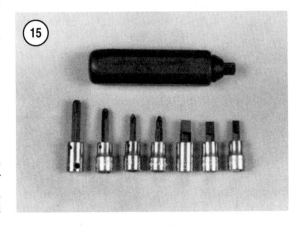

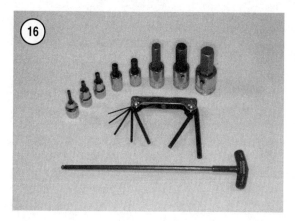

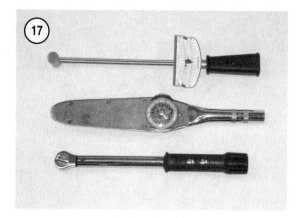

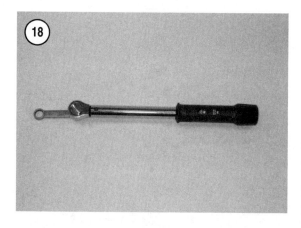

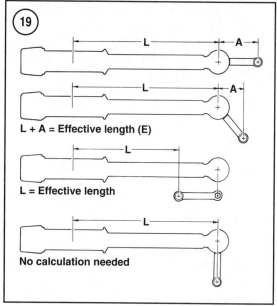

L + A = Effective length (E)

L = Effective length

No calculation needed

the torque value are the deflecting beam, the dial indicator and the audible click (**Figure 17**).

When choosing a torque wrench, consider the torque range, drive size and accuracy. The torque specifications in this manual provide an indication of the range required.

A torque wrench is a precision tool that must be properly cared for to remain accurate. Store torque wrenches in cases or separate padded drawers within a toolbox. Follow the manufacturer's instructions for their care and calibration.

**Torque Adapters**

Torque adapters or extensions extend or reduce the reach of a torque wrench. The torque adapter shown in **Figure 18** is used to tighten a fastener that cannot be reached because of the size of the torque wrench head, drive and socket. If a torque adapter changes the effective lever length (**Figure 19**), the torque reading on the wrench does not equal the actual torque applied to the fastener. It is necessary to recalibrate the torque setting on the wrench to compensate for the change of lever length. When using a torque adapter at a right angle to the drive head, calibration is not required because the effective length has not changed.

To recalculate a torque reading when using a torque adapter, use the following formula and refer to **Figure 19**:

$$TW = \frac{TA + L}{L + A}$$

*TW* is the torque setting or dial reading on the wrench.

when working on most motorcycles. Allen bolts are sometimes called socket bolts.

**Torque Wrenches**

Use a torque wrench with a socket, torque adapter or similar extension to tighten a fastener to a measured torque. Torque wrenches come in several drive sizes (1/4, 3/8, 1/2 and 3/4) and have various methods of reading the torque value. The drive size indicates the size of the square drive that accepts the socket, adapter or extension. Common methods of reading

*TA* is the torque specification and the actual amount of torque that is applied to the fastener.

*A* is the amount the adapter increases (or in some cases reduces) the effective lever length as measured along the centerline of the torque wrench.

*L* is the lever length of the wrench as measured from the center of the drive to the center of the grip.

The effective length is the sum of *L* and *A*.

Example:

TA = 20 ft.-lb.
A = 3 in.
L = 14 in.
$$TW = \frac{20 + 14}{14 + 3} = \frac{280}{17} = 16.5 \text{ ft.-lb.}$$

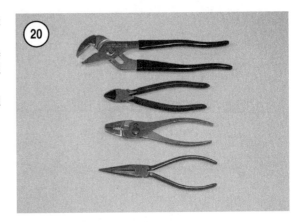

In this example, the torque wrench should be set to the calculated torque value of 16.5 ft.-lb. Although the torque wrench is set to 16.5 ft.-lb., the applied torque is 20 ft.-lb. When using a beam-type wrench, tighten the fastener until the pointer aligns with 16.5 ft.-lb.

### Pliers

Pliers come in a wide range of types and sizes. Pliers are useful for holding, cutting, bending and crimping. Do not use them to turn fasteners. **Figure 20** and **Figure 21** show several types of useful pliers. Each design has a specialized function. Slip-joint pliers are general-purpose pliers used for gripping and bending. Diagonal cutting pliers are needed to cut wire and can be used to remove cotter pins. Use needlenose pliers to hold or bend small objects. Locking pliers (**Figure 21**), sometimes called Vise-Grips, are used to hold objects very tightly. They have many uses ranging from holding two parts together, to gripping the end of a broken stud. Use caution when using locking pliers because the sharp jaws damage the objects they hold.

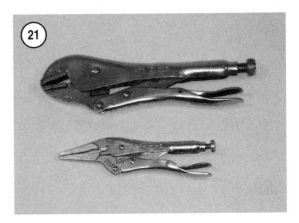

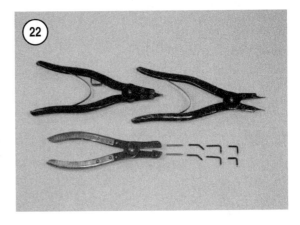

### Snap Ring Pliers

> *WARNING*
> *Snap rings can slip and fly off when removing and installing them. Also, the snap ring pliers' tips may break. Always wear eye protection when using snap ring pliers.*

Snap ring pliers are specialized pliers with tips that fit into the ends of snap rings to remove and install them.

Snap ring pliers (**Figure 22**) are available with a fixed action (either internal or external) or convertible (one tool works on both internal and external snap rings). They may have fixed tips or interchangeable ones of various sizes and angles. For general use, select a convertible type pliers with interchangeable tips (**Figure 22**).

### Hammers

> *WARNING*
> *Always wear eye protection when using hammers. Make sure the hammer face is in good condition and the handle is not cracked. Select the correct hammer for the job, and strike the object*

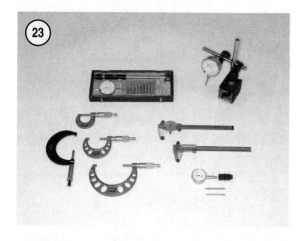

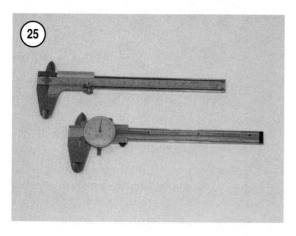

## MEASURING TOOLS

The ability to accurately measure components is essential to perform many of the procedures described in this manual. Equipment is manufactured to close tolerances, and obtaining consistently accurate measurements is essential to determine which components require replacement or further service.

Each type of measuring instrument (**Figure 23**) is designed to measure a dimension with a certain degree of accuracy and within a certain range of measurement. When selecting the measuring tool, make sure it is applicable to the task.

As with all tools, measuring tools provide the best results if cared for properly. Improper use can damage the tool and cause inaccurate results. If any measurement is questionable, verify the measurement using another tool. A standard gauge is usually provided with micrometers to check accuracy and calibrate the tool if necessary.

Precision measurements can vary according to the experience of the person taking the measurement. Accurate results are possible only if the mechanic possesses a feel for using the tool. Heavy-handed use of measuring tools produces inaccurate results. Hold the tool gently by the fingertips to easily feel the point at which the tool contacts the object. This feel for the equipment produces more accurate measurements and reduces the risk of damaging the tool or component. Refer to the following subsections for specific measuring tools.

### Feeler Gauge

Use feeler, or thickness, gauges (**Figure 24**) for measuring the distance between two surfaces.

A feeler gauge set consists of an assortment of steel strips of graduated thickness. Each blade is marked with its thickness. Blades can be of various lengths and angles for different procedures.

A common use for a feeler gauge is to measure valve clearance. Use wire (round) type gauges to measure spark plug gap.

### Calipers

Use calipers (**Figure 25**) for obtaining inside, outside and depth measurements. Although not as precise as a micrometer, they typically measure to within 0.05 mm (0.001 in.). Most calipers have a range up to 150 mm (6 in.).

Calipers are available in dial, vernier or digital versions. Dial calipers have a dial readout that provides convenient reading. Vernier calipers have marked

*squarely. Do not use the handle or the side of the hammer to strike an object.*

Various types of hammers are available to fit a number of applications. Use a ball-peen hammer to strike another tool, such as a punch or chisel. Use soft-faced hammers when a metal object must be struck without damaging it. *Never* use a metal-faced hammer on engine and suspension components because damage occurs in most cases.

scales that must be compared to determine the measurement. The digital caliper uses a liquid-crystal display (LCD) to show the measurement.

Properly maintain the measuring surfaces of the caliper. There must not be any dirt or burrs between the tool and the measured object. Never force the caliper to close around an object. Close the caliper around the highest point so it can be removed with a slight drag. Some calipers require calibration. Always refer to the manufacturer's instructions when using a new or unfamiliar caliper.

To read a vernier caliper, refer to **Figure 26**. The fixed scale is marked in 1 mm increments. Ten individual lines on the fixed scale equal 1 cm. The movable scale is marked in 0.05 mm (five-hundredth) increments. To obtain a reading, establish the first number by the location of the 0 line on the movable scale in relation to the first line to the left on the fixed scale. In this example, the number is 10 mm. To determine the next number, note which of the lines on the movable scale align with a mark on the fixed scale. A number of lines will seem close, but only one will align exactly. In this case, 0.50 mm is the reading to add to the first number. The result of adding 10 mm and 0.50 mm is a measurement of 10.50 mm.

## Micrometers

Use a micrometer for linear measurement. Although many types and styles of micrometers are available, most of the procedures in this manual call for an outside micrometer. Use an outside micrometer to measure the outside diameter of cylindrical forms and the thickness of materials.

When combined with a telescoping gauge or small hole gauge, a micrometer can obtain inside diameter measurements.

A micrometer's size indicates the minimum and maximum size of a part that it can measure. The usual sizes (**Figure 27**) are 0-25 mm (0-1 in.), 25-50 mm (1-2 in.), 50-75 mm (2-3 in.) and 75-100 mm (3-4 in.).

Micrometers that cover a wider range of measurements are available. These use a large frame with interchangeable anvils of various lengths. This type of micrometer offers a cost savings, but its overall size may make it less convenient.

### *Adjustment*

Before using a micrometer, check its adjustment as follows:

1. Clean the anvil and spindle faces.
2A. To check a 0-25 mm or 0-1 in. micrometer:

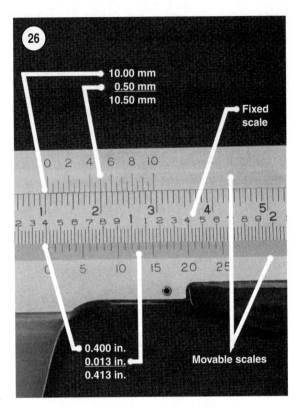

a. Turn the thimble until the spindle contacts the anvil. If the micrometer has a ratchet stop, use it to make sure the proper amount of pressure is applied.

b. If the adjustment is correct, the 0 mark on the thimble aligns exactly with the 0 mark on the sleeve line. If the marks do not align, the micrometer is out of adjustment.

c. Follow the manufacturer's instructions to adjust the micrometer.

2B. To check a micrometer larger than 25 mm or 1 in., use the standard gauge supplied by the manufacturer. A standard gauge is a steel block, disc or rod that is machined to an exact size.

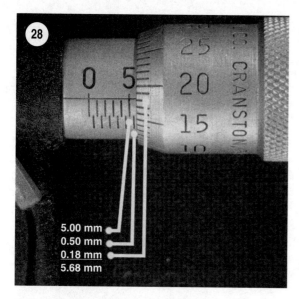

5.00 mm
0.50 mm
0.18 mm
5.68 mm

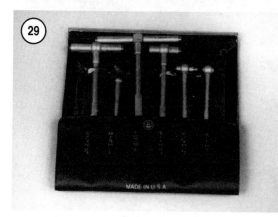

a. Place the standard gauge between the spindle and anvil and measure the outside diameter or length. If the micrometer has a ratchet stop, use it to make sure that the proper amount of pressure is applied.

b. If the adjustment is correct, the 0 mark on the thimble aligns exactly with the 0 mark on the sleeve line. If the marks do not align, the micrometer is out of adjustment.

c. Follow the manufacturer's instructions to adjust the micrometer.

### Care

Micrometers are precision instruments. They must be used and maintained with great care. Note the following:

1. Store micrometers in protective cases or separate padded drawers in a toolbox.

2. When in storage, make sure the spindle and anvil faces do not contact each other or another object. If they do, temperature changes and corrosion may damage the contact faces.

3. Do not clean a micrometer with compressed air. Dirt forced into the tool causes wear.

4. Lubricate micrometers with a light tool oil to prevent corrosion.

### Reading

The standard metric micrometer is accurate to one one-hundredth of a millimeter (0.01 mm). The sleeve line is graduated in millimeter and half millimeter increments. The marks on the upper half of the sleeve line equal 1.00 mm. Each fifth mark above the sleeve line is identified with a number. The number sequence depends on the size of the micrometer. A 0-25 mm micrometer, for example, has sleeve marks numbered 0 through 25 in 5 mm increments. This numbering sequence continues with larger micrometers. On all metric micrometers, each mark on the lower half of the sleeve equals 0.50 mm.

The tapered end of the thimble has 50 lines marked around it. Each mark equals 0.01 mm. One complete turn of the thimble aligns its 0 mark with the first line on the lower half of the sleeve line, or 0.50 mm.

When reading a metric micrometer, add the number of millimeters and half-millimeters on the sleeve line to the number of one one-hundredth millimeters on the thimble. To read a standard metric micrometer, refer to **Figure 28** and perform the following:

1. Read the upper half of the sleeve line and count the number of lines visible. Each upper line equals 1 mm.

2. See if a half-millimeter line is visible on the lower sleeve line. If so, add 0.50 mm to the reading in Step 1.

3. Read the thimble mark that aligns with the sleeve line. Each thimble mark equals 0.01 mm. If a thimble mark does not align exactly with the sleeve line, estimate the amount between the lines. For accurate readings in two-thousandths of a millimeter (0.002 mm), use a metric vernier micrometer.

4. Add the readings from Steps 1-3.

### Telescoping and Small Hole Gauges

Use telescoping gauges (**Figure 29**) and small hole gauges (**Figure 30**) to measure bores. Neither gauge has a scale for direct readings. Use an outside micrometer to determine the reading.

To use a telescoping gauge, select the correct size gauge for the bore. Compress the movable post and carefully insert the gauge into the bore. Carefully move the gauge in the bore to make sure it is centered. Tighten the knurled end of the gauge to hold the movable post in position. Remove the gauge and measure the length of the posts. Telescoping gauges are typically used to measure cylinder bores.

To use a small hole gauge, select the correct size gauge for the bore. Carefully insert the gauge into the bore. Tighten the knurled end of the gauge to carefully expand the gauge fingers to the limit within the bore. Do not overtighten the gauge because there is no built-in release. Excessive tightening can damage the bore surface and the tool. Remove the gauge and use a micrometer to measure the outside dimension (**Figure 31**). Small hole gauges are typically used to measure valve guides.

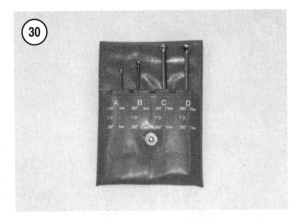

### Dial Indicator

A dial indicator (**Figure 32**) is a gauge with a dial face and needle used to measure variations in dimensions and movements. Measuring brake rotor runout is a typical use for a dial indicator.

Dial indicators are available in various ranges and graduations and with three basic types of mounting bases: magnetic (B, **Figure 32**), clamp or screw-in stud. When purchasing a dial indicator, select one with a continuous dial (A, **Figure 32**).

### Cylinder Bore Gauge

A cylinder bore gauge is similar to a dial indicator. The gauge set shown in **Figure 33** consists of a dial indicator, handle and different length adapters (anvils) to fit the gauge to various bore sizes. The bore gauge is used to measure bore size, taper and out-of-round. When using a bore gauge, follow the manufacturer's instructions.

### Compression Gauge

A compression gauge (**Figure 34**) measures combustion chamber (cylinder) pressure, usually in psi or kg/cm$^2$. The gauge adapter is either inserted or screwed into the spark plug hole to obtain the reading. Disable the engine so it does not start and hold the throttle in the wide-open position when performing a compression test. An engine that does not have adequate compression cannot be properly tuned. Refer to Chapter Three.

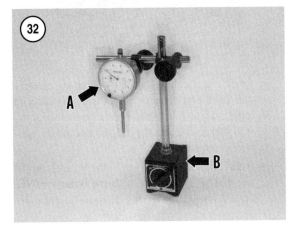

### Multimeter

A multimeter (**Figure 35**) is an essential tool for electrical system diagnosis. The voltage function indicates the voltage applied or available to various electrical components. The ohmmeter function tests circuits for continuity and measures the resistance of a circuit.

Some manufacturers' specifications for electrical components are based on results using a specific test meter. Results may vary if a meter not recommended by the manufacturer is used. Such requirements are noted when applicable.

Each time an analog ohmmeter is used or if the scale is changed, the ohmmeter must be calibrated. Refer to the manufacturer's instructions.

1

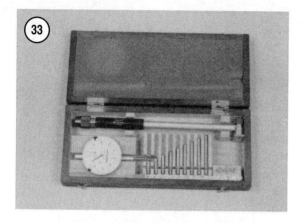

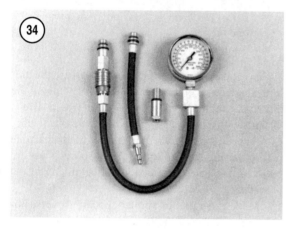

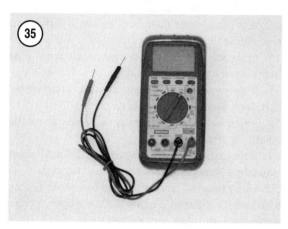

## ELECTRICAL SYSTEM FUNDAMENTALS

A thorough study of the many types of electrical systems used in today's motorcycles is beyond the scope of this manual. However, a basic understanding of voltage, resistance and amperage is necessary to perform diagnostic tests.

Refer to Chapter Two for troubleshooting. Refer to Chapter Nine for specific system test procedures.

### Voltage

Voltage is the electrical potential or pressure in an electrical circuit and is expressed in volts. The more pressure (voltage) in a circuit, the more work can be performed.

Direct current (DC) voltage means the electricity flows in one direction. All circuits powered by a battery are DC circuits.

Alternating current (AC) means the electricity flows in one direction momentarily and then switches to the opposite direction. Alternator output is an example of AC voltage. This voltage must be changed or rectified to direct current to operate in a battery-powered system.

### Resistance

Resistance is the opposition to the flow of electricity within a circuit or component. It is measured in ohms. Resistance causes a reduction in available current and voltage.

Resistance is measured in an inactive circuit with an ohmmeter. The ohmmeter sends a small amount of current into the circuit and measures how difficult it is to push the current through the circuit.

An ohmmeter, although useful, is not always a good indicator of a circuit's actual ability under operating conditions. This is because of the low voltage (6-9 volts) the meter uses to test the circuit. The voltage in an ignition coil secondary winding can be several thousand volts. Such high voltage can cause the coil to malfunction, even though it tests acceptable during a resistance test.

Resistance generally increases with temperature. Perform all testing with the component or circuit at room temperature. Resistance tests performed at high temperatures may indicate high resistance readings and cause unnecessary replacement of a component.

### Amperage

Amperage is the unit of measurement for the amount of current within a circuit. Current is the actual flow of electricity. The higher the current, the more work can be performed up to a given point. If the current flow exceeds the circuit or component capacity, it damages the system.

## SERVICE METHODS

Most of the procedures in this manual are straightforward and can be performed by anyone reasonably competent with tools. However, consider personal capabilities carefully before attempting any operation involving major disassembly.

1. In this manual, the term *Front* refers to the front of the motorcycle. The front of any component is the end closest to the front of the motorcycle. *Left* and *right* refer to the position of the parts as viewed by the rider sitting on the seat facing forward.

2. Whenever servicing an engine or suspension component, secure the motorcycle in a safe manner.

3. Tag all similar parts for location and mark all mating parts for position. Record the number and thickness of any shims when removing them. Identify parts by placing them in sealed and labeled plastic sandwich bags.

4. Label disconnected wires and connectors with masking tape and a marking pen. Connectors must be reconnected to their mates. Do not rely on memory alone.

5. Protect finished surfaces from physical damage or corrosion. Keep gasoline and other chemicals off painted surfaces.

6. Use penetrating oil on frozen or tight bolts. Avoid using heat where possible. Heat can warp, melt or affect the temper of parts. Heat also damages the finish of paint and plastics.

7. When a part is a press fit or requires a special tool for removal, the information or type of tool is identified in the text. Otherwise, if a part is difficult to remove or install, determine the cause before proceeding.

8. To prevent objects or debris from falling into the engine, cover all openings.

9. Read each procedure thoroughly and compare the illustrations to the actual components before starting the procedure. Perform the procedure in sequence.

10. Recommendations are occasionally made to refer service to a dealership or specialist. In these cases, the work can be performed more economically by the specialist than by the home mechanic.

11. The term *replace* means to discard a defective part and replace it with a new part. *Overhaul* means to remove, disassemble, inspect, measure, repair and/or replace parts as required to recondition an assembly.

12. Some operations require using a hydraulic press. If a press is not available, have these operations performed by a shop equipped with the necessary equipment. Do not use makeshift equipment that may damage the motorcycle.

*CAUTION*
*Do not direct high-pressure water at steering bearings, fuel hoses, wheel bearings, suspension and electrical components. Water may force grease*

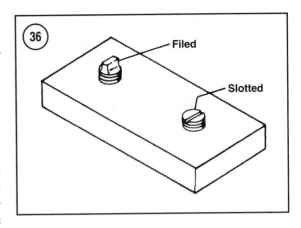

*out of the bearings and possibly damage the seals.*

13. Repairs are much faster and easier if the motorcycle is clean before starting work. Degrease the motorcycle with a commercial degreaser; follow the directions on the container for the best results. Clean all parts with cleaning solvent when removing them.

14. If special tools are required, have them available before starting the procedure. When special tools are required, they are described at the beginning of the procedure.

15. Make diagrams of similar-appearing parts. For instance, crankcase bolts are often not the same lengths. Do not rely on memory alone. Carefully laid out parts can become disturbed, making it difficult to reassemble the components correctly.

16. Make sure all shims and washers are reinstalled in the same location and position.

17. Whenever rotating parts contact a stationary part, look for a shim or washer.

18. Use new gaskets if there is any doubt about the condition of old ones.

19. Replace self-locking fasteners. Do not install standard fasteners in place of self-locking ones.

20. Use grease to hold small parts in place if they tend to fall out during assembly. Do not apply grease to electrical or brake components.

**Heating Components**

*WARNING*
*Wear protective gloves to prevent injury when heating parts.*

A heat gun or propane torch is required to disassemble, assemble, remove and install many parts and components in this manual. Read the safety and operating information supplied by the manufacturer of the heat gun or propane torch while also noting the following:

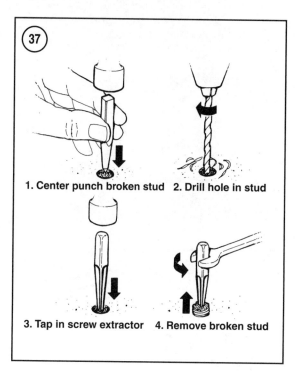

**37**

1. Center punch broken stud  2. Drill hole in stud

3. Tap in screw extractor  4. Remove broken stud

*CAUTION*
*Do not use a welding torch when heating parts in this manual. A welding torch applies excessive heat to a small area very quickly, which can rapidly damage parts.*

1. The work area should be clean and dry. Wipe up all grease, oil and other fluids from parts.

2. Never use a gas torch near the battery, fuel tank, fuel lines or other flammable materials.

3. Check for leaking or damaged fuel system components. Repair or remove these parts before beginning work.

4. Before heating a part installed on the motorcycle, check areas around the part and hidden areas that could be damaged or possibly ignite. Do not heat surfaces than can be damaged by heat. Shield materials, such as cables and wiring harnesses, near the part or area to be heated.

5. Before heating a part, read the procedure through to see what other tools, such as a hammer and bearing driver, will be required and have them at hand. This will allow you to work quickly while the part is at optimum temperature.

6. The amount of heat required to loosen or install a critical part will be listed in the text. To prevent damaging a part, monitor temperature with heat sticks or an infrared thermometer if possible. Another way, though not as accurate, is to place tiny drops of water on the part. When the water starts to sizzle, bead and jump, the part is hot enough.

7. Keep the heat in motion to prevent overheating.

8. When the temperature is monitored, the careful use and application of the heat should not be injurious to the part. However, before heating other parts not recommended in the text, consider the effects of heat applied to the part.

9. Remove all combustible components and materials from the work area.

10. When using a heat gun, remember that the heat is flameless and can be in excess of 1000° F (540° C).

11. Have an ABC fire extinguisher near the job.

12. Always wear protective goggles and gloves when heating parts.

**Removing Frozen Fasteners**

If a fastener cannot be removed, several methods may be used to loosen it. First apply penetrating oil liberally and let it penetrate for 10-15 minutes. Rap the fastener several times with a small hammer. Do not hit it hard enough to cause damage. Reapply the penetrating oil if necessary.

For frozen screws, apply penetrating oil as described, and then insert a screwdriver into the slot and rap the top of the screwdriver with a hammer. This loosens the rust so the screw can be removed in the normal way. If the screw head is too damaged to use this method, grip the head with locking pliers and twist the screw out.

Avoid applying heat unless specifically instructed. Heat may melt, warp or remove the temper from parts.

**Removing Broken Fasteners**

If the head breaks off a screw or bolt, several methods are available for removing the remaining portion. If a large portion of the remainder projects out, try gripping it with locking pliers. If the projecting portion is too small, file it to fit a wrench or cut a slot in it to fit a screwdriver (**Figure 36**).

If the head breaks off flush, use a screw extractor (**Figure 37**). To do this, centerpunch the exact center of the remaining portion of the screw or bolt. Drill a small hole into the screw and tap the extractor into the hole. Back the screw out using a wrench on the extractor.

**Repairing Damaged Threads**

Occasionally, threads are stripped through carelessness or impact damage. Often the threads can be repaired by running a tap (for internal threads on nuts) or die (for external threads on bolts) through the

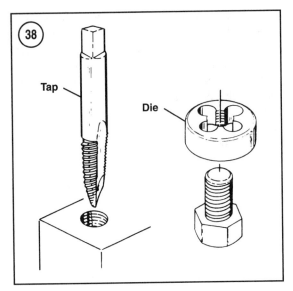

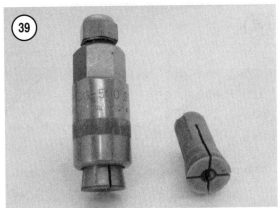

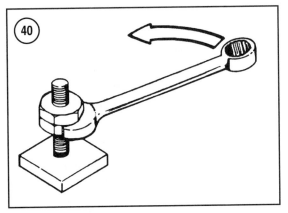

threads (**Figure 38**). To clean or repair spark plug threads, use a spark plug tap.

If an internal thread is damaged, it may be necessary to install a Helicoil or some other type of thread insert. Follow the manufacturer's instructions when installing their insert.

If it is necessary to drill and tap a hole, refer to **Table 3** for metric tap and drill sizes.

### Stud Removal/Installation

A stud removal tool (**Figure 39**) is available from most tool suppliers. This tool makes the removal and installation of studs easier. If one is not available, thread two nuts onto the stud and tighten them against each other. Remove the stud by turning the lower nut (**Figure 40**). Install the stud by turning the top nut.

1. Measure the height of the stud above the surface.

2. Thread the stud removal tool onto the stud and tighten it, or thread two nuts onto the stud.

3. Remove the stud by turning the stud remover or the lower nut.

4. Remove any threadlocking compound from the threaded hole. Clean the threads with an aerosol parts cleaner.

5. Install the stud removal tool onto the new stud, or thread two nuts onto the stud.

6. Apply threadlocking compound to the threads of the stud.

7. Install the stud and tighten with the stud removal tool or the top nut.

8. Install the stud to the height noted in Step 1 or its torque specification.

9. Remove the stud removal tool or the two nuts.

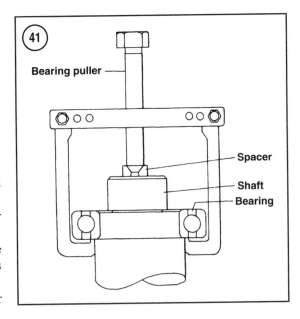

### Removing Hoses

When removing stubborn hoses, do not exert excessive force on the hose or fitting. Remove the hose clamp and carefully insert a small screwdriver or pick tool between the fitting and hose. Apply a spray lubricant under the hose and carefully twist the hose off

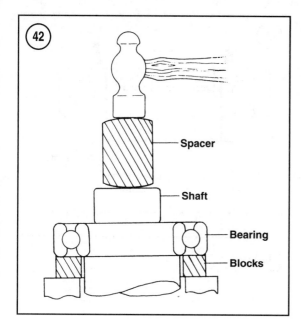

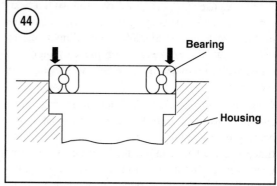

damaged, there may be times when it is necessary to remove a bearing that is in good condition. However, improper bearing removal damages the bearing and possibly the shaft or case. Bearing replacement procedures are included in the individual chapters where applicable; however, use the following procedure as a guideline.

*NOTE*
*Unless otherwise specified, install bearings with the manufacturer's mark or number facing outward.*

1. When using a puller to remove a bearing from a shaft, take care that the shaft is not damaged. Always place a piece of metal as a spacer between the end of the shaft and the puller screw. In addition, place the puller arms next to the inner bearing race. Refer to **Figure 41**.

2. When using a hammer to remove a bearing from a shaft, do not strike the hammer directly against the shaft. Instead, use a brass or aluminum rod between the hammer and shaft (**Figure 42**). Make sure to support both bearing races with wooden blocks as shown.

3. The ideal method of bearing removal is with a hydraulic press. Note the following when using a press:

   a. Always support the inner and outer bearing races with a suitable size wooden or aluminum spacer (**Figure 43**). If only the outer race is supported, pressure applied against the balls and/or the inner race damages them.

   b. Always make sure the press ram (**Figure 43**) aligns with the center of the shaft. If the ram is not centered, it may damage the bearing and/or shaft.

   c. The moment the shaft is free of the bearing, it drops to the floor. Secure or hold the shaft to prevent it from falling.

4. When installing a bearing into a housing, apply pressure to the *outer* bearing race (**Figure 44**). When installing a bearing onto a shaft, apply pressure to the *inner* bearing race (**Figure 45**).

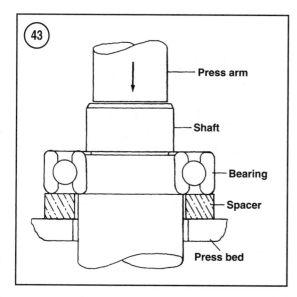

the fitting. Clean any corrosion or rubber hose material from the fitting with a wire brush. Clean the inside of the hose thoroughly. Do not use any lubricant when installing the hose (new or old). The lubricant may allow the hose to come off the fitting, even with the clamp secure.

## Bearings

### Removal/installation

Bearings are precision parts and must be maintained with proper lubrication and service. If a bearing is damaged, replace it immediately. When installing a new bearing, make sure not to damage it. While bearings are normally removed only when

5. Always use some type of driver to install a bearing. Never strike the bearing directly with a hammer or it damages the bearing. When installing a bearing over a shaft, for example, use a piece of pipe or a driver with a diameter that matches the bearing inner race (**Figure 46**).

6. Step 1 describes how to install a bearing into a case half or over a shaft. However, when installing a bearing over a shaft and into a housing at the same time, a tight fit is required for both outer and inner bearing races. In this situation, install a spacer underneath the driver tool so pressure is applied evenly across both races. Refer to **Figure 47**. If the outer race is not supported as shown, the balls push against the outer bearing race and damage it.

### Interference fit

1. Follow this procedure when installing a bearing over a shaft. When a tight fit is required, the bearing inside diameter is smaller than the shaft. In this case, driving the bearing onto the shaft using normal methods may cause bearing damage. Instead, heat the bearing before installation. Note the following:

   a. Secure the shaft so it is ready for bearing installation.

   b. Clean all residues from the bearing surface of the shaft. Remove burrs with a file or sandpaper.

   c. Fill a suitable pot or beaker with clean mineral oil. Place a thermometer rated above 120° C (248° F) in the oil. Support the thermometer so it does not rest on the bottom or side of the pot.

   d. Remove the bearing from its wrapper and secure it with a piece of heavy wire bent to hold it in the pot. Hang the bearing in the pot so it does not touch the bottom or sides of the pot.

   e. Turn the heat on and monitor the thermometer. When the oil temperature rises to approximately 120° C (248° F), remove the bearing from the pot and quickly install it. If necessary, place a socket on the inner bearing race and tap the bearing into place. As the bearing chills, it tightens on the shaft, so installation must be done quickly. Make sure the bearing is installed completely.

2. Follow this step when installing a bearing into a housing. Bearings are generally installed in a housing with a slight interference fit. Driving the bearing into the housing using normal methods may damage the housing or cause bearing damage. Instead, heat the housing before the bearing is installed. Note the following:

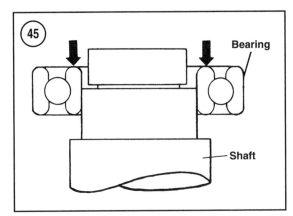

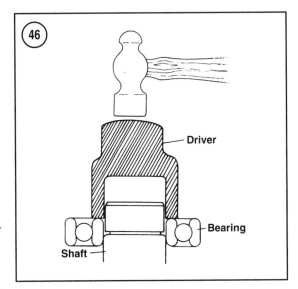

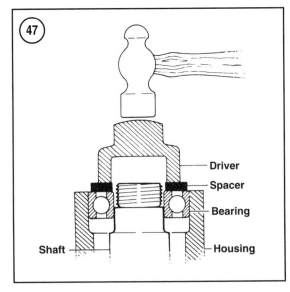

   a. Wash the housing thoroughly with detergent and water. Rinse and rewash as required to remove all traces of oil and other chemical deposits.

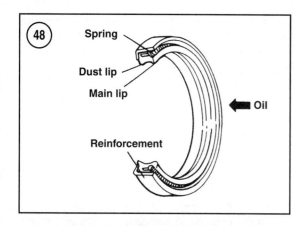

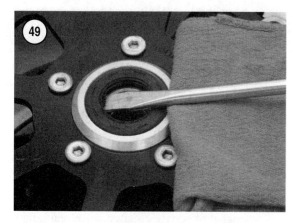

b. Heat the housing to approximately 100° C (212° F) in an oven or on a hot plate. Do not heat the housing with a propane or acetylene torch. To check the temperature, fling tiny drops of water on the housing. If they sizzle and evaporate immediately, the temperature is correct. Heat only one housing at a time.

c. Remove the housing from the oven or hot plate, and hold onto the housing with welding gloves.

d. Hold the housing with the bearing side down and tap the bearing out. Repeat for all bearings in the housing.

e. Before heating the bearing housing, place the new bearing in a freezer, if possible. Chilling a bearing slightly reduces its outside diameter while the heated bearing housing assembly is slightly larger due to heat expansion. This makes bearing installation easier.

f. While the housing is still hot, install the new bearing(s) into the housing. Install the bearings by hand, if possible. If necessary, lightly tap the bearing(s) into the housing with a driver placed on the outer bearing race (**Figure 44**). Do not install new bearings by driving on the inner bearing race. Install the bearing until it seats completely.

**Seal Replacement**

Seals (**Figure 48**) contain oil, water, grease or combustion gasses in a housing or shaft. Improperly removing a seal can damage the housing or shaft. Improperly installing the seal can damage the seal. Note the following:

1. Prying is generally the easiest and most effective method of removing a seal from the housing. However, always place a rag under the pry tool (**Figure 49**) to prevent damage to the housing. Note the seal's installed depth or if it is installed flush.

2. Pack waterproof grease into the seal lips before the seal is installed.

3. In most cases, install seals with the manufacturer's numbers or marks facing out.

4. Install seals with a socket or driver placed on the outside of the seal as shown in **Figure 50**. Drive the seal squarely into the housing until it is to the correct depth or flush (**Figure 51**) as noted during removal. Never install a seal by hitting against the top of it with a hammer.

**STORAGE**

Several months of non-use can cause a general deterioration of the motorcycle. This is especially true in areas of extreme temperature variations. This deterioration can be minimized with careful preparation for storage. A properly stored motorcycle is much easier to return to service.

### Storage Area Selection

When selecting a storage area, consider the following:

1. The storage area must be dry. A heated area is best but not necessary. It should be insulated to minimize extreme temperature variations.
2. If the building has large window areas, mask them to keep sunlight off the motorcycle.
3. Avoid buildings in industrial areas where corrosive emissions may be present. Avoid areas close to saltwater.
4. Consider the area's risk of fire, theft or vandalism. Check with an insurer regarding motorcycle coverage while in storage.

### Preparing the Motorcycle for Storage

The amount of preparation a motorcycle should undergo before storage depends upon the expected length of non-use, storage area conditions and personal preference. Consider the following list the minimum requirement:

1. Wash the motorcycle thoroughly. Make sure all dirt, mud and road debris are removed.
2. Start the engine and allow it to reach operating temperature. Drain the engine oil regardless of the riding time since the last service. Fill the engine with the recommended type of oil.

3. Fill the fuel tank with fuel mixed with a fuel stabilizer. Mix the fuel and stabilizer in the ratio recommended by the stabilizer manufacturer. Run the engine for a few minutes so the stabilized fuel can enter the fuel injection system.
4. Remove the spark plugs and pour a tablespoon (45-60 ml) of engine oil into each cylinder. Place a rag over the openings and slowly turn the engine over to distribute the oil. Reinstall the spark plugs.
5. Remove the battery. Store the battery in a cool and dry location. Charge the battery once a month.
6. Cover the exhaust and intake openings.
7. Apply a protective substance to the plastic and rubber components. Make sure to follow the manufacturer's instructions for each type of product being used.
8. Place the motorcycle on its centerstand. Rotate the front tire periodically to prevent a flat spot from developing and damaging the tire.
9. Cover the motorcycle with old bed sheets or something similar. Do not cover it with any plastic material that traps moisture.

### Returning the Motorcycle to Service

The amount of service required when returning a motorcycle to service after storage depends on the length of non-use and storage conditions. In addition to performing the reverse of the above procedures, make sure the brakes, clutch, throttle and engine stop switch work properly before operating the motorcycle. Refer to Chapter Three and evaluate the service intervals to determine which areas require service.

### Table 1 MOTORCYCLE DIMENSIONS AND WEIGHT

| | |
|---|---|
| **Dry mass** | |
| 1999-2000 models | |
| All models except California | 215 kg (473 lb.) |
| California models | 216 kg (476 lb.) |
| 2001-on models | |
| All models except California | 217 kg (478 lb.) |
| California models | 218 kg (480 lb.) |
| **Ground clearance** | 120 mm (4.7 in.) |
| **Overall height** | 1155 mm (45.5 in.) |
| **Overall length** | |
| 1999 models | |
| All models except Switzerland | 2140 mm (84.3 in.) |
| Switzerland models | 2180 mm (85.8 in.) |
| 2000-on models | 2140 mm (84.3 in.) |
| **Overall width** | 740 mm (29.1 in.) |
| **Seat height** | 805 mm (31.7 in.) |
| **Wheelbase** | 1485 mm (58.5 in.) |

## Table 2 METRIC, INCH AND FRACTIONAL EQUIVALENTS

| mm | in. | Nearest fraction | mm | in. | Nearest fraction |
|----|-----|------------------|----|-----|------------------|
| 1 | 0.0394 | 1/32 | 26 | 1.0236 | 1 1/32 |
| 2 | 0.0787 | 3/32 | 27 | 1.0630 | 1 1/16 |
| 3 | 0.1181 | 1/8 | 28 | 1.1024 | 1 3/32 |
| 4 | 0.1575 | 5/32 | 29 | 1.1417 | 1 5/32 |
| 5 | 0.1969 | 3/16 | 30 | 1.1811 | 1 3/16 |
| 6 | 0.2362 | 1/4 | 31 | 1.2205 | 1 7/32 |
| 7 | 0.2756 | 9/32 | 32 | 1.2598 | 1 1/4 |
| 8 | 0.3150 | 5/16 | 33 | 1.2992 | 1 5/16 |
| 9 | 0.3543 | 11/32 | 34 | 1.3386 | 1 11/32 |
| 10 | 0.3937 | 13/32 | 35 | 1.3780 | 1 3/8 |
| 11 | 0.4331 | 7/16 | 36 | 1.4173 | 1 13/32 |
| 12 | 0.4724 | 15/32 | 37 | 1.4567 | 1 15/32 |
| 13 | 0.5118 | 1/2 | 38 | 1.4961 | 1 1/2 |
| 14 | 0.5512 | 9/16 | 39 | 1.5354 | 1 17/32 |
| 15 | 0.5906 | 19/32 | 40 | 1.5748 | 1 9/16 |
| 16 | 0.6299 | 5/8 | 41 | 1.6142 | 1 5/8 |
| 17 | 0.6693 | 21/32 | 42 | 1.6535 | 1 21/32 |
| 18 | 0.7087 | 23/32 | 43 | 1.6929 | 1 11/16 |
| 19 | 0.7480 | 3/4 | 44 | 1.7323 | 1 23/32 |
| 20 | 0.7874 | 25/32 | 45 | 1.7717 | 1 25/32 |
| 21 | 0.8268 | 13/16 | 46 | 1.8110 | 1 13/16 |
| 22 | 0.8661 | 7/8 | 47 | 1.8504 | 1 27/32 |
| 23 | 0.9055 | 29/32 | 48 | 1.8898 | 1 7/8 |
| 24 | 0.9449 | 15/16 | 49 | 1.9291 | 1 15/16 |
| 25 | 0.9843 | 31/32 | 50 | 1.9685 | 1 31/32 |

## Table 3 METRIC TAP AND DRILL SIZES

| Metric tap | Drill bit | Decimal (in.) | Nearest fraction |
|------------|-----------|---------------|------------------|
| 3 × 0.50 | No. 39 | 0.0995 | 3/32 |
| 3 × 0.60 | 3/32 | 0.0937 | 3/32 |
| 4 × 0.70 | No. 30 | 0.1285 | 1/8 |
| 4 × 0.75 | 1/8 | 0.125 | 1/8 |
| 5 × 0.80 | No. 19 | 0.166 | 11/64 |
| 5 × 0.90 | No. 20 | 0.161 | 5/32 |
| 6 × 1.00 | No. 9 | 0.196 | 13/64 |
| 7 × 1.00 | 16/64 | 0.234 | 15/64 |
| 8 × 1.00 | J | 0.277 | 9/32 |
| 8 × 1.25 | 17/64 | 0.265 | 17/64 |
| 9 × 1.00 | 5/16 | 0.3125 | 5/16 |
| 9 × 1.25 | 5/16 | 0.3125 | 5/16 |
| 10 × 1.25 | 11/32 | 0.3437 | 11/32 |
| 10 × 1.50 | R | 0.339 | 11/32 |
| 11 × 1.50 | 3/8 | 0.375 | 3/8 |
| 12 × 1.50 | 13/32 | 0.406 | 13/32 |
| 12 × 1.75 | 13/32 | 0.406 | 13/32 |

## Table 4 CONVERSION FORMULAS

| Multiply: | By: | To get the equivalent of: |
|-----------|-----|---------------------------|
| Length | | |
| Inches | 25.4 | Millimeter |
| Inches | 2.54 | Centimeter |

(continued)

## Table 4 CONVERSION FORMULAS (continued)

| Multiply: | By: | To get the equivalent of: |
|---|---|---|
| Length (continued) | | |
| Miles | 1.609 | Kilometer |
| Feet | 0.3048 | Meter |
| Millimeter | 0.03937 | Inches |
| Centimeter | 0.3937 | Inches |
| Kilometer | 0.6214 | Mile |
| Meter | 3.281 | Feet |
| Fluid volume | | |
| U.S. quarts | 0.9463 | Liters |
| U.S. gallons | 3.785 | Liters |
| U.S. ounces | 29.573529 | Milliliters |
| Imperial gallons | 4.54609 | Liters |
| Imperial quarts | 1.1365 | Liters |
| Liters | 0.2641721 | U.S. gallons |
| Liters | 1.0566882 | U.S. quarts |
| Liters | 33.814023 | U.S. ounces |
| Liters | 0.22 | Imperial gallons |
| Liters | 0.8799 | Imperial quarts |
| Milliliters | 0.033814 | U.S. ounces |
| Milliliters | 1.0 | Cubic centimeters |
| Milliliters | 0.001 | Liters |
| Torque | | |
| Foot-pounds | 1.3558 | Newton-meters |
| Foot-pounds | 0.138255 | Meters-kilograms |
| Inch-pounds | 0.11299 | Newton-meters |
| Newton-meters | 0.7375622 | Foot-pounds |
| Newton-meters | 8.8507 | Inch-pounds |
| Meters-kilograms | 7.2330139 | Foot-pounds |
| Volume | | |
| Cubic inches | 16.387064 | Cubic centimeters |
| Cubic centimeters | 0.0610237 | Cubic inches |
| Temperature | | |
| Fahrenheit | $(°F - 32) \times 0.556$ | Centigrade |
| Centigrade | $(°C \times 1.8) + 32$ | Fahrenheit |
| Weight | | |
| Ounces | 28.3495 | Grams |
| Pounds | 0.4535924 | Kilograms |
| Grams | 0.035274 | Ounces |
| Kilograms | 2.2046224 | Pounds |
| Pressure | | |
| Pounds per square inch | 0.070307 | Kilograms per square centimeter |
| Kilograms per square centimeter | 14.223343 | Pounds per square inch |
| Kilopascals | 0.1450 | Pounds per square inch |
| Pounds per square inch | 6.895 | Kilopascals |
| Speed | | |
| Miles per hour | 1.609344 | Kilometers per hour |
| Kilometers per hour | 0.6213712 | Miles per hour |

## Table 5 TECHNICAL ABBREVIATIONS

| | |
|---|---|
| A | Amp |
| AC | Alternating current |
| A.h. | Ampere hour |
| AP sensor | Atmospheric pressure sensor |
| ATDC | After top dead center |
| BDC | Bottom dead center |
| BTDC | Before top dead center |
| C | Celsius (centigrade) |

(continued)

## Table 5 TECHNICAL ABBREVIATIONS (continued)

| | |
|---|---|
| cc | Cubic centimeters |
| cid | Cubic inch displacement |
| CDI | Capacitor discharge ignition |
| CKP sensor | Crankshaft position sensor |
| cm | Centimeter |
| CMP sensor | Camshaft position sensor |
| cu. in. | Cubic inches |
| DC | Direct current |
| ECM | Electronic control module |
| ECT sensor | Engine coolant temperature sensor |
| F | Fahrenheit |
| fl. oz. | Fluid ounce |
| ft. | Feet |
| ft.-lb. | Foot-pounds |
| gal. | Gallons |
| GP sensor | Gear position sensor |
| H/A | High altitude |
| hp | Horsepower |
| IAP sensor | Intake air pressure sensor |
| IAT sensor | Intake air temperature sensor. |
| I.D. | Inside diameter |
| in. | Inches |
| in. Hg | Inches of mercury |
| in.-lb. | Inch-pounds |
| kg | Kilograms |
| kg/cm$^2$ | Kilograms per square centimeter |
| kgm | Kilogram meters |
| km | Kilometer |
| km/h | Kilometer per hour |
| kPa | Kilopascals |
| L | Liter |
| m | Meter |
| ml | Milliliter |
| mm | Millimeter |
| N•m | Newton-meters |
| O.D. | Outside diameter |
| oz. | Ounces |
| PAIR | Pulsed air injection |
| psi | Pounds per square inch |
| pt. | Pint |
| qt. | Quart |
| rpm | Revolutions per minute |
| TDC | Top dead center |
| TP sensor | Throttle position sensor |
| TO sensor | Tip over sensor |
| V | Volt |
| VCSV | Vacuum control solenoid valve |
| VTV | Vacuum transmitting valve |
| W | Watt |

## Table 6 TORQUE RECOMMENDATIONS*

| Thread diameter | N•m | in.-lb. | ft.-lb. |
|---|---|---|---|
| 5 mm | | | |
|   Bolt and nut | 5 | 44 | – |
|   Screw | 4 | 35 | – |
| 6 mm | | | |
|   Bolt and nut | 10 | 89 | – |
|   Screw | 9 | 80 | – |
| (continued) | | | |

**Table 6 TORQUE RECOMMENDATIONS\* (continued)**

| Thread diameter | N•m | in.-lb. | ft.-lb. |
| --- | --- | --- | --- |
| 6 mm (continued) | | | |
|   6 mm flange bolt and nut | 12 | 106 | – |
|   6 mm bolt with 8 mm head | 9 | 80 | – |
| 8 mm | | | |
|   Bolt and nut | 22 | – | 16 |
|   Flange bolt and nut | 27 | – | 20 |
| 10 mm | | | |
|   Bolt and nut | 35 | – | 26 |
|   Flange bolt and nut | 40 | – | 30 |
| 12 mm | | | |
|   Bolt and nut | 55 | – | 41 |

\*Torque recommendations for fasteners without a specification. Refer to the torque specification table(s) at the end of the respective chapter(s) for specific applications.

# CHAPTER TWO

# TROUBLESHOOTING

The troubleshooting procedures described in this chapter provide typical symptoms and logical methods for isolating the cause(s). There may be several ways to solve a problem, but only a systematic approach will be successful in avoiding wasted time and possibly unnecessary parts replacement. Gather as much information as possible to aid in diagnosis. Never assume anything and do not overlook the obvious. Make sure the kill switch is in the run position and there is fuel in the tank.

An engine needs three basics to run properly: correct air/fuel mixture, compression and a spark at the correct time. If any of these is missing, the engine will not run.

Learning to recognize symptoms makes troubleshooting easier. In most cases, expensive and complicated test equipment is not needed to determine whether repairs can be performed at home. On the other hand, be realistic and do not start procedures that are beyond your experience and the equipment available. If the motorcycle requires the attention of a professional, describe symptoms and conditions accurately and fully. The more information a technician has available, the easier it is to diagnose the problem.

## ENGINE STARTING

*CAUTION*
*Do not operate the starter for more than 5 seconds at a time. Wait approximately 10 seconds between starting attempts.*

### Starting System Operation

1. A sidestand ignition cutoff system is used on all models. The position of the sidestand affects engine starting. If the engine will not start, check the condition of the sidestand switch (**Figure 1**) as follows:

    a. The engine cannot start when the sidestand is down and the transmission is in gear.

    b. The engine can start when the sidestand is down and the transmission is in neutral. The engine stops, however, if the transmission is put in gear while the sidestand is down.

    c. The engine can start when the sidestand is up and the transmission is in neutral.

    d. If the sidestand is up, the engine also starts if the transmission is in gear and the clutch lever is pulled in.

2. Before starting the engine, shift the transmission into neutral and confirm that the engine stop switch (A, **Figure 2**) is set to run.

> *WARNING*
> *The warning lights should go off after a few seconds or after the engine starts. If a light stays on, turn the ignition switch off and check the oil level and coolant level as described in Chapter Three.*

3. The following indicator lights should function when the ignition switch is turned on.
    a. The neutral indicator light (when the transmission is in neutral).
    b. Oil pressure indicator.
    c. Low fuel indicator.
    d. Coolant temperature indicator.
    e. Fuel injection indicator.
    f. The needle on each gauge swings to its maximum setting and then returns to zero.

4. The engine is now ready to start. Refer to the starting procedure in this section that best describes the air temperature and engine conditions.

5. If the engine idles at a fast speed for more than 5 minutes or if the throttle is repeatedly snapped on and off at normal air temperatures, the exhaust pipes may discolor.

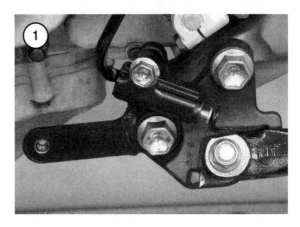

## Cold Engine

1. Shift the transmission into neutral.
2. Move the fast idle lever to on. Close the throttle completely.
3. Make sure the engine stop switch (A, **Figure 2**) is in the run position.
4. Turn the ignition switch on.

> *NOTE*
> *When a cold engine is started with the throttle open and the fast idle lever on, a lean mixture results and causes difficult starting.*

5. Depress the starter button (B, **Figure 2**) and start the engine. Do not open the throttle when pressing the starter button.
6. Once the engine has started, adjust the fast idle lever to keep the engine idling between 2000 and 2500 rpm.
7. After approximately 30 seconds, move the fast idle lever to off. In cold weather, the fast idle lever may need to remain on for a slightly longer period.
8. The engine is warm when it cleanly responds to the throttle.

## Warm or Hot Engine

1. Shift the transmission into neutral.
2. Turn the ignition switch on.
3. Make sure the fast idle lever is off.
4. Make sure the engine stop switch (A, **Figure 2**) is in the run position.
5. Close the throttle and depress the starter button (B, **Figure 2**).

## Flooded Engine

If the engine does not start and if a strong gasoline smell is present, the engine is probably flooded. To start a flooded engine:

1. Turn the engine stop switch to off.
2. Push the fast idle lever to its fully closed position.
3. Open the throttle fully.
4. Turn the ignition switch to on and operate the starter button for 5 seconds. Close the throttle.
5. Wait 10 seconds and turn the engine stop switch to on.
6. Open the throttle slightly, and press the starter button. Do not operate the fast idle lever.

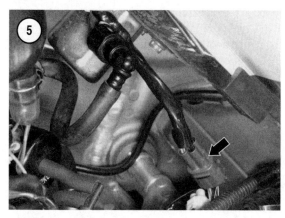

## ENGINE WILL NOT START

### Identifying the Problem

If the engine does not start, perform the following steps in order. Because there are so many things that can cause a starting problem, it is important to narrow the possibilities by following a specific troubleshooting procedure. If the engine fails to start after performing these checks, refer to the troubleshooting procedures indicated in the steps. If the engine starts, but idles or runs roughly, refer to *Engine Performance* in this chapter. Perform each step in order. If

the engine still does not start, refer to the appropriate troubleshooting procedures in this section.

1. Refer to *Engine Starting* in this chapter to make sure all switches and starting procedures are correct.
2. If the starter does not operate, refer to *Starting System* in this chapter.
3. If the starter operates, and the engine seems flooded, refer to *Flooded Engine* in this chapter. If the engine is not flooded, continue with Step 4.
4. Make sure there is sufficient fuel in the tank. Turn the ignition switch on and check the low fuel indicator light. The fuel level is low (less than 3.5 liters [0.9 U.S. gal.]) if the light remains on.
5. Support the fuel tank, and remove the air filter housing (Chapter Eight). Make sure each 2-pin electrical connector (**Figure 3**) is securely connected to its ignition coil/spark plug cap. If necessary, carefully push and slightly rotate each direct ignition coil to assure it is securely connected to its spark plug. If the engine does not start, continue with Step 6.
6. Test the ignition system by performing the spark test described in this section. If the test produces a good spark, proceed with Step 7. If the spark is weak, or if there is no spark, refer to *Diagnostic System* in Chapter Eight.
7. Check engine compression as described in Chapter Three. If the compression is low, check for one or more of the following:
   a. Leaking cylinder head gasket(s).
   b. Cracked or warped cylinder head(s).
   c. Worn piston rings, pistons and cylinders.
   d. Valve stuck open.
   e. Worn or damaged valve seat(s).
   f. Incorrect valve timing.

### Spark Test

A spark test determines if the ignition system is producing adequate spark. The following procedure uses a Motion Pro spark tester (part No. 08-0122). If a tester is not available, use a new spark plug.

1. Raise and support the fuel tank, and then remove the air filter housing as described in Chapter Eight.

*WARNING*
*Step 2 must be performed to disable the fuel system. Otherwise, fuel enters into the cylinders when the engine is turned over during the spark test, flooding the cylinders and creating explosive fuel vapors.*

2. Disconnect the fuel pump connector (1999 and 2000 models: **Figure 4**; 2001-on models: **Figure 5**) from its harness mate.

3. Remove the spark plugs (Chapter Three).

*CAUTION*
*Do not ground the spark plug to the cylinder head cover, clutch cover, starter clutch cover, idler gear cover or the alternator cover. An electrical spark damages these magnesium covers.*

4. Set the spark tester gap to 8.0 mm (0.3 in.), and insert the spark tester into the direct ignition coil/spark plug cap. Place the tester base on a good engine ground. Position the tester so the electrode can be seen.

5. Shift the transmission into neutral, turn the ignition switch on and place the engine stop switch in the run position.

*WARNING*
*Do not hold the spark plugs, tester, wire or connector. Serious electrical shock may result.*

*NOTE*
*Make sure the throttle bodies are clear.*

6. Operate the starter button to turn the engine over. A fat blue spark must be evident across the spark plug electrodes or between the tester terminals. Repeat for each cylinder.

7. If the spark is good at each spark plug, the ignition system is functioning properly. Check for one or more of the following possible malfunctions:
   a. Faulty fuel system component. Refer to *Fuel System* in this chapter.
   b. Engine damage (low compression).
   c. Engine flooded.

8A. If there is no spark or a weak spark on all plugs, check the following:
   a. Fouled spark plug(s).
   b. Damaged spark plug(s).
   c. Loose or damaged spark plug wire(s).
   d. Loose or damaged spark plug cap(s).
   e. Damaged ECM.
   f. Defective crankshaft position (CKP) sensor, camshaft position (CMP) sensor or tip-over (TO) sensor.
   g. Faulty direct ignition coil(s).
   h. Damaged engine stop switch.
   i. Damaged ignition switch.
   j. Dirty or loose-fitting terminals.

8B. If there is no spark at only one spark plug, the spark plug is probably faulty, or there is a problem with the ignition coil/spark plug cap. Retest with a spark tester or use a new spark plug.

   a. If there is still no spark at that one plug, make sure the ignition coil/ plug cap is installed correctly.
   b. Refer to *Diagnostic System* in Chapter Eight to troubleshoot the ignition system.

9. Install the spark plugs (Chapter Three).

10. Install the air filter housing and fuel tank (Chapter Eight).

**Engine Is Difficult to Start**

1. After attempting to start the engine, remove one of the spark plugs as described in Chapter Three. Check for the presence of fuel on the plug tip. Note the following:
   a. If there is no fuel visible on the plug, remove another spark plug. If there is no fuel on this plug, perform Step 2.
   b. If there is some fuel on the plug tip, go to Step 5.
   c. If there is an excessive amount of fuel on the plug, check for a clogged air filter, incorrect fast idle valve operation/adjustment or incorrect throttle valve operation (stuck open).

2. Perform the *Fuel Pump Operation Test* described in Chapter Eight. Note the following:
   a. If the fuel pump operation is correct, go to Step 3.
   b. If the fuel pump operation is faulty, perform the fuel pump relay test (Chapter Eight) and troubleshoot the tip-over (TO) sensor. Refer to *Diagnostic System* in Chapter Eight. If both components are within specification, replace the fuel pump.

3. Perform the *Fuel Pump Discharge Test* described in Chapter Eight.
   a. If the fuel flow is low, check for a clogged fuel filter or replace the fuel pump.
   b. If fuel flow is within specification, proceed to Step 4.

4. Perform the *Fuel Pressure Test* described in Chapter Eight.
   a. If fuel pressure is within specification, proceed to Step 5.
   b. If fuel pressure is low, check for a leak in the fuel system, a clogged fuel filter or faulty pressure regulator or fuel pump.
   c. If fuel pressure is high, check for a clogged fuel line or faulty fuel pump check valve or pressure regulator.

5. Perform the spark test (this section). If the spark is good, go to Step 6.

6. If the engine turns over but does not start, the engine compression is probably low. Check for the following possible malfunctions:

a. Leaking cylinder head gasket.
b. Valve clearance too tight.
c. Bent or stuck valve(s).
d. Incorrect valve timing. Worn cylinders and/or pistons rings.
e. Improper valve-to-seat contact.
7. If the spark is good, try starting the engine by following normal starting procedures. If the engine starts but then stops, check for the following conditions:
a. Incorrect fast idle valve operation.
b. Leaking or damaged intake manifold.
c. Contaminated fuel.
d. Incorrect ignition timing due to failed ignition system component.

## Engine Does Not Crank

If the engine does not turn over, check for one or more of the following:
1. Blown fuse.
2. Discharged battery.
3. Defective starter, starter relay or starter switch.
4. Faulty starter clutch.
5. Seized pistons(s).
6. Seized crankshaft bearings.
7. Broken connecting rod.
8. Locked-up transmission or clutch assembly.

## ENGINE PERFORMANCE

If the engine runs, but performance is unsatisfactory, refer to the following procedure that best describes the symptom(s).

## Engine Will Not Idle

1. Incorrect valve adjustment.
2. Poor valve seating.
3. Worn valve guide.
4. Worn camshaft.
5. Fouled or improperly gapped spark plug(s).
6. Leaking head gasket, intake manifold or vacuum hose.
7. Faulty ECM, crankshaft position sensor or throttle position sensor.
8. Faulty ignition coil/spark plug cap.
9. Faulty fuel pump.
10. Improperly synchronized throttle bodies.
11. Clogged air filter element.
12. Incorrect idle speed adjustment.
13. Incorrect throttle cable free play.
14. Low engine compression.
15. Obstructed or defective fuel injector(s).

## Poor Overall Performance

1. Securely support the motorcycle with the rear wheel off the ground, and spin the rear wheel by hand. If the wheel spins freely, perform Step 2. If the wheel does not spin freely, check for the following conditions:
a. Dragging rear brake.
b. Excessive rear axle torque.
c. Damaged rear axle/bearing.
d. Damaged drive chain (swollen O-rings).
2. Check the clutch adjustment and operation. If the clutch slips, refer to *Clutch* in this chapter.
3. If Step 1 and Step 2 did not locate the problem, test ride the motorcycle and accelerate lightly. If the engine speed increases according to throttle position, perform Step 4. If the engine speed does not increase, check for one or more of the following problems:
a. Clogged air filter or air ducts.
b. Restricted fuel flow.
c. Pinched fuel tank breather hose.
d. Clogged or damaged muffler.
4. Check for one or more of the following problems:
a. Low engine compression.
b. Worn or fouled spark plugs.
c. Incorrect spark plug heat range.
d. Clogged or defective fuel injector(s).
e. Incorrect ignition timing due to a faulty ignition component, damaged ECM or crankshaft position sensor.
f. Incorrect oil level (too high or too low).
g. Contaminated oil.
h. Worn or damaged valve train assembly.
i. Engine overheating. Refer to *Engine Overheating* in this section.
5. If the engine knocks when it accelerates or when running at high speed, check for one or more of the following possible malfunctions:
a. Incorrect type of fuel.
b. Lean fuel mixture.
c. Advanced ignition timing due to a damaged ignition system component.
d. Excessive carbon buildup in the combustion chamber(s).
e. Worn pistons and/or cylinder bores.

## Poor Idle or Low Speed Performance

1. Check the valve clearance. Adjust the valves as necessary.
2. Check for damaged intake manifolds and loose throttle body or air filter clamps.

3. Check the fuel pump circuit and the fuel injectors (Chapter Eight).

4. Perform the spark test described in this chapter. If the spark is weak, troubleshoot the ignition system as described in *Diagnostic System* (Chapter Eight).

## Poor High Speed Performance

1. Faulty engine or electrical component.
   a. Weak valve springs.
   b. Worn camshaft.
   c. Improper valve timing.
   d. Spark plug gap too narrow.
   e. Insufficiently advanced ignition timing.
   f. Defective ignition coil.
   g. Faulty crankshaft position sensor.
   h. Faulty ECM.
   i. Clogged air filter element.
   j. Clogged fuel line.
   k. Faulty fuel pump.
   l. Defective throttle position sensor.
2. Air flow fault.
   a. Clogged air filter element.
   b. Faulty throttle valve.
   c. Leaking intake manifold.
   d. Defective ECM.
   e. Faulty vacuum control solenoid valve or intake air control valve actuator.
3. Control circuit fault.
   a. Low fuel pressure.
   b. Faulty throttle position sensor.
   c. Faulty intake air temperature sensor.
   d. Faulty camshaft position sensor.
   e. Faulty crankshaft position sensor.
   f. Faulty gear position sensor.
   g. Faulty intake air pressure sensor.
   h. Faulty atmospheric pressure sensor.
   i. Faulty ECM.
   j. Improperly synchronized throttle valves.

## Engine Lacks Power

1. Faulty engine or electrical part.
   a. Improperly adjusted valve.
   b. Weakened valve springs.
   c. Improperly timed valves.
   d. Worn piston rings or cylinder.
   e. Uneven valve seating.
   f. Fouled or incorrect spark plug.
   g. Plugged or leaking fuel injector.
   h. Misadjusted adjusted throttle position sensor.
   i. Clogged air filter element.
   j. Throttle valves out of sync.
   k. Leaking throttle valve or vacuum hose.

l. Excessively high engine oil level.
   m. Faulty fuel pump or ECM.
   n. Faulty crankshaft position sensor and ignition coil.
2. Faulty control circuit.
   a. Low fuel pressure.
   b. Throttle position sensor failure.
   c. Intake air temperature sensor failure.
   d. Camshaft position sensor failure.
   e. Crankshaft position sensor failure.
   f. Gear position sensor failure.
   g. Intake air pressure sensor failure.
   h. Atmospheric pressure sensor failure.
   i. ECM failure.
   j. Throttle valves not synchronized.

## Engine Stalls

1. Faulty air/fuel mixture.
   a. Clogged fuel filter.
   b. Faulty intake air pressure sensor.
   c. Defective fuel pump or pressure regulator.
   d. Leaking vacuum hose.
   e. Faulty engine coolant temperature sensor or thermostat.
   f. Faulty intake air temperature sensor.
2. Faulty fuel injector.
   a. Defective injector.
   b. Poor signal from ECM.
   c. Wiring or connector fault.
   d. Defective or low battery.
3. Control circuit failure.
   a. Faulty ECM.
   b. Faulty fuel pressure regulator.
   c. Poorly adjusted or faulty throttle position sensor.
   d. Intake air temperature sensor fault.
   e. Camshaft position sensor fault.
   f. Crankshaft position sensor fault.
   g. Engine coolant temperature sensor fault.
   h. Fuel pump relay failure.
4. Faulty engine or electrical component.
   a. Fouled spark plugs.
   b. Faulty crankshaft position sensor or ECM.
   c. Clogged fuel hose.
   d. Poorly adjusted valves.

## Engine Overheating

1. Cooling system malfunction.
   a. Low coolant level.
   b. Air in cooling system.
   c. Clogged radiator, hose or engine coolant passages.

    d. Thermostat stuck closed.

    e. Clogged or damaged oil cooler.

    f. Worn or damaged radiator cap.

    g. Damaged water pump.

    h. Damaged fan thermo switch.

    i. Damaged fan motor.

    j. Damaged temperature gauge.

    k. Defective coolant temperature sensor.

2. Lean air/fuel mixture.

    a. Short in the intake air pressure sensor or its wire.

    b. Short in the intake air temperature sensor or its wire.

    c. Air leak through intake manifold.

    d. Defective fuel injector.

    e. Defective engine coolant temperature sensor.

    f. Clogged or faulty fuel pressure vacuum hose.

3. Other causes.

    a. Engine coolant temperature sensor fault.

    b. Gear position sensor fault.

    c. Crankshaft position sensor fault.

    d. Faulty ECM.

    e. Drive chain too tight.

## Engine Not Reaching Operating Temperature

1. Thermostat stuck open.
2. Defective fan thermo switch.
3. Inaccurate temperature gauge.
4. Defective coolant temperature sensor.

## Engine Backfires

1. Improper ignition timing caused by faulty ignition system component.
2. Incorrect throttle body adjustment.
3. Lean fuel mixture.

## Engine Misfires During Acceleration

1. Improper ignition timing caused by faulty ignition system component.
2. Excessively worn or defective spark plug(s).
3. Incorrect throttle body adjustment.

## Engine Noises

Unusual noises are often the first indication of a developing problem. Investigate any new noises as soon as possible. Something that may be a minor problem, if corrected, could prevent the possibility of more extensive damage.

Use a mechanic's stethoscope or a small section of hose held near your ear (not directly on your ear) with the other end close to the source of the noise to isolate the location. Determining the exact cause of a noise can be difficult. If this is the case, consult with a professional mechanic to determine the cause. Do not disassemble major components until all other possibilities have been eliminated.

Consider the following when troubleshooting engine noises:

1. Knocking or pinging during acceleration is caused by the use of a lower octane fuel than recommended. It may also be caused by poor fuel, a spark plug of the wrong heat range or carbon buildup in the combustion chamber. Refer to *Spark Plugs, Selection* and *Compression Test* in Chapter Three.

2. Slapping or rattling noises at low speed or during acceleration may be caused by excessive piston-to-cylinder clearance (piston slap). Piston slap is easier to detect when the engine is cold and before the pistons have expanded. Once the engine has warmed up, piston expansion reduces piston-to-cylinder clearance.

3. Knocking or rapping while decelerating is usually caused by excessive connecting rod bearing clearance.

4. Persistent knocking and vibration during every crankshaft rotation is usually caused by a worn connecting rod or main bearing(s). This can also be caused by broken piston rings or damaged piston pins.

5. Rapid on-off squeal indicates a compression leak around the cylinder head gasket or spark plug(s).

6. To troubleshoot a valve train noise, check for the following:

    a. Excessive valve clearance.

    b. Excessively worn or damaged camshaft.

    c. Damaged cam chain tensioner.

    d. Worn or damaged valve lifters and/or shims.

    e. Damaged valve bore(s) in cylinder head.

    f. Valve sticking in guide.

    g. Broken valve spring.

    h. Low oil pressure.

    i. Clogged cylinder oil hole or oil passage.

    j. Excessively worn or damaged cam chain.

    k. Damaged cam chain sprockets.

7. For rattles, start checking where the sound is coming from. This may require the removal of fairing components (Chapter Fifteen).

## LUBRICATION SYSTEM

An improperly operating engine lubrication system quickly leads to engine seizure. Check the engine oil level before each ride and top off the oil as described in Chapter Three. Oil pump service is described in Chapter Five.

## Oil Consumption High or Engine Smokes Excessively

1. Worn valve guides, valve stem or valve seal.
2. Worn or damaged piston rings or cylinders.
3. Scuffed cylinder walls.
4. Too much oil in the crankcase.

## Oil Leaks

1. Clogged air filter housing breather hose.
2. Loose engine parts.
3. Damaged gasket sealing surfaces.

## Low Oil Pressure

1. Low oil level.
2. Worn or damaged oil pump.
3. Clogged oil strainer screen.
4. Clogged oil filter.
5. Clogged oil cooler.
6. Internal oil leaks.
7. Incorrect type of engine oil.
8. Oil pressure relief valve stuck open.

## High Oil Pressure

1. Clogged oil filter.
2. Clogged oil cooler.
3. Clogged oil gallery or metering orifices.
4. Incorrect type of engine oil.

## No Oil Pressure

1. Damaged oil pump.
2. Low oil level.
3. Damaged oil pump drive shaft.
4. Damaged oil pump drive sprocket.
5. Incorrect oil pump installation.

## Oil Level Too Low

1. Insufficient amount of oil.
2. Worn piston rings.
3. Worn cylinder(s).
4. Worn valve guides.
5. Worn valve stem seals.
6. Piston rings incorrectly installed during engine overhaul.
7. External oil leaks.

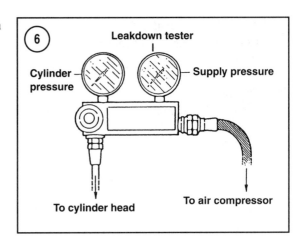

8. Oil leaking into the cooling system.

## Oil Contamination

1. Blown head gasket allowing coolant to leak into the engine.
2. Water contamination.
3. Oil and filter not changed at specified intervals or when operating conditions demand more frequent changes.

## LEAKDOWN TEST

A cylinder leakdown test can locate engine problems from leaking valves, blown head gasket or broken, worn or stuck piston rings. This test is performed by applying compressed air to the cylinder and then measuring the leak percentage or pressure loss.

A cylinder leakdown tester (**Figure 6**) and an air compressor are needed to perform this test.

1. Run the engine until it is warm, and then turn the engine off.
2. Remove the air filter housing as described in Chapter Eight. Secure the throttle at its wide-open position.
3. Set the No. 1 cylinder to top dead center on the compression stroke as described in *Valve Clearance* in Chapter Three.

> *WARNING*
> *Because the crankshaft may spin when compressed air is applied to the cylinder, remove any tools attached to the end of the crankshaft. To prevent the engine from turning over as compressed air is applied to the cylinder, shift the transmission into sixth gear and have an assistant apply the rear brake.*

4. Remove the spark plug from the No. 1 cylinder.

5. Thread the tester's 10 mm adapter into the No. 1 cylinder spark plug hole following the manufacturer's instructions. Connect the leakdown tester onto the adapter. Connect an air compressor hose onto the tester's fitting.

6. If the engine is not too hot, remove the radiator cap.

7. Apply compressed air to the leakdown tester and perform a cylinder leakdown test following the manufacturer's instructions. Read the rate of leakage on the gauge. Note the following:

   a. For a new or rebuilt engine, a pressure loss of 0 to 5 percent per cylinder is desirable. 6 to 14 percent is acceptable and means the engine is in good condition.

   b. Note the difference between the cylinders. On a used engine, a difference of 10 percent or less between cylinders is satisfactory. A pressure loss exceeding 10 percent between cylinders points to an engine that is in very poor condition and requires further inspection and possible engine repair.

8. With air pressure still applied to the combustion chamber, listen for air escaping from the following areas:

   a. Air leaking through the exhaust pipe indicates a leaking exhaust valve.

   b. Air leaking through the throttle bodies indicates a leaking intake valve.

   c. Air leaking through the crankcase breather suggests worn piston rings or a worn cylinder bore.

   d. Bubbles in the cooling system indicate a blown head gasket.

9. Remove the leakdown tester and repeat these steps for each cylinder.

## CLUTCH

Clutch service is covered in Chapter Six.

### Rough Clutch Operation

Check for worn, grooved or damaged clutch hub and clutch housing slots.

### Clutch Slip

If the engine speed increases without a related increase in motorcycle speed, the clutch is probably slipping. Inspect for the following:

1. Weak clutch springs.
2. Worn plates or friction discs.

3. Damaged pressure plate.
4. Clutch contaminated by engine oil additive.

### Clutch Drag

If the clutch does not disengage, or if the motorcycle creeps with the transmission in gear and the clutch disengaged, the clutch is dragging. Check for:

1. Warped plain plates.
2. Damaged clutch lifter assembly.
3. Engine oil additive being used.
4. Damaged pressure plate, clutch hub splines or clutch housing slots.

## GEARSHIFT LINKAGE

The gearshift linkage assembly connects the shift pedal to the shift drum (internal shift mechanism). The external shift mechanism can be examined after the shift mechanism cover has been removed. The internal shift mechanism can only be accessed by splitting the crankcase.

### Transmission Jumps Out of Gear

1. Loose stopper lever mounting bolt.
2. Damaged stopper lever.
3. Weak or damaged stopper lever spring.
4. Incorrect shift pedal position.
5. Bent or worn shift fork(s).
6. Bent shift fork shaft.
7. Gear groove worn.
8. Damaged stopper bolt.
9. Worn gear dogs or slots.
10. Damaged shift drum grooves.
11. Weak or damaged gearshift linkage springs.
12. Worn shift cam.

### Difficult Shifting

1. Improperly assembled clutch.
2. Incorrect engine oil viscosity.
3. Loose or damaged stopper lever assembly.
4. Bent shift fork shaft(s).
5. Bent or damaged shift fork(s).
6. Worn gear dogs or slots.
7. Damaged shift drum grooves.
8. Weak or damaged gearshift linkage springs.
9. Worn or broken shift cam.

### Shift Pedal Does Not Return

1. Bent shift shaft.

2. Weak or damaged shift shaft return spring.
3. Shift shaft incorrectly installed.
4. Improper shift pedal linkage adjustment.
5. Bent shift fork shaft.
6. Damaged shift fork.
7. Seized transmission gear.
8. Improperly assembled transmission.

## TRANSMISSION

Transmission symptoms are sometimes difficult to distinguish from clutch symptoms. Before working on the transmission, make sure the clutch and gearshift linkage assemblies are working properly. Refer to Chapter Seven for transmission service procedures.

### Jumps Out of Gear

1. Improperly adjusted shift pedal position.
2. Loose or damaged shift drum stopper lever.
3. Bent or damaged shift fork(s).
4. Bent shift fork shaft(s).
5. Damaged shift drum grooves.
6. Worn shift cam.
7. Worn gear dogs or slots.
8. Worn sliding gear on mainshaft or countershaft.

### Incorrect Shift Lever Operation

1. Bent shift pedal or linkage.
2. Stripped shift lever splines.
3. Damaged shift lever linkage.
4. Improperly adjusted shift pedal.

### Excessive Gear Noise

1. Worn bearings.
2. Worn or damaged gears.
3. Excessive gear backlash.

## FUEL SYSTEM

### Engine Does Not Start

If the engine does not start and the electrical and mechanical systems are operating correctly, check the following:
1. Air leak at the intake manifold, air filter or throttle body assembly.
2. Contaminated or old fuel.
3. Clogged fuel line.
4. Clogged fuel injector filter.

5. Sticking or damaged fuel injector needle.
6. Damaged fuel pump.
7. Faulty fuel pump system.

### Poor Fuel Mileage and Engine Performance

1. Infrequent tune-ups. Compare the service records with the recommended service intervals in Chapter Three.
2. Clogged air filter.
3. Clogged fuel system.
4. Damaged pressure regulator.
5. Faulty fuel pump.
6. Faulty sensor.

### Engine Backfires or Misfires During Acceleration

1. Lean/rich fuel mixture.
2. Incorrect throttle body adjustment.
3. Ignition system malfunction.
4. Faulty vacuum hoses.
5. Vacuum leaks at the throttle body and/or intake manifold(s).
6. Fouled spark plug(s).

## FUEL PUMP

When troubleshooting the fuel pump, first perform the fuel pump operation test described in Chapter Eight. If the fuel pump is operational, the problem is in the fuel pump system circuit. Troubleshoot the circuit by following the fuel-pump-circuit troubleshooting procedures listed below. Refer to the wiring diagram at the end of this manual.

### Fuel Pump Circuit Troubleshooting

Perform these test procedures in sequence. Each test presumes that the components tested in the earlier steps are working properly. The tests can yield invalid results if they are performed out of sequence. If a test indicates that a component is working properly, reconnect the electrical connections and proceed to the next step.
1. Inspect the main, fuel and ignition fuses as described Chapter Nine.
2. Check the battery (Chapter Nine).
3. Check the continuity of the main switch (Chapter Nine).
4. Check the continuity of the engine stop switch (Chapter Nine).
5. Perform the fuel pump relay test (Chapter Eight).

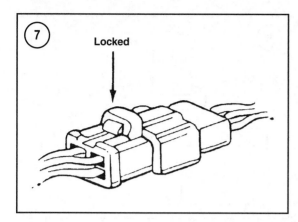

⑦    **Locked**

6. Check the tip over sensor as described in Chapter Eight.

7. Perform the fuel pump operation test (Chapter Eight).

8. Perform the fuel pump discharge test (Chapter Eight).

9. Perform the fuel pressure test (Chapter Eight).

10. Check the wiring and connectors in the circuit.

## ELECTRICAL TESTING

This section describes basic electrical testing. Refer to *Electrical Systems* in this chapter for specific system testing and Chapter Nine for specific component testing.

Electrical troubleshooting can be very time-consuming and frustrating without proper knowledge and a suitable plan. Refer to the color wiring diagrams at the end of the manual for component and connector identification. Use the wiring diagrams to determine how the circuit should work by tracing the current paths from the power source through the circuit components to ground. Also, check any circuits that share the same fuse, ground or switch. If the other circuits work properly and the shared wiring is good, the cause must be in the wiring used only by the suspect circuit. If all related circuits are faulty at the same time, the probable cause is a poor ground connection or a blown fuse(s).

As with all troubleshooting procedures, analyze typical symptoms in a systematic manner. Never assume anything and do not overlook the obvious like a blown fuse or an electrical connector that has separated. Test the simplest and most obvious items first and try to make tests at easily accessible points on the bike.

### Preliminary Checks and Precautions

Start electrical troubleshooting by performing the following:

1. Check the main fuse (Chapter Nine). If the fuse is blown, replace it.

2. The various circuit fuses are mounted in the fuse box (Chapter Nine). Inspect the fuse protecting the suspect circuit, and replace the fuse as necessary.

3. Inspect the battery (Chapter Nine). Make sure it is fully charged. Make sure the battery cables are clean and securely attached to the battery terminals.

4. Disconnect each electrical connector in the suspect circuit, and examine the terminals. They must be straight. A bent terminal will not connect to its mate, causing an open circuit.

5. Make sure the terminals are pushed all the way into the connector. If not, carefully push them in with a narrow blade screwdriver.

6. Check the wires where they join with the terminals.

7. Make sure all electrical terminals within the housing are clean and free of corrosion. Clean them, if necessary, and pack the connectors with dielectric grease.

8. Push the connector halves together. Make sure the halves are fully engaged and locked together (**Figure 7**).

9. Never pull the electrical wires when disconnecting an electrical connector. Only pull the connector housing.

10. Never use a self-powered test light on circuits that contain solid-state devices. The solid-state device may be damaged.

### Back Probing a Connector

Some tests, such as voltage or peak voltage tests, require back probing a connector. In these instances, insert a small wire, or a back probe pin, into the connector at the indicated terminal. Connect the multimeter test probe to the back probe pin. The pin must not exceed 0.5 mm (0.02 in.) in diameter.

Make sure the back probe pin contacts the metal part of the terminal. Exercise caution so the pin does not deform either the male or female terminals in the connector.

### Electrical Component Replacement

Most motorcycle dealerships and parts suppliers do not accept the return of any electrical part. If the exact cause of an electrical system malfunction cannot be determined, have a dealership retest the specific system to verify the test results. If a new component does not resolve the problem, in all likelihood, it cannot be returned for a refund.

Consider any test results carefully before replacing a component that tests only slightly out of specification, especially resistance. A number of variables can affect test results dramatically. These include the test meter's internal circuitry, ambient temperature and the conditions under which the machine has been operated. All instructions and specifications have been checked for accuracy. However, successful test results depend to a great degree upon individual accuracy.

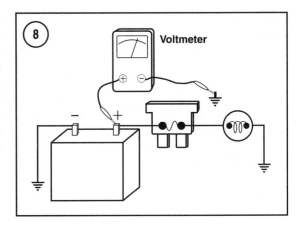

## Test Light or Voltmeter

Construct a test light from a 12-volt light bulb with a pair of test leads carefully soldered to the bulb. To check for battery voltage in a circuit, attach one lead to ground and the other lead to various points along the circuit. The bulb lights when voltage is present.

A voltmeter is used in the same manner as the test light to find out if battery voltage is present in any given circuit. The voltmeter, unlike the test light, also indicates how much voltage is present at each test point. When using a voltmeter, attach the positive test lead to the component or wire to be checked and the negative test lead to a good ground (**Figure 8**).

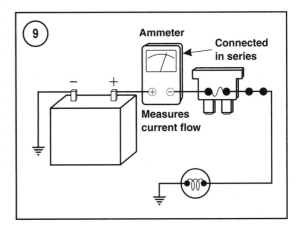

## Ammeter

Use an ammeter to measure the flow of current (amps) in a circuit. When connected in series in a circuit (**Figure 9**), the ammeter determines if current is flowing through the circuit and if that current flow is excessive because of a short in the circuit. Current flow is often referred to as current draw. Comparing actual current draw in the circuit or component to the current draw specifications (if specified by the manufacturer) provides useful diagnostic information.

## Self-Powered Test Light

A self-powered test light can be constructed from a 12-volt light bulb, a pair of test leads and a 12-volt battery. When the test leads are touched together the light bulb should go on.

Use a self-powered test light as follows:
1. Touch the test leads together to make sure the light bulb turns on. If not, correct the problem before using the test light in a test procedure.
2. Disconnect the motorcycle's battery or remove the fuse(s) that protects the circuit to be tested.
3. Select two points within the circuit where there should be continuity.
4. Attach one lead of the self-powered test light to each test point.

5. If there is continuity, the self-powered test light bulb turns on.
6. If there is no continuity, the self-powered test light bulb does not come on, indicating an open circuit.

## Ohmmeter

*CAUTION*
*Never connect an ohmmeter to a circuit that has power applied to it. Always disconnect the battery negative lead before using an ohmmeter.*

Use an ohmmeter to measure the resistance (in ohms) to current flow in a circuit or component.

Ohmmeters may be analog (needle scale) or digital (LCD or LED readout). Both types of ohmmeters have a switch that selects different resistance ranges for accurate readings. The analog ohmmeter also has a set-adjust control, which is used to zero or calibrate the meter (digital ohmmeters do not require calibration). Refer to the manufacturer's instructions to determine the correct scale setting. If the specification has a *K* after it, multiply it by 1000.

An ohmmeter is used by connecting its test leads to the terminals or leads of the item to be tested (**Fig-**

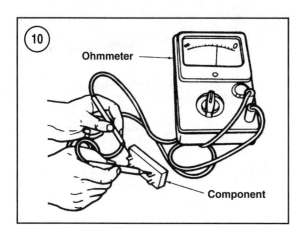

**Ohmmeter**

**Component**

2. Install insulated boots over alligator clips. This prevents accidental grounding, sparks or possible shock when working in cramped quarters.

3. Jumper wires are temporary test measures only. Do not leave a jumper wire installed as a permanent solution. This creates a hazard that could damage the wiring harness.

4. When using a jumper wire always install an inline fuse/fuse holder (available at most auto supply stores or electronic supply stores) to the jumper wire.

5. Never use a jumper wire across any load (a component that is connected and turned on). This would cause a direct short and blow the fuse(s).

ure 10). If an analog meter is used, it must be calibrated by touching the test leads together and turning the set-adjust knob until the meter needle reads zero. When the leads are uncrossed, the needle should move to the other end of the scale indicating infinite resistance.

During a continuity test, a reading of infinity indicates there is an open in the circuit or component. A reading of zero indicates continuity, which means there is no measurable resistance in the circuit or component being tested.

## Jumper Wire

Use a jumper wire to bypass a potential problem and isolate it to a particular point in a circuit. If a faulty circuit works properly with a jumper wire installed, an open exists between the two jumped points in the circuit.

To troubleshoot with a jumper wire, first use the wire to determine if the problem is on the ground side or the load side of a device. Test the ground by connecting a jumper between the lamp and a good ground. If the lamp comes on, the problem is the connection between the lamp and ground. If the lamp does not come on with the jumper installed, the lamp's connection to ground is good so the problem is between the lamp and the power source.

To isolate the problem, connect the jumper between the battery and the lamp. If it comes on, the problem is between these two points. Next, connect the jumper between the battery and the fuse side of the switch. If the lamp comes on, the switch is good. By successively moving the jumper from one point to another, the problem can be isolated to a particular place in the circuit.

Note the following when using a jumper wire:

1. Make sure the jumper wire gauge (thickness) is the same as that used in the circuit being tested. A smaller gauge wire could overheat and melt.

## Voltage Test

Unless otherwise specified, all voltage tests are made with the electrical connectors still connected. Insert 0.5 mm (0.02 in.) back probe pins (test leads) into the backside of the connector. Make sure the back probe pin touches the electrical wire or metal terminal within the connector housing. Touching the wire insulation yields a false reading.

Always check both sides of a connector because one side may be loose or corroded thus preventing electrical flow through the connector. This type of test can be performed with a test light or a voltmeter.

1. Attach the voltmeter negative test lead to a good ground. If possible, use the battery ground connection. Make sure the part is not insulated with a rubber gasket or rubber grommet.

2. Attach the voltmeter positive test lead to the point being tested (**Figure 8**).

3. Turn the ignition switch on. If using a test light, the test light comes on if voltage is present. If using a voltmeter, note the voltage reading. The reading should be within one volt of battery voltage. If the voltage is less, a problem exists in the circuit.

## Voltage Drop Test

The wires, cables, connectors and switches in the electrical circuit are designed to carry current with low resistance. This ensures current can flow through the circuit with a minimum loss of voltage. Voltage drop indicates where there is resistance in a circuit. A higher-than-normal amount of resistance in a circuit decreases the flow of current and causes the voltage to drop between the source and destination in the circuit.

Because resistance causes voltage to drop, a voltmeter is used to measure voltage drop when current is running through the circuit. If the circuit has no resistance, there is no voltage drop so the voltmeter indicates 0 volts. The greater the resistance in a circuit, the greater the voltage drop reading.

To perform a voltage drop:

1. Connect the positive meter test lead to the electrical source (where electricity is coming from).

2. Connect the voltmeter negative test lead to the electrical load (where the electricity is going). Refer to **Figure 11**.

3. If necessary, activate the component(s) in the circuit.

4. Read the voltage drop (difference in voltage between the source and destination) on the voltmeter. Note the following:

   a. The voltmeter should indicate 0 volts. If there is a drop of 1 volt or more, there is a problem within the circuit. A voltage drop reading of 12 volts indicates an open in the circuit.

   b. A voltage drop of 1 or more volts indicates that a circuit has excessive resistance.

   c. For example, consider a starting problem where the battery is fully charged but the starter turns over slowly. Voltage drop would be the difference in the voltage at the battery (source) and the voltage at the starter (destination) as the engine is being started (current is flowing through the battery cables). A corroded battery cable would cause a high voltage drop (high resistance) and slow engine cranking.

   d. Common sources of voltage drop are loose or contaminated connectors and poor ground connections.

## Peak Voltage Test

A peak voltage test checks the voltage output of a component at normal cranking speed. This test accurately measures a component's output voltage under operating conditions.

All peak voltage specifications are minimum values. If the measured voltage meets or exceeds this specification, the test results are satisfactory. In some instances, the measured voltage may greatly exceed the minimum specification.

The multicircuit tester (Suzuki part No. 09900-25008) with the peak voltage adapter, or an equivalent multimeter and peak voltage adapter, are needed to perform a peak voltage test. Refer to the manufacturer's instructions when using these tools.

## Continuity Test

A continuity test is used to determine the integrity of a circuit, wire or component. A circuit has continuity if it forms a complete circuit; that is if there are no opens in either the electrical wires or components

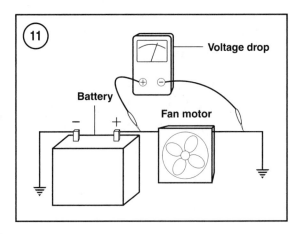

within the circuit. An open circuit, on the other hand, has no continuity.

A continuity test can be performed with a self-powered test light or an ohmmeter.

1. Disconnect the negative battery cable.

2. Attach one test lead to one end of the part of the circuit to be tested.

3. Attach the other test lead to the other end of the part or the circuit to be tested.

4. The self-powered test light comes on if there is continuity. An ohmmeter reads zero or very low resistance if there is continuity. A reading of infinite resistance indicates no continuity; the circuit is open.

## Testing for a Short with a Self-Powered Test Light or Ohmmeter

1. Disconnect the negative battery cable.

2. Remove the blown fuse from the fuse panel.

3. Connect one test lead of the test light or ohmmeter to the load side (battery side) of the fuse terminal in the fuse panel.

4. Connect the other test lead to a good ground. Make sure the part is not insulated.

5. With the self-powered test light or ohmmeter attached to the fuse terminal and ground, wiggle the wiring harness of the suspect circuit at 15.2 cm (6 in.) increments. Start next to the fuse panel and work away from the fuse panel.

6. Watch the self-powered test light or ohmmeter and progress along the harness. If the test light blinks or the ohmmeter needle moves when the harness is wiggled, there is a short-to-ground at that point in the harness.

## Testing For a Short with a Test Light or Voltmeter

1. Remove the blown fuse from the fuse panel.

2. Connect the test light or voltmeter across the fuse terminals in the fuse panel. Turn the ignition switch on and check for battery voltage.

3. With the test light or voltmeter attached to the fuse terminals, wiggle the wiring harness of the suspect circuit at 15.2 cm (6 in.) intervals. Start next to the fuse panel and work away from the panel.

4. Watch the test light or voltmeter while moving along the harness. If the test light blinks or if the needle on the voltmeter moves when the harness is wiggled, there is a short-to-ground at that point in the harness.

## ELECTRICAL SYSTEMS

When troubleshooting an electrical problem, locate the procedures for the affected system. Start with the first inspection in the list, and perform the indicated check(s). If a test indicates that a component is working properly, reconnect the electrical connections and proceed to the next step. Systematically work through the procedure until the source of the problem is identified. Repair or replace faulty parts as described in the appropriate chapter.

### Charging System

A malfunction in the charging system generally causes the battery to remain undercharged.

1. Check the connections at the battery. If polarity is reversed, check for a damaged regulator/rectifier.

2. Check for loose or corroded battery cable connectors.

3. Check battery condition. Clean and recharge as required.

4. Perform the *Current Draw Test* (Chapter Nine).
   a. If current draw is excessive, check for a short in the wiring harness, loose or dirty connectors or a faulty battery.
   b. If current draw is within specification, proceed to Step 5.

5. Perform the *Regulated Voltage Test* (Chapter Nine).
   a. If voltage is within specification, the battery is faulty.
   b. If voltage is out of specification, proceed Step 6.

6. Perform the *Stator Assembly Resistance Test* (Chapter Nine).
   a. If stator resistance is out of specification, replace the stator.
   b. If resistance is within specification, proceed to Step 7.

7. Perform the *No-load Voltage Test* (Chapter Nine).

a. If the voltage is out of specification, the alternator is faulty. Replace the stator and retest. If the problem persists, the rotor is faulty.
   b. If voltage is within specification, proceed to Step 8.

8. Perform the *Voltage Regulator/Rectifier Voltage Test* (Chapter Nine).
   a. If test result is out of specification, replace the regulator/rectifier.
   b. If the test readings are within specification, proceed to Step 9.

9. Inspect the charging system wiring for a short or for corroded connectors.
   a. Repair the wiring or connector.
   b. If the wiring is good, replace the battery.

### Ignition System

Refer to *Diagnostic System* in Chapter Eight.

### Starting System

1. Check the main fuse.

2. Check the battery as described in Chapter Three.

3. With the transmission in neutral and engine stop switch in the run position, disengage the clutch and turn the ignition switch on. Listen for the operation of the starter relay. The relay should click.
   a. If the relay clicks, perform Step 4.
   b. If a click is not heard, perform Step 5.

4. Perform the starter operational test (Chapter Nine).
   a. If the starter does not run, replace it.
   b. If the starter runs, check the starter lead for a loose or corroded connection. If the starter lead is in good condition, perform Step 5.

5. Perform the starter relay input voltage test (Chapter Nine).
   a. If the relay has battery voltage, perform Step 6.
   b. If it does not have battery voltage, perform Step 7.

6. Perform the starter relay operational test (Chapter Nine).
   a. If the relay tests within specification, check for poor contacts at the starter relay.
   b. If the relay is out of specification, replace the relay.

7. Check the continuity of the ignition switch (Chapter Nine).

8. Check the continuity of the engine stop switch (Chapter Nine).

9. Check the continuity of the clutch switch (Chapter Nine).

10. Check the continuity of the starter button (Chapter Nine).

11. Perform the sidestand switch diode test (Chapter Nine).

12. Check the gear position sensor by performing the gear position sensor voltage test and the gear position sensor continuity test (Chapter Nine).

13. Perform the sidestand relay test and the diode test (Chapter Nine).

14. Check the wiring and each connector in the starting circuit.

## STEERING AND SUSPENSION

### Steering is Sluggish

1. Incorrect steering stem adjustment (too tight).
2. Improperly installed upper or lower fork bridge.
3. Damaged steering head bearings.
4. Incorrect tire pressure.
5. Worn or damaged tire.

### Wobbly Handlebars

1. Uneven front fork adjustment.
2. Bent or damaged front fork.
3. Bend or damaged front axle or front wheel.
4. Loose steering stem nut.
5. Incorrect fork oil viscosity.

### Motorcycle Steers to One Side

1. Bent front or rear axle.
2. Bent frame or fork(s).
3. Worn or damaged wheel bearings.
4. Worn or damaged swing arm pivot bearings.
5. Damaged steering head bearings.
6. Bent swing arm.
7. Incorrectly installed wheels.
8. Front and rear wheels are not aligned.
9. Uneven front fork adjustment.
10. Front fork legs positioned unevenly in the fork bridges.
11. Incorrect drive chain adjustment.

### Suspension Noise

1. Loose mounting fasteners.
2. Damaged fork(s) or rear shock absorber.
3. Incorrect fork oil level.
4. Loose or damaged fairing mounts.

### Wheel Wobble/Vibration

1. Loose wheel axle.
2. Loose or damaged wheel bearing(s).
3. Damaged wheel rim(s).
4. Damaged tire(s).
5. Unbalanced tire and wheel assembly.
6. Loose swing arm pivot bolt.
7. Worn swing arm bearings.
8. Incorrect fork oil level.
9. Loose fasteners.

### Hard Suspension
### (Front Fork)

1. Incorrectly adjusted fork.
2. Incorrect front tire pressure.
3. Bent fork tubes.
4. Binding slider.
5. Incorrect fork oil viscosity.
6. Incorrect fork oil level.
7. Plugged fork oil passage.
8. Worn or damaged fork tube bushing or slider bushing.
9. Damaged damper rod.
10. Bent front axle.

### Hard Suspension
### (Rear Shock Absorber)

1. Incorrect excessive rear tire pressure.
2. Bent or damaged shock absorber.
3. Incorrect shock adjustment.
4. Worn swing arm pivot bearings.
5. Worn suspension linkage bearings.
6. Damaged suspension linkage component.
7. Poorly lubricated suspension components.

### Soft Suspension
### (Front Fork)

1. Incorrectly adjusted fork.
2. Incorrect front tire pressure.
3. Incorrect fork oil level.
4. Incorrect fork oil viscosity.
5. Weak or damaged fork springs.

### Soft Suspension
### (Rear Shock Absorber)

1. Incorrectly adjusted rear shock.
2. Incorrect rear tire pressure.
3. Weak or damaged shock absorber spring.
4. Damaged shock absorber.

5. Leaking damper unit.

## BRAKE SYSTEM

The brake system is critical to riding performance and safety. Inspect the front and rear brakes frequently. Repair any problem immediately. When adding or changing the brake fluid, use only DOT 4 brake fluid from a sealed container. Refer to Chapter Fourteen for additional information on brake fluid selection and brake service.

### Brake Drag

Brake drag occurs when the brake pads cannot move away from the brake disc once the brake lever or pedal is released. Any of the following can cause brake drag:
1. Warped or damaged brake disc(s).
2. Sticking or damaged brake caliper pistons.
3. Contaminated brake pads and disc(s).
4. Plugged master cylinder port.
5. Contaminated brake fluid and hydraulic passages.
6. Restricted brake hose joint.
7. Loose brake disc mounting bolts.
8. Damaged wheel(s).
9. Incorrect wheel alignment.
10. Incorrectly installed brake caliper.
11. Poorly lubricated brake-lever or brake-pedal.

### Brake Grab

1. Damaged brake pad pin. Look for steps or cracks along the pad pin surface.
2. Contaminated brake pads and disc(s).
3. Incorrect wheel alignment.
4. Warped or damaged brake disc(s).
5. Loose brake disc mounting bolts.
6. Mismatched brake pads.
7. Damaged wheel bearings.

### Brake Squeal or Chatter

1. Contaminated brake pads and disc(s).

2. Incorrectly installed brake caliper.
3. Warped brake disc(s).
4. Loose wheel axle.
5. Mismatched brake pads.
6. Incorrectly installed brake pads.
7. Contaminated brake fluid.
8. Clogged master cylinder return port.

### Soft or Spongy Brake Lever or Pedal

If the fluid level in the reservoir drops too low, air can enter the hydraulic system through the master cylinder. Air can also enter the system from loose or damaged hose fittings. If air has entered the hydraulic system, flush the brake system and bleed the brakes as described in Chapter Fourteen.
1. Air in brake hydraulic system.
2. Low brake fluid level.
3. Leaking brake hydraulic system.
4. Clogged brake hydraulic system.
5. Worn brake caliper seals.
6. Worn master cylinder seals.
7. Sticking caliper piston.
8. Sticking master cylinder piston.
9. Damaged front brake lever.
10. Damaged rear brake pedal.
11. Contaminated brake pads and disc(s).
12. Excessively worn brake disc(s) or pad(s).
13. Warped or damaged brake disc(s).

### Hard Brake Lever or Pedal Operation

1. Clogged brake hydraulic system.
2. Sticking caliper piston.
3. Sticking master cylinder piston.
4. Glazed or worn brake pads.
5. Mismatched brake pads.
6. Damaged front brake lever.
7. Damaged rear brake pedal.
8. Brake caliper not sliding correctly.
9. Worn or damaged brake caliper seals.

# CHAPTER THREE

# LUBRICATION, MAINTENANCE AND TUNE-UP

This chapter describes the lubrication, maintenance and tune-up procedures.

Refer to *Safety* in Chapter One before performing the procedures in this chapter. Refer to **Table 1** for service intervals. Refer to **Tables 2-5** for specifications.

## CYLINDER NUMBERING AND FIRING ORDER

The cylinders are numbered one through four from left to right. The No. 1 cylinder sits on the left side (alternator side). The No. 4 cylinder is on the right side (starter clutch side). Refer to **Figure 1**. Left and right refer to a rider's point of view while sitting on the seat facing forward.

The cylinder firing order is 1-2-4-3.

Normal engine rotation is *clockwise* when viewed from the right side of the engine (starter clutch side). Use the starter clutch bolt to rotate the crankshaft. Always turn the crankshaft clockwise.

## MAINTENANCE INTERVALS

Refer to **Table 1** for the recommended maintenance and service intervals. Adherence to these rec-

ommendations helps ensure a long life for the motorcycle. If the motorcycle is operated in extreme conditions, perform the services more frequently.

Most of the procedures are described in this chapter. Those procedures that require more than minor disassembly or adjustment are covered in the appropriate chapter in the manual. Refer to the Table of Contents or the Index to locate a particular procedure.

## TUNE-UP

Inspect the following items and perform the service as described in this chapter:

1. Air filter.
2. Spark plugs.
3. Valve clearance.
4. Compression test.
5. Throttle valve synchronization.
6. Engine oil and filter.
7. Brake system.
8. Suspension components.
9. Tires and wheels.
10. Drive chain.
11. Fasteners.

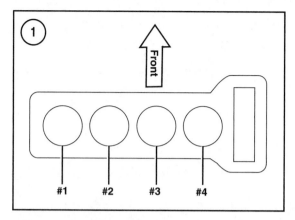

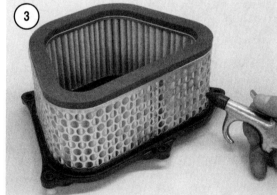

## AIR FILTER REPLACEMENT

Remove, clean and inspect the air filter element at the interval specified in **Table 1**. Replace the air filter if it is soiled, severely clogged or broken in any area.

1. Raise and support the fuel tank as described in Chapter Eight.

2. Remove the air filter screws (**Figure 2**), and lift the filter from the air filter housing.

3. Place a clean shop cloth over the housing opening to keep debris out of the engine.

4. Gently tap the air filter to loosen the trapped dirt and dust.

> *CAUTION*
> *In the next step, do not apply compressed air toward the inside of the filter. Air directed at this side forces the dirt and dust into the pores of the element thus restricting air flow.*

5. Apply compressed air to the *outside* (**Figure 3**) of the air filter element, and remove all loosened dirt and dust.

6. Thoroughly and carefully inspect the filter element. If it is torn or broken in any area, replace the air filter. Do not run the motorcycle with a damaged air filter element. It may admit dirt into the engine. If the element is in good condition, it can be used until the indicated replacement time.

7. Remove the drain plug (**Figure 4**) from the rear of the housing, and drain away any accumulated moisture. Wipe out the interior of the air filter housing (**Figure 5**) with a shop rag dampened in cleaning solvent. Remove any debris that may have passed through a broken filter element.

8. Installation is the reverse of removal. Make sure the air filter components are properly installed and that the housing is sealed.

## COMPRESSION TEST

The compression gauge set (Suzuki part No. 09915-64510) and adapter (part No. 09913-10750), or equivalent tools (**Figure 6**), are needed to perform this test.

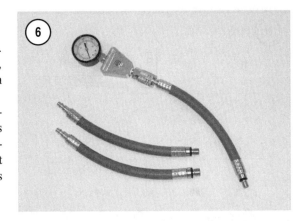

An engine compression test is a quick way to evaluate the condition of the rings, head gasket, pistons and cylinders. Always record the compression readings taken during each tune-up. Compare the current reading with those taken during earlier tests. This helps identify any developing problems.

1. Before starting this test, confirm that:
    a. The cylinder head bolts are tightened to specification (Chapter Four).
    b. The valves are properly adjusted as described in this chapter.
    c. The battery is fully charged to ensure proper cranking speed.

2. Warm the engine to normal operating temperature, and turn the engine off.

3. Raise and support the fuel tank (Chapter Eight).

4. Remove the spark plugs as described in this chapter.

> *WARNING*
> *Step 5 must be performed to disable the fuel system. Otherwise, fuel enters the cylinders when the engine is turned over during the compression test, flooding the cylinders and creating explosive fuel vapors.*

5. Disconnect the 2-pin fuel pump connector (1999 and 2000 models: **Figure 7**; 4-pin, 2001-on models: **Figure 8**).

6. Turn the compression gauge into one cylinder following the manufacturer's instructions. Make sure the gauge is properly seated in the spark plug hole.

7. Check that the engine stop switch is in the run position, turn the ignition switch on and open the throttle completely. Use the starter button to crank the engine until there is no further rise in pressure. Maximum pressure is usually reached within a few seconds of engine cranking. Record the reading and cylinder number.

8. Repeat Step 6 and Step 7 for the remaining cylinders.

9. Standard compression pressure is specified in **Table 4**. When interpreting the results, note any difference between the cylinders. Large differences indicate worn or broken rings, leaky or sticky valves, blown head gasket or a combination of these items.
    a. If a cylinder's reading is less than the service limit, it indicates valve or ring trouble. To determine which, pour about a teaspoon of engine

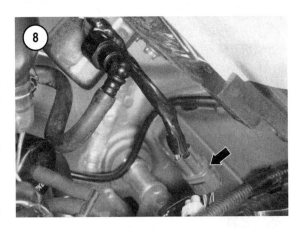

oil through the spark plug hole onto the piston crown. Perform another compression test and record the reading. If the compression returns to normal, the rings are worn or defective. If compression does not increase, the valves are leaking.

b. If the difference between cylinder compression readings is less than the specified maximum allowable, the rings and valves are in good condition.

c. If a compression reading exceeds the standard pressure specification, check for excessive car-

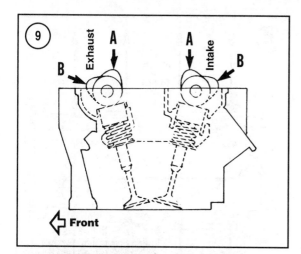

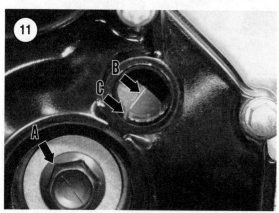

bon deposits in the cylinder head, or on the piston crown and valves.

10. Connect the fuel pump connector.

11. Install the spark plugs as described in this chapter.

12. Install the fuel tank as described in Chapter Eight.

## IGNITION TIMING

The ignition timing is not adjustable.

## VALVE CLEARANCE

### Measurement

Perform the valve clearance measurement and adjustment with the engine cold (below 35° C [95° F]).

Refer to **Table 4** for specifications.

In this procedure, the engine is shown removed from the frame for clarity. Valve clearance can be checked with the engine in the frame.

> *CAUTION*
> *For this procedure, the camshaft lobes must point away from the tappets as shown in either position A or B, **Figure 9**. Clearance measurements taken with the lobes in any other position give false readings leading to incorrect valve clearance adjustment and possible engine damage.*

1. Remove both fairing side panels (Chapter Fifteen).

2. Remove the cylinder head cover (Chapter Four).

3. Remove all four spark plugs (this chapter) so the engine can easily be turned by hand.

4. Remove the timing inspection cap (A, **Figure 10**) and the starter clutch bolt cap (B) from the starter clutch cover.

> *NOTE*
> *In Step 5, both the index line on the starter clutch and the camshaft notches on the left side must be correctly aligned and positioned. Several complete engine revolutions may be necessary to achieve this correct alignment.*

> *NOTE*
> *If the engine is mounted in the frame, use a mirror to see the camshaft notches on the left side.*

5. Correctly position the camshafts as follows:

  a. Use the starter clutch bolt (A, **Figure 11**) to rotate the engine *clockwise*, as viewed from the right side, until the index line (B) on the starter clutch aligns with the index mark (C) of the timing inspection window.

  b. At the same time, this brings the camshaft notches, on the left side of each camshaft, to the positions shown in **Figure 12**. If the camshaft notches are not positioned as shown, rotate the engine clockwise 360° (one full revolution) until the camshaft notches are positioned correctly.

  c. If it was necessary to rotate the engine an additional revolution, recheck that the index line

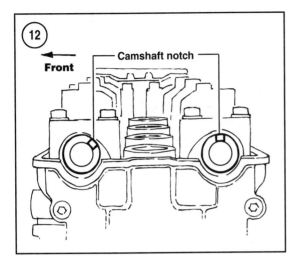

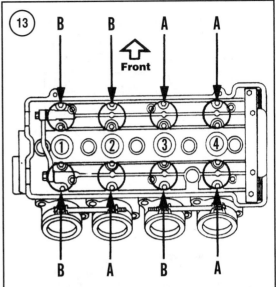

(B, **Figure 11**) on the starter clutch once again aligns with the index mark (C) on the timing inspection window. Realign this mark if necessary.

6. With the engine in this position, check the valve clearance on the indicated valves (A, **Figure 13**).

    a. No. 2 cylinder: Intake valves.

    b. No. 3 cylinder: Exhaust valves.

    c. No. 4 cylinder: Intake and exhaust valves.

7. Check the clearance by inserting a flat metric feeler gauge (**Figure 14**) between the lifter and the camshaft lobe. Repeat this process until a slight resistance is felt on the feeler gauge when it is inserted and withdrawn, indicating the clearance is correct. Record the clearance for each valve. Identify each valve by its cylinder number and by intake or exhaust valve.

8. To measure the remaining valves, perform the following:

    a. Use the starter clutch mounting bolt (A, **Figure 11**) and rotate the engine 360° (one full revolution) *clockwise*, when viewed from the right side. Rotate the engine until the index line on the starter clutch (B, **Figure 11**) once again aligns with the index mark (C) on the timing inspection window.

    b. At the same time, this brings the camshaft notches to the position shown in **Figure 15**.

9. With the engine in this position, repeat the procedure described in Step 7 to check the valve clearance on the indicated valves. Refer to B, **Figure 13**:

    a. No. 1 cylinder: Intake and exhaust valves.

    b. No. 2 cylinder: Exhaust valves.

    c. No. 3 cylinder: Intake valves.

10. If any valve is out of specification, adjust the clearance as described in this chapter.

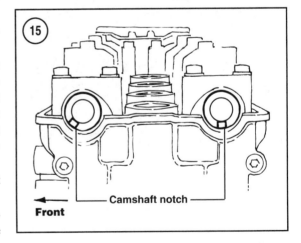

### Adjustment

To adjust the valve clearance, the shim located under the lifter must be replaced with a shim of a different thickness. The camshaft(s) must be removed to

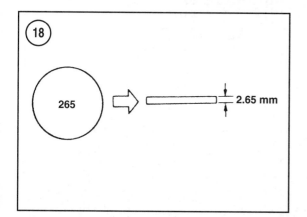

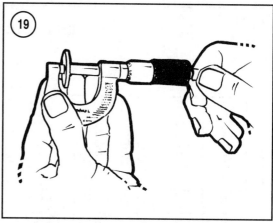

4. Use needlenose pliers or tweezers to remove the shim (**Figure 17**) from the top of the valve spring retainer.

5. Check the number on the shim. This number indicates the shim thickness (**Figure 18**). If the number is no longer legible, measure the shim with a micrometer (**Figure 19**).

6. Use the number on the installed shim and the measured valve clearance to select the new shim by performing the following:

    a. Refer to the appropriate chart for the valve being serviced. Use the chart in **Figure 20** to select new shims for intake valves; refer to **Figure 21** for exhaust valves.

    b. The correct number for a new shim is listed at the intersection of the installed shim number column and the measured clearance row in each chart.

    c. For *example*, if the measured clearance for an intake valve is 0.23 mm and the installed shim number is 270 (2.70 mm), locate the 270 column and the 0.21-0.25 mm row on the intake valve chart (**Figure 20**). The new shim number is indicated at the intersection of the column and row. In this example, install a new No. 280 shim (2.80 mm).

    d. Replacing a 270 shim with a 280 shim increases shim thickness by 0.10 mm. This decreases the clearance from 0.23 mm to 0.13 mm, bringing it within specification.

7. Apply clean engine oil to both sides of the new shim and to the receptacle on top of the valve spring retainer. Position the shim so the side with the printed number faces up, and install the shim (**Figure 17**) into the recess in the valve spring retainer.

8. Apply clean engine oil to the lifter (**Figure 16**), and install it into the cylinder head.

9. Repeat this procedure for all valve assemblies that are out of specification.

gain access to the shims. Shims are available from a dealership in thickness increments of 0.05 mm, and range from 2.30 mm to 3.50 mm. Measure the thickness of the old shim with a micrometer to determine the exact thickness of the shim. If the shim is worn to less than the indicated thickness, use the measured thickness to select the new shim. Also measure the new shim to make sure it is marked correctly.

1. Remove the camshaft(s) as described in Chapter Four.

2. To avoid confusion adjust one valve at a time.

3. Remove the valve lifter (**Figure 16**) for the valve requiring adjustment.

**20**     **INTAKE VALVE SHIM SELECTION**

*Valve clearance specification (cold): 0.10-0.20 mm (0.004-0.008 in.)

**VALVE CLEARANCE SPECIFICATION***

| Measured clearance (mm) / Installed shim No. (Shim size mm) | 230 | 235 | 240 | 245 | 250 | 255 | 260 | 265 | 270 | 275 | 280 | 285 | 290 | 295 | 300 | 305 | 310 | 315 | 320 | 325 | 330 | 335 | 340 | 345 | 350 |
|---|---|---|---|---|---|---|---|---|---|---|---|---|---|---|---|---|---|---|---|---|---|---|---|---|---|
| 0.00-0.04 | | | 2.30 | 2.35 | 2.40 | 2.45 | 2.50 | 2.55 | 2.60 | 2.65 | 2.70 | 2.75 | 2.80 | 2.85 | 2.90 | 2.95 | 3.00 | 3.05 | 3.10 | 3.15 | 3.20 | 3.25 | 3.30 | 3.35 | 3.40 |
| 0.05-0.09 | | 2.30 | 2.35 | 2.40 | 2.45 | 2.50 | 2.55 | 2.60 | 2.65 | 2.70 | 2.75 | 2.80 | 2.85 | 2.90 | 2.95 | 3.00 | 3.05 | 3.10 | 3.15 | 3.20 | 3.25 | 3.30 | 3.35 | 3.40 | 3.45 |
| 0.10-0.20 | | | | | | | | | | | | | | | | | | | | | | | | | |
| 0.21-0.25 | 2.40 | 2.45 | 2.50 | 2.55 | 2.60 | 2.65 | 2.70 | 2.75 | 2.80 | 2.85 | 2.90 | 2.95 | 3.00 | 3.05 | 3.10 | 3.15 | 3.20 | 3.25 | 3.30 | 3.35 | 3.40 | 3.45 | 3.50 | 3.50 | |
| 0.26-0.30 | 2.45 | 2.50 | 2.55 | 2.60 | 2.65 | 2.70 | 2.75 | 2.80 | 2.85 | 2.90 | 2.95 | 3.00 | 3.05 | 3.10 | 3.15 | 3.20 | 3.25 | 3.30 | 3.35 | 3.40 | 3.45 | 3.50 | 3.50 | | |
| 0.31-0.35 | 2.50 | 2.55 | 2.60 | 2.65 | 2.70 | 2.75 | 2.80 | 2.85 | 2.90 | 2.95 | 3.00 | 3.05 | 3.10 | 3.15 | 3.20 | 3.25 | 3.30 | 3.35 | 3.40 | 3.45 | 3.50 | 3.50 | | | |
| 0.36-0.40 | 2.55 | 2.60 | 2.65 | 2.70 | 2.75 | 2.80 | 2.85 | 2.90 | 2.95 | 3.00 | 3.05 | 3.10 | 3.15 | 3.20 | 3.25 | 3.30 | 3.35 | 3.40 | 3.45 | 3.50 | 3.50 | | | | |
| 0.41-0.45 | 2.60 | 2.65 | 2.70 | 2.75 | 2.80 | 2.85 | 2.90 | 2.95 | 3.00 | 3.05 | 3.10 | 3.15 | 3.20 | 3.25 | 3.30 | 3.35 | 3.40 | 3.45 | 3.50 | 3.50 | | | | | |
| 0.46-0.50 | 2.65 | 2.70 | 2.75 | 2.80 | 2.85 | 2.90 | 2.95 | 3.00 | 3.05 | 3.10 | 3.15 | 3.20 | 3.25 | 3.30 | 3.35 | 3.40 | 3.45 | 3.50 | 3.50 | | | | | | |
| 0.51-0.55 | 2.70 | 2.75 | 2.80 | 2.85 | 2.90 | 2.95 | 3.00 | 3.05 | 3.10 | 3.15 | 3.20 | 3.25 | 3.30 | 3.35 | 3.40 | 3.45 | 3.50 | 3.50 | | | | | | | |
| 0.56-0.60 | 2.75 | 2.80 | 2.85 | 2.90 | 2.95 | 3.00 | 3.05 | 3.10 | 3.15 | 3.20 | 3.25 | 3.30 | 3.35 | 3.40 | 3.45 | 3.50 | 3.50 | | | | | | | | |
| 0.61-0.65 | 2.80 | 2.85 | 2.90 | 2.95 | 3.00 | 3.05 | 3.10 | 3.15 | 3.20 | 3.25 | 3.30 | 3.35 | 3.40 | 3.45 | 3.50 | 3.50 | | | | | | | | | |
| 0.66-0.70 | 2.85 | 2.90 | 2.95 | 3.00 | 3.05 | 3.10 | 3.15 | 3.20 | 3.25 | 3.30 | 3.35 | 3.40 | 3.45 | 3.50 | 3.50 | | | | | | | | | | |
| 0.71-0.75 | 2.90 | 2.95 | 3.00 | 3.05 | 3.10 | 3.15 | 3.20 | 3.25 | 3.30 | 3.35 | 3.40 | 3.45 | 3.50 | 3.50 | | | | | | | | | | | |
| 0.76-0.80 | 2.95 | 3.00 | 3.05 | 3.10 | 3.15 | 3.20 | 3.25 | 3.30 | 3.35 | 3.40 | 3.45 | 3.50 | 3.50 | | | | | | | | | | | | |
| 0.81-0.85 | 3.00 | 3.05 | 3.10 | 3.15 | 3.20 | 3.25 | 3.30 | 3.35 | 3.40 | 3.45 | 3.50 | 3.50 | | | | | | | | | | | | | |
| 0.86-0.90 | 3.05 | 3.10 | 3.15 | 3.20 | 3.25 | 3.30 | 3.35 | 3.40 | 3.45 | 3.50 | 3.50 | | | | | | | | | | | | | | |
| 0.91-0.95 | 3.10 | 3.15 | 3.20 | 3.25 | 3.30 | 3.35 | 3.40 | 3.45 | 3.50 | 3.50 | | | | | | | | | | | | | | | |
| 0.96-1.00 | 3.15 | 3.20 | 3.25 | 3.30 | 3.35 | 3.40 | 3.45 | 3.50 | 3.50 | | | | | | | | | | | | | | | | |
| 1.01-1.05 | 3.20 | 3.25 | 3.30 | 3.35 | 3.40 | 3.45 | 3.50 | 3.50 | | | | | | | | | | | | | | | | | |
| 1.06-1.10 | 3.25 | 3.30 | 3.35 | 3.40 | 3.45 | 3.50 | 3.50 | | | | | | | | | | | | | | | | | | |
| 1.11-1.15 | 3.30 | 3.35 | 3.40 | 3.45 | 3.50 | 3.50 | | | | | | | | | | | | | | | | | | | |
| 1.16-1.20 | 3.35 | 3.40 | 3.45 | 3.50 | 3.50 | | | | | | | | | | | | | | | | | | | | |
| 1.21-1.25 | 3.40 | 3.45 | 3.50 | 3.50 | | | | | | | | | | | | | | | | | | | | | |
| 1.26-1.30 | 3.45 | 3.50 | 3.50 | | | | | | | | | | | | | | | | | | | | | | |
| 1.31-1.35 | 3.50 | 3.50 | | | | | | | | | | | | | | | | | | | | | | | |
| 1.36-1.40 | 3.50 | | | | | | | | | | | | | | | | | | | | | | | | |

## ㉑ EXHAUST VALVE SHIM SELECTION

*Valve clearance specification (cold): 0.20–0.30 mm (0.008–0.012 in.)

VALVE CLEARANCE SPECIFICATION* (spec range 0.20–0.30 mm — no shim change required)

| Measured clearance (mm) / Installed shim No. | 230 | 235 | 240 | 245 | 250 | 255 | 260 | 265 | 270 | 275 | 280 | 285 | 290 | 295 | 300 | 305 | 310 | 315 | 320 | 325 | 330 | 335 | 340 | 345 | 350 |
|---|---|---|---|---|---|---|---|---|---|---|---|---|---|---|---|---|---|---|---|---|---|---|---|---|---|
| **Shim size (mm)** | 2.30 | 2.35 | 2.40 | 2.45 | 2.50 | 2.55 | 2.60 | 2.65 | 2.70 | 2.75 | 2.80 | 2.85 | 2.90 | 2.95 | 3.00 | 3.05 | 3.10 | 3.15 | 3.20 | 3.25 | 3.30 | 3.35 | 3.40 | 3.45 | 3.50 |
| 0.00–0.04 |  |  |  |  | 2.30 | 2.35 | 2.40 | 2.45 | 2.50 | 2.55 | 2.60 | 2.65 | 2.70 | 2.75 | 2.80 | 2.85 | 2.90 | 2.95 | 3.00 | 3.05 | 3.10 | 3.15 | 3.20 | 3.25 | 3.30 |
| 0.05–0.09 |  |  |  | 2.30 | 2.35 | 2.40 | 2.45 | 2.50 | 2.55 | 2.60 | 2.65 | 2.70 | 2.75 | 2.80 | 2.85 | 2.90 | 2.95 | 3.00 | 3.05 | 3.10 | 3.15 | 3.20 | 3.25 | 3.30 | 3.35 |
| 0.10–0.14 |  |  | 2.30 | 2.35 | 2.40 | 2.45 | 2.50 | 2.55 | 2.60 | 2.65 | 2.70 | 2.75 | 2.80 | 2.85 | 2.90 | 2.95 | 3.00 | 3.05 | 3.10 | 3.15 | 3.20 | 3.25 | 3.30 | 3.35 | 3.40 |
| 0.15–0.19 |  | 2.30 | 2.35 | 2.40 | 2.45 | 2.50 | 2.55 | 2.60 | 2.65 | 2.70 | 2.75 | 2.80 | 2.85 | 2.90 | 2.95 | 3.00 | 3.05 | 3.10 | 3.15 | 3.20 | 3.25 | 3.30 | 3.35 | 3.40 | 3.45 |
| 0.20–0.30 |  |  |  |  |  |  |  |  |  |  |  |  |  |  |  |  |  |  |  |  |  |  |  |  |  |
| 0.31–0.35 | 2.35 | 2.40 | 2.45 | 2.50 | 2.55 | 2.60 | 2.65 | 2.70 | 2.75 | 2.80 | 2.85 | 2.90 | 2.95 | 3.00 | 3.05 | 3.10 | 3.15 | 3.20 | 3.25 | 3.30 | 3.35 | 3.40 | 3.45 | 3.50 |  |
| 0.36–0.40 | 2.40 | 2.45 | 2.50 | 2.55 | 2.60 | 2.65 | 2.70 | 2.75 | 2.80 | 2.85 | 2.90 | 2.95 | 3.00 | 3.05 | 3.10 | 3.15 | 3.20 | 3.25 | 3.30 | 3.35 | 3.40 | 3.45 | 3.50 |  |  |
| 0.41–0.45 | 2.45 | 2.50 | 2.55 | 2.60 | 2.65 | 2.70 | 2.75 | 2.80 | 2.85 | 2.90 | 2.95 | 3.00 | 3.05 | 3.10 | 3.15 | 3.20 | 3.25 | 3.30 | 3.35 | 3.40 | 3.45 | 3.50 |  |  |  |
| 0.46–0.50 | 2.50 | 2.55 | 2.60 | 2.65 | 2.70 | 2.75 | 2.80 | 2.85 | 2.90 | 2.95 | 3.00 | 3.05 | 3.10 | 3.15 | 3.20 | 3.25 | 3.30 | 3.35 | 3.40 | 3.45 | 3.50 |  |  |  |  |
| 0.51–0.55 | 2.55 | 2.60 | 2.65 | 2.70 | 2.75 | 2.80 | 2.85 | 2.90 | 2.95 | 3.00 | 3.05 | 3.10 | 3.15 | 3.20 | 3.25 | 3.30 | 3.35 | 3.40 | 3.45 | 3.50 |  |  |  |  |  |
| 0.56–0.60 | 2.60 | 2.65 | 2.70 | 2.75 | 2.80 | 2.85 | 2.90 | 2.95 | 3.00 | 3.05 | 3.10 | 3.15 | 3.20 | 3.25 | 3.30 | 3.35 | 3.40 | 3.45 | 3.50 |  |  |  |  |  |  |
| 0.61–0.65 | 2.65 | 2.70 | 2.75 | 2.80 | 2.85 | 2.90 | 2.95 | 3.00 | 3.05 | 3.10 | 3.15 | 3.20 | 3.25 | 3.30 | 3.35 | 3.40 | 3.45 | 3.50 |  |  |  |  |  |  |  |
| 0.66–0.70 | 2.70 | 2.75 | 2.80 | 2.85 | 2.90 | 2.95 | 3.00 | 3.05 | 3.10 | 3.15 | 3.20 | 3.25 | 3.30 | 3.35 | 3.40 | 3.45 | 3.50 |  |  |  |  |  |  |  |  |
| 0.71–0.75 | 2.75 | 2.80 | 2.85 | 2.90 | 2.95 | 3.00 | 3.05 | 3.10 | 3.15 | 3.20 | 3.25 | 3.30 | 3.35 | 3.40 | 3.45 | 3.50 |  |  |  |  |  |  |  |  |  |
| 0.76–0.80 | 2.80 | 2.85 | 2.90 | 2.95 | 3.00 | 3.05 | 3.10 | 3.15 | 3.20 | 3.25 | 3.30 | 3.35 | 3.40 | 3.45 | 3.50 |  |  |  |  |  |  |  |  |  |  |
| 0.81–0.85 | 2.85 | 2.90 | 2.95 | 3.00 | 3.05 | 3.10 | 3.15 | 3.20 | 3.25 | 3.30 | 3.35 | 3.40 | 3.45 | 3.50 |  |  |  |  |  |  |  |  |  |  |  |
| 0.86–0.90 | 2.90 | 2.95 | 3.00 | 3.05 | 3.10 | 3.15 | 3.20 | 3.25 | 3.30 | 3.35 | 3.40 | 3.45 | 3.50 |  |  |  |  |  |  |  |  |  |  |  |  |
| 0.91–0.95 | 2.95 | 3.00 | 3.05 | 3.10 | 3.15 | 3.20 | 3.25 | 3.30 | 3.35 | 3.40 | 3.45 | 3.50 |  |  |  |  |  |  |  |  |  |  |  |  |  |
| 0.96–1.00 | 3.00 | 3.05 | 3.10 | 3.15 | 3.20 | 3.25 | 3.30 | 3.35 | 3.40 | 3.45 | 3.50 |  |  |  |  |  |  |  |  |  |  |  |  |  |  |
| 1.01–1.05 | 3.05 | 3.10 | 3.15 | 3.20 | 3.25 | 3.30 | 3.35 | 3.40 | 3.45 | 3.50 |  |  |  |  |  |  |  |  |  |  |  |  |  |  |  |
| 1.06–1.10 | 3.10 | 3.15 | 3.20 | 3.25 | 3.30 | 3.35 | 3.40 | 3.45 | 3.50 |  |  |  |  |  |  |  |  |  |  |  |  |  |  |  |  |
| 1.11–1.15 | 3.15 | 3.20 | 3.25 | 3.30 | 3.35 | 3.40 | 3.45 | 3.50 |  |  |  |  |  |  |  |  |  |  |  |  |  |  |  |  |  |
| 1.16–1.20 | 3.20 | 3.25 | 3.30 | 3.35 | 3.40 | 3.45 | 3.50 |  |  |  |  |  |  |  |  |  |  |  |  |  |  |  |  |  |  |
| 1.21–1.25 | 3.25 | 3.30 | 3.35 | 3.40 | 3.45 | 3.50 |  |  |  |  |  |  |  |  |  |  |  |  |  |  |  |  |  |  |  |
| 1.26–1.30 | 3.30 | 3.35 | 3.40 | 3.45 | 3.50 |  |  |  |  |  |  |  |  |  |  |  |  |  |  |  |  |  |  |  |  |
| 1.31–1.35 | 3.35 | 3.40 | 3.45 | 3.50 |  |  |  |  |  |  |  |  |  |  |  |  |  |  |  |  |  |  |  |  |  |
| 1.36–1.40 | 3.40 | 3.45 | 3.50 |  |  |  |  |  |  |  |  |  |  |  |  |  |  |  |  |  |  |  |  |  |  |
| 1.41–1.45 | 3.45 | 3.50 |  |  |  |  |  |  |  |  |  |  |  |  |  |  |  |  |  |  |  |  |  |  |  |
| 1.46–1.50 | 3.50 |  |  |  |  |  |  |  |  |  |  |  |  |  |  |  |  |  |  |  |  |  |  |  |  |

**3**

10. Install the camshaft(s) as described in Chapter Four.

11. Use the starter clutch mounting bolt (A, **Figure 11**) to rotate the engine several complete revolutions *clockwise* (when viewed from the right side). This seats the new shims.

12. Recheck all valve clearances. If any clearance is outside the specified range, repeat this process until all clearances are correct.

13. Install the cylinder head cover as described in Chapter Four.

14. Install the spark plugs as described in this chapter.

15. Install new O-rings onto the timing inspection cap and the starter clutch bolt cap. Lubricate each O-ring with engine oil, and install the caps into the clutch cover. Tighten the timing inspection cap (A, **Figure 10**) to 23 N•m (17 ft.-lb.) and the starter clutch bolt cap (B) to 11 N•m (97 in.-lb.).

16. Install the side fairings as described in Chapter Fifteen.

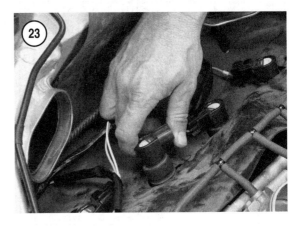

## SPARK PLUGS

### Removal

*NOTE*
*The spark plugs can be serviced with the heat shield installed.*

1. Raise and support the fuel tank as described in Chapter Eight.

2. Remove the air filter housing (Chapter Eight).

*CAUTION*
*Whenever the spark plug is removed, dirt around it can fall into the plug hole. This can cause engine damage. Use compressed air to remove all loose debris from the heat shield and spark plug tunnels before removing the plug.*

3. Blow away all loose dirt and wipe off the top surface of the heat shield.

*CAUTION*
*Remove the electrical connector before removing the ignition coil/plug cap. Do not remove the ignition coil/plug cap with the electrical connector attached.*

4. Disconnect the 2-pin connector (**Figure 22**) from each ignition coil/spark plug cap. Label each connector, if necessary. The connectors must be reinstalled on the correct coil.

5. The ignition coil/plug caps form a tight seal on the cylinder head cover as well as the spark plugs. Grasp the ignition coil/plug cap (**Figure 23**) and carefully

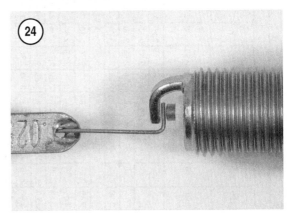

pull it straight up and off the spark plug. *Do not* use any tool to pry the ignition coil/plug cap from the spark plug.

*CAUTION*
*Do not drop or roughly handle the ignition coil/plug cap assemblies. They will become damaged, leading to an open or short within their circuit.*

6. Label each ignition coil/plug cap with its cylinder number so it can be reinstalled onto the same spark plug.

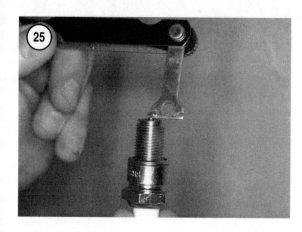

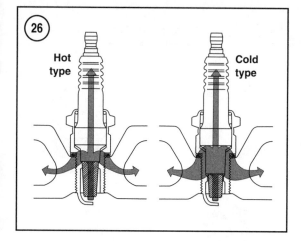

### Installation

1. Apply a light coat of antiseize compound to the threads of the spark plug before installing it. Do not use engine oil on the plug threads.

> *CAUTION*
> *The cylinder head is aluminum. The spark plug hole threads can be easily damaged by cross-threading the spark plug.*

2. Use the same tool set-up used during removal to hand tighten the plug until it seats. Tighten the spark plug to 11 N•m (97 in.-lb.). Do not overtighten the plug.

3. Refer to the marks made during removal, and then install each ignition coil/plug cap onto the correct spark plug. Press ignition coil/plug cap (**Figure 23**) into the spark plug tunnel and onto the spark plug. Rotate the assembly slightly in both directions and make sure it is firmly attached to the spark plug.

4. Carefully connect each 2-pin connector (**Figure 22**) to the correct ignition coil/plug cap.

5. Make sure the electrical connectors are free of corrosion and are on tight.

6. Install the air filter housing (Chapter Eight).

### Gap

Carefully gap the spark plugs to ensure a reliable, consistent spark. Always use a spark plug gapping tool and a wire feeler gauge to measure and adjust the gap.

1. Remove the new spark plugs from the boxes. If installed, unscrew the terminal nut from the end of the plug.

2. Insert a wire feeler gauge between the center and side electrode of the plug (**Figure 24**). The specified gap is in **Table 4**. If the gap is correct, a slight drag is felt as the wire is pulled through the gap. If there is no drag or if the gauge does not pass through the gap, set the gap to specification by bending the side electrode with a gaping tool (**Figure 25**).

### Selection

The manufacturer provides three spark plug heat ranges (**Table 4**). If necessary, select a different heat range from the standard recommendation to accommodate for load and temperature conditions under which the motorcycle is operated. Refer to **Figure 26**.

In general, use a hot plug for low speeds and low temperatures. Use a cold plug for high speeds, high engine loads and high temperatures. A plug should

7. Use compressed air to blow debris from the spark plug tunnels.

8. Using a spark plug socket equipped with a rubber insert, install it onto the spark plug. Make sure it is correctly seated on the plug. Install the socket handle, and turn out the spark plug about halfway from its hole in the cylinder head. Repeat for each plug.

9. Use compressed air to blow out the spark plug tunnels to remove any debris that was trapped below the spark plug hex fitting.

10. Remove each spark plug. Mark the spark plug with its cylinder number.

11. Inspect the plugs carefully. Look for a broken center porcelain insulator, excessively eroded electrodes and excessive carbon or oil fouling.

12. Inspect the ignition coil/plug caps for damage. If visibly damaged, test the assembly as described in Chapter Nine.

13. Inspect each electrical connector and wiring for corrosion and/or damage. The wiring and electrical connectors are part of the main wiring harness and cannot be replaced separately.

14. Measure the spark plug gap (this section). Adjust the gap as necessary.

operate hot enough to burn off unwanted deposits, but not so hot that it is damaged or causes preignition. To determine if plug heat range is correct, remove each spark plug and examine the insulator when reading the spark plugs.

Do not change the spark plug heat range to compensate for adverse engine or fuel system conditions. A plug with an incorrect heat range can foul, overheat or cause piston damage.

When replacing plugs, make sure the reach (**Figure 27**) is correct. A plug could interfere with the piston and cause engine damage.

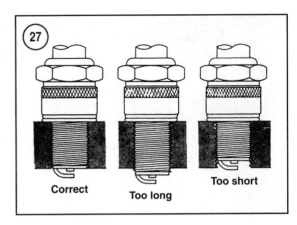

Correct  Too long  Too short

### Reading

Reading the spark plugs can provide information about spark plug operation, air/fuel mixture composition and engine conditions (such as oil consumption or pistons). Before checking the spark plugs, operate the motorcycle under a medium load for approximately 10 km (6 miles). Avoid prolonged idling before shutting off the engine. Remove the spark plugs as described in this section. Examine each plug and compare it to those shown in **Figure 28**.

#### Normal condition

A light tan- or gray-colored deposit on the firing tip and no abnormal gap wear or erosion indicate good engine, ignition and air/fuel mixture conditions. A plug with the proper heat range is being used. It may be serviced and returned to use.

#### Carbon fouled

Soft, dry and sooty deposits covering the entire firing end of the plug are evidence of incomplete combustion. Even though the firing end of the plug is dry, the deposits decrease the plug's insulation. The carbon forms an electrical path that bypasses the electrodes causing a misfire. One or more of the following conditions can cause carbon fouling:
1. Rich air/fuel mixture.
2. Spark plug heat range too cold.
3. Clogged air filter.
4. Improperly operating ignition component.
5. Ignition component failure.
6. Low engine compression.
7. Prolonged idling.

#### Oil fouled

An oil fouled plug has a black insulator tip, a damp oily film over the firing end and a carbon layer over

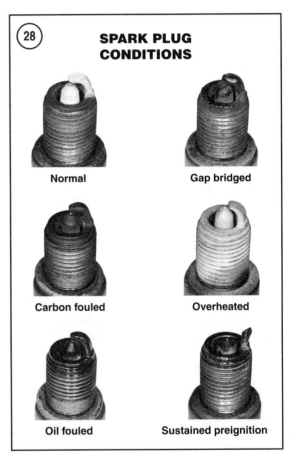

**SPARK PLUG CONDITIONS**

Normal  Gap bridged

Carbon fouled  Overheated

Oil fouled  Sustained preignition

the entire nose. The electrodes are not worn. Oil fouled plugs can be cleaned in an emergency, but it is better to replace them. Correct the cause of the fouling before returning the engine to service. Common causes for this condition are:
1. Incorrect air/fuel mixture.
2. Faulty fuel injection system.
3. Low idle speed or prolonged idling.
4. Ignition component failure.
5. Spark plug heat range too cold.
6. Engine still being broken in.
7. Valve guides worn.

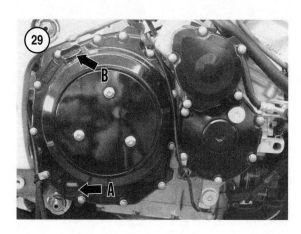

8. Piston rings worn or broken.

### Gap bridging

Plugs with this condition have deposits building up between the electrodes. The deposits reduce the gap and eventually close it entirely. If this condition is encountered, check for excessive carbon or oil in the combustion chamber. Make sure to locate and correct the cause of this condition.

### Overheating

Badly worn electrodes and premature gap wear (along with a gray or white blistered porcelain insulator surface) are signs of overheating. This condition is commonly caused by a spark plug with a heat range that is too hot. If the spark plug heat range is correct, consider the following causes:
1. Lean air/fuel mixture.
2. Faulty fuel injection operation.
3. Improperly operating ignition component.
4. Engine lubrication system malfunction.
5. Cooling system malfunction.
6. Engine air leak.
7. Improper spark plug installation (overtightening).
8. No spark plug gasket.

### Worn out

Corrosive gasses formed by combustion and high voltage sparks have eroded the electrodes. A spark plug in this condition requires more voltage to fire under hard acceleration. Install a new spark plug.

### Preignition

If the electrodes are melted, preignition is almost certainly the cause. Check for throttle body mounting or intake manifold leaks and advanced ignition tim-

ing. The plug heat range may also be too hot. Find the cause of the preignition before returning the engine into service. For additional information on preignition, refer to Chapter Two.

## ENGINE OIL AND FILTER

The recommended oil and filter change interval is in **Table 1**. This assumes the motorcycle is operated in moderate climates. If it is operated under dusty conditions, the oil gets dirty more quickly and should be changed more frequently than recommended.

### Engine Oil Level Check

The engine oil level is checked at the oil inspection window on the clutch cover.
1. Start the engine and warm it up for several minutes.
2. Securely support the motorcycle in an upright position on a level surface.
3. Shut off the engine and let the oil settle for approximately 3 minutes.

> *CAUTION*
> *Do not take this oil level reading with the motorcycle on the sidestand because the oil flows away from the window giving a false reading.*

4. Have an assistant sit on the bike to hold it vertically on level ground.
5. Check the engine oil level in the oil inspection window (A, **Figure 29**) on the clutch cover. The oil level must be between the full and low lines on the clutch cover.
6. If the oil level is low, unscrew the oil filler cap (B, **Figure 29**) from the clutch cover. Insert a small funnel into the hole. Add the recommended oil (**Table 3**) to correct the oil level.
7. If the oil level is too high, remove the oil filler cap and draw out the excess oil with a syringe or another suitable pump.
8. Inspect the O-ring seal on the oil filler cap. Replace the O-ring if it is starting to deteriorate or harden.
9. Install the oil filler cap, and tighten it securely.
10. Recheck the oil level, and adjust if necessary.

### Engine Oil and Filter Change

> *NOTE*
> *Some service stations and oil retailers accept used engine oil for recycling. Do*

*not discard oil with the household trash or pour it onto the ground.*

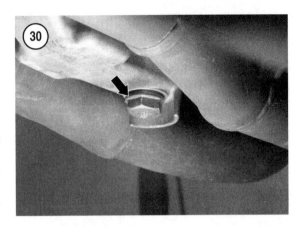

*NOTE*
*Warming the engine heats up the oil so it flows freely and carries out contaminants and sludge.*

1. Remove the rear lower panel and the fairing side panels (Chapter Fifteen).
2. Start the engine and warm it up for several minutes. Shut the engine off.
3. Securely support the motorcycle in an upright position on a level surface.
4. Place a drain pan under the engine.
5. Remove the oil drain bolt (**Figure 30**) and gasket from the bottom of the oil pan.
6. Loosen the oil filler cap (B, **Figure 29**). This speeds up the flow of oil.
7. Let the oil completely drain from the engine.

*WARNING*
*The exhaust system must be completely cool before oil filter removal. Hot oil cooler and exhaust system parts surround the oil filter, making the work area small. Protect your hands accordingly.*

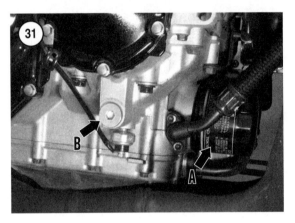

8. To replace the oil filter, perform the following:
   a. Move the drain pan under the oil filter (A, **Figure 31**) so it catches oil that drains from the filter.
   b. Install a socket-type oil filter wrench (Suzuki part No. 09915-40610) onto the oil filter (**Figure 32**) and turn the filter *counterclockwise* until oil begins to run out. Wait until the oil stops, and then loosen the filter until it is easy to turn.
   c. Because of limited space, remove the oil filter wrench from the end of the filter and completely unscrew and remove the filter. Hold it with the open end facing up.
   d. Hold the filter over the drain pan and pour out any remaining oil. Place the old filter in a plastic bag. Discard the old filter properly.
   e. Thoroughly clean the oil filter sealing surface on the crankcase.
   f. Apply a light coat of clean engine oil to the rubber seal on the new filter.
   g. Spin a new oil filter onto the threaded stud.
   h. Tighten the filter by hand until the rubber gasket contacts the crankcase sealing surface, and then tighten it an additional two full turns.
9. Inspect the drain plug gasket for damage. Replace the gasket if necessary.
10. Install the oil drain bolt (**Figure 30**) and its gasket. Tighten the oil drain bolt to 23 N•m (17 ft.-lb.).

11. Insert a funnel into the oil filler hole, and add the amount of oil specified in **Table 3**.
12. Remove the funnel and screw in the oil filler cap (B, **Figure 29**) securely.
13. Usually some oil finds its way onto the exhaust pipes during this procedure. Wipe off as much as possible with a shop rag, and spray an aerosol parts cleaner onto the pipes. This removes most of the oil residue and helps eliminate the burned oil smoke and smell when the motorcycle is started.
14. Start the engine and let it idle.
15. Check the oil filter and drain plug for leaks. Tighten either if necessary.
16. Turn off the engine and check the engine oil level as described in this section. Adjust the oil level if necessary.
17. Install the fairing side panels and rear lower panel (Chapter Fifteen).

## ENGINE OIL PRESSURE TEST

1. The following Suzuki tools or equivalents are required to check the oil pressure:
   a. Oil pressure gauge hose: part No. 09915-74520.

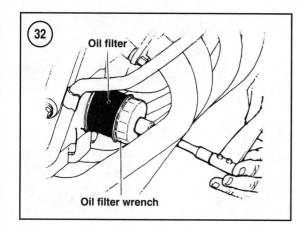

Oil filter

Oil filter wrench

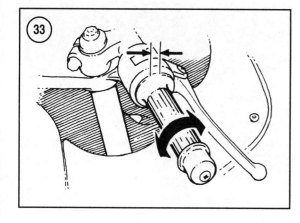

b. Oil pressure gauge attachment: part No. 09915-74540.

c. Meter (for high pressure): part No. 09915-77330.

2. Remove the fairing side panel from the right side (Chapter Fifteen).

3. Check the engine oil level described in this chapter. Add oil if necessary.

4. Place a drain pan under the 16 mm oil gallery plug (B, **Figure 31**) to catch the oil that drains out during the test.

5. Unscrew and remove the 16 mm oil gallery plug from the crankcase.

6. Install the adapter, hose and then the gauge into the main oil gallery. Make sure the fitting is tight to avoid oil loss.

> *WARNING*
> *Keep the gauge hose away from the exhaust pipe during this test. Contact with the hot exhaust may melt the hose, allowing oil to leak onto the pipes and start a fire.*

7. Start the engine and warm it up. During summer months, run the engine at 2000 rpm for 10 minutes. During the winter, run it at 2000 rpm for 20 minutes.

8. Increase engine speed to 3000 rpm. The oil pressure should be with the range specified in **Table 4** when the oil temperature is 140° F (60° C).

9. If the oil pressure is lower than specified, check the following:

  a. Clogged oil filter.
  b. Oil leaking from an oil passage.
  c. Damaged oil seal(s).
  d. Defective oil pump.
  e. Combination of the above.

10. If the oil pressure is higher than specified check the following:

  a. Oil viscosity too high (drain oil and install lighter weight oil).
  b. Clogged oil passage.
  c. Combination of the above

11. Shut off the engine and remove the test equipment.

12. Apply a light coat of gasket sealer to the 16 mm oil gallery plug and install the plug (B, **Figure 31**). Tighten it to 35 N•m (26 ft.-lb.).

13. Check the oil level and adjust if necessary.

14. Install the side panel as described in Chapter Fifteen.

## THROTTLE CABLE ADJUSTMENT

> *WARNING*
> *With the engine running at idle speed, turn the handlebars from side to side. If the idle speed increases during this movement, either the throttle cables need adjusting or they may be incorrectly routed through the frame. Correct this problem immediately. Do not ride the motorcycle in this unsafe condition.*

Measure throttle cable free play at the throttle grip (**Figure 33**).

### Minor Adjustment

1. At the handlebar, loosen the locknut (A, **Figure 34**) on the return cable, and turn its adjuster (B) all the way in.

2. Loosen the locknut (C, **Figure 34**) on the pull cable.

3. Turn the pull cable adjuster (D, **Figure 34**) until the free play is within the range specified in **Table 4**.

4. Hold the pull cable adjuster (D, **Figure 34**) and tighten the locknut (C).

5. Hold the throttle grip fully closed, and turn out the return cable adjuster (B, **Figure 34**) until slight resis-

tance is felt. Tighten the locknut (A, **Figure 34**) while holding the adjuster.

6. Start the engine and let it idle. Turn the handlebar from side to side and listen to the engine speed. Make sure it does not increase.

### Major Adjustment

1. Raise and support the fuel tank (Chapter Eight).
2. Loosen the return cable locknut (A, **Figure 35**), and turn the adjuster (B) to remove any slack from the return cable.
3. Loosen the pull cable locknut (C, **Figure 35**) and turn the adjuster (D) until throttle cable free play is within specification (**Table 4**).
4. Hold the pull cable adjuster (D, **Figure 35**) and tighten the locknut (C).
5. Hold the throttle grip in its fully closed position, and turn the return cable adjuster (B, **Figure 35**) until the slack in the return cable equals 1.0 mm (0.04 in.) as shown in **Figure 35**.
6. Tighten the return cable locknut (A, **Figure 35**) securely.
7. Start the engine and let it idle. Turn the handlebar from side to side and listen to the engine speed. Make sure the idle speed does not increase.

### IDLE SPEED ADJUSTMENT

*WARNING*
*With the engine running at idle speed, turn the handlebars from side to side. If the idle speed increases during this movement, either the throttle cables need adjusting or they may be incorrectly routed through the frame. Correct this problem immediately. Do not ride the motorcycle in this unsafe condition.*

Before adjusting idle speed, clean or replace the air filter, test the engine compression and synchronize the throttle bodies (this chapter). Idle speed cannot be properly adjusted if these items are not within specification.

1. Securely support the motorcycle on a level surface.
2. Make sure the throttle cable free play is adjusted correctly. Check and adjust as described in this chapter.
3. Start the engine and warm it to normal operating temperature. Turn off the engine.
4. Raise and support the fuel tank (Chapter Eight).
5. Start the engine and let it idle. Turn the throttle stop screw until engine idle speed is within specification (**Table 4**). On 1999-2000 models, the throttle stop screws sits on the top of the clutch cover (**Figure**

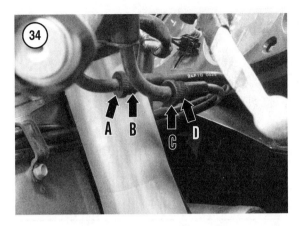

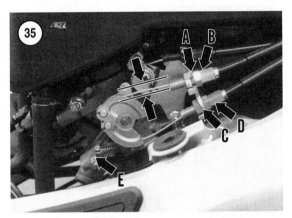

36). On 2001-on models, it is on the throttle wheel (E, **Figure 35**).

6. Rev the engine a couple times to see if it settles down to the set speed. Readjust if necessary.
7. Shut off the engine.

### FAST IDLE SPEED ADJUSTMENT

The fast idle system is similar to a starter system. This system operates the fast idle cam, which opens the throttle valve to increase idle speed until the engine warms up.

**3**

1. Securely support the motorcycle in an upright position.

2. Start the engine, and warm it up to normal operating speed.

3. Adjust the idle speed as described in this chapter.

4. Move the fast idle lever (on the left handlebar switch) rearward to fully on and note the engine speed. It should equal the fast idle specification in **Table 4**.

5. If fast idle speed is out of specification, perform the following:

    a. Raise and support the fuel tank (Chapter Eight).

    b. Start the engine and let it idle. If necessary, adjust the engine idle speed as described in this chapter.

    c. Move the fast idle level rearward to fully on.

    d. Turn the fast idle screw (**Figure 37**) until fast idle speed is within specification.

    e. If necessary, adjust the idle speed as described in this chapter.

## THROTTLE VALVE
## SYNCHRONIZATION

*CAUTION*
*Label the vacuum hoses before removal. Each hose must be reconnected*

*to the correct throttle body once synchronization is completed.*

Throttle valve synchronization ensures that each cylinder receives the same air/fuel mixture by synchronizing the vacuum in each throttle intake port.

Before synchronizing the throttle valves, make sure the air filter element is clean and the valve clearances are correct.

A vacuum gauge set that can simultaneously measure the vacuum in each cylinder is required to synchronize the throttle bodies.

1. Start the engine and warm it to normal operating temperature.

2. Use the throttle stop screw (**Figure 36** or E, **Figure 35**) to set the idle speed to 1150 rpm. Shut off the engine.

3. Raise and support the fuel tank (Chapter Eight).

*NOTE*
*On 1999-2001 models, remove the intake air temperature and intake air pressure sensors from the air filter housing and reconnect their electrical connectors so they are in the loop while the throttle valves are synchronized. On 2002-on models, only the intake air temperature sensor must be in the loop.*

4A. On 1999-2001 models, remove the intake air pressure sensor mounting screw, and lower the sensor from the air filter housing. Keep the electrical connector and hose connected to the intake air pressure sensor.

4B. On 2002-on models, disconnect the electrical connector from the intake air pressure sensor.

5. Remove the air filter housing (Chapter Eight).

6. Remove the intake air temperature sensor from the air filter housing. Reconnect the electrical connector to the sensor and place the intake air temperate sensor onto the frame.

7. Synchronize the vacuum gauge following the tool manufacturer's instructions.

8A. On 1999-2001 models, connect the vacuum gauges to the throttle bodies by performing the following:

    a. Disconnect the hose or cap from the left vacuum nipple on the No. 1 throttle body.

    b. Connect the hose from the No. 1 vacuum gauge (A, **Figure 38**) to this nipple on the No. 1 body.

    c. Repeat substep a and substep b for each remaining vacuum gauge.

8B. On 2002-on models, connect the vacuum gauges to the throttle bodies by performing the following:

    a. Disconnect the hose or cap from the right nipple on the No. 1 throttle body.

b. Connect the hose from the No. 1 vacuum gauge (A, **Figure 39**) to this nipple on the No. 1 body.

c. Repeat substep a and substep b for each remaining vacuum gauge.

9. Start the engine and let it idle. If necessary, use the throttle stop screw to adjust the idle speed to 1150 rpm.

10. With the engine running at the idle, check the gauge readings. The throttle valves are balanced if the gauge readings are the same for all cylinders.

11. If the readings vary, use the balance adjust screws to synchronize the throttle valves. Perform the following:

a. Use the left balance adjust screw (B, **Figure 38** or **Figure 39**) to synchronize the No. 1 and No. 2 throttle bodies.

b. Use the right screw (C, **Figure 38** or **Figure 39**) to synchronize the No. 3 and No. 4 bodies.

c. Synchronize the left pair and right pair with the middle balance adjust screw (D, **Figure 38** or **Figure 39**).

12. Rev the throttle a few times and recheck the synchronization readings after all throttle valves have been adjusted. Readjust synchronization if required.

13. Check the idle speed. If necessary, adjust it as described in this chapter.

14. Stop the engine and detach the equipment.

15. Reconnect the vacuum lines and/or caps.

16. Install the intake air temperature sensor, air filter housing and intake air pressure sensor (Chapter Eight).

17. Lower the fuel tank, start the engine and check the engine idle speed.

18. If necessary, adjust the throttle cable free play as described in this chapter.

## FUEL LINE INSPECTION

Inspect the fuel hoses at the intervals specified in **Table 1**.

1. Raise and support the fuel tank as described in Chapter Eight.

2. Inspect the fuel hose(s) for leaks, hardness, deterioration or other damage.

3. Make sure the hoses are securely attached to their respective fittings.

4. Make sure the fuel supply hose is attached correctly.

5. Replace damaged fuel hose(s) as needed.

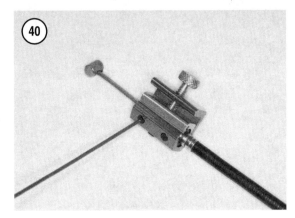

## EMISSION CONTROL SYSTEM INSPECTION

### PAIR System

The PAIR, or pulsed air injection, system injects fresh air into the cylinder exhaust port, thus reducing the amount of unburned hydrocarbons in the exhaust.

At the service intervals in **Table 1**, inspect all PAIR hoses for deterioration, damage or loose connections. Replace any parts or hoses as required. Check the tightness of the fittings and clamps.

Remove and inspect the PAIR control valve and the reed valves as described in Chapter Eight.

### Evaporative Emission Control System (California Models)

All models sold in California are equipped with an evaporative emission control system. EVAP hose routing label is on the frame inside the tail piece.

At the service intervals in **Table 1**, check all the emission control lines and the EVAP canister for loose connections or damage. Also check the EVAP canister housing for damage. Replace any parts or hoses as required. Refer to Chapter Eight for additional information.

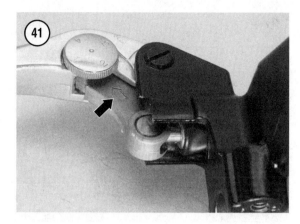

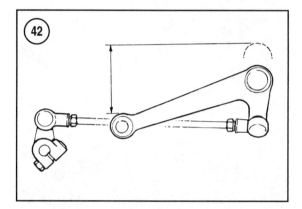

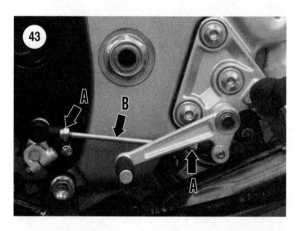

1. Disconnect each throttle cable or disconnect the fast idle cable as described in Chapter Eight.

2. Attach a cable lubricator (**Figure 40**) to the cable, following the manufacturer's instructions.

3. Insert the nozzle of the lubricant can into the lubricator. Press the button on the can and hold it down until the lubricant begins to flow out of the other end of the cable. If the lubricant flows out from the cable lubricator, the lubricator is not installed properly onto the cable end. Remove and reinstall the lubricator until it seals. Place a shop cloth at the end of the cable(s) to catch lubricant as it flows out.

*NOTE*
*If lubricant does not flow out the end of the cable, check the entire cable for damage.*

4. Remove the lubricator and wipe excess lubricant from the cable. Place a dab of grease onto the cable end before reconnecting it.

5. Install the cables as described in Chapter Eight.

6. Adjust the throttle cables as described in this chapter.

## CLUTCH LEVER ADJUSTMENT

Adjust the distance between the clutch lever and the hand grip to suit the rider's preference.

1. Push the clutch lever forward away from the handle grip.

2. Rotate the adjusting dial until the desired setting is opposite the arrow on the bracket (**Figure 41**). Setting No. 1 moves the clutch lever to the furthest position away from the hand grip, setting No. 4 to the closest. The default setting is No. 2.

3. Make sure the stop on the clutch lever holder engages the detent in the adjusting dial.

4. After adjusting the lever position, check for any clutch slip. Readjust as necessary.

## CABLE LUBRICATION

Lubricate the non-nylon lined control cables with a cable lubricant and cable lubricator (**Figure 40**) during cable adjustment or if a cable becomes stiff or sluggish. During cable lubrication, inspect the cables for fraying, and check the sheath for chafing. Replace any defective cables immediately.

*CAUTION*
*Most nylon-lined cables do not require lubrication. When servicing nylon-lined and other aftermarket cables, follow the cable manufacturer's instructions.*

## SHIFT PEDAL HEIGHT ADJUSTMENT

1. Securely support the motorcycle on a level surface.

2. Measure the distance from the top of the footrest to the top of the shift pedal (**Figure 42**). The specified shift pedal height is in **Table 4**.

3. Adjust the pedal height by performing the following:

   a. Loosen the locknut (A, **Figure 43**) at each end of the shift rod (B).

   b. Turn the shift rod until the shift pedal moves to the desired height.

   c. Tighten each locknut securely.

## COOLING SYSTEM

*WARNING*
*When performing any service work on the engine or cooling system, never remove the radiator cap or disconnect any coolant hose while the engine and radiator are hot. Scalding fluid and steam may be forced out under pressure and cause serious injury.*

*WARNING*
*Never discharge coolant into storm sewers, septic systems, waterways or onto the ground. Pour used coolant into the original container and dispose of it according to local regulations. Do not store coolant where it is accessible to children or pets.*

*CAUTION*
*Make sure not to spill coolant onto painted surfaces. It damages the surface. Wash immediately with soapy water and rinse thoroughly.*

Check, inspect and service the cooling system at the intervals specified in **Table 1**.

### Coolant Type

*CAUTION*
*Many coolant solutions contain silicate inhibitors to protect aluminum parts from corrosion damage. However, silicate inhibitors cause premature wear of water pump seals. Do not use coolants that contain silicate inhibitors.*

Use only a high quality, ethylene-glycol based coolant specifically designed for aluminum engines. Mix the coolant with distilled water in a 50:50 ratio. *Never* use tap water when mixing coolant with water. The minerals in the water damage engine parts.

Cooling system capacities are in **Table 3**.

### Coolant Level

Check the coolant level when the engine is cold. The coolant reservoir mounts to the left side of the frame. The coolant can be checked with the fairing side panel in place.

When the coolant level is low, add coolant to the reservoir, not the radiator.

1. Securely support the motorcycle on a level surface.

2. Check the coolant level in the coolant reservoir. It should be between the UPPER and LOWER level lines on the reservoir cover (**Figure 44**).

3. If necessary, add coolant to the reservoir by performing the following:

   a. Remove the left fairing side panel (Chapter Fifteen).

   b. Remove the reservoir cap (**Figure 45**) and add coolant to bring the level to the UPPER level line.

4. Reinstall the reservoir tank cap and side panel.

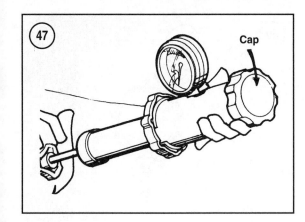

47

Cap

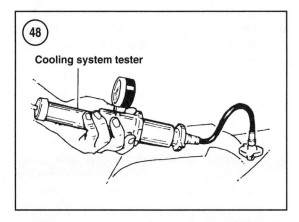

48

Cooling system tester

49

A    B

## Cooling System Inspection

1. Remove the fairing side panel from each side (Chapter Fifteen).

2. Check all cooling system hoses for damage or deterioration. Replace any questionable hose. Make sure all hose clamps are tight.

3. Carefully clean any dirt and debris from the radiator core. Use a whiskbroom, compressed air or low-pressure water. If an object has hit the radiator, carefully straighten the fins with a screwdriver.

4. Pressure test the radiator cap by performing the following:

a. Remove the radiator cap (**Figure 46**) from the radiator.

b. Use a cooling system tester to pressure test the radiator cap (**Figure 47**) following the tester manufacturer's instructions. Slowly pressurize the cap and stop when the pressure is within the radiator cap opening pressure specified in **Table 4**. Replace the radiator cap if it does not hold pressure or if release pressure is outside the specified range.

*CAUTION*
*Do not exceed the indicated test pressure. If test pressure exceeds the specifications, the radiator may be damaged.*

5. Pressure test the cooling system by performing the following:

a. Leave the radiator cap off and install the cooling system pressure tester onto the cap fitting on the radiator filler neck (**Figure 48**).

b. Pressurize the cooling system to the specified pressure in **Table 4**. If the pressure does not hold steady, check the system for leaks. Replace or repair any component that fails this test.

6. Reinstall the radiator cap.

## Coolant Change and Air Bleeding

Drain and refill the cooling system at the interval in **Table 1**.

At times, the cooling system must be drained when another part of the engine is being serviced. If the coolant is still in good condition, it can be reused if it is not contaminated. In these instances, drain the coolant into a clean pan and pour the coolant into a clean container for storage.

Perform the following procedure when the engine is cold:

1. Securely support the motorcycle on a level surface.

2. Remove the fairing side panel from the each side (Chapter Fifteen).

3. Remove the coolant reservoir (Chapter Ten), and pour out its contents.

4. Place a drain pan under the water pump. Clean out the reservoir, and reinstall it onto the motorcycle.

5. Release the clamp and disconnect the radiator hose (A, **Figure 49**) from the water pump input fitting. Let the coolant drain from the system.

6. Slowly remove the radiator cap (**Figure 46**) and let the coolant completely drain from the system.

7. Reinstall the radiator hose (A, **Figure 49**) so its indexing dot aligns with the raised indexing line (B) on the pump input fitting. Tighten the clamp securely.

8. Place a funnel into the radiator filler neck and slowly refill the radiator and engine with a 50:50 mixture of coolant and distilled water. Add the mixture slowly so it expels as much air as possible from the cooling system.

9. Sit on the motorcycle and slowly rock it from side to side to help expel air bubbles from the engine, radiator and coolant hoses.

10. Top off the radiator as necessary.

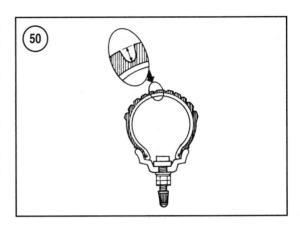

> *WARNING*
> *Do not start and run the motorcycle in an enclosed area. The exhaust gasses contain carbon monoxide, a colorless, odorless and poisonous gas. Carbon monoxide levels build quickly in a small, enclosed area and can cause unconsciousness and death in a short time.*

11. After filling the radiator, leave the radiator cap off and bleed the cooling system by performing the following:

    a. Start the engine and let it idle for 2-3 minutes.

    b. Snap the throttle a few times to bleed air from the cooling system. When the coolant level drops in the radiator, add coolant to raise the level to the bottom of the filler neck.

12. Once the coolant level has stabilized, install the radiator cap (**Figure 46**). Turn the radiator cap clockwise to the first stop. Then push the cap down and turn it clockwise until it stops.

13. Fill the coolant reservoir to the UPPER level line.

14. Start the engine and run it at idle speed until the engine reaches normal operating temperature. Snap the throttle several times, and turn off the engine.

15. Wait several minutes so the coolant can settle, and check the coolant level in the reservoir (**Figure 44**). If necessary, add coolant to the reservoir, not the radiator.

16. Install both fairing side panels (Chapter Fifteen).

17. Test ride the motorcycle and readjust the coolant level in the reservoir as required.

## TIRES AND WHEELS

### Tire Inspection

Refer to Chapter Eleven for tire changing and repair information.

1. Check and adjust the tire pressure (**Table 2**) to maintain tire profile, good handling and to get the maximum mileage out of the tire. Check the tire pressure when the tires are cold. Never release air pressure from a warm tire to match the recommended tire pressure. Doing so causes an under-inflated tire. Use an accurate tire pressure gauge to measure tire pressure, and reinstall the air valve cap.

2. Periodically inspect the tires for the following:

    a. Deep cuts and imbedded objects, such as nails and stones. If a nail or other object is in a tire, mark its location with a light crayon before removing it. This helps to locate the hole for repair.

    b. Flat spots.

    c. Cracks.

    d. Separating plies.

    e. Sidewall damage.

### Tire Wear Analysis

Analyze abnormal tire wear to determine the cause. Common causes are:

1. Incorrect tire pressure. Check the tire pressure and examine the tire tread as follows:

    a. Measure the tread depth in the center of the tire using a small ruler or a tread depth gauge (**Figure 50**). Replace the original equipment tires if the center tread depth has worn to the minimum tread depth in **Table 2** or if the wear bars are showing.

    b. Compare the wear in the center of the contact patch with the wear at the edge of the contact patch.

    c. If the tire shows excessive wear at the edge of the contact patch but the wear at the center of the contact patch is normal, the tire has been under-inflated. Under-inflated tires cause higher tire temperatures, hard or imprecise steering and abnormal wear.

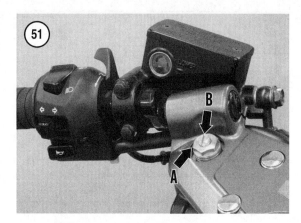

d. If the tire shows excessive wear in the center of the contact patch but wear at the edge of the contact patch is normal, the tire has been over-inflated. Over-inflated tires cause a hard ride and abnormal wear.

e. The tires are also designed with tread wear indicators that appear when the tires are worn out. When these are visible, the tires are no longer safe.

2. Overloading.

3. Incorrect wheel alignment.

4. Incorrect wheel balance. Balance the tire/wheel assembly when installing a new tire, and then rebalance each time the tire is removed.

5. Worn or damaged wheel bearings.

## Wheel Inspection

Frequently inspect the wheel for cracks, warping or dents. A damaged wheel may cause an air leak or steering vibration. If the rim portion of an alloy wheel is damaged, the wheel must be replaced. It *cannot* be serviced or repaired.

Wheel runout is the amount of wobble a wheel shows as it rotates. To quickly check runout, support the motorcycle with the wheel off the ground. Slowly rotate the wheel while holding a pointer solidly against a fork leg or the swing arm with the other end against the rim. For more precise inspection, remove the wheel and check the axial and radial runout as described in Chapter Eleven.

## FRONT SUSPENSION

### Fork Oil Change

The manufacturer does not provide an oil change interval for the front fork. Nonetheless, it is a good practice to change the fork oil once a year. If the fork oil becomes contaminated with dirt or water, change it immediately.

Changing the fork oil requires disassembling and assembling the fork legs. Refer to Chapter Twelve.

### Front Fork Inspection

Inspect the front fork at the intervals specified in **Table 1**.

1. Using a soft wet cloth, wipe the fork tubes to remove any debris. As this debris moves against the fork seals, it eventually damages the seals and causes an oil leak.

2. Check the fork sliders for any oil leaks or signs of damage.

3. Apply the front brake and pump the fork up and down. Check for smooth operation.

4. Refer to the specifications in **Table 5**, and check the tightness of the following items:

a. Lower fork bridge clamp bolt.

b. Upper fork bridge clamp bolt.

c. Handlebar clamp bolt.

d. Handlebar holder nut.

e. Front axle.

f. Front axle clamp bolt.

5. Adjust the front fork settings.

### Front Fork Adjustment

*WARNING*
*The spring preload, rebound damping and compression damping settings on the left fork leg must match the settings on the right fork leg. If they do not, the motorcycle's handling will be adversely affected, which could lead to loss of steering control.*

#### Spring preload

Adjust the spring preload by turning the hex-shaped preload adjuster (A, **Figure 51**) on the top of each fork cap. The adjuster is marked with eight (0-8) equally spaced grooves. Position 0 provides the maximum spring preload; position 8 provides the minimum. Position 5 is the standard setting (**Figure 52**).

The preload is set to a particular setting when the adjuster groove aligns with the top of the hexagon surface on the fork cap. Turn the preload adjuster (A, **Figure 51**) clockwise to increase preload. Turn the adjuster counterclockwise to decrease preload. Use the grooves to make sure that the spring preload is set to the same level on each fork leg.

## Rebound damping

Rebound damping affects the speed at which the front suspension returns to the fully extended position after compression.

Each front fork is equipped with a rebound damping adjuster (B, **Figure 51**) in the middle of the spring preload adjuster. The top of the adjuster is marked with a directional arrow and an *S* (soft) and *H* (hard) designations.

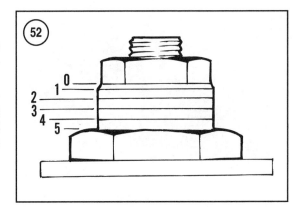

> *CAUTION*
> *Do not turn the rebound damping adjuster past the point where it stops at its full clockwise or full counterclockwise positions. Doing so damages the adjuster screw.*

1. To set the rebound damping to the standard setting, perform the following:
   a. Turn the rebound damping adjuster clockwise until it stops. This is the hardest setting.
   b. Turn the adjuster counterclockwise, and back it out three clicks. The rebound damping is now adjusted to the standard setting.
2. To further adjust the rebound damping, perform the following:
   a. To reduce rebound damping, turn the adjuster counterclockwise toward the *S*.
   b. To increase rebound damping, turn the adjuster clockwise toward the *H*.
3. Repeat this process on the other fork leg. The rebound damping must be adjusted to the same setting on both fork legs.

## Compression damping

Compression damping affects the speed at which the front suspension compresses when the wheel hits a bump. The compression damping adjuster is mounted in the rear side of each fork leg (**Figure 53**).

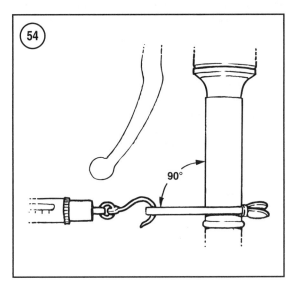

> *CAUTION*
> *Do not turn the compression damping adjuster past the point where it stops at its full clockwise or full counterclockwise positions. Doing so damages the adjuster screw.*

1. To set the compression damping to the standard setting, perform the following:
   a. Turn the compression damping adjuster clockwise until it stops. This is the hardest setting.
   b. Turn the adjuster counterclockwise, and back it out the nine clicks. The compression damping is now adjusted to the standard setting.

2. To further adjust the compression damping, perform the following:
   a. To reduce compression damping, turn the adjuster counterclockwise.
   b. To increase compression damping, turn the adjuster clockwise.
3. Repeat this process on the other fork leg. Make sure the compression damping is adjusted to the same setting on both fork legs.

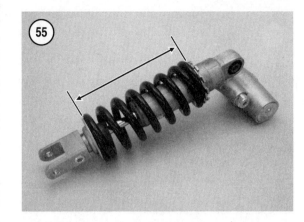

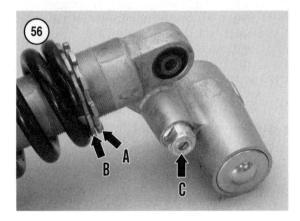

## Steering Tension Inspection

1. Securely support the motorcycle on a level surface with the front wheel off the ground.

2. Remove the steering damper as described in Chapter Twelve.

3. Check that the control cables and wiring harness are properly routed.

4. Connect a spring scale (Suzuki part No. 09940-92720 or equivalent) to the end of the handlebar grip. Position the spring scale so it forms a right angle with the handlebar. Refer to **Figure 54**.

5. Position the front wheel so it points straight ahead.

6. Pull the spring scale rearward, and note the reading on the scale when the handlebar first begins to move.

7. Repeat Steps 4-6 on the other handlebar.

8. Each reading should be within the steering tension range specified in **Table 4**.

9. If either reading is outside the specified range, adjust the steering head bearings as described in Chapter Twelve.

10. Grasp the lower end of both fork legs, and rock the steering head back and forth. Adjust the steering head bearings (Chapter Twelve) if excessive movement is noted.

## REAR SUSPENSION

### Inspection

1. Securely support the motorcycle with both wheels on the ground. Check the shock absorber by bouncing on the seat several times.

2. Securely support the motorcycle with the rear wheel off the ground.

3. While an assistant steadies the motorcycle, push hard on the rear wheel (sideways) to check for side play in the rear swing arm bearings.

4. Check the shock absorber for oil leaks or other damage.

5. Check the shock absorber, suspension linkage, rear axle and swing arm hardware. Make sure all fasteners are tight.

### Shock Absorber Adjustment

The rear shock can be adjusted to suit the load and rider preference. The spring preload rebound damping and compression damping can be adjusted on the shock absorber. To access the shock, remove the fairing side panels (Chapter Fifteen).

#### Spring preload

A pair of ring nut wrenches is required for this adjustment.

Set the spring preload by adjusting the spring installed length (**Figure 55**). A longer spring length provides a softer ride; a shorter spring length provides a stiffer ride. There must be preload on the spring at all times. Never ride the motorcycle without some spring preload. Doing so could cause loss of control. The standard, maximum and minimum preload specifications appear in **Table 4**.

1. Securely support the motorcycle on a level surface.

2. Loosen the locknut (A, **Figure 56**).

3. Turn the adjust nut (B, **Figure 56**) clockwise to increase preload, counterclockwise to reduce preload.

4. Hold the adjust nut, and tighten the locknut securely.

5. Measure the spring length. It must be between the minimum and maximum specified in **Table 4**.

#### Compression damping

Compression damping affects the rate at which the shock compresses when the rear wheel hits a bump. This adjustment does not affect the action of the shock absorber on rebound.

1. Set the compression damping to the standard set-ting and perform the following:

   a. Turn the compression damping adjuster (C, **Figure 56**) clockwise until it stops. This is the hardest setting.

   b. Back the adjuster out (counterclockwise) eight clicks. The compression damping is now adjusted to the standard setting.

   c. Fine tune the setting by turning the adjuster slightly until the two indexing dots align.

2. To further adjust the compression damping, set the damping to the standard setting and then perform the following:

*NOTE*
*When adjusting the compression damp-ing, do so gradually. Turn the compres-sion damping adjuster in one-click increments and then test ride the motor-cycle.*

   a. To reduce the compression damping, turn the adjuster counterclockwise toward the *S* (soft) marked on the shock housing.

   b. To increase the compression damping, turn the adjuster clockwise toward the *H* (hard) mark on the shock housing

### Rebound damping

Rebound damping affects the rate at which the shock absorber returns to its extended position after compression. Rebound damping does not affect the action of the shock on compression.

*NOTE*
*When turning the adjuster, make sure it clicks into one of the detent positions. Otherwise, the adjuster automatically sets to the stiffest position.*

1. Set the rebound damping to the standard setting and perform the following:

   a. Turn the rebound adjuster (**Figure 57**) clock-wise until it stops. This is the hardest setting.

   b. Back the adjuster out (counterclockwise) 11 clicks. The rebound damper is now adjusted to the standard setting.

   c. Fine tune the setting by turning the adjuster slightly until the two indexing dots align.

2. To further adjust the rebound damping, set the damping to the standard setting and then perform the following:

*NOTE*
*When adjusting the rebound damping, do so gradually. Turn the rebound*

*damping adjuster in one-click incre-ments, and then test ride the motorcycle.*

   a. To reduce the rebound damping, turn the ad-juster counterclockwise toward the *S* (soft) marked on the shock housing.

   b. To increase the rebound damping, turn the ad-juster clockwise toward the *H* (hard) mark on the shock housing

### DRIVE CHAIN

### Drive Chain Lubrication

Lubricate the drive chain at the interval indicated in **Table 1**. To prevent the side plates and rollers from rusting, the actual chain lubrication is enclosed within the chain by the O-rings (**Figure 58**).

A properly maintained drive chain provides maxi-mum service life and reliability. Use a chain lube de-signed for O-ring chains.

Not all commercial chain lubricants are recom-mended for use on O-ring drive chains. Read the product label to make sure it is formulated for O-ring chains.

1. Ride the motorcycle a few miles to warm up the drive chain. A warm chain increases lubricant pene-tration.

2. Securely support the motorcycle on a level surface with the rear wheel off the ground.

3. Oil the bottom chain run with a chain lubricant rec-ommended for use on O-ring drive chains. Concen-trate on getting the oil down between the side plates on both sides of the chain. Do not over lubricate.

4. Rotate the wheel and continue lubricating the chain until the entire chain has been lubricated.

5. Turn the rear wheel slowly and wipe excess oil from the chain with a shop cloth. Also, wipe any spilt lubricant from the rear hub, wheel and tire.

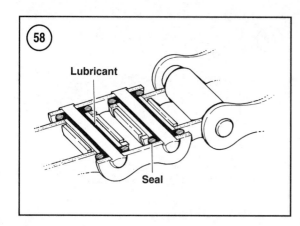

**58**

Lubricant

Seal

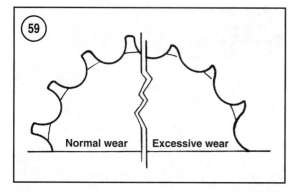

**59**

Normal wear | Excessive wear

## Drive Chain Cleaning

Clean the drive chain after riding in dusty or sandy conditions. A properly maintained chain provides maximum service life and reliability.

> *CAUTION*
> *Clean the chain only with kerosene. Solvents and gasoline cause the O-rings to swell. The drive chain then becomes so stiff it cannot move or flex. If this happens, the drive chain must be replaced. High-pressure washers, steam cleaning and coarse brushes also damage the O-rings.*

Because all models are equipped with an endless drive chain, it is not practical to break the chain to clean it. This section describes how to clean the drive chain while it is mounted on both sprockets.

1. Ride the motorcycle a few miles to warm up the drive chain.
2. Securely support the motorcycle on a level surface with the rear wheel off the ground.
3. Place some stiff cardboard and a drain pan beneath the drive chain.

> *WARNING*
> *Wear rubber gloves when cleaning the drive chain. To avoid catching your fin-*

gers and the rag between the chain and sprocket, do not rotate the rear wheel when wiping the chain. Clean one section of the chain at a time.

4. Soak a thick rag in kerosene and wipe it against the exposed section of the lower chain run. When this section of the chain is clean, turn the rear wheel to expose the next section and clean it. Repeat this process until all the chain is clean. To remove stubborn dirt, scrub the rollers and side plates with a soft brush.
5. Turn the rear wheel slowly, and wipe the drive chain dry with a thick shop cloth.
6. Clean any kerosene residue from the rear swing arm, wheel sprocket, chain guard, wheel and tire.
7. Lubricate the drive chain as described in this section.

## Drive Chain and Sprocket Inspection

Frequently check the chain and both sprockets for wear and damage.

1. Clean the drive chain as described in this chapter.
2. Securely support the motorcycle on a level surface with the rear wheel off the ground.
3. Turn the rear wheel and inspect both sides of the chain for missing or damaged O-rings.
4. Inspect the inner plate chain faces. They should be polished on both sides. If they show considerable uneven wear on one side, the sprockets are not aligned properly. Excessive wear requires replacement of not only the drive chain, but also of the engine and rear sprockets.
5. Inspect the engine and rear sprockets for the following defects:
   a. Undercutting or sharp teeth (**Figure 59**).
   b. Broken teeth.
6. Check the engine sprocket nut and the rear sprocket nuts for looseness. If loose, tighten them to the specification in **Table 5**.
7. If excessive chain or sprocket wear is evident, replace the drive chain and both sprockets as a complete set. If only the drive chain is replaced, the worn sprockets cause rapid chain wear.
8. At the rear sprocket, pull one of the links away from the sprocket. If the link pulls back more than 1/2 the height of the sprocket tooth (**Figure 60**), the chain is excessively worn. Confirm this by performing Step 9.
9. Measure the drive chain 21-pin length as follows:
   a. Loosen the rear axle nut.
   b. Loosen the rear torque arm nut (**Figure 61**).
   c. Loosen the drive chain adjuster locknut (A, **Figure 62**) located at the swing arm on both sides of the motorcycle.
   d. Tighten both swing arm adjuster bolts (B, **Figure 62**) an equal number of turns until the

lower chain run is straight. Make sure each chain puller aligns with the same swing arm indexing mark (C, **Figure 62**) on both sides of the motorcycle.

e. Use a vernier caliper to measure the distance between the 21 pins on the lower chain run (**Figure 63**). If this distance exceeds the specification in **Table 4**, the chain is excessively worn and must be replaced.

### Drive Chain Adjustment

Check and adjust the drive chain at the intervals specified in **Table 1**. If the motorcycle is operated at sustained high speeds or if it is repeatedly accelerated very hard, inspect the drive chain adjustment more often. A properly lubricated and adjusted drive chain provides maximum service life and reliability.

When adjusting the chain, check the free play at several places along its length by rotating the rear wheel. A chain rarely wears uniformly and as a result is tighter at some places than others. Measure the chain free play halfway between the sprockets (**Figure 64**). The chain free play at the tightest place on the chain must be within the range specified in **Table 4**.

1. Turn the engine off and shift the transmission into neutral.

2. Securely support the motorcycle on a level surface with the rear wheel off the ground.

3. Turn the rear wheel slowly, then stop it and check the chain tightness. Continue until the tightest point is located. Mark this spot with chalk and turn the wheel so the mark is located on the lower chain run midway between both sprockets. Check the chain at this point. If it is outside the specified range, adjust the drive chain as follows.

> *NOTE*
> *If the drive chain is kinked or feels tight, it may require cleaning and lubrication. Clean and lubricate the drive chain as described in this chapter.*

4. On U.S., California and Canada models, remove the cotter pin from the rear axle nut.

5. Loosen the rear axle nut.

6. Loosen the rear torque arm nut (**Figure 61**).

7. Loosen the chain adjuster locknut (A, **Figure 62**) on each side of the swing arm. Turn both adjuster bolts (B, **Figure 62**) an equal number of turns to obtain the correct drive chain slack. Check that each chain puller aligns with the same index mark (C, **Figure 62**) on the swing arm.

8. Recheck the chain free play in the middle of the lower run (**Figure 64**).

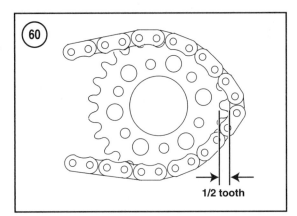

60

1/2 tooth

61

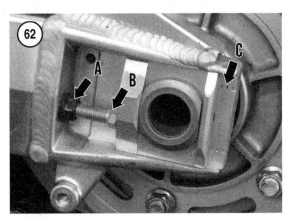

62

A  B  C

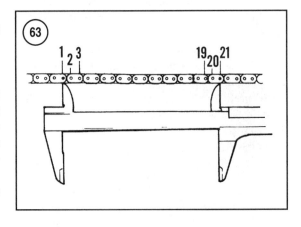

63

1 2 3          19 20 21

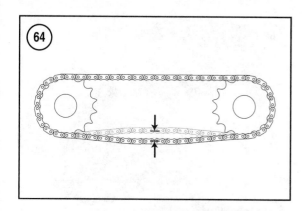

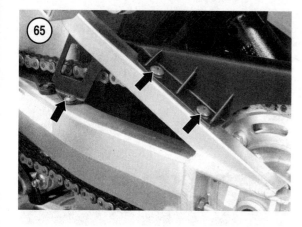

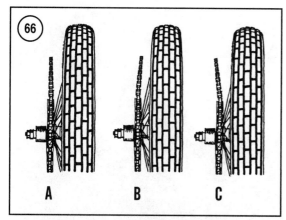

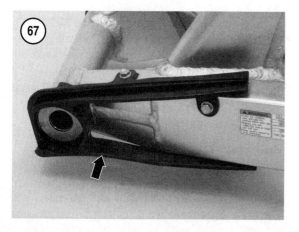

9. To verify the swing arm adjuster marks, remove the chain guard (**Figure 65**) from the swing arm. Check the rear wheel alignment by sighting along the drive chain as it runs over the rear sprocket. It should leave the rear sprocket in a straight line heading toward the engine sprocket as shown in A, **Figure 66**. If the chain veers to one side or the other (B or C, **Figure 66**), perform the following:

    a. Check that the chain pullers are set to the same index mark on each side of the swing arm.

    b. If not, readjust the drive chain to achieve the same position on both sides as well as maintain the correct free play. Tighten each drive chain adjuster locknut (A, **Figure 62**) securely.

10. Tighten the rear axle nut to 100 N•m (74 ft.-lb.). On U.S., California and Canada models, install a new cotter pin.

11. Tighten the rear torque arm nut (**Figure 61**) to 35 N•m (26 ft.-lb.).

### Drive Chain Slider Inspection

A slider is installed on the left side of the swing arm (**Figure 67**) to protect the swing arm from chain damage. Inspect the slider frequently for advanced wear or damage that would allow the chain to contact and damage the swing arm. Replace the slider if it is worn to the limit line. Replace the slider after removing the swing arm as described in Chapter Thirteen.

## BRAKE SYSTEM

### Brake Hoses

Check the brake hoses between the master cylinder and each brake caliper. If there are any leaks, tighten the connections and bleed the brakes as described in Chapter Fourteen. If this does not stop the leak or if a line is obviously damaged, cracked or chafed, replace the hose(s) and then bleed the brakes.

### Brake Fluid Change

Refer to Chapter Fourteen.

### Checking Brake Fluid Level

> **WARNING**
> *Use DOT 4 brake fluid. Others may vaporize and cause brake failure. Do not mix different brands or different types of brake fluid. They may not be compatible with one another.*

Keep the fluid level above the lower mark on the reservoir. If the brake fluid level reaches the lower level mark (front: **Figure 68**, rear: **Figure 69**), correct the fluid level by adding brake fluid.

1. Securely support the motorcycle on level ground.

2. When adding fluid to the front master cylinder, turn the handlebars so the master cylinder reservoir is level. For the rear master cylinder, position the motorcycle so the top of the reservoir is level.

3. Clean any dirt from the area around the top cover before removing the cover.

4. Remove the top cover, diaphragm plate (front master cylinder) and diaphragm.

*CAUTION*
*Be careful when handling brake fluid. Do not spill it on painted, plated surfaces or plastic parts. It damages the surfaces. Wash the area immediately with soapy water and thoroughly rinse.*

5. Add brake fluid.

6. Reinstall the diaphragm, diaphragm plate (front master cylinder) and top cover.

## Brake Pad Inspection

Refer to Chapter Fifteen.

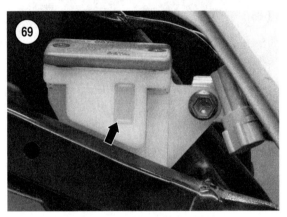

## Brake Lever Position

Adjust the distance between the front brake lever and the hand grip to suit the rider's preference.

1. Push the brake lever forward away from the handle grip.

2. Rotate the adjusting dial until the desired setting is opposite the arrow on the bracket (**Figure 70**). Setting No. 1 moves the brake lever to the furthest position away from the hand grip, setting No. 6 to the closest position.

3. Make sure the stop on the brake lever holder engages the detent in the adjusting dial.

4. After adjusting the lever position, spin the wheel and check for any brake drag. Readjust as necessary.

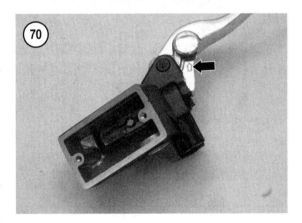

## Brake Pedal Height Adjustment

The pedal height is the distance from the top of the brake pedal to the top of the footpeg (**Figure 71**). If the brake pedal height is outside the range specified in **Table 4**, adjust the height by performing the following:

1. Securely support the motorcycle on a level surface.

2. Make sure the brake pedal is in the at-rest position.

3. Loosen the rear brake master cylinder locknut (A, **Figure 72**) and turn the pushrod (B) in either direction until the brake pedal height equals the dimension specified in **Table 4**.

4. Tighten the rear brake master-cylinder-rod locknut (A, **Figure 72**) to 18 N•m (13 ft.-lb.).

## Rear Brake Light Switch Adjustment

1. Turn the ignition switch on.

2. Depress the brake pedal and watch the brake light. The brake light should come on just before pressure

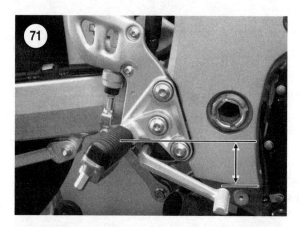

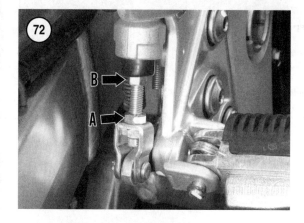

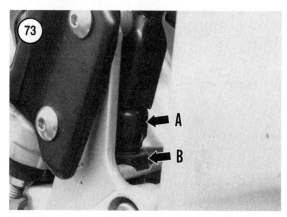

is felt at the brake pedal. If necessary, adjust the rear brake light switch as follows.

   a. Hold the switch body (A, **Figure 73**) and turn the adjusting locknut (B).

   b. To make the light come on earlier, turn the adjusting locknut and move the switch body *up*. Move the switch body *down* to delay the light.

   c. Make sure the brake light comes on when the pedal is depressed and goes off when the pedal is released. Readjust if necessary.

3. Turn the ignition switch off.

## GENERAL LUBRICATION

### Swing Arm Bearings

Lubricate the swing arm bearings at the rear suspension inspection intervals specified in **Table 1**. The swing arm must be removed to service the bearings. Refer to Chapter Thirteen.

### Steering Head Bearings

Remove, clean and lubricate the steering head bearings at the steering inspection interval specified in **Table 1**. Refer to the procedure in Chapter Twelve.

### Wheel Bearings

Worn wheel bearings cause excessive wheel play that causes vibration and other steering troubles. Inspect and lubricate the wheel bearings regularly as described in Chapter Eleven.

### Miscellaneous

Unless otherwise indicated, lubricate the following items with Suzuki Super Grease A or its equivalent: O-rings, seal lips, shift pedal pivot, brake pedal pivot, footrest pivot, clutch lever pivot, front brake lever pivot, sidestand pivot and control cable ends.

## FASTENER INSPECTION

Check the tightness of all fasteners, especially those on:

1. Engine mounting hardware.
2. Engine crankcase covers.
3. Handlebar and front fork.
4. Gearshift lever.
5. Drive chain components.
6. Brake pedal and lever.
7. Exhaust system.
8. Lighting equipment.

**Tables 1-5 are on the following pages.**

3

**Table 1  MAINTENANCE SCHEDULE**

Initial 600 miles (1000 km) or 1 month
  Change engine oil and replace oil filter.
  Check idle speed; adjust if necessary.
  On California models, synchronize the throttle bodies.
  Check throttle cable free play; adjust and lubricate as necessary.
  Clean and lubricate drive chain.
  Check drive chain and sprockets for wear or damage.
  Check drive chain free play; adjust if necessary.
  Check brake pads for wear.
  Check brake discs thickness; replace if necessary.
  Check brake discs for rust and corrosion; clean if necessary.
  Check steering play; lubricate components and adjust if necessary.
  Check and tighten all nuts, bolts and fasteners on exhaust system.
  Check tightness of all chassis fasteners; tighten if necessary.


Every 4000 miles (6000 km) or 6 months
  Check air filter element for contamination; clean or replace if necessary.
  Check spark plugs; replace if necessary.
  Check all fuel system hoses for leaks; repair or replace if necessary.
  Change engine oil.
  Check idle speed; adjust if necessary.
  Check throttle cable free play; adjust and lubricate as necessary.
  Check the clutch hose for leaks or wear; replace as necessary.
  Check the fluid level in the clutch master cylinder; adjust as necessary.
  Check radiator and all coolant hoses for leakage.
  Check drive chain and sprockets for wear or damage.
  Check drive chain free play; adjust if necessary.
  Clean and lubricate drive chain.
  Check brake pads for wear.
  Check brake discs thickness; replace if necessary.
  Check brake discs for rust and corrosion; clean if necessary.
  Check brake hoses for leakage; repair if necessary.
  Bleed the brake and check brake fluid level in both reservoirs; add fluid if necessary.
  Check tire and wheel rim condition.
  Check tightness of all chassis fasteners; tighten if necessary.


Every 7500 miles (12,000 km) or 12 months
  Check air filter element for contamination; clean or replace if necessary.
  Replace spark plugs.
  Change engine oil.
  Check the engine idle speed; adjust as necessary.
  Check all fuel system hoses for leakage; repair or replace if necessary.
  Synchronize the throttle bodies.
  Check EVAP (California models) and PAIR systems.
  Check throttle cable free play; adjust and lubricate as necessary.
  Check the clutch hose for leaks or wear; replace as necessary.
  Check the fluid level in the clutch master cylinder; adjust as necessary.
  Check radiator and all coolant hoses for leaks.
  Check drive chain and sprockets for wear or damage.
  Check drive chain free play; adjust if necessary.
  Clean and lubricate drive chain.
  Check brake pads for wear.
  Check brake discs thickness; replace if necessary.
  Check brake discs for rust and corrosion; clean if necessary.
  Check brake system for leaks; repair if necessary.
  Bleed the brake and check brake fluid level in both reservoirs; add fluid if necessary.
  Check tire and wheel rim condition.
  Check front fork operation and for leaks.
  Check steering play; lubricate components and adjust if necessary.
  Check and lubricate rear suspension components. Inspect the shock absorber for leaks.
  Check the tightness of an exhaust system fasteners; tighten as necessary.
  Check tightness of all chassis fasteners; tighten if necessary.

(continued)

## Table 1 MAINTENANCE SCHEDULE (continued)

Every 11,000 miles (18,000 km) or 18 months
   All 4000 miles (6000 km) or 6 month interval checks, and perform the following:
   Replace air filter element.
   Change engine oil, and replace oil filter.

Every 15,000 miles (24,000 km) or 24 months
   All 7500 miles (12,000 km) or 12 month interval checks, and perform the following:
   Check valve clearance; adjust if necessary.

Every 2 years
   Replace the engine coolant and hoses.
   Replace the brake fluid.
   Replace the clutch fluid.

Every 4 years*
   Replace all brake hoses.
   Replace the clutch hose.
   Replace the fuel hoses.
   Replace the EVAP hoses (California models).

*Manufacturer's recommendation.

## Table 2 TIRE SPECIFICATIONS

| Item | Front | Rear |
|---|---|---|
| Type | Tubeless | Tubeless |
| Size | 120/70 ZR17 (58W) | 190/50 ZR17 (73W) |
| Inflation pressure (cold)* | | |
|   Solo | 290 kPa (42 psi) | 290 kPa (42 psi) |
|   Rider and passenger | 290 kPa (42 psi) | 290 kPa (42 psi) |
| Minimum tread depth | 1.6 mm (0.06 in.) | 2.0 mm (0.08 in.) |

*Tire inflation pressure is for original equipment tires only. Aftermarket tires may require different inflation pressure.

## Table 3 RECOMMENDED LUBRICANTS AND FLUIDS

| | |
|---|---|
| Brake fluid | DOT 4 |
| Coolant | |
|   Type | Antifreeze/coolant compatible with aluminum radiator |
|   Ratio | Mixed with distilled water @ 50:50 ratio |
|   Capacity | |
|     Engine | Approx. 2700 ml (2.9 U.S. qt.) |
|     Reservoir | Approx. 250 ml (0.3 U.S. qt. ) |
| Engine oil | |
|   Classification | API SF or SG |
|   Viscosity | SAE 10W-40 |
|   Capacity | |
|     Oil change only | 3.3 liters (3.5 U.S. qt.) |
|     Oil and filter change | 3.5 liters (3.7 U.S. qt.) |
|     When engine completely dry | 4.2 liters (4.4 U.S. qt.) |
| Fork oil | |
|   Viscosity | Suzuki L01 fork oil or equivalent |
|   Capacity per leg | 480 ml (16.2 U.S. oz. ) |
| Fuel | Unleaded |
|   U.S., California, and Canada models | |
|     Pump octane - (R+M) / 2 method | 87 or higher |
| | (continued) |

**Table 3 RECOMMENDED LUBRICANTS AND FLUIDS (continued)**

| | |
|---|---|
| Fuel | |
| U.S., California, and Canada models (continued) | |
| Research octane | 91 or higher |
| All models except U.S., California and Canada | 91 or higher |
| Fuel tank capacity (total) | |
| 1999-2000 models | |
| California models | 20 liters (5.3 U.S. gal. ) |
| All models except California | 22 liters (5.8 U.S. gal. ) |
| 2001-on models | |
| California models | 19 liters (5.0 U.S. gal.) |
| All models except California | 21 liters (5.5 U.S. gal.) |

**Table 4 MAINTENANCE AND TUNE-UP SPECIFICATIONS**

| | |
|---|---|
| Battery | |
| Type | YT12A-BS Maintenance free (sealed) |
| Capacity | 12 volt 36 kC (10 amp hour)/10 HR |
| Brake pedal height | 55-65 mm (2.2-2.6 in.) below the footpeg |
| Compression pressure (at sea level) | |
| Standard | 1200-1600 kPa (174-232 psi) |
| Service limit | 900 kPa (131 psi) |
| Maximum difference between cylinders | 200 kPa (29 psi) |
| Cooling system test pressure | 120 kPa (17 psi) |
| Drive chain 21-pin length | 319.4 mm (12.6 in.) |
| Drive chain free play | 20-30 mm (0.8-1.2 in.) |
| Engine oil pressure @ 60° C (140° F) | 200-500 kPa (29-73 psi) @ 3000 rpm |
| Fast idle speed | 3500 rpm (when engine is warm) |
| Front fork adjustments | |
| Spring preload | 5th groove from top |
| Rebound damping | 3 clicks out |
| Compression damping | 9 clicks out |
| Idle speed | |
| 1999-2003 models | |
| Switzerland models | 1100-1200 rpm |
| All models except Switzerland | 1050-1250 rpm |
| 2004-on models | 1050-1250 rpm |
| Ignition timing* | |
| 1999 models | 4° BTDC @ 1150 rpm |
| 2000 models | |
| Cylinders Nos. 1 and 4 | 11° BTDC @ 1150 rpm |
| Cylinders Nos. 2 and 3 | 3° BTDC @ 1150 rpm |
| 2001-on models | |
| U.S., California and Canada models | 4° BTDC @ 1200 rpm |
| All models except U.S., California and Canada | |
| Cylinders Nos. 1 and 4 | 11° BTDC @ 1150 rpm |
| Cylinders Nos. 2 and 3 | 3° BTDC @ 1150 rpm |
| Radiator cap opening pressure | 95-125 kPa (14-18 psi) |
| Shift pedal height | 50-60 mm (2.0-2.4 in.) below the footpeg |
| Shock absorber | |
| Spring preload (spring set length) | |
| Standard setting | 183 mm (7.2 in.) |
| Softest setting | 180 mm (7.1 in.) |
| Stiffest setting | 190 mm (7.5 in.) |
| Rebound damping | 11 clicks out |
| Compression damping | 8 clicks out |
| Spark plug | |
| Gap | 0.7-0.8 (0.028-0.031) |
| Heat range | |
| Standard | NGK: CR9E, Denso: U27ESR-N |
| Hotter | NGK: CR8E, Denso: U24ESR-N |

(continued)

**Table 4 MAINTENANCE AND TUNE-UP SPECIFICATIONS (continued)**

| | |
|---|---|
| Spark plug | |
|   Heat range (continued) | |
|     Colder | NGK: CR10E, Denso:U31ESR-N |
| Steering tension | 200-500 grams (7.1-17.6 oz.) |
| Throttle cable free play | 2.0-4.0 mm (0.08-0.16 in.) |
| Valve clearance (cold) | |
|   Intake | 0.10-0.20 mm (0.004-0.008 in.) |
|   Exhaust | 0.20-0.30 mm (0.008-0.012 in.) |
| Wheel runout limit | |
|   Axial | 2.0 mm (0.08 in.) |
|   Radial | 2.0 mm (0.08 in.) |

*Not adjustable.

**Table 5 MAINTENANCE AND TUNE-UP TORQUE SPECIFICATIONS**

| Item | N•m | in.-lb. | ft.-lb. |
|---|---|---|---|
| Cylinder head cover bolt | 14 | – | 10 |
| Engine sprocket nut | 145 | – | 107 |
| Exhaust header bolt | 23 | – | 17 |
| Exhaust pipe hanger bolt | 23 | – | 17 |
| Fork bridge clamp bolt | | | |
|   Lower | 23 | – | 17 |
|   Upper | 23 | – | 17 |
| Front axle | 100 | – | 74 |
| Front axle clamp bolt | 23 | – | 17 |
| Handlebar clamp bolt | 10 | 89 | – |
| Handlebar holder nut | 35 | – | 26 |
| Muffler connecting nut | 25 | – | 18 |
| Muffler hanger nut | 23 | – | 17 |
| Muffler pipe clamp bolt | 23 | – | 17 |
| Oil line banjo bolt | | – | |
|   6 mm | 10 | 89 | – |
|   14 mm | 28 | – | 21 |
| Oil drain bolt | 23 | – | 17 |
| Oil gallery plug | | | |
|   6 and 8 mm | 18 | – | 13 |
|   10 mm | 16 | – | 12 |
|   16 mm | 35 | – | 26 |
| Oil pan bolt | 10 | 89 | – |
| Rear axle nut | 100 | – | 74 |
| Rear brake master-cylinder-rod locknut | 18 | – | 13 |
| Rear sprocket nuts | 60 | – | 44 |
| Starter clutch bolt cap | 11 | 97 | – |
| Spark plug | 11 | 97 | – |
| Timing inspection cap | 23 | – | 17 |
| Torque arm nut | | | |
|   Front | 28 | – | 21 |
|   Rear | 35 | – | 26 |

# CHAPTER FOUR

# ENGINE TOP END

This chapter covers the engine top end components. These include the camshafts, timing gears, valves, cylinder head, pistons and cylinder block. Valve adjustment procedures are in Chapter Three.

The Suzuki Hayabusa GSX1300R features a liquid-cooled, four-valve, in-line four cylinder engine. Valves are operated by dual camshafts driven by a single cam chain. Cam chain tension is maintained by an automatic, spring-loaded tensioner that bears against the rear run of the cam chain.

The engine and transmission share a common case and the same wet-sump oil supply. The flywheel and crankshaft position sensor are on the left side of the crankshaft. The clutch and timing rotor are on the right.

Specifications are in **Tables 1-3** at the end of the chapter.

## CYLINDER HEAD COVER

The cylinder head cover can be removed with the engine installed in the frame. The procedure is shown with the engine removed for photographic clarity.

### Removal/Installation

1. Securely support the motorcycle on a level surface.

2. Remove each fairing side panel (Chapter Fifteen).
3. Remove the battery (Chapter Nine).
4. Remove the fuel tank and air filter housing (Chapter Eight).
5. Disconnect the 2-pin connector (A, **Figure 1**) from the camshaft position sensor.
6. Disconnect the 2-pin connector (B, **Figure 1**) from each ignition coil/plug cap. Label the connector and ignition coil/ plug cap so they can be reinstalled in their original locations.
7. Remove the heat shield (Chapter Eight).

*NOTE*
*Before removing an ignition coil/plug cap, twist it to break the mating seal.*

8. Pull straight up and remove the ignition coil/ plug cap (**Figure 2**) from each spark plug.
9. Using a crisscross pattern, evenly loosen and remove the cylinder head cover bolts (**Figure 3**). Remove the cover bolts and their gaskets. Discard the bolt gaskets (**Figure 4**). They must be replaced to prevent an oil leak.
10. Pull the cover straight up and off the cylinder head.
11. Remove the dowels (**Figure 5**).
12. The cylinder head gasket usually remains attached to the cylinder head cover. Remove and dis-

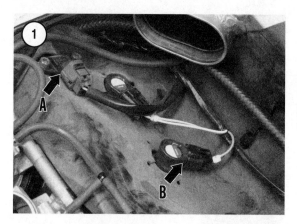

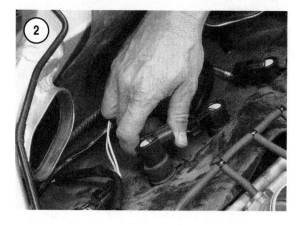

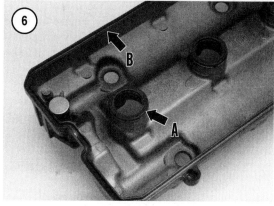

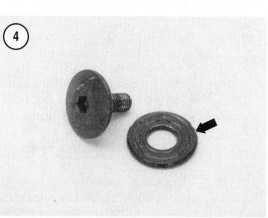

card the gasket even if it appears to be in good condition. The cylinder head gasket must be replaced.

13. Watch for the rubber gaskets (A, **Figure 6**) on each spark plug tower.

14. Installation is the reverse of removal. Note the following:

  a. Install the locating dowels (A, **Figure 5**).

  b. Fill the voids in the cylinder head with clean engine oil.

  c. Install a new cylinder head cover gasket into the groove (B, **Figure 6**) in the cover. Make sure the gasket is completely seated in the groove.

  d. Install a new rubber gasket onto each spark plug tower (A, **Figure 6**) in the cylinder head cover.

  e. Apply a light coat of Suzuki Bond No. 1207B, or an equivalent sealant, to the crescent-shaped portions of the gasket. This ensures an oil-tight seal between the cylinder head cover and the cylinder head.

  f. Set the cylinder head cover onto the cylinder head so the four crescent-shaped portions of the cover gasket properly engage the crescent-shaped areas of the cylinder head.

g. Install a new gasket (**Figure 4**) onto each cylinder head cover bolt.

h. Evenly tighten the cylinder head cover bolts in a crisscross pattern to 14 N•m (10 ft.-lb.).

### Inspection

1. Remove any old gasket material from the cylinder head and cover.

2. Remove all old gasket sealer residue from the gasket sealing surface around the perimeter of the cylinder head. Make sure to clean off all old sealant from the crescent-shaped surfaces at each end of the cylinder head.

3. Make sure the gasket groove (B, **Figure 6**) in the cylinder head cover is clean and free of any oil buildup from a previously leaking gasket. This surface must be clean and smooth to provide an oil-tight seal.

4. Check the cylinder head cover (**Figure 7**) for warping, cracks or damage. Replace the cover if necessary.

5. Inspect the cover bolts for thread damage. Replace as necessary.

### CAMSHAFT

*NOTE*
*The camshafts can be removed and installed with the engine in the frame. However, timing the camshafts is difficult because the frame restricts vision. The following procedure is shown with the engine removed from the frame.*

### Removal

1. Remove the engine (Chapter Five).

2. Remove the cylinder head cover.

3. Remove all four spark plugs (Chapter Three) so the engine can be easily rotated by hand.

4. Remove the timing inspection cap (A, **Figure 8**) and the starter clutch bolt cap (B) from the starter clutch cover.

5. Set the No. 1 cylinder to top dead center (TDC) on the compression stroke by performing the following:

a. Use the starter clutch bolt (A, **Figure 9**) to rotate the engine *clockwise*, when viewed from the right side, until the index line (B) on the starter clutch aligns with cutout (C) in the timing inspection window.

b. Check the timing mark on the exhaust camshaft sprocket. The No. 1 arrow on the exhaust sprocket should point forward and align with the top edge of the cylinder head. Refer to **Figure 10**.

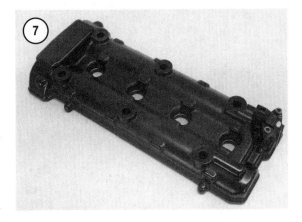

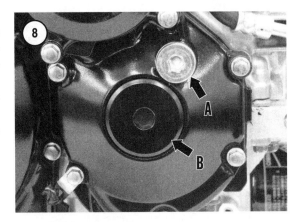

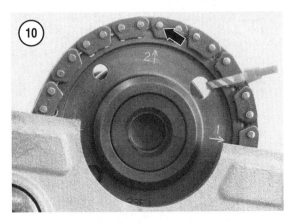

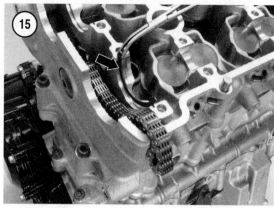

4

c. If the No. 1 arrow is not positioned as shown, rotate the engine one full revolution clockwise (360°) until the index line on the starter clutch once again aligns cutout (C, **Figure 9**) in the timing inspection window. The No. 1 arrow on the exhaust cam sprocket should now point forward and align with the cylinder head.

6. Remove the cam chain tensioner as described in this chapter.

7. Remove the upper cam chain guide bolts (A, **Figure 11**) and remove the upper guide (B).

8. Remove each oil pipe bolt (A and B, **Figure 12**) and its washer. Lower the oil pipe from the fitting on each cam shaft holder. Note that the oil pipe bolt on the exhaust side (A, **Figure 12**) is slightly longer that the intake-side bolt (B).

9. Tie one end of a safety wire to the cam chain and secure the other end to the exterior of the engine.

10. Reverse the tightening sequence stamped on the intake camshaft holder, and evenly loosen the camshaft holder bolts (A, **Figure 13**). Remove the bolts. Note that the two bolts (B, **Figure 13**) at the ball bearing end of (cam chain side) of the camshaft holder are longer than the other bolts.

11. Lift the intake camshaft holder (C, **Figure 13**) straight up, and remove it from the cylinder head. Watch for the dowels (A, **Figure 14**) beneath the intake camshaft holder.

12. Repeat Step 10 and Step 11, and remove the exhaust camshaft holder (D, **Figure 13**). Watch for the dowels (B, **Figure 14**) beneath this holder also.

13. Disengage the cam chain from the intake camshaft sprocket, and remove the intake camshaft. (C, **Figure 14**). Repeat this procedure, and remove the exhaust camshafts (D, **Figure 14**) from the cylinder head. Watch for the C-ring (**Figure 15**) in each bearing boss in the head.

*CAUTION*
*If the crankshaft must be rotated while the camshafts are removed, pull up on*

*the cam chain so it properly engages the timing sprocket. Hold the chain taut on the timing sprocket while rotating the crankshaft. If this is not done, the cam chain could become kinked and damage the chain, timing sprocket or crankcase.*

**Installation**

*NOTE*
*The camshafts and camshaft holders are identified by an IN or EX. Refer to A, **Figure 16**. Install a camshaft and its holder on the correct side of the cylinder head.*

1. Pull up on the cam chain so it properly meshes with the timing sprocket.
2. If necessary, use the starter clutch bolt (A, **Figure 9**) to rotate the engine clockwise, when viewed from the right side, until the index line on the starter clutch (B) aligns with the cutout (C) in the starter clutch cover. Hold the cam chain taut against the timing sprocket when rotating the engine.
3. Lubricate all bearing surfaces in the cylinder head (A, **Figure 17**) and camshaft holders (**Figure 18**) with clean engine oil.
4. Install a C-ring (**Figure 15**) into the bearing boss on each side of the cylinder head.
5. Apply Suzuki Moly Paste (part No. 99000-25140), or its equivalent, to the camshaft journals and cam lobes.

*CAUTION*
*The front run of the cam chain must be taut against the timing sprocket during camshaft installation. Any slack in the cam chain must be on the rear run of the chain (the chain tensioner side).*

6. Set the exhaust camshaft into the cam chain and lower the camshaft onto the cylinder head bearing surfaces. Lift the chain and rotate the exhaust camshaft until the No. 1 arrow points forward and aligns with the top surface of the cylinder head. The No. 2 arrow should also point straight up. Refer to **Figure 10**.
7. Properly mesh the cam chain with the sprocket, and use a cable tie to secure the cam chain to the cam sprocket.
8. Fit the intake camshaft (A, **Figure 19**) through the cam chain and lower the camshaft into the cylinder head.
9. Note the No. 2 arrow on the exhaust cam sprocket points to a pin (**Figure 10**) on the cam chain. Mark this pin. It is the first pin (**Figure 20**).

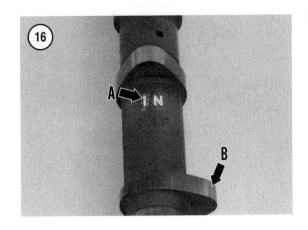

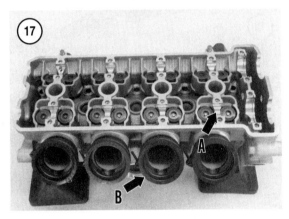

10. Starting at this first pin, count back to the 15th pin. Mark this pin as well. Properly mesh the cam chain onto the intake cam sprocket so this 15th pin (B, **Figure 19**) sits opposite the No. 3 arrow on the intake cam sprocket. Secure the cam chain to the intake sprocket with a cable tie.

*CAUTION*
*Damage could result from improper cam chain/camshaft installation. Recheck the work several times to ensure correct alignment.*

*NOTE*
*The cam chain is now meshed with the timing sprocket, the exhaust camshaft sprocket and the intake camshaft sprocket. Do not disturb the crankshaft or camshafts until the camshaft holders and cam chain tensioner are properly installed.*

11. Install the camshaft holder dowels (A and B, **Figure 14**) into the cylinder head.
12. Refer to the *IN* or *EX* marks on the camshaft holders, and set the exhaust camshaft holder (D, **Figure 13**) into the front of the engine. Fit the intake camshaft holder (C, **Figure 13**) into the rear side.

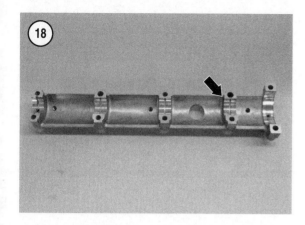

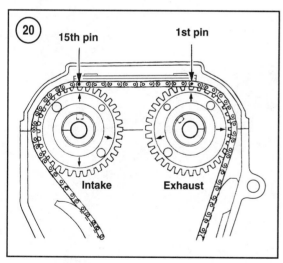

**CAUTION**
*If the camshaft holder bolts require replacement, do not substitute another type of bolt. It does not have the holding capability of these bolts. The use of a substitute bolt design may cause engine damage.*

13. Install and finger-tighten the camshaft holder bolts (A and B, **Figure 13**) into each holder. Install

the two longer camshaft holder bolts (B, **Figure 13**) into the ball bearing end of each holder.

**CAUTION**
*Failure to tighten the bolts in the specified order damages the bearing surfaces in the cylinder head and camshaft holders.*

14. Tighten the camshaft holder bolts on one holder by performing the following:
   a. Following the sequence on the camshaft holder, evenly tighten the bolts in ascending order.
   b. Tighten the bolts in stages to slowly pull the camshaft holder down onto its camshaft.
   c. Tighten the camshaft holder bolts to 10 N•m (89 in.-lb.) on the final pass.

15. Repeat Step 14 for the other camshaft holder.

16. Install the cam chain tensioner as described in this chapter.

17. Recheck the timing marks. All marks must still be properly aligned as shown in **Figure 9** and **Figure 20**. If incorrect, reposition the cam chain on the sprockets.

18. Clip the cable tie from each camshaft sprocket.

**CAUTION**
*If there is any binding while rotating the crankshaft, **stop**. Determine the cause before proceeding.*

19. Use the starter clutch mounting bolt (A, **Figure 9**) to rotate the engine clockwise when viewed from the right side of the motorcycle. Rotate the crankshaft through several complete revolutions, and check the operation of the top end.

20. Fit the oil pipe onto the fittings on the left end of the camshaft holders. Secure the oil pipe to the fittings on the ends of the camshaft holders with the oil pipe bolts (A and B, **Figure 12**) and washers. Install the longer oil pipe bolt (A, **Figure 12**) into the exhaust side. Tighten the oil pipe bolts to 10 N•m (89 in.-lb.).

21. Install the upper cam chain guide (B, **Figure 11**) into the cylinder head. Tighten the upper cam chain guide bolts (A, **Figure 11**) to 10 N•m (89 in.-lb.).

22. Adjust the valves as described in Chapter Three.

23. Install the timing inspection cap (A, **Figure 8**) and the starter clutch bolt cap (B). Lubricate a new O-ring with engine oil, and install an O-ring onto each cap. Tighten the timing inspection cap to 23 N•m (17 in.-lb.). Tighten the starter clutch bolt cap to 11 N•m (97 in.-lb.).

24. Install the cylinder head cover as described in this chapter.

25. Install the spark plugs as described in Chapter Three.

26. Install the engine as described in Chapter Five.

### Inspection

1. Check the camshaft lobes (B, **Figure 16**) for wear. The lobes should not be scored and the edges should be square.

2. Measure the height of each lobe (**Figure 21**) with a micrometer. Replace the camshaft if any lobe is out of specification.

3. Check each camshaft journal for wear and scoring.

4. Measure the outside diameter of each camshaft journal (**Figure 22**) with a micrometer. Record each measurement for use when checking camshaft oil clearance. Replace the camshaft if any journal diameter is out of specification.

5. If the journals are excessively worn or damaged, check the bearing surfaces in the cylinder head (A, **Figure 17**) and in the camshaft holders (**Figure 18**). They should not be scored or excessively worn. If any of the bearing surfaces are worn or scored, the cylinder head assembly and camshaft holders must be replaced as a set.

6. Place each camshaft on a set of V-blocks, and check its runout with a dial indicator. Replace the camshaft if its runout exceeds the service limit (**Table 2**).

7. Inspect the camshaft sprocket (A, **Figure 23**) for broken or chipped teeth. Also check the teeth for cracking or rounding. If either of the camshaft sprockets is damaged or excessively worn, replace the camshaft. Also inspect the timing rotor as described in this chapter.

> *NOTE*
> *If the camshaft sprockets are worn, check the cam chain, chain guides and chain tensioner for damage.*

8. Manually spin the camshaft ball bearing (B, **Figure 23**). It should turn smoothly without noise or binding.

9. Inspect the sliding surface of the upper cam chain guide (**Figure 24**) for wear or damage. Replace the upper guide as necessary.

10. Make sure the oil pipe (**Figure 25**) is clear. Clean it with solvent and blow clear if necessary.

### *Oil clearance*

Before installing the camshafts, wipe all oil residue from each camshaft journal and from the bearing surfaces of the cylinder head and camshaft holders.

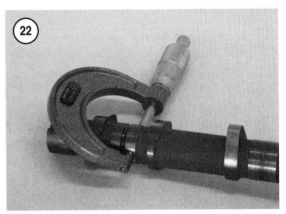

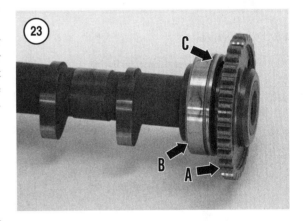

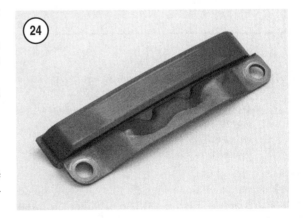

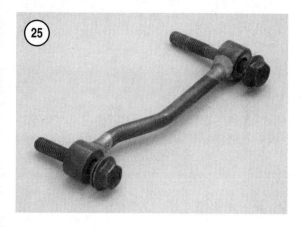

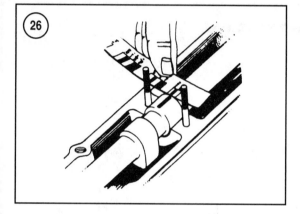

6. Refer to the *IN* or *EX* mark on each camshaft holder, and set the correct camshaft holder into place in the cylinder head (**Figure 27**).

7. Loosely install the camshaft holder bolts (A and B, **Figure 27**). Install the two longer camshaft holder bolts (B, **Figure 27**) at the bearing end of the holder.

8. Following the sequence on the camshaft holder, evenly tighten the camshaft holder bolts in ascending order. Tighten the bolts in stages to slowly pull the camshaft holder down onto its camshaft. Tighten the camshaft holder bolts to 10 N•m (89 in.-lb.) on the final pass.

> *CAUTION*
> *Do not rotate the camshafts with the Plastigage in place.*

9. Reverse the order of the tightening sequence and evenly loosen the camshaft holder bolts in 2-3 stages.

10. Pull straight up and carefully remove the camshaft holder.

11. Measure the flattened Plastigage (**Figure 26**) at its widest point according to the manufacturer's instructions. Record the measurement.

> *CAUTION*
> *Make sure to remove all traces of Plastigage from the camshaft holders and from the camshaft journals. If any Plastigage is left in the engine, it can plug an oil control orifice and cause engine damage.*

12. Remove *all* Plastigage from the camshaft and camshaft holders.

13. Repeat Steps 1-12 for the other camshaft.

14. If the camshaft oil clearance is greater than the service limit (**Table 2**), perform the following to determine which component requires replacement:

   a. With the camshafts removed from the cylinder head, install the camshaft holders. Install the two longer camshaft holder bolts (B, **Figure 27**) at the bearing end of the holder.

   b. Follow the tightening sequence on each holder, and evenly tighten the camshaft holder bolts in 2-3 stages. Tighten the bolts to 10 N•m (89 in.-lb.) on the final pass.

   c. Use a telescoping gauge to measure the inside diameter of the each camshaft bearing (**Figure 28**). Record the readings.

   d. Measure the outside diameter of each camshaft journal (**Figure 22**). Record the readings.

   e. Compare a camshaft journal's outside diameter and the inside diameter of its related camshaft bearing. If the inside diameter of the camshaft bearing exceeds specification, replace the cyl-

1. Do not install the cam chain onto the camshafts for this procedure.

2. Install a C-ring (**Figure 15**) into the bearing boss on the correct side of the cylinder head.

3. Refer to the *IN* and *EX* marks (**Figure 16**) on the camshaft, and set the camshaft into its correct location in the cylinder head. Make sure the slot (C, **Figure 23**) in the bearing engages the C-ring.

4. Install the camshaft holder dowels (A or B, **Figure 14**) into the cylinder head.

5. Place a strip of Plastigage onto each camshaft journal so the Plastigage parallels the camshaft (**Figure 26**).

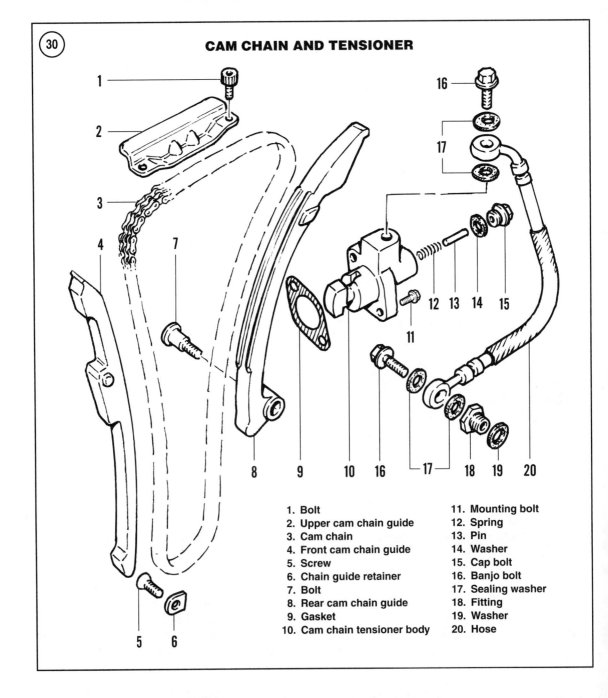

**CAM CHAIN AND TENSIONER**

1. Bolt
2. Upper cam chain guide
3. Cam chain
4. Front cam chain guide
5. Screw
6. Chain guide retainer
7. Bolt
8. Rear cam chain guide
9. Gasket
10. Cam chain tensioner body
11. Mounting bolt
12. Spring
13. Pin
14. Washer
15. Cap bolt
16. Banjo bolt
17. Sealing washer
18. Fitting
19. Washer
20. Hose

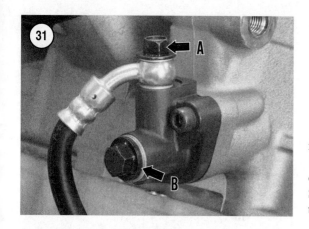

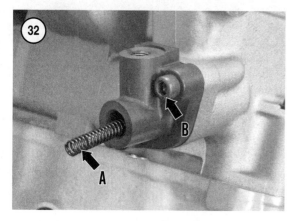

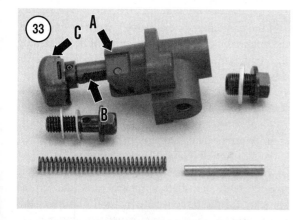

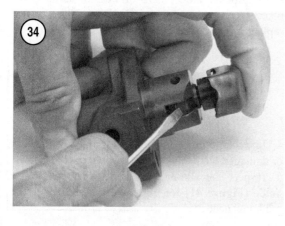

inder head and camshaft holders as a set. If the camshaft journal outside diameter is out of specification, replace the camshaft.

## CAM CHAIN TENSIONER

The following procedure covers the oil-dampened ratchet tensioner installed on 2001-on models. If a 1999-2000 model is still equipped with an old-style original cam chain tensioner (**Figure 29**), have a Suzuki dealership replace it. Do not operate the motorcycle with the old-style tensioner.

### Removal/Inspection/Installation

Refer to **Figure 30** for this procedure.

> *CAUTION*
> *The cam chain tensioner is a non-return type. After the tensioner mounting bolts are loosened, the tensioner assembly must be **completely removed** and the plunger reset. If the mounting bolts are loosened, do not simply retighten them. The plunger has already moved out to an extended position and exerts too much pressure on the cam chain leading to engine damage.*

1. Remove the fuel tank and air filter housing as described in Chapter Eight.
2. Remove the banjo bolt (A, **Figure 31**), and separate the oil line from the cam chain tensioner. Watch for the sealing washer on each side of the oil line fitting.
3. Remove the cap bolt (B, **Figure 31**) and its washer.
4. Remove the spring (A, **Figure 32**) from the tensioner body. Watch for the pin behind the spring.
5. Remove the mounting bolts (B, **Figure 32**), and pull the cam chain tensioner and its gasket from the cylinder head.
6. Inspect the housing (A, **Figure 33**) for cracks or other damage. Replace the tensioner assembly if necessary.
7. Inspect the tensioner rack (B, **Figure 33**) for chipped or missing teeth.
8. Check the plunger end (C, **Figure 33**) for damage.
9. Release the ratchet lock and press the plunger into the tensioner body (**Figure 34**).
10. Apply molybdenum disulfide grease to the plunger end. Fit the tensioner body, along with a new gasket, into place in the cylinder head.

11. Apply Suzuki Thread Lock 1342, or its equivalent, to the mounting bolt threads, and install the bolts (B, **Figure 32**). Tighten the cam chain tensioner mounting bolts to 10 N•m (89 in.-lb.).

12. Set the oil line onto the tensioner. Place a new sealing washer onto each side of the oil fitting, and loosely install the banjo bolt (A, **Figure 31**).

13. Position the oil fitting so its neck forms a 45° angle with the center of the tensioner body as shown in **Figure 35**.

14. If removed, connect the lower oil fitting to the crankcase. Route the oil line as shown in **Figure 36**. Make sure the fitting neck does not contact the crankcase. Install a sealing washer onto each side of the fitting.

15. Tighten the banjo bolt(s) to 12 N•m (106 in.-lb.).

16. Fit the adjusting pin into the spring (**Figure 37**), and install the spring/pin assembly into the tensioner body (A, **Figure 32**).

17. Install the cam chain tensioner cap bolt (B, **Figure 31**) along with its washer. Tighten securely.

## CAM CHAIN AND CHAIN GUIDES

A continuous cam chain is used on all models. Do not cut the chain; replacement links are not available.

### Removal/Installation

Refer to **Figure 30**.

1. Remove the cylinder head as described in this chapter.

2. Remove the starter clutch (Chapter Five).

3. Pull the front cam chain guide straight up and remove it from the cylinder block. Note how the stop (**Figure 38**) on the guide engages the boss in the cylinder block.

4. Remove the cam chain guide bolt (A, **Figure 39**) and lift the rear cam chain guide from the cylinder block.

5. Disengage the cam chain (B, **Figure 39**) from the timing sprocket and lift the chain from the cam chain tunnel.

6. If necessary, remove the timing sprocket as described in *Crankshaft Inspection* in Chapter Five.

7. Inspect the cam chain, guides and timing sprocket as described in this section.

8. Also check the cam chain guide retainer screw (C, **Figure 39**). If necessary, apply Suzuki Thread Lock 1342 to the screw, and tighten the retainer screw to 8 N•m (71 in.-lb.).

9. Installation is the reverse of removal. Note the following:

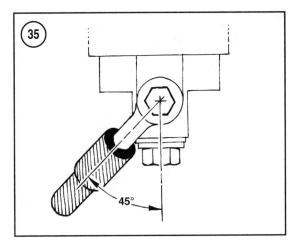

a. Make sure the cam chain properly engages the timing sprocket.

b. Apply Suzuki Thread Lock 1342 to the threads of the cam chain guide bolt (A, **Figure 39**), and tighten the bolt to 10 N•m (89 in.-lb.).

c. When installing the front cam chain guide, seat its upper stop into the boss (**Figure 38**) in the cylinder block. When properly installed, the guide's lower end sits inside the retainer as shown in **Figure 40**.

### Inspection

If the cam chain is excessively worn or damaged, the automatic chain tensioner may not be tensioning the chain properly. Refer to *Cam Chain Tensioner* in this chapter.

1. Clean the cam chain (**Figure 41**) in solvent. Blow it dry with compressed air.

2. Check the cam chain for:

a. Worn or damaged pins and rollers.

b. Cracked or damaged side plates.

3. If the cam chain is excessively worn or damaged, inspect both camshaft sprockets and the timing sprocket for the same wear condition. If either camshaft sprocket shows signs of wear or damage, replace them both. If the timing sprocket is worn, replace it.

> *CAUTION*
> *If the cam chain, timing sprocket or either camshaft sprocket requires replacement, replace them as a set. The old parts quickly wear out the new one.*

4. Inspect the timing sprocket (**Figure 42**) for worn or damaged teeth.

5. Inspect the sliding surface of each cam chain guide (**Figure 41**) for excessive wear. Replace the guides as needed.

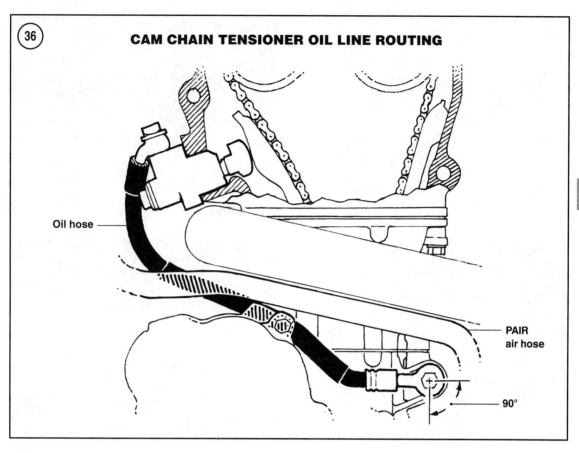

**36**

## CAM CHAIN TENSIONER OIL LINE ROUTING

Oil hose

PAIR
air hose

90°

4

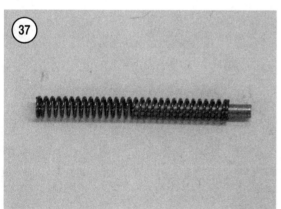

**37**

**39**

A

B

C

**38**

**40**

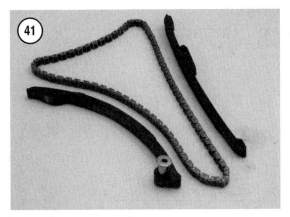

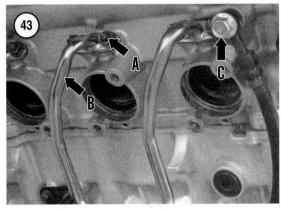

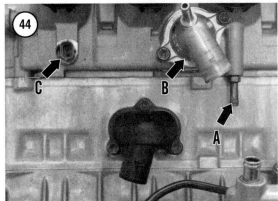

## CYLINDER HEAD

### Removal

1. Remove the engine (Chapter Five).

2. Remove the cylinder head cover, both camshafts and the cam chain tensioner (this chapter).

3. Tie one end of a safety wire to the cam chain and secure the other end to the outside of the engine.

4. Remove the mounting nuts (A, **Figure 43**) and disconnect each PAIR valve pipe (B) from its fitting on the cylinder head.

5. Remove the banjo bolt (C, **Figure 43**) and disconnect the oil hose from the fitting on the cylinder head. Secure the hose in a plastic bag so oil does not leak. Watch for the sealing washer on each side of the oil line fitting.

6. Disconnect the bypass hose from the coolant bypass fitting (A, **Figure 44**) on the rear of the head.

7. Remove the thermostat cover (B, **Figure 44**) and the thermostat (Chapter Ten). Disconnect the 2-pin connector from the coolant temperature sensor (C, **Figure 44**).

8. Unscrew and remove the cylinder head side bolt (A, **Figure 45**) and its washer. Note that the metal side of the washer (**Figure 46**) faces out toward the

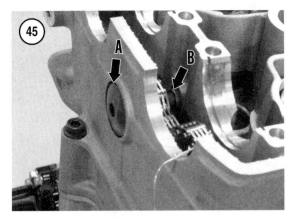

**4**

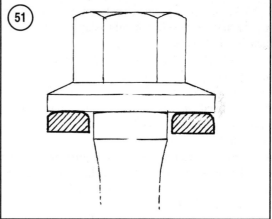

locations in the head could become un-
clear.

9. If the cylinder head is going to be inspected and/or
serviced, remove the valve lifters and shims before
removing the head. Refer to *Valve Lifters and Shims,
Removal/Installation* in this chapter.

10. Make a cardboard template of the cylinder head.
Punch a hole in the template for each bolt location,
and then mark the bolt number next to the hole. As
the bolt is removed, place it into its proper hole in the
template. This makes installation much easier.

11. On the right side, remove the 6-mm cylinder
head bolts (**Figure 47**).

12. Loosen the cylinder nuts (**Figure 48**) on the right
side.

13. Reverse the tightening sequence shown in **Figure 49**, and evenly loosen the 10-mm cylinder head
bolts (**Figure 50**) in two-to-three stages.

14. Remove the bolts and washers. Note that the cylinder head bolt washers are directional. The rounded
side of the washer faces the bolt head (**Figure 51**).

15. Break the cylinder head free from the cylinder
block by tapping around the perimeter with a rubber

bolt head. The washer must be reinstalled with this
orientation during assembly.

> *CAUTION*
> *If the cylinder head is not going to be
> serviced, leave the valve lifters and
> shims in place. **Do not** turn the cylinder
> head over. The valve lifters and shims
> will fall out. If this happens, these parts
> could be damaged, and their original*

or soft faced mallet. If necessary, *gently* pry the cylinder head loose with a broad tipped screwdriver.

16. Lift the cylinder head straight up and off the cylinder block. Guide the cam chain through the tunnel in the cylinder head, and retie the safety wire to the outside of the engine.

17. Remove the cylinder head gasket (A, **Figure 52**) and locating dowels (B). Discard the gasket.

18. Place a clean shop cloth into the cam chain tunnel and cover the cylinder block with another clean shop rag.

### Installation

1. Make sure the cylinder head and cylinder block mating surfaces are clean of all gasket residue. Clean them again if necessary.

2. If removed, install the coolant bypass fitting (A, **Figure 44**). Apply Suzuki Bond 1207B to the threads of the fitting, and tighten the fitting to 14 N•m (10 ft.-lb.).

3. If removed, install the engine coolant temperature sensor (C, **Figure 44**). Tighten the sensor to 18 N•m (13 ft.-lb.).

4. Install the locating dowels (B, **Figure 52**) into the cylinder block, and install a new cylinder head gasket (A). Make sure all the holes in the gasket align with those in the cylinder block.

5. Position the cylinder head over the cylinder block, and run the cam chain through the cam chain tunnel.

6. Carefully lower the cylinder head onto the engine, and seat the cylinder head onto the cylinder block so the locating dowels engage the cylinder head.

7. Pull up on the cam chain and make sure it properly engages the timing sprocket before continuing. Tie the cam chain's safety wire to the outside of the engine.

8. Fit a washer onto each cylinder head bolt so the round side of washer faces the bolt head as shown in **Figure 51**.

9. Install the 10-mm cylinder head bolts (**Figure 50**). Apply clean engine oil to the bolt threads and bottom side of the washer. Install each bolt into the correct location in the cylinder head. Start each bolt by hand to make sure it is not cross-threaded.

10. Following the tightening sequence shown in **Figure 49**, evenly tighten the 10-mm cylinder head bolts in two-to-three stages.

11. Tighten the bolts to 25 N•m (18 ft.-lb.), and then to 52 N•m (38 ft.-lb.). Follow the tightening sequence (**Figure 49**) each time.

12. On the right side, install the 6-mm cylinder head bolts (**Figure 47**). Tighten these bolts to 10 N•m (89 in.-lb.).

13. Tighten the cylinder nuts (**Figure 48**) to 10 N•m (89 in.-lb.).

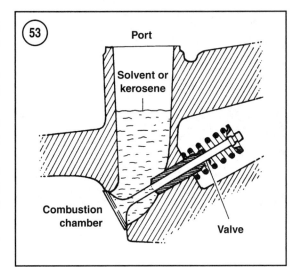

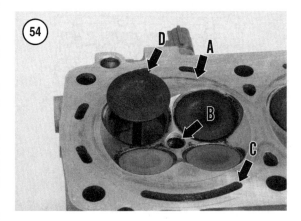

14. Pull up on the cam chain, and install the cylinder head side bolt (A, **Figure 45**). Make sure the bolt passes between the cam chain runs (B, **Figure 45**) and that the metal side of the washer (**Figure 46**) faces the bolt head. Tighten the cylinder head side bolt to 14 N•m (10 ft.-lb.).

15. If the valve lifters and shims were removed, install them as described in *Valve Lifters and Shims* (this chapter).

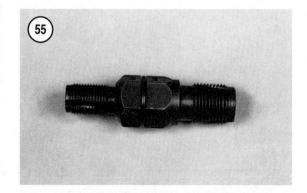

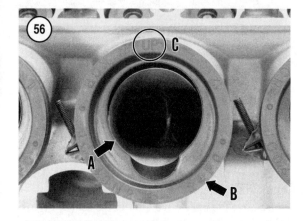

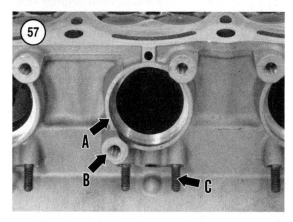

16. Install the thermostat and cover (B, **Figure 44**) as described in Chapter Ten.

17. Connect the bypass hose to the coolant bypass fitting (A, **Figure 44**).

18. Connect the oil hose to the oil port on the head. Apply a new sealing washer to each side of the oil hose fitting, and tighten the oil hose banjo bolt (C, **Figure 43**) to 20 N•m (15 ft.-lb.).

19. Connect each PAIR valve pipe (B, **Figure 43**) to its fitting on the cylinder head. Use a new gasket, and tighten each PAIR valve pipe nut (A, **Figure 43**) to 10 N•m (89 in.-lb.).

20. Install the camshafts, cam chain tensioner, and cylinder head cover (this chapter).

## Inspection

1. Before removing the valves or cleaning the cylinder head, perform a cylinder head leak test.

   a. If still installed, remove the valve lifters and shims as described in this chapter.

   b. Position the cylinder head so the exhaust ports faces up. Pour solvent or kerosene into each exhaust port opening (**Figure 53**).

   c. Turn the head over slightly, and check each exhaust valve area on the combustion chamber side. If the valve and seats are in good condition, no leaking past the valve seats will be found. If any area is wet, the valve seat is not sealing correctly. This can be caused by a damaged valve seat and/or valve face or by a bent or damaged valve. Remove the valve, and then inspect the valve and seat for wear or damage.

   d. Pour solvent into the intake ports, and then check the intake valves.

2. Remove all traces of gasket residue from the cylinder head and cylinder block mating surfaces. Do not scratch the gasket surfaces.

> *CAUTION*
> *Cleaning the combustion chamber with the valves removed can damage the valve seat surfaces. A damaged or even slightly scratched valve seat causes poor valve seating.*

3. Without removing the valves, remove all carbon deposits from the combustion chamber (A, **Figure 54**). Use a fine wire brush dipped in solvent or make a scraper from hardwood. Make sure not to damage the head, valves or spark plug threads.

4. Examine the spark plug threads (B, **Figure 54**) in the cylinder head for damage. If damage is minor or if the threads are dirty or clogged with carbon, use a spark plug thread tap (**Figure 55**) to clean the threads following the manufacturer's instructions. If thread damage is excessive, the threads can be restored by installing a steel thread insert.

5. Clean the entire head in solvent. Blow it dry with compressed air.

6. Inspect the intake manifolds (B, **Figure 56**) for cracks or other damage that would allow unfiltered air into the engine. If necessary, replace the intake manifolds.

7. Check for cracks in the combustion chambers (A, **Figure 54**), the intake ports (A, **Figure 56**) and the exhaust ports (A, **Figure 57**). A cracked head must be replaced if it cannot be repaired by welding.

8. Make sure all coolant passageways (C, **Figure 54**) are clear. If necessary, blow them clear with compressed air.

9. Inspect the threads on the exhaust pipe mounting holes (B, **Figure 57**) and PAIR studs (C) for damage. Clean them with an appropriate size metric tap or die if damaged.

*NOTE*
*If the cylinder head is bead-blasted, clean the head thoroughly with solvent and then with hot soapy water. Also chase each exposed thread with a tap to remove grit between the threads so they are not be damaged later. Residual grit left in the engine contaminates the oil and causes premature wear.*

10. After the head has been thoroughly cleaned, place a straightedge across the gasket surface at several points. Measure warp by inserting a feeler gauge between the straightedge and cylinder head at each location (**Figure 58**). Maximum allowable warp is in **Table 2**. Warp or nicks in the cylinder head surface could cause an air leak and overheating. If warp exceeds the limit, the cylinder head must be resurfaced or replaced. Consult a Suzuki dealership or machine shop.

11. Make sure all engine mounting bolt holes are in good condition. Clean them out with an appropriate size metric tap if necessary.

12. If removed, install each intake manifold in its original location. The UP mark on the manifold must face up (C, **Figure 56**), and the cutout in the manifold must engage the boss on the cylinder head. Tighten the clamp screw securely. Position each intake manifold clamp so it forms the angle shown in **Figure 59**, and then tighten the clamp securely.

## VALVE LIFTERS AND SHIMS

Refer to **Figure 60**.

If the cylinder head is going to be inspected and/or serviced, remove the valve lifters and shims before removing the head. To avoid mixing up the parts, work with the lifters from one cylinder at a time and systematically perform the following procedure.

### Removal/Installation

1. Make a holder for the valve lifters and shims. Identify it by the cylinder number and whether it is from the intake or exhaust side. The cylinders are numbered one through four from left to right. The No.1 cylinder is on the left side (alternator side) of the motorcycle. The term *left* refers to a rider's point-of-view while seated on the seat facing forward.

*NOTE*
*The shim may stick to the bottom of the valve lifter or it may remain in the valve spring retainer. Remove each lifter carefully so the shim does not fall into the engine.*

2. Remove a valve lifter (A, **Figure 61**) and then its shim (**Figure 62**) from the first cylinder. Place both of them in the correct location in the holder. Keep each shim together with its lifter.

3. Remove the next valve lifter in the set (B, **Figure 61**) and its shim. Set them together in the correct location in the holder.

4. Repeat this process for the other set of valve lifters and shims (C, **Figure 61**) in the same cylinder.

5. Repeat Steps 2-4 for the remaining three cylinders.

6. Inspect the valve lifters and shims for wear or heat damage. Service specifications for the outside diameter of the lifter and the inside diameter of the lifter bore in the cylinder head are not available. The lifter (with clean oil applied to its sides) should move up and down in the cylinder head bore with no binding or chatter. If the side of the lifter is scuffed or scratched, replace it.

*NOTE*
*To avoid mixing up the parts, work with one cylinder at a time. Position the holder containing the valve lifters and shims with the same orientation as the cylinder head. Make sure the lifter and shims for the No. 1 cylinder face the left side of the engine.*

7. Working with one cylinder at a time, first install the shim onto the top of the valve spring retainer. Make sure it is seated correctly. The side of the shim with the size stamp must face up (**Figure 62**).

8. Apply clean engine oil to the sides of the valve lifter and install it (A, **Figure 61**).

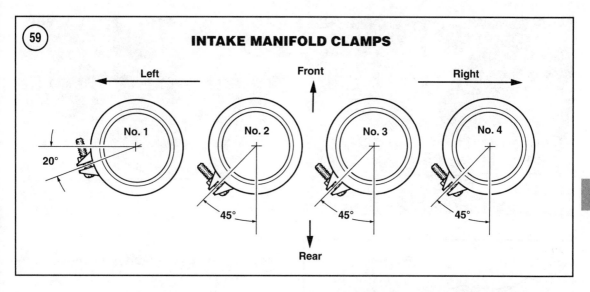

**59** **INTAKE MANIFOLD CLAMPS**

Left Front Right

No. 1 No. 2 No. 3 No. 4

20° 45° 45° 45°

Rear

**4**

**60** **VALVES**

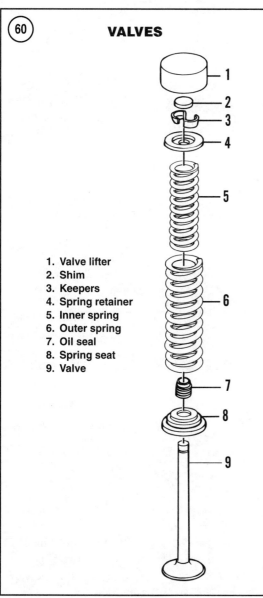

1. Valve lifter
2. Shim
3. Keepers
4. Spring retainer
5. Inner spring
6. Outer spring
7. Oil seal
8. Spring seat
9. Valve

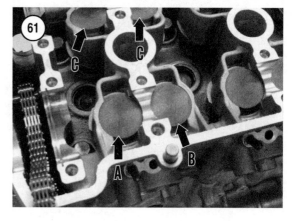

**61**

9. After the valve lifter has been installed, rotate the lifter by hand to make sure it is seated correctly and rotates freely.

10. Repeat Steps 7-9, and install all remaining shims and lifters into that cylinder. Continue with each successive cylinder until the process is completed.

## VALVES AND VALVE COMPONENTS

Refer to **Figure 60**.

**Valve Removal**

1. Remove the cylinder head, valve lifters and shims as described in this chapter.

2. Protect the walls of the valve bore during valve removal by performing the following:

    a. Cut the bottom out of a plastic 35-mm film canister.

    b. Cut open the side of the canister so it is flexible.

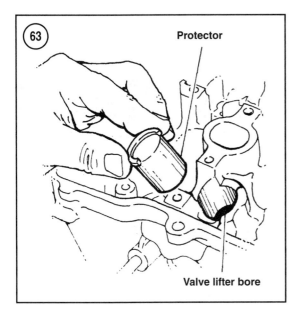

Protector

Valve lifter bore

   c. Insert the modified film canister between the
      valve assembly and the valve bore (**Figure 63**)
      during valve spring removal and installation.

3. Install a valve spring compressor squarely over
the valve spring retainer, and place the other end of
tool against the valve head.

*CAUTION*
*To avoid loss of spring tension, do not
compress the spring any more than necessary to remove the valve keepers.*

4. Tighten the valve spring compressor until the
valve keepers separate from the valve stem. Lift the
valve keepers (**Figure 64**) out through the valve
spring compressor with a magnet or needlenose pliers.

5. Gradually loosen the valve spring compressor,
and remove it from the cylinder head.

6. Remove the spring retainer (**Figure 65**), inner
spring (**Figure 66**) and outer spring (**Figure 67**).

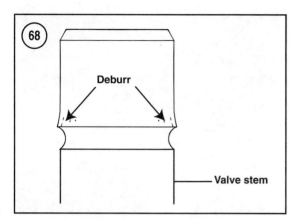

> *CAUTION*
> *Remove any burrs from the valve stem groove before removing the valve (**Figure 68**). Burrs damage the valve guide as the valve stem passes through the guide.*

7. Remove the valve (D, **Figure 54**) from the cylinder while rotating it slightly.

8. Pull the oil seal (**Figure 69**) from the valve guide. Discard the oil seal.

9. Remove the spring seat (**Figure 70**).

> *CAUTION*
> *Keep all components of each valve assembly together (**Figure 71**). Place each set in a divided carton or small reclosable plastic bags. Label each valve set. Identify a valve set by its cylinder number and whether it is an intake or exhaust valve.*

10. Repeat Steps 3-9 and remove the remaining valves. Keep all valve sets separate.

**Valve Installation**

1. Clean the end of the valve guide.

2. Install the spring seat (**Figure 70**) over the valve guide.

3. Apply molybdenum disulfide oil to a new oil seal (**Figure 72**), and seat the seal onto the end of the valve guide. (**Figure 69**).

4. Coat the valve stem with molybdenum disulfide oil. Install the valve (D, **Figure 54**) part way into the guide. Slowly turn the valve as it enters the oil seal, and continue turning it until the valve is completely installed.

5. Install the outer valve spring (**Figure 67**) and the inner valve spring (**Figure 66**). Install each spring so its closer wound coils (**Figure 73**) face down into the cylinder head. If the paint mark is still visible on the

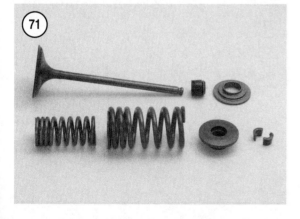

spring, the end with the paint should face up out of the head.

6. Install the spring retainer (**Figure 65**), and seat it onto the valve spring.

7. Protect the valve lifter bore with the same modified 35-mm film canister used during removal (**Figure 63**).

> *CAUTION*
> *To avoid loss of spring tension, do not compress the springs any more than necessary to install the valve keepers.*

8. Compress the valve spring with a valve spring compressor and install the valve keepers (**Figure 64**).

9. Make sure both keepers are seated around the valve stem before releasing the compressor.

10. Slowly release the compressor and remove it. Inspect the valve keepers to make sure they are properly seated (**Figure 74**). Tap the end of the valve stem with a drift and hammer. This ensures the keepers are properly seated (**Figure 75**).

11. Repeat Steps 1-10 for the remaining valves.

12. Install the shims and valve lifters (this chapter).

13. Install the cylinder head and camshafts (this chapter).

14. Adjust the valve clearance (Chapter Three).

**Valve Inspection**

When measuring the valves and valve components in this section, compare any measurements to the specifications in **Table 2**. Replace parts that are out of specification or show damage as described in this section.

1. Clean valves in solvent. Do not gouge or damage the valve seating surface.

2. Inspect the valve face (**Figure 76**). Minor roughness and pitting can be removed by lapping the valve as described in this section. Excessive unevenness on the contact surface is an indication that the valve is not serviceable.

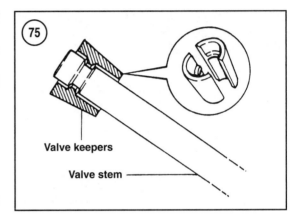

Valve keepers

Valve stem

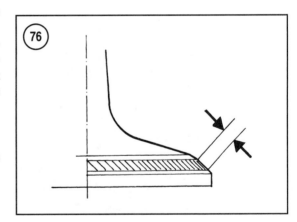

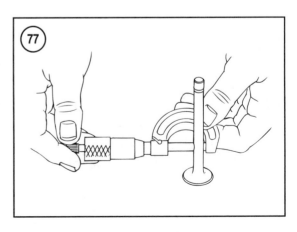

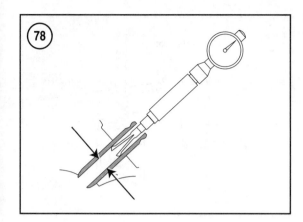

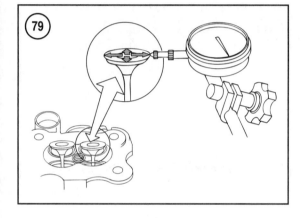

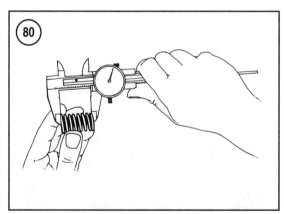

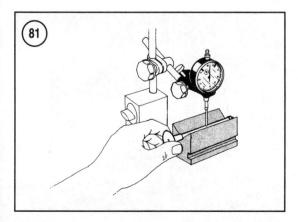

3. Inspect the valve stem for wear and roughness. Measure the valve stem outside diameter (**Figure 77**) with a micrometer.

4. Remove all carbon and varnish from the valve guides with a stiff spiral wire brush.

5. Measure the valve guide inside diameter with a small hole gauge (**Figure 78**). Measure the guide at the top, center and bottom positions. Measure the small hole gauge, and compare the readings to the specifications in **Table 2**.

6. Subtract the valve stem outside diameter (the Step 3 measurement) from the valve guide inside diameter (the Step 5 measurement). The difference is the valve stem-to-guide clearance. If the clearance is out of specification, examine the valve stem outside diameter and the valve guide inside diameter measurements. If the outside diameter is out of specification, replace the valve. If the inside diameter is out of specification, replace the valve guide.

7. If the valve guide inside diameter cannot be measured, measure the valve stem deflection by performing the following:

   a. Hold the valve approximately 10 mm (0.39 in.) off its seat.

   b. Attach a dial indicator to the valve head (**Figure 79**).

   c. Rock the valve sideways in two directions 90° to each other.

   d. If the valve stem deflection in either direction exceeds the service limit in **Table 2**, examine the valve stem outside diameter measurement taken earlier.

   e. If the outside diameter is out of specification, replace the valve. If the outside diameter is within specification, replace the valve guide. However, as a final check, take the cylinder head to a dealership or machine shop and have the valve guides measured.

8. Check each valve spring by performing the following:

   a. Visually inspect the valve spring for damage.

   b. Measure the valve spring free length (**Figure 80**).

9. Check the valve spring seats and valve keepers for cracks or other damage.

10. Check the valve stem runout with a V-block and dial indicator as shown in **Figure 81**. Replace the valve if the valve stem runout exceeds the service limit in **Table 2**.

11. Measure valve head radial runout with a V-block and dial indicator as shown in **Figure 82**. Replace the valve if the valve head radial runout exceeds the service limit in **Table 2**.

12. Measure the valve head thickness (A, **Figure 83**) with a vernier caliper. Replace the valve if the valve head thickness is less than the limit in **Table 2**.

13. Visually inspect the valve seats (**Figure 84**) in the cylinder head. If worn or burned, they may be reconditioned as described in this section. Seats and valves in near-perfect condition can be reconditioned by lapping with fine Carborundum paste. Check the valve seats as described in *Valve Seat Inspection* in this chapter.

### Valve Guide Replacement

#### Tools

The following Suzuki tools, or their equivalent, are required to perform this task.

1. Valve guide remover/installer: part No. 09916-44310.

2. Attachment: part No. 09916-53350.

3. Valve guide reamer (10.8 mm): part No. 09916-34580 (for reaming the valve guide bores).

4. Valve guide reamer (5.0 mm): part No. 09916-34570 (for reaming the installed valve guide).

5. Valve guide reamer handle: part No. 09916-34542.

#### Procedure

1. Place the new valve guides in a freezer.

2. Remove the intake manifolds (B, **Figure 52**), coolant bypass fitting (A, **Figure 85**) and coolant temperature sensor (C) from the cylinder head.

3. Remove the thermostat cover (B, **Figure 85**) and thermostat (Chapter Ten).

> *CAUTION*
> *Do not heat the cylinder head with a torch. Never bring a flame into contact with the cylinder head. Direct heat can warp the cylinder head.*

> *NOTE*
> *The odor of residual oil or solvent may remain in the oven after heating the cylinder head.*

4. Place the cylinder head in a shop oven and warm it to 212° F (100° C). To check the temperature, flick tiny drops of water onto the cylinder head. The head is heated to the proper temperature if the drops sizzle and evaporate immediately.

> *WARNING*
> *Wear heavy gloves when performing this procedure. The cylinder head is very hot.*

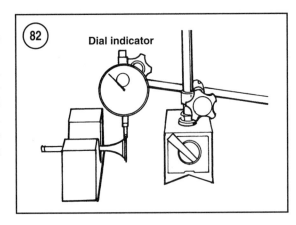

(82) Dial indicator

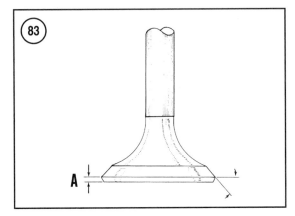

(83)

A

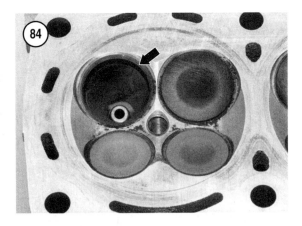

(84)

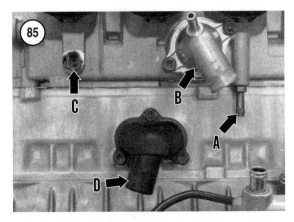

(85)

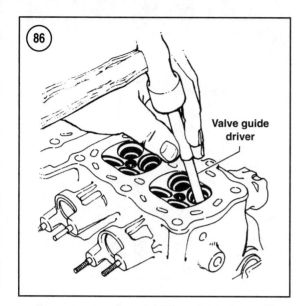

**Valve guide driver**

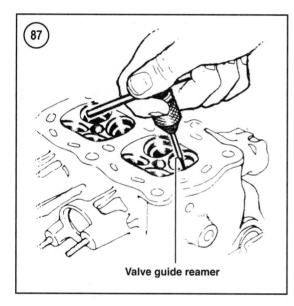

**Valve guide reamer**

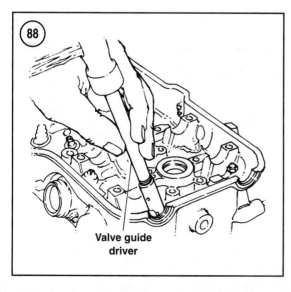

**Valve guide driver**

5. Using heavy gloves or kitchen pot holders, remove the cylinder head from the oven and place it onto wooden blocks with the combustion chamber facing up.

6. From the combustion side of the head, drive the old valve guide out of the cylinder head with the valve guide installer/remover (**Figure 86**) and a hammer.

7. Remove and discard the valve guide. *Never* reinstall a used valve guide. It is no longer true nor within tolerance.

> *NOTE*
> *Only oversized valve guides are available from Suzuki.*

8. After the cylinder head has cooled, ream the valve guide bore as follows:

   a. Apply cutting oil to both the valve guide bore and to the 10.8-mm valve guide reamer.

> *CAUTION*
> *Always rotate the valve guide reamer clockwise. The valve guide will be damaged if the reamer is rotated counter-clockwise.*

   b. Insert the valve guide reamer from the combustion chamber side (**Figure 87**), and rotate the reamer clockwise. Continue to rotate the reamer and work it down through the entire length of the valve guide bore. Apply additional cutting oil as needed during this procedure.

   c. Rotate the reamer *clockwise* until it has traveled all the way through the bore.

   d. Rotate the reamer clockwise, and completely withdraw the reamer from the valve guide.

9. Reheat the cylinder head as described in Step 4.

10. Using heavy gloves or kitchen pot holders, remove the cylinder head from the oven and place it onto wooden blocks with the combustion chamber facing down.

11. Remove one valve guide from the freezer.

> *CAUTION*
> *Failure to lubricate the new valve guide and guide bore damages the cylinder head and/or valve guide.*

12. Apply clean engine oil to the new valve guide and to the valve guide bore in the cylinder head.

13. From the top side of the cylinder head (camshaft side), drive the new valve guide into the cylinder head with a hammer, the valve guide installer/remover and the valve guide attachment. (**Figure 88**). Drive the valve guide into the bore until the attachment bottoms in the cylinder head, which sets the guide to the specified height (**Figure 89**).

14. After the cylinder head has cooled, ream the new valve guide as follows:

    a. Apply cutting oil to both the new valve guide and to the 5-mm valve guide reamer.

> *CAUTION*
> *Always rotate the valve guide reamer clockwise. The valve guide is damaged if the reamer is rotated counterclockwise.*

    b. Insert the 5-mm valve guide reamer from the combustion chamber side (**Figure 87**), and rotate the reamer *clockwise*. Continue to rotate the reamer and work it down through the entire length of the new valve guide. Apply additional cutting oil as needed.

    c. Rotate the reamer clockwise until it has traveled all the way through the new valve guide.

    d. Rotate the reamer *clockwise*, and completely withdraw the reamer from the valve guide.

    e. Measure the inside diameter of the valve guide with a small hole gauge (**Figure 78**). Measure the gauge with a micrometer, and compare the measurement to the specification in **Table 2**. Replace the valve guide if it is not within specification.

15. If necessary, repeat Steps 1-14 for any other valve guide.

16. Thoroughly clean the cylinder head and valve guides with solvent to wash out all metal particles. Dry the head with compressed air.

17. Lightly oil the valve guides to prevent rust.

18. Reface the valve seats as described in this section.

19. Install the intake manifolds in their original locations. The UP mark on the manifold must face up (C, **Figure 56**), and the cutout in the manifold must engage the boss on the cylinder head. Tighten the clamp screw securely. Position each intake manifold clamp so it forms the angle show in **Figure 59**, and tighten the clamp securely.

20. Install the coolant temperature sensor (C, **Figure 85**) and the bypass fitting (A) as described in *Cylinder Head, Installation*.

21. Install the thermostat and thermostat cover (B, **Figure 85**). Refer to Chapter Ten.

**Valve Seat Inspection**

1. Remove the valves as described in this section.

2. Thoroughly clean all carbon deposits from each valve face with solvent or detergent. Completely dry the valve face.

3. Spread a thin layer of marking compound evenly on a valve face, and insert that valve into its guide.

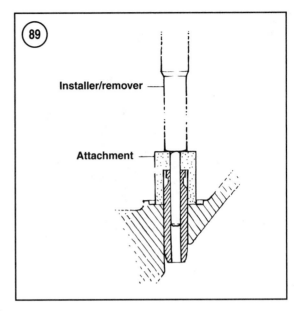

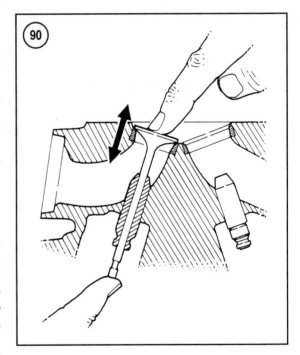

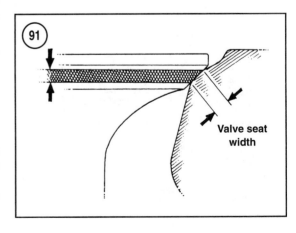

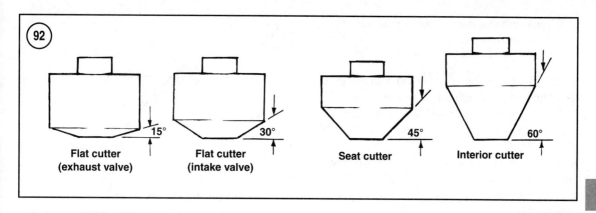

Flat cutter (exhaust valve) — 15°
Flat cutter (intake valve) — 30°
Seat cutter — 45°
Interior cutter — 60°

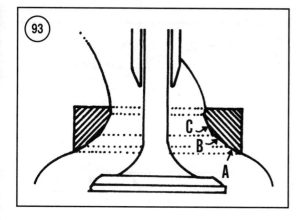

C
B
A

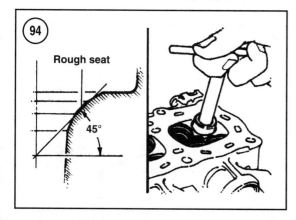

Rough seat
45°

4. Support the valve by hand (**Figure 90**), and tap the valve up and down in the cylinder head. Do not rotate the valve; a false impression results.

5. Remove the valve and examine the pattern left by the marking compound. The pattern left in the dye (on the valve or in the cylinder head) should be even and continuous, and the valve seat width (**Figure 91**) should be within specification (**Table 2**).

6. Closely examine the valve seat in the cylinder head (**Figure 84**). It should be smooth, even and have a polished seating surface.

7. Measure the valve seat width (**Figure 91**) with a vernier caliper.

8. If the valve seat is within specification, install the valves as described in this section.

9. If the valve seat is not correct, recondition the valve seat in the cylinder head as described in this section.

**Valve Seat Reconditioning**

*Tools*

The following Suzuki tools (**Figure 92**), or their equivalents, are needed to recondition the valve seats:

1. The valve cutter set (part No. 09916-21111):
   a. A 15° cutter for the area below the valve contact surface (A, **Figure 93**) on an exhaust valve.
   b. A 45° cutter for the valve contact surface (B, **Figure 93**) on an exhaust valve.
   c. A 60° cutter for the interior angle above the contact surface (C, **Figure 93**) on an exhaust valve.

2. A 30°/45° valve seat cutter (part No. 09916-22430) for the 30° angle below the valve contact surface (A, **Figure 93**) of an intake valve. The same cutter also cuts the 45° contact surface (B, **Figure 93**) on an intake valve.

3. A 60° cutter for the interior angle above the contact surface (C, **Figure 93**) on an intake valve.

4. A solid pilot (part No. 09916-24311).

5. An appropriate handle for the cutters.

*Procedure*

1. Carefully rotate and insert the solid pilot into the valve guide. Make sure the pilot is correctly seated.

2. Install the 45° cutter onto the solid pilot. Descale and clean the valve seat with one or two turns (**Figure 94**).

*CAUTION*
*Measure the valve seat contact area in the cylinder head after each cut to make sure the contact area is correct and to*

*prevent removing too much material. If too much material is removed, the cylinder head must be replaced.*

3. If the seat is still pitted or burned, turn the 45° cutter additional turns until the surface is clean.

4. Measure the valve seat with a vernier caliper (**Figure 91**). Record the measurement to use a reference point.

5. Install the 15° cutter (exhaust valve) or the 30° cutter (intake valve) onto the solid pilot, and lightly cut the seat to remove 1/4 of the existing valve seat (**Figure 95**).

6. Install the 60° cutter onto the solid pilot, and lightly cut the seat to remove 1/4 of the existing valve seat (**Figure 96**).

7. Measure the valve seat width with a vernier caliper. Fit the 45° cutter onto the solid pilot, and cut the valve seat to the specified width (**Table 2**).

8. Inspect and measure the valve seat width as described in *Valve Seat Inspection* in this section.

9. If the contact area is too wide or too high on the valve face (**Figure 97**), use the 15° cutter (for an exhaust valve) or the 30° cutter (for an intake valve) to lower and narrow the contact area.

10. If the contact area is too wide or too low on the valve face, use the 60° cutter to raise and narrow the contact area.

11. If the contact area is too narrow or too low on the valve face (**Figure 98**), use the 45° cutter to remove a portion of the valve seat material and increase the contact area.

12. After the desired valve seat contact position and width are obtained, use the 45° cutter and very lightly clean away any burrs that may have been caused by the previous cuts. Remove only enough material as necessary.

13. Check that the finish has a smooth and velvety surface (**Figure 84**). It should *not* be shiny or highly polished. The final seating takes place when the engine is first run.

14. Repeat Steps 1-12 for all remaining valve seats.

15. After the valve seat has been reconditioned, lap the valve and seat as described in this section.

## Valve Seat Lapping

Valve lapping can restore the valve seat without machining if the amount of wear or distortion is not too great. Lapping is recommended after the valve seat has been refaced or when a new valve and valve guide have been installed.

1. Smear a light coating of fine grade valve lapping compound onto the seating surface of the valve.

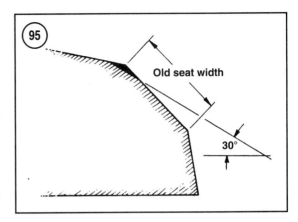

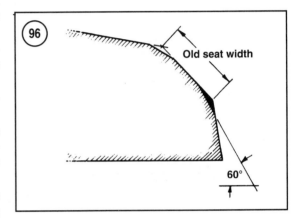

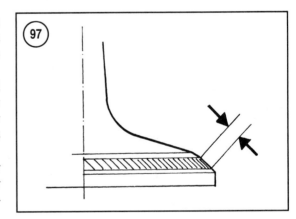

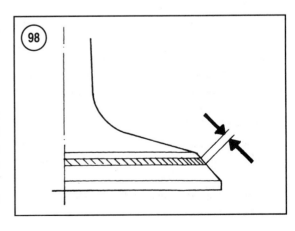

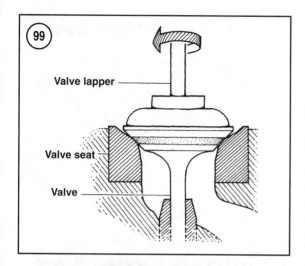

Valve lapper

Valve seat

Valve

B  A                              A

2. Apply molybdenum disulfide oil to the valve stem, and insert the valve into the cylinder head.

3. Wet the suction cup of the valve lapping tool and stick it onto the valve head.

4. Lap the valve to the valve seat as follows (**Figure 99**):

   a. Lap the valve by rotating the lapping stick between your hands in both directions.

   b. Every 5 to 10 seconds, stop and rotate the valve 180° in the valve seat.

   c. Continue lapping until the contact surfaces of the valve and the valve seat in the cylinder head are a uniform gray. Stop as soon as they turn this color to avoid removing too much material.

5. Thoroughly clean the cylinder head and all valve components in solvent, followed by a wash with detergent and hot water.

6. After the lapping has been completed and the valve assemblies have been reinstalled into the cylinder head, test the valve seat for leaks as described in *Cylinder Head, Inspection* (this chapter). If fluid leaks past any of the seats, disassemble that valve assembly and repeat the lapping procedure until there are no leaks.

7. After the cylinder head and valve components are cleaned in detergent and hot water, apply a light coat of engine oil to all bare metal surfaces to prevent rust.

## CYLINDER BLOCK

### Removal

1. Remove the engine as described in Chapter Five.

2. Remove the cylinder head (this chapter).

3. Disconnect the water pump hose from the water jacket fitting (D, **Figure 85**) on the cylinder block.

4. Remove the cylinder nuts (**Figure 100**) from the right side.

5. Loosen the cylinder by tapping around its perimeter with a plastic or rubber mallet.

6. Lift the block straight up and remove it from the crankcase.

7. Remove the dowels (A, **Figure 101**), and discard the base gasket (B).

8. If necessary, remove the pistons as described in this chapter.

9. Cover the crankcase opening to prevent debris from falling into the crankcase.

### Installation

Four 10 × 9.25 mm studs installed in the outside corners of the crankcase greatly ease cylinder block installation. The studs guide the block as it is lowered into place, and they keep the cylinders properly aligned with their respective pistons.

If proper sized studs are unavailable, purchase four cylinder head bolts and cut off their heads.

1. If removed, install the water jacket fitting (D, **Figure 85**) onto the rear of the cylinder block. Install a new O-ring onto the fitting. Install and tighten the fitting bolts to 10 N•m (89 in.-lb.).

2. Make sure the crankcase and cylinder block mating surfaces are clean and dry.

3. Install the dowels (A, **Figure 101**) and a new base gasket (B) onto the crankcase. Make sure the holes in the gasket align with those in the crankcase.

4. Have an assistant pull up on the cam chain so it sits taut against the timing sprocket during the next step.

5. Using the starter clutch bolt, slowly rotate the engine clockwise, when viewed from the right side of the engine. Guide the No. 2 and No. 3 pistons down into the upper crankcase and rotate the engine until the pistons are positioned at BDC. This also positions the No. 1 and No. 4 pistons at TDC and makes cylinder block installation easier.

6. Turn each $10 \times 9.25$ mm stud (A, **Figure 102**) into an outside cylinder head bolt hole in the crankcase.

7. Lubricate the cylinder walls, pistons and rings liberally with clean engine oil.

8. Carefully lower the cylinder block over the four studs, and align the cylinder block with the two raised pistons. Have an assistant guide the cam chain guide and the cam chain (B, **Figure 102**) through the cam chain tunnel.

9. Slowly slide the cylinder block down onto the No. 1 and No. 4 pistons until the block *lightly* bottoms on each top piston ring.

10. Carefully align the pistons with their respective cylinder bores, and lower the cylinder block over pistons No. 1 and No. 4 until all the piston rings are inside the cylinder. Manually compress each piston ring as it enters its cylinder (**Figure 103**).

11. Use the starter clutch bolt to rotate the crankshaft clockwise and raise the No. 2 and No. 3 pistons. Hold the cam chain taut on the timing sprocket when rotating the crankshaft.

12. Slowly lower the cylinder block and insert the No. 2 and No. 3 pistons into their cylinder bores. Compress each piston ring as it enters the cylinder bore.

13. Carefully push the cylinder block down until it bottoms on the upper crankcase (**Figure 104**). Make sure the locating dowels correctly engage the cylinder block.

14. Loosen and remove the four guide studs (**Figure 104**).

15. Secure the cam chain safety wire to the outside of the engine.

16. On the right side, install the two cylinder nuts (**Figure 100**). Finger-tighten the nuts at this time.

17. Connect the water pump hose to the water jacket fitting (D, **Figure 85**) on the rear of the cylinder block.

18. Install the cylinder head as described in this chapter.

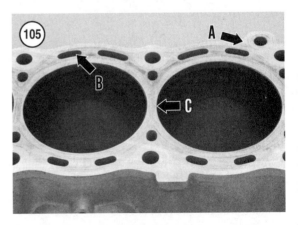

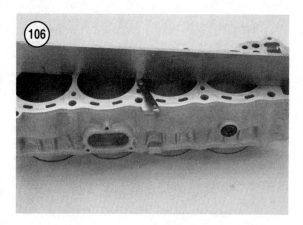

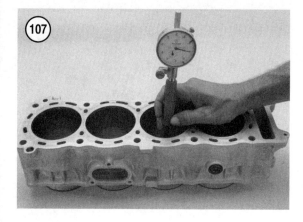

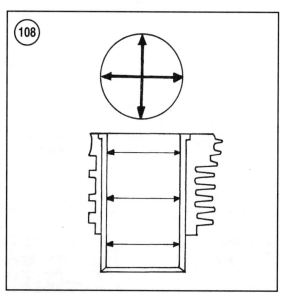

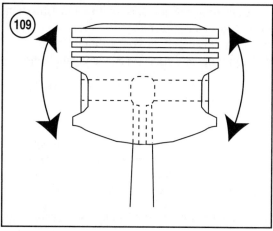

4. Use a straightedge and flat feeler gauge (**Figure 106**) to check the top of the cylinder block for warp. Check this at several places across the cylinder block. Replace the cylinder block if warp exceeds the service limit in **Table 2**.

5. Measure the diameter of each cylinder with a cylinder bore gauge (**Figure 107**). Measure the bore at the top, middle and bottom of a cylinder as shown in **Figure 108**. At each height, measure the bore across two axes: one parallel to the crankshaft and the other 90° to the crankshaft. Replace the cylinder block if a cylinder is out of specification. The cylinders cannot be bored or honed.

6. Lubricate the cylinder walls with clean engine oil so they do not rust.

## PISTON AND PISTON RINGS

### Piston Removal

1. Remove the cylinder head and cylinder block (this chapter).

2. Make sure each piston and its connecting rod is marked with its cylinder number. These marks help ensure the pistons are reinstalled onto the correct connecting rods.

3. Cover the area below the pistons with clean shop rags so a circlip cannot fall into the crankcase.

4. Before removing the piston, hold the rod tightly and rock the piston (**Figure 109**). Any rocking motion (do not confuse with the normal sliding motion) indicates wear on the piston pin, rod bushing, pin bore, or more likely, a combination of all three.

5. Remove the circlip (**Figure 110**) from one side of the piston pin bore. Discard the circlip.

6. From the other side, push the piston pin (**Figure 111**) from the piston by hand. If the pin is tight, use a homemade tool (**Figure 112**) and remove it. Do not

### Inspection

1. Check the cylinder block surfaces (A, **Figure 105**) for cracks or damage.

2. Check the water jacket passages (B, **Figure 105**). Clean out any noted debris or residue.

3. Check the cylinder walls (C, **Figure 105**) for deep scratches, signs of seizure or other damage.

drive out the piston pin. This action could damage the piston pin, connecting rod or piston.

7. Lift the piston off the connecting rod.

8. Inspect the pistons as described in this section.

### Piston Installation

> *CAUTION*
> *Each piston must be reinstalled onto its original connecting rod. Refer to the cylinder number placed on each piston and connecting rod during removal.*

1. Select the No. 1 piston and the No. 1 connecting rod.

2. Apply molybdenum disulfide oil to the piston pin bore in the piston, piston pin and connecting rod bushing.

3. Install a new circlip into one side of the piston. Make sure the circlip end gap is not seated in the piston's notch (A, **Figure 113**).

4. Slide the piston pin into the piston until the pin end is flush with the inside of the piston pin boss.

5. Set the piston onto the connecting rod so the indexing dot (A, **Figure 111**) on the piston crown faces the exhaust side of the engine.

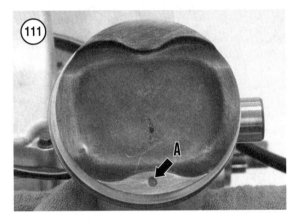

6. Align the piston pin with the hole in the connecting rod. Push the piston pin through the connecting rod until the pin lightly bottoms against the piston pin clip in the opposite side.

7. Install a *new* piston pin circlip (B, **Figure 113**) into the piston. Make sure the circlip is properly seated in the piston groove. The circlip end gap must not align with the piston's notch (A, **Figure 113**).

8. Check the installation of the piston.

9. Repeat Steps 1-8 for each remaining piston.

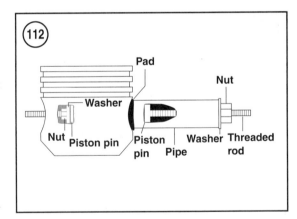

### Piston Inspection

1. If necessary, remove the piston rings as described in this section.

2. Carefully clean the carbon from the piston crown (**Figure 114**) with a soft scraper or wire wheel mounted in a drill. Large carbon accumulation reduces piston cooling and causes detonation and piston damage. Re-number the piston crown as soon as it is cleaned.

> *CAUTION*
> *Make sure not to gouge or otherwise damage the piston when removing carbon. Never use a wire brush to clean the piston skirt or ring grooves. Do not remove carbon from the sides of the piston above the top ring or from the*

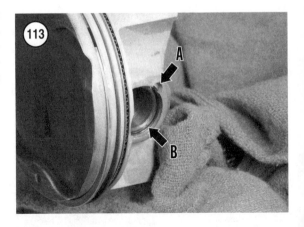

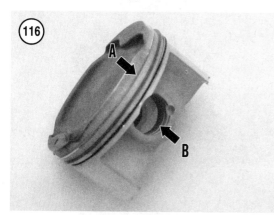

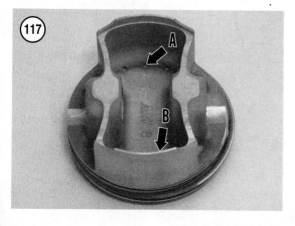

*cylinder bore near the top. Removal of carbon from these two areas may cause increased oil consumption.*

3. After cleaning the piston, examine the crown (**Figure 115**). The crown should exhibit no signs of wear or damage. If a crown appears pecked or spongy-looking, also check the spark plug, valves and combustion chamber for aluminum deposits. If these deposits are found, the engine is overheating.

4. Examine each ring groove (A, **Figure 116**) for burrs, dented edges or other damage. Pay particular attention to the top compression ring groove. It usually wears more than the others. Because the oil rings are constantly bathed in oil, these rings and grooves wear little compared to compression rings and their grooves. If there is evidence of oil ring groove wear or if the oil ring assembly is tight and difficult to remove, the piston skirt may have collapsed due to excessive heat and is permanently deformed. Replace the piston.

5. Check the oil control holes (A, **Figure 117**) in the piston for carbon or oil sludge buildup. Clean the holes with wire and blow them clear with compressed air.

6. Check the piston skirt (B, **Figure 117**) for cracks or other damage. If a piston shows signs of partial seizure (bits of aluminum build-up on the piston skirt), replace the piston to reduce the possibility of engine noise and further piston seizure. If the piston skirt is worn or scuffed unevenly from side-to-side, the connecting rod may be bent or twisted.

7. Check the circlip groove (B, **Figure 116**) on each side for wear, cracks or other damage. If a groove is questionable, check the circlip fit by installing a new circlip. Try to move the circlip from side-to-side. If the circlip has any side play, the groove is worn and the piston must be replaced.

8. Measure piston-to-cylinder clearance as described in this section.

9. If damage or wear call for piston replacement, select a new piston as described in *Piston Clearance*. If the piston, rings and cylinder are not damaged and are dimensionally correct, they can be reused.

**Piston Pin Inspection**

1. Clean the piston pin in solvent and dry it thoroughly.

2. Inspect the piston pin for chrome flaking or cracks. Replace the pin if necessary.

3. Oil the piston pin. Install it into the connecting rod, and check for excessive play (**Figure 118**).

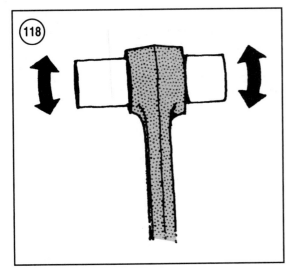

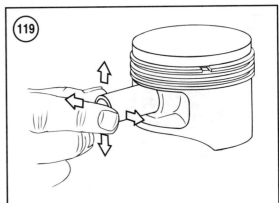

4. Oil the piston pin and partially install it into the piston. Check the piston pin for excessive play (**Figure 119**).

5. Measure the piston pin outside diameter with a micrometer (**Figure 120**). Measure the diameter at three places along the piston pin. If any measurement is less than the service limit in **Table 2**, replace the piston pin.

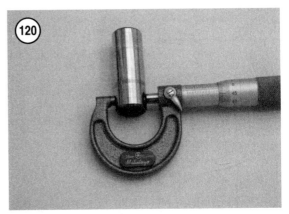

6. Measure the inside diameter of the piston pin bore (**Figure 121**) with a small hole gauge. Measure the small hole gauge with a micrometer. If the measurement exceeds the service limit in **Table 2**, replace the piston.

7. Replace the piston pin, piston or connecting rod as necessary.

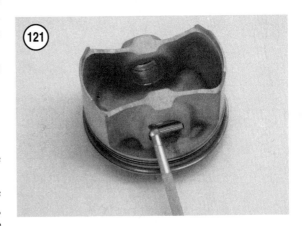

**Piston Clearance**

1. Make sure the piston skirt and cylinder wall are clean and dry.

2. Measure the cylinder bore with a cylinder bore gauge (**Figure 107**). Measure the bore at the top, middle and bottom of a cylinder as shown in **Figure 108**. At each height, measure the bore across two axes: one parallel to the crankshaft and the other 90° to the crankshaft.

3. Measure the piston outside diameter with a micrometer (**Figure 122**) at a right angle to the piston pin bore. Measure the piston at a point 15 mm (0.590 in.) above the bottom edge of the piston skirt.

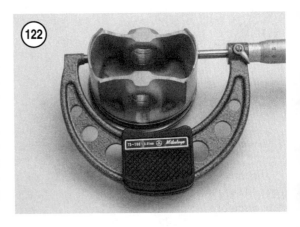

4. Subtract the piston outside diameter from the largest cylinder bore inside diameter (Step 2). The difference is the piston-to-cylinder clearance. If this clearance exceeds the service limit in **Table 2**, replace the pistons and cylinder block. The cylinders in this engine cannot be bored or honed.

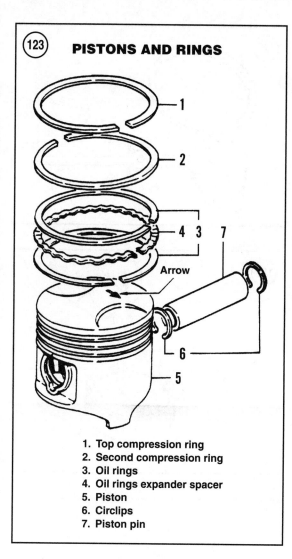

(123) **PISTONS AND RINGS**

Arrow

1. Top compression ring
2. Second compression ring
3. Oil rings
4. Oil rings expander spacer
5. Piston
6. Circlips
7. Piston pin

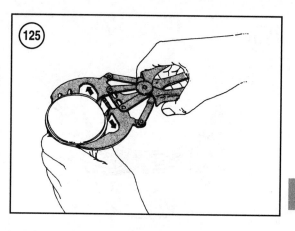

(125)

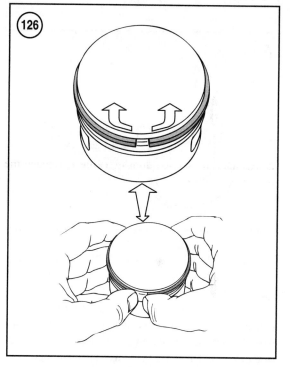

(126)

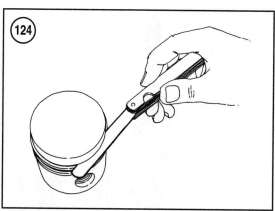

(124)

**Piston Ring**

*Removal/inspection*

The three-ring assembly (**Figure 123**) consists of top and second compression rings and an oil control ring assembly.

When inspecting the piston rings and piston in this section, compare the measurements to specifications in **Table 2**. Replace parts that are out of specification or show damage.

1. Measure the ring-to-groove clearance of each compression ring in its groove with a flat feeler gauge (**Figure 124**). If the clearance is greater than specified, replace the rings. If the clearance is still excessive with the new rings installed, replace the piston.

> *WARNING*
> *The edges of all piston rings are very sharp. Avoid cuts by handling the rings carefully.*

2. Spread each compression ring with a ring expander tool (**Figure 125**) or by hand (**Figure 126**) and then lift the ring up and off the piston.

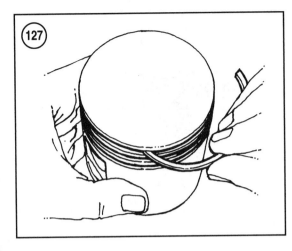

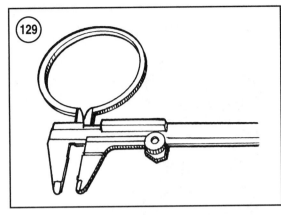

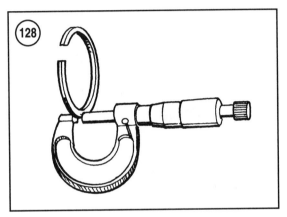

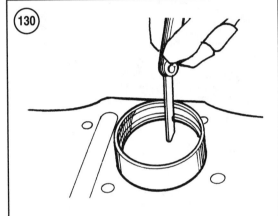

3. Remove the oil ring assembly by first removing the upper and then the lower ring rails. Then remove the expander spacer.

4. Using a broken piston ring, carefully remove carbon and oil residue from the piston ring grooves (**Figure 127**). Do not remove aluminum material from the ring grooves. This increases ring side clearance.

5. Measure each ring groove width with a vernier caliper at several points around the piston. Replace the piston if any groove width is outside the specified range.

6. Inspect the ring grooves carefully for burrs, nicks, and broken or cracked lands. Replace the piston if necessary.

7. Measure the thickness of each compression ring with a micrometer (**Figure 128**). If the thickness is less than specified, replace the ring(s).

8. Measure the free end gap with a vernier caliper (**Figure 129**). Replace the ring(s) if free end gap exceeds the specified service limit.

9. Insert the ring into the bottom of the cylinder bore. Square the ring with the cylinder wall by tapping the ring with the piston. Measure the end gap with a feeler gauge (**Figure 130**). Replace the rings if the end gap equals or exceeds service limit. Also measure the end gap when installing new piston rings. If

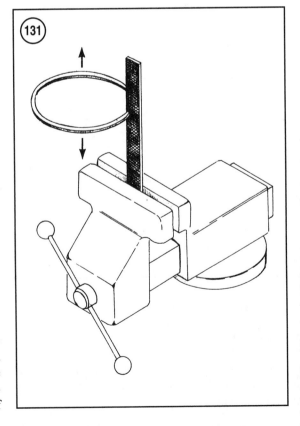

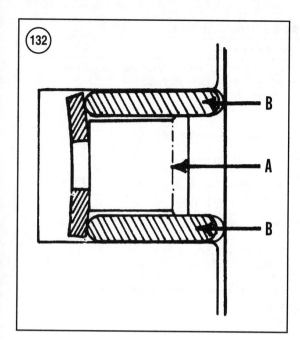

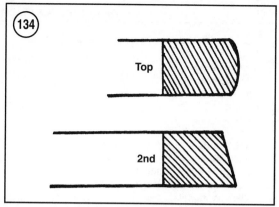

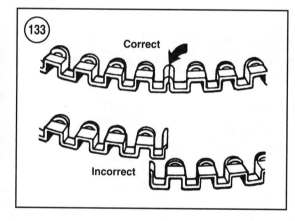

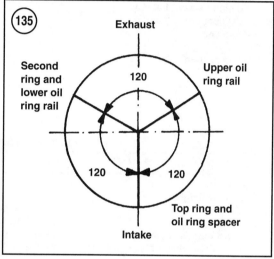

the gap on a new compression ring is smaller than specified, hold a small file in a vise, grip the ends of the ring, and enlarge the gap (**Figure 131**).

### Installation

1. Clean the piston and rings. Dry them with compressed air.

2. Install piston rings as follows:

   a. Install the oil control ring assembly into the bottom ring groove. Install the oil ring expander spacer first (A, **Figure 132**), and then install each ring rail (B). Make sure the ends of the expander spacer butt together (**Figure 133**).

They should not overlap. If reassembling used parts, install the ring rails as they were removed.

   b. Install the second or middle compression ring with the manufacturer's *RN* mark facing up. This ring has a slight taper (**Figure 134**).

   c. Install the top compression ring with the manufacturer's *R* mark facing up.

3. Make sure the rings are seated completely in their grooves all the way around the piston. Distribute the end gaps around the piston as shown in **Figure 135**. The piston ring gaps must not align with each other. This prevents compression pressures from escaping past them.

4. If new parts were installed, follow the *Engine Break-In* procedure in Chapter Five.

**Tables 1-3 are on the following pages.**

## Table 1 GENERAL ENGINE SPECIFICATIONS

| Item | Specification |
|------|---------------|
| Type | 4-stroke, DOHC, 4-valve head, inline 4-cylinder |
|   Bore × stroke | 81.0 × 63.0 mm (3.189 × 2.480 in.) |
|   Displacement | 1299 cc (79.3 cu. in.) |
|   Compression ratio | 11.0:1 |
| Ignition | |
|   Type | Electronic (Transistorized) |
|   Timing | |
|     1999 models | 4° BTDC @ 1150 rpm |
|     2000 models | |
|       Cylinders Nos. 1 and 4 | 11° BTDC @ 1150 rpm |
|       Cylinders Nos. 2 and 3 | 3° BTDC @ 1150 rpm |
|     2001-on models | |
|       U.S., California and Canada models | 4° BTDC @ 1200 rpm |
|       All models except U.S., California and Canada | |
|       Cylinders Nos. 1 and 4 | 11° BTDC @ 1150 rpm |
|       Cylinders Nos. 2 and 3 | 3° BTDC @ 1150 rpm |
| Firing order | 1-2-4-3 |
| Rotation | Clockwise, viewed from the right side |
| Cooling system | Liquid |
| Lubrication system | Wet sump |

## Table 2 ENGINE TOP END SPECIFICATIONS

| Item | Standard mm (in.) | Service limit mm (in.) |
|------|-------------------|------------------------|
| Camshaft | | |
|   Cam lobe height | | |
|     Intake | 36.780-36.848 (1.4480-1.4507) | 36.48 (1.436) |
|     Exhaust | 35.480-35.548 (1.3968-1.3995) | 35.18 (1.385) |
|   Journal outside diameter | 23.959-23.980 (0.9433-0.9441) | – |
|   Camshaft bearing inside diameter | 24.012-24.025 (0.9454-0.9459) | – |
|   Camshaft runout | – | 0.10 (0.004) |
|   Camshaft oil clearance | 0.032-0.066 (0.0013-0.0026) | 0.15 (0.006) |
|   Cylinder head warp | – | 0.20 (0.008) |
| Valves and valve springs | | |
|   Valve clearance (cold) | | |
|     Intake | 0.10-0.20 (0.004-0.008) | – |
|     Exhaust | 0.20-0.30 (0.008-0.012) | – |
|   Valve stem outside diameter | | |
|     Intake | 4.975-4.990 (0.1959-0.1965) | – |
|     Exhaust | 4.955-4.970 (0.1951-0.1957) | – |
|   Valve stem deflection | – | 0.35 (0.014) |
|   Valve stem runout | – | 0.05 (0.002) |
|   Valve guide inside diameter | 5.000-5.012 (0.1969-0.1973) | |
|   Valve stem-to-guide clearance | | |
|     Intake | 0.010-0.037 (0.0004-0.0015) | – |
|     Exhaust | 0.030-0.057 (0.0012-0.0022) | – |
|   Valve diameter | | |
|     Intake | 33 (1.30) | – |
|     Exhaust | 27.5 (1.08) | – |
|   Valve head thickness | – | 0.5 (0.02) |
|   Valve head radial runout | – | 0.03 (0.001) |
|   Valve seat width | 0.9-1.1 (0.035-0.043) | – |
|   Valve seat cutter angle | | |
|     Intake | 30°, 45°, 60° | |
|     Exhaust | 15°, 45°, 60° | |
|   Valve spring free length | | |
|     Inner spring | – | 35.1 (1.38) |
|     Outer spring | – | 45.2 (1.78) |

(continued)

**Table 2 ENGINE TOP END SPECIFICATIONS (continued)**

| Item | Standard mm (in.) | Service limit mm (in.) |
|---|---|---|
| Valves and valve springs (continued) | | |
| Valve spring tension | | |
| Inner spring | 3.1-3.5 kg @ 33.1 mm | – |
| | (6.83-7.72 lb. @ 1.30 in.) | |
| Valves and valve springs | | |
| Valve spring tension (continued) | | |
| Outer spring | 15.5-17.9 kg @ 36.6 mm | – |
| | (34.17-39.46 lb. @ 1.44 in.) | |
| Cylinder | | |
| Bore | 81.000-81.015 (3.1890-3.1896) | Nicks or scratches |
| Warp | – | 0.20 (0.008) |
| Compression pressure | 1200-1600 kPa (174-232 psi) | 900 kPa (131 psi) |
| Maximum difference | 200 kPa (29 psi) | |
| between cylinders | | |
| Piston | | |
| Outside diameter* | 80.975-80.990 (3.1880-3.1886) | 80.880 (3.1842) |
| Piston-to-cylinder clearance | 0.020-0.030 (0.0008-0.0012) | 0.120 (0.0047) |
| Piston-pin bore inside diameter | 20.002-20.008 (0.7875-0.7877) | 20.030 (0.7886) |
| Piston pin outside diameter | 19.995-20.000 (0.7872-0.7874) | 19.980 (0.7866) |
| Piston rings | | |
| Ring-to groove clearance | | |
| Top | – | 0.180 (0.0071) |
| Second | – | 0.150 (0.0059) |
| Ring thickness | | |
| Top | 1.17-1.19 (0.0461-0.0469) | – |
| Second | 0.97-0.99 (0.0382-0.0390) | – |
| Piston ring groove width | | |
| Top | 1.21-1.23 (0.0476-0.0484) | – |
| Second | 1.01-1.03 (0.0398-0.0406) | – |
| Oil ring | 2.01-2.03 (0.0791-0.0799) | – |
| Ring end gap (installed) | | |
| Top | 0.08-0.20 (0.003-0.008) | 0.50 (0.020) |
| Second | 0.08-0.20 (0.003-0.008) | 0.50 (0.020) |
| Ring free gap | | |
| First | Approx. 7.3 (0.29) | 5.8 (0.23) |
| Second | | |
| 1999 models | Approx. 8.1 (0.32) | 6.4 (0.25) |
| 2000-on models | Approx. 11.4 (0.45) | 9.1 (0.36) |

*Measured 15 mm (0.6 in.) from skirt bottom.

**Table 3 ENGINE TOP END TORQUE SPECIFICATIONS**

| Item | N•m | in.-lb. | ft.-lb. |
|---|---|---|---|
| Cam chain guide bolt | 10 | 89 | – |
| Cam chain guide retainer screw | 8 | 71 | – |
| Camshaft holder bolt | 10 | 89 | – |
| Cam chain oil line banjo bolt | 12 | 106 | – |
| Cam chain tensioner mounting bolt | 10 | 89 | – |
| Coolant bypass fitting | 14 | – | 10 |
| Cylinder head cover bolt | 14 | – | 10 |
| Cylinder head bolt | | | |
| 6 mm | 10 | 89 | – |
| 10 mm | | | |
| Initial | 25 | – | 18 |
| Final | 52 | – | 38 |
| Cylinder head side bolt | 14 | – | 10 |
| Cylinder nut | 10 | 89 | – |
| Engine coolant temperature sensor | 18 | – | 13 |

(continued)

**Table 3 ENGINE TOP END TORQUE SPECIFICATIONS (continued)**

| Item | N•m | in.-lb. | ft.-lb. |
|------|-----|---------|---------|
| Oil hose banjo bolt | 20 | – | 15 |
| Oil pipe bolt | 10 | 89 | – |
| PAIR valve pipe nut | 10 | 89 | – |
| Spark plug | 11 | 97 | – |
| Starter clutch bolt cap | 11 | 97 | |
| Timing inspection cap | 23 | – | 17 |
| Upper cam chain guide mounting bolt | 10 | 89 | – |
| Water jacket fitting bolt | 10 | 89 | – |

# CHAPTER FIVE

# ENGINE LOWER END

This chapter covers the engine lower end components. This chapter also includes removal and installation procedures for the transmission, but service procedures for it appear in Chapter Seven.

Refer to **Tables 1-7** at the end of this chapter for specifications.

## ENGINE

### Removal

1. Note the following when removing/installing the engine:
   a. A hydraulic floor jack and at least two people are needed to remove or install the engine.
   b. Cover the O-ring chain before degreasing the engine. The chemicals in the degreaser cause O-ring swelling, which permanently damages the chain.
   c. Electrical connectors and hoses must be reinstalled in their original locations. Use tape and a permanent marking pen to label them during disassembly. Locate and mark any mounts or holders securing these items before disconnecting.
   d. Study the engine mounts closely. Make notes or take photographs of the mounting bolts,

clamp bolts and adjusters. Note their positions on the motorcycle and keep the various components separate.
   e. The Suzuki engine mounting thrust adjuster socket wrench (**Figure 1**, part No. 09940-14990, or its equivalent) is needed to tighten the thrust adjusters.
   f. To decrease the weight of the engine, remove as many engine subassemblies as possible before removing the engine from the frame.

2. Move the motorcycle to a level surface, and securely support it on a swing arm stand. Block both sides of the front wheel so it cannot roll in either direction.

3. Remove the seats, the front and rear lower panels, both fairing side panels and the sidestand (Chapter Fifteen).

4. Disconnect the negative battery cable.

5. Drain the engine oil, remove the oil filter and drain the coolant (Chapter Three)

6. Remove the oil cooler (this chapter). Also remove the oil cooler lines from the crankcase so they are not damaged.

7. Remove the radiator assembly and the coolant reservoir (Chapter Ten).

8. Remove the radiator and oil cooler brackets from the front of the engine.

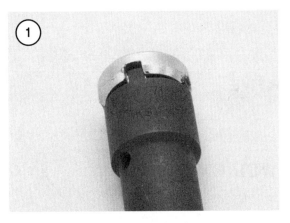

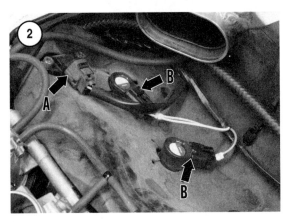

9. Remove the fuel tank, air filter housing, throttle bodies, mufflers and exhaust header pipes (Chapter Eight).

10. Disconnect the 2-pin connector (A, **Figure 2**) from the camshaft position sensor, and then disconnect the 2-pin connector (B) from each ignition coil/plug cap.

11. Pull back the rubber boot from the starter terminal, and disconnect the starter cable from the terminal (A, **Figure 3**). Also disconnect the ground terminal from the rear starter bolt (B, **Figure 3**).

12. Remove the engine sprocket cover and the engine sprocket (Chapter Seven).

13. Remove the left clutch pushrod (**Figure 4**) from the mainshaft so it is not damaged.

14. Remove the coolant hose (A, **Figure 5**) and by-pass hose (B) from the thermostat housing.

15. Disconnect the 2-pin connector (C, **Figure 5**) from the engine coolant temperature sensor.

16. Disconnect the vacuum hose (A, **Figure 6**) and the air filter housing hose (B) from the PAIR valve.

17. Disconnect the electrical wire from the terminal (A, **Figure 7**) on the oil pressure switch. Release any wire clamps (B, **Figure 7**) that secure the wire to the engine.

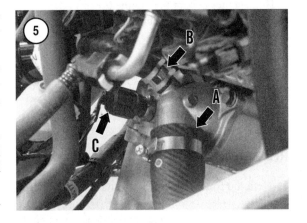

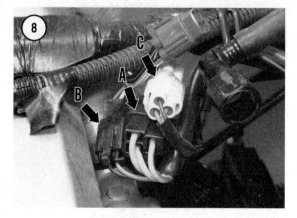

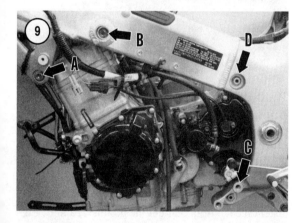

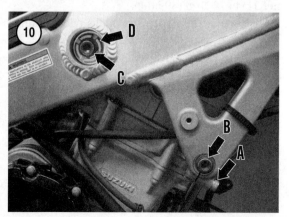

18. Disconnect the following electrical connectors. Follow each wire and release it from any holder or clamp securing it to the engine or frame. Refer to **Figure 8**.

    a. The 2-pin crankshaft position sensor connector (A, **Figure 8**).

    b. The 3-pin stator connector (B, **Figure 8**).

    c. The 3-pin gear position sensor connector (C, **Figure 8**).

19. If disassembling the engine, remove the following subassemblies:

    a. Flywheel (this chapter).

    b. Clutch (Chapter Six).

    c. Starter motor (Chapter Nine).

20. Move all electrical wires, harnesses and hoses out of the way.

21. Support the engine with a hydraulic jack. Raise the jack and place tension against the engine to ease mounting bolt removal.

*NOTE*
*The front and middle mounting bolts on the left side are not the same length as those used on the right side. Label these bolts as they are removed so they can be identified and replaced correctly during assembly.*

22. Remove the front engine mounting bolt (A, **Figure 9**) and middle mounting bolt (B) from the left side.

23 On the right side, loosen the engine mounting clamp bolt (A, **Figure 10**) and remove the front engine mounting bolt (B). Note the spacer installed in this mount.

24. Remove the right middle engine mounting bolt (C, **Figure 10**). Use the thrust adjuster socket wrench to remove the thrust adjuster locknut (D, **Figure 10**) from the right middle engine mount.

25. Use the socket wrench to loosen the thrust adjuster on the left middle engine mount.

26. Perform the following on the right lower rear engine mount (A, **Figure 11**):

a. Remove and discard the self-locking nut (1, **Figure 12**).

b. Use the socket wrench to remove the rear lower thrust adjuster locknut (2, **Figure 12**).

c. Use the socket wrench to loosen the lower thrust adjuster (3, **Figure 12**).

27. Repeat Step 25 on the right upper rear engine mount (B, **Figure 11**).

28. Make sure the floor jack is still positioned correctly against the engine.

29. Slowly withdraw the lower rear mounting bolt (C, **Figure 9**) from the right side.

30. Have an assistant steady the engine, and then withdraw the left upper rear mounting bolt (D, **Figure 9**). Watch for the spacer (**Figure 13**) installed between the thrust adjuster and the engine lug on this bolt.

31. Lower the jack and engine from the frame. Make sure the drive chain clears the countershaft.

32. Roll the jack and engine from the frame. Carefully remove the engine from the jack, and support the engine on wooden blocks.

33. Remove the spacer from the front engine mount on the right side of the frame so it is not lost.

34. Refer to *Cleaning and Inspection* in this section.

### Installation

1. Install the spacer into the front engine mount on the right side.

2. Check that a thrust adjuster (**Figure 14**) is in place in the right side of each rear frame mount (A and B, **Figure 11**) and the middle mount (D, **Figure 10**). If necessary, turn a thrust adjuster counterclockwise, and seat it against the frame. This provides maximum clearance for engine installation.

3. With the help of an assistant, set the engine on a hydraulic floor jack.

4. Carefully maneuver the engine until it is centered beneath the frame.

5. Slowly raise the engine and align the rear engine mounts between their mates in the frame. Set the drive chain onto the countershaft.

6. Install the lower rear mounting bolt (C, **Figure 9**) from the left side. Make sure the bolt emerges from its thrust adjuster on the right side.

7. Install the upper rear mounting bolt (D, **Figure 9**) from the left side. The bolt must pass through the spacer (**Figure 13**) and then emerge from its thrust adjuster on the right side.

8. On the right side, make sure the collar is in place in the front engine mount. Install the front engine mounting bolt (B, **Figure 10**) and the middle mounting bolt (C). Hand-tighten the bolts at this time.

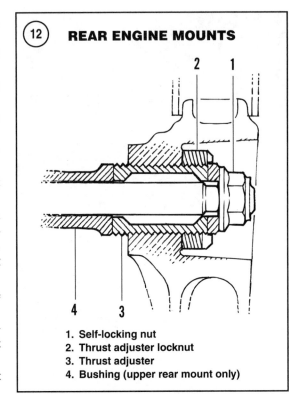

(12) **REAR ENGINE MOUNTS**

1. Self-locking nut
2. Thrust adjuster locknut
3. Thrust adjuster
4. Bushing (upper rear mount only)

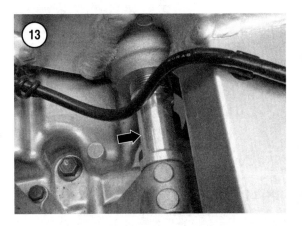

(13)

9. Use the socket wrench to tighten the thrust adjuster on each right rear engine mount (A and B, **Figure 11**) to 10 N•m (89 in.-lb.).

10. Torque the thrust adjuster on the middle engine mount to 10 N•m (89 in.-lb.).

11. Turn a thrust adjuster locknut (A, **Figure 15**) onto the thrust adjuster on each right rear engine mount and the right middle engine mount (D, **Figure 10**). Use the socket wrench to tighten each thrust adjuster locknut to 45 N•m (33 ft.-lb.).

> *CAUTION*
> *Self-locking nuts are used on the rear engine mounting bolts. Do not reuse a self-locking nut, and do not substitute another type of nut.*

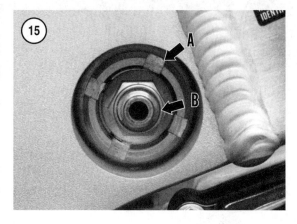

12. Install a *new* self-locking nut (B, **Figure 15**) onto each right rear engine mounting bolt (A and B, **Figure 11**). Tighten each self-locking nut to 75 N•m (55 ft.-lb.).

13. Tighten the middle engine mounting bolt (C, **Figure 10**) on the right side to 55 N•m (41 ft.-lb.).

14. On the left side, tighten the front (A, **Figure 9**) and middle engine mounting bolts (B) to 55 N•m (41 ft.-lb.).

15. On the right side, tighten the front engine mounting bolt (B, **Figure 10**) to 55 N•m (41 ft.-lb.) and tighten the clamp bolt (A, **Figure 11**) to 35 N•m (26 ft.-lb.).

16. If removed, install the following sub-assemblies:
   a. Flywheel (this chapter).
   b. Clutch (Chapter Six).
   c. Starter (Chapter Nine).

17. Connect the following electrical connectors. Secure each wire to any wire holder noted during removal.
   a. The 2-pin crankshaft position sensor connector (A, **Figure 8**).
   b. The 3-pin stator connector (B, **Figure 8**).
   c. The 3-pin gear position sensor connector (C, **Figure 8**).

18. Connect the electrical wire to the terminal (A, **Figure 7**) on the oil pressure switch. Secure the wire

with any wire clamps (B, **Figure 7**) noted during removal.

19. Connect the 2-pin connector (C, **Figure 5**) to the engine coolant temperature sensor.

20. Connect the coolant hose (A, **Figure 5**) and bypass hose (B) to their respective fittings on the thermostat housing.

21. Connect the vacuum hose (A, **Figure 6**) and the air filter housing hose (B) to the PAIR valve.

22. Lubricate the left clutch pushrod (**Figure 4**) with Suzuki Super Grease A, and slide the rod into the mainshaft.

23. Install the engine sprocket and the engine sprocket cover (Chapter Seven).

24. If still disconnected, connect the ground terminal onto the rear starter bolt (B, **Figure 3**), and then connect the starter cable to the starter motor terminal (A). Fit the rubber boot over the terminal.

25. Connect the 2-pin connector (A, **Figure 2**) to the camshaft position sensor, and then connect each 2-pin connector (B) to its ignition coil/plug cap.

26. Install the exhaust header pipes, mufflers, throttle bodies, air filter housing and fuel tank (Chapter Eight).

27. Install the radiator and oil cooler brackets onto the front of the engine.

28. Install the radiator and the coolant reservoir (Chapter Ten).

29. Install the oil cooler (this chapter) and secure the oil pipes to their respective fittings on the crankcase.

30. Install a new oil filter and add engine oil (Chapter Three).

31. Add engine coolant (Chapter Three).

32. Connect the negative battery cable.

33. Start the engine, and check for oil and coolant leaks. Bleed the cooling system as described in Chapter Three.

34. Check and adjust the engine idle speed and throttle body synchronization (Chapter Three).

35. Shift the transmission through each gear, and check the operation of the clutch and transmission.

36. Install the sidestand, fairing side panels, front and rear lower panels and seats (Chapter Sixteen).

37. Slowly test ride the motorcycle to ensure all systems operate properly.

**Cleaning and Inspection**

1. Check the mounting hardware for thread damage or wear. Remove any corrosion from the engine mounting bolts with a wire wheel.

2. Clean and dry the engine mounting bolts, nuts, thrust adjusters, spacers and locknuts.

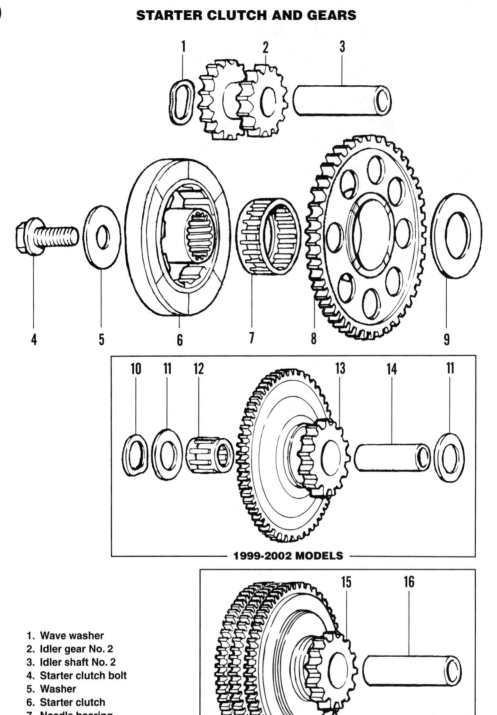

(16) **STARTER CLUTCH AND GEARS**

**1999-2002 MODELS**

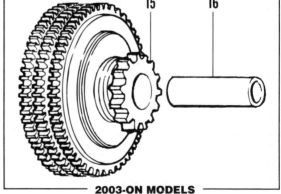

**2003-ON MODELS**

1. Wave washer
2. Idler gear No. 2
3. Idler shaft No. 2
4. Starter clutch bolt
5. Washer
6. Starter clutch
7. Needle bearing
8. Starter clutch driven gear
9. Washer
10. Wave washer
11. Washer
12. Needle bearing
13. Idler gear No. 1 (1999-2002 models)
14. Idler shaft No. 1 (1999-2002 models)
15. Idler gear No. 1 (2003-on models)
16. Idler shaft No. 1 (2003-on models)

3. Clean the thrust adjuster's mating threads in the frame.

4. Replace any damaged fastener.

5. Check the coolant hoses for cracks, leaks or other damage. Replace any hose as needed.

6. Check the wiring harness for chafing or other damage. Replace any wire holders or clamps as needed.

7. Clean the electrical connectors with contact cleaner.

8. Check the engine and frame mounts for cracks or other damage.

9. Inspect the exposed portion of the frame for cracks or wear.

## STARTER IDLER GEAR NO. 1

Refer to **Figure 16**.

**Removal/Installation**

1. Remove the fairing side panel from the right side (Chapter Fifteen).

2. Turn out the bolts (**Figure 17**), and remove the starter idler cover. Watch for the dowels (A, **Figure 18**) behind the cover.

3. Pull the dowels (A, **Figure 18**) and gasket (B). Discard the gasket.

4A. On 1999-2002 models, perform the following:

   a. Remove the wave washer (A, **Figure 19**) and flat washer (B).

   b. Remove starter idler gear No. 1 (**Figure 20**) from the starter idler shaft.

   c. Slide the needle bearing (A, **Figure 21**) and thrust washer (B) off the shaft.

4B. On 2003-on models, slide starter idler gear No. 1 off the shaft and remove it.

5. Remove the starter idler shaft (**Figure 22**) from its boss in the crankcase.

6. Inspect the components as described in *Starter Clutch and Gear Inspection* in this chapter.

7. Installation is the reverse of removal. Note the following:

   a. Install a new cover gasket (B, **Figure 18**) and the dowels (A).
   b. Torque the starter idler cover bolts (**Figure 17**) to 10 N•m (89 in.-lb.).

### Torque Limiter Inspection
### (2003-on Models)

1. Insert starter idler gear No.1 into the starter torque limiter holder (Suzuki part No. 09930-73170) and secure the holder in a vise.

2. Using the starter torque limiter socket (Suzuki part No. 09930-73140) and a beam-type torque wrench, rotate the torque limiter and measure the starter slip torque.

3. Replace the starter idler gear No. 1 if the starter slip torque is out of specification (**Table 1**).

### STARTER CLUTCH AND GEARS

The starter clutch holder (Suzuki part No. 09920-34830), or an equivalent holder, is needed to remove and install the starter clutch.

Refer to **Figure 16**.

### Removal

1. Remove the fairing side panel from the right side (Chapter Fifteen).

2. Remove starter idler gear No. 1 (this chapter).

3. Remove the starter clutch cover bolts (**Figure 23**). Discard the gasket washer installed on bolt A (**Figure 23**). Also note the cable clamp installed behind bolt B (**Figure 23**).

4. Remove the starter clutch cover (C, **Figure 23**) from the crankcase. Watch for the dowels (A, **Figure**

24) and the wave washer (A, **Figure 25**) behind the cover.

5. Remove the dowels (A, **Figure 24**) and the gasket (B) from the crankcase. Discard the gasket.

6. Slide the wave washer (A, **Figure 25**) and idler gear No. 2 (B) from the idler shaft No. 2 (C). Then pull the shaft from its boss in the crankcase.

7. Hold the starter clutch with the starter clutch holder, and remove the starter clutch bolt (D, **Figure 25**) and its washer.

8. Note the indexing line (A, **Figure 26**) on the starter clutch aligns with the indexing dot (B) on the crankshaft.

9. Remove the starter clutch (C, **Figure 26**) from the crankshaft, and remove the washer (**Figure 27**).

10. Set the starter clutch on the bench so the driven gear (A, **Figure 28**) faces up.

11. Hold the clutch housing and rotate the driven gear. It should rotate freely when turned clockwise but lock when turned counterclockwise. Replace the starter clutch if it fails either portion of this test.

### Installation

1. Install the washer (**Figure 27**) onto the crankshaft.

2. Slide the starter clutch onto the crankshaft splines so the indexing line (A, **Figure 26**) on the starter clutch aligns with the indexing dot (B) on the crankshaft.

3. Install the washer and starter clutch bolt (D, **Figure 25**).

4. Hold the starter clutch with the holder and tighten the starter clutch bolt to 55 N•m (41 ft.-lb.). Refer to **Figure 29**.

5. Lubricate idler shaft No. 2 (C, **Figure 25**) with clean engine oil.

6. Fit starter idler gear No. 2 (B, **Figure 25**) into the crankcase so the teeth on its inner gear engage those on the starter clutch driven gear.

7. Install idler shaft No. 2 (C, **Figure 25**) through idler gear No. 2, and seat the shaft into its boss in the crankcase.

8. Install the wave washer (A, **Figure 25**) onto the shaft, and seat it within the recess in idler gear No. 2.

9. Clean all gasket residue from the crankcase.

10. Apply Suzuki Bond 1207B, or an equivalent sealant, to the seams formed by the crankcase mating surfaces (**Figure 30**).

11. Install the dowels (A, **Figure 24**) and a new gasket (B).

12. Fit the starter clutch cover (C, **Figure 23**) into place and hand-tighten the starter cover bolts. Install a new gasket washer onto cover bolt A (**Figure 23**), and install the wire clamp behind bolt B.

13. Tighten the starter clutch cover bolts to 10 N•m (89 in.-lb.).

14. Install idler gear No. 1 (this chapter).

### Inspection

1. Remove the needle bearing (B, **Figure 28**) from the starter clutch.

2. Remove the starter clutch driven gear (A, **Figure 28**) by rotating the gear clockwise and simultaneously lifting it from the starter clutch.

3. Clean all parts in solvent and dry them with compressed air.

4. Inspect the starter clutch driven gear (A, **Figure 31**), idler gear No. 1 (A, **Figure 32**), and idler gear No. 2 (A, **Figure 33**) for worn, chipped or cracked teeth. Replace any gear as necessary.

5. Inspect each idler gear shaft (B, **Figure 33** and B, **Figure 32**) for scoring or other signs of wear.

6A. On 1999-2002 models, inspect the idler gear needle bearing (C, **Figure 32**) for scoring or other signs of wear.

6B. On 2003-on models, perform the test described in *Torque Limiter Inspection*.

7. Inspect the starter clutch needle bearing (**Figure 34**) for scoring or other signs of wear.

8. Inspect the splines of the starter clutch (A, **Figure 35**) for excessive wear. If any is noted, also inspect the splines on the crankshaft.

9. Inspect the rollers (B, **Figure 35**) in the starter clutch for burrs, wear or damage. Replace if necessary.

10. Inspect the bearing surface (B, **Figure 31**) of the driven gear for scoring or other signs of wear.

11. Inspect the shaft bosses in the right crankcase, starter idler cover and in the starter clutch cover for wear or damage.

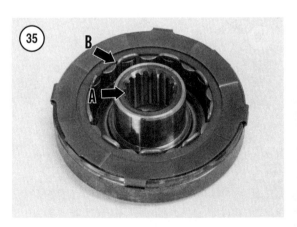

## ALTERNATOR COVER

### Removal/Installation

1. Disconnect the negative battery cable.
2. Remove the side fairing panel from the left side.
3. Disconnect the 3-pin stator connector (B, **Figure 36**) and the 2-pin crankshaft position sensor (A).
4. Place an oil pan beneath the alternator cover.
5. Remove the alternator cover bolts (A, **Figure 37**), and remove the cover (B). Watch for the dowels (A, **Figure 38**) behind the cover.
6. Remove the dowels (A, **Figure 38**) and gasket (B) from the crankcase. Discard the gasket.
7. Installation is the reverse of removal. Note the following:
   a. Clean all gasket residue from the gasket mating surfaces of the crankcase and cover.
   b. Apply Suzuki Bond 1207B, or an equivalent sealant, to the seams (A, **Figure 39**) formed by the mating surfaces of the crankcase.
   c. Install the dowels (A, **Figure 38**), and then install a new cover gasket (B).
   d. Tighten the alternator cover bolts to 10 N•m (89 in.-lb.).

## FLYWHEEL

### Removal/Installation

1. Remove the alternator cover as described in this chapter.
2. Hold the flywheel with a rotor holder (Suzuki part No. 09930-44530), the sheave holder or with a 32-mm wrench. Remove the flywheel bolt (B, **Figure 39**) and washer.
3. Turn the rotor remover (Suzuki part No. 09930-30450) into the crankshaft.
4. Hold the flywheel with the same tool used in Step 2, and turn the rotor remover until the flywheel releases from the crankshaft taper.
5. Turn out the rotor remover, and then remove the flywheel from the taper.
6. Remove the Woodruff key (A, **Figure 40**) from the crankshaft.
7. Installation is the reverse of removal. Note the following:
   a. Clean the crankshaft taper (B, **Figure 40**) and the flywheel tapered bore (A, **Figure 41**) so they are free of oil and contaminants.
   b. Install the Woodruff key (A, **Figure 40**) into the crankshaft.
   c. Hold the flywheel with the same tool used in Step 2 (**Figure 42**), and tighten the flywheel bolt (B, **Figure 39**) to 120 N•m (89 ft.-lb.).

## Inspection

*WARNING*
*Replace a cracked or chipped flywheel.*
*At high engine speeds, a damaged fly-*
*wheel can fly apart and scatter metal*
*fragments into the engine. Do not re-*
*pair a damaged flywheel.*

1. Clean the flywheel in solvent and dry it with compressed air.
2. Check the flywheel for cracks or other signs of damage.
3. Check the flywheel tapered bore (A, **Figure 41**) and the crankshaft taper (B, **Figure 40**) for damage.
4. Inspect the flywheel magnet (B, **Figure 41**) for metal debris it may have attracted. Remove all debris.

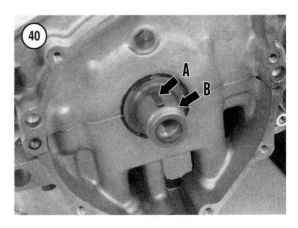

## OIL PUMP

The oil pump (**Figure 43**) is located behind the clutch. The oil pump can be removed with the engine mounted in the frame. With the exception of the driven gear, replacement parts are not available. If the oil pump is not operating properly, the entire oil pump assembly must be replaced.

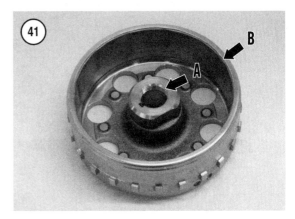

## Removal

1. Remove the clutch as described in Chapter Six.
2. Cover the crankcase opening to keep debris out of the crankcase.
3. Remove the snap ring (**Figure 44**) securing the driven gear to the oil pump shaft.
4. Rotate the driven gear (**Figure 45**) so the pin sits horizontally. The pin is less likely to fall into the crankcase when seated in this position. Remove the driven gear from the oil pump shaft.
5. Remove the pin (A, **Figure 46**) and washer (B) from the oil pump shaft.
6. Remove the oil pump mounting bolts (C, **Figure 46**).
7. Withdraw the oil pump assembly from the crankcase (D **Figure 46**). Remove and discard the O-ring (A, **Figure 47**) from the inboard side of the pump.
8. Inspect the oil pump as described in this section.

## Installation

1. Apply Suzuki Super Grease A to a new O-ring (A, **Figure 47**), and install it into the oil pump.
2. Apply clean engine oil to the oil pump housing and to the crankcase.
3. Cover the crankcase opening to keep parts out of the crankcase.

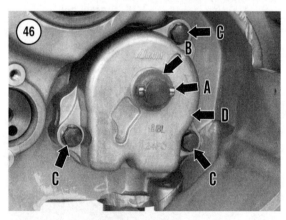

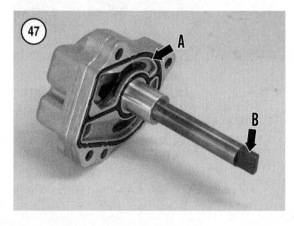

4. Insert the oil pump into the crankcase. Align the male end (B, **Figure 47**) of the oil pump shaft with the female end of water pump shaft, and push the oil pump into the crankcase until it bottoms. Make sure the oil pump shaft engages the water pump shaft.

5. Apply Suzuki Thread Lock 1342, or its equivalent, to the threads of the oil pump mounting bolts, and then install the bolts (C, **Figure 46**). Evenly tighten the oil pump mounting bolts to 10 N•m (89 in.-lb.).

6. Install the washer (B, **Figure 46**) onto the oil pump drive shaft.

7. Install the pin (A, **Figure 42**) through the hole in the drive shaft. Center the pin in the shaft.

8. Align the pin receptacle in the driven gear with the pin on the drive shaft, and install the driven gear (**Figure 45**).

9. Secure the gear in place with a new snap ring (**Figure 44**). Make sure the entire snap ring sits within the groove on the drive shaft.

10. Install the clutch as described in Chapter Six.

**Inspection**

1. Check pump operation by rotating its drive shaft. Replace the pump if the shaft does not turn smoothly.

2. Inspect the male slot (B, **Figure 47**) on the end of the drive shaft.

3. Visually inspect the oil pump for wear, cracks or damage. Check the inner wall for scuff marks.

### OIL COOLER

Refer to **Figure 48**.

**Removal/Installation**

1. Remove both fairing side panels and the lower front panel (Chapter Fifteen).

2. Drain the engine oil (Chapter Three).

3. Place the oil pan beneath the fitting on the right side of the oil cooler.

4. Remove each oil cooler pipe bolt (A, **Figure 49**), and separate the oil pipe (B) from the fitting on the oil cooler. Watch for the O-ring installed in the fitting.

5. Remove the oil pipe fitting on the left side of the oil cooler by repeating Step 3 and Step 4.

6. Remove the upper oil cooler mounting bolts (A, **Figure 50**) that secure the oil cooler to the radiator. Watch for the collar and damper (A, **Figure 51**) installed with each mount.

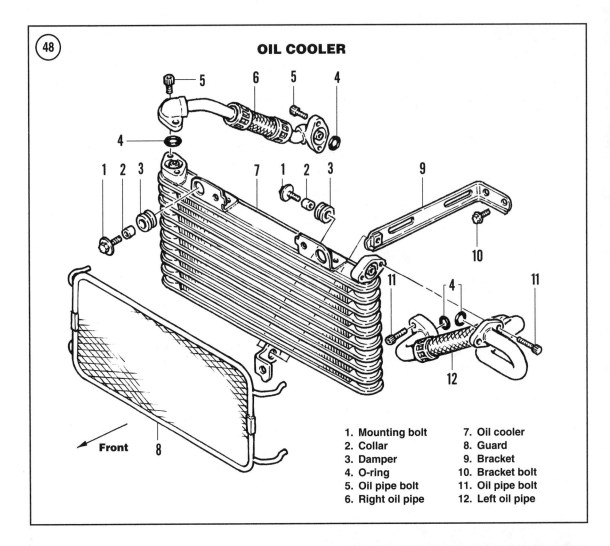

**48** **OIL COOLER**

Front 8

1. Mounting bolt
2. Collar
3. Damper
4. O-ring
5. Oil pipe bolt
6. Right oil pipe
7. Oil cooler
8. Guard
9. Bracket
10. Bracket bolt
11. Oil pipe bolt
12. Left oil pipe

7. Remove the lower oil cooler mounting bolt (B, **Figure 50**). Watch for the collar and damper installed within the mount.

> *CAUTION*
> *Exercise caution when spreading the oil cooler pipes during removal or installation.*

8. Lower the oil cooler from its mounting bracket and remove the cooler from the motorcycle. Gently spread the oil cooler pipes as necessary.

9. If necessary, remove the oil cooler pipes from the crankcase (A, **Figure 52**) by repeating Step 3 and Step 4.

10. Remove and discard the O-ring (B, **Figure 51**) from the fitting. New O-rings must be installed during installation.

11. Installation is the reverse of removal. Note the following:

    a. Make sure the collar and damper (A, **Figure 51**) are in place on each mount.

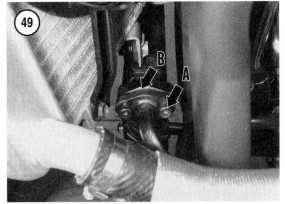

**49**

    b. Lubricate new O-rings with Suzuki Super Grease A, and install an O-ring into the fitting (B, **Figure 51**).

    c. If removed, install each oil cooler pipe (A, **Figure 52**) onto its fitting on the crankcase. Apply Suzuki Thread Lock 1342 to the threads of the oil cooler pipe bolts, and tighten the bolts to 10 N•m (89 in.-lb.).

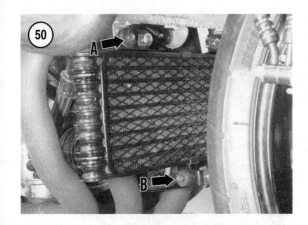

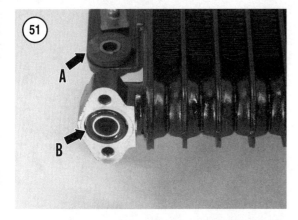

5

d. Gently spread the oil cooler pipes, and fit the oil cooler into place. Make sure the fitting on the end of each oil pipe sits opposite the fitting on each side of the oil cooler.

e. Install the oil cooler mounting bolts. Finger-tighten the mounting bolts (A and B, **Figure 50**).

f. Secure the oil cooler fittings to the oil cooler. Apply Suzuki Thread Lock 1342 to the threads of the oil cooler pipe bolts (A, **Figure 49**), and tighten the bolts to 10 N•m (89 in.-lb.).

g. Tighten the oil cooler mounting bolts securely.

h. Fill the engine with clean oil (Chapter Three).

i. Start the engine and check for oil leaks. Make any necessary repairs.

**Inspection**

1. Remove the guard from the oil cooler.

2. Wash the exterior of the oil cooler (**Figure 53**) and guard with a water hose on low pressure. Spray both the front and back to remove all debris. Carefully use a whiskbroom or stiff paintbrush to remove any stubborn debris.

> *CAUTION*
> *Do not press too hard on the cooling fins and tubes. The resultant damage could cause a leak.*

3. Carefully straighten out any bent cooling fins (A, **Figure 53**) with a broad-tipped screwdriver.

4. Inspect the oil cooler for cracks or other signs of damage. Pay particular attention to the cooler pipes and fittings.

5. Check the mounting bracket (B, **Figure 52**) and oil cooler mounts (B, **Figure 53**) for cracks or damage.

6. Inspect the dampers (A, **Figure 51**) for hardness or deterioration. Replace a damper as necessary.

7. To prevent oxidation to the oil cooler, touch up any area where the paint is worn off.

**OIL CATCH TANK (1999 MODELS)**

1. Raise and support the fuel tank (Chapter Eight).

2. Disconnect the crankcase breather hose (A, **Figure 54**) and air filter housing breather (B) from the oil catch tank (C). Label each hose and its fitting so the hoses can be reinstalled in their original locations.

3. Remove the mounting bolt and pull the tank.

4. Installation is the reverse of removal. Connect each hose to the correct fitting.

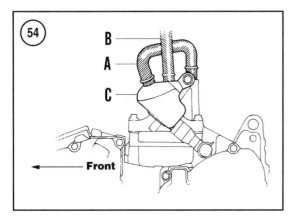

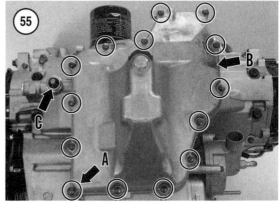

## OIL PAN AND STRAINER

### Removal

1. Remove the engine (this chapter).

2. Evenly loosen the oil pan bolts, and remove the bolts. Discard the gasket washer installed on the bolt (A, **Figure 55**) indicated.

3. Lift the oil pan (B, **Figure 55**) from the crankcase.

4. Remove and discard the oil pan gasket (**Figure 56**).

5. Remove the mounting bolts (A, **Figure 57**), and remove the oil strainer (B) from the crankcase.

6. Remove and discard the oil strainer O-ring (A, **Figure 58**) from the port in the crankcase.

7. Remove the mounting bolt (B, **Figure 58**), and lift the breather pipe (C) from its crankcase port.

> *NOTE*
> *A replacement O-ring for the oil pressure regulator is not available from the manufacturer. Do not remove the regulator unless necessary.*

8. If necessary, pull the oil pressure regulator (**Figure 59**) from its port in the crankcase.

9. If necessary, turn out and remove the oil pressure switch (C, **Figure 55**) from the crankcase.

### Installation

1. Thoroughly clean the mating surfaces of the crankcase and oil pan with an aerosol electrical contact cleaner.

2. If removed, install the oil pressure switch by performing the following:

> *CAUTION*
> *Do not apply sealant to the port in the switch.*

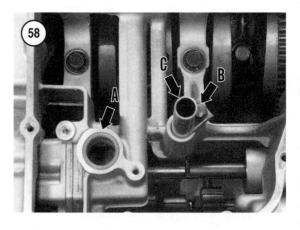

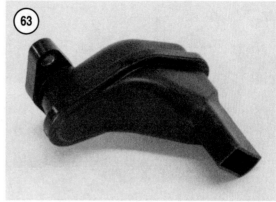

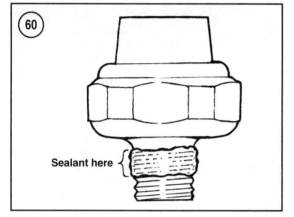

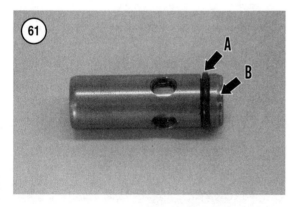

Sealant here

a. Apply Suzuki Bond 1207B, or an equivalent sealant, to the portion of the threads on the oil pressure switch shown in **Figure 60**.

b. Turn the oil pressure switch (C, **Figure 55**) into the crankcase. Then tighten it to 14 N•m (10 ft.-lb.).

c. Attach the electrical lead to the terminal on the switch.

3. If removed, install the oil pressure regulator by performing the following:

a. Lubricate the pressure regulator O-ring (A, **Figure 61**) with Suzuki Super Grease A.

b. Press the regulator (**Figure 59**) into its crankcase port until it bottoms.

4. Insert the breather pipe (C, **Figure 58**) into its port in the crankcase. Apply Suzuki Thread Lock 1342 to the threads of the bolt and tighten the breather pipe mounting bolt (B, **Figure 58**) to 10 N•m (89 in.-lb.).

5. Lubricate a new oil strainer O-ring with Suzuki Super Grease A, and seat the O-ring (A, **Figure 58**) into the crankcase port.

6. Install the oil strainer (B, **Figure 57**). Apply Suzuki Thread Lock 1342 to the threads of the oil strainer bolts (A, **Figure 57**) and tighten the bolts to 10 N•m (89 in.-lb.).

7. Install a new oil pan gasket (**Figure 56**).

8. Install the oil pan and oil pan bolts. Install a gasket washer under the bolt (A, **Figure 55**) indicated. Evenly tighten the bolts to 10 N•m (89 in.-lb.).

### Inspection

1. Clean all parts in solvent and dry them with compressed air.

2. Visually inspect the oil pan (**Figure 62**) and oil breather pipe for cracks or other signs of damage.

3. Inspect the oil strainer (**Figure 63**) for signs of wear or damage. Clean any debris from the strainer as necessary.

4. Use a wooden rod to check the operation of the pressure regulator. Insert the rod into the regulator (B, **Figure 61**), and press the piston into the regulator. The piston must slide smoothly and return to the fully closed position when released. If operation is not smooth, clean the pressure regulator in solvent and thoroughly dry it with compressed air.

5. Replace any worn or damaged part.

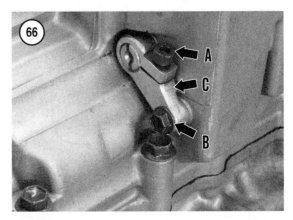

## CRANKCASE

The two-piece crankcase is made of thin-walled, precision-cast aluminum alloy. The case halves are assembled without a gasket. Only sealant is needed during assembly. The upper and lower case halves are a matched set. If one is excessively damaged, both must be replaced as a set.

To avoid damaging the components, do not hammer or pry any of the interior or exterior projected walls. Excessive force damages these areas.

During the following procedures, the terms *right* and *left* refer to the engine as it sits in the frame not as it sits on the bench. Keep this in mind when the crankcase is sitting upside down on the workbench.

### Separation

1. Remove the engine (this chapter.)

2. Remove the cylinder head, cylinder block and pistons (Chapter Four).

3. Place the engine upside down on the bench. Set the engine on a wooden block, and remove the oil pan, oil strainer and breather pipe (this chapter).

4. Remove the balancer by performing the following:

    a. Remove the balancer cover bolts (A, **Figure 64**), and lift the balancer cover (B) from the lower case half.

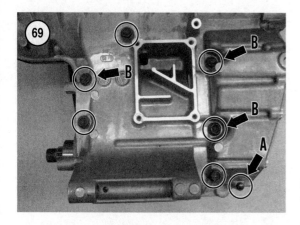

b. Note that the indexing dot (A, **Figure 65**) and the indexing line (B) on the balancer assembly align with the pointer (C) on the crankcase.

c. Loosen the balancer arm clamp bolt (A, **Figure 66**), remove the balancer arm bolt (B) and slide the balancer arm (C) from the balancer shaft.

d. Pull the balancer shaft (**Figure 67**) and lift the balancer assembly from the lower case half. Watch for the washer (**Figure 68**) on each end of the assembly.

5. Turn the engine over and place it upright on the wooden blocks.

*NOTE*
*Draw an outline of each crankcase half on a piece of cardboard. Number and punch holes in the template that correspond with each bolt location. As a bolt is removed, insert it into its appropriate location in the template. Keep any washer or cable clamp on its respective bolt.*

6. Evenly loosen the upper crankcase bolts (**Figure 69**) in a crisscross pattern. Remove the 6-mm bolt (A, **Figure 69**) first, and then remove the remaining 8-mm bolts. Watch for a copper washer under the three bolts (B, **Figure 69**) indicated.

7. Turn the engine over, and place it upside down on the wooden blocks.

8. Following a crisscross pattern, evenly loosen the lower crankcase bolts shown in **Figure 70** and **Figure 71**.

9. Remove each bolt, and insert it in the appropriate place in the template. Remove the PAIR bracket installed beneath the two bolts (A, **Figure 71**) indicated.

10. Reverse the tightening sequence shown in **Figure 72**, and evenly loosen the 9-mm bolts. Remove the bolts. Watch for the copper washer installed under each of the four outside bolts (Nos. 7-10).

11. Tap around the perimeter of the sealing surfaces of the crankcase with a soft-faced mallet and separate the case halves.

*CAUTION*
*Used bearing inserts must be reinstalled in their original bearing boss in the crankcase.*

12. Lift the lower case half from the upper case half. Watch for any loose main bearing inserts (A, **Figure 73**). If a bearing insert falls out, immediately reinstall it into its original place in the lower crankcase.

13. Remove the dowels (**Figure 74**) from the upper case half.

14. Disassemble and inspect the crankcase as described in this section.

## Joining

Assemble the crankcase as described in this section.
1. Set the upper case half upside down on wooden blocks.
2. Install the dowels (A, **Figure 74**) into place in the upper case half.
3. Set the lower case half upright on the bench.
4. Lightly lubricate each main bearing insert (A, **Figure 73**) and crankshaft journal (B, **Figure 74**) with molybdenum disulfide oil.

> *CAUTION*
> *Keep sealant away from any oil hole, oil groove or bearing.*

5. Apply a thin coat of Suzuki Bond 1207B sealant, or its equivalent, to the portions of the upper and lower case halves shown in **Figure 75**. Make the coating as thin as possible, but make sure the sealant completely covers the entire mating surface.

> *CAUTION*
> *When properly aligned, the lower case half slides over the crankshaft and seats against the upper case half. If the crankcase halves do not fit together completely, do not pull them together with the crankcase bolts. Separate the case halves and investigate the cause of the interference. Check the gears for proper installation.*

6. Turn the lower case half upside down and slowly lower it onto the upper case half. Properly align the shift forks with the grooves of their respective transmission gears. Push the lower case half down until it seats on the entire perimeter of the upper case half.
7. Join both case halves and tap them together lightly with a soft-faced mallet. Do not use a metal hammer.
8. Slowly spin the countershaft and shift the transmission through all of the gears. Make sure the transmission operates properly before proceeding.

> *CAUTION*
> *Before tightening the crankcase bolts, set all bolts into place. Make sure the bolt heads are the same distance up from the bolt boss on the crankcase. If any bolts are higher or lower than the others, switch the bolts around until all*

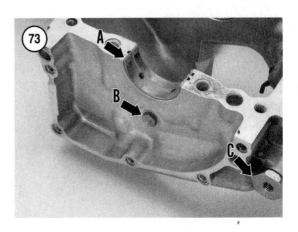

*are the same height, which indicates the bolts are in their correct locations.*

9. Remove the 9-mm lower crankcase bolts from the cardboard template, and install them into the correct locations in the lower case half (**Figure 72**). Apply engine oil to the bolt threads, and include a copper washer under each of the four outside bolts (Nos. 7-10).
10. Following the tightening sequence shown in **Figure 72**, evenly tighten the 9-mm crankcase bolts in two or three stages until all the bolts are snug. In sequence, tighten all the 9-mm bolts to 18 N•m (13 ft.-lb.) and then to 32 N•m (24 ft.-lb.).
11. Remove the remaining lower crankcase bolts (6-, 8- and 10-mm) from the template, and install them into the correct locations in the lower case half (**Figure 71** and **Figure 72**). Include the PAIR bracket under the correct bolts (A, **Figure 71**). Apply Suzuki Thread Lock 1342 to the threads of the bolts (A, B and C, **Figure 71**) indicated.
12. Evenly tighten these bolts (**Figure 70** and **Figure 71**) in two or three stages until all are snug.
13. Tighten the 10-mm bolt (A, **Figure 70**) to 28 N•m (21 ft.-lb.) and then tighten it to 50 N•m (37 ft.-lb.).
14. Tighten the 8-mm bolts (A and B, **Figure 71**) to 13 N•m (115 in.-lb.) and then to 26 N•m (19 ft.-lb.).

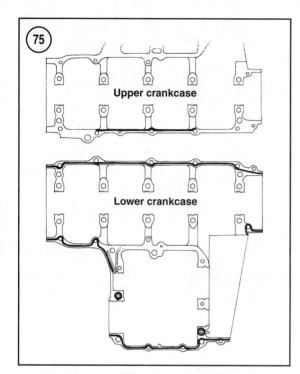

15. Tighten the 6-mm bolts to 6 N•m (53 in.-lb.) and then to 11 N•m (97 in.-lb.).

16. Turn the crankcase over, and set it upright on the wooden blocks.

17. Remove the upper crankcase bolts from the template, and turn them into place in the crankcase (**Figure 69**). Apply engine oil to the threads of all the bolts and install a copper washer under the bolts (B, **Figure 69**) indicated.

18. Evenly tighten the bolts until all are snug.

19. Tighten each 8-mm bolt to 13 N•m (115 in.-lb.) and then to 26 N•m (19 ft.-lb.).

20. Tighten the 6-mm bolt (A, **Figure 69**) to 6 N•m (53 in.-lb.) and then to 11 N•m (97 in.-lb.).

21. Temporarily install the starter clutch and starter clutch cover (this chapter).

22. Set the engine to TDC by using the starter clutch bolt (A, **Figure 76**) to rotate the engine *clockwise*, as viewed from the starter-clutch side, until the index line (B) on the starter clutch aligns with cutout (C) in the timing inspection window.

23. Turn the crankcase upside down, and set it on the wooden blocks. Check the timing marks. The engine must be at the top dead center for balancer installation.

24. Install the balancer assembly by performing the following:

a. Holding the washer (**Figure 68**) on each end of the balancer assembly, lower the balancer into the lower crankcase until the balancer gear engages the drive gear on the crankshaft.

b. Make sure the indexing dot (A, **Figure 65**) and the indexing line (B) on the balancer assembly align with the pointer (C) on the crankcase.

c. Apply molybdenum disulfide oil to the balancer shaft (**Figure 67**) and install the shaft until it bottoms in the crankcase (**Figure 77**).

d. Slip the balancer arm onto the balancer shaft, and install the balancer arm clamp bolt (B, **Figure 66**). Apply Suzuki Thread Lock 1342 to the threads, and then tighten the balancer arm clamp bolt to 10 N•m (89 in.-lb.).

e. Set the balancer cover (B, **Figure 64**) into place, and install the bolts (B). Apply Suzuki Thread Lock 1342 to the threads, and then tighten the balancer cover bolts to 10 N•m (89 in.-lb.).

25. Set the balancer to the standard setting by performing the following:

a. Use a screwdriver to turn the balancer shaft clockwise until it stops.

b. Note the position of the screwdriver slot relative to the graduations on the balancer arm (**Figure 78**).

c. Rotate the balancer shaft counterclockwise 1.5 or 2 graduations. Tighten the balancer arm clamp bolt (A, **Figure 66**) securely.

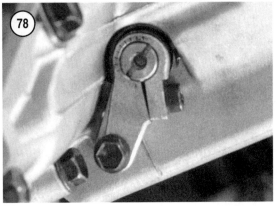

d. If the balancer is noisy once the engine is started, reduce the gear noise by turning the balancer shaft in (clockwise) or out (counterclockwise) within 1 graduation of the standard setting.

26. Install the breather pipe, oil strainer and oil pan (this chapter).

27. Install the pistons, cylinder and cylinder head (Chapter Four).

**Disassembly**

1. Set the engine upside down on the wooden block.

2. Separate the crankcase as previously described in this section.

3. If still installed, remove the dowels (A, **Figure 74**) from the upper case half.

4. Remove the external shift mechanism (Chapter Seven).

5. Remove the countershaft assembly (A, **Figure 79**) and the mainshaft assembly (B) from the upper crankcase half. Make sure the seal (C, **Figure 79**) remains with the mainshaft. Place each shaft assembly in a labeled, reclosable plastic bag until it is serviced.

6. Remove the dowel (A, **Figure 80**) from the small bearing bosses for each shaft. Remove the C-ring (B, **Figure 80**) from the large bearing boss for the mainshaft.

7. Remove the internal shift mechanism (Chapter Seven).

8. Remove the crankshaft (this chapter).

9. Remove the oil spray jet (**Figure 81**) from the countershaft boss in the upper crankcase half.

10. Remove the alternator oil jet (B, **Figure 73**) from the upper crankcase.

11. Remove the transmission oil jet (**Figure 82**) from the upper crankcase.

12. Remove the bolt (A, **Figure 83**) and each piston oil jet (B) from the upper case half. Watch for the O-ring (A, **Figure 84**) behind each jet.

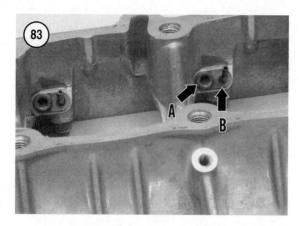

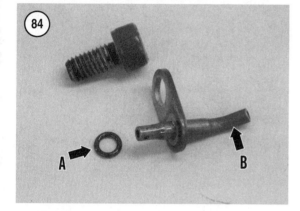

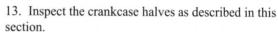

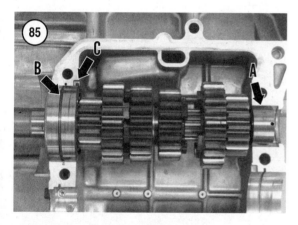

13. Inspect the crankcase halves as described in this section.

**Assembly**

1. Install each piston oil jet by performing the following:
   a. Install a new O-ring (**Figure 84**) onto the jet.
   b. Fit the jet into place in the upper crankcase so the jet's nozzle (B, **Figure 84**) points toward the crankcase-to-cylinder mating surface.
   c. Apply Suzuki Thread Lock 1342 to the threads of the bolt and tighten the piston oil jet bolt (A, **Figure 83**) to 10 N•m (89 in.-lb.).
   d. Repeat substeps a-c for the three remaining piston oil jets.

2. Install the alternator oil jet (B, **Figure 73**). Tighten the jet to 5 N•m (44 in.-lb.).

3. Install the transmission oil jet (**Figure 82**) and the oil spray jet (**Figure 81**) in the upper crankcase.

4. If removed, install each crankshaft main bearing insert (A, **Figure 73**) into its original location in the crankcase halves as described in this chapter.

5. Install the crankshaft (this chapter).

6. Install the internal shift mechanism (Chapter Seven).

7. Install a dowel (A, **Figure 80**) into the small bearing boss for each transmission shaft.

8. Slip the C-ring (B, **Figure 80**) into the large bearing boss for the mainshaft. A C-ring is not needed for the countershaft.

9. Lower the mainshaft into the upper crankcase half so the hole in the needle bearing (A, **Figure 85**) engages the dowel, the slot in the bearing (B) engages the C-clip, and the pin in the ball bearing rests in the cutout (C) in the bearing boss.

10. Install the seal onto the end of the mainshaft so the seal sits inside the lip on the crankcase (**Figure 86**).

11. If removed, install the seal (**Figure 87**) onto the countershaft.

12. Install the countershaft so the hole in its needle bearing engages the dowel, the full-round clip (D, **Figure 79**) on the bearing engages the slot in the bearing boss and the pin on the bearing rests in the cutout in the boss.

13. Install the external shift mechanism (Chapter Seven).

14. Install the dowels (A, **Figure 74**) into the upper crankcase.

15. Join the crankcase halves as described in this chapter.

**Inspection**

1. Remove the crankshaft main bearing inserts as described in *Crankshaft* in this chapter.

2. Remove the oil gallery plugs (C, **Figure 73** and **Figure 88**) from the crankcase halves.

3. Clean both crankcase halves, inside and out, and clean all crankcase bearing inserts with solvent. Thoroughly dry all components with compressed air. Make sure no solvent remains in the crankcase. It contaminates the engine oil.

4. Apply compressed air to the oil galleries and blow out any accumulated residue. If necessary, rinse out the gallery with solvent. Use compressed air to thoroughly dry the galleries.

5. Using a scraper, *carefully* remove any remaining sealant residue from all crankcase mating surfaces.

6. Visually inspect the mating surface of each crankcase half. Check for gouges or nicks that may lead to an oil leak.

7. Install the oil gallery plugs (C, **Figure 73** and **Figure 88**) with new sealing washers. Tighten them as specified in **Table 7**.

8. Clean the oil jets with compressed air.

9. Inspect each crankcase half for cracks and fractures, especially in the lower areas. Check the areas around the stiffening ribs, bearing bosses and threaded holes for damage. If damage is found, have it repaired by a shop specializing in the repair of precision aluminum castings or replace the crankcase.

10. Check the threaded holes in both cases halves for thread damage, dirt or oil buildup. If necessary, clean or repair the threads with a suitable size metric tap. Coat the tap threads with kerosene or an aluminum tap fluid before use.

11. Rotate the shift drum bearing (A, **Figure 89**) and shift shaft bearing (B) by hand. Each bearing should turn smoothly and quietly. Replace any worn or damaged bearing as necessary.

    a. Use a blind bearing puller (C, **Figure 89**) to remove a bearing from the crankcase.

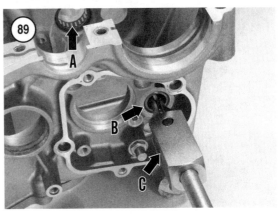

    b. Position a new bearing so the side with the manufacturer's marks face the outside of the crankcase.

    c. Lubricate the bearing and bearing bore with clean engine oil.

    d. Use a bearing driver that matches the outside diameter of the bearing to drive the new bearing into place.

12. If the shift shaft bearing (B, **Figure 89**) in the crankcase requires replacement, also inspect the oil seal (A, **Figure 90**) and bearing (B) in the shift mechanism cover. Replace either part as necessary.

**BALANCER**

**Disassembly/Assembly**

1. Remove the balancer assembly as described in *Crankcase* in this chapter.

2. Note that the indexing dot (A, **Figure 91**) on the balancer drive gear aligns with the indexing line on the balancer web. These must align during assembly.

3. Remove the washer (A, **Figure 92**) from each side of the balancer. Note that the shouldered side of each washer faces the balancer.

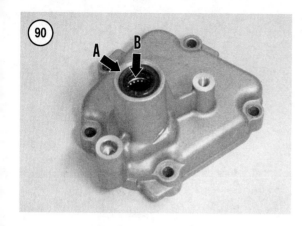

4. Remove each needle bearing (B, **Figure 92**) and the spacer (C) from the balancer (D).

5. Pull the balancer driven gear (E, **Figure 92**) from the balancer, and remove the dampers.

6. Assembly is the reverse of disassembly. Note the following:

    a. Lubricate all parts with molybdenum disulfide oil before installation.

    b. Insert two dampers in each space between the splines in the balancer driven gear.

    c. Install the gear onto the balancer so the splines on the balancer fit between two adjacent dampers in the driven gear. The indexing dot (A, **Figure 91**) on the gear must align with the indexing line (B) on the web.

    d. Install each washer (A, **Figure 92**) so its shouldered side faces in toward the balancer.

    e. Install and adjust the balancer as described in *Crankcase* in this chapter.

### Inspection

1. Inspect the dampers (F, **Figure 92**) for wear or damage.

2. Clean the balancer and gear in solvent. Dry them completely with compressed air.

3. Inspect the balancer shaft (**Figure 93**) for scoring or signs of abrasion.

4. Inspect the teeth of the balancer driven gear (E, **Figure 92**) for cracked or broken teeth. If damage is found, replace the gear and inspect the balancer drive gear on the crankshaft.

5. Inspect the needle bearings (B, **Figure 92**) and spacer (C) for signs of wear or heat damage.

6. Replace any part as needed.

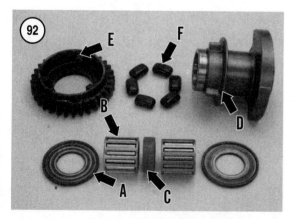

### CRANKSHAFT

#### Removal/Installation

1. Remove the engine and split the crankcase (this chapter).

2. Measure the crankshaft thrust clearance as described later in this section.

3. Rotate the crankshaft so the two outside connecting rods are at the top dead center (**Figure 94**) and carefully lift the crankshaft from the crankcase. Watch for any loose main bearing inserts in the upper case half. Immediately reinsert a loose insert into its original bearing boss.

4. Remove the two thrust bearings (**Figure 95**) from the upper case half. The right bearing is identified by green paint. If this mark is illegible, label the back of

each bearing (left or right) so it can be reinstalled in its original location.

5. Installation is the reverse of removal. Note the following:

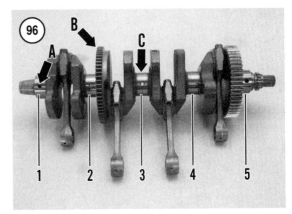

> *CAUTION*
> *If reusing the old main bearing inserts, make sure they are installed in their original locations as noted during removal. Apply molybdenum disulfide oil to all bearing surfaces.*

a. Install the crankshaft main bearing inserts into the upper case half as described in this section.

b. Apply a light coat of grease to the backside of each thrust bearing and install them onto the upper case half bearing boss. Make sure to install each thrust bearing (**Figure 95**) so the side with the grooves faces out.

### Inspection

1. Clean the crankshaft thoroughly with solvent. Clean the crankshaft oil passageways (A, **Figure 96**) with compressed air. If necessary, clean them with rifle cleaning brushes, and then flush the passageways with solvent. Dry the crankshaft with compressed air. Lubricate all bearing surfaces with a light coat of engine oil.

2. Inspect each crankshaft journal (1-5, **Figure 96**) for scratches, ridges, scoring, nicks or heat discoloration. Replace the crankshaft if any journal is scored or pitted.

3. Measure the outside diameter of each crankshaft journal (A, **Figure 97**). Record each reading.

4. Measure crankshaft runout as follows:

a. Set the crankshaft on V-blocks so the two outside journals rest on the blocks.

b. Position a dial indicator so its stem rests against the center journal (C, **Figure 96**). Zero the dial gauge.

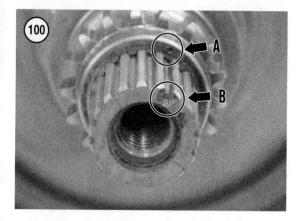

c. Slowly turn the crankshaft while reading the dial gauge. Record the runout.

d. If the runout exceeds the service limit (**Table 1**), replace the crankshaft.

5. Inspect the crankshaft taper (B, **Figure 97**) for scoring or signs of heat damage. If the taper shows damage, also inspect the inside taper on the flywheel.

6. Inspect the crankshaft splines (A, **Figure 98**). If damaged, the crankshaft must be replaced. If the crankshaft splines are damaged, also inspect the inner splines on the timing sprocket and starter clutch. They are probably damaged also.

7. Inspect the timing sprocket (B, **Figure 98**) for worn or damaged teeth. If necessary, replace the timing sprocket by performing the following:

*CAUTION*
*Replace the timing sprocket, cam chain and camshaft sprockets as a set. Otherwise, the old parts quickly wear out the new ones.*

a. Use a universal puller to pull the timing sprocket (**Figure 99**) from the crankshaft. Note that the timing dot (A, **Figure 100**) on the sprocket aligns with the timing dot (B) on the crankshaft. These marks must be aligned during assembly.

b. Use the appropriate size bearing driver (**Figure 101**) to drive the timing sprocket onto the crankshaft. Make sure he timing dots align as shown in **Figure 100**.

8. Inspect the teeth on primary drive gear (C, **Figure 98**). If the primary drive gear is damaged, replace the crankshaft and inspect the primary driven gear on the clutch housing. Refer to Chapter Six.

9. Inspect the teeth on balancer drive gear (B, **Figure 96**). If the balancer drive gear is damaged, replace the crankshaft and inspect the gear on the balancer shaft.

**Main Bearing Removal/Installation**

If the crankshaft main bearing inserts are reused, they must be reinstalled into their original locations in the upper or lower case halves. The crankshaft main bearing bosses are identified as No. 1-5 counting from left-to-right (alternator side to clutch side). Refer to **Figure 102**.

When removing bearing inserts, mark the backside of each insert with a 1, 2, 3, 4 or 5 and a U (upper case half) or L (lower case half) as it is removed. This ensures the insert can be properly identified for assembly.

1. Remove the main bearing inserts from the upper and lower case halves by performing the following:

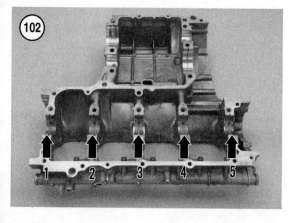

a. Remove the leftmost bearing (alternator side) from one crankcase.

b. Use a permanent marker to label the backside of the insert with a 1 and either a U (upper crankcase) or an L (lower crankcase).

c. Systematically work across the crankcase until each insert is removed and properly labeled.

d. Repeat substeps a-c for the other case half.

2. Install the crankshaft main bearing inserts as follows:

a. Make sure each bearing boss (A, **Figure 103**) in the upper and lower case halves is clean and its oil control hole (B) is clear.

b. Wipe both sides of the bearing insert (**Figure 104**) with a lint-free cloth.

c. If reusing the old bearing inserts, refer to the marks made during removal. Used bearings must be reinstalled in their original locations.

d. Starting with the left most bearing boss in a crankcase (alternator side), insert the No. 1 main bearing insert into the No. 1 bearing boss, the No. 2 main bearing insert into the No. 2 bearing boss, etc. Refer to **Figure 102**.

e. Install an insert into its correct location and carefully press the insert into position by hand. Make sure tab of each insert locks into place in the bearing boss. (**Figure 105**).

**Main Bearing Oil Clearance**

1. Check each crankshaft main bearing insert for evidence of wear, abrasion and scoring. If the bearing inserts are good, they may be reused. If any insert is questionable, replace the entire set.

2. Clean the bearing surfaces of the crankshaft journals and main bearing inserts.

3. Place the upper and lower case halves on the workbench with the bearing boss sides facing up.

4. If removed, install all existing crankshaft main bearing inserts into their original locations. Make sure each bearing is locked into its bearing boss (**Figure 105**).

5. Install the crankshaft (A, **Figure 106**) into the upper case half.

6. Place a piece of Plastigage over each crankshaft journal so the Plastigage parallels the crankshaft as shown in **Figure 107**.

*CAUTION*
*Do not rotate the crankshaft while the Plastigage is in place.*

7. Install the dowels (B, **Figure 106**) into the upper crankcase.

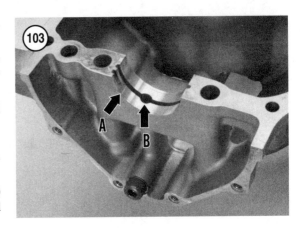

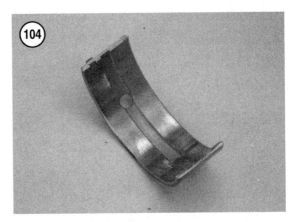

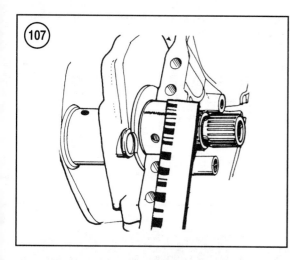

*CAUTION*
*Before tightening the crankcase bolts, set all bolts into place. Check that all the bolt heads are the same distance up from the bolt boss on the crankcase. If any bolts are higher or lower than the others, switch the bolts around until all are the same height, which indicates the bolts are in their correct locations.*

9. Remove the 9-mm bolts from the template and install them into the correct location in the lower case half (**Figure 108**). Apply engine oil to the bolt threads. Install a copper washer under the four outside bolts (Nos. 7-10).

10. Following the sequence shown in **Figure 108**, evenly tighten the 9-mm crankcase bolts in two or three stages until all the bolts are snug. In sequence, tighten the 9-mm crankcase bolts to 18 N•m (13 ft.-lb.) and then tighten to 32 N•m (24 ft.-lb.).

11. Reverse the sequence shown in **Figure 108**, and loosen the bolts in the 9-mm crankcase bolts in descending order. Evenly loosen all bolts in two or three stages, and then remove the bolts. Insert each bolt into its place in the template.

12. Lift the lower case half off the upper case half. If any bearing insert falls from the lower case half, immediately reinstall it into its original location.

13. Measure the width of the flattened Plastigage according to the manufacturer's instructions (**Figure 107**). Measure both ends of the Plastigage strip. A difference of 0.025 mm (0.001 in.) or more indicates a tapered journal. Confirm this by measuring the journal outside diameter with a micrometer.

14. If the widest part of any Plastigage exceeds the crankshaft journal oil clearance, refer to *Main Bearing Selection* in this section and install a new set of crankshaft main bearings.

15. Remove all Plastigage material from the crankshaft journals and bearing inserts.

**Main Bearing Selection**

1. The crankshaft journal outside diameter codes (A, B and C) are stamped on the outside crankweb (A, **Figure 109**) at the alternator end of the crankshaft. These codes correspond to the outside diameter of the crankshaft main journals in the sequence shown in **Figure 110**.

2. The crankcase inside diameter codes (A or B) are stamped on the rear side of the upper case half (**Figure 111**). These codes correspond to the inside diameter of the main bearing bosses in the crankcase.

3. Identify the code for each crankshaft journal and its related bearing boss.

*CAUTION*
*When properly aligned, the lower case half slides over the crankshaft assembly and seats against the upper case half. If the case halves do not fit together completely, do not pull them together with the crankcase bolts. Separate the case halves and investigate the cause of the interference.*

8. Set the lower case half onto the upper case half.

4. Select new bearings by cross-referencing the crankshaft outside diameter codes in the horizontal row of **Table 2** with the crankshaft bearing boss inside diameter codes in the vertical column. The intersection of the appropriate row and column indicates the color of the new bearing insert. **Table 3** lists bearing color, part number and thickness for the inserts. Always replace all 10 crankshaft bearing inserts as a set.

5. After new bearing inserts have been installed, recheck the clearance by measuring the crankshaft main bearing oil clearance as described in this section. If the oil clearance is still out of specification, measure the outside diameter of the crankshaft journals (**Figure 98**). Identify each journal's outside diameter code (**Figure 110**) and compare the measurement to the specification for the indicated code (**Table 1**). Replace the crankshaft if a journal's outside diameter is less than the range specified in **Table 1**. If the journals are within specification, replace the crankcases.

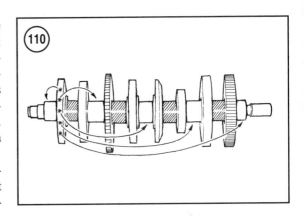

**Thrust Clearance**

1. Separate the crankcase as described in this chapter.

2. Push the crankshaft assembly all the way toward the alternator side (left side) until there is no clearance between the crankshaft and the right thrust bearing (**Figure 112**).

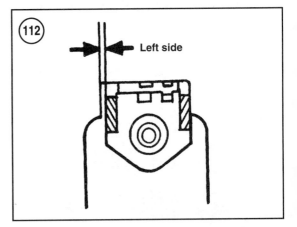

3. Measure the thrust clearance by inserting a flat feeler gauge between the crankshaft web thrust surface and the left thrust bearing as shown in **Figure 113**. Compare the reading to the crankshaft thrust clearance in **Table 1**.

4. If the thrust clearance is outside the specified range, perform the following.

   a. Remove the right thrust bearing, and measure its thickness with a micrometer (**Figure 114**). Compare to the reading to the bearing thickness specified in **Table 1**.

   b. If the thickness is within the specified range, reinstall the right thrust bearing and proceed to Step 5.

   c. If the thickness is less than specified, install a new right thrust bearing and then repeat Step 2 and Step 3.

5. Remove the left thrust bearing.

6. Measure the left thrust clearance by inserting a flat feeler gauge between the left surface of the crankcase and the machined surface of the crankshaft (**Figure 115**).

7. Refer to **Table 6** and use the clearance measured in Step 6 to select the correct left thrust bearing.

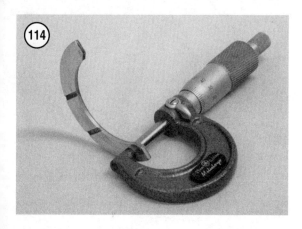

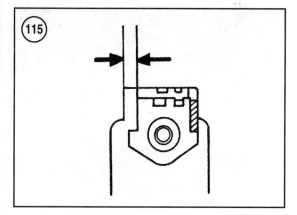

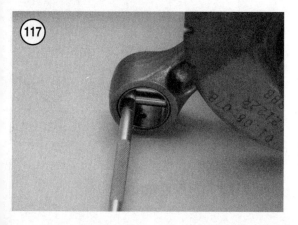

Thrust bearings are identified by the color painted on the end of the bearing.

8. Install the new left thrust bearing. Measure the thrust clearance by repeating Step 2 and Step 3.

9. If the clearance cannot be brought into specification with the new thrust bearings, replace the crankshaft.

10. After the clearance has been correctly adjusted, remove both thrust bearings and apply a coat of molybdenum disulfide grease to each side of the bearings. Install both bearings into the crankcase with their oil grooves facing out toward the crankshaft web (**Figure 95**).

## CONNECTING ROD

### Removal

1. Remove the crankshaft as described in this chapter.

> *CAUTION*
> *Before proceeding, mark the connecting rods and caps with their cylinder number, counting from the left to right (alternator taper to timing sprocket side).*

2. Measure the big end side clearance of each connecting rod by performing the following:

   a. Starting with the No. 1 connecting rod, insert a flat feeler gauge between the connecting rod big end and the machined surface of the crankweb (**Figure 116**).

   b. Record the big end side clearance.

   c. Repeat this for each remaining connecting rod. These measurements are used during connecting rod inspection.

3. Measure the small end inside diameter (**Figure 117**) of each connecting rod with a small hole gauge. Record the reading for each connecting rod.

> *CAUTION*
> *The connecting rod weight mark (**Figure 118**) faces rearward toward the intake side of the engine. The rods must be reinstalled with this orientation. Keep each bearing insert in its original location in the connecting rod or cap. If reused, the inserts must be reinstalled in their original locations.*

4. Remove a connecting rod by performing the following:

   a. Use a 12-mm, 12-point socket to remove the connecting rod cap bolts (A, **Figure 119**) from one connecting rod.

b. Remove the cap (B, **Figure 119**) from the rod. If the bearing insert falls from the cap, immediately reinsert it into the cap.

c. Remove the connecting rod (**Figure 120**) from its crankpin. Watch for the bearing insert. Reinstall it into the rod, if necessary.

d. Fit the rod cap back onto the connecting rod (**Figure 121**). Loosely install the rod bolts. The weight mark on the cap should align with the mark on its connecting rod (**Figure 118**).

e. Repeat substeps a-d for each remaining connecting rod.

5. Inspect the connecting rods and bearing inserts as described in this section.

6. Measure the connecting rod oil clearance as described in this section.

### Installation

1. Make sure the bearing inserts are locked into place in the rod cap (**Figure 122**) and connecting rod.

2. Apply molybdenum disulfide oil to the crankpins and to the connecting rod bearing inserts.

> *NOTE*
> *The connecting rod and rod cap are mated. When installed on its mate, the weight mark on the rod cap aligns with the weight mark on the connecting rod as shown in **Figure 118**. Use the cylinder numbers marked during removal to identify the correct cap for each connecting rod.*

3. Slip a connecting rod (**Figure 120**) onto its crankpin so the rod's weight mark (**Figure 118**) faces the intake side of the engine (the rear).

4. Fit the rod cap onto the connecting rod. Push the cap until it bottoms on the connecting rod. The weight marks on the cap and connecting rod should align (**Figure 118**). If they do not, the wrong cap has been used. Correct this immediately.

5. Apply molybdenum disulfide oil to the threads and seating surface of each cap bolt, and install the bolts. Use a 12-point, 12-mm socket to tighten the connecting rod cap bolts in two steps to 35 N•m (26 ft.-lb.) and then to 67 N•m (49 ft.-lb.).

6. Make sure the weight marks (**Figure 118**) face the intake side (rear) of the engine. If they do not, the connecting rod has been installed backwards. Remove it and correct the problem.

7. Apply engine oil to the big end surfaces, and check the movement of the connecting rod on the crankpin.

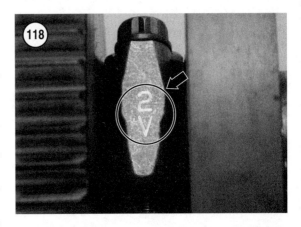

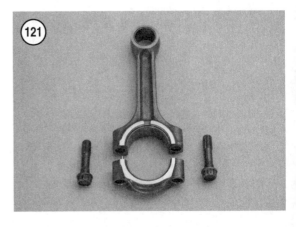

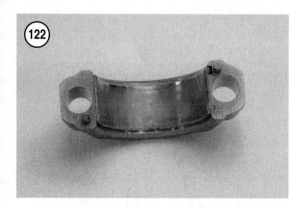

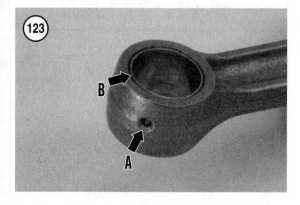

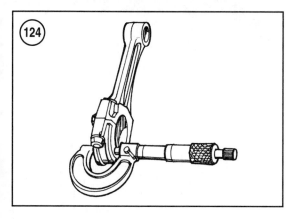

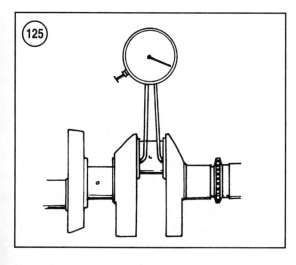

8. Repeat Steps 3-7 for the remaining connecting rods.

**Inspection**

1. Check each connecting rod assembly (**Figure 121**) for obvious damage such as cracks or burns.

2. Make sure the small end oil hole (A, **Figure 123**) is open. Clean it out if necessary. Inspect the bushing (B, **Figure 123**) for signs of scoring, wear or signs of heat damage.

3. Take the connecting rods to a Suzuki dealership or machine shop and have them check the alignment.

4. Examine the bearing inserts (**Figure 122**) for wear, scoring or burned surfaces. They are reusable if in good condition. When discarding a bearing, note the bearing color identification.

5. Compare the small end inside diameter measurement taken during removal with the specification in **Table 1**. Replace a connecting rod if the inside diameter is worn to the service limit.

6. Compare the connecting rod big end side clearance measurement taken during removal to the specification in **Table 1**. If the side clearance exceeds the service limit, perform the following:

    a. Measure the width of the connecting rod big end with a micrometer (**Figure 124**). If the width is less than the value specified in **Table 1**, replace the connecting rod assembly.

    b. Measure the crankpin width with a dial caliper or vernier caliper (**Figure 125**). Compare the measurement to the dimension in **Table 1**. If the width is greater than specified, replace the crankshaft.

**Oil Clearance**

1. Check each connecting rod bearing insert for evidence of wear, abrasion and scoring. Inserts in good condition can be reused. If either insert is questionable, replace both as a set.

2. Clean the crankpins and check for signs of scoring or abrasion.

3. If removed, install the existing bearing inserts into the connecting rod and cap. Each insert must be locked into place (**Figure 122**).

4. Place a piece Plastigage across the relevant crankpin (**Figure 126**). Do not place Plastigage across an oil hole. Make sure the Plastigage parallels the crankpin.

*CAUTION*
*The connecting rod and rod cap are mated. When installed on its mate, the*

5

*weight mark on the rod cap aligns with the weight mark on the connecting rod as shown in* **Figure 118***. Use the cylinder numbers marked during removal to identify the correct cap for each connecting rod.*

5. Install the connecting rod as described in Steps 3-5 of *Installation*.

6. Loosen the cap bolts (A, **Figure 119**). Carefully lift the cap (B, **Figure 115**) straight up and off the connecting rod.

7. Measure the width of the flattened Plastigage according to the manufacturer's instructions (**Figure 126**). Measure both ends of the Plastigage strip.

   a. A difference of 0.025 mm (0.001 in.) or more indicates a tapered journal. Confirm this by measuring the crankpin outside diameter with a micrometer (**Figure 127**).

   b. If the connecting rod oil clearance is greater than the service limit specified in **Table 1**, select new bearings as described in this section.

8. Repeat Steps 1-7 for the remaining connecting rods.

9. Remove all of the Plastigage from the crankpins or rod caps.

**Bearing Selection**

1. A numeric code (1, 2 or 3) stamped into the counterbalance web (B, **Figure 109**) coincides with the crankpin outside diameter as shown in **Figure 128**.

2. A numeric weight code (1 or 2) marked on the side of the connecting rod (**Figure 118**) coincides with the inside diameter of the connecting rod big end.

3. Select new bearings by cross-referencing the crankpin outside diameter code in the top row of **Table 4** with the connecting rod inside diameter code in the left column of the table. The intersection of the appropriate row and column indicates the color of the new bearing inserts. Refer to **Table 5** for bearing color, part number and thickness. Always replace all connecting rod bearing inserts as a set.

4. After new bearing inserts have been installed, recheck the clearance by repeating the *Oil Clearance* procedure. If the clearance is still out of specification, either the crankshaft or the connecting rod(s) is worn to the service limit and requires replacement. Measure the inside diameter of the connecting rod big end and measure the outside diameter of the crankpin. Compare the measurements to the specifications in **Table 1**. Replace the component that is out of specification

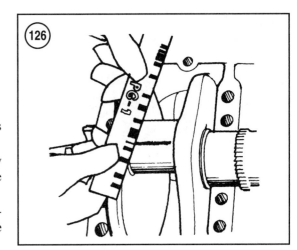

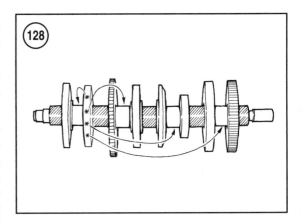

## ENGINE BREAK-IN

During break-in, oil consumption is higher than normal. It is important to check and correct the oil level frequently (Chapter Three). Never allow the oil level to drop below the minimum level.

The manufacturer designates the first 1600 km (1000 miles) of operation as the break-in period. During the first 800 km (500 miles), do not exceed 5500 rpm. In the period between 800-1600 km (500-1000 miles), do not exceed 8000 rpm.

Vary the engine speed during the break-in period. Avoid prolonged operation at any one engine speed.

After the break-in period, change the engine oil and filter as described in Chapter Three.

### Table 1 ENGINE LOWER END SPECIFICATIONS

| Item | Standard mm (in.) | Service limit mm (in.) |
|---|---|---|
| Connecting rod | | |
| Small end inside diameter | 20.010-20.018 (0.7878-0.7881) | 20.040 (0.7890) |
| Big end side clearance | 0.10-0.20 (0.004-0.008) | 0.30 (0.012) |
| Big end width | 20.95-21.00 (0.825-0.827) | – |
| Big end inside diameter | | |
| Code 1 | 41.000-41.008 (1.6142-1.6145) | – |
| Code 2 | 41.008-41.016 (1.6145-1.6148) | – |
| Big end oil clearance | 0.032-0.056 (0.0013-0.0022) | 0.080 (0.0032) |
| Crankshaft | | |
| Crankpin width | 21.10-21.15 (0.831-0.833) | – |
| Crankpin outside diameter | | – |
| Standard | 37.976-38.000 (1.4951-1.4961) | – |
| Code 1 | 37.992-38.000 (1.4957-1.4961) | – |
| Code 2 | 37.984-37.992 (1.4954-1.4957) | – |
| Code 3 | 37.976-37.984 (1.4951-1.4954) | – |
| Crankshaft journal outside diameter | | – |
| Standard | 39.976-40.000 (1.5739-1.5748) | – |
| Code A | 39.992-40.000 (1.5745-1.5748) | – |
| Code B | 39.984-39.992 (1.5742-1.5745) | – |
| Code C | 39.976-39.984 (1.5739-1.5742) | – |
| Crankshaft journal oil clearance | 0.016-0.040 (0.0006-0.0016) | 0.080 (0.0032) |
| Main bearing boss inside diameter | | |
| Code A | 43.000-43.008 (1.6929-1.6932) | – |
| Code B | 43.008-43.016 (1.6932-1.6935) | – |
| Crankshaft runout | – | 0.05 (0.002) |
| Crankshaft thrust clearance | 0.055-0.110 (0.0022-0.0043) | – |
| Crankshaft thrust bearing thickness | | |
| Right side | 2.425-2.450 (0.0955-0.0965) | – |
| Left side | 2.350-2.500 (0.0925-0.0984) | – |
| Oil pressure @ 60° C (140° F) | 200-500 kPa (29-73 psi) @ 3000 rpm | |
| Starter slip torque | 33-52 N•m (24-38 ft.-lb.) | |

### Table 2 CRANKSHAFT MAIN BEARING INSERT SELECTION

| Bearing boss inside diameter code | Crankshaft outside diameter code | | |
|---|---|---|---|
| | A | B | C |
| A | Green | Black | Brown |
| B | Black | Brown | Yellow |

### Table 3 CRANKSHAFT BEARING INSERT DIMENSIONS

| Color (part No.) | Specification mm (in.) |
|---|---|
| Green (12229-24F00-0A0) | 1.488-1.492 (0.0586-0.0587) |
| Black (12229-24F00-0B0) | 1.492-1.496 (0.0587-0.0589) |
| Brown (12229-24F00-0C0) | 1.496-1.500 (0.0589-0.0591) |
| Yellow (12229-24F00-0D0) | 1.500-1.504 (0.0591-0.0592) |

**Table 4 CONNECTING ROD BEARING INSERT SELECTION**

| Connecting rod inside diameter code | Crankpin outside diameter code | | |
|---|---|---|---|
| | 1 | 2 | 3 |
| 1 | Green | Black | Brown |
| 2 | Black | Brown | Yellow |

**Table 5 CONNECTING ROD BEARING INSERT DIMENSIONS**

| Color (part No.) | Specification mm (in.) |
|---|---|
| Green (12164-46E01-0A0) | 1.480-1.484 (0.0583-0.0584) |
| Black (12164-46E01-0B0) | 1.484-1.488 (0.0584-0.0586) |
| Brown (12164-46E01-0C0) | 1.488-1.492 (0.0586-0.0587) |
| Yellow (12164-46E01-0D0) | 1.492-1.496 (0.0587-0.0589) |

**Table 6 THRUST BEARING SELECTION**

| Clearance without left thrust bearing mm (in.) | Color (part number) | Thrust bearing thickness mm (in.) | Thrust Clearance mm (in.) |
|---|---|---|---|
| 2.560-2.585 (0.1008-0.1018) | White (12228-24F00-0F0) | 2.475-2.500 (0.0974-0.0984) | 0.060-0.110 (0.0024-0.0043) |
| 2.535-2.560 (0.0998-0.1008) | Yellow (12228-24F00-0E0) | 2.450-2.475 (0.0965-0.0974) | 0.060-0.110 (0.0024-0.0043) |
| 2.510-2.535 (0.0988-0.0998) | Green (12228-24F00-0D0) | 2.425-2.450 (0.0955-0.0965) | 0.060-0.110 (0.0024-0.0043) |
| 2.485-2.510 (0.0978-0.0988) | Blue (12228-24F00-0C0) | 2.400-2.425 (0.0945-0.0955) | 0.060-0.110 (0.0024-0.0043) |
| 2.460-2.485 (0.0969-0.0978) | Black (12228-24F00-0B0) | 2.375-2.400 (0.0935-0.0945) | 0.060-0.110 (0.0024-0.0043) |
| 2.430-2.460 (0.0957-0.0969) | Red (12228-24F00-0A0) | 2.350-2.375 (0.0925-0.0935) | 0.055-0.110 (0.0022-0.0043) |

**Table 7 ENGINE LOWER END TORQUE SPECIFICATIONS**

| Item | N•m | in.-lb. | ft.-lb. |
|---|---|---|---|
| Alternator cover bolt | 10 | 89 | – |
| Balancer arm bolt | 10 | 89 | – |
| Balancer cover bolt | 10 | 89 | – |
| Breather pipe | 10 | 89 | – |
| Connecting rod cap bolt | | | |
| Initial | 35 | – | 26 |
| Final | 67 | – | 49 |
| Coolant bypass fitting | 14 | – | 10 |
| Crankcase bolts | | | |
| Initial torque | | | |
| 6 mm | 6 | 53 | – |
| 8 mm | 13 | 115 | – |
| 9 mm | 18 | – | 13 |
| 10 mm | 28 | – | 21 |
| Final torque | | | |
| 6 mm | 11 | 97 | – |

(continued)

**Table 7 ENGINE LOWER END TORQUE SPECIFICATIONS (continued)**

| Item | N•m | in.-lb. | ft.-lb. |
|---|---|---|---|
| Crankcase bolts | | | |
| Final torque (continued) | | | |
| 8 mm | 26 | – | 19 |
| 9 mm | 32 | – | 24 |
| 10 mm | 50 | – | 37 |
| Engine mounting hardware | | | |
| Engine mounting clamp bolt | 35 | – | 26 |
| Engine mounting thrust adjuster | 10 | 89 | |
| Engine mounting thrust adjuster locknut | 45 | – | 33 |
| Front engine mounting bolt | 55 | – | 41 |
| Middle engine mounting bolt | 55 | – | 41 |
| Rear mount self-locking nut | 75 | – | 55 |
| Engine sprocket nut | 145 | – | 107 |
| Flywheel bolt | 120 | – | 89 |
| Gearshift cover bolt | 10 | 89 | – |
| Oil cooler pipe bolt | 10 | 89 | – |
| Oil drain bolt | 23 | – | 17 |
| Oil gallery plug | | | |
| 6 mm, 8 mm | 18 | – | 13 |
| 10 mm | 16 | – | 12 |
| 16 mm | 35 | – | 26 |
| Oil pan bolt | 10 | 89 | – |
| Oil line banjo bolt | | – | |
| 6 mm | 10 | 89 | – |
| 14 mm | 28 | – | 21 |
| Cam chain tensioner oil hose (2001-on models) | 12 | 106 | – |
| Oil pump mounting bolt | 10 | 89 | – |
| Oil strainer bolt | 10 | 89 | – |
| Oil pressure switch | 14 | – | 10 |
| Oil jets | | | |
| Alternator oil jet | 5 | 44 | – |
| Piston oil jet bolt | 10 | 89 | – |
| Shift cam stopper bolt | 10 | 89 | – |
| Shift cam stopper plate bolt | 10 | 89 | – |
| Starter clutch bolt | 55 | – | 41 |
| Starter clutch cover bolt | 10 | 89 | – |
| Starter idler cover bolt | 10 | 89 | – |
| Stator bolt | 10 | 89 | – |
| Speed sensor rotor bolt | 23 | – | 17 |
| Valve timing inspection cap | 23 | – | 17 |

5

# CHAPTER SIX

# CLUTCH

This chapter covers the clutch and the clutch release mechanism. Refer to **Tables 1-2** at the end of the chapter for specifications.

The clutch is a wet multiplate type mounted on the right end of the transmission mainshaft. The clutch housing, which is driven by the crankshaft primary drive gear, rotates freely on the mainshaft. The clutch hub, however, is splined to the mainshaft.

The hydraulic release mechanism acts upon two clutch pushrods that ride within a channel in the transmission mainshaft. The movements of the pushrods disengage and engage the clutch.

## CLUTCH HYDRAULIC SYSTEM

### Bleeding

The clutch system uses DOT 4 brake fluid. Before servicing the clutch hydraulic system, refer to Chapter Fourteen. The bleeding and fluid information also applies to the clutch.

The clutch can be bled manually or with the use of a vacuum pump. Both methods are described here.

1. Remove the fairing side panel from the left side (Chapter Fifteen) and remove the coolant reservoir (Chapter Ten).

2. Check all banjo bolts in the system. They must be tight.

3. Remove the dust cap (**Figure 1**) from the bleed valve on the clutch slave cylinder. Fit a box-end wrench onto the valve.

4. Clean all debris from the top of the clutch master cylinder reservoir, and remove the top cover, diaphragm plate and the diaphragm from the reservoir.

5. Add brake fluid to the reservoir until the fluid level reaches the reservoir upper limit. Loosely install the diaphragm and the cover. Leave them in place during this procedure to keep dirt out of the system and so brake fluid cannot spurt out of the reservoir.

6A. When manually bleeding the system, perform the following:

    a. Connect a length of clear tubing to the bleed valve (**Figure 2**). Place the other end of the tube into a clean container. Fill the container with enough brake fluid to keep the end submerged. The tube should be long enough so its loop is higher than the bleed valve. This prevents air from being drawn back through the bleed valve.

    b. Pump the clutch lever a few times. Then apply the clutch lever until it stops, and hold it in this position.

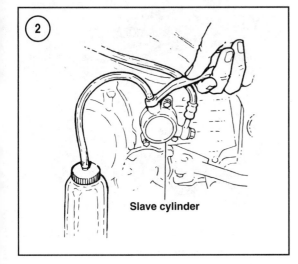

Slave cylinder

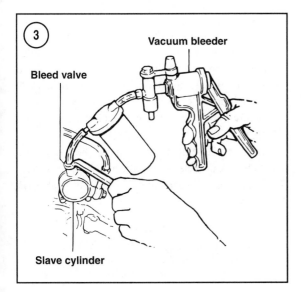

Bleed valve

Vacuum bleeder

Slave cylinder

*NOTE*
*As brake fluid enters the system, the level in the reservoir drops. Add brake fluid as necessary to keep the fluid level 10 mm (3/8 in.) below the reservoir top so air is not drawn into the system.*

c. Open the bleed valve with the wrench. Let the clutch lever move to the limit of its travel, and then close the bleed valve. Do not release the lever while the bleed valve is open.

d. Repeat substep b and substep c until the fluid flowing from the hose is clear and free of air.

6B. If vacuum bleeding, perform the following:

a. Assemble the vacuum tool following the manufacturer's instructions.

b. Connect the pump's catch hose to the bleed valve on the slave cylinder (**Figure 3**).

*NOTE*
*When using a vacuum pump, keep an eye on the fluid level in the reservoir. It drops rapidly. Stop often and check the clutch fluid level. Maintain the level at 10 mm (3/8 in.) from the top of the reservoir so air is not drawn into the system.*

c. Operate the vacuum pump to create vacuum in the hose.

d. Use a wrench to open the bleed valve. The vacuum pump should pull fluid from the system. Close the bleed valve before the fluid stops flowing from the system (low vacuum pressure) or before the clutch master cylinder reservoir runs empty. Add fluid to the reservoir as necessary.

e. Operate the clutch lever a few times, and release it.

f. Repeat substeps c-e until the fluid leaving the bleed valve is clear and free of air bubbles.

7. If the system is difficult to bleed, tap the master cylinder and slave cylinder housing with a soft mallet to release trapped air bubbles.

8. Test the feel of the clutch lever. It should feel firm and offer the same resistance each time it is operated. If the lever feels soft, air is still trapped in the system. Continue bleeding.

*NOTE*
*The setting on the clutch lever adjuster affects bleeding. Initially bleed the clutch with the adjuster turned to the No. 4 setting. Once the clutch feel solid, check the feel with the adjuster in several different settings. If the lever feels soft at any setting or if the lever hits the handlebar, air is still trapped in the system. Continue bleeding.*

9. When bleeding is complete, disconnect the hose from the bleed valve. Tighten the bleed valve to 7.5 N•m (66 in.-lb.).

10. Add brake fluid to the reservoir and adjust the fluid level.

11. Install the diaphragm, diaphragm plate and top cap. Make sure the cap is secured in place.

12. Test ride the motorcycle slowly at first to make sure the clutch operates properly.

### Draining

Always drain the fluid from the system before disconnecting a clutch hose. Draining reduces the amount of fluid that can spill out when system components are removed.

This section describes two methods for draining the clutch system: manual and vacuum. An empty bottle and a length of clear hose are needed to drain the fluid manually. A hand-operated vacuum pump is needed with the vacuum method.

1. Remove the dust cap (**Figure 1**) from the bleed valve on the slave cylinder. Fit a box-end wrench onto the bleed valve. Remove all debris from the valve and its outlet port.

2A. To manually drain the clutch, perform the following:

    a. Connect a length of clear hose to the bleed valve. Insert the other end into a container (**Figure 2**).

    b. Apply the clutch lever until it stops. Hold the lever in this position.

    c. Open the bleed valve with a wrench, and let the lever move to the limit of its travel. Close the bleed valve.

    d. Release the lever, and repeat substep b and substep c until brake fluid stops flowing from the bleed valve.

2B. To drain the clutch with a hand-operated vacuum pump, perform the following:

    a. Connect the pump's catch hose to the bleed valve on the slave cylinder (**Figure 3**).

    b. Operate the vacuum pump to create vacuum in the hose.

    c. Use a wrench to open the bleed valve. The vacuum pump should pull fluid from the system.

    d. When fluid has stopped flowing through the hose, close the bleed valve.

    e. Repeat substeps b-d until brake fluid no longer flows from the bleed valve.

3. Discard the drained fluid.

### CLUTCH COVER

### Removal

1. Securely support the motorcycle on a level surface.

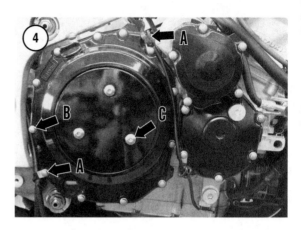

2. Remove the fairing side panel from the right side as described in Chapter Fifteen.

3. Drain the engine oil (Chapter Three).

4. Release the hoses and oil pressure switch wire from the cable holders (A, **Figure 4**). Note how the wire and hoses are routed so they can be rerouted along the same path. Also note where each holder is installed on the clutch cover. The holders must be installed behind the original bolts during assembly.

5. Evenly loosen and remove the clutch cover bolts (B, **Figure 4**).

6. Remove the clutch cover from the crankcase. Watch for the dowels (A, **Figure 5**) behind the cover.

7. Remove and discard the clutch cover gasket (B, **Figure 5**).

> *NOTE*
> *The clutch outer cover is strictly cosmetic. Removal is unnecessary unless the outer cover needs replacing.*

8. If necessary, remove the outer cover bolts (C, **Figure 4**) and remove the outer cover and the damper from the clutch cover. Watch for the stepped washer installed with each outer cover bolt (**Figure 6**).

9. Installation is the reverse of removal. Note the following:

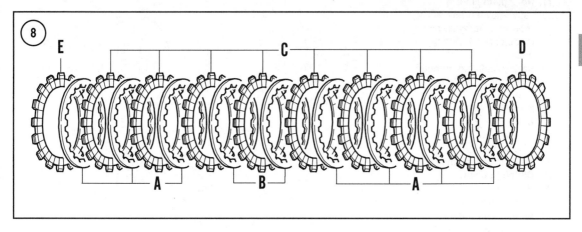

a. If removed, install the damper and outer cover onto the clutch cover. Include a stepped washer with each outer cover bolt (**Figure 6**).

b. Apply Suzuki Bond 1270B, or an equivalent sealant, to the crankcase seams (A, **Figure 7**).

c. Make sure the grommet (B, **Figure 7**) for the gear position sensor wire is properly seated in the crankcase.

d. Install the dowels (A, **Figure 5**) and a new gasket (B).

e. Install the cable holders (A, **Figure 4**) behind the bolts noted during removal.

f. Tighten the clutch cover bolts (B, **Figure 4**) to 10 N•m (89 in.-lb.).

g. Secure the oil pressure switch wire and the hoses behind the cable holders. Route these lines as noted during removal.

h. Add engine oil (Chapter Three). Start the engine and check for oil leaks.

## CLUTCH

### Plates and Discs

The clutch uses nine plain plates and 10 friction discs.

The No. 1 plain plate (A, **Figure 8**) and No. 2 plain plate (B) are used in the clutch. A No. 1 plain plate is 2.0 mm thick; a No. 2 plain plate is 2.3 mm thick. A total of seven No. 1 plain plates (A, **Figure 8**) are used in all models. Two No. 2 plain plates (B, **Figure 8**) are used.

The clutch on 1999-2001 models, uses a No. 1 friction disc (C, **Figure 8**) and No. 2 friction disc (D and E, **Figure 8**).

The clutch on 2002-on models, however, has a No. 1 friction disc (C, **Figure 8**), No. 2 friction disc (D) and No. 3 friction disc (E). The No. 2 and No. 3 friction discs are identical except for their inside diameters. The inside diameter of a No. 3 friction disc is larger than that of a No. 2 disc.

On all clutches, the two outside friction discs (D and E, **Figure 8**) are steel discs. The eight inside friction discs (C, **Figure 8**) are aluminum.

Note the quantity and relative position of each type of plain plate and friction disc. During disassembly, stack all parts in their order of removal. If the friction discs and plain plates are reused, they must be reinstalled in their original locations.

### Removal/Disassembly

Refer to **Figure 9**.

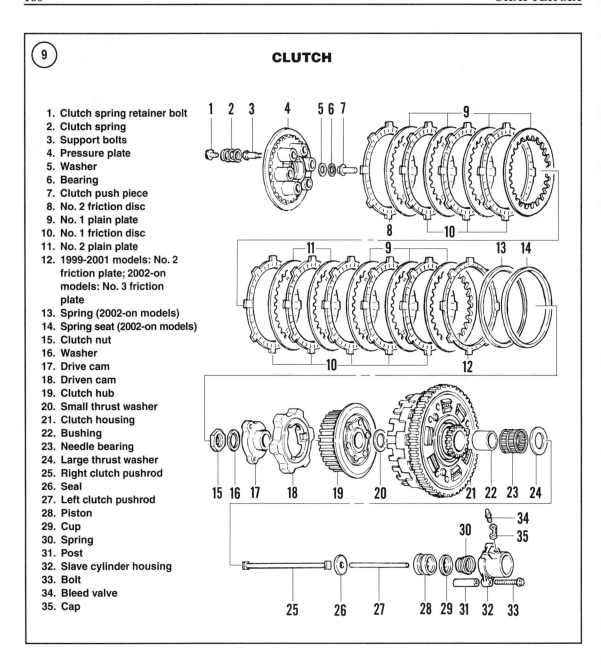

⑨ **CLUTCH**

1. Clutch spring retainer bolt
2. Clutch spring
3. Support bolts
4. Pressure plate
5. Washer
6. Bearing
7. Clutch push piece
8. No. 2 friction disc
9. No. 1 plain plate
10. No. 1 friction disc
11. No. 2 plain plate
12. 1999-2001 models: No. 2 friction plate; 2002-on models: No. 3 friction plate
13. Spring (2002-on models)
14. Spring seat (2002-on models)
15. Clutch nut
16. Washer
17. Drive cam
18. Driven cam
19. Clutch hub
20. Small thrust washer
21. Clutch housing
22. Bushing
23. Needle bearing
24. Large thrust washer
25. Right clutch pushrod
26. Seal
27. Left clutch pushrod
28. Piston
29. Cup
30. Spring
31. Post
32. Slave cylinder housing
33. Bolt
34. Bleed valve
35. Cap

The clutch can be serviced while the engine is in the frame. The procedure is shown with the engine removed for photographic clarity.

1. Remove clutch cover as described in this chapter.

2. Hold the clutch with a clutch holding tool.

3. Evenly loosen the clutch spring retainer bolts (C, **Figure 7**) in a crisscross pattern. Once all the bolts are loose, remove each bolt and the clutch spring (**Figure 10**).

4. Remove the pressure plate (**Figure 11**) from the clutch.

5. Slide the thrust washer (A, **Figure 12**) and the bearing (B) off the clutch push piece (C).

6. Remove the clutch push piece and the right clutch pushrod from the mainshaft (**Figure 13**).

7. Remove the outside friction disc (A, **Figure 14**), and set it on the bench. Note the tabs of this friction disc fit in the short slots of the clutch housing. Also note the tabs of all the other friction discs fit into the long slots (B, **Figure 14**). Each friction disc must be installed in the correct slots during assembly.

8. Remove the outside plain plate (**Figure 15**), and set it on the first friction disc.

9. Continue to remove a friction disc and then a plain plate. Set each part atop the stack as it is removed. The last part removed should be a friction disc (**Figure 16**).

10. On 2002-on models, remove the spring (**Figure 17**) and spring seat from the clutch hub. Note the concave side of the spring faces out away from the clutch

6

housing. A spring and spring seat are not used on 1999-2001 models.

11. Unstake the clutch nut (**Figure 18**). Hold the clutch hub with a clutch holder, and remove the clutch nut from the mainshaft.

12. Remove the washer (**Figure 19**) from the mainshaft.

13. Remove the clutch hub (**Figure 20**) along with the clutch drive cam and driven cam.

14. Remove the small thrust washer (**Figure 21**), the bushing (**Figure 22**) and the needle bearing (A, **Figure 23**) from the clutch housing.

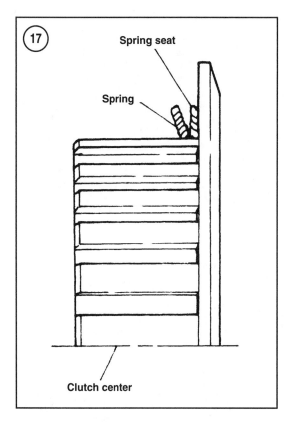

Spring seat

Spring

Clutch center

15. Remove the clutch housing (B, **Figure 23**) from the mainshaft, and then remove the large thrust washer (**Figure 24**). If necessary, rotate the crankshaft so the primary driven gear on the clutch housing does not strike the crankweb during removal.

**Installation/Assembly**

> *CAUTION*
> *If installing new friction discs, soak them in clean engine oil for at least 20 minutes before installation.*

1. Install the large thrust washer (**Figure 24**) onto the mainshaft so its chamfered side faces into the crankcase.

2. Install the clutch housing (B, **Figure 23**) into the mainshaft. Position the housing so the primary driven gear on the clutch housing aligns the primary drive gear (B, **Figure 24**) on the crankshaft and so the oil pump drive gear on the housing aligns the oil pump driven gear (C) on the oil pump shaft. Rotate the crankshaft or the oil pump driven gear as necessary to align the gears, and then press the clutch housing onto the mainshaft until the housing bottoms.

3. Support the housing, and install the needle bearing (A, **Figure 23**) and the bushing (**Figure 22**). Apply clean engine oil to each part, and seat them within the housing.

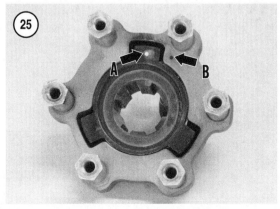

4. Use a screwdriver to wiggle the oil pump driven gear (C, **Figure 24**). Make sure it still engages the oil pump drive gear on the back of the clutch housing.

5. Install the small thrust washer (**Figure 21**).

6. Install the clutch drive cam into the clutch driven cam. Align the punch mark on the drive cam (A, **Figure 25**) with the mark on the driven cam (B).

7. Install the clutch cam assembly into the clutch hub.

8. Align the splines of the clutch hub with those of the mainshaft, and install the hub (**Figure 20**).

9. Install the washer (**Figure 19**) so its concave side faces in toward the clutch hub.

10. Install a new clutch nut (**Figure 18**) onto the mainshaft.

11. Hold the clutch hub with a clutch holder and tighten the clutch nut to 95 N•m (75 ft.-lb.).

12. Stake the clutch nut to lock it into place.

13. On 2002-on models, install the spring seat and spring (**Figure 26**) onto the clutch hub. The concave side of the spring must face away from the spring seat as shown in **Figure 17**.

> *CAUTION*
> *If reinstalling used friction discs and plain plates, install them in the reverse of their removal order. Used discs and plates must be reinstalled in their original locations within the clutch housing.*

14. Install the first friction disc (E, **Figure 8**) into the clutch housing so the tabs (**Figure 16**) of the disc fit into the long slots in the clutch housing as noted during removal. On 1999-2001 models, this disc is a No. 2 friction disc; on 2002-on models, it is a No. 3 friction disc.

15. Install a plain plate (**Figure 15**) so its splines engage those in the clutch hub.

16. Install the next friction disc (No. 1 friction disc) and then install another plain plate. Install the friction

disc so its tabs fit in the long slots of the clutch housing.

17. Repeatedly install a friction disc and then another plain plate until all the plain plates are installed. The first three plates should be No. 1 plates (A, **Figure 8**), followed by two No. 2 plates (B), followed by four No. 1 plates (A). Install each friction disc so its tabs fit into the long slots (B, **Figure 14**) in the clutch housing.

18. End by installing a No. 2 friction disc (D, **Figure 8**). This disc must be staggered. Fit this final disc into place so its tabs engage the short slots in the housing as shown in A, **Figure 14**.

19. Install the right clutch pushrod (**Figure 13**) and then the push piece (C, **Figure 12**) into the mainshaft.

20. Install the bearing (B, **Figure 12**) and thrust washer (A) onto the clutch push piece.

21. Install the pressure plate (**Figure 11**).

22. Fit a spring (**Figure 10**) over each clutch support bolt, and install the clutch spring retainer bolts (C, **Figure 7**). Evenly tighten the bolts in a crisscross pattern. Tighten the clutch spring retainer bolts to 10 N•m (89 in.-lb.).

**Inspection**

Inspect all parts and compare measurements to specifications in **Table 1**. Replace any that are worn, damaged or out of specification. If any friction disc is damaged or out of specification, replace all discs as a set.

1. If still installed, remove the clutch drive and driven cams from the clutch hub.

2. Clean all clutch parts in a petroleum-based solvent, such as kerosene. Thoroughly dry them with compressed air.

3. Measure the thickness of each friction disc at several places around the disc as shown in **Figure 27**.

4. Measure the width of all claws on each friction disc as shown in **Figure 28**.

5. Visually inspect the friction material for cracks, uneven wear or damage. Also check the disc tangs for surface damage.

6. Check the plain plates for warp with a flat feeler gauge on a surface plate or a piece of plate glass (**Figure 29**).

7. Visually inspect the plain plates for cracks, damage or color change. Blue discoloration indicates overheated clutch plates.

8. Check the clutch plates for an oil glaze. Remove any buildup by lightly sanding both sides of the plate with 4000-grit sandpaper placed on a surface plate.

9. Inspect the inner teeth on the plain plates. The tooth contact surfaces must be smooth.

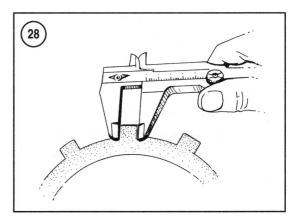

10. Inspect the splines (A, **Figure 30**) of the clutch hub for rough spots or chatter marks. Repair minor damage with a file or oil stone.

11. Inspect the drive cam ramps (B, **Figure 30**) for damage or excessive wear.

12. Inspect the slots (A, **Figure 31**) in the clutch housing for cracks, nicks or galling where they contact the friction disc tabs. Inspect both the long and the short slots in the housing. If excessive damage is evident on any slot, the housing must be replaced.

13. Check the bearing surface (B, **Figure 31**) of the clutch housing for signs of wear or damage.

14. Inspect the teeth of the primary driven gear (A, **Figure 32**) and the oil pump drive gear (B) on the clutch housing for damage. Remove any small nicks with an oil stone. If damage is excessive, replace the gear.

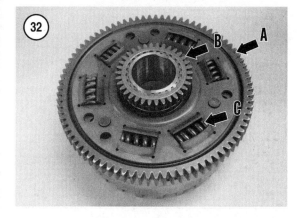

15. Inspect the damper springs (C, **Figure 32**) for cracks or other signs of fatigue. Replace the clutch housing if they are sagging or broken.

16. Inspect the bearing surfaces of the clutch drive and driven cam. If either cam is worn, replace both as a set.

17. Visually inspect the clutch spring support bolts (**Figure 33**) for wear. Replace all the bolts if any one is worn. Apply Suzuki Thread Lock Super 1303 to the threads of the new bolts, and tighten each clutch spring support bolt to 23 N•m (17 ft.-lb.).

18. Check the needle bearing (A, **Figure 34**). It must turn smoothly without excessive play or noise.

19. Check the inner and outer surfaces of the bushing (B, **Figure 34**) for signs of wear or damage.

20. Install the bushing into the needle bearing. Rotate the bushing, and check for wear. Replace either/or both parts if necessary.

21. Inspect the pressure plate for wear or damage (**Figure 35**).

22. Check the clutch push piece (A, **Figure 36**) for wear or damage. Pay attention to the end that rides against the right clutch pushrod.

23. Check the clutch push piece bearing (B, **Figure 36**). Make sure it rotates smoothly.

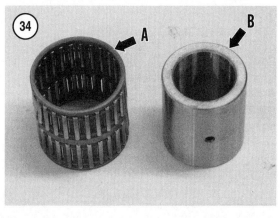

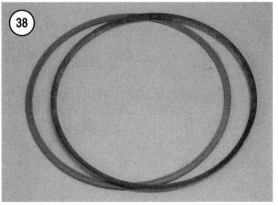

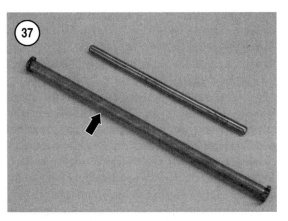

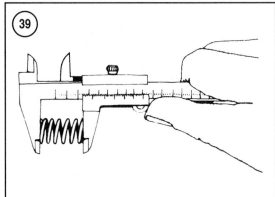

24. Install the bearing and washer onto the push piece. Rotate them by hand. Make sure all parts rotate smoothly.

25. Inspect the right clutch pushrod (**Figure 37**) for bending. Roll the rod along a surface plate or piece of plate glass. If the rod is bent or deformed in any way, it must be replaced. Otherwise it may hang up within the mainshaft tunnel, causing erratic clutch operation.

26. On 2002-on models, inspect the spring and spring seat (**Figure 38**) for cracks, warp or other damage.

27. Measure the free length of each clutch spring (**Figure 39**). Replace all the clutch springs if any one is less than the service limit (**Table 1**).

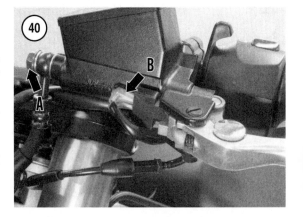

## CLUTCH MASTER CYLINDER

### Removal

> *CAUTION*
> *Cover the fuel tank and front fairing to protect them from brake fluid. Wash any spilled brake fluid from the motorcycle with soapy water.*

1. If servicing the clutch master cylinder, perform the following:

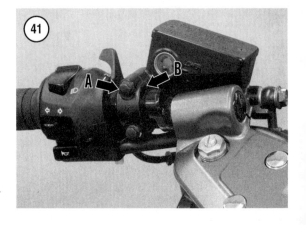

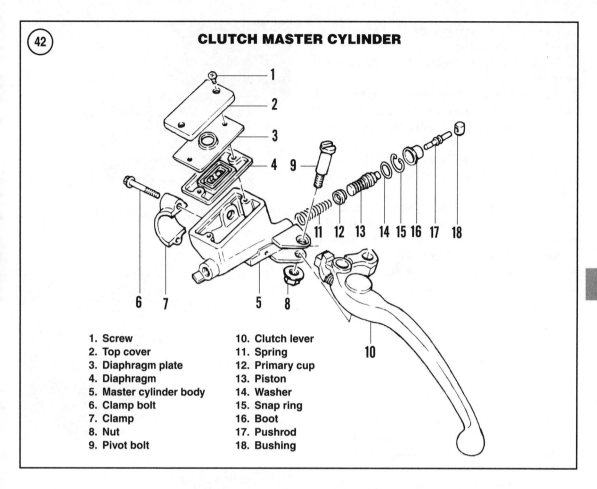

**CLUTCH MASTER CYLINDER**

42

1. Screw
2. Top cover
3. Diaphragm plate
4. Diaphragm
5. Master cylinder body
6. Clamp bolt
7. Clamp
8. Nut
9. Pivot bolt
10. Clutch lever
11. Spring
12. Primary cup
13. Piston
14. Washer
15. Snap ring
16. Boot
17. Pushrod
18. Bushing

a. Drain the fluid from the clutch as described in this chapter.

b. Clean the top of the master cylinder.

c. Remove the top cover, diaphragm plate and diaphragm from the master cylinder reservoir.

d. Place a rag beneath the banjo bolt, and remove the bolt (A, **Figure 40**). Separate the clutch hose from the master cylinder. Watch for the two sealing washers, one on each side of the clutch hose fitting.

e. Secure the loose end of the clutch hose in a plastic bag to prevent brake fluid from leaking onto the motorcycle. Suspend the loose end of the hose from the handlebar.

2. Disconnect the electrical connector (B, **Figure 40**) from the clutch switch.

3. Remove the master cylinder clamp bolts (A, **Figure 41**), and remove the master cylinder from the handlebar.

4. If servicing the master cylinder, drain any residual brake fluid from the master cylinder and reservoir. Watch for the protector inside the reservoir.

**Installation**

1. Set the master cylinder onto the left handlebar so its clamp mating surface (B, **Figure 41**) aligns with the indexing dot on the handlebar.

2. Mount the clamp with the UP mark facing up, and install the master cylinder clamp bolts. Tighten the upper clamp bolt first (A, **Figure 41**) and then the lower bolt leaving a gap at the bottom. Tighten the clutch master cylinder clamp bolts to 10 N•m (89 in.-lb.).

3. Connect the electrical connector (B, **Figure 40**) to the clutch switch.

4. Fit the clutch hose onto the master cylinder so the hose neck seats against the front side of the stop post. Install a new sealing washer onto each side of the hose fitting and tighten the banjo bolt (A, **Figure 40**) to 23 N•m (17 ft.-lb.).

5. Refill the master cylinder reservoir, and bleed the clutch system as described in this chapter.

**Disassembly**

Refer to **Figure 42**.

1. Remove the master cylinder as described in this section.

2. Turn out the mounting screw (A, **Figure 43**) and remove the clutch switch.

3. Remove the nut (B, **Figure 43**) from the clutch lever pivot bolt.

4. Remove the clutch lever pivot bolt (A, **Figure 44**), and slide the lever from the master cylinder bracket. Watch for the bushing (B, **Figure 44**) in the clutch lever.

5. Roll the rubber boot (**Figure 45**) from the cylinder bore, and remove the pushrod/boot assembly from the master cylinder.

6. Press the piston into the cylinder bore, and use snap ring pliers to remove the internal snap ring (**Figure 46**).

7. Remove the washer (**Figure 47**).

8. Remove the piston (A, **Figure 48**) and the spring assemblies (B) from the cylinder bore.

9. Remove the protector from the bottom of the reservoir. Note the position of the protector in the reservoir. It must be reinstalled with this same orientation.

**Assembly**

Refer to **Figure 42**.

1. Soak the new cups in brake fluid for at least 15 minutes to make them pliable. Coat all parts and the inside of the cylinder bore with brake fluid before assembly.

2. Install the new primary cup (C, **Figure 48**) onto the tapered end of the spring (B). Roll the new secondary cup (D, **Figure 48**) onto the piston (A).

> *CAUTION*
> *Carefully install the piston assembly so the cups do not turn inside out.*

3. Install the spring/primary cup assembly (B, **Figure 48**) into the master cylinder bore.

4. Lubricate the piston (A, **Figure 48**) with brake fluid, and install it into the cylinder bore.

5. Install the washer (**Figure 47**) into the cylinder bore and onto the end of the piston.

6. Press the piston into the bore. Secure it in place with a new snap ring (**Figure 46**). The snap ring (A, **Figure 49**) must be fully seated in the groove inside the cylinder bore.

7. Install the pushrod and boot by performing the following:

   a. Install the boot over the pushrod so the end of the boot sits within the pushrod groove (A, **Figure 50**).

   b. Set the pushrod/boot assembly into the cylinder bore so the round end of the pushrod engages the bore in the piston end (B, **Figure 49**). Center the pushrod in the bore.

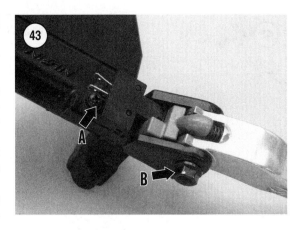

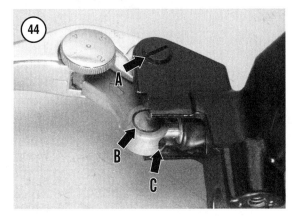

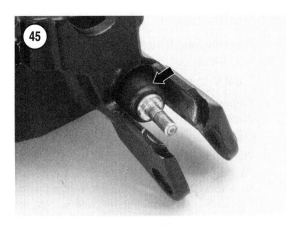

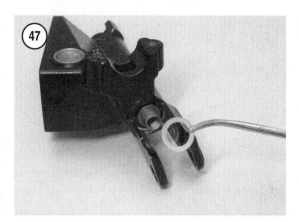

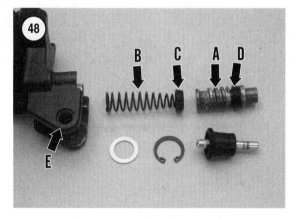

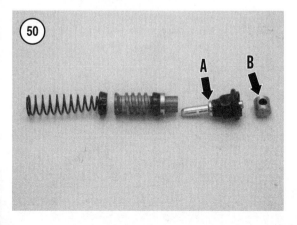

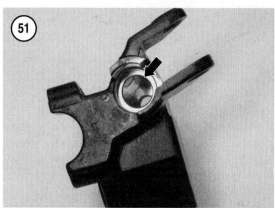

c. Press the pushrod into the cylinder.

d. While holding the pushrod in the cylinder, push the boot into the cylinder until its lip is seated in the bore (**Figure 45**).

e. Slowly release the pushrod. Make sure the boot remains seated in the cylinder bore.

8. Apply a light coat of Suzuki Super Grease A to the inside of the pivot-bolt hole and the bushing hole in the clutch lever.

9. Install the clutch lever as follows:

a. Install the bushing (B, **Figure 50**) into the hole in the clutch lever. Rotate the bushing so its hole sits within the lever's cutout (C, **Figure 44**).

b. Set the clutch lever into position in the master cylinder body. Make sure the end of the pushrod passes through the lever cutout (C, **Figure 44**) and engages the hole in the bushing (B).

c. Position the clutch lever so the pivot bolt hole aligns with the pivot boss in the master cylinder body, and install the pivot bolt (A, **Figure 44**).

d. Install the nut (B, **Figure 43**) onto the pivot bolt, and tighten the nut securely.

10. Fit the clutch switch into position, and secure it with the mounting screw (A, **Figure 43**).

11. Operate the clutch lever, making sure it pivots smoothly and that the pushrod engages the bushing.

12. Seat the protector over the port in the bottom of the reservoir as noted during removal.

13. Install the master cylinder as described in this section.

**Inspection**

Compare any measurements to the specifications in **Table 1**. Replace any worn, damaged or out-of-specification part.

1. Clean all parts in brake fluid or in isopropyl alcohol.

2. Inspect the cylinder bore surface (**Figure 51**) for signs of wear, corrosion or damage. If less than per-

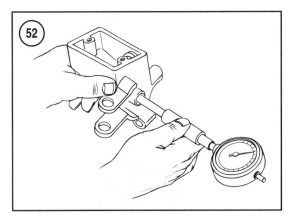

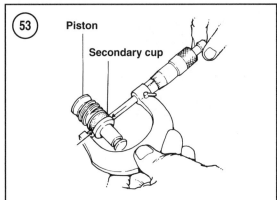

fect, replace the master cylinder assembly. *Do not* hone the master cylinder bore.

3. Measure the clutch master cylinder bore with a bore gauge (**Figure 52**) or vernier caliper.

4. Inspect the piston cups (C and D, **Figure 48**) for signs of wear and damage. If less than perfect, replace the master piston assembly. Cups are not available individually.

5. Inspect the contact surfaces of the piston (A, **Figure 48**) for signs of wear and damage. If less than perfect, replace the master piston assembly.

6. Check the end of the piston for wear caused by the pushrod. If worn, replace the master piston assembly.

7. Measure the outside diameter of the clutch master cylinder piston with a micrometer (**Figure 53**).

8. Check the lugs (E, **Figure 48**) on the clutch lever boss for cracks or elongation.

9. Inspect the pivot hole (A, **Figure 54**) in the clutch lever and the hole in the bushing (B, **Figure 50**) for cracks or elongation.

10. Check for plugged supply and relief ports in the reservoir (**Figure 55**).

11. Check the top cover, diaphragm and diaphragm plate for damage and deterioration. Replace as necessary.

12. Inspect the adjuster (B, **Figure 54**) on the hand lever. If worn or damaged, replace the hand lever as an assembly.

13. Check the threads on the banjo bolt and in the fluid port (**Figure 56**) on the master cylinder. Dress the threads or replace the bolt and master cylinder as necessary.

14. Inspect the clutch hose/pipe assembly for damage and deterioration.

## CLUTCH SLAVE CYLINDER

The clutch slave cylinder sits within the engine sprocket cover.

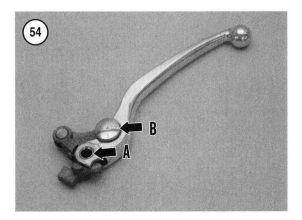

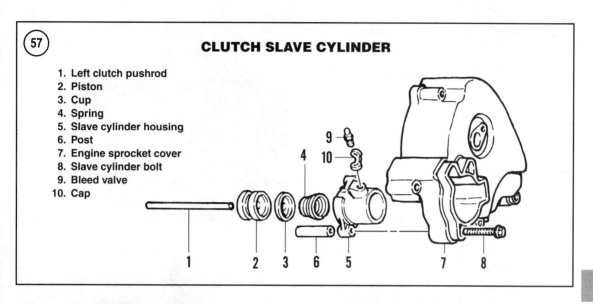

**CLUTCH SLAVE CYLINDER**

1. Left clutch pushrod
2. Piston
3. Cup
4. Spring
5. Slave cylinder housing
6. Post
7. Engine sprocket cover
8. Slave cylinder bolt
9. Bleed valve
10. Cap

Watch for the sealing washer on either side of the hose fitting. Insert the clutch hose end into a plastic bag, and seal the bag with a rubber band.

4. Loosen, but do not remove, the clutch slave cylinder bolts (B, **Figure 58**).

5. Remove the engine sprocket cover (Chapter Seven).

6. Remove the bleed valve (A, **Figure 59**) and the slave cylinder bolts (B).

7. Remove the slave cylinder (**Figure 60**) from the inboard side of the engine sprocket cover. Watch for the dowels (**Figure 61**) behind the slave cylinder.

8. Installation is the reverse of removal. Note the following:

    a. Install the dowels (**Figure 61**) into the inside of the engine sprocket cover.

    b. Set the slave cylinder (**Figure 60**) into the cover so the cylinder engages the dowels.

    c. Tighten the slave cylinder bolts (B, **Figure 59**) to 10 N•m (89 in.-lb.). Tighten the bleed valve (A, **Figure 59**) to 7.5 N•m (66 in.-lb.).

    d. Install the engine sprocket cover (Chapter Seven).

**Removal/Installation**

Refer to **Figure 57**.

1. Remove the fairing side panel from the left side as described in Chapter Fifteen.

2. Drain the fluid from the clutch system (this chapter).

3. Remove the banjo bolt (A, **Figure 58**), and disconnect the clutch hose from the slave cylinder. Be prepared to catch brake fluid that leaks from the hose.

e. Install the brake hose so its neck rests against the outboard side of the post. Use a new sealing washer on each side of the hose fitting and tighten banjo bolt (A, **Figure 58**) to 23 N•m (17 ft.-lb.).

f. Add brake fluid to the clutch reservoir and bleed the system (this chapter).

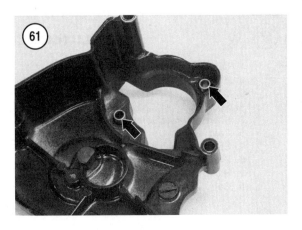

**Disassembly/Inspection/Assembly**

1. Manually pull the piston (**Figure 62**) from the slave cylinder bore. If necessary, used compressed air to remove the piston by performing the following:

a. Support the slave cylinder on wooden block with the piston facing down.

b. Pad the area beneath the piston with a shop cloth.

> *WARNING*
> *The piston may shoot out of the slave cylinder with considerable force. Make sure the piston faces down onto the bench. Keep your hands out of the way.*

c. Apply short bursts of low pressure compressed air to the banjo bolt fitting. Hold the air nozzle away from the fitting so excessive pressure is not applied.

2. Remove the spring (C, **Figure 63**) from the piston (A).

3. Clean all parts in brake fluid. Place the components on a clean lint-free cloth after cleaning them.

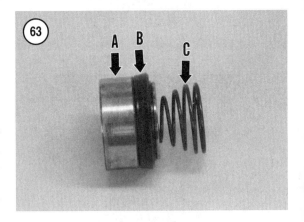

> *NOTE*
> *Do not remove the piston seal unless replacing it.*

4. Inspect the piston seal (B, **Figure 63**) for cuts or other damage. If necessary, install a new piston seal so the lip faces toward the spring side of the piston. Coat the new piston seal with brake fluid

5. Check the piston surface (A, **Figure 63**) for scoring or damage.

6. Check the cylinder bore surface (**Figure 64**) for scoring or damage.

7. Blow through the body with compressed air so all ports are clear. Replace the slave cylinder body if necessary.

8. Clean the banjo bolt with compressed air.

9. Insert the small end of the spring onto the piston as shown in **Figure 63**.

10. Apply brake fluid to the piston, seal and cylinder bore.

11. Install the spring/piston assembly into the cylinder bore (spring first), and push the piston all the way into the cylinder as shown in **Figure 62**.

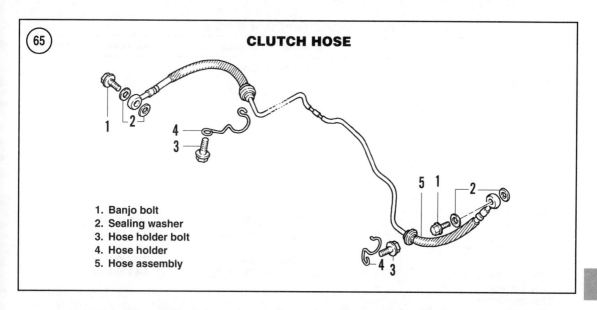

**CLUTCH HOSE**

1. Banjo bolt
2. Sealing washer
3. Hose holder bolt
4. Hose holder
5. Hose assembly

6

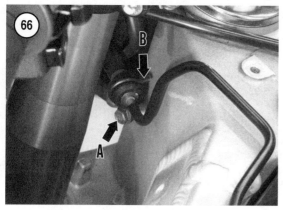

12. Install the slave cylinder onto the engine sprocket cover as described in this section.

## CLUTCH HOSE REPLACEMENT

The clutch hose assembly (**Figure 65**) consists of two hoses permanently bonded to a metal pipe.

1. Remove the left fairing side panel and the front fairing as described in Chapter Fifteen.

2. Remove the coolant reservoir (Chapter Ten).

3. Drain the fluid from the clutch system (this chapter).

4. Note how the clutch hose assembly is routed through and secured to the motorcycle. The new hose must be rerouted along the same path.

5. Remove the banjo bolt (A, **Figure 40**) from the hose fitting on the clutch master cylinder. Insert the hose end into a plastic bag and seal the bag with a rubber band. Discard the two sealing washers. New washers must be installed during installation.

6. Disconnect the hose fitting (A, **Figure 58**) from the clutch slave cylinder.

7. Remove the holder bolt (A, **Figure 66**) and lower the clutch hose holder (B) from the damper on each hose/pipe union.

8. Release the pipe from the holder (**Figure 67**) on the left side of the frame.

9. Remove the clutch hose assembly from the motorcycle.

10. Installation is the reverse of removal. Note the following:

   a. Route the new clutch hose assembly along the same path noted during removal. Secure the assembly to the frame with the holders noted during removal. Tighten each hose holder bolt securely.

   b. Install a new sealing washer onto each side of the clutch hose fittings. Tighten the banjo bolts to 23 N•m (17 ft.-lb.).

   c. Refill the clutch reservoir with brake fluid, and bleed the clutch (this chapter).

**Tables 1-2 are on the following page.**

### Table 1 CLUTCH SPECIFICATIONS

| Item | Standard mm (in.) | Service limit mm (in.) |
|---|---|---|
| Fluid type | DOT 4 brake fluid | |
| Friction discs | | |
|   Quantity | | |
|     1999-2001 models | | |
|       No. 1 disc | 8 | – |
|       No. 2 disc | 2 | – |
|     2002-on models | | |
|       No. 1 disc | 8 | – |
|       No. 2 disc | 1 | – |
|       No. 3 disc | 1 | |
|   Thickness | | |
|     1999-2001 models | | |
|       No. 1 disc | 2.92-3.08 (0.115-0.121) | 2.62 (0.103) |
|       No. 2 disc | 3.72-3.88 (0.146-0.153) | 3.42 (0.135) |
|     2002-on models | | |
|       No. 1 disc | 2.92-3.08 (0.115-0.121) | 2.62 (0.103) |
|       No. 2 and No. 3 discs | 3.72-3.88 (0.146-0.153) | 3.42 (0.135) |
|   Inside diameter | | |
|     2002-on models | | |
|       No. 1 disc | N.A. | – |
|       No. 2 disc | 127 (4.99) | – |
|       No. 3 disc | 135 (5.32) | – |
|   Claw width | | |
|     No. 1 disc | 13.85-13.96 (0.545-0.550) | 13.05 (0.514) |
|     No. 2 and No. 3 discs | 13.90-14.00 (0.547-0.551) | 13.10 (0.516) |
| Master cylinder bore | 14.000-14.043 (0.5512-0.5529) | – |
| Master cylinder piston outside diameter | 13.957-13.984 (0.5495-0.5506) | – |
| Plain plates | | |
|   Quantity | | |
|     No. 1 plate | 7 | – |
|     No. 2 plate | 2 | – |
|   Thickness | | |
|     No. 1 plate | 2.0 (0.08) | – |
|     No. 2 plate | 2.3 (0.09) | – |
|   Plate warp | – | 0.10 (0.004) |
| Slave cylinder bore | | |
|   1999-2001 models | 38.100-38.162 (1.5000-1.5024) | – |
|   2002-on models | 35.700-35.762 (1.4055-1.4080) | – |
| Slave cylinder piston outside diameter | | |
|   1999-2001 models | 38.042-38.075 (1.4977-1.4990) | – |
|   2002-on models | 35.650-35.675 (1.4035-1.4045) | – |
| Spring free length | | |
|   1999 models | 24.88 (0.980) | 23.7 (0.93) |
|   2000-2004 models | 28.96 (1.140) | 27.6 (1.09) |

### Table 2 CLUTCH TORQUE SPECIFICATIONS

| Item | N•m | in.-lb. | ft.-lb. |
|---|---|---|---|
| Banjo bolt | 23 | – | 17 |
| Bleed valve | 7.5 | 66 | – |
| Clutch nut | 95 | – | 70 |
| Clutch cover bolt | 10 | 89 | – |
| Clutch master cylinder clamp bolt | 10 | 89 | – |
| Clutch spring retainer bolt | 10 | 89 | – |
| Clutch spring support bolt | 23 | – | 17 |
| Slave cylinder bolt | 10 | 89 | – |

# CHAPTER SEVEN

# TRANSMISSION, SHIFT MECHANISM AND ENGINE SPROCKET

This chapter covers procedures for the transmission shaft, shift mechanism and engine sprocket. Refer to Chapter Five for transmission shaft removal. Refer to **Tables 1-3** at the end of this chapter for specifications.

## ENGINE SPROCKET COVER

### Removal/Installation

1. Securely support the motorcycle on a level surface.

2. Raise and support the fuel tank as described in Chapter Eight.

3. Remove the fairing side panel from the left side (Chapter Fifteen).

4. Remove the coolant reservoir (Chapter Ten).

5. On 1999 models, release the oil-catch-tank drain hose from its clamp.

6. Loosen the clamp bolt (A, **Figure 1**) on the shift lever, and slide the lever from the shaft. Note that the slot on the shift lever aligns with the indexing dot (B, **Figure 1**) on the shift shaft. If the indexing dot is not plainly visible, make a new one.

7. Follow the speed sensor cable (A, **Figure 2**) to its 3-pin connector. Disconnect the speed sensor connector (**Figure 3**).

8. Remove the engine sprocket cover bolts (B, **Figure 2**).

9. Lift the engine sprocket cover from the crankcase. Suspend the cover from the motorcycle. Do not excessively strain the clutch hose.

10. Remove the protector (**Figure 4**) from the cover bolt boss directly behind the shift shaft. The protector must be reinstalled on this boss during assembly.

11. Remove the left clutch pushrod (A, **Figure 5**) from the mainshaft so the rod is not damaged.

12. Installation is the reverse of removal. Note the following:

   a. Lubricate the left clutch pushrod (A, **Figure 5**) with Suzuki Super Grease A, and install the rod into the mainshaft.

   b. Set the protector (**Figure 4**) into place on the bolt boss noted during removal.

   c. Align the hole (**Figure 6**) in the clutch slave cylinder piston with the end of the left clutch pushrod, and set the engine sprocket cover onto the crankcase. Make sure the clutch pushrod sits in the hole in the piston.

d. Slide the shift lever onto the shift shaft. The slot in the lever must align with the indexing dot (B, **Figure 1**) on the shift shaft. Tighten the clamp bolt (A, **Figure 1**) securely.

e. If necessary, adjust the shift pedal height (Chapter Three).

## ENGINE SPROCKET

1. Securely support the motorcycle on a level surface with the rear wheel off the ground. Shift the transmission into gear.

2. Remove the engine sprocket cover (this chapter).

3. Remove the speed sensor rotor bolt (B, **Figure 5**) and remove the speed sensor rotor (C).

4. Remove the engine sprocket nut (A, **Figure 7**) and its washer.

5. On USA, California and Canada models, remove the cotter pin from the rear axle nut.

6. Loosen the rear axle nut (A, **Figure 8**), and loosen the brake torque arm nut (B).

7. Loosen the chain adjuster locknut (A, **Figure 9**), and then loosen the chain adjuster (B) on each side of the swing arm.

8. Slide the wheel far enough forward to slacken the chain.

9. Pull the engine sprocket (B, **Figure 7**) and drive chain off the countershaft. Remove the sprocket from between the chain runs.

10. Installation is the reverse of removal. Note the following:

a. Fit the engine sprocket between the chain runs, and then slide the sprocket onto the countershaft.

b. Install the sprocket washer onto the countershaft.

c. Apply Suzuki Thread Lock 1342, or its equivalent, to the threads of the countershaft. Install the engine sprocket nut (A, **Figure 7**) so the side with the raised lip faces out. Tighten the sprocket nut to 145 N•m (107 ft.-lb.).

d. Apply Suzuki Thread Lock 1342, or its equivalent, to the threads of the speed sensor rotor bolt. Tighten the bolt to 18 N•m (13 ft.-lb.).

e. Tighten the rear torque arm nut (B, **Figure 8**) to 35 N•m (26 ft.-lb.).

f. Adjust the chain as described in Chapter Three.

## Inspection

1. Inspect the teeth of the engine sprocket for any worn, chipped or missing teeth (**Figure 10**). Replace the engine sprocket if wear is noted.

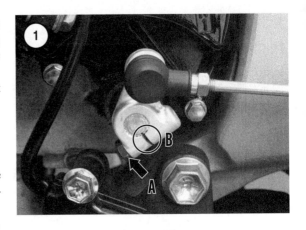

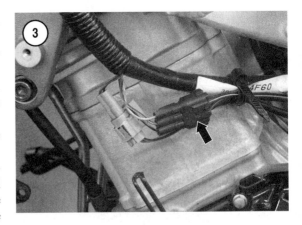

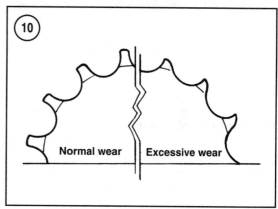

7

*CAUTION*
*If the engine sprocket is replaced, also replace the wheel sprocket and the drive chain. Never install a new drive chain over worn sprockets or a worn chain over new sprockets. The old parts prematurely wear out the new ones.*

2. If the engine sprocket requires replacement, also inspect the drive chain and the wheel sprocket (Chapter Eleven).

3. Inspect the splines of the engine sprocket for excessive wear. If wear is noted, also inspect the splines on the countershaft.

**SHIFT PEDAL**

**Removal/Installation**

1. Loosen the clamp bolt (A, **Figure 1**) on the shift lever.

2. Slide the shift lever from the shift shaft. Note that the slot in the lever aligns with the indexing dot (B, **Figure 1**) on the shift shaft.

3. Remove the snap ring (A, **Figure 11**) and its washer from the shift pedal pivot.

4. Slide the shift pedal off the pivot.

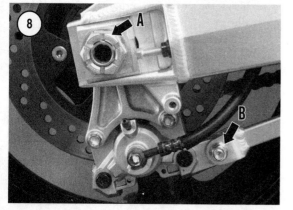

5. If necessary, loosen the shift rod locknut, and then remove the shift rod from the fitting (B, **Figure 11**) on the shift pedal.

6. Installation is the reverse of removal. Note the following:

   a. Apply Suzuki Super Grease A to the shift pedal pivot.

   b. Make sure the snap ring (A, **Figure 11**) is completely seated within the groove in the shift pedal pivot.

   c. Align the shift lever slot with the indexing dot (B, **Figure 1**) on the shift shaft. Tighten the clamp bolt (A, **Figure 1**) securely.

   d. Adjust the shift pedal height (Chapter Three).

### EXTERNAL SHIFT MECHANISM

#### Removal/Installation

Refer to **Figure 12**.

1. Remove the engine as described in Chapter Five.

2. If still installed, remove the engine sprocket cover (this chapter) and the water pump (Chapter Ten).

3. Remove the shift mechanism cover bolts (A, **Figure 13**), and pull the cover (B) from the crankcase. Watch for the dowels (A, **Figure 14**) behind the cover.

4. Remove the dowels (A, **Figure 14**) and the gasket (B). Discard the gasket.

5. Withdraw the shift shaft assembly from the crankcase. Note that the arms of the shift shaft spring straddle the stopper bolt (C, **Figure 14**).

6. Watch for the washer (A, **Figure 15**). It should come out with the shift shaft.

7. Installation is the reverse of removal. Note the following:

   a. Make sure the inboard washer (A, **Figure 15**) is in place on the shift shaft.

   b. Slide the shift shaft into the shift shaft bearing (A, **Figure 16**) in the left side of the lower crankcase.

   c. Make sure the shift shaft spring straddles the stopper bolt (C, **Figure 14**).

   d. Rotate the shift cam (D, **Figure 14**) as necessary so the shift pawls (D and E, **Figure 15**) engage the shift cam.

   e. If removed, install the outboard washer onto the shift shaft.

   f. Fit the dowels (A, **Figure 14**) and a new cover gasket (B) into place in the crankcase.

   g. Apply Suzuki Super Grease A to the lips of the oil seal (A, **Figure 17**) in the shift mechanism cover, and install the cover. Tighten the shift

mechanism cover bolts (A, **Figure 13**) to 10 N•m (89 ft.-lb.).

#### Inspection

1. Clean all parts in solvent, and dry them with compressed air.

2. Inspect the shift shaft spring (B, **Figure 15**) on the shift shaft assembly. If the spring is broken or weak, replace it by performing the following:

   a. Remove the inboard washer (A, **Figure 18**) and snap ring from the shift shaft, and slide the shift shaft spring (B) from the shaft.

   b. Install the new shift shaft spring so its arms straddle the tang (C, **Figure 15**) on the secondary plate (E, **Figure 18**).

   c. Seat a new snap ring into the groove on the shift shaft, and install the inboard washer (A, **Figure 15**).

3. Inspect the shift pawls (D, **Figure 15**) on the shift plate for excessive wear or damage. If necessary, replace the shift plate by performing the following:

   a. Remove the outboard washer (C, **Figure 18**), snap ring, washer, shift plate spring (F) and the shift plate (D) from the end of the shift shaft.

   b. Install the new shift plate so its hole engages the post of the secondary plate (E, **Figure 18**).

   c. Install the shift plate spring (F, **Figure 18**) and washer (C).

   d. Seat a new snap ring into the groove at the end of the shift shaft, and install the outboard washer (C, **Figure 18**).

4. Inspect the shift shaft for bending, wear or other damage.

5. Inspect the splines on the end of the shift shaft for damage.

6. Inspect the pawls (E, **Figure 15**) on the secondary plate.

7. Inspect the shift plate spring (F, **Figure 18**) for cracks or fatigue.

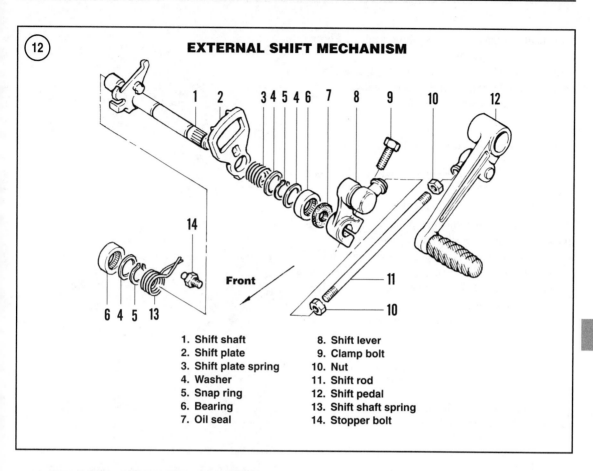

**EXTERNAL SHIFT MECHANISM**

1. Shift shaft
2. Shift plate
3. Shift plate spring
4. Washer
5. Snap ring
6. Bearing
7. Oil seal
8. Shift lever
9. Clamp bolt
10. Nut
11. Shift rod
12. Shift pedal
13. Shift shaft spring
14. Stopper bolt

7

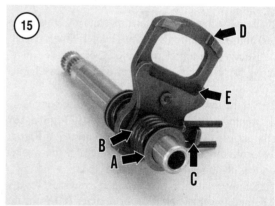

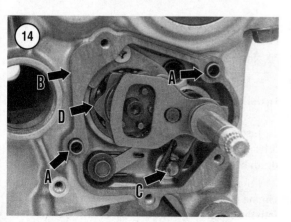

8. Visually inspect the shift shaft oil seal (A, **Figure 17**) for wear or signs of leaking.

9. Rotate the shift shaft bearing (B, **Figure 17**) by hand. It should rotate smoothly and quietly.

10. Replace any worn or damaged part.

**Shift Shaft Seal/Bearing Replacement**

1. Remove the shift mechanism cover as described in this section.

2. Pry the oil seal (A, **Figure 17**) from the cover.

3. Use a drift and hammer to tap the bearing (B, **Figure 17**) from the cover. Tap on the bearing outer race.

4. Lubricate the new bearing and cover with engine oil. Select a socket or bearing driver that matches the outside diameter of the bearing, and drive the new bearing into the cover (**Figure 19**).

5. Use the same driver to install a new oil seal. Make sure the manufacturer marks face out.

## INTERNAL SHIFT MECHANISM

The internal shift mechanism (**Figure 20**) includes the shift drum and the shift forks.

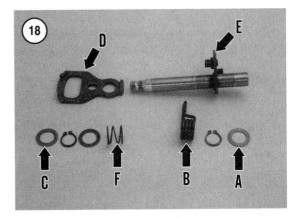

**Removal**

1. Remove the external shift mechanism (this chapter) and gear position switch (Chapter Nine).

2. Remove the engine, separate the crankcase and remove the transmission shafts as described in Chapter Five.

3. Set the lower crankcase upright on the bench.

4. Remove the stopper lever bolt (B, **Figure 16**), stopper lever (C) and stopper lever spring (A, **Figure 21**) from the lower crankcase. Watch for the washer on the inboard side of the stopper lever.

5. Remove the shift drum retainer screws (B, **Figure 21**), and lower the shift drum retainer (C) from the crankcase.

6. Note the position of the mainshaft and countershaft shift forks (A and B, **Figure 22**). Each shift fork must be reinstalled with the same orientation in its original location.

7. Partially remove the countershaft shift fork shaft (A, **Figure 22**) from the lower crankcase, and remove the right shift fork (B). Mark this fork *R*.

8. Pull the countershaft shift fork shaft from the crankcase, and remove the left shift fork (B, **Figure 22**). Mark this shift fork *L*.

9. Slide the mainshaft shift fork shaft (A, **Figure 23**) from the crankcase, and lift out the center shift fork (B). Mark this fork *C*.

10. Pull the shift drum (A, **Figure 24**) from the lower crankcase.

11. Inspect the components as described in this section.

**Installation**

1. Insert the shift drum (A, **Figure 24**) through the left side of the lower crankcase, and seat it in the shift drum bearing (B) in opposite side of the case.

2. Lubricate the mainshaft shift fork shaft with clean engine oil. Insert the shift fork shaft (A, **Figure 23**) into the crankcase, slide the center shift fork (B) onto

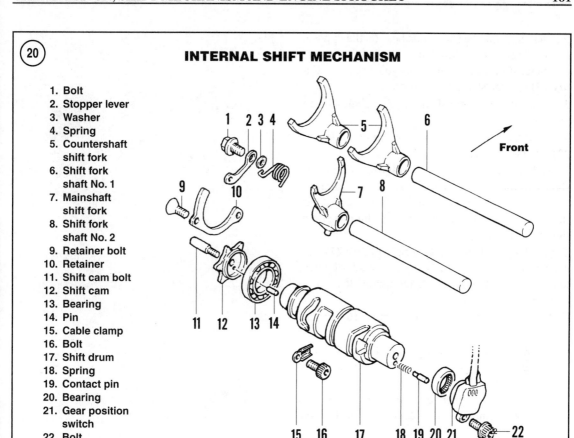

**INTERNAL SHIFT MECHANISM**

1. Bolt
2. Stopper lever
3. Washer
4. Spring
5. Countershaft shift fork
6. Shift fork shaft No. 1
7. Mainshaft shift fork
8. Shift fork shaft No. 2
9. Retainer bolt
10. Retainer
11. Shift cam bolt
12. Shift cam
13. Bearing
14. Pin
15. Cable clamp
16. Bolt
17. Shift drum
18. Spring
19. Contact pin
20. Bearing
21. Gear position switch
22. Bolt

Front

7

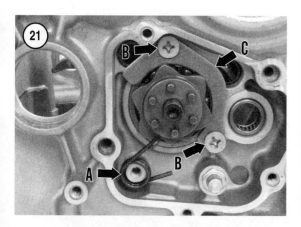

the shaft and seat the shaft in its boss on the opposite side of the crankcase. Install the shift fork in the position noted during removal. Fit its guide post (C, **Figure 23**) into the slot in the shift drum.

3. Lubricate the countershaft shift fork shaft with engine oil.

4. Insert the countershaft shift fork shaft (C, **Figure 22**) into the crankcase.

5. Slide the left shift fork (B, **Figure 22**) and the right shift fork (A) onto the countershaft, and seat the shaft in its boss. Position each shift fork as noted during removal, and seat each guide post into its slot in the shift drum.

6. Install the shift drum retainer (C, **Figure 21**). Apply Suzuki Thread Lock 1342 to the threads of the retainer screws (B, **Figure 21**), and tighten the screws to 8 N•m (71 in.-lb.).

7. Install the stopper lever (C, **Figure 16**) by performing the following:

   a. Fit the stopper lever spring (A, **Figure 21**) onto the mounting boss so its straight arm faces the crankcase.

   b. Install the stopper lever bolt (A, **Figure 25**) through the stopper lever, and install the washer (B) onto the bolt.

   c. Apply Suzuki Thread Lock 1342 to the threads of the stopper lever bolt.

   d. Position the stopper lever into the crankcase so the spring tang engages the cutout in the stopper lever, and loosely install the stopper lever bolt.

   e. Press down the stopper lever and rotate the shift drum as necessary so the lever's bearing (D, **Figure 16**) engages the neutral detent in the shift cam.

   f. Tighten the stopper lever bolt (B, **Figure 16**) to 10 N•m (89 in.-lb.).

8. Install the external shift mechanism (this chapter) and the gear position sensor (Chapter Nine).

### Inspection

During inspection, replace any part that is worn, damaged or out of specification.

1. Clean all parts in solvent, and thoroughly dry them with compressed air.

2. Inspect each shift fork for signs of wear or cracking. Check for any burned marks on the fingers of the shift forks (A, **Figure 26**).

3. Check the guide post (B, **Figure 26**) on each shift fork for wear or damage.

4. Check the bore (C, **Figure 26**) of each shift fork and the faces of the shift fork shafts for burrs, wear or pitting.

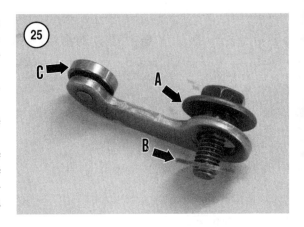

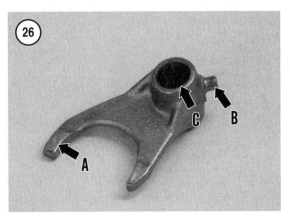

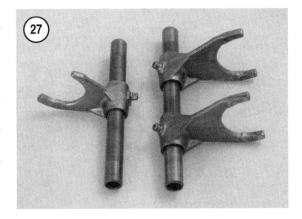

5. Install each shift fork onto its shaft (**Figure 27**). Make sure each fork slides freely on its shaft.

6. Roll each shift fork shaft on a flat surface such as a surface plate or a piece of plate glass. If a shaft is bent, it must be replaced.

7. Check the grooves in the shift drum (A, **Figure 28**) for wear or roughness. If any of the groove profiles have excessive wear or damage, replace the shift drum.

8. Rotate the shift drum bearing (B, **Figure 28**). Make sure it operates smoothly with no signs of wear or damage. Replace as necessary.

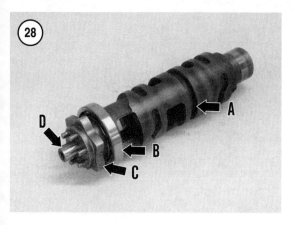

9. Inspect the ramps and posts on the shift cam (C, **Figure 28**). If wear is noted, replace the shift cam by performing the following:

    a. Remove the shift cam bolt (D, **Figure 28**), and remove the shift cam from the shift drum. Watch for the locating pin behind the shift cam.

    b. Insert the locating pin into the shift drum. Fit the shift cam into place so its hole engages the locating pin in the shift drum.

    c. Apply Suzuki Thread Lock 1342 to the threads of the shift cam bolt (D, **Figure 28**), and tighten the bolt to 10 N•m (89 in.-lb.).

*CAUTION*
*Worn forks can cause the transmission*
*to slip out of gear, leading to damage.*

10. Install each shift fork into the groove in its respective gear. Use a flat feeler gauge and measure the clearance between the fork and the groove as shown in **Figure 29**. If the shift fork-to-groove clearance exceeds the service limit in **Table 2**, perform the following:

    a. Measure the thickness of the shift fork fingers with vernier calipers. Replace the shift fork if the thickness is outside the range specified in **Table 2**.

    b. Use a vernier caliper to measure the width of the shift fork groove in the gear. Replace the gear if the groove width is outside the range specified in **Table 2**.

11. Inspect the bearing (C, **Figure 25**) on the stopper lever. It should turn smoothly with no binding.

12. Inspect the stopper lever spring (A, **Figure 21**).

## TRANSMISSION

During the following procedures, the term *mainshaft* refers to the transmission input shaft. The mainshaft is connected to the clutch hub, which is driven by the crankshaft primary drive gear and the primary driven gear on the clutch housing.

The term *countershaft* refers to the output shaft of the transmission. The countershaft drives the engine sprocket.

The manufacturer refers to the transmission input shaft as the countershaft and the output shaft as the driveshaft. Note that this differs from the terminology used in this manual. Note these differences when ordering parts.

### Removal/Installation

Remove and install the transmission mainshaft and countershaft assemblies as described in Chapter Five.

### Preliminary Inspection

Clean and inspect the transmission assemblies before disassembling them. Thoroughly clean each shaft assembly with a solvent and a stiff brush. Dry the assembly with compressed air or let it air dry. Repeat this for the other shaft assembly.

1. After the shaft assemblies have been cleaned, visually inspect the components for excessive wear. Any burrs, pitting or roughness on the teeth of a gear cause wear on its mated gear. Minor roughness can be removed with an oilstone. If gear replacement is required, replace mating gear pairs.

2. Carefully check the engagement dogs. If any dog is chipped, worn, rounded or missing, then the affected gear must be replaced.

3. Rotate the transmission bearings (**Figure 30**) by hand. Check for roughness, noise and radial play. Any suspect bearing should be replaced.

4. Slide the clutch pushrods into the mainshaft and check for binding. If binding occurs, check the pushrods for bending or damage. Also inspect the mainshaft tunnel for debris. Clean out the tunnel if necessary.

7

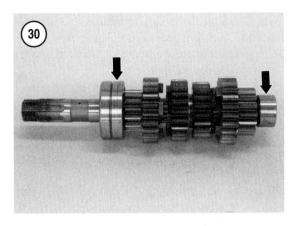

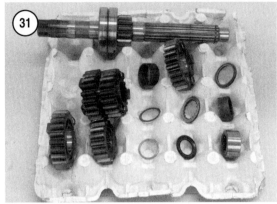

5. If the transmission shafts are satisfactory and are not disassembled, apply clean engine oil to all components, and reinstall them into the crankcase as described in Chapter Five.

## Transmission Service

1. As a part is removed from a shaft, set it into an egg crate (**Figure 31**) in the exact order of removal and with the same orientation the part had when installed on the shaft.

2. Note any additional shims not shown in the figures. These shims may have been installed during a previous repair. If the transmission is reassembled with the old parts, install all the parts in their original locations, including the additional shims. If new parts are installed in place of the original, discard the shims.

3. The snap rings fit tightly on the transmission shafts. All snap rings must be replaced during assembly.

4. Snap rings turn and fold over, making removal and installation difficult. To ease replacement, open a snap ring with a pair of snap ring pliers while at the same time holding the back of the snap ring with a pair of pliers.

5. When installing a snap ring, align the gap in the snap ring with a groove in the shaft as shown in **Figure 32**.

6. Snap rings have one flat edge and one rounded edge. Install a snap ring so the sharp edge faces away from the gear producing the thrust (**Figure 33**).

7. When installing a splined gear or splined bushing onto a shaft, align the oil hole in the gear or bushing with the oil holes in the shaft. Refer to **Figure 34**.

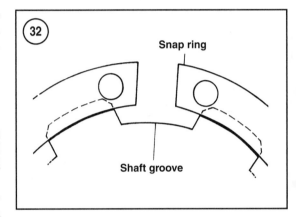

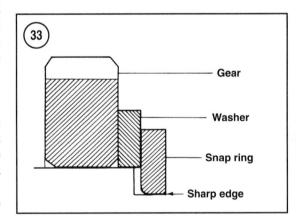

## Mainshaft Disassembly

Refer to **Figure 35** and **Figure 36**.

1. Slide the needle bearing and seal off the mainshaft.

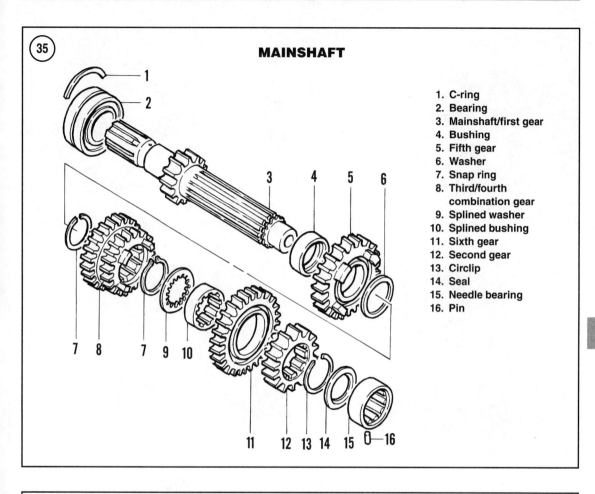

**MAINSHAFT**

1. C-ring
2. Bearing
3. Mainshaft/first gear
4. Bushing
5. Fifth gear
6. Washer
7. Snap ring
8. Third/fourth combination gear
9. Splined washer
10. Splined bushing
11. Sixth gear
12. Second gear
13. Circlip
14. Seal
15. Needle bearing
16. Pin

7

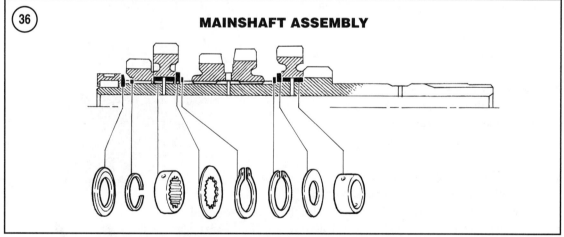

**MAINSHAFT ASSEMBLY**

*NOTE*
*The circlip (**Figure 37**) at the end of the mainshaft sits beneath second gear. The sixth gear snap ring must be removed from its groove so sixth and second gears can be moved to provide access to this circlip.*

2. Slide the third/fourth combination (A, **Figure 38**) toward first gear to expose the sixth gear snap ring

(B). Release the snap ring from its groove and move the snap ring down the shaft toward the third/fourth combination gear.

3. Slide the sixth (C, **Figure 38**) and second gears toward the third/fourth combination gear (A).

*NOTE*
*The circlip can be difficult to remove. Carefully pry the circlip from the mainshaft groove with a scribe.*

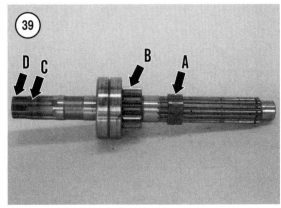

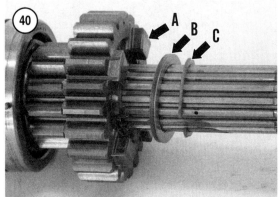

4. Use a scribe to pry one end of the circlip (**Figure 37**) from the outermost groove on the mainshaft. Grasp this end with needlenose pliers. Working around the shaft with the scribe, pry the circlip from the groove and remove it. Discard the circlip.

5. Slide second gear from the mainshaft.

6. Remove sixth gear and sixth gear bushing.

7. Remove the splined washer and the snap ring.

8. Slide the third/fourth combination gear from the mainshaft.

9. Remove the snap ring and washer.

10. Slide off fifth gear and the fifth gear bushing.

11. Keep the parts in the exact order of removal and with the same orientation they had while installed on the mainshaft as shown in **Figure 31**.

12. Inspect the mainshaft components as described in this section.

### Mainshaft Assembly

1. Apply a light coat of clean engine oil to all sliding surfaces before installing any part.

2. Slide the fifth gear bushing (A, **Figure 39**) onto the mainshaft and seat it against first gear.

3. Slide fifth gear (A, **Figure 40**) onto the mainshaft so its engagement dogs face out away from first gear. Seat the gear over its bushing, and install the washer (B, **Figure 40**).

4. Install a new snap ring (C, **Figure 40**) so its flat side faces out away from the washer. Make sure the snap ring (**Figure 41**) is properly seated in the mainshaft groove.

5. Position the third/fourth combination gear (**Figure 42**) so the larger fourth gear faces in toward fifth gear. Align the oil hole in the gear with a hole in the mainshaft, slide the combination gear onto the shaft and seat the gear up against fifth gear.

*NOTE*
*The snap ring installed in Step 6 must be positioned down on the shaft so the circlip can be installed in Step 10.*

6. Slide a new snap ring (A, **Figure 43**) onto the mainshaft, but do not seat the snap ring in its groove at this time. Instead, slide the snap ring toward the third/fourth combination gear. The flat side of this snap ring must face in toward third/fourth combination gear.

7. Install the splined washer (B, **Figure 43**) and the splined bushing (**Figure 44**). Align the oil hole in the bushing with a hole in the mainshaft.

8. Install sixth gear (**Figure 45**) so its engagement dogs face in toward the third/fourth combination gear. Seat the sixth gear onto the sixth gear bushing.

9. Install second gear so its shouldered side faces in toward sixth gear (**Figure 46**).

10. Install a *new* circlip, and seat it in the groove on the end of the mainshaft (**Figure 37**).

11. Push sixth (A, **Figure 47**) and second gears toward the end of the mainshaft.

12. Move the snap ring (B, **Figure 47**), installed in Step 6, into its correct groove next to sixth gear. Make sure the snap ring (B, **Figure 38**) is completely seated in the groove.

13. Press the oil seal onto the mainshaft so its concave side faces out (**Figure 48**), and push the seal up against the circlip.

14. Install the needle bearing (**Figure 49**).

15. Refer to **Figure 30** for correct placement of all gears. Make sure all snap rings and circlips are completely seated in their respective grooves.

16. After both transmission shafts have been assembled, mesh the two assemblies together in the correct position (**Figure 50**). Confirm that each gear properly engages its adjoining gear, where applicable. Check the shaft assemblies now before installing them into the crankcase.

### Countershaft Disassembly

Refer to **Figure 51** and **Figure 52**.

1. Slide the needle bearing and washer from the countershaft.

2. Remove first gear and the first gear bushing.

3. Remove the washer and fifth gear.

4. Remove the snap ring and the splined washer.

5. Pull fourth gear and the splined bushing from the countershaft.

6. Remove the splined washer, third gear, the splined bushing and another splined washer.

7. Remove the snap ring and sixth gear.

8. Remove the snap ring, washer, second gear and the second gear splined bushing.

9. Keep the parts in the exact order of removal and with the same orientation they had while installed on the countershaft.

10. Inspect the countershaft components as described in this section.

### Countershaft Assembly

1. Apply a light coat of clean engine oil to all sliding surfaces before installing any part.

2. Slide the second gear bushing (A, **Figure 53**) onto the countershaft, and seat it against the shoulder on the shaft.

3. Install second gear (B, **Figure 53**) so its engagement slots face out away from the bearing.

4. Slide the washer (A, **Figure 54**) onto the countershaft, and then install a new snap ring (B) with its flat side facing out away from the washer. Seat the snap ring (**Figure 55**) in the groove next to second gear.

5. Install sixth gear (**Figure 56**) so its shift fork groove faces away from second gear. Align the oil hole in the gear with an oil hole in the countershaft.

6. Install the new snap ring (A, **Figure 57**) so its flat side faces in toward sixth gear. Seat the snap

ring in the countershaft groove, and install a splined washer (B).

7. Install a splined bushing (**Figure 58**) onto the countershaft so the oil hole in the bushing aligns with an oil hole in the countershaft.

*NOTE*
*Third gear (29 teeth) and fourth gear (27 teeth) are similar. Do not confuse them during assembly.*

8. Install third gear (**Figure 59**) so its flat side faces out. Seat the gear on the splined bushing.

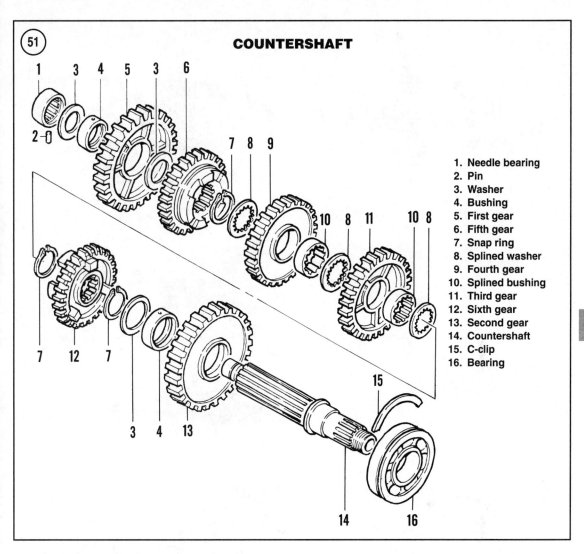

**COUNTERSHAFT**

1. Needle bearing
2. Pin
3. Washer
4. Bushing
5. First gear
6. Fifth gear
7. Snap ring
8. Splined washer
9. Fourth gear
10. Splined bushing
11. Third gear
12. Sixth gear
13. Second gear
14. Countershaft
15. C-clip
16. Bearing

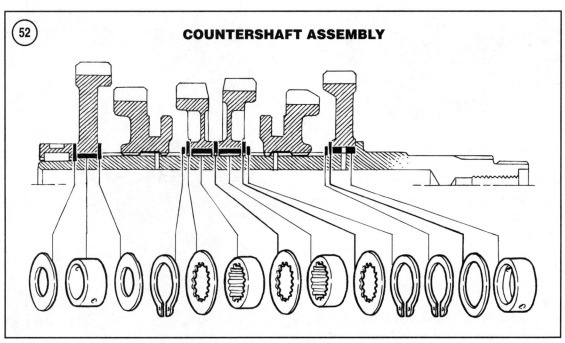

**COUNTERSHAFT ASSEMBLY**

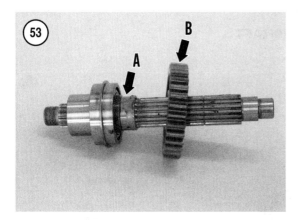

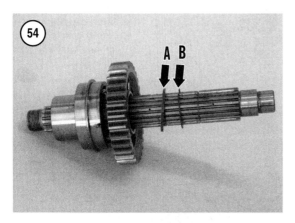

9. Install a splined washer (A, **Figure 60**) and splined bushing (B). The oil hole in the bushing must align with an oil hole in the countershaft.

10. Install fourth gear (**Figure 61**) so that it seats on the splined bushing with its engagement slots facing out away from third gear.

11. Install a splined washer (A, **Figure 62**) and new snap ring (B). Position the snap ring so its flat side faces out away from the washer, and seat the snap ring in its groove.

12. Install fifth gear (**Figure 63**) so the side with the shift fork groove faces in toward fourth gear. Align

7

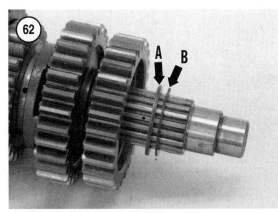

the oil hole in the gear with an oil hole in the countershaft.

13. Slide the washer (A, **Figure 64**) and first gear bushing (B) onto the shaft.

14. Install first gear (A, **Figure 65**) over the bushing so its engagement slots face in toward fifth gear, and install the washer (B).

15. Install the needle bearing (**Figure 66**).

16. Refer to **Figure 50** for correct placement of all gears. Make sure all snap rings are completely seated in their respective grooves.

17. After both transmission shafts have been assembled, mesh the two assemblies together in the correct position (**Figure 50**). Confirm that each gear properly engages its adjoining gear, where applicable. Make sure they are correctly assembled.

**Transmission Inspection**

Replace any part that is worn, damaged or out of specification. When replacing a defective gear, also replace its mate on the opposite shaft even through the mate may not show as much damage or wear. The old gear will rapidly wear down the new gear.

1. Check each gear for excessive wear, burrs or pitting and for chipped or missing teeth (A, **Figure 67**).
2. Inspect the engagement slots (B, **Figure 67**) and the engagement dogs (A, **Figure 68**) for wear or damage.
3. Check the inner splines (B, **Figure 68**) on sliding gears for excessive wear or damage. Replace the gear if necessary.
4. Inspect the bearing surfaces (C, **Figure 67**) on rotating gears for wear, pitting or damage.
5. Check each bushing (**Figure 69**) for excessive wear, pitting or damage. Replace the bushing if necessary.
6. Inspect the inner splines on splined washers (**Figure 70**) and splined bushings for excessive wear.
7. Inspect the washers for wear or damage. Replace if necessary.
8. Measure the shift fork-to-groove clearance as described in *Internal Shift Mechanism* in this chapter.

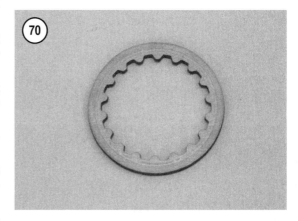

9. Inspect the snap ring grooves (A, **Figure 71**) and the shaft splines (B) on each shaft.
10. Inspect the teeth of first gear (B, **Figure 39**) on the mainshaft.
11. Inspect the clutch hub splines (C, **Figure 39**) and clutch nut threads (D) on the mainshaft. Also inspect the engine sprocket splines (C, **Figure 71**) and engine sprocket nut threads (D) on the countershaft. If

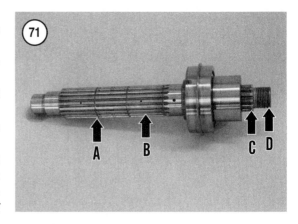

any spline is damaged, the shaft must be replaced. If the threads have burrs or other minor damage, clean them with a properly sized metric thread die. If the threads are excessively worn, replace the shaft.

12. Check all oil holes on the shafts, gears and bushings. Blow them clear with compressed air as necessary.
13. Make sure all gears and bushings slide smoothly along their respective shafts.

### Table 1 TRANSMISSION SPECIFICATIONS

| Item | Standard |
|------|----------|
| Transmission gear ratios | |
| 1st gear | 2.615 (34/13) |
| 2nd gear | 1.937 (31/16) |
| 3rd gear | 1.526 (29/19) |
| 4th gear | 1.285 (27/21) |
| 5th gear | 1.136 (25/22) |
| 6th gear | 1.043 (24/23) |
| Primary reduction ratio | 1.596 (83/52) |
| Secondary reduction ratio | 2.353 (40/17) |

### Table 2 SHIFT MECHANISM SPECIFICATIONS

| Item | Standard mm (in.) | Service limit mm (in.) |
|------|-------------------|------------------------|
| Shift fork-to-groove clearance | 0.10-0.30 (0.004-0.012) | 0.50 (0.020) |
| Shift fork groove width | 5.0-5.1 (0.197-0.201) | – |
| Shift fork finger thickness | 4.8-4.9 (0.189-0.193) | – |
| Shift pedal height | 50-60 (2.0-2.4) | – |

### Table 3 SHIFT MECHANISM TORQUE SPECIFICATIONS

| Item | N•m | in.-lb. | ft.-lb. |
|------|-----|---------|---------|
| Engine sprocket nut | 145 | – | 107 |
| Front footrest bracket bolt | 26 | – | 19 |
| Rear axle nut | 100 | – | 74 |
| Shift cam bolt | 10 | 89 | – |
| Shift drum retainer screw | 8 | 71 | – |
| Shift mechanism cover bolt | 10 | 89 | – |
| Speed sensor rotor bolt | 18 | – | 13 |
| Stopper bolt | 19 | – | 14 |
| Stopper lever bolt | 10 | 89 | – |
| Torque arm nut | | | |
| Front | 28 | – | 21 |
| Rear | 35 | – | 26 |

7

# CHAPTER EIGHT

# AIR, FUEL INJECTION, EMISSIONS AND EXHAUST SYSTEMS

This chapter covers the air and fuel systems, emissions systems and the exhaust system.

Refer to **Tables 1-3** at the end of the chapter for specifications.

## DEPRESSURIZING THE FUEL SYSTEM (1999-2000 MODELS)

*WARNING*
*Fuel drains from the system during this procedure. Do not allow smoking or any open flame in the vicinity of the motorcycle when depressurizing the fuel system.*

The fuel system on 1999 and 2000 models must be depressurized before any component is removed or disconnected. With 2001-on models, excess fuel pressure vents directly into the fuel tank so depressurization is not necessary.

1. Lift and support the fuel tank as described in this chapter.
2. Remove the cover from the fuel pump.
3. Place a rag beneath the fuel pressure check bolt (A, **Figure 1**).
4. Loosen the check bolt and bleed the pressure from the system.

5. Tighten the fuel pressure check bolt to 10 N•m (89 in.-lb.).

## FUEL TANK

### Raising the Tank

1. Securely support the motorcycle on a level surface.
2. Remove both seats as described in Chapter Fifteen.
3. Remove the tank prop from the storage compartment.
4. Remove each fuel tank mounting bolt (**Figure 2**) and its washer. Watch for the collar and damper installed on each front tank mount.
5. Raise the front of the fuel tank and support the tank with the prop rod.
6. Reverse the procedure to lower and install the fuel tank.

### Removal/Installation

The rear of the fuel tank bracket rests against the battery. Removing the battery eases fuel tank removal.

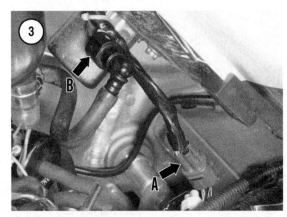

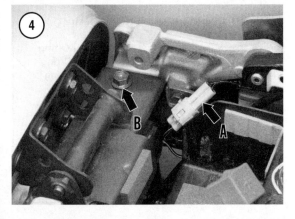

1. Remove the battery (Chapter Nine).
2. Raise and support the fuel tank (this section).

*WARNING*
*Be prepared to catch fuel leaking from a hose or its fitting when disconnecting fuel hoses.*

*NOTE*
*As a hose is removed, label the hose and its fitting. Hoses must be reconnected to their original fittings.*

3A. On 1999-2000 models, perform the following:
   a. Disconnect the 2-pin fuel level sender connector.
   b. Depressurize the fuel system as described in this chapter.
   c. Place a rag under the fuel valve on the tank. Disconnect the fuel hose from the fuel valve.
   d. Place a rag under the return port on the tank. Disconnect the return hose from the return port.
   e. Remove the plugs from the top of the rear fender and fit them onto the fuel valve and the return port on the tank.
   f. On 2000 models, note that the white or red marks on the fuel and return hoses face the left side. They must be reinstalled with this same orientation.
3B. On 2001-on models, perform the following:
   a. Disconnect the 4-pin fuel pump connector (A, **Figure 3**).
   b. Press the release tabs in the fuel hose connector (B, **Figure 3**), and disconnect the fuel hose from the output port on the fuel pump. Be prepared to catch residual fuel.
4. Disconnect the 2-pin tip-over sensor connector (A, **Figure 4**).
5. Remove the fuel tank bracket bolt (B, **Figure 4**) from each side.
6. Lift the fuel tank slightly and disconnect the fuel tank drain hose and breather hose from their fittings (**Figure 5**) on the fuel tank.
7. Installation is the reverse of removal. Tighten each bolt securely, and connect each hose to its original fitting.

## FUEL PUMP

The fuel pump operates whenever the ignition switch is turned on.

On 1999-2000 models, the pump mounts to the throttle body assembly, directly behind the No. 4 throttle body. If fuel pressure becomes excessive, a

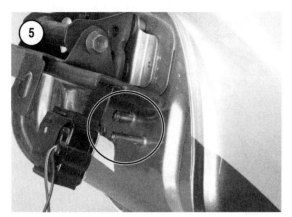

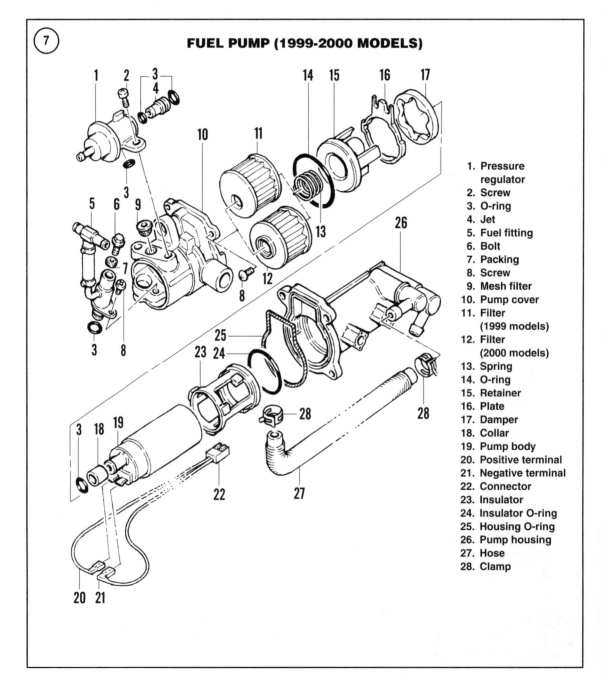

**FUEL PUMP (1999-2000 MODELS)**

1. Pressure regulator
2. Screw
3. O-ring
4. Jet
5. Fuel fitting
6. Bolt
7. Packing
8. Screw
9. Mesh filter
10. Pump cover
11. Filter (1999 models)
12. Filter (2000 models)
13. Spring
14. O-ring
15. Retainer
16. Plate
17. Damper
18. Collar
19. Pump body
20. Positive terminal
21. Negative terminal
22. Connector
23. Insulator
24. Insulator O-ring
25. Housing O-ring
26. Pump housing
27. Hose
28. Clamp

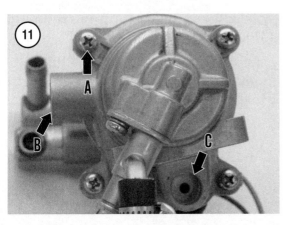

check valve in the pressure regulator opens so fuel flows through the return hose and back into the fuel tank.

On 2001-on models, the fuel pump is inside the fuel tank. If fuel pressure becomes excessive, the check valve in the pressure regulator releases excess fuel directly into the tank, which eliminates the need for a fuel return hose.

### Removal/Installation (1999-2000 Models)

The fuel pump can be removed with the throttle bodies or independently.

1. Raise and support the fuel tank. Depressurize the fuel system as described in this chapter.
2. Disconnect the fuel hose and the return hose from the fuel tank. Retrieve the plugs from the top of the rear fender, and plug the ports on the fuel tank.
3. Disconnect the 2-pin fuel pump connector (B, **Figure 1**).
4. Disconnect the vacuum hose from the top of the pressure regulator (A, **Figure 6**).
5. Disconnect the fuel line from the fitting on the fuel rail (B, **Figure 6**).
6. Remove the fuel pump bracket screws (C, **Figure 6**) from each bracket. Pull the fuel pump rearward, and remove it along with its bracket.
7. Installation is the reverse of removal. Tighten the fuel pump bracket screws (C, **Figure 6**) to 5 N•m (44 in.-lb.).

### Disassembly (1999-2000 Models)

The fuel pump O-rings must be replaced during assembly. Do not begin this procedure unless replacement O-rings are on hand. Some of these O-rings are easily damaged during pump disassembly. Assembling the pump with a damaged O-ring causes reduced fuel pressure.

Refer to **Figure 7**.

1. Remove the fuel pump (this chapter).
2. Remove the pump mounting screws (**Figure 8**) from each side, and remove each bracket from the fuel pump.
3. Remove the pressure regulator screws (A, **Figure 9**). Lift the pressure regulator (B, **Figure 9**) and its jet from the fuel filter cover.
4. Pull the jet (**Figure 10**) from the pressure regulator.
5. Remove the cover screws (A, **Figure 11**), and lift the fuel filter cover (B) from the pump housing. Watch for the O-ring (A, **Figure 12**) in the housing.
6. Carefully pull the retainer (A, **Figure 13**) from the filter cover.

**8**

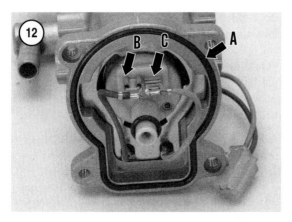

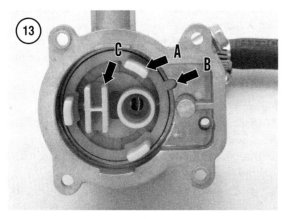

7. Remove the spring (A, **Figure 14**) and filter (B) from the cover. Watch for the filter's rubber washer (**Figure 15**). It may remain behind in the cover.

8. Disconnect the connectors (B and C, **Figure 12**) from the pump terminals. Note that one wire's connector faces inward; the other outward.

9. Pull the plate (**Figure 16**) from the pump housing.

10. Remove the damper (**Figure 17**) from the pump housing. Note the damper's concave side faces the pump.

11. Slide the fuel pump (A, **Figure 18**) from the pump housing. Note the pump's input port (B, **Figure 18**) faces the wires in the housing.

12. Remove the O-ring (A, **Figure 19**) and collar (B) from the pump's input port. Note that the collar's concave end faces the pump body.

13. Slide the insulator (C, **Figure 19**) from the pump body.

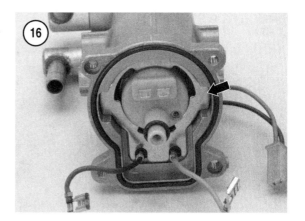

### Assembly (1999-2000 Models)

Lubricate each O-ring with engine oil before installation.

1. Install the collar (B, **Figure 19**) onto the pump's input port. Make sure the collar's concave end faces in toward the pump.

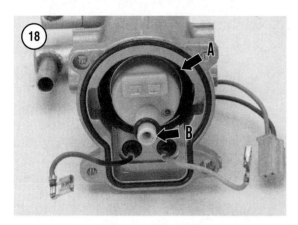

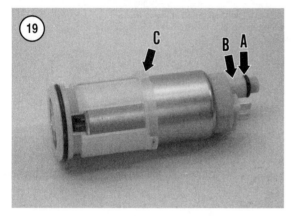

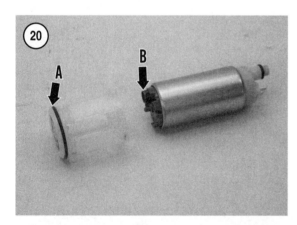

8

2. Lubricate a new O-ring (A, **Figure 19**) with clean engine oil, and install it on the input port.

3. Lubricate a new O-ring (A, **Figure 20**), and install it onto the insulator.

4. Install the insulator (C, **Figure 19**) onto the end of the pump so the pump's output port (B, **Figure 20**) mates with the port in the insulator.

5. Slide the pump into the housing so the pump's input port (B, **Figure 18**) faces the wires in the housing.

6. Install the damper (**Figure 17**) into the pump housing with its concave side facing the pump.

7. Install the plate (**Figure 16**) so its ears engage the slots in the pump housing.

8. Connect the wires (B and C, **Figure 12**) to the pump terminals so one connector faces inward while the other faces outward. Connect the gray wire (B, **Figure 12**) to the negative terminal, tan wire (C) to the positive terminal.

9. Lubricate a new O-ring (A, **Figure 12**) with engine oil, and install it into the pump housing.

10. Set the rubber washer (**Figure 15**) into the filter port, and install the filter (B, **Figure 14**) so its port side faces into the filter cover.

11. Install the spring (A, **Figure 14**) so it sits around the nub on the filter end.

12. Lubricate a new O-ring with clean engine oil, and install the O-ring (**Figure 21**) onto the retainer.

13. Set the retainer into the filter cover. Evenly press the retainer (A, **Figure 13**) into place so its tab (B) engages the cutout in the cover. Exercise caution so the retainer's O-ring is not torn or nicked.

14. Lower the filter cover into the pump housing. When properly installed, the *H-boss* on the retainer (C, **Figure 13**) straddles the two terminals (B and C, **Figure 12**) in the pump.

15. Install the fuel filter cover screws (A, **Figure 11**). Tighten them to 3 N•m (27 in.-lb.).

16. Install new O-rings into the pressure regulator and onto the regulator jet (**Figure 22**). Lubricate the O-rings with engine oil.

17. Press the narrow end of the jet into the pressure regulator until the jet bottoms (**Figure 10**).

18. Lower the pressure regulator (B, **Figure 9**) into place so the jet sits into the port on the filter cover (C, **Figure 11**).

19. Secure the regulator in place with the regulator screws (A, **Figure 9**).

20. Fit the pump brackets into place on each side of the pump, and install the pump mounting screws (**Figure 8**). Tighten the screws securely.

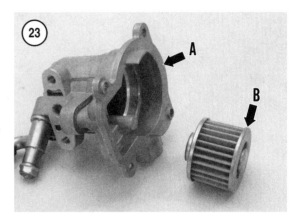

### Inspection (1999-2000 Models)

1. Remove and discard each O-ring. New O-rings must be installed during assembly.

2. Clean any sediment from the fuel filter cover (**Figure 23**) or pump housing (**Figure 24**).

3. Clean the mesh filter (**Figure 25**) in the cover. Blow it clear with compressed air if necessary.

4. Inspect the fuel filter (B, **Figure 23**) for tears or excessive dirt. Replace the filter as necessary.

5. Clean the mesh filter in the end of the insulator (C, **Figure 19**). Replace the insulator as necessary.

6. Clean the ports in the pump (**Figure 26**).

7. Inspect the damper (**Figure 27**) for nicks or tears. Replace the damper if it is brittle.

### Removal/Installation
### (2001-on Models)

1. Remove the fuel tank as described in this chapter. Drain the fuel into a suitable container.

2. Set the fuel tank on towels or a blanket on the workbench.

3. Evenly loosen the fuel pump bolts (**Figure 28**) in a crisscross pattern and remove the bolts.

4. Pull the fuel pump assembly from the tank. The fuel sender (A, **Figure 29**) sits on the pump. Watch for the fuel sender float (B, **Figure 29**) and float arm during removal.

5. Remove the fuel pump O-ring from the fuel tank. Discard the O-ring.

6. Installation is the reverse of removal. Note the following:

    a. Apply Suzuki Super Grease A to a new O-ring, and fit the O-ring into the channel in the tank.

    b. Apply Suzuki Thread Lock 1342, or its equivalent, to the threads of the fuel pump bolts (**Figure 28**) and install the bolts.

    c. Evenly tighten the bolts in a crisscross pattern. Tighten the fuel pump bolts to 10 N•m (89 in.-lb.).

7. Install the fuel tank (this chapter).

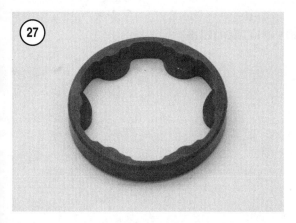

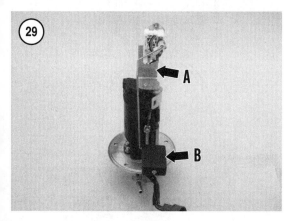

**Disassembly (2001-on Models)**

Refer to **Figure 30**.

1. Remove the fuel pump as described in this chapter.

2. Remove the nut and split washer from each terminal (A, B, and C, **Figure 31**), and disconnect the electrical leads from their respective terminals. Label each wire and its terminal so there is no confusion during assembly. Watch for the split washer at the bottom of each terminal.

3. Remove the screws (A, **Figure 32**), and lift the fuel level sender (B) from the cartridge assembly.

4. Remove the screws from the upper (A, **Figure 33**) and lower mounting arms on the pump base. Watch for the special nut installed on each arm. Note that the black fuel pump wire (negative wire) mounts to the upper mounting arm (B, **Figure 33**).

5. Slide the fuel pump/cartridge assembly (A, **Figure 34**) from the pump base (B).

6. Release the pump retainer (**Figure 35**) from the tabs on the pump, and remove the retainer.

7. Remove the damper (**Figure 36**), and pull the fuel filter (**Figure 37**) from the pump.

8. Release the safety clip (**Figure 38**) from the tab on the cartridge, and pull the clip from the pressure regulator.

9. Pull the pressure regulator (**Figure 39**) from the cartridge. Remove and discard the regulator O-ring (A, **Figure 40**).

10. Slide the fuel pump (A, **Figure 41**) from the cartridge (B). Note that the fuel pump wires (C, **Figure 41**) cross behind the pump. The wires must be rerouted in the same fashion during assembly.

11. Slide the grommet from the cartridge port or remove the grommet from the fitting on the fuel pump.

12. Discard the O-ring (A, **Figure 42**) from the fitting on the pump base.

**Assembly (2001-on Models)**

1. Slide the grommet into the port in the cartridge.

2. Slide the fuel pump (A, **Figure 41**) into the cartridge (B) so the pump's fitting engages grommet in the cartridge port. Make sure the pump wires (C, **Figure 41**) cross behind the pump.

3. Lubricate a new O-ring (A, **Figure 40**) with engine oil, and install it onto the pressure regulator (B).

4. Seat the pressure regulator (**Figure 39**) in the regulator port on the cartridge.

5. Install the safety clip (**Figure 38**) so it locks onto the cartridge tab.

6. Install the fuel filter (**Figure 37**) so it engages the indexing post in the pump.

7. Seat the damper (**Figure 36**) onto the pump.

8. Install the retainer (**Figure 35**) so it locks onto the pump tabs.

9. Lubricate a new O-ring (A, **Figure 42**) with engine oil, and install it onto the fitting on the pump base.

10. Lower the pump/cartridge assembly (A, **Figure 34**) onto the pump base so the cartridge port engages the base fitting (A, **Figure 42**).

11. Install the special nut onto each mounting arm, and install the screw. Secure the black, fuel pump negative wire (B, **Figure 33**) behind the screw on the upper mounting arm (A).

8

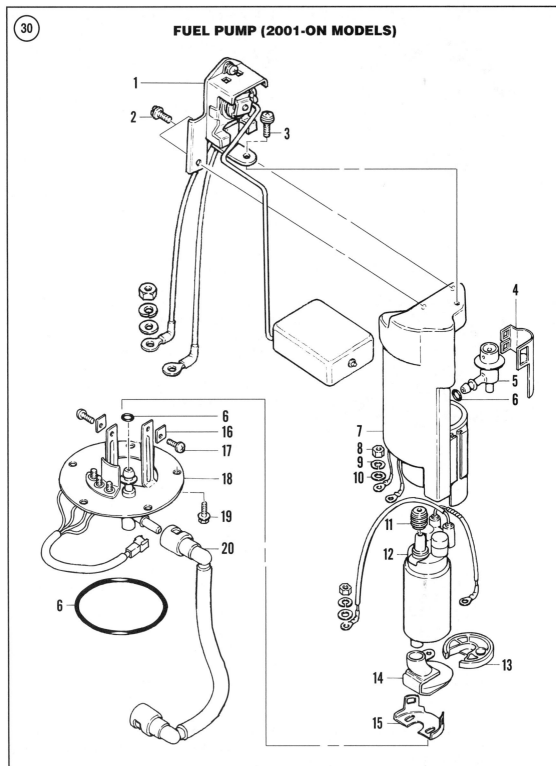

**FUEL PUMP (2001-ON MODELS)**

1. Fuel level sender
2. Screw
3. Screw
4. Safety clip
5. Pressure
   regulator
6. O-ring
7. Fuel pump case/
   cartridge assembly
8. Nut
9. Lockwasher
10. Washer
11. Bushing
12. Fuel pump
13. Fuel pump
    damper
14. Mesh filter
15. Fuel pump holder
16. Special nut
17. Screw
18. Fuel pump base
19. Bolt
20. Fuel line

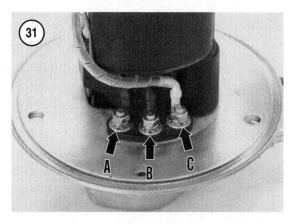

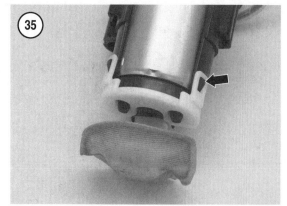

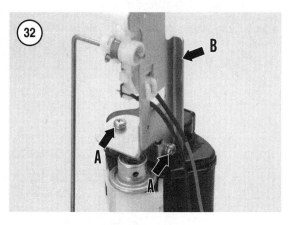

8

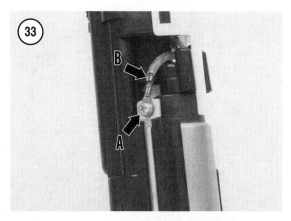

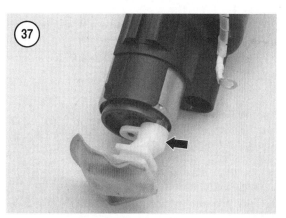

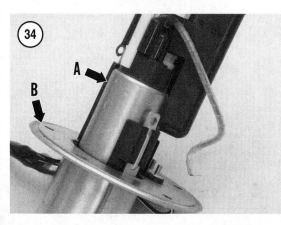

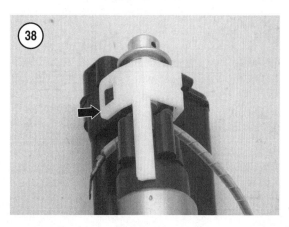

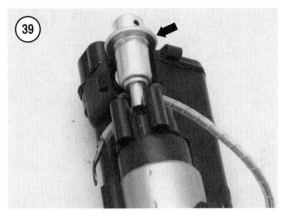

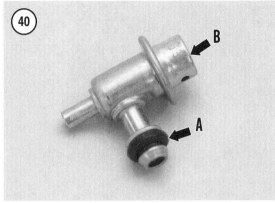

12. Install the black wire (negative wire for the fuel level sender) onto the left terminal (A, **Figure 31**) in the fuel pump base. Set a star washer onto the terminal, followed by the wire connector, split washer and nut. Tighten the nut securely.

13. Repeat Step 12 and connect the red wire (positive wire for the fuel level sender) to the middle terminal (B, **Figure 31**) and the blue wire (positive wire for the fuel pump) to the right terminal (C).

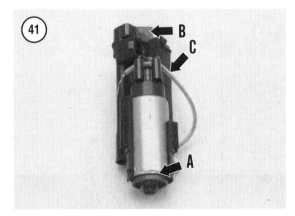

### Inspection (2001-on Models)

1. Clean any sediment from the fuel pump base (B, **Figure 42**).

2. Clean the mesh filter (**Figure 43**). Replace the mesh filter if it remains clogged.

3. Clear the ports in the pump and cartridge assembly.

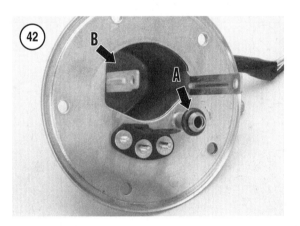

### Fuel Pressure Test

#### Tools

The following Suzuki tools, or their equivalents, are required to perform this test:

1. Fuel pressure gauge adapter: part No. 09949-40210 (1999-2000 models).

2. Fuel pressure gauge adapter: part No. 09940-40211 (2001-on models).

3. Fuel pressure gauge hose attachment: part No. 09940-40220 (2001-on models).

4. Oil pressure gauge: part No. 09915-77330 (all models).

5. Oil pressure gauge hose: part No. 09915-74520 (all models).

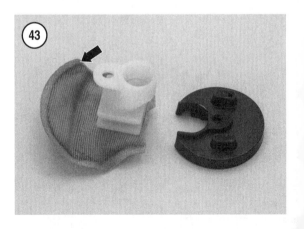

#### 1999-2000 models

1. Raise and support the fuel tank. Depressurize the fuel system as described in this chapter.

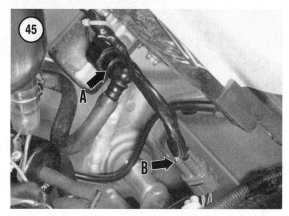

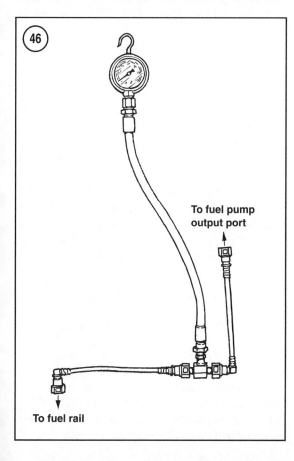

**To fuel pump output port**

**To fuel rail**

2. Remove the fuel pressure check bolt (A, **Figure 44**) from the port on the fuel pump.

3. Connect a fuel pressure gauge to the fuel pump port.

4. Turn on the ignition switch, and check the reading on the gauge. Fuel pressure should equal the fuel pump output pressure specified in **Table 1**.

    a. If fuel pressure is less than specified, check for a leak in the fuel system, a clogged fuel filter, faulty pressure regulator or faulty fuel pump.

    b. If fuel pressure exceeds specification, check the fuel pump check valve or the pressure regulator.

### *2001-on models*

1. Raise and support the fuel tank as described in this chapter.

2. Disconnect the fuel hose (A, **Figure 45**) from the output port on the fuel pump. Be prepared to catch residual gasoline.

3. Use the adapter to install the gauge inline between the fuel pump and the fuel rail. Follow the manufacturer's instructions. Refer to **Figure 46**.

4. Turn the ignition switch on, and read the fuel pressure. It should equal the fuel pump output pressure specified in **Table 1**.

    a. If fuel pressure is less than specified, check for a leak in the fuel system, a clogged fuel filter, faulty pressure regulator or faulty fuel pump.

    b. If fuel pressure exceeds specification, check the fuel pump check valve or the pressure regulator.

5. Disassemble the fuel pump and visually inspect the components. Replace any part as needed. The check valve is an integral part of the fuel pump and cannot be replaced separately.

### Fuel Pump Operation Test (All Models)

1. Turn the ignition switch on and listen for the operation of the fuel pump.

2. If no sound is heard, test the fuel pump relay and the tip over sensor as described in this chapter. If both of these components are within specification, replace the fuel pump.

### Fuel Pump Discharge Test (1999-2000 Models)

1. Siphon fuel from the fuel tank until the fuel indicator light turns on.

2. Raise and support the fuel tank (this chapter).

3. Disconnect the fuel pump connector (B, **Figure 44**).

**8**

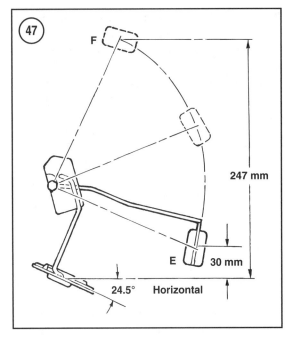

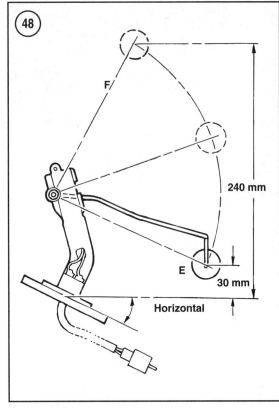

4. Disconnect the return hose from the fitting on the fuel tank. Be prepared to catch residual gasoline.

5. Remove the plug from the top of the rear fender, and install the plug onto the fuel tank return port.

6. Connect a secondary hose to the end of the fuel return hose. Feed the opposite end of the secondary hose into a graduated cylinder. Route this hose from the rear of the tank so it is not pinched when the tank is lowered.

7. Remove the prop rod and lower the fuel tank.

8. Apply battery voltage directly to the fuel pump for 30 seconds by performing the following:

    a. Use a jumper to connect the battery positive terminal to the brown/black wire in the pump side of the fuel pump connector (B, **Figure 44**). Connect the negative battery terminal to the black/white terminal in the pump side of the connector.

    b. Keep the jumpers connected to the terminals for 30 seconds, and then disconnect them from the connector and from the battery terminal.

9. Measure the amount of fuel in the graduated cylinder. It should equal the fuel pump output volume specified in **Table 1**. The fuel pump is faulty if the volume is significantly less than specified.

### Fuel Pump Discharge Test (2001-on Models)

1. Raise and support the fuel tank (this chapter).

2. Disconnect the 4-pin fuel pump connector (B, **Figure 45**).

3. Disconnect the fuel hose (A, **Figure 45**) from the output port on the fuel pump. Be prepared to catch residual gasoline.

4. Connect a secondary hose to the fuel pump output port, and feed the opposite end of this hose into the graduated cylinder.

5. Apply battery voltage directly to the fuel pump for 30 seconds by performing the following:

    a. Use a jumper to connect the battery positive terminal to the yellow/red wire in the pump side of the fuel pump connector. Connect the negative battery terminal to the black/white terminal in the pump side of the connector.

    b. Keep the jumpers connected to the terminals for 30 seconds, and then disconnect them from the connector and from the battery terminal.

6. Measure the amount of fuel in the graduated cylinder. It should equal the fuel pump output volume specified in **Table 1**. The fuel pump is faulty if the volume is significantly less than specified.

### FUEL LEVEL SENDER

#### Removal/Installation (1999-2000 Models)

1. Remove the fuel tank as described in this chapter. Drain the fuel into a suitable container.

2A. On 1999 models, remove the fuel level sender bolts, and pull the fuel sender from the fuel tank.

2B. On 2000 models, remove the fuel level sender nuts, and pull the sender from the fuel tank.

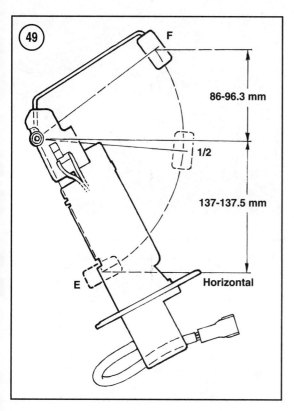

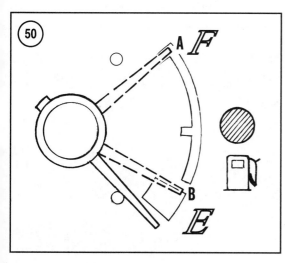

2. Remove the terminal nuts (A and B, **Figure 31**) and disconnect each fuel level sender lead from its terminal on the fuel pump base. Mark the terminals and leads.

3. Remove the fuel level sender screws (A, **Figure 32**), and lift the fuel level sender (B) from the cartridge assembly.

4. Installation is the reverse of removal. Note the following:

    a. Install the black, negative wire onto the left terminal (A, **Figure 31**) in the fuel pump base. Set a star washer onto the terminal, followed by the wire connector, split washer and nut. Tighten the nut securely.

    b. Repeat substep a, and connect the red positive wire to the middle terminal (B, **Figure 31**).

**Fuel Level Sender Resistance Test**

1A. On 1999 and 2000 models, perform the following:

    a. Remove the fuel level sender (this chapter).

    b. Connect the test probes of an ohmmeter to the terminals in the sender side of the 2-pin fuel level sender connector.

1B. On 2001-on models, perform the following:

    a. Remove the fuel pump (this chapter).

    b. Connect test probes of an ohmmeter to the black/light green and red/black terminals in the pump side of the 4-pin fuel pump connector (B, **Figure 45**).

2. Position the fuel sender or fuel pump as shown in **Figure 47** (1999 models), **Figure 48** (2000 models) or **Figure 49** (2001-on models).

3. Move the float to the full and empty positions and note the resistance. On 2001-on models, also measure the resistance when the float is in the half-full position.

4. Replace the fuel sender if any reading is outside the range specified in **Table 2**.

**Fuel Gauge Test (1999-2000 Models)**

1. Remove the fuel level sender as described in this section.

2. Connect the 2-pin fuel level sender connector to it harness mate.

3. Position the fuel level sender as shown in **Figure 47** (1999 models) or **Figure 48** (2000 models).

4. Turn the ignition switch on.

5. Move the float to the full position, and watch the fuel gauge. The needle should move to the position shown in A, **Figure 50** and the LED should be off.

3. Installation is the reverse of removal. Note the following:

    a. Evenly tighten the bolts or nuts in a crisscross pattern.

    b. On 1999 models, tighten the fuel level sender bolts to 4 N•m (35 in.-lb.).

    c. On 2000 models, tighten the fuel level sender nuts to 6 N•m (53 in.-lb.).

**Removal/Installation (2001-on Models)**

1. Remove the fuel pump (this chapter).

8

6. Move the float to the empty position, and watch the fuel gauge. The needle should move to the position shown in B, **Figure 50** and the LED should turn on.

## FUEL PUMP RELAY

### Removal/Installation

1. Disconnect the negative battery cable.
2. Remove the passenger seats and tail piece as described in Chapter Fifteen.
3. Disconnect the 4-pin connector (**Figure 51**) from the relay, and remove the fuel pump relay.
4. Installation is the reverse of removal.

### Test

1. Remove the relay from the motorcycle as described in this section.
2. Check the continuity between the A and B terminals on the relay (**Figure 52**). The relay should not have continuity.
3. Use jumpers to connect the positive terminal of a 12-volt battery to the C terminal on the relay (**Figure 52**). Connect the negative battery terminal to the D relay terminal.
4. Check the continuity between the relay's A and B terminals. The relay should have continuity while voltage is applied.
5. Replace the relay if it fails either portion of this test.

## FUEL PRESSURE REGULATOR

The fuel pressure regulator is part of the fuel pump assembly. Refer to *Fuel Pump* (this chapter) when servicing the pressure regulator.

## AIR FILTER HOUSING

### Removal/Installation

1. Raise and support the fuel tank as described in this chapter.
2. On the left side of the housing, disconnect the 2-pin connector (A, **Figure 53**) from the intake air temperature (IAT) sensor.
3. On the rear of the housing, disconnect the 3-pin connector (A, **Figure 54**) and the vacuum hose (B) from the intake air pressure (IAP) sensor.
4. Disconnect the PAIR hose (C, **Figure 54**) from the port on the air filter housing.
5A. On 1999 models, disconnect the oil-catch-tank breather hose from the air filter housing.

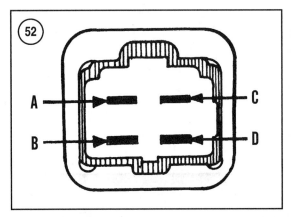

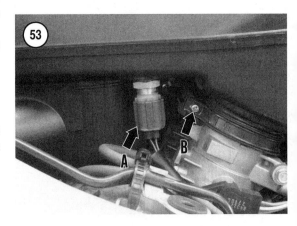

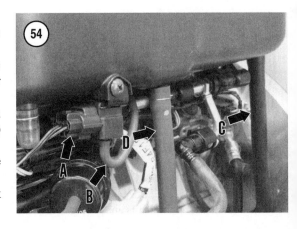

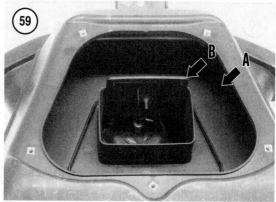

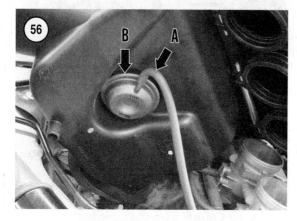

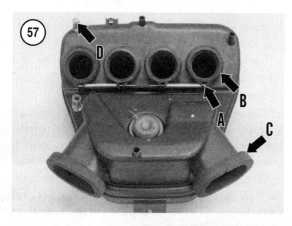

5B. On 2000-on models, disconnect the crankcase breather hose (D, **Figure 54**) from the air filter housing.

*NOTE*
*A single clamp screw (B, **Figure 53**) loosens the two outside throttle body clamps on each side of the motorcycle.*

6. Loosen the throttle body clamp screw (B, **Figure 53**) on each side of the motorcycle.
7. Remove the air filter housing bolt (A, **Figure 55**).
8. Disengage each air filter housing port from its respective throttle body, and rotate the air filter housing to expose its bottom.
9. Disconnect the vacuum hose (A, **Figure 56**) from the intake air control valve actuator (B) on the bottom of the housing, and remove the air filter housing.
10. Cover each throttle body inlet to keep debris out of the throttle bodies.
11. Inspect the air filter housing as described in this section.
12. Install the air filter housing by reversing the removal steps. Note the following:
   a. If removed, install each pair of throttle body clamps (A, **Figure 57**) onto the housing output ports so the clamp screw faces the outboard side.
   b. Make sure each output port (B, **Figure 57**) securely engages its throttle body intake.
   c. The foam seal (**Figure 58**) on each intake duct must seal against the frame duct.

**Inspection**

1. Remove the air filter screws (B, **Figure 55**) and lift the air filter from the housing.
2. Inspect the air filter element as described in Chapter Three.
3. Wipe out the interior of the housing (A, **Figure 59**).
4. Inspect the air filter housing and the intake ducts for cracks, wear or damage. If any damage is noted,

8

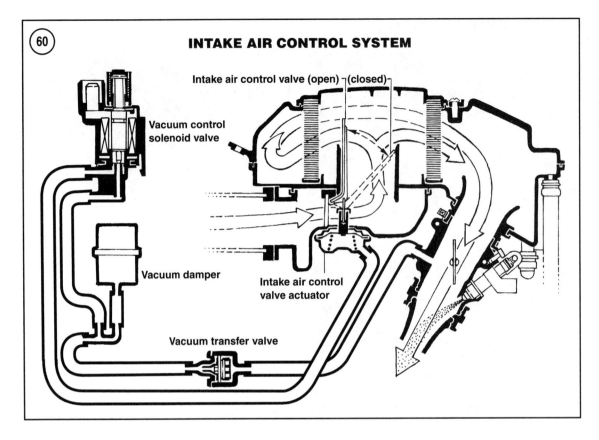

## INTAKE AIR CONTROL SYSTEM

(60)

Intake air control valve (open) ⌐(closed)⌐

Vacuum control
solenoid valve

Vacuum damper

Intake air control
valve actuator

Vacuum transfer valve

replace the housing to keep unfiltered air out of the engine.

5. Inspect the foam seal (C, **Figure 57**) on each housing intake duct. Replace the seals if they are worn, broken or starting to deteriorate.

6. Inspect the housing output fittings (B, **Figure 57**) for hardness, deterioration or damage. Replace them as necessary.

7. Remove the drain plug (D, **Figure 57**) and clean out all residue from the plug and air box. Reinstall the drain plug.

## INTAKE AIR CONTROL SYSTEM

The intake air control system (**Figure 60**) adjusts the intake air flow at various throttle settings. When the engine operates at low to medium speeds, a signal from the ECM opens the vacuum control solenoid valve. Vacuum from the throttle bodies flows through the solenoid valve and is applied to the intake air control valve actuator (B, **Figure 56**). This vacuum acts on the diaphragm in the actuator, and closes the intake air control valve.

During medium- to high-speed operation, the ECM closes the solenoid valve. This interrupts the vacuum being applied to the intake control valve actuator so the spring in the actuator opens the intake air control valve (B, **Figure 59**) for maximum air flow.

### Intake Air Control System Inspection

1. Raise and support the fuel tank as described in this chapter.

2. Remove the air filter screws (B **Figure 55**), and lift the air filter from the housing.

3. Start the engine.

4. Gradually open the throttle and watch the intake air control valve (B, **Figure 59**). Note the engine speed when the control valve begins to open. It should open when engine speed exceeds 2500 rpm.

5. Once the valve is open, gradually close the throttle. Note the engine speed when the intake air control valve begins to close. It should close when speed drops below 2200 rpm.

6. If the valve does not operate as indicated, check the vacuum hoses for damage or clogs. Also inspect the vacuum control solenoid valve, vacuum transfer valve, intake air control valve actuator and vacuum damper as described in this section.

### Vacuum Control Solenoid Valve
### (VCSV) Inspection

1. Support the fuel tank as described in this chapter.

2. Disconnect the 2-pin connector (A, **Figure 61**) from the VCSV (B).

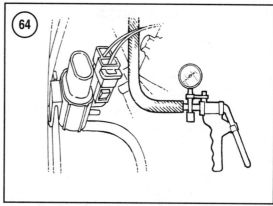

3. Replace the vacuum damper as necessary.

## Vacuum Transfer Valve (VTV) Inspection

1. Support the fuel tank as described in this chapter.
2. Disconnect each hose from the VTV (**Figure 62**) and remove the valve. Note that the orange side of the valve faces the rear of the motorcycle. The valve must be reinstalled with this same orientation.
3. Blow into the orange side of the VTV (**Figure 63**). Air should flow out the opposite side.
4. Blow into the non-orange side of the VTV. Air should not flow out the orange side.
5. Replace the VTV if it fails either portion of this test.

## Intake Air Control Valve Actuator Inspection

A hand-operated vacuum pump with a gauge is needed to perform this test.
1. Remove the air filter screws (B, **Figure 55**) and lift the air filter from the housing.
2. Disconnect the vacuum hose from the upper fitting on the vacuum control solenoid valve (B, **Figure 61**).
3. Connect the vacuum pump to the disconnected vacuum hose (**Figure 64**).

*CAUTION*
*Do not apply more than 24 kPa (180 mm Hg) of vacuum. The diaphragm in the actuator could be damaged.*

4. Operate the vacuum pump and gradually apply vacuum to the actuator. The intake air control valve (B, **Figure 59**) should close when vacuum is applied to the actuator.
5. Replace the intake air control valve actuator (B, **Figure 56**) if the intake air control valve does not close.

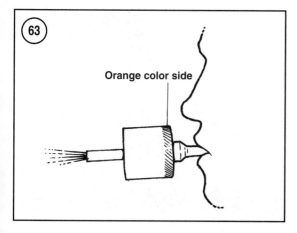

Orange color side

3. Connect the probes of an ohmmeter to the two terminals in the VCSV (B, **Figure 61**). The resistance should be within the range specified in **Table 2**.
4. If the resistance is out of specification, replace the VSCV.

## Vacuum Damper Inspection

1. Support the fuel tank as described in this chapter.
2. Visually inspect the vacuum damper (C, **Figure 61**) for damage or dents.

## HEAT SHIELD

### Removal/Installation

1. Raise and support the fuel tank as described in this chapter. Remove the air filter housing.

2. Disconnect the 2-pin connector from the camshaft position sensor (A, **Figure 65**), and disconnect the 2-pin connector from each ignition coil/spark plug cap (B).

3. Blow away all loose dirt, and then wipe off the top surface of the heat shield. Remove all loose debris that could fall into the cylinder head spark plug tunnels.

4. Remove each ignition coil/plug cap (**Figure 66**) as described in Chapter Nine. Label each coil/plug cap so it can be reinstalled into the correct cylinder.

5. Note how the shield is seated and where various wires and clamps pass through it. Remove the heat shield from the cylinder head cover (**Figure 67**).

6. Installation is the reverse of removal. Make sure the edges of the head shield sit below each intake port (C, **Figure 65**) in the frame.

## THROTTLE BODIES

Refer to **Figure 68** for 1999 and 2000 models and to **Figure 69** for 2001-on models.

### Removal/Installation

1. Remove the fuel tank and air filter housing as described in this chapter.

2. Loosen the locknuts (A, **Figure 70**) on the throttle pull cable, and disconnect the cable end (B) from the throttle wheel.

3. Disconnect the throttle return cable end (C, **Figure 70**) from the throttle wheel, and the fast idle cable (D) from the fast idle cam. Repeat Step 2 for each cable.

4. On 1999 and 2000 models, perform the following:
   a. Depressurize the fuel system (this chapter).
   b. Release the throttle stop screw (**Figure 71**) from its holder.

5. Disconnect the PAIR hose (**Figure 72**) from its fitting on the No. 4 throttle body.

6. Disconnect the hose (**Figure 73**) from its fitting on the No. 1 throttle body.

7. Disconnect the throttle body subharness connector (A, **Figure 74**).

8. On California models, disconnect the EVAP purge hose from the throttle body fitting.

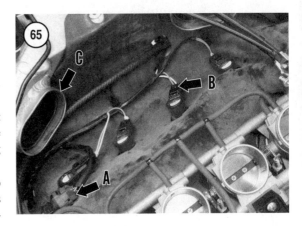

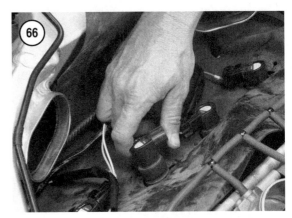

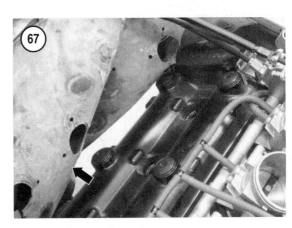

*NOTE*
*A single clamp screw loosens the two outside intake manifold clamps on each side of the motorcycle.*

9. Insert a long screwdriver through the hole in one side of the frame (**Figure 75**), and loosen the intake manifold clamp screw on that side. Repeat this on the other side of the motorcycle.

10. Lift the throttle body assembly, disengage each throttle body from its intake manifold and remove the assembly. On 1999 and 2000 models, the fuel pump comes out with the throttle bodies.

(68) **THROTTLE BODY ASSEMBLY (1999-2000 MODELS)**

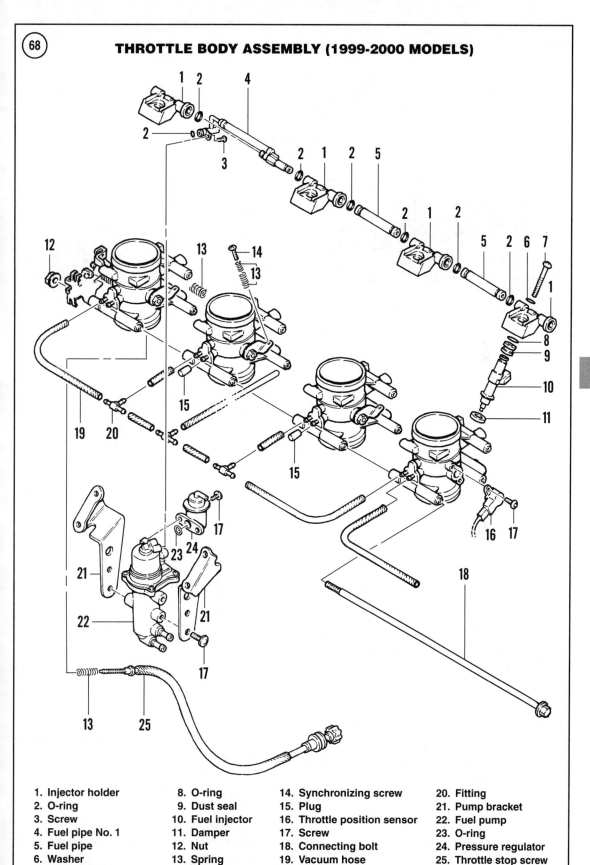

| | | | |
|---|---|---|---|
| 1. Injector holder | 8. O-ring | 14. Synchronizing screw | 20. Fitting |
| 2. O-ring | 9. Dust seal | 15. Plug | 21. Pump bracket |
| 3. Screw | 10. Fuel injector | 16. Throttle position sensor | 22. Fuel pump |
| 4. Fuel pipe No. 1 | 11. Damper | 17. Screw | 23. O-ring |
| 5. Fuel pipe | 12. Nut | 18. Connecting bolt | 24. Pressure regulator |
| 6. Washer | 13. Spring | 19. Vacuum hose | 25. Throttle stop screw |
| 7. Injector holder screw | | | |

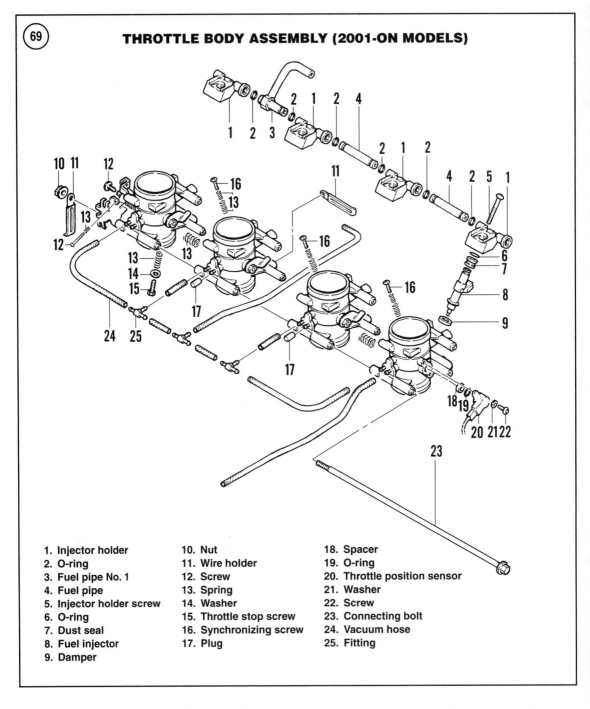

**THROTTLE BODY ASSEMBLY (2001-ON MODELS)**

1. Injector holder
2. O-ring
3. Fuel pipe No. 1
4. Fuel pipe
5. Injector holder screw
6. O-ring
7. Dust seal
8. Fuel injector
9. Damper
10. Nut
11. Wire holder
12. Screw
13. Spring
14. Washer
15. Throttle stop screw
16. Synchronizing screw
17. Plug
18. Spacer
19. O-ring
20. Throttle position sensor
21. Washer
22. Screw
23. Connecting bolt
24. Vacuum hose
25. Fitting

11. Installation is the reverse of removal. Note the following:

　a. Lubricate each intake manifold with a soap solution to ease installation.

　b. Fully seat each throttle body into its intake manifold. A solid bottoming is felt when a throttle body is correctly seated.

　c. Tighten the intake manifold clamp screws securely (**Figure 75**).

　d. Add fuel, start the engine and check for fuel leaks.

　e. Adjust the throttle cable free play, idle speed and fast idle speed as described in Chapter Three.

**Disassembly**

1. On 1999 and 2000 models, perform the following:

　a. Disconnect the 2-pin fuel pump connector (A, **Figure 76**).

　b. Disconnect the hose (B, **Figure 76**) from the fuel rail fitting.

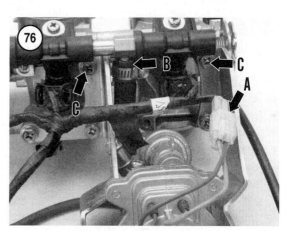

8

c. Remove the fuel pump bracket screws (C, **Figure 76**) from each bracket, and remove the fuel pump assembly.

2. Disconnect each vacuum hose from its fitting on the throttle bodies. Refer to **Figure 77**. Label each hose and its fitting. Hoses must be reinstalled onto their original fittings during assembly.

3. Remove the fuel rail and injectors as described in this chapter.

4. Remove the throttle position sensor (A, **Figure 78**) as described in this chapter.

5. Remove the nut (**Figure 79**) from each connecting bolt.

6. Pull the connecting bolts (B, **Figure 78**) from the throttle body assembly.

7. Pull one throttle body from its adjacent body, and separate the throttle levers. Watch for the springs on the synchronizing screw (A, **Figure 80**) between these two bodies.

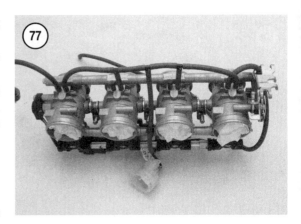

## Assembly

1. Join the throttle bodies together by performing the following:

   a. Apply Suzuki Super Grease A to the throttle levers, synchronizing screw and springs.

   b. Set the throttle bodies adjacent to one another on a surface plate or piece of glass.

   c. Slide the No. 1 and No. 2 bodies together so the throttle lever in one body mates with lever in the other. Make sure the throttle lever sits between the synchronizing springs (A, **Figure 80**) as noted during disassembly.

   d. Repeat substep c and join No. 3 and No. 4 throttle bodies.

   e. Repeat substep c and join the first pair of throttle bodies (Nos. 1 and 2) to the second pair (Nos. 3 and 4).

   f. Install the connecting bolts (B, **Figure 78**) through the throttle bodies.

   g. Install the nuts (**Figure 79**) onto the connecting bolts. Evenly tighten the nuts securely.

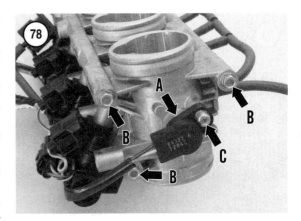

2. Install the throttle position sensor (A, **Figure 78**) as described in this chapter.

3. Install the fuel rail and injectors as described in this chapter.

4. Connect each vacuum hose (**Figure 77**) to the fitting noted during removal.

5. On 1999 and 2000 models, perform the following:

   a. Fit the fuel pump assembly onto the throttle bodies, and install the fuel pump bracket screws (C, **Figure 76**). Tighten the screws to 5 N•m (44 in.-lb.).

   b. Connect the fuel hose (B, **Figure 76**) to the fuel rail fitting.

   c. Connect the 2-pin fuel pump connector (A, **Figure 76**).

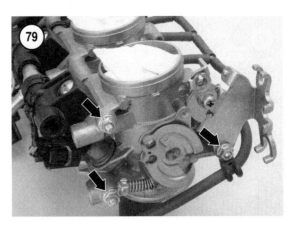

## Inspection

> *CAUTION*
> *Do not use wires to clean passages in*
> *the throttle bodies.*

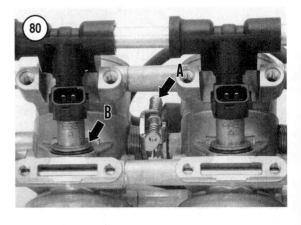

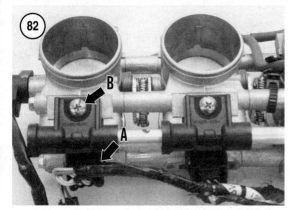

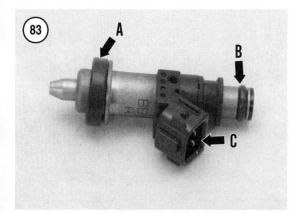

1. Clean the throttle bodies with an aerosol carburetor cleaner. Dry the bodies and all passages with compressed air.

2. Visually inspect the throttle bodies for cracks or other damage that could admit unfiltered air.

3. Operate the throttle valves. They must move smoothly.

4. Check the operation of the throttle wheel and the fast idle cam assembly. Each must operate smoothly.

5. Inspect the hoses for cracks or other signs of damage. Replace any hose that is becoming brittle.

6. Inspect the fuel rail and injectors as described in this chapter.

7. Inspect the fittings (**Figure 81**) on each throttle body. Blow them clear with compressed air.

8. Replace any part that is worn or damaged.

## FUEL INJECTORS

*NOTE*
*The fuel injectors can be removed while the throttle bodies are installed in the engine. The procedure is shown with the bodies removed for photographic clarity.*

**Removal**

1. Raise and support the fuel tank (this chapter).

2. Disconnect the negative battery terminal cable.

3. Remove the air filter housing (this chapter).

4. Disconnect the 2-pin injector connector (A, **Figure 82**) from each fuel injector. Label each injector and its connector.

5. Remove the injector holder screws (B, **Figure 82**) from each injector holder.

6. Pull the fuel rail, disengage each injector from its throttle body, and remove the fuel rail/injectors. Watch for the damper on each fuel injector. It could come out with the injector (A, **Figure 83**) or remain behind in the throttle body port (**Figure 84**). Discard each damper.

7. Remove each fuel injector from its holder (**Figure 85**).

8. Remove and discard the O-ring (B, **Figure 83**) from each injector.

9. Pull apart the fuel rail and disengage the fuel pipes (A, **Figure 86**) from the injector holders (B). Discard the O-ring (C, **Figure 86**) from each end of the fuel pipe.

## Installation

1. Apply clean engine oil to new fuel pipe O-rings, and install an O-ring (C, **Figure 86**) onto each end of each fuel delivery pipe (A).

2. Assemble the fuel rail by pressing an injector holder (B, **Figure 86**) onto one end of a fuel pipe (A) until the pipe bottoms. Assemble the fuel rail so the fuel pipe with the fuel hose fitting sits between bodies No. 3 and No. 4.

3. Oil the new fuel injector O-rings, and install an O-ring (B, **Figure 83**) onto each injector.

4. Oil the new fuel injector dampers, and install a damper (A, **Figure 83**) onto each injector.

5. Press each fuel injector straight into its injector holder (**Figure 85**). Do not turn an injector during installation.

6. Position the fuel rail/injector assembly so each fuel injector rests in its throttle body port (**Figure 87**). Gently press the fuel rail down until each injector bottoms (B, **Figure 80**).

7. Install the injector holder screw (B, **Figure 82**) into each holder. Evenly tighten the screws to 5 N•m (44 in.-lb.).

8. Refer to the wiring diagrams to identify the proper injector connectors by wiring color. Connect each 2-pin connector (A, **Figure 82**) to the correct fuel injector.

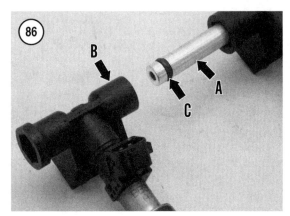

## Inspection

1. Visually inspect the fuel injectors (**Figure 83**) for damage. Inspect the injector nozzle for carbon buildup or damage.

2. Check the terminals of each fuel injector connector (C, **Figure 83**) and subharness connector for corrosion or damage.

3. Blow the fuel delivery pipes (A, **Figure 86**) and the injector holders (B) clear with compressed air.

4. Inspect the injector ports (**Figure 84**) in the throttle body for contamination.

5. Replace any worn or damaged part.

### *Resistance test*

1. Turn the ignition switch off.

2. Raise and support the fuel tank as described in this chapter.

3. Disconnect the connector (A, **Figure 82**) from the No. 1 fuel injector.

4. Use an ohmmeter to measure the resistance between the two terminals in the fuel injector. The resistance should be within the range specified in **Table 2**.

5. Repeat this test for each of the remaining fuel injectors.

### *Continuity test*

1. Perform Steps 1-3 of the injector resistance test.

2. Check the continuity between each terminal in injector No. 1 and ground. No continuity (infinity) should be indicated.

3. Repeat this test for each remaining fuel injector.

### *Voltage test*

1. Perform Steps 1-3 of the injector resistance test.

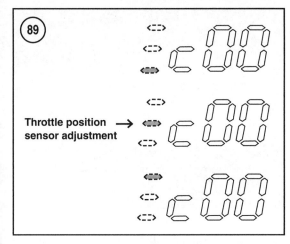

Throttle position sensor adjustment →

2. Connect a voltmeter positive test probe to the yellow/red wire in the injector connector; connect the negative test probe to a good ground.

*NOTE*
*Injector voltage is present for only 3 seconds after the ignition switch is turned on. If necessary, turn the switch off and then back on.*

3. Turn the ignition switch on and measure the voltage. It should equal battery voltage.
4. Repeat this test for each of the remaining fuel injectors.

## THROTTLE POSITION (TP) SENSOR

### Removal/Installation

A Torx wrench (Suzuki part No. 09930-11960 [1999-2001 models] or part No. 09930-11950 [2002-on models]) is needed to perform this procedure.
1. Disconnect the electrical lead from the negative battery terminal (Chapter Nine).

2. Raise and support the fuel tank as described in this chapter.
3. Disconnect the 3-pin throttle position sensor connector (B, **Figure 74**).
4. Scribe an indexing line across the sensor (A, **Figure 78**) and throttle body so the sensor can be reinstalled in the same position during assembly.
5. Use the Torx wrench to remove the throttle position sensor screw(s) (C, **Figure 78**), pull the TP sensor (A) from the throttle shaft and remove the sensor. Note how the throttle position sensor engages the throttle shaft.
6. Installation is the reverse of removal. Note the following:
   a. Apply Suzuki Super Grease A to the end of the throttle shaft.
   b. Align the end of the throttle shaft with the slot in the throttle position sensor, and slide the sensor onto the shaft.
   c. Position the sensor so the indexing mark made on the sensor aligns with the mark on the throttle body.
   d. Install the throttle position sensor screw(s). On 1999-2001 models, tighten the screws securely. On 2002-on models, tighten the screw to 3.5 N•m (31 in.-lb.).

### Adjustment

The mode select switch (Suzuki part No. 09930-82710) and a Torx wrench (part No. 09930-11960 [1999-2001 models] or part No. 09930-11950 [2002-on models]) or their equivalents are needed to perform this procedure.

*CAUTION*
*Do not perform this procedure without the mode select switch. Shorting the terminals in the dealer mode connector could damage the ECM.*

1. Start the engine and check the idle speed. If necessary, adjust the idle to specification as described in Chapter Three.
2. Stop the engine.
3. Remove the rider's seat and the passenger seat as described in Chapter Fifteen. Connect the mode select switch to the dealer mode connector on the frame rail. Refer to **Figure 88**.
4. Turn the model select switch on.
5. The malfunction code cOO should appear in the meter display. The dash before the code indicates the state of the TP sensor adjustment. When correctly adjusted, the dash should be in the middle position as shown in **Figure 89**. If the dash is in the upper or

lower position, adjust the sensor by performing the following:

   a. Raise and support the fuel tank as described in this chapter.

   b. Loosen the throttle position sensor screw(s) (C, **Figure 78**).

   c. Rotate the throttle position sensor (A, **Figure 78**) until the dash moves to the center position.

   d. On 1999-2001 models, tighten the throttle position sensor screws securely. On 2002-on models, tighten the screw to 3.5 N•m (31 in.-lb.).

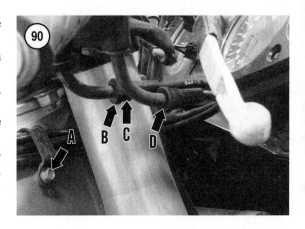

### Continuity Test

1. Turn the ignition switch off.

2. Raise and support the fuel tank as described in this chapter.

3. Disconnect the 3-pin throttle position sensor connector (B, **Figure 74**).

4. Check the continuity between the yellow terminal in the sensor side of the connector and a good ground.

5. Reverse the test probes, and check the continuity in the opposite direction.

6. Both readings should indicate no continuity (infinity).

### Resistance Test

1. Perform Steps 1-3 of the TP sensor continuity test.

2. Connect an ohmmeter's positive test probe to the yellow terminal in the sensor side of the connector. Connect the negative test probe to the black (or black/brown) terminal in the sensor side of the connector.

3. Read the resistance when the throttle is fully closed and fully open. Record each reading.

4. The fully open and fully closed resistance should be within the range specified in **Table 2**.

### Input Voltage Test

1. Perform Steps 1-3 of the TP sensor continuity test.

2. Connect a voltmeter's positive test probe to the blue or red terminal in the harness side of the TP sensor connector. Connect the voltmeter's negative probe to ground.

3. Turn the ignition switch on, and measure the input voltage. It should be within the range specified in **Table 2**.

4. Connect the voltmeter's positive test probe to the blue or red terminal in the harness side of the TP sensor connector. Connect the negative test probe to the

black/brown terminal in the harness side of the connector.

5. The input voltage should be within the range specified in **Table 2**.

### Output Voltage Test

1. Raise and support the fuel tank (this chapter).

2. Make sure the throttle position sensor connector is connected to its harness mate.

3. Connect a voltmeter positive test probe to the yellow terminal in the harness side of the connector. Connect the negative test probe to the black/brown terminal in the harness side of the connector. Use 0.5-mm back probe pins to back probe the harness side of the connector during this test.

4. Turn the ignition switch on.

5. Measure the output voltage when the throttle valve is fully closed and fully opened. Each measurement should be within the range specified in **Table 2**.

## THROTTLE CABLE REPLACEMENT

All models are equipped with two throttle cables: the pull (or accelerator) cable and the return (or decelerator) cable. These cables are not the same. Use

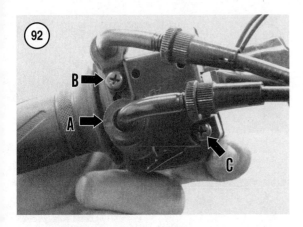

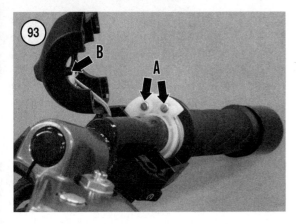

masking tape to label the old cables before removal. Replace both cables as a set.

1. Disconnect the negative battery cable.

2. Raise and support the fuel tank as described in this chapter. Remove the air filter housing if more work room is desired.

3. Note how the throttle cables are routed from the right handlebar switch housing, through the clamp on the right side of the frame (A, **Figure 90**) and on to the throttle wheel. Make a drawing so the new cables can be rerouted along the same path followed by the old cables. Also note where the cables are secured to the motorcycle. The new cables must pass through the same holders/cable ties as the originals.

4. At the throttle grip, loosen the return cable locknut (B, **Figure 90**) and turn the adjuster (C) in toward the switch assembly to allow maximum slack in the cable. Repeat this procedure for the pull cable (D, **Figure 90**).

5. At the throttle body assembly, loosen both locknuts (A and B, **Figure 91**) on the pull cable, and disconnect the cable end (C) from the throttle wheel. Disengage the pull cable from the throttle cable bracket.

6. Loosen both locknuts on the return cable, and disconnect its cable end (D, **Figure 91**) from the throttle

wheel. Disengage the return cable from the throttle cable bracket.

7. At the right handlebar switch, unthread the return cable clamp nut (A, **Figure 92**), and lower it from the switch housing.

8. Remove the front switch housing screw (B, **Figure 92**) and lower the pull cable clamp from the switch housing.

9. Remove the rear switch housing screw (C, **Figure 92**), and separate the housing halves (**Figure 93**).

10. Disconnect each cable end (A, **Figure 93**) from the throttle drum, and feed the cables through the lower housing half.

*CAUTION*
*Do not lubricate nylon-lined cables. Nylon-lined cables are generally used dry. Oil and most cable lubricants cause liner expansion, pinching the liner against the cable. When installing nylon-lined and other aftermarket cables, follow the cable manufacturer's instructions.*

11. Lubricate the new cables as described in Chapter Three. Do not lubricate any cable with a nylon liner.

12. Route the new cables along the same path as the old cables.

13. At the right handlebar, feed the return cable through the rear port in the lower switch half. Tighten the return cable clamp nut (A, **Figure 92**) in toward the switch housing.

14. Feed the pull cable through the front port in the lower switch half.

15. Apply grease to the cable ends, and connect each cable end to the throttle drum (A, **Figure 93**). Make sure each cable is securely seated in the throttle drum channel.

16. Lower the upper switch half over the throttle drum so the indexing pin (B, **Figure 93**) engages the hole in the handlebar, and install the switch housing screws (B and C, **Figure 92**). Secure the pull cable clamp under the forward screw (B, **Figure 92**). Tighten the screws evenly.

17. At the throttle body assembly, turn the forward locknut (B, **Figure 91**) on the pull cable against the cable adjuster (E). Repeat this for the return cable.

18. Apply grease to the ends of both throttle cables, and then connect the return cable end (D, **Figure 91**) to the throttle wheel, and fit the cable onto the bracket. Make sure a locknut sits on each side of the bracket.

19. Repeat Step 19 and install the pull cable (C, **Figure 91**). Make sure each cable is securely seated in the throttle wheel channel.

20. Tighten the rear locknut (A, **Figure 91**) on each cable against the cable bracket.

8

21. Operate the throttle drum on the handlebar and make sure the throttle wheel operates correctly with no binding. If any drag or binding is noted, carefully check that the cables are attached correctly and there are no tight bends in either cable.

22. Adjust the cable free play as described in Chapter Three.

23. Install the fuel tank.

> *WARNING*
> *An improperly adjusted or incorrectly routed throttle cable can cause the throttle to hang open and lead to a crash. Do not ride the motorcycle until the throttle cable operation is correct.*

24. Start the engine and let it idle. Turn the handlebar from side to side and listen to the engine speed. Make sure the idle speed does not increase. If it does, the throttle cables are incorrectly adjusted or improperly routed. Find and correct the source of the problem before riding.

## FAST IDLE (CHOKE)

The fuel system includes a cable-adjusted fast idle cam that adjusts throttle valve position during cold starts and engine warm-up. When the fast idle lever on the left handlebar switch is operated, the fast idle cam opens and closes the throttle valves.

### Adjustment

Refer to *Fast Idle Speed Adjustment* in Chapter Three.

### Cable Replacement

1. Raise and support the fuel tank as described in this chapter. Remove the air filter housing if more work room is desired.

2. Note how the fast idle cable is routed from the left handlebar switch housing, through the clamp on the right side of the frame (A, **Figure 90**), and on to the fast idle cam on the side of the No. 4 throttle body. Make a drawing so the new cable can be rerouted along the same path followed by the old cable. Also note where the cable is secured to the motorcycle. The new cable must pass through the same holders/cable ties as the originals.

3. At the throttle body assembly, loosen both locknuts (F, **Figure 91**) on the fast idle cable. Disconnect the cable end (G, **Figure 91**) from the fast idle cam and disengage the cable from the bracket.

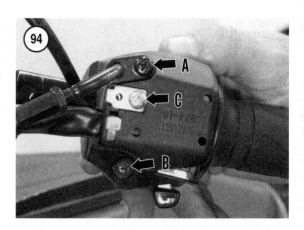

4. At the left handlebar switch, remove the forward switch housing screw (A, **Figure 94**), and then lower the fast idle cable clamp from the housing.

5. Remove the rear switch housing screw (B, **Figure 94**) and separate the housing halves.

> *NOTE*
> *The middle screw (C, **Figure 94**) in the switch housing is a friction adjuster for the fast idle lever.*

6. Disconnect the cable end (**Figure 95**) from the fast idle lever, and feed the cable through the lower housing half.

> *CAUTION*
> *Do not oil a nylon-lined cable. Nylon-lined cables are generally used dry. Oil and most cable lubricants cause liner expansion, pinching the liner against the cable. When installing nylon-lined and other aftermarket cables, follow the cable manufacturer's instructions.*

7. Lubricate the new cable as described in Chapter Three. Do not lubricate any cable with a nylon liner.

8. Route the cable along the same path as the old cable.

9. At the handlebar, feed the cable through the port in the lower switch half.

10. Apply grease to the cable end, position the lower switch half onto the handlebar, and connect the cable end (**Figure 95**) to the fast idle lever.

11. Install the upper switch half over the handlebar. Make sure its pin engages the hole in the handlebar, and install the switch housing screws (A and B, **Figure 94**). Secure the cable clamp under the front switch housing screw (A, **Figure 94**). Tighten the screws evenly.

12. At the throttle body assembly, apply grease to the end of the fast idle cable.

13. Connect the cable end (G, **Figure 91**) to the fast idle cam, and fit the cable onto the bracket. Make sure a locknut (F, **Figure 91**) sits on each side of the bracket.

14. Turn the forward locknut so it sits against the cable adjuster, and tighten the rear locknut against the cable bracket.

15. Operate the fast idle lever on the handlebar and make sure the fast idle cam operates correctly with no binding. If operation is incorrect or if there is binding, carefully check that the cable is attached correctly and there are no tight bends in the cable.

16. Install the fuel tank. Start the engine and check the fast idle adjustment as described in Chapter Three. Adjust the fast idle speed as necessary.

### ATMOSPHERIC PRESSURE (AP) SENSOR

#### Removal/Installation

1. Raise and support the fuel tank as described in this chapter.

2. Disconnect the negative battery cable.

3. Disconnect the 3-pin connector (A, **Figure 96**) from the atmospheric pressure sensor.

4. Remove the screws (B, **Figure 96**), and lower the sensor from the frame.

5. Installation is the reverse of removal.

#### Input Voltage Test

1. Raise and support the fuel tank as described in this chapter.

2. Disconnect the 3-pin connector (A, **Figure 96**) from the atmospheric pressure sensor.

3. Connect a voltmeter's positive test probe to the red terminal in the harness-side connector. Connect the negative test probe to ground.

4. Turn the ignition switch on, and measure the voltage. It should be within the input voltage range specified in **Table 2**.

5. Turn the ignition switch off.

6. Connect the voltmeter's positive test probe to the red terminal in the harness-side connector. Connect the negative test probe to the black/brown terminal in the harness-side connector.

7. Turn the ignition switch on and measure the voltage. It should be within the input voltage range specified in **Table 2**.

#### Output Voltage Test

1. Make sure the AP sensor connector (A, **Figure 96**) is securely connected to the AP sensor.

2. Connect a voltmeter's positive test probe to the green/yellow terminal in the AP sensor connector. Connect the negative test probe to the black/brown terminal. Use 0.5-mm back probe pins to back probe the connector during this test.

3. Turn the ignition switch on and measure the voltage. It should equal the output voltage value specified in **Table 2**.

#### Vacuum Test

1. Remove the atmospheric pressure sensor as described in this section. Make sure the sensor's air passage is clear.

2. Connect a vacuum pump and gauge to the sensor's air passage (**Figure 97**).

3. Connect three new 1.5-volt batteries in series as shown in **Figure 97**. Measure the total voltage of the batteries. The voltage must be 4.5-5 volts. Replace the batteries if necessary.

4. Connect the battery positive terminal to the Vcc terminal in the sensor. Connect the battery negative terminal to the ground terminal in the sensor.

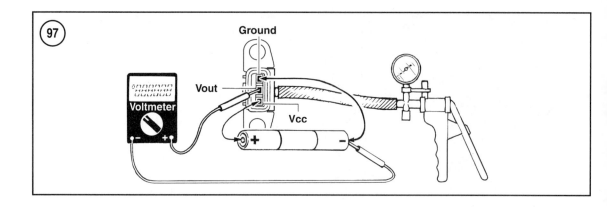

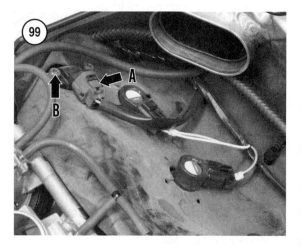

**AP SENSOR AND IAP SENSOR VOUT VOLTAGE**

| Reference altitude m (ft.) | Atmospheric pressure kPa (mm Hg) | Vout Voltage |
|---|---|---|
| 0-610 (0-2000) | 100-94 (760-707) | 3.1-3.6 |
| 611-1524 (2001-5000) | 94-85 (707-634) | 2.8-3.4 |
| 1525-2438 (5001-8000) | 85-76 (634-567) | 2.6-3.1 |
| 2439-3048 (8001-10,000) | 76-70 (567-526) | 2.4-2.9 |

5. Connect the voltmeter's positive test probe to the Vout terminal in the sensor. Connect the negative test probe to the battery negative terminal.

6. Note the voltage reading. It should be within the Vout voltage range specified in **Table 2**.

7. Use the vacuum pump to apply vacuum to the sensor's air passage, and note the changes in the voltage reading. The voltage should decrease as vacuum increases up to 53 kPa (400 mm Hg.) Refer to **Figure 98**.

## CAMSHAFT POSITION (CMP) SENSOR

### Removal/Installation

1. Disconnect the negative battery cable.

2. Raise and support the fuel tank as described in this chapter.

3. Remove the air filter housing (this chapter).

4. Disconnect the 2-pin connector (A, **Figure 99**) from the camshaft position sensor.

5. Remove the mounting bolts (B, **Figure 99**), and lift the sensor from the cylinder head cover. Watch for the O-ring behind the sensor

6. Installation is the reverse of removal. Note the following:

    a. Install a new O-ring with the sensor.

    b. Tighten the camshaft position sensor bolts (B, **Figure 99**) to 8 N•m (71 in.-lb.).

### Resistance Test

1. Turn the ignition switch off, and perform Steps 2-4 of the CMP sensor removal procedure.

2. Connect the positive test probe to the black/yellow terminal in the sensor. Connect the negative test probe to the sensor's brown terminal.

3. The resistance should be within the range specified in **Table 2**.

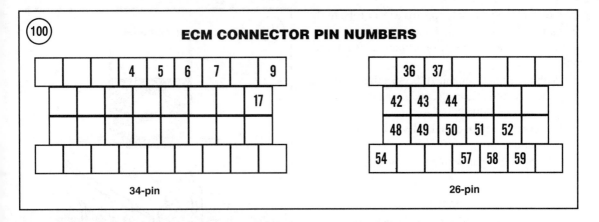

**ECM CONNECTOR PIN NUMBERS**

34-pin

26-pin

## Continuity Test

1. Turn the ignition switch off, and perform Steps 2-4 of the CMP sensor removal procedure.

2. Check the continuity between each terminal in the sensor and ground.

3. No continuity (infinity) should be indicated during either portion of the test.

## Peak Voltage Test

A multicircuit tester (Suzuki part No. 09900-25008 or equivalent) with the peak voltage adapter is needed to perform this test.

Refer to *Peak Voltage Test* in Chapter Two.

1. Turn the ignition switch off, and perform Steps 2-4 of the CMP sensor removal procedure.

2. Connect the peak voltage adapter to the voltmeter following the manufacturer's instructions.

3. Connect the positive test probe to the black/yellow terminal in the sensor. Connect the negative test probe to the sensor's brown terminal.

4. Turn the ignition switch on and shift the transmission to neutral.

5. Crank the engine for a few seconds.

6. The peak voltage reading should equal or exceed the value specified in **Table 2**.

7. Connect the CMP sensor connector to the sensor, and disconnect the 26-pin connector from the ECM.

8. Connect the positive test probe to the black/yellow terminal (37, **Figure 100**) in the harness side of the ECM's 26-pin connector. Connect the negative test probe to the brown terminal (44, **Figure 100**) in the harness connector.

9. Repeat Steps 4-6 to measure the peak voltage.

### ENGINE COOLANT TEMPERATURE (ECT) SENSOR

#### Removal/Installation

1. Disconnect the negative battery cable.

2. Drain the coolant as described in Chapter Three.

3. Remove the air filter housing (this chapter). Remove the throttle bodies if necessary.

4. Disconnect the 2-pin connector (A, **Figure 101**) from the ECT sensor (B).

*CAUTION*
*The engine coolant temperature sensor is sensitive to shock. Exercise caution when handling the sensor.*

5. Remove the ECT sensor (B, **Figure 101**) from the back of the cylinder head. Watch for the sealing washer installed with the sensor.

6. Installation is the reverse of removal. Note the following:

   a. Include a new sealing washer, and tighten the ECT sensor to 18 N•m (13. ft.-lb.)

#### Resistance Test

1. Turn the ignition switch off, and perform Step 3 and Step 4 of the ECT sensor removal procedure.

2. Connect the ohmmeter positive test probe to the black/blue terminal in the sensor. Connect the negative test probe to the sensor's black/brown terminal.

3. With the engine coolant at the specified temperature, measure the resistance, and compare this to the specification in **Table 2**.

4. If necessary, remove the ECT sensor as described in this section.

5. Fill a beaker or pan with oil, and place it on a stove or hot plate.

> *NOTE*
> *The thermometer and the sensor must not touch the container sides or bottom. If either does, test readings are inaccurate.*

6. Place a thermometer in the pan of oil.

7. Mount the ECT sensor so the temperature sensing tip and the threaded portion of the body are submerged as shown in **Figure 102**.

8. Attach an ohmmeter to the sensor terminals as shown in **Figure 102**. Check the resistance as follows:

   a. Gradually heat the oil to the temperatures specified in **Table 2**.

   b. Note the resistance of the sensor when the oil temperature reaches the specified values.

   c. Replace the ECT sensor if any reading equals infinity or is considerably different than the specified resistance at a given temperature.

**Voltage Test**

1. Turn the ignition switch off. Perform Step 3 and Step 4 of the ECT sensor removal procedure.

2. Connect the voltmeter positive test probe to the black/blue terminal in the 2-pin connector. Connect the negative test probe to a good ground.

3. Turn on the ignition switch and measure the voltage. It should be within the range specified in **Table 2**.

4. Connect the voltmeter positive test probe to the black/blue terminal in the 2-pin connector. Connect the negative test probe to the black/brown terminal in the connector.

5. Turn on the ignition switch. The voltage should be within the specified range.

**Gauge Test**

Before performing this test, perform the *Resistance Test* described in this section. Replace the sensor if it

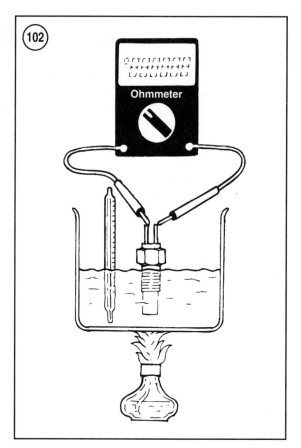

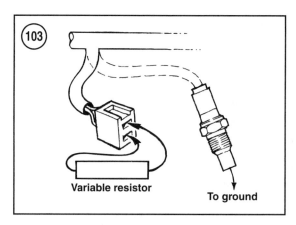

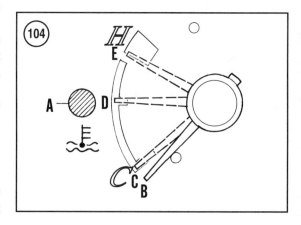

**COOLANT TEMPERATURE GAUGE TEST**

| Resistance | LED (A) | Needle position | Coolant Temperature |
|---|---|---|---|
| Over 2.45 k ohms | on | B | – |
| Approx. 0.811 k ohms | off | C | Approx. 50° C (122° F) |
| Approx. 0.142 k ohms | off | D | Approx. 110° C (230° F) |
| Approx. 0.1 ohms | on | E | Approx. 123° C (253° F) |

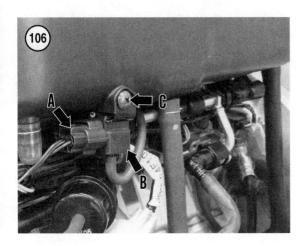

is out of specification. If the display is still not working, perform the following test:

1. Raise and support the fuel tank (this chapter).

2. Disconnect the 2-pin connector (A, **Figure 101**) from the ECT sensor (B).

3. Connect a variable resistor across the two terminals in the harness side of the ECT sensor connector (**Figure 103**).

> *NOTE*
> *If the engine stop switch is off when the ignition switch is turned on, the meter LED (A, **Figure 104**) turns on, the needle moves to high position (E, **Figure 104**) and CHECK appears in the LCD. This is normal. The system is indicating that no signal is reaching the ECM. Turn the engine stop switch on, and retry.*

4. Turn the ignition switch on.

5. Refer to **Figure 105**. Set the resistor to each indicated resistance, and check the operation of the gauge. The gauge LED (A, **Figure 104**) should turn on or off, and the needle should move to the indicated points (B-E).

6. Replace the meter assembly if the gauge fails any portion of this test.

## INTAKE AIR PRESSURE (IAP) SENSOR

### Removal/Installation

1. Disconnect the negative battery cable.

2. Raise and support the fuel tank as described in this chapter.

3. Disconnect the 3-pin connector (A, **Figure 106**) from the intake air pressure sensor (B).

4. Remove the vacuum hose from the sensor (B, **Figure 106**).

5. Remove the mounting screw (C, **Figure 106**) and lower the sensor (B) from the air filter housing.

6. Installation is the reverse of removal.

### Input Voltage Test

1. Turn the ignition switch off, and perform Step 2 and Step 3 of the IAP sensor removal procedure.

2. Connect a voltmeter's positive test probe to the red terminal in the 3-pin connector. Connect the negative test probe to ground.

3. Turn the ignition switch on and measure the voltage. It should be within the input voltage range specified in **Table 2**.

4. Turn the ignition switch off.

5. Connect the voltmeter's positive test probe to the red terminal in the 3-pin connector. Connect the negative test probe to the black/brown terminal in the connector.

6. Turn the ignition switch on and measure the voltage. It should be within the input voltage specified range.

### Output Voltage Test

1. Make sure the IAP sensor connector (A, **Figure 106**) is securely mated to the IAP sensor (B).

2. Connect a voltmeter's positive test probe to the green/black terminal in the connector. Connect the

**8**

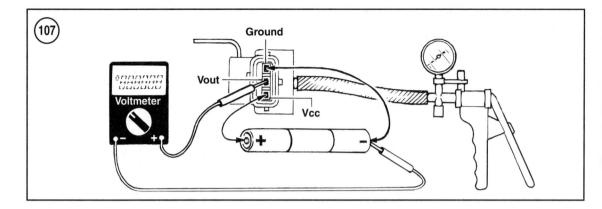

negative test probe to the black/brown terminal. Use 0.5-mm back probe pins to back probe the IAP connector during this test.

3. Start the engine, run it at idle and measure the voltage. It should equal the output voltage specified in **Table 2**.

### Vacuum Test

1. Remove the intake air pressure sensor as described in this chapter.

2. Make sure the sensor's air passage is clear, and connect a vacuum pump and gauge to the air passage (**Figure 107**).

3. Connect three new 1.5-volt batteries in series as shown in **Figure 107**. Measure the total voltage of the batteries. The voltage must be 4.5-5.0 volts. Replace the batteries if necessary.

4. Connect the battery positive termnal to the Vcc terminal in the sensor. Connect the battery negative terminal to the ground terminal in the sensor.

5. Connect the voltmeter's positive test probe to the Vout terminal in the sensor. Connect the negative test probe to the battery negative terminal.

6. Note the voltage reading. It should be within the Vout voltage range specified in **Table 2**.

7. Use the vacuum pump to apply vacuum to the sensor's air passage, and note the changes in the voltage reading. The voltage should decrease as vacuum increases up to 53 kPa (400 mm Hg.) Refer to **Figure 98**.

### INTAKE AIR TEMPERATURE (IAT) SENSOR

#### Removal/Installation

1. Disconnect the negative battery cable.

2. Raise and support the fuel tank.

3. Disconnect the 2-pin connector (A, **Figure 108**) from the IAT sensor (B).

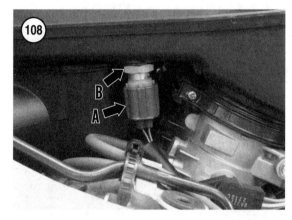

4. Remove the sensor from the air filter housing. Discard the sensor's O-ring.

5. Installation is the reverse of removal. Note the following:

    a. Install a new O-ring onto the sensor.

    b. Tighten the IAT sensor to 18 N•m (13 ft.-lb.).

#### Resistance Test

1. Turn the ignition switch off, and perform Step 2 and Step 3 of the IAT sensor removal procedure.

2. Connect the ohmmeter positive test probe to the dark green terminal in the sensor. Connect the negative test probe to the sensor's black/brown terminal.

3. With the air temperature at the specified value, measure the resistance and compare this to the specification in **Table 2**.

4. Remove the IAT sensor as described in this section.

5. Fill a beaker or pan with oil, and place it on a stove or hot plate.

*NOTE*
*The thermometer and the sensor must not touch the container sides or bottom. If either does, it causes a false reading.*

6. Place a thermometer in the pan of oil.

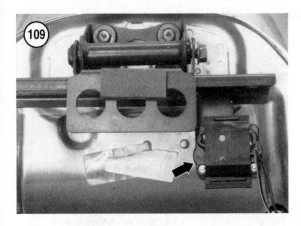

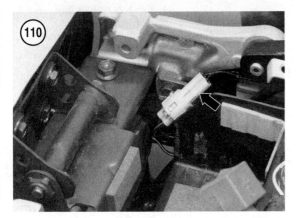

7. Mount the IAT sensor so the temperature sensing tip and the threaded portion of the body are submerged as shown in **Figure 102**.

8. Attach an ohmmeter to the sensor terminals as shown in **Figure 102**. Check the resistance as follows:

    a. Gradually heat the oil to the temperatures specified in **Table 2**. Note the resistance of the sensor when the oil temperature reaches the specified values.

    b. Replace the IAT sensor if any reading equals infinity or is considerably different than the specified resistance at a given temperature.

**Voltage Test**

1. Turn the ignition switch off, and perform Step 2 and Step 3 of the IAT sensor removal procedure.

2. Connect the voltmeter positive test probe to the dark green terminal in the 2-pin connector. Connect the negative test probe to a good ground.

3. Turn on the ignition switch and measure the voltage. It should be within the range specified in **Table 2**.

4. Connect the voltmeter positive test probe to the dark green terminal in the 2-pin connector. Connect

the negative test probe to the black/brown terminal in the connector.

5. Turn on the ignition switch. The voltage should be within the specified range.

## TIP OVER (TO) SENSOR

Whenever the TO sensor is activated, the ECM cuts off power to the fuel pump, fuel injectors and ignition coils.

**Removal/Installation**

1. Remove the fuel tank (this chapter).

2. Remove the sensor (**Figure 109**) from its mounting tangs on the fuel tank bracket. Disconnect the 2-pin TO sensor connector (**Figure 110**).

3. Installation is the reverse of removal. Make sure the side marked UPPER sits up.

**Resistance Test**

1. Remove the rider's seat (Chapter Fifteen).

2. Disconnect the 2-pin TO sensor connector (**Figure 110**).

3. Connect the ohmmeter test probes to the black terminal and to the black/white terminal in the sensor side of the connector. Read the resistance.

4. The resistance should be within the range specified in **Table 2**.

**Voltage Test**

1. Remove the TO sensor as described in this section.

2. Reconnect the TO sensor connector (**Figure 110**).

3. Reinstall the battery (Chapter Nine).

4. Connect the voltmeter positive test probe to black terminal in the harness side of the connector. Connect the negative test probe to the black/brown terminal (harness side). Use 0.5-mm back probe pins to back probe the harness side of the connector during this test.

5. Turn the ignition switch on.

6. Hold the sensor so it is horizontal with the side marked UPPER facing up. Read the voltage.

7. Measure the voltage while tilting the sensor more than 43° from horizontal. Lean the TO sensor to the right and to the left. Note the voltage reading each time.

8. Each reading should be within specification (**Table 2**).

8

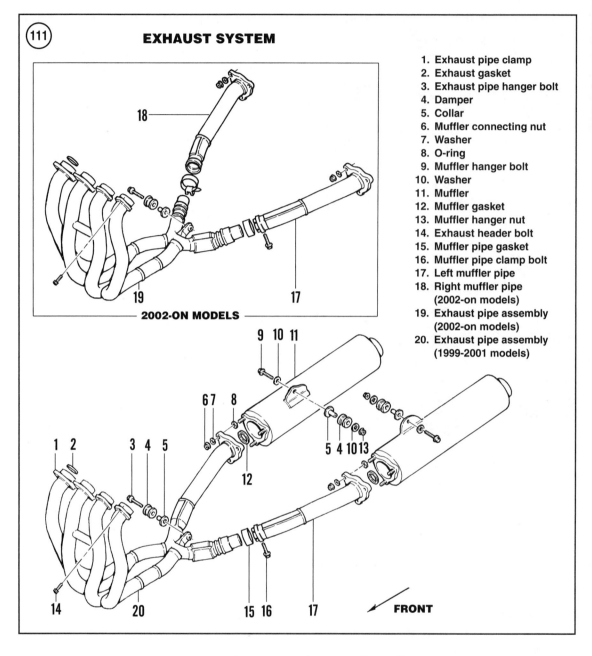

# EXHAUST SYSTEM

1. Exhaust pipe clamp
2. Exhaust gasket
3. Exhaust pipe hanger bolt
4. Damper
5. Collar
6. Muffler connecting nut
7. Washer
8. O-ring
9. Muffler hanger bolt
10. Washer
11. Muffler
12. Muffler gasket
13. Muffler hanger nut
14. Exhaust header bolt
15. Muffler pipe gasket
16. Muffler pipe clamp bolt
17. Left muffler pipe
18. Right muffler pipe (2002-on models)
19. Exhaust pipe assembly (2002-on models)
20. Exhaust pipe assembly (1999-2001 models)

**2002-ON MODELS**

FRONT

## EXHAUST SYSTEM

Refer to **Figure 111**.

### Muffler Removal/Installation

1. Remove the muffler connecting nuts (A, **Figure 112**) and washers from the muffler studs.

2. Remove the nut from behind the muffler hanger bolt (B, **Figure 112**).

3. Remove the hanger bolt and washers from the footpeg bracket. Note that a washer sits on either side of the footpeg bracket.

4. Lower the muffler from the footpeg bracket, and pull the muffler from the muffler pipe.

5. Discard the O-ring on each muffler stud, and discard muffler gasket (A, **Figure 113**). New ones must be installed during assembly.

6. Inspect the muffler.

7. Installation is the reverse of removal. Note the following:

   a. Apply engine oil to the new muffler stud O-rings, and install an O-ring onto each stud.

   b. Seat a new muffler gasket (A, **Figure 113**) onto the muffler pipe.

   c. Tighten the muffler hanger bolt/nut (B, **Figure 112**) to 23 N•m (17 ft.-lb.).

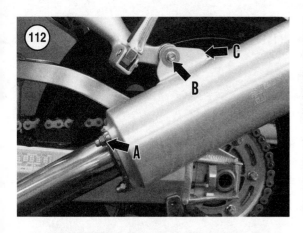

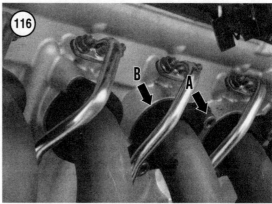

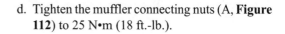

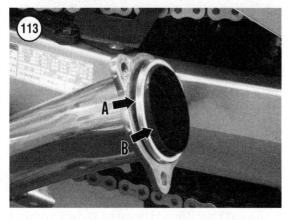

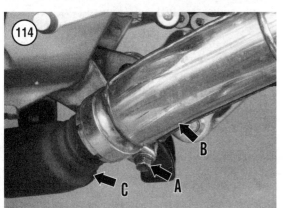

d. Tighten the muffler connecting nuts (A, **Figure 112**) to 25 N•m (18 ft.-lb.).

**Exhaust Pipe Assembly
Removal/Installation**

1. Remove the fairing side panel from each side (Chapter Fifteen).

2. Remove the oil cooler (Chapter Five) and the radiator (Chapter Ten).

3. Perform the following on the left side of the motorcycle:

   a. Loosen the muffler pipe clamp bolt (A, **Figure 114**).

   b. Remove the nut from behind the muffler hanger bolt (B, **Figure 112**).

   c. Remove the hanger bolt and washers from the footpeg bracket. Note that a washer sits on each side of the footpeg bracket.

   d. Disengage the muffler pipe (B, **Figure 114**) from the exhaust pipe assembly (C), and remove the muffler/muffler pipe assembly from the left side. Discard the muffler pipe gasket. A new one must be installed during assembly.

4A. On 1999-2001 models, remove the right muffler as described in this section.

4B. On 2002-on models, repeat Step 3 and remove the right muffler/muffler pipe assembly.

5. Remove the exhaust pipe hanger bolt (**Figure 115**). Watch for the damper and collar installed in the mount.

6. Remove each exhaust pipe header bolt (A, **Figure 116**), and lower each pipe clamp (B).

7. Disengage the exhaust pipes from the exhaust ports, and remove the pipe assembly.

8. Remove the gaskets from each exhaust port.

9. Inspect the exhaust system.

10. Installation is the reverse of removal. Note the following:

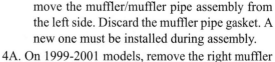

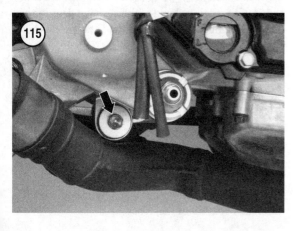

**8**

a. Install a new exhaust gasket into each exhaust port in the cylinder head.

b. Install a new muffler pipe gasket into each muffler pipe fitting. Apply Permatex 1372 Exhaust Gas Sealer to the inside and outside surfaces of each muffler pipe gasket.

c. Install the entire assembly and hand-tighten all hardware.

d. Tighten the hardware in order.

e. Tighten the exhaust pipe (A, **Figure 116**) header bolts to 23 N•m (17 ft.-lb.).

f. Tighten the exhaust pipe hanger bolt (**Figure 115**) to 23 N•m (17 ft.-lb.).

g. Tighten the muffler connecting nut (A, **Figure 112**) to 25 N•m (18 ft.-lb.).

h. Tighten the muffler pipe clamp bolt (A, **Figure 114**) to 23 N•m (17 ft.-lb.).

i. Tighten the muffler hanger bolt/nut (B, **Figure 112**) to 23 N•m (17 ft-lb.).

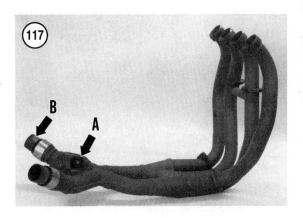

**Exhaust System Inspection**

1. Inspect all hanger brackets (A, **Figure 117** and C, **Figure 112**) for cracks or damage.

2. Inspect the exhaust pipe-to-cylinder head fittings (**Figure 118**) for corrosion, burned areas or damage.

3. Inspect the fitting on the exhaust pipe (B, **Figure 117**) and its mate in the muffler pipe for corrosion or damage.

4. Inspect the fitting on the muffler pipe (B, **Figure 113**) and its mate in the muffler for corrosion or damage.

5. Inspect all welds for leaks or corrosion.

6. Check the damper in the muffler mount on the footpeg bracket. Replace as necessary.

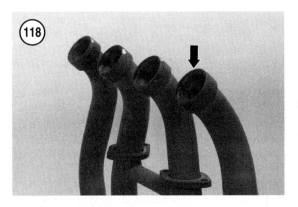

## EVAPORATIVE EMISSIONS CONTROL SYSTEM (CALIFORNIA MODELS)

*WARNING*
*Because the evaporative emission control system stores fuel vapor, the work area must be free of flames or sparks during EVAP system service.*

*NOTE*
*Label each hose and its fitting before removal so they can be identified during assembly. Hoses must be reinstalled onto the correct fittings during assembly.*

All California models are equipped with an evaporative emission control system (EVAP), which consists of a charcoal canister, fuel shutoff valve, pressure control valve, assorted hoses, and modified throttle bodies and fuel tank (**Figure 119**).

The EVAP system captures fuel tank vapor and stores it in the charcoal canister. When the motorcycle is ridden, these vapors are routed to the throttle bodies and drawn into the engine where they are burned. The gravity-operated fuel shutoff valve, which sits in line between the fuel tank and charcoal canister, ensures the fumes remain in the canister until they can be burned.

Refer to the vacuum hose routing label on the left side of the rear frame rail. Make sure the hoses are correctly routed and attached to the right components. Inspect the hoses and replace any if necessary.

On most models, the hoses and fittings are color coded with labels or bands. If these have deteriorated or are missing, mark the hose and the fittings with masking tape and a marker. There are many vacuum hoses on these models. Without clear identification marks, reconnecting the hoses can be very time consuming.

Refer to **Figure 120**.

**Maintenance/Service**

1. Make sure the ignition switch is turned off.

2. Check the canister mounting and inspect the condition and routing of the hoses.

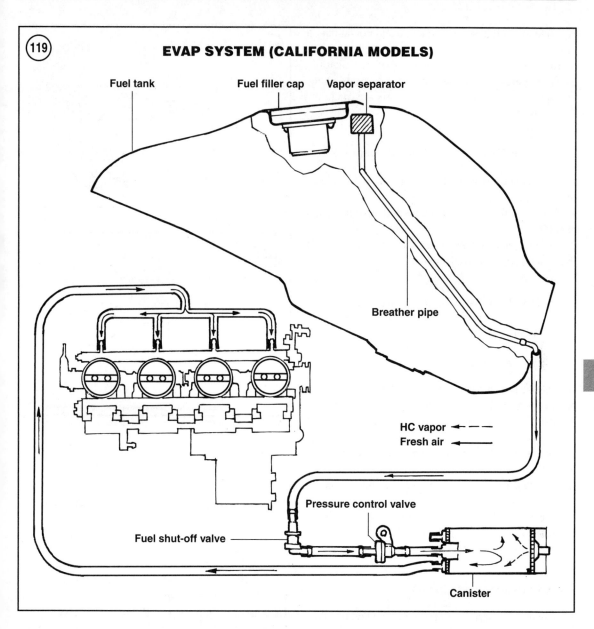

(119)

## EVAP SYSTEM (CALIFORNIA MODELS)

Fuel tank

Fuel filler cap

Vapor separator

Breather pipe

HC vapor

Fresh air

Pressure control valve

Fuel shut-off valve

Canister

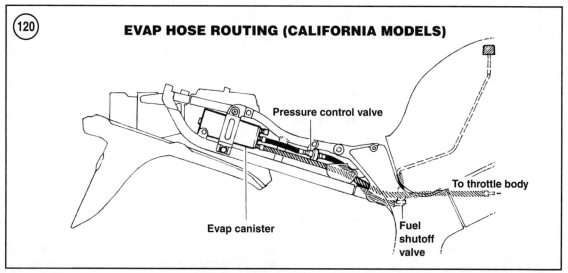

(120)

## EVAP HOSE ROUTING (CALIFORNIA MODELS)

Pressure control valve

To throttle body

Evap canister

Fuel shutoff valve

8

3. Make sure all hoses are attached and not damaged or pinched.

4. Replace any worn or damaged part immediately.

5. When purchasing replacement parts (throttle bodies and fuel tank), make sure the parts are made for California models.

### Fuel Shutoff Valve Removal/Installation

The fuel shutoff valve is beneath the right side of the fuel tank.

1. Raise and support the fuel tank as described in this chapter.

2. Remove any clamps. Then label and disconnect the hose(s) from the fuel shutoff valve.

> *NOTE*
> *The shutoff valve is directional. Note that the larger side of the valve sits below the clamp (**Figure 121**). The shutoff valve must be reinstalled with this same orientation.*

3. Release the clamp securing the shutoff valve, and remove it from the motorcycle.

4. Install by reversing these removal steps. Note the following:

    a. Hoses must be reinstalled onto the correct fitting.

    b. Install the shutoff valve so it is positioned as noted during removal.

    c. Connect the canister and tank hose to their respective fittings on the valve.

    d. Secure each hose with a clamp.

### Canister Removal/Installation

1. Securely support the motorcycle on a level surface with the rear wheel off the ground.

2. Remove the tail piece as described in Chapter Fifteen.

> *NOTE*
> *The charcoal canister mounts on the right side of the rear frame member.*

3. Remove the mounting bolt and lower the charcoal canister from the mount.

4. Label and disconnect the EVAP hoses from the fittings on the canister.

5. Release the clamp and lower the canister from the frame.

6. Install by reversing these removal steps. Note the following:

    a. Connect each hose to the correct fitting on the EVAP canister.

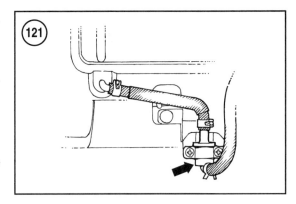

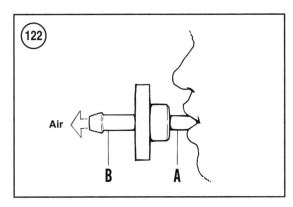

    b. Fit the charcoal canister into the frame mount.

    c. Tighten the mounting bolts securely.

### Pressure Control Valve Removal/Installation

1. Remove the tail piece (Chapter Fifteen).

2. The pressure control valve connects to the surge hose, inline between the fuel tank and the canister. Locate the valve on the surge hose.

3. Label and remove the hoses from the fittings on the pressure control valve. Remove the valve.

4. Test the pressure control valve by performing the following:

    a. Blow into the A side of the valve as shown in **Figure 122**. Air should flow out of the B port on the opposite end.

    b. Reverse the valve and blow into the B side. Air should not flow out of the A port.

    c. Replace the valve if it fails either portion of this test.

5. Installation is the reverse of removal. Install the valve so the A side faces the canister.

### PAIR (AIR SUPPLY) SYSTEM

The PAIR, or pulsed air injection, system lowers emissions by introducing fresh air into the exhaust ports. The PAIR system consists of a PAIR control

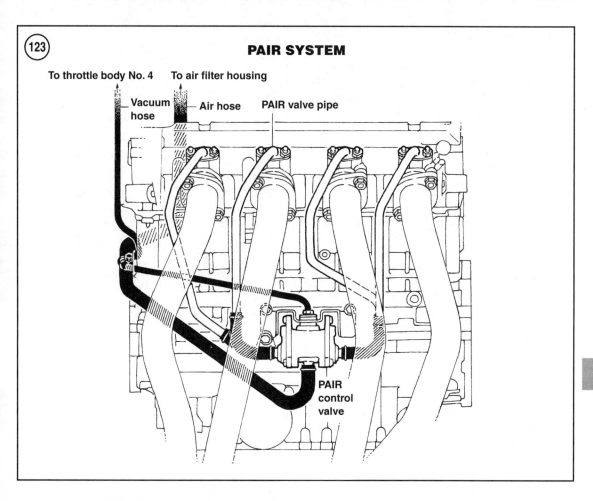

**PAIR SYSTEM**

To throttle body No. 4    To air filter housing

Vacuum hose — Air hose    PAIR valve pipe

PAIR control valve

valve, two reed valves, a vacuum hose, air hose and outlet hoses and pipes (**Figure 123**). The system does not pressurize air, but uses the momentary pressure variations created by exhaust gas pulses to introduce fresh air into the exhaust ports.

**PAIR Control Valve**
**Removal/Inspection/Installation**

1. Remove the exhaust pipes as described in this chapter.
2. Disconnect the vacuum hose (A, **Figure 124**) from the upper fitting on the PAIR control valve.
3. Disconnect the air hose (B, **Figure 124**) from the lower fitting of the PAIR control valve.
4. Disconnect each hose (C, **Figure 124**) from each reed valve cover. Label each hose and its fitting on the cover. The hoses must be reconnected to the proper fitting.
5. Remove the PAIR bracket bolts (D, **Figure 124**), and lower the bracket and PAIR control valve from the crankcase.
6. Remove the bolt(s) (A, **Figure 125**), and then separate the valve from its bracket.

7. Inspect the PAIR control valve by performing the following:

    a. Blow air into the air inlet port on the bottom of the control valve (**Figure 126**).

    b. Air should flow from the each outlet port. Replace the control valve if it does not.

    c. Connect a vacuum pump to the vacuum fitting on the top of the control valve. Refer to **Figure 127**.

*CAUTION*
*Vacuum pressure applied in the following step should not exceed the value specified in **Table 1**. The control valve could be damaged if excessive vacuum is applied.*

    d. Slowly apply vacuum to the control valve until the vacuum pressure equals the PAIR control valve vacuum specified in **Table 1**.

    e. Blow into the control valve inlet port. Air should not flow from the outlet ports when the applied vacuum equals specification.

    f. Replace the PAIR control valve if it fails either portion of this test.

8. If necessary, remove each PAIR valve pipe nut (A, **Figure 128**) and lower the pipe (B) from the cylinder head. Discard the PAIR valve pipe gasket. A new one must be installed during assembly.

9. Installation is the reverse of removal. Connect each hose to the proper fitting.

10. If the PAIR valve pipes were removed, install them by performing the following:

    a. Connect each PAIR valve pipe (B, **Figure 128**) to its fitting on the cylinder head. Install a new gasket with each pipe.

    b. Tighten each PAIR valve pipe nut (A, **Figure 128**) to 10 N•m (89 in.-lb.).

## Reed Valve
## Removal/Inspection/Installation

1. Remove the PAIR control valve.

2. Remove the cover bolts (B, **Figure 125**) from the reed valve cover.

3. Carefully lift the cover from the PAIR control valve.

4. Inspect the reed valve (**Figure 129**) for carbon deposits.

    a. Replace the reed valve if deposits are found.

    b. Note how the reed valve is installed, and then carefully pry it from the PAIR control valve.

5. Installation is the reverse of removal. Make sure each hose is reconnected to its original port on the control valve.

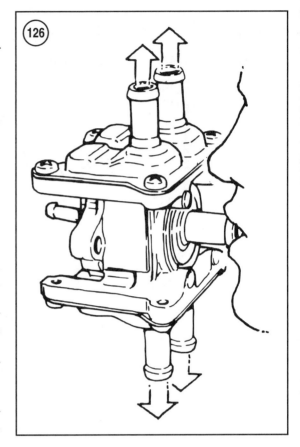

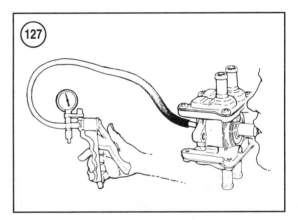

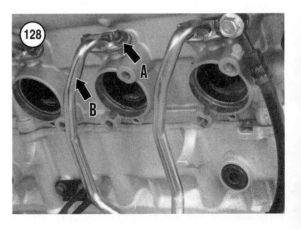

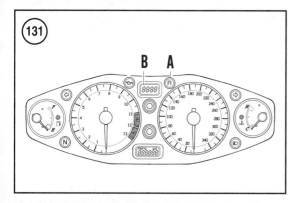

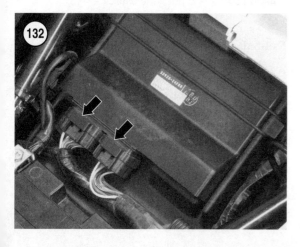

## CRANKCASE BREATHER

On 1999 models, the crankcase breather hose connects to the oil catch tank. On all other models, the breather hose connects to the air filter housing.

1. Raise and support the fuel tank (this chapter). If necessary, remove the air filter housing.
2. Disconnect the crankcase breather hose from the fitting (A, **Figure 130**) on the breather cover.
3. Remove the cover bolts (B, **Figure 130**), and lift the crankcase breather cover from the crankcase. Discard the gasket. A new gasket must be installed during assembly.
4. Installation is the reverse of removal.

## DIAGNOSTIC SYSTEM

The self-diagnostic electronic control module (ECM) monitors the fuel injection and ignition system sensors and actuators. If an error is detected in a system component, the ECM records the malfunction and sets a malfunction code. Malfunction codes can be retrieved by entering the dealer mode.

If a malfunction code is set, the system uses the FI LED (A, **Figure 131**) and the clock/FI LCD (B) in the meter assembly to alert the rider. If the FI LED turns on and the LCD alternates between FI and the clock display, an error is detected, and the engine operates in fail-safe mode. If the FI LED flashes and FI remains in the clock/FI LCD, an error that disables the engine has occurred.

The meter assembly also indicates if no signal is received from the ECM. CHEC appears in the clock/FI LCD (B, **Figure 131**) when the meter assembly does not receive a signal from the ECM within 5 seconds after the ignition switch is turned on. The engine will not operate if CHEC is displayed.

Note that CHEC indicates a communication problem, not a malfunction in the fuel injection system. No malfunction code is set. Make sure the engine stop switch is in the run position and that the meter assembly connector is properly engaged. Also check the wiring between the ECM and meter assembly. If these items are in proper working order, then check for a faulty engine stop switch, a malfunction in the starting interlock system or a damaged ignition fuse.

### ECM Connectors

Some wiring colors are used more than once in the 34-pin and 26-pin ECM connectors (**Figure 132**). To ensure the correct wire is tested, the test procedures include the wire color and pin location to describe a

8

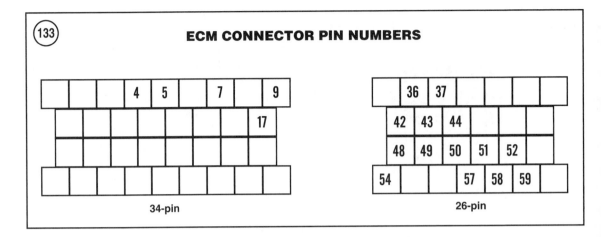

test point. The number in parentheses after the wiring color refers to the pin number. Refer to **Figure 133** to determine the terminal location in the relevant ECM connector.

A number of troubleshooting tests also require back probing a connector. Always back probe the harness side of a connector with a probe pin that is 0.5 mm (0.02 in.) in diameter or less. Refer to *Back Probing a Connector* in Chapter Two.

### Dealer Mode

When the system is shifted into the dealer mode, any stored malfunction code is displayed in the clock/FI LCD (B, **Figure 131**) portion of the meter assembly.

The mode select switch (Suzuki part No. 09930-82710) is needed to enter the dealer mode.

*CAUTION*
*Do not perform this procedure without the mode select switch. Shorting the terminals in the dealer mode connector could damage the ECM.*

1. Remove the passenger seat as described in Chapter Fifteen.

2. Connect the mode select switch (**Figure 134**) to the dealer mode connector on the frame rail.

3. Run the engine for 4 seconds. If the engine does not start, crank the engine for 4 seconds.

4. After 4 seconds, turn the mode select switch on. The system enters the dealer mode and displays a stored malfunction code(s) in the clock/FI LCD (B, **Figure 131**). If more than one code is stored, codes are displayed in numeric order starting with the lowest numbered code. Each code is displayed for 2 seconds.

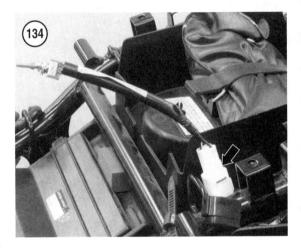

*NOTE*
*Record any malfunction codes before disconnecting the ECM connectors, the ECM ground wire from the wiring harness or engine, the electrical leads from the battery or before pulling the main fuse. Any of these actions erases the malfunction code(s) from memory.*

5. Record the codes. Refer to **Figure 135** for malfunction codes and probable causes.

### Fail-Safe Operation

For some malfunctions, the ECM establishes a preset value for the input so the motorcycle can still operate. This fail-safe operation gives a rider the opportunity to get home or to a service shop. Refer to **Figure 136** to determine if a malfunction code has a fail-safe operation.

If the motorcycle continues to run with a malfunction code stored, troubleshoot the system and eliminate the problem immediately. If the problem cannot be solved, take the motorcycle to a dealership.

# MALFUNCTION CODES

| Malfunction Code | Related Item | Detected Failure | Probable Cause |
|---|---|---|---|
| c00 | No error | – | – |
| c11 | Camshaft position sensor | The ECM does not receive a signal from the camshaft position sensor 2 seconds after it received the start signal. | Faulty camshaft position sensor, intake cam pin, sensor wiring and/or connector. |
| c12 | Crankshaft position sensor | The ECM does not receive a signal from the crankshaft position sensor 2 seconds after it received the start signal. | Faulty crankshaft position sensor, wiring or connector. |
| c13 | Intake air pressure sensor | The sensor's voltage is outside the range of 0.5-4.5 volts. | Faulty intake air pressure sensor, wiring or connector. |
| c14 | Throttle position sensor | The sensor's voltage is outside the range of 0.2-4.8 volts. | Faulty throttle position sensor, wiring or connector. |
| c15 | Engine coolant temperature sensor | The sensor's voltage is outside the range of 0.15-4.85 volts. | Faulty engine coolant temperature sensor, wiring or connector. |
| c21 | Intake air temperature sensor | The sensor's voltage is outside the range of 0.15-4.85 volts. | Faulty intake air temperature sensor, wiring or connector. |
| c22 | Atmospheric pressure sensor | The sensor's voltage is outside the range of 0.5-4.85 volts. | Faulty atmospheric pressure sensor, wiring or connector. |
| c23 | Tip over sensor | Three seconds after the ignition switch has been turned on, the sensor's voltage is less than 4.85 volts. | Faulty tip over sensor, wiring or connector. |
| c24 (No. 1), c25 (No. 2), c26 (No. 3), or c27 (No. 4) | Ignition system malfunction | The ECM does not receive a proper signal from an ignition coil. | Faulty ignition coil, wiring or connector. Faulty power supply from the battery. |
| c31 | Gear position signal | The gear position sensor's voltage is less than 0.6 volts for 3 or more seconds. | Faulty gear position sensor, wiring, connector or faulty shift cam. |
| c32 (No. 1), c33 (No. 2), c34 (No. 3), or c35 (No. 4) | Fuel injector | The ECM does not receive a proper signal from the fuel injector. | Faulty fuel injector, wiring or connector. Faulty power supply to the injector. |
| c41 | Fuel pump relay | The ECM does not receive a signal from the fuel pump relay. | Faulty fuel pump relay, wiring or connector. Faulty power supply to the fuel pump relay or injectors. |

(continued)

(135)

## MALFUNCTION CODES (CONTINUED)

| c42 | Ignition switch signal (antitheft) | The ECM does not receive a signal from the ignition switch. | Faulty ignition switch, wiring or connector. |
|-----|------------------------------------|-------------------------------------------------------------|-----------------------------------------------|
| c92 | Fuel lever sender | The ECM does not receive a signal from the fuel level sender. | Faulty fuel level sender, wiring or connector. |

(136)

## FAIL-SAFE ACTION

| Failed Item | Fail-safe Action* | Operation Status |
|-------------|-------------------|------------------|
| Camshaft position sensor. | The ECM defaults to the cylinder identification data noted before the failure. | Engine continues operating; cannot restart. |
| Crankshaft position sensor. | The motorcycle stops. | Engine stops operating; cannot restart. |
| Intake air pressure sensor. | Intake air pressure is set to 760 mm Hg (29.92 in. Hg). | Engine continues operating; can restart. |
| Throttle position sensor. | Throttle valve is set to its fully open position. Ignition timing is set to a present value. | Engine continues operating; can restart. |
| Enginge coolant temperature sensor. | Engine coolant temperature is set to 176° F (80° C). | Engine continues operating; can restart. |
| Intake air temperature sensor. | Intake air temperature is set to 104° F (40° C). | Engine continues operating; can restart. |
| Atmospheric pressure sensor. | Atmospheric pressure sensor is set to 760 mm Hg (29.92 in. Hg). | Engine continues operating; can restart. |
| Ignition signal, cylinder No. 1. | No spark at cylinder No. 1. | Cylinder Nos. 2, 3 and 4 continue operating; can restart. |
| Ignition signal; cylinder No. 2. | No spark at cylinder No. 2. | Cylinder Nos. 1, 3 and 4 continue operating; can restart. |
| Ignition signal; cylinder No. 3. | No spark at cylinder No. 3. | Cylinder Nos. 1, 2 and 4 continue operating; can restart. |
| Ignition signal; cylinder No. 4. | No spark at cylinder No. 4. | Cylinder Nos. 1, 2 and 3 continue operating; can restart. |
| Fuel injector No. 1. | Fuel cut off to injector No. 1. | Cylinder Nos. 2, 3 and 4 continue operating; can restart. |
| Fuel injector No. 2. | Fuel cut off to injector No. 2. | Cylinder Nos. 1, 3 and 4 continue operating; can restart. |
| Fuel injector No. 3. | Fuel cut off to injector No. 3. | Cylinder Nos. 1, 2 and 4 continue operating; can restart. |

(continued)

## FAIL-SAFE ACTION (CONTINUED)

| Fuel injector No. 4. | Fuel cut off to injector No. 4. | Cylinder Nos. 1, 2 and 3 continue operating; can restart. |
| Gear position signal. | Gear position signal set to sixth gear. | Engine continues operating; can restart. |

*The engine will not run or restart if two ignition codes or two fuel injector codes are set.

## ⒀⑦ TROUBLESHOOTING CHART

| Malfunction Code | Diagnostic Flow Chart |
| --- | --- |
| c00 | No fault detected |
| c11 | Figure 138 |
| c12 | Figure 139 |
| c13 | Figure 140 |
| c14 | Figure 141 |
| c15 | Figure 142 |
| c21 | Figure 143 |
| c22 | Figure 144 |
| c23 | Figure 145 |
| c24, c25, c26 or c27 | Figure 146 |
| c31 | Figure 147 |
| c32, c33, c34 or c35 | Figure 148 |
| c41 | Figure 149 |
| c42 | Figure 150 |
| c92 | Figure 151 |

### Troubleshooting

Perform the following to troubleshoot a problem with the fuel injection and ignition systems.

1. Enter the dealer mode as described in this section.
2. Record any displayed malfunction code(s).
3. Refer to **Figure 137**, and identify the relevant diagnostic flow chart (**Figures 138-151**) for each malfunction code.
4. Perform the test procedures in order until the problem is resolved.
5. Once a fault has been corrected, reset the self-diagnostic system as described in this section.

### Resetting

Perform the following to reset the system once a fuel injection/ignition system malfunction has been corrected.

1. While in the dealer mode, turn the ignition switch off and then back on.
2. The clock/FI LCD (B, **Figure 131**) should display the no fault code: c00.
3. Turn the dealer mode switch off (**Figure 134**), and disconnect the switch from the dealer mode connector.
4. Reinstall the seat.

**Figures 138-151 are on the following pages.**

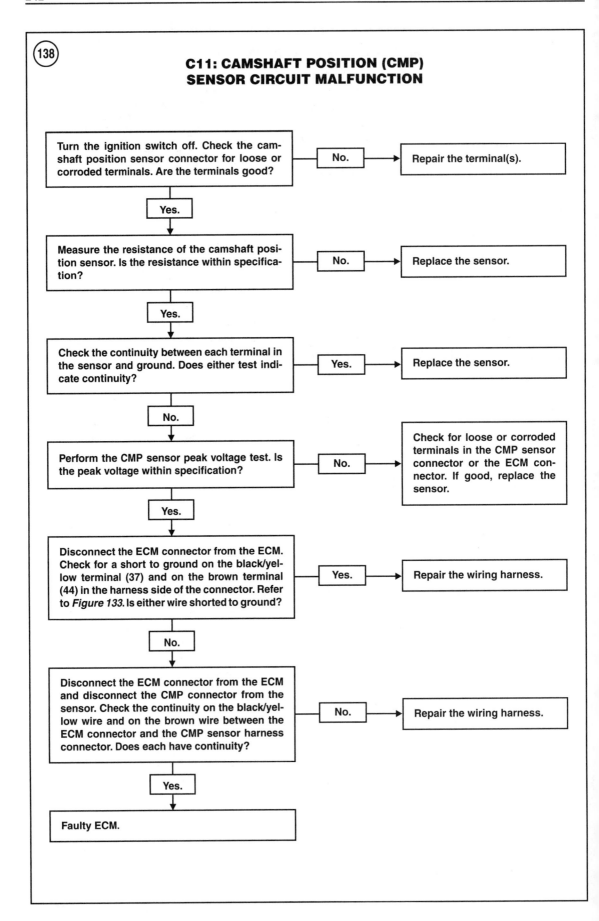

(138)

## C11: CAMSHAFT POSITION (CMP) SENSOR CIRCUIT MALFUNCTION

Turn the ignition switch off. Check the camshaft position sensor connector for loose or corroded terminals. Are the terminals good? → No. → Repair the terminal(s).

Yes. ↓

Measure the resistance of the camshaft position sensor. Is the resistance within specification? → No. → Replace the sensor.

Yes. ↓

Check the continuity between each terminal in the sensor and ground. Does either test indicate continuity? → Yes. → Replace the sensor.

No. ↓

Perform the CMP sensor peak voltage test. Is the peak voltage within specification? → No. → Check for loose or corroded terminals in the CMP sensor connector or the ECM connector. If good, replace the sensor.

Yes. ↓

Disconnect the ECM connector from the ECM. Check for a short to ground on the black/yellow terminal (37) and on the brown terminal (44) in the harness side of the connector. Refer to *Figure 133.* Is either wire shorted to ground? → Yes. → Repair the wiring harness.

No. ↓

Disconnect the ECM connector from the ECM and disconnect the CMP connector from the sensor. Check the continuity on the black/yellow wire and on the brown wire between the ECM connector and the CMP sensor harness connector. Does each have continuity? → No. → Repair the wiring harness.

Yes. ↓

Faulty ECM.

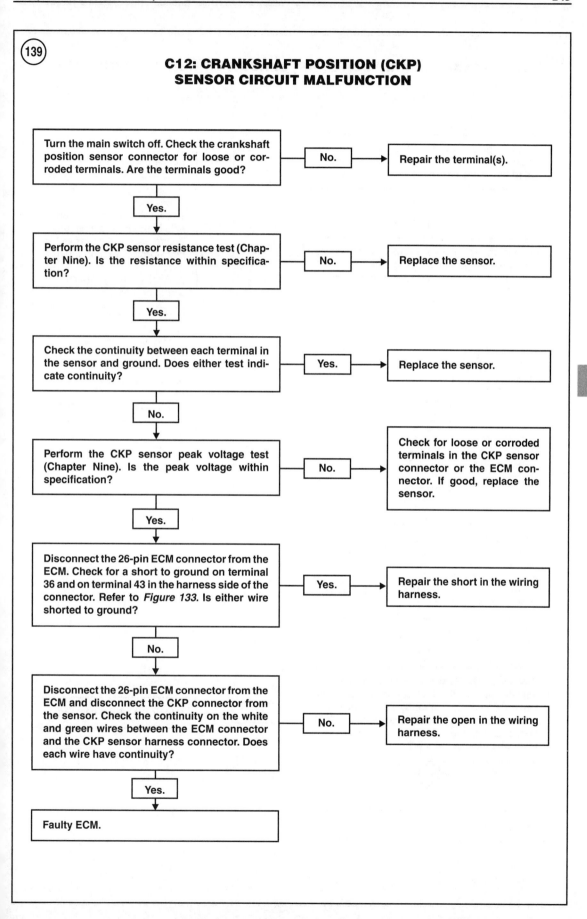

(139)

## C12: CRANKSHAFT POSITION (CKP)
## SENSOR CIRCUIT MALFUNCTION

Turn the main switch off. Check the crankshaft position sensor connector for loose or corroded terminals. Are the terminals good? — **No.** → Repair the terminal(s).

**Yes.**

Perform the CKP sensor resistance test (Chapter Nine). Is the resistance within specification? — **No.** → Replace the sensor.

**Yes.**

Check the continuity between each terminal in the sensor and ground. Does either test indicate continuity? — **Yes.** → Replace the sensor.

**No.**

Perform the CKP sensor peak voltage test (Chapter Nine). Is the peak voltage within specification? — **No.** → Check for loose or corroded terminals in the CKP sensor connector or the ECM connector. If good, replace the sensor.

**Yes.**

Disconnect the 26-pin ECM connector from the ECM. Check for a short to ground on terminal 36 and on terminal 43 in the harness side of the connector. Refer to *Figure 133*. Is either wire shorted to ground? — **Yes.** → Repair the short in the wiring harness.

**No.**

Disconnect the 26-pin ECM connector from the ECM and disconnect the CKP connector from the sensor. Check the continuity on the white and green wires between the ECM connector and the CKP sensor harness connector. Does each wire have continuity? — **No.** → Repair the open in the wiring harness.

**Yes.**

Faulty ECM.

8

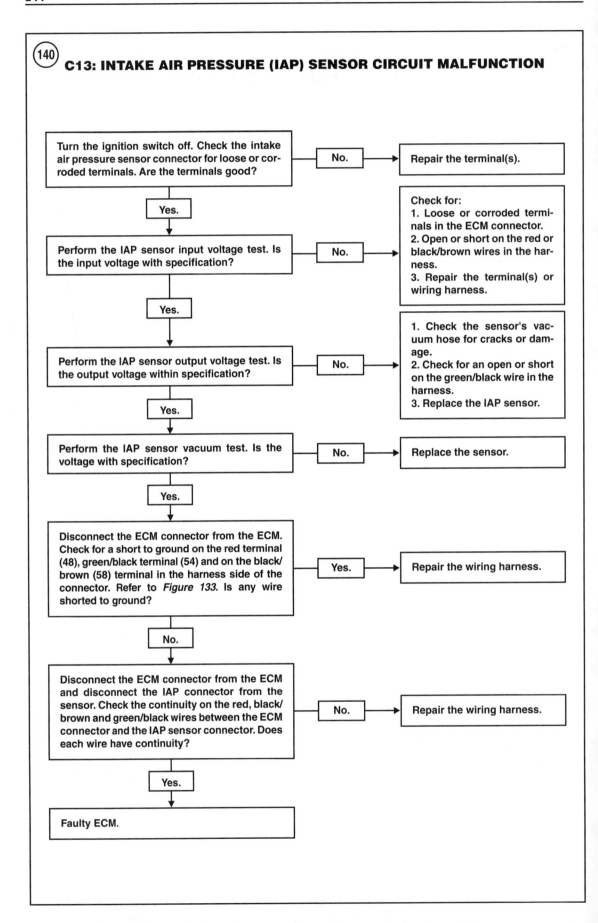

**140** **C13: INTAKE AIR PRESSURE (IAP) SENSOR CIRCUIT MALFUNCTION**

Turn the ignition switch off. Check the intake air pressure sensor connector for loose or corroded terminals. Are the terminals good?

→ No. → Repair the terminal(s).

↓ Yes.

Perform the IAP sensor input voltage test. Is the input voltage with specification?

→ No. → Check for:
1. Loose or corroded terminals in the ECM connector.
2. Open or short on the red or black/brown wires in the harness.
3. Repair the terminal(s) or wiring harness.

↓ Yes.

Perform the IAP sensor output voltage test. Is the output voltage within specification?

→ No. → 1. Check the sensor's vacuum hose for cracks or damage.
2. Check for an open or short on the green/black wire in the harness.
3. Replace the IAP sensor.

↓ Yes.

Perform the IAP sensor vacuum test. Is the voltage with specification?

→ No. → Replace the sensor.

↓ Yes.

Disconnect the ECM connector from the ECM. Check for a short to ground on the red terminal (48), green/black terminal (54) and on the black/brown (58) terminal in the harness side of the connector. Refer to *Figure 133.* Is any wire shorted to ground?

→ Yes. → Repair the wiring harness.

↓ No.

Disconnect the ECM connector from the ECM and disconnect the IAP connector from the sensor. Check the continuity on the red, black/brown and green/black wires between the ECM connector and the IAP sensor connector. Does each wire have continuity?

→ No. → Repair the wiring harness.

↓ Yes.

Faulty ECM.

(141)

# C14: THROTTLE POSITION (TP) SENSOR CIRCUIT MALFUNCTION

| | | |
|---|---|---|
| Turn the main switch off. Check the throttle position sensor connector for loose or corroded terminals. Are the terminals good? | No. → | Repair the terminal(s). |

Yes. ↓

| | | |
|---|---|---|
| Perform the TP sensor input voltage test. Is the voltage within specification? | No. → | 1. Check for loose or corroded terminals in the ECM connector.<br>2. Check for an open or short on the blue or black.brown wires in the harness<br>3. Repair the terminal(s) or wiring harness. |

Yes. ↓

| | | |
|---|---|---|
| Perform the TP sensor continuity test and the TP sensor resistance test. Are both continuity and resistance within specification? | No. → | 1. Readjust the throttle position sensor (this chapter).<br>2. Replace the sensor. |

Yes. ↓

| | | |
|---|---|---|
| Perform the TP sensor output voltage test. Is the voltage within specification? | No. → | Replace the throttle position sensor. |

Yes. ↓

| | | |
|---|---|---|
| Disconnect the ECM connector from the ECM. Check for a short to ground on the red (48), pink/black (49) and on the black/brown (54) terminals in the harness side of the connector. Refer to *Figure 133*. Is any wire shorted to ground? | Yes. → | Repair the wiring harness. |

No. ↓

| | | |
|---|---|---|
| Disconnect the ECM connector and the throttle body subharness connector. Check the continuity on the red, pink/black and black/brown wires between the ECM connector and the subharness connector. Does each wire have continuity? | No. → | Repair the wiring. |

Yes. ↓

(continued)

8

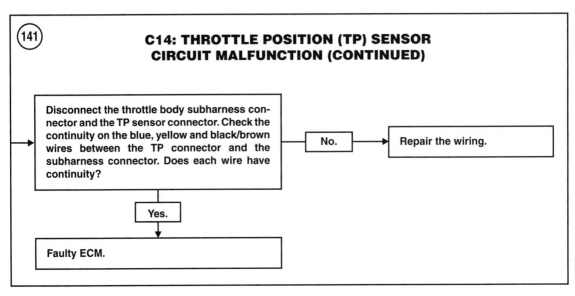

## C14: THROTTLE POSITION (TP) SENSOR
## CIRCUIT MALFUNCTION (CONTINUED)

(141)

Disconnect the throttle body subharness connector and the TP sensor connector. Check the continuity on the blue, yellow and black/brown wires between the TP connector and the subharness connector. Does each wire have continuity?

**No.** → Repair the wiring.

**Yes.**

Faulty ECM.

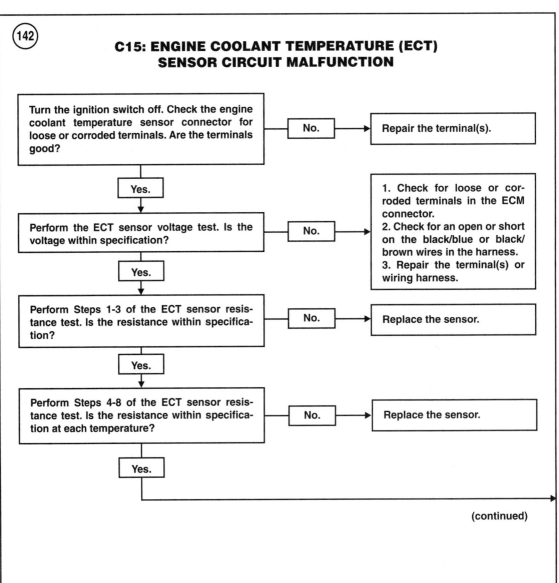

## C15: ENGINE COOLANT TEMPERATURE (ECT)
## SENSOR CIRCUIT MALFUNCTION

(142)

Turn the ignition switch off. Check the engine coolant temperature sensor connector for loose or corroded terminals. Are the terminals good?

**No.** → Repair the terminal(s).

**Yes.**

Perform the ECT sensor voltage test. Is the voltage within specification?

**No.** →
1. Check for loose or corroded terminals in the ECM connector.
2. Check for an open or short on the black/blue or black/brown wires in the harness.
3. Repair the terminal(s) or wiring harness.

**Yes.**

Perform Steps 1-3 of the ECT sensor resistance test. Is the resistance within specification?

**No.** → Replace the sensor.

**Yes.**

Perform Steps 4-8 of the ECT sensor resistance test. Is the resistance within specification at each temperature?

**No.** → Replace the sensor.

**Yes.**

(continued)

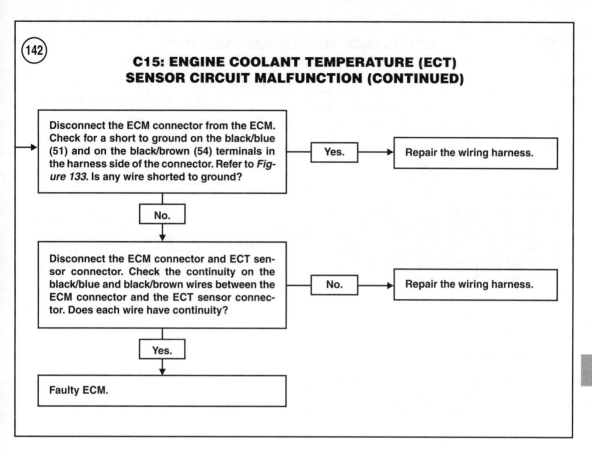

**(142)**

## C15: ENGINE COOLANT TEMPERATURE (ECT) SENSOR CIRCUIT MALFUNCTION (CONTINUED)

Disconnect the ECM connector from the ECM. Check for a short to ground on the black/blue (51) and on the black/brown (54) terminals in the harness side of the connector. Refer to *Figure 133*. Is any wire shorted to ground? → Yes. → Repair the wiring harness.

No.

Disconnect the ECM connector and ECT sensor connector. Check the continuity on the black/blue and black/brown wires between the ECM connector and the ECT sensor connector. Does each wire have continuity? → No. → Repair the wiring harness.

Yes.

Faulty ECM.

8

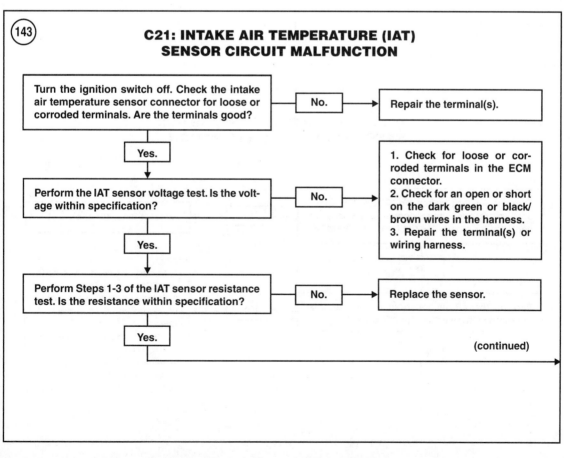

**(143)**

## C21: INTAKE AIR TEMPERATURE (IAT) SENSOR CIRCUIT MALFUNCTION

Turn the ignition switch off. Check the intake air temperature sensor connector for loose or corroded terminals. Are the terminals good? → No. → Repair the terminal(s).

Yes.

Perform the IAT sensor voltage test. Is the voltage within specification? → No. →
1. Check for loose or corroded terminals in the ECM connector.
2. Check for an open or short on the dark green or black/brown wires in the harness.
3. Repair the terminal(s) or wiring harness.

Yes.

Perform Steps 1-3 of the IAT sensor resistance test. Is the resistance within specification? → No. → Replace the sensor.

Yes.

(continued)

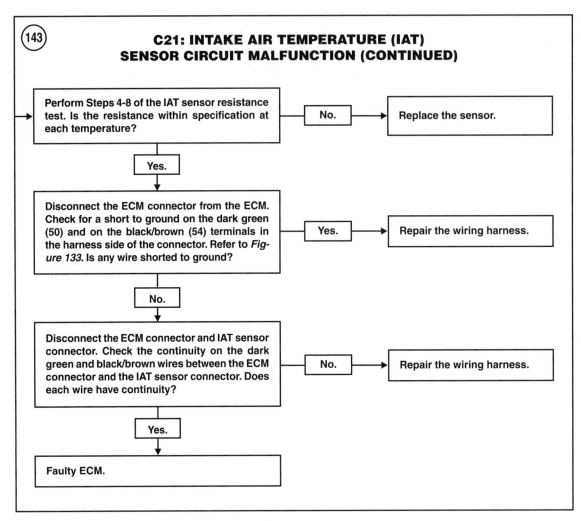

(143)

## C21: INTAKE AIR TEMPERATURE (IAT)
## SENSOR CIRCUIT MALFUNCTION (CONTINUED)

Perform Steps 4-8 of the IAT sensor resistance test. Is the resistance within specification at each temperature? → No. → Replace the sensor.

Yes. ↓

Disconnect the ECM connector from the ECM. Check for a short to ground on the dark green (50) and on the black/brown (54) terminals in the harness side of the connector. Refer to *Figure 133*. Is any wire shorted to ground? → Yes. → Repair the wiring harness.

No. ↓

Disconnect the ECM connector and IAT sensor connector. Check the continuity on the dark green and black/brown wires between the ECM connector and the IAT sensor connector. Does each wire have continuity? → No. → Repair the wiring harness.

Yes. ↓

Faulty ECM.

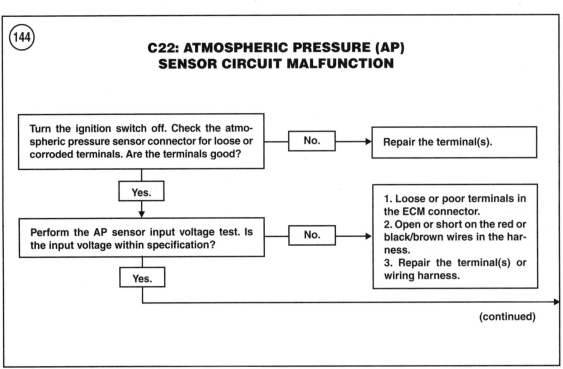

(144)

## C22: ATMOSPHERIC PRESSURE (AP)
## SENSOR CIRCUIT MALFUNCTION

Turn the ignition switch off. Check the atmospheric pressure sensor connector for loose or corroded terminals. Are the terminals good? → No. → Repair the terminal(s).

Yes. ↓

Perform the AP sensor input voltage test. Is the input voltage within specification? → No. →
1. Loose or poor terminals in the ECM connector.
2. Open or short on the red or black/brown wires in the harness.
3. Repair the terminal(s) or wiring harness.

Yes. ↓

(continued)

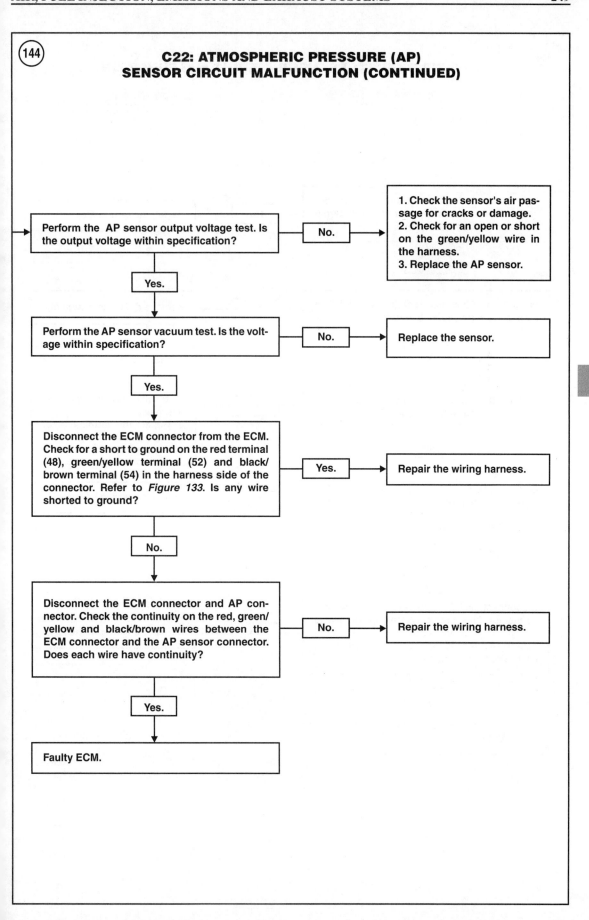

(144)

## C22: ATMOSPHERIC PRESSURE (AP)
## SENSOR CIRCUIT MALFUNCTION (CONTINUED)

Perform the AP sensor output voltage test. Is the output voltage within specification?

No.

1. Check the sensor's air passage for cracks or damage.
2. Check for an open or short on the green/yellow wire in the harness.
3. Replace the AP sensor.

Yes.

Perform the AP sensor vacuum test. Is the voltage within specification?

No.

Replace the sensor.

Yes.

Disconnect the ECM connector from the ECM. Check for a short to ground on the red terminal (48), green/yellow terminal (52) and black/brown terminal (54) in the harness side of the connector. Refer to *Figure 133*. Is any wire shorted to ground?

Yes.

Repair the wiring harness.

No.

Disconnect the ECM connector and AP connector. Check the continuity on the red, green/yellow and black/brown wires between the ECM connector and the AP sensor connector. Does each wire have continuity?

No.

Repair the wiring harness.

Yes.

Faulty ECM.

8

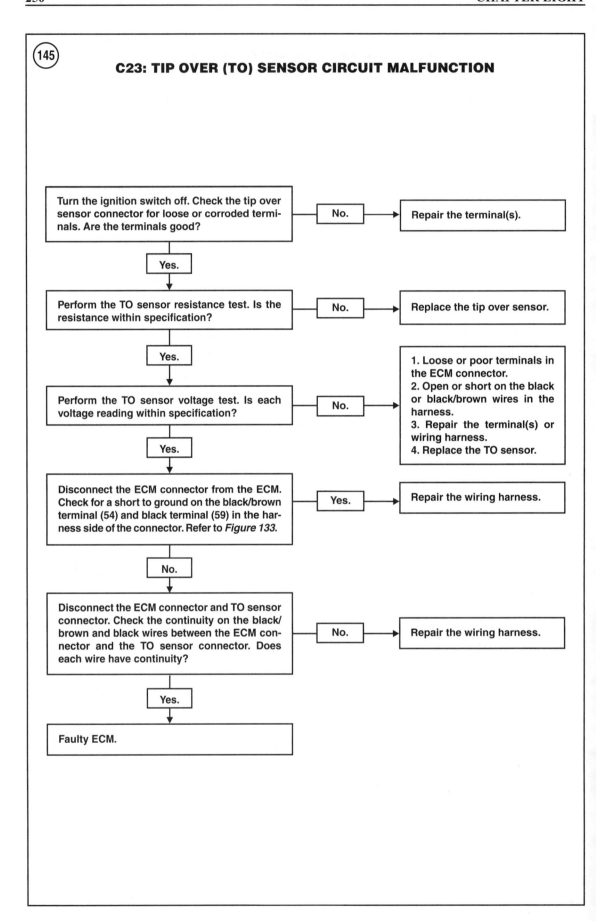

## C23: TIP OVER (TO) SENSOR CIRCUIT MALFUNCTION

Turn the ignition switch off. Check the tip over sensor connector for loose or corroded terminals. Are the terminals good? — **No.** → Repair the terminal(s).

**Yes.**

Perform the TO sensor resistance test. Is the resistance within specification? — **No.** → Replace the tip over sensor.

**Yes.**

Perform the TO sensor voltage test. Is each voltage reading within specification? — **No.** →
1. Loose or poor terminals in the ECM connector.
2. Open or short on the black or black/brown wires in the harness.
3. Repair the terminal(s) or wiring harness.
4. Replace the TO sensor.

**Yes.**

Disconnect the ECM connector from the ECM. Check for a short to ground on the black/brown terminal (54) and black terminal (59) in the harness side of the connector. Refer to *Figure 133*. — **Yes.** → Repair the wiring harness.

**No.**

Disconnect the ECM connector and TO sensor connector. Check the continuity on the black/brown and black wires between the ECM connector and the TO sensor connector. Does each wire have continuity? — **No.** → Repair the wiring harness.

**Yes.**

Faulty ECM.

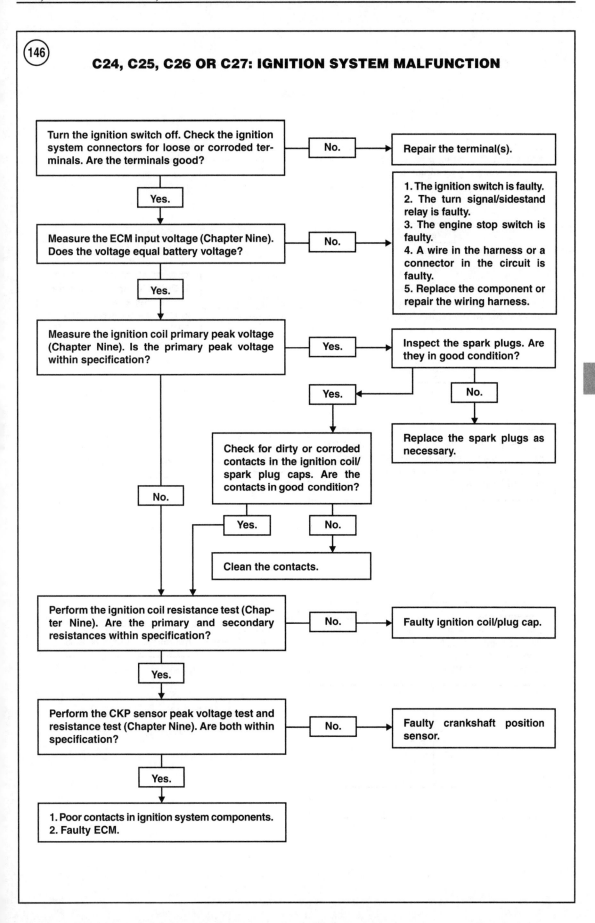

**146**

## C24, C25, C26 OR C27: IGNITION SYSTEM MALFUNCTION

Turn the ignition switch off. Check the ignition system connectors for loose or corroded terminals. Are the terminals good? — **No.** → Repair the terminal(s).

**Yes.**

Measure the ECM input voltage (Chapter Nine). Does the voltage equal battery voltage? — **No.** →
1. The ignition switch is faulty.
2. The turn signal/sidestand relay is faulty.
3. The engine stop switch is faulty.
4. A wire in the harness or a connector in the circuit is faulty.
5. Replace the component or repair the wiring harness.

**Yes.**

Measure the ignition coil primary peak voltage (Chapter Nine). Is the primary peak voltage within specification? — **Yes.** → Inspect the spark plugs. Are they in good condition?

**Yes.** ← **No.**

**No.** (from primary peak voltage)

Replace the spark plugs as necessary.

Check for dirty or corroded contacts in the ignition coil/spark plug caps. Are the contacts in good condition?

**Yes.** / **No.**

Clean the contacts.

Perform the ignition coil resistance test (Chapter Nine). Are the primary and secondary resistances within specification? — **No.** → Faulty ignition coil/plug cap.

**Yes.**

Perform the CKP sensor peak voltage test and resistance test (Chapter Nine). Are both within specification? — **No.** → Faulty crankshaft position sensor.

**Yes.**

1. Poor contacts in ignition system components.
2. Faulty ECM.

**8**

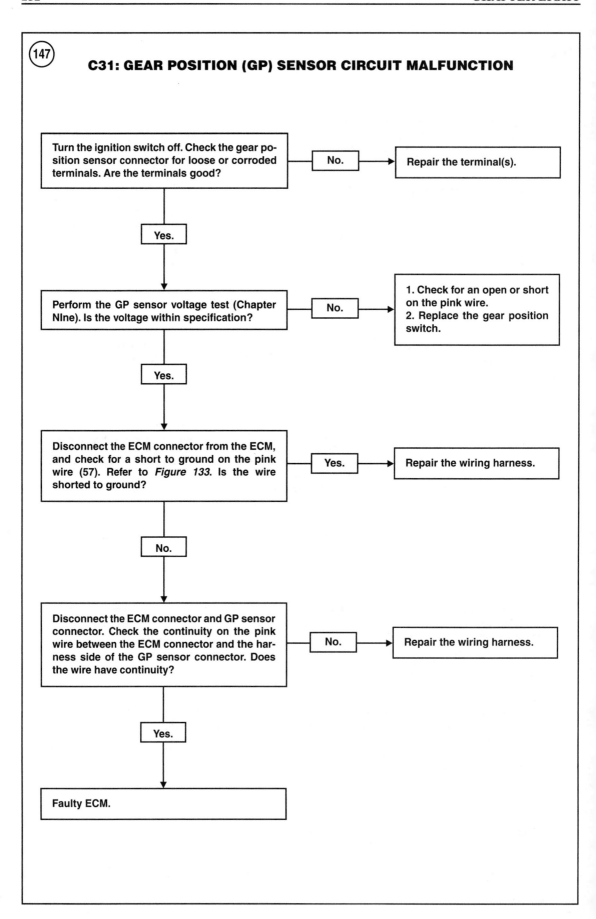

**(147)**

## C31: GEAR POSITION (GP) SENSOR CIRCUIT MALFUNCTION

Turn the ignition switch off. Check the gear position sensor connector for loose or corroded terminals. Are the terminals good? — **No.** → Repair the terminal(s).

**Yes.**

Perform the GP sensor voltage test (Chapter Nine). Is the voltage within specification? — **No.** → 1. Check for an open or short on the pink wire.
2. Replace the gear position switch.

**Yes.**

Disconnect the ECM connector from the ECM, and check for a short to ground on the pink wire (57). Refer to *Figure 133*. Is the wire shorted to ground? — **Yes.** → Repair the wiring harness.

**No.**

Disconnect the ECM connector and GP sensor connector. Check the continuity on the pink wire between the ECM connector and the harness side of the GP sensor connector. Does the wire have continuity? — **No.** → Repair the wiring harness.

**Yes.**

Faulty ECM.

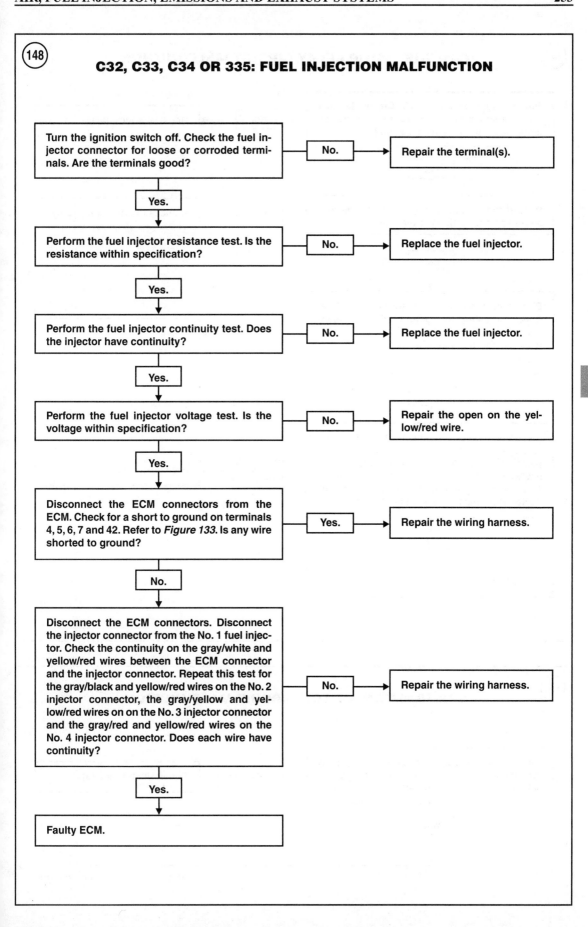

(148)

## C32, C33, C34 OR 335: FUEL INJECTION MALFUNCTION

Turn the ignition switch off. Check the fuel injector connector for loose or corroded terminals. Are the terminals good? → No. → Repair the terminal(s).

Yes.

Perform the fuel injector resistance test. Is the resistance within specification? → No. → Replace the fuel injector.

Yes.

Perform the fuel injector continuity test. Does the injector have continuity? → No. → Replace the fuel injector.

Yes.

Perform the fuel injector voltage test. Is the voltage within specification? → No. → Repair the open on the yellow/red wire.

Yes.

Disconnect the ECM connectors from the ECM. Check for a short to ground on terminals 4, 5, 6, 7 and 42. Refer to *Figure 133.* Is any wire shorted to ground? → Yes. → Repair the wiring harness.

No.

Disconnect the ECM connectors. Disconnect the injector connector from the No. 1 fuel injector. Check the continuity on the gray/white and yellow/red wires between the ECM connector and the injector connector. Repeat this test for the gray/black and yellow/red wires on the No. 2 injector connector, the gray/yellow and yellow/red wires on on the No. 3 injector connector and the gray/red and yellow/red wires on the No. 4 injector connector. Does each wire have continuity? → No. → Repair the wiring harness.

Yes.

Faulty ECM.

8

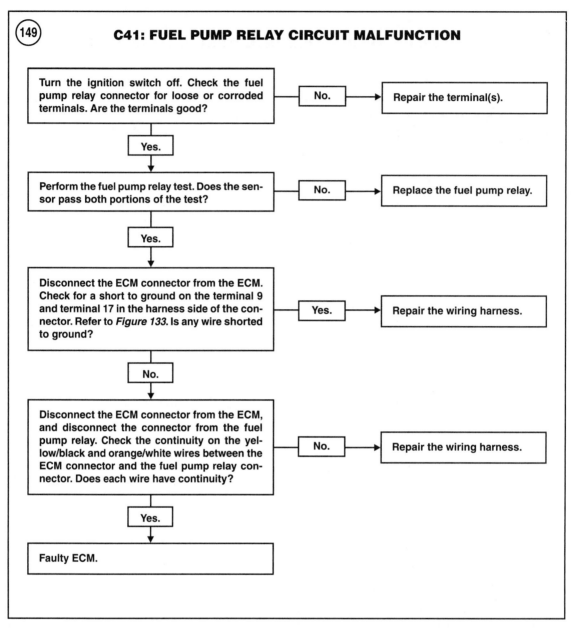

(149)

## C41: FUEL PUMP RELAY CIRCUIT MALFUNCTION

Turn the ignition switch off. Check the fuel pump relay connector for loose or corroded terminals. Are the terminals good? → No. → Repair the terminal(s).

Yes. ↓

Perform the fuel pump relay test. Does the sensor pass both portions of the test? → No. → Replace the fuel pump relay.

Yes. ↓

Disconnect the ECM connector from the ECM. Check for a short to ground on the terminal 9 and terminal 17 in the harness side of the connector. Refer to *Figure 133*. Is any wire shorted to ground? → Yes. → Repair the wiring harness.

No. ↓

Disconnect the ECM connector from the ECM, and disconnect the connector from the fuel pump relay. Check the continuity on the yellow/black and orange/white wires between the ECM connector and the fuel pump relay connector. Does each wire have continuity? → No. → Repair the wiring harness.

Yes. ↓

Faulty ECM.

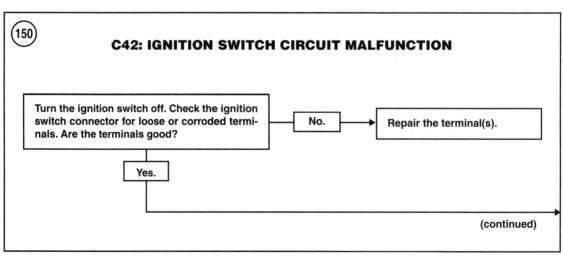

(150)

## C42: IGNITION SWITCH CIRCUIT MALFUNCTION

Turn the ignition switch off. Check the ignition switch connector for loose or corroded terminals. Are the terminals good? → No. → Repair the terminal(s).

Yes. ↓

(continued)

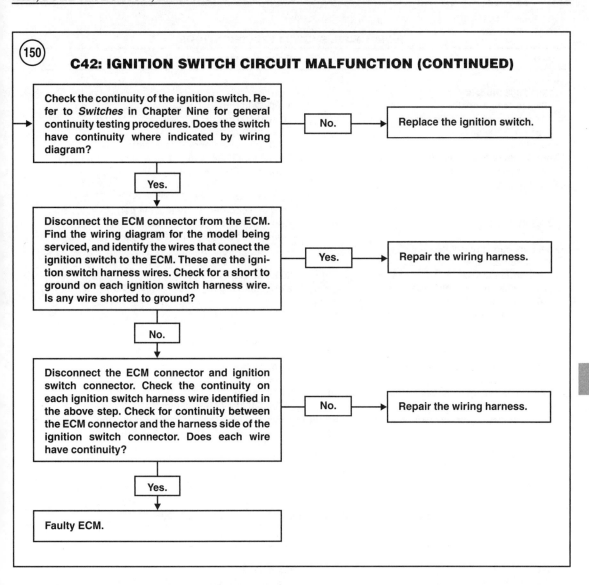

(150)

## C42: IGNITION SWITCH CIRCUIT MALFUNCTION (CONTINUED)

Check the continuity of the ignition switch. Refer to *Switches* in Chapter Nine for general continuity testing procedures. Does the switch have continuity where indicated by wiring diagram?

No. → Replace the ignition switch.

Yes.

Disconnect the ECM connector from the ECM. Find the wiring diagram for the model being serviced, and identify the wires that conect the ignition switch to the ECM. These are the ignition switch harness wires. Check for a short to ground on each ignition switch harness wire. Is any wire shorted to ground?

Yes. → Repair the wiring harness.

No.

Disconnect the ECM connector and ignition switch connector. Check the continuity on each ignition switch harness wire identified in the above step. Check for continuity between the ECM connector and the harness side of the ignition switch connector. Does each wire have continuity?

No. → Repair the wiring harness.

Yes.

Faulty ECM.

8

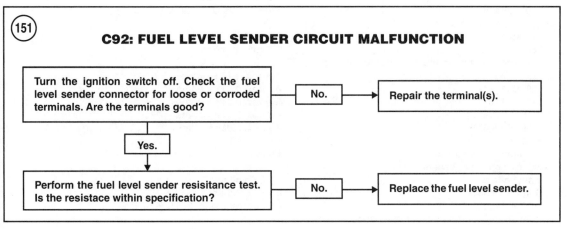

(151)

## C92: FUEL LEVEL SENDER CIRCUIT MALFUNCTION

Turn the ignition switch off. Check the fuel level sender connector for loose or corroded terminals. Are the terminals good?

No. → Repair the terminal(s).

Yes.

Perform the fuel level sender resisitance test. Is the resistace within specification?

No. → Replace the fuel level sender.

**Tables 1-3 are on the following pages.**

## Table 1 FUEL SYSTEM SPECIFICATIONS

| Item | Specification |
| --- | --- |
| Idle speed | |
| 1999-2003 models | |
| Switzerland models | 1100-1200 rpm |
| All models except Switzerland | 1050-1250 rpm |
| 2004-on models | 1050-1250 rpm |
| Fast idle speed | 3500 rpm (when engine is warm) |
| Throttle cable free play | 2.0-4.0 mm (0.08-0.16 in.) |
| Fuel pump output pressure | Approx. 300 kPa (44 psi) |
| Fuel pump output volume | |
| 1999-2000 models | Approx. 458 ml (15.5 U.S. oz.) per 30 seconds @ 300 kPa (44 psi) |
| 2001-on models | Approx. 1200 ml (40.6 U.S. oz.) per 30 seconds @ 300 kPa (44 psi) |
| Fuel tank capacity (total) | |
| 1999-2000 models | |
| California models | 20 L (5.3 U.S. gal. ) |
| All models except California | 22 L (5.8 U.S. gal. ) |
| 2001- models | |
| California models | 19 L (5.0 U.S. gal. ) |
| All models except California | 21 L (5.5 U.S. gal.) |
| Fuel | Unleaded |
| U.S., California, and Canada models | |
| Pump octane - (R +M) / 2 method | 87 or higher |
| Research octane | 91 or higher |
| All models except USA, California and Canada | 91 or higher |
| PAIR control valve vacuum | 44.0-65.3 kPa (330-490 mm Hg) |

## Table 2 FUEL SYSTEM ELECTRICAL SPECIFICATIONS*

| Item | Specification |
| --- | --- |
| Atmospheric pressure sensor | |
| Input voltage | 4.5-5.5 volts |
| Output voltage | Approx. 3.6 volts @ 100 kPa (750 mm Hg) |
| Vout voltage | 4.5-5.0 volts @ 20-30° C (68-86° F) |
| Camshaft position sensor | |
| Resistance | 0.9-1.3 k ohms |
| Peak voltage | 0.7 volts or higher |
| Engine coolant temperature sensor resistance | |
| 20° C (68° F) | Approx. 2.45 k ohms |
| 50° C (122° F) | Approx. 0.811 k ohms |
| 80° C (176° F) | Approx. 0.318 k ohms |
| 110° C (230° F) | Approx. 0.142 k ohms |
| 130° C (266° F) | Approx. 0.088 k ohms |
| Voltage | 4.5-5.5 volts |
| Fuel injector resistance | 11-16 ohms @ 20° C (68° F) |
| Intake air pressure sensor | |
| Input voltage | 4.5-5.5 volts |
| Output voltage | Approx. 2.5 volts @ idle |
| Vout voltage | 4.5-5.0 volts @ 20-30° C (68-86° F) |
| Intake air temperature sensor resistance | |
| 20° C (68° F) | Approx. 2.45 k ohms |
| 50° C (122° F) | Approx. 0.808 k ohms |
| 80° C (176° F) | Approx. 0.322 k ohms |
| 110° C (230° F) | Approx. 0.148 k ohms |
| Voltage | 4.5-5.5 volts |

(continued)

Table 2 FUEL SYSTEM ELECTRICAL SPECIFICATIONS* (continued)

| Item | Specification |
|---|---|
| Oxygen sensor | |
|   Output voltage | 0.4 volts or less @ 1150 rpm (engine warm) |
|   Resistance | 4-5 k ohms @ 23° C (73° F) |
| Throttle position sensor | |
|   Resistance | |
|     Fully closed | Approx. 1.3 k ohms |
|     Fully open | Approx. 4.5 k ohms |
|   Input voltage | 4.5-5.5 volts |
|   Output voltage | |
|     Fully closed | Approx. 1.1 volts |
|     Fully open | Approx. 4.3 volts |
| Tip over sensor | |
|   Resistance | 60-64 k ohms |
|     Upright voltage | Approx. 2.5 volts |
|     Leaning voltage (43°) | 0 volts |
| VCSV resistance | 36-44 ohms |
| Intake air control valve operating rpm | |
|   Open | above 2500 rpm |
|   Close | below 2200 rpm |
| Fuel sender resistance | |
|   Float in full position | 11-13 ohms |
|   Float in half-full position (2001-on models) | 70-77 ohms |
|   Float in empty position | |
|     1999-2000 models | 130-133 ohms |
|     2001-on models | 130-135 ohms |

*k × 1000.

8

Table 3 FUEL AND EXHAUST SYSTEM TORQUE SPECIFICATIONS

| Item | N•m | in.-lb. | ft.-lb. |
|---|---|---|---|
| Camshaft position sensor bolt | 8 | 71 | – |
| Crankshaft position sensor bolt | 8 | 71 | – |
| Engine coolant temperature sensor | 18 | – | 13 |
| Exhaust pipe header bolt | 23 | – | 17 |
| Exhaust pipe hanger bolt | 23 | – | 17 |
| Fuel filter cover screw (1999-2000 models) | 3 | 27 | – |
| Fuel pressure check bolt (1999-2000 models) | 10 | 89 | – |
| Fuel pressure regulator mounting screw | 3 | 27 | – |
| Fuel pump bracket screw (1999-2000 models) | 5 | 44 | – |
| Fuel pump bolts (2001-on models) | 10 | 89 | – |
| Fuel sender bolt (1999 models) | 4 | 35 | – |
| Fuel sender nut (2000 models) | 6 | 53 | – |
| Intake air temperature sensor | 18 | – | 13 |
| Injector holder screw | 5 | 44 | |
| Muffler connecting nut | 25 | – | 18 |
| Muffler hanger bolt/nut | 23 | – | 17 |
| Muffler pipe clamp bolt | 23 | – | 17 |
| PAIR-valve pipe nut | 10 | 89 | – |
| Throttle position sensor screw | | | |
|   2002-on models | 3.5 | 31 | – |

# CHAPTER NINE

# ELECTRICAL SYSTEM

This chapter contains service and test procedures for the electrical system.

Before working on any part of the electrical system, refer to *Electrical System Fundamentals* in Chapter One and *Electrical Testing* in Chapter Two.

The fuel system and cooling system are addressed in Chapter Eight and Chapter Ten respectively. Refer to Chapter Three for spark plug information.

When inspecting electrical components, compare any measurements to the specifications in **Table 1** at the end of this chapter. During assembly, tighten fasteners to the specified torque.

Refer to the appropriate wiring diagram at the end of this manual when working on the electrical system.

## ELECTRICAL COMPONENT REPLACEMENT

Most motorcycle dealerships and parts suppliers do not accept the return of any electrical part. If the exact cause of an electrical system malfunction cannot be determined, have a dealership retest the specific system to verify test results. If a new electrical component is installed and the system still does not work, the unit, in all likelihood, cannot be returned for a refund.

## ELECTRICAL CONNECTORS

To prevent corrosion, pack electrical connectors with dielectric grease when reconnecting them. Dielectric grease does not interfere with current flow, and it seals and waterproofs electrical connectors. Only use this compound or an equivalent sealant designed for electrical use. Other materials may interfere with the current flow. Do not use silicone sealant.

In addition to packing electrical connectors, also regularly check the ground connections. Loose or dirty ground terminals are often the source of electrical problems.

The position of electrical connectors can vary between model years, and a connector may have been repositioned during a previous repair. Refer to the wiring diagram for a particular model. Check the wiring colors to confirm a connector has been correctly identified. Follow the electrical cable from the specific component to where it connects to the wiring harness or to another electrical component.

## BATTERY

A sealed, maintenance-free battery is used on all models. The battery electrolyte cannot be serviced. Never remove the sealing cap from the top of a maintenance-free battery.

When replacing the battery, use a sealed type. Do not install a non-sealed battery.

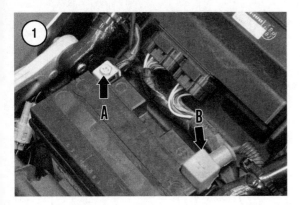

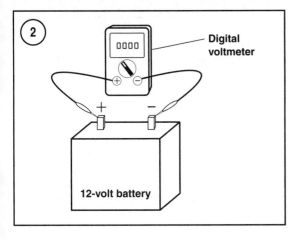

To prevent accidental shorts during electrical service, always disconnect the negative battery cable (A, **Figure 1**) before beginning work.

## Precautions

Observe the following precautions when servicing the battery:

1. Always wear safety glasses when servicing the battery.

2. Do not smoke or permit any open flame near a battery being charged or one that has been recently charged.

3. Do not disconnect active circuits at the battery. A spark usually occurs when a live circuit is broken.

4. When removing the battery, always disconnect the negative battery cable first and then the positive cable.

5. Exercise caution when connecting or disconnecting a battery charger. Turn the power switch off before making or breaking connections.

6. Keep children and pets away from the charging equipment and the battery.

## Removal/Installation

1. Turn the ignition switch off.

2. Remove the rider's seat (Chapter Fifteen).

3. Disconnect the negative battery cable (A, **Figure 1**).

4. Move the red protective cover (B, **Figure 1**), and disconnect the positive cable.

5. Lift the battery from the battery box.

6. Inspect the pads in the battery box for wear or deterioration. Replace any if necessary.

7. Install the battery by reversing the removal steps. Note the following:

    a. Install the battery so that the terminals face rearward. Refer to **Figure 1**.

> *CAUTION*
> *Make sure each battery cable is connected to the correct battery terminal. Connecting the cables backwards reverses the polarity and damages the rectifier and ignition system.*

    b. First connect the positive battery cable (B, **Figure 1**), and then connect the negative cable (A).

    c. Coat the battery connections with dielectric grease.

    d. Install the red protective cap back over the positive terminal.

## Inspection and Testing

1. Remove the battery as described in this section. Do not clean the battery while it is mounted in the frame.

2. Set the battery on a stack of newspapers or shop cloths to protect the workbench surface.

3. Inspect the battery pads in the battery box for contamination or damage. Clean the pads and compartment with a solution of baking soda and water.

4. Check the entire battery case for cracks or other damage. If the battery case is warped, discolored or has a raised top, the battery has been overcharging or overheating.

5. Check the battery terminals and bolts for corrosion or damage. Clean parts thoroughly with a solution of baking soda and water. Replace excessively corroded or damaged parts.

6. If corroded, clean the top of the battery with a stiff bristle brush using the baking soda and water solution.

7. Check the cable terminals for corrosion and damage. If corrosion is minor, clean the cable terminals with a stiff wire brush. Replace excessively worn or damaged cables or terminals.

> *NOTE*
> *Test the battery at 20° C (68° F).*

8. Check the state of charge by connecting a digital voltmeter across the battery terminals (**Figure 2**).

a. The battery is fully charged if voltage equals 13.0-13.2 volts.

b. If the battery voltage is less than 12.5 volts, the battery is undercharged and requires charging.

c. If battery voltage is less than 12.5 volts after charging, replace the battery.

## Charging

A digital voltmeter and a charger with an adjustable amperage output are required when charging a maintenance-free battery. If this equipment is not available, have the battery charged by a shop with the proper equipment. Excessive voltage and amperage from an unregulated charger can damage the battery and shorten its service life.

A battery self-discharges approximately one percent of its capacity each day. If a battery not in use (without any loads connected) loses its charge within a week after charging, the battery is defective.

When a motorcycle is not used for long periods of time, connect it to an automatic battery charger with variable voltage and amperage outputs for optimum battery service life.

1. Remove the battery from the motorcycle as described in this section.

2. Connect the positive charger lead to the positive battery terminal. Connect the negative charger lead to the negative battery terminal.

3. Set the charger to 12 volts. If the output of the charger is variable, it is best to select the low setting. Normally, a battery should be charged at one-tenth of its rated capacity.

*CAUTION*
*Never set the battery charger to more than 4 amps. The battery is damaged if the charge rate exceeds 4 amps.*

4. Turn the charger on. Charging time depends upon the discharged condition of the battery. A battery charging at 1.2 amps takes between 5-10 hours to charge.

5. After the battery has been charged, turn the charger off and disconnect the leads.

6. Wait 30 minutes, and then measure the battery voltage.

a. If the battery voltage equals 13.0-13.2 volts, the battery is fully charged.

b. If the battery voltage is 12.5 volts or less, charge the battery again.

c. If the battery voltage is still 12.5 volts or less after the second charge, replace the battery.

7. If the battery remains stable for one hour, the battery is charged.

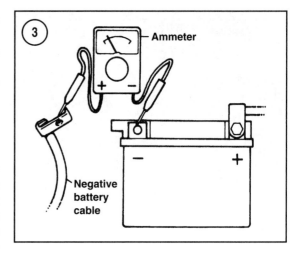

8. Install the battery into the motorcycle as described in this section.

## Battery Initialization

When replacing the old battery, make sure the new battery is charged completely before installing it. Using a new battery without a complete charge causes permanent battery damage. Charging a new battery after it has been used does not bring its charge to 100 percent. When purchasing a new battery, verify its charge status.

*NOTE*
***Recycle the old battery.*** *Most motorcycle dealerships accept an old battery in trade when a new battery is purchased. Never place an old battery in the trash. It is illegal to place any acid or lead contents in landfills.*

## CHARGING SYSTEM

The charging system consists of the battery, alternator and a voltage regulator/rectifier. A 30-amp main fuse protects the circuit.

Alternating current generated by the alternator is rectified to direct current. The voltage regulator maintains the voltage to the battery and additional electrical loads, such as the lights and ignition system, at a constant voltage regardless of variations in engine speed and load.

## Precautions

To prevent damage to the alternator and the regulator/rectifier when servicing the charging system, note the following:

1. Always disconnect the negative battery cable before removing a component from the charging system.

2. When charging the battery, remove it from the motorcycle and follow the charging procedures described in this chapter.

3. Inspect the physical condition of the battery. Look for bulges or cracks in the case, leaking electrolyte or corrosion build-up.

4. Check the wiring in the charging system for signs of chafing, deterioration or other damage.

5. Check the wiring, including ground connections, for corroded or loose connections. Clean, tighten or reconnect as required.

### Troubleshooting

Refer to Chapter Two for troubleshooting procedures. Before troubleshooting the charging system, make sure the battery is fully charged and in good condition. Clean and test the battery as described in this chapter. Make sure all electrical connectors are tight and free of corrosion.

### Current Draw Test

Perform this test before performing the regulated voltage test:

1. Turn the ignition switch off.

2. Remove the rider's seat as described in Chapter Fifteen.

3. Disconnect the negative battery cable (A, **Figure 1**).

> *CAUTION*
> *Before connecting the ammeter to the circuit in Step 4, set the meter to its highest amperage scale. This prevents a possible large current flow from damaging the meter or blowing the meter's fuse.*

4. Connect the ammeter between the battery negative cable and the negative battery terminal (**Figure 3**).

5. Switch the ammeter from its highest to lowest amperage scale while reading the meter. The reading must not exceed the battery maximum current draw specified in **Table 1**.

6. If the current draw is excessive, check for the following:

    a. Damaged battery.

    b. Short circuit in the system.

    c. Loose, dirty or faulty electrical system connectors in the charging system wiring harness(es).

    d. Aftermarket electrical accessory added to the system.

7. To find the source of a current draw, disconnect individual circuits at connectors or fuses and monitor the current draw. When the current draw returns to the specified level, the faulty circuit is indicated. Refer to the wiring diagrams and test the circuit further to isolate the problem.

8. Disconnect the ammeter test leads, and reconnect the negative battery cable.

### Regulated Voltage Test

1. Start the engine and let it reach normal operating temperature. Turn off the engine.

2. Remove the rider's seat (Chapter Fifteen).

3. On models with a headlight switch, turn the switch on.

4. Turn the headlight dimmer switch to the HI position.

5. Connect a voltmeter positive test lead to the positive battery terminal and connect the negative test lead to the negative battery terminal.

6. Turn on the engine, and run it at 5000 rpm. The voltage reading should be within the regulated voltage range specified in **Table 1**. If the voltage is outside the specified range, inspect the alternator and the voltage regulator as described in this chapter.

7. If the voltage is too high, the voltage regulator/rectifier is probably at fault.

### No-Load Voltage Test

1. Raise and support the fuel tank (Chapter Eight).

2. Disconnect the 3-pin stator connector (A, **Figure 4**). If necessary, follow the electrical cable from the alternator cover to the connector.

3. Start the engine and let it idle.

4. Connect the voltmeter test probes to a pair of terminals in the alternator side of the connector. Select the proper test range on the voltmeter as necessary.

5. Increase engine speed to 5000 rpm and check the voltage on the meter. Record the voltage for that pair of terminals.

6. Repeat Step 4 and Step 5 and measure the voltage between each of the remaining terminal pairs. Take a total of three readings. Refer to **Figure 5**.

7. If the voltage in any test is less than the no-load voltage specified in **Table 1**, the alternator is faulty and must be replaced.

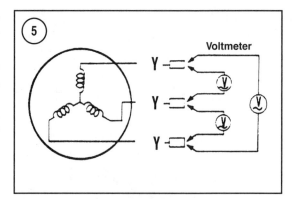

## VOLTAGE REGULATOR/RECTIFIER

### Removal/Installation

1. Remove both seats and tail piece (Chapter Fifteen).

2. Disconnect the negative battery cable.

3. Disconnect the 5-pin regulator/rectifier connector (A, **Figure 6**).

4. Remove the two mounting nuts (B, **Figure 6**), and remove the regulator/rectifier from the bracket

5. Carefully pull the electrical wiring harness out through the frame while noting its path. Remove the voltage regulator/rectifier assembly from the frame.

6. Install by reversing the removal steps. Note the following:

   a. Tighten the mounting nuts securely.

   b. Route the wiring along the path noted during removal.

   c. Make sure the electrical connector is tight and free of corrosion.

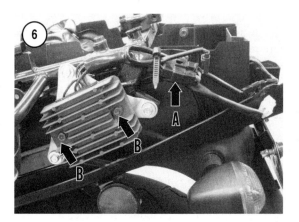

### Voltage Test

A multicircuit tester (Suzuki part No. 09900-25008) is required to test the regulator/rectifier unit. If this tester is not available, take the regulator/rectifier to a dealership for testing.

1. Perform Steps 1-3 of the regulator/rectifier removal procedures.

2. Set the tester to the diode setting.

3. **Figure 7** identifies the terminals in the regulator/rectifier connector. Connect the tester probes to the terminals indicated in **Figure 8**, and check the voltage across each pair of terminals.

4. If any voltage reading differs from the stated value, replace the regulator/rectifier.

## STATOR ASSEMBLY

### Removal/Installation

The stator assembly consists of the stator and crankshaft position sensor. Both parts are replaced as a set.

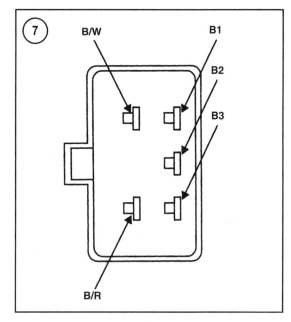

1. Raise and support the fuel tank (Chapter Eight).

2. Remove the fairing side panel from the left side (Chapter Fifteen).

3. Disconnect the 3-pin stator connector (A, **Figure 4**) and the 2-pin crankshaft position sensor connector (B).

4. Remove the alternator cover (Chapter Five).

**⑧** REGULATOR/RECTIFIER TEST

| | | + Probe of tester to: | | | | |
|---|---|---|---|---|---|---|
| | | B/R | B1 | B2 | B3 | B/W |
| − Probe of tester to: | B/R | | ∞ | ∞ | ∞ | ∞ |
| | B1 | 1 - 10 V | | ∞ | ∞ | ∞ |
| | B2 | 1 - 10 V | ∞ | | ∞ | ∞ |
| | B3 | 1 - 10 V | ∞ | ∞ | | ∞ |
| | B/W | 1 - 20 V | 1 - 10 V | 1 - 10 V | 1 - 10 V | |

**⑨**

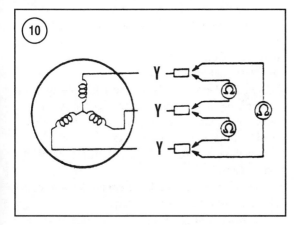

**⑩**

5. Carefully pull the rubber grommet (A, **Figure 9**) from the alternator cover. Note how the wiring is routed through the cover.

6. Remove the crankshaft position sensor bolts (B, **Figure 9**). Lift the sensor and clamp (C, **Figure 9**) from the mount in the cover. The clamp secures the wires in the alternator cover so they are not damaged by the spinning rotor.

7. Loosen and remove the stator bolts (D, **Figure 9**).

8. Remove the stator assembly from the alternator cover.

9. Install the stator assembly by reversing these removal steps. Note the following:

   a. The clamp (C, **Figure 9**) must secure the wiring in the cover as noted during removal.

   b. Apply Suzuki Thread Lock 1342 to the threads of the stator bolts (D, **Figure 9**) and the crankshaft position sensor bolts.

   c. Torque the stator bolts to 10 N•m (89 in.-lb.).

   d. Torque the crankshaft position sensor bolts (B, **Figure 9**) to 5.5 N•m (49 in.-lb.).

   e. Completely seat the grommet (A, **Figure 9**) in the alternator cover.

**Resistance Test**

1. Raise and support the fuel tank as described in Chapter Eight.

2. Disconnect the 3-pin stator connector (A, **Figure 4**). If necessary, follow the electrical cable from the alternator cover to the connector.

3. Connect the ohmmeter test probes to a pair of terminals in the stator side of the connector.

4. Check the reading on the meter and record the resistance for that pair of terminals.

5. Repeat Step 3 and Step 4 and measure the resistance between each of the remaining terminal pairs. Take a total of three readings. Refer to **Figure 10**.

6. The stator is faulty and must be replaced if any resistance is outside the specified range (**Table 1**).

7. Use the ohmmeter to check the continuity between each terminal in the stator side of the connector and ground. If any reading indicates continuity, one or more of the stator wires is shorted to ground. Replace the stator.

**9**

## IGNITION SYSTEM

*WARNING*
*High voltage is present during ignition system operation. Do not touch any ignition component, wire or test lead while cranking or running the engine.*

The ignition system consists of a crankshaft position (CKP) sensor, camshaft position (CMP) sensor, engine control module (ECM) and four ignition coil/spark plug caps.

During operation, the ECM uses input from the CKP sensor, CMP sensor, throttle position (TP) sensor, engine coolant temperature (ECT) sensor and gear position (GP) sensor to calculate the best ignition timing for the current operating conditions.

The ECM then sends a signal to the power source, which sends its energy to the primary side of the ignition coil. This induces a high voltage in the coil's secondary windings and fires the spark plug.

The ECM also includes an rpm limiter. On 1999-2000 models, the ECM shuts off the primary current to the ignition coil/spark plug caps if the engine speed exceeds 10,600 rpm. On 2001-on models, however, the ECM alters the fuel injection duration as engine speed approaches 10,089 rpm when the engine is in sixth gear.

### Troubleshooting

Refer to *Diagnostic System* in Chapter Eight.

## CRANKSHAFT POSITION (CKP) SENSOR

### Removal/Installation

The CKP sensor is part of the stator assembly. Refer to *Stator Assembly, Removal/Installation* in this chapter.

### Resistance Test

1. Raise and support the fuel tank (Chapter Eight).
2. Disconnect the 2-pin crankshaft position sensor connector (B, **Figure 4**).
3. Use an ohmmeter to measure the resistance between the two terminals in the sensor side of the connector.
4. The resistance should be within the range specified in **Table 1**.
5. Check the continuity between the green terminal in the sensor side of the connector and a good ground. No continuity (infinity) should be indicated.

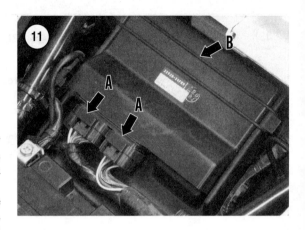

6. Check the continuity between the white (or blue) terminal in the sensor side of the connector and a good ground. No continuity (infinity) should be indicated.

### Peak Voltage Test

A multicircuit tester (Suzuki part No. 09900-25008) with the peak voltage adapter, or an equivalent multimeter and peak voltage adapter, are needed to perform this test.

Refer to *Peak Voltage Test* in Chapter Two.

1. Raise and support the fuel tank (Chapter Eight).
2. Disconnect the 2-pin crankshaft position sensor connector (B, **Figure 4**).
3. Connect the peak voltage adapter to the voltmeter following the manufacturer's instructions.
4A. On 1999-2000 models, connect the positive test probe to the green terminal in the sensor side of the connector. Connect the negative test probe to the white terminal in the sensor side.
4B. On 2001-on models, connect the positive test probe to the blue terminal in the sensor side of the connector. Connect the negative test probe to the green terminal in the sensor side.
5. Turn the ignition switch on and shift the transmission to neutral.
6. Use the starter to crank the engine for a few seconds. Record the highest reading.
7. The peak voltage reading should equal or exceed the value specified in **Table 1**.
   a. If the peak voltage is within specification, continue with Step 8 and measure the peak voltage at the ECM connector.
   b. If peak voltage is out of specification, check for loose or corroded contacts in the crankshaft position sensor connector. Repair the connector as necessary. If the connectors are good, replace the sensor.
8. Connect the crankshaft position sensor connector.

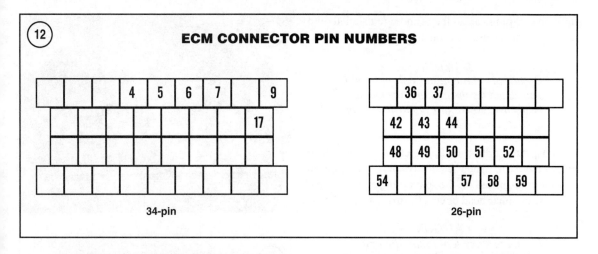

9. Disconnect the 26-pin connector from the ECM.

*NOTE*
*Some wiring colors are used more than once in the 34-pin and 26-pin ECM connectors (A, **Figure 11**). To ensure that the correct wire is tested, some test procedures include the wire color and pin location to describe a test point. The number in parentheses after the wiring color refers to that wire's pin number. Refer to **Figure 12** to determine where that terminal is located in the relevant ECM connector. Refer to **Diagnostic System** in Chapter Eight for more details.*

10. Connect the positive test probe to green terminal (36, **Figure 12**) in the ECM connector. Connect the negative test probe to the white terminal (43, **Figure 12**) in the connector.

11. Repeat Steps 5-7 and measure the peak voltage at the 26-pin ECM connector. Peak voltage should be within specification. If peak voltage is out of specification, check the wiring between the ECM and the CKP sensor connectors.

## ENGINE CONTROL MODULE (ECM)

### Removal/Installation

1. Remove the rider's seat as described in Chapter Fifteen.
2. Disconnect the electrical cable from the battery negative terminal.
3. Disconnect the 26-pin and the 34-pin connectors (A, **Figure 11**) from the ECM.
4. Remove the securing band (B, **Figure 11**) and lift the ECM from the motorcycle.
5. Installation is the reverse of removal. Secure the ECM in place with the band.

### Input Voltage Test

1. Disconnect both ECM connectors.
2. Connect the voltmeter negative test probe to a black/white terminal in the ECM connector. Connect the voltmeter positive test probe to the orange/white terminal.
3. Turn the ignition switch on, and measure the voltage. It should equal battery voltage

## IGNITION COIL/PLUG CAP

### Removal/Installation

1. Raise and support the fuel tank (Chapter Eight).
2. Remove the air filter housing (Chapter Eight.).

*CAUTION*
*Always disconnect the 2-pin connector (**Figure 13**) from an ignition coil/plug cap before removing the coil/plug cap.*

3. Disconnect the 2-pin connector (**Figure 13**) from the ignition coil/plug cap. Mark each connector and

ignition coil/plug cap so they can be reinstalled onto the correct spark plug during assembly.

> *CAUTION*
> *Do not pry the ignition coil/plug cap. This damages the coil and the cylinder head cover. Make sure not to drop a coil once it is removed.*

4. Grasp the ignition coil/plug cap, and twist it to break the seal. Then carefully pull the ignition coil/plug cap up and off the spark plug, and remove it from the cylinder head cover (**Figure 14**).

> *CAUTION*
> *Do not use any tool to tap the ignition coil/plug cap assembly onto the spark plug. Striking the cap causes damage. Install the coil/plug cap by hand.*

> *NOTE*
> *Push the ignition coil/plug cap all the way down to make full contact with the spark plug post. If each coil/cap does not make full contact with the spark plug, the engine may cut out.*

5. Refer to the marks made during removal, and then press each ignition coil/plug cap onto the correct spark plug. Make sure the coil/plug cap attaches to the spark plug and seals against the cylinder head cover.
6. Carefully connect each 2-pin connector (**Figure 13**) onto its related ignition coil/plug cap. Position the electrical coupler so it does not contact the raised portion of the cylinder head cover.

### Ignition Coil Primary Peak Voltage Test

A multicircuit tester (Suzuki part No. 09900-25008) with the peak voltage adapter, or an equivalent multimeter and peak voltage adapter, are needed to perform this test.

Refer to *Peak Voltage Test* in Chapter Two.
1. Connect the peak voltage adapter to the meter according to the manufacturer's instructions.
2. Perform Steps 1-4 of the *Ignition Coil/Plug Cap Removal*, and remove each ignition coil/plug cap from its spark plug.
3. Insert a new spark plug into the cap.

> *CAUTION*
> *Do not ground the spark plugs to the cylinder head cover. An electrical spark damages the magnesium cover.*

4. Connect each 2-pin connector (**Figure 13**) to its respective ignition coil/plug cap, and ground the

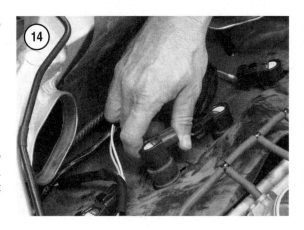

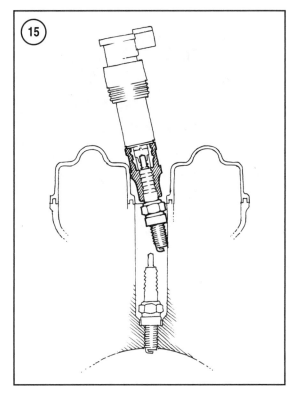

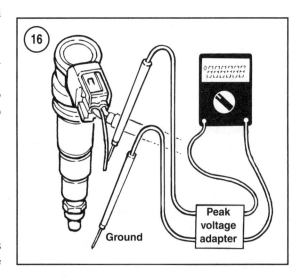

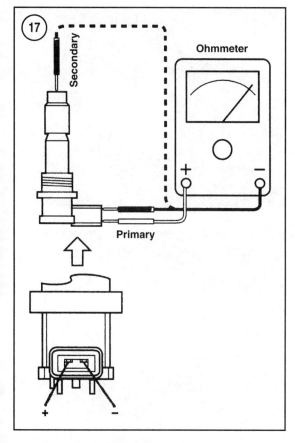

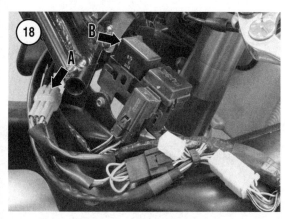

spark plug against the cylinder head as shown in **Figure 15**.

5. Backprobe the white/blue terminal of the No. 1 ignition coil/spark plug cap, and connect the positive test probe to a 0.5-mm back probe pin. Connect the negative test lead to a good ground. Refer to **Figure 16**.

6. Shift the transmission into neutral and turn the ignition switch on.

7. Press the starter button and crank the engine for a few seconds while reading the meter. Note the meter's highest reading.

8. Repeat Step 7 a few times. Note the highest reading.

9. Repeat Steps 5-8 for each of the remaining ignition coils. When testing the No. 2 ignition coil, connect the positive test probe to a back probe pin in the connector's black terminal. Connect the positive test probe to the yellow terminal on the No. 3 coil or the green terminal on the No. 4 coil.

10. Compare the readings to the ignition coil primary peak voltage specification is in **Table 1**. The individual peak voltage reading for each ignition coil can vary as long as the voltage meets or exceeds the specified value.

11. If the ignition coil primary peak voltage at the ignition coil/plug cap is less than the specified value, perform the ignition coil resistance test.

### Ignition Coil Resistance Test

1. Perform Steps 1-4 of the *Ignition Coil/Plug Cap Removal*, and remove each ignition coil/plug cap from its spark plug.

2. Connect the ohmmeter test probes to the two terminals in the ignition coil/plug cap, and measure the primary coil resistance as shown in **Figure 17**. Compare the reading to the primary coil resistance specified in **Table 1**.

3. Move the negative test probe to the spark plug connector in the ignition coil/plug cap, and measure the secondary coil resistance as shown in **Figure 17**. Compare the reading to the secondary coil resistance specified in **Table 1**.

4. Repeat Step 2 and Step 3 for the other three ignition coils.

5. If a coil's resistance does not meet (or come close to) either of these specifications, replace the coil. If the coil exhibits visible damage, replace it.

### IGNITION SWITCH

#### Removal/Installation

A JT40H Torx bit (Suzuki part No.: 09930-11920) and bit holder (part No.: 09930-11940), or equivalent tools, are needed to perform this procedure.

1. Remove the front fairing (Chapter Fifteen).

2. Disconnect the 6-pin ignition switch connector (A, **Figure 18**).

3. Remove the bolts under the ignition switch, and lower the switch (**Figure 19**) from the upper fork bridge assembly.

4. Installation is the reverse of removal. Apply Suzuki Thread Lock 1342 to the threads of the ignition switch bolts. Tighten the bolts securely.

9

## STARTING SYSTEM

The starting system consists of the starter, starter gears, ignition switch, engine stop switch, starter relay, clutch switch, gear position sensor, sidestand switch, turn signal/sidestand relay and starter button. When the starter button is pressed, it engages the starter relay and completes the circuit allowing electricity to flow from the battery to the starter.

The starting system includes an interlock system that interrupts current flow to the starter relay unless certain conditions are met. The engine does not crank unless the transmission is in neutral, and the clutch is disengaged, or the transmission is in gear, the clutch is disengaged, and the sidestand is up.

> **CAUTION**
> *During starting, do not operate the starter for more than 5 seconds at a time. Let it cool 10 seconds between attempts.*

### Troubleshooting

Refer to Chapter Two.

### STARTER

#### Operation Test

1. Securely support the motorcycle on level ground.
2. Raise and support the fuel tank, and then remove the air filter housing (Chapter Eight).
3. Pull back the rubber boot from the starter motor terminal.
4. Remove the starter terminal nut (A, **Figure 20**), and disconnect the starter cable from the starter terminal.

> **WARNING**
> *The jumper wire in Step 5 must be as large as the battery lead to handle the current flow from the battery. If the wire is too small, it could melt.*

> **WARNING**
> *The test in the next step produces sparks. Make sure no flammable materials are in the vicinity.*

5. Pull back the cover from the battery positive terminal. Apply battery voltage directly to the starter by connecting a jumper from the battery positive terminal to the starter terminal (A, **Figure 20**). The starter should operate.
6. If the starter does not operate when battery voltage is applied, repair or replace the motor.

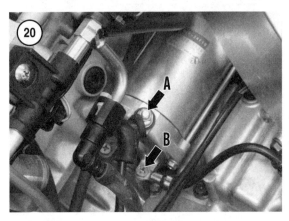

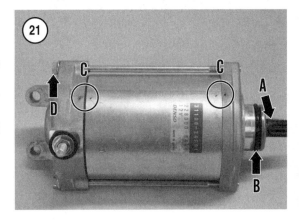

#### Removal/Installation

> **NOTE**
> *Refer to Chapter Five for starter gear service procedures*

1. Securely support the motorcycle on level ground.
2. Disconnect the negative battery cable.
3. Raise and support the fuel tank, and then remove the air filter housing (Chapter Eight).
4. Pull back the rubber boot from the starter terminal.
5. Remove the starter terminal nut (A, **Figure 20**) and disconnect the starter cable from the terminal.

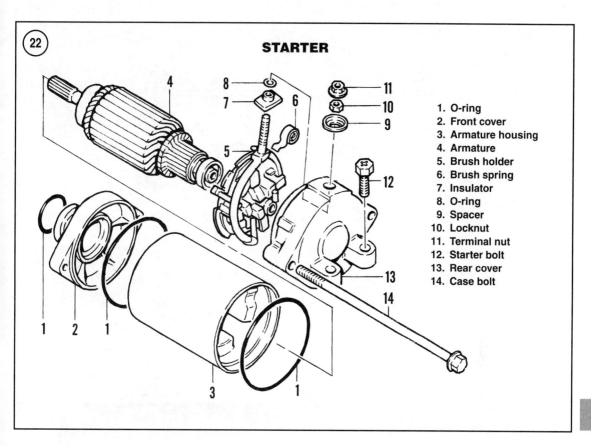

**STARTER**

22

1. O-ring
2. Front cover
3. Armature housing
4. Armature
5. Brush holder
6. Brush spring
7. Insulator
8. O-ring
9. Spacer
10. Locknut
11. Terminal nut
12. Starter bolt
13. Rear cover
14. Case bolt

9

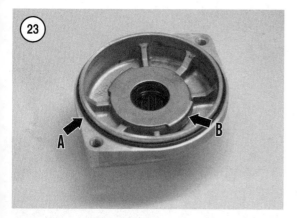

23

10. Push the starter into the starter gear housing so the teeth on the armature shaft (A, **Figure 21**) engage the starter reduction gear.

11. Install the starter bolts with the ground wire beneath the rear starter bolt (B, **Figure 20**). Tighten the bolts securely.

12. Secure the starter cable to the starter terminal (A, **Figure 20**). Tighten the starter terminal nut securely, and press the rubber boot back into position.

13. Install the air filter housing and fuel tank (Chapter Eight).

14. Connect the negative battery cable.

**Disassembly**

As the starter (**Figure 22**) is disassembled, lay each part out in the order of removal.

1. Make an alignment dot on the front cover and housing and on the rear cover and housing (C, **Figure 21**) so each cover can be properly aligned with the housing during assembly.

2. Remove each case bolt (D, **Figure 21**).

3. Pull the front cover from the armature housing. Discard the O-ring (A, **Figure 23**). New O-rings must be installed during assembly.

4. Slide the armed washer (B, **Figure 23**) and the thin washer (**Figure 24**) from the armature shaft.

6. Remove the starter bolts (B, **Figure 20**). Note the ground wire secured beneath the rear bolt (B, **Figure 20**). The wire must be reinstalled under this bolt during assembly.

7. Pull the starter toward the left side, disengage the armature shaft (A, **Figure 21**) from the starter reduction gear and remove the starter from the starter gear housing.

8. Thoroughly clean the starter mounting pads on the crankcase and the mounting lugs on the starter.

9. Install a new starter O-ring (B, **Figure 21**) onto the front cover. Apply Suzuki Super Grease A to the O-ring before installing the starter.

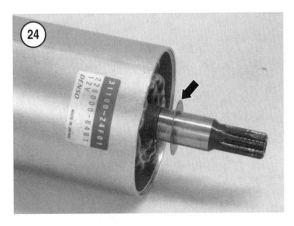

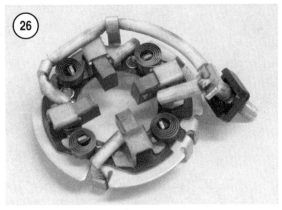

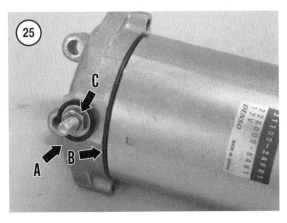

5. Remove the rear cover (A, **Figure 25**) from the armature housing. Discard the O-ring (B, **Figure 25**).

6. Press the armature from the housing.

7. Remove the locknut (C, **Figure 25**) and spacer from the terminal bolt. Remove the brush holder (**Figure 26**) from the rear cover.

8. Further disassembly is unnecessary. The brushes and brush holder are sold as an assembly.

> *CAUTION*
> *Do not immerse the armature in solvent because the insulation may be damaged. Wipe the windings with a cloth lightly moistened with solvent. Dry thoroughly.*

9. Clean all grease, dirt and carbon from all components.

10. Inspect all starter components as described in this section.

## Assembly

1. Install a new O-ring on the lip of the rear cover. Lubricate the O-ring with Suzuki Super Grease A.

2. Install the brush holder onto the armature so the brushes engage the commutator (A, **Figure 27**).

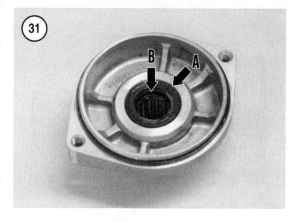

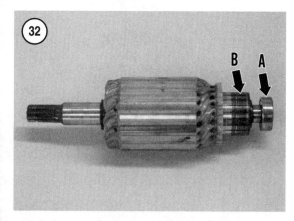

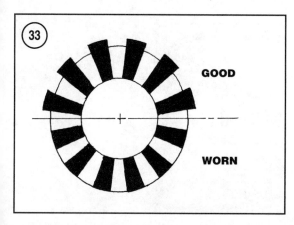

3. Insert the terminal bolt (A, **Figure 28**) through the hole in the rear cover, and seat the brush holder in the cover (**Figure 29**). Note the following:

    a. The armature bearing (B, **Figure 27**) must sit in the bearing boss (B, **Figure 28**) in the rear cover.

    b. The tab in the brush holder must engage the rear cover slot (A, **Figure 29**).

4. Install a new O-ring (B, **Figure 29**) onto the terminal bolt.

5. Install the spacer (A, **Figure 30**) and locknut (B).

6. Lower the rear cover/armature assembly into the armature housing. Make sure the brush holder fork (C, **Figure 30**) engages the tab in the housing.

7. Install the thin washer (**Figure 24**) onto the armature shaft.

8. Apply Suzuki Super Grease A to the lips of the seal (A, **Figure 31**) in the front cover.

9. Install the armed washer (B, **Figure 23**) into the front cover so the arms engage the large slots in the cover.

10. Lubricate a new O-ring with Suzuki Super Grease A, and install it onto the lip of the front cover (A, **Figure 23**).

11. Fit the front cover onto the armature housing so the indexing dot on the cover aligns with the dot on the housing (C, **Figure 21**).

12. Install the case bolts (D, **Figure 21**). Tighten the bolts securely.

13. Apply Suzuki Super Grease A to a new O-ring, and install the O-ring (B, **Figure 21**) onto the front cover.

**Inspection**

1. Inspect each brush for cracks or abnormal wear. Service specifications are not available. Replace the brush holder if any brush is excessively worn.

2. Check the entire length of the armature (**Figure 32**) for straightness or heat damage.

3. Inspect the bearing (A, **Figure 32**) on the armature shaft for wear or damage. If it is damaged, replace the starter.

4. Inspect the commutator (B, **Figure 32**). The mica in a good commutator sits below the surface of the copper bars. On a worn commutator, the mica and copper bars may be worn to the same level (**Figure 33**). If necessary, have the commutator serviced by a dealership or electrical repair shop.

5. Inspect the commutator copper bars for discoloration. If a pair of bars are discolored, grounded armature coils are indicated.

6. Use an ohmmeter and perform the following:

a. Check for continuity between the commutator bars (**Figure 34**). There should be continuity (zero or low resistance) between pairs of bars.

b. Check for continuity between the commutator bars and the shaft (**Figure 35**). There should be no continuity (infinite resistance).

c. The armature is faulty if it fails either of these tests. Replace the starter.

7. Inspect the seal (A, **Figure 31**) in the front cover for wear, hardness or damage. Replace the cover as necessary.

8. Inspect the needle bearing (B, **Figure 31**) in the front cover. It must turn smoothly without excessive play or noise. Replace the cover as necessary.

9. Inspect the magnets (**Figure 36**) within the armature housing. Remove any small metal particles. Also inspect the armature housing for loose, chipped or damaged magnets.

10. Inspect both front and rear covers for wear or damage. Replace either cover as necessary.

11. Check the long case screws for thread damage. Clean the threads with the appropriate size metric die if necessary.

### STARTER RELAY

#### Removal/Installation

1. Remove the tail piece as described in Chapter Fifteen.

2. Disconnect the negative battery cable.

3. Remove the starter relay from its mounting tangs (A, **Figure 37**), and pull the cover (B) from the relay.

4. Disconnect the 4-pin primary connector (A, **Figure 38**) from the relay.

5. Disconnect the starter lead (B, **Figure 38**) and the battery lead (C) from the starter relay, and remove the relay

6. Install by reversing these removal steps while noting the following:

a. Securely install the starter (B, **Figure 38**) and battery leads (C) to their original terminals.

b. Make sure the primary connector (A, **Figure 38**) is tight and the cover is properly installed to keep out moisture.

#### Operational Test

1. Remove the starter relay.

> *CAUTION*
> *Do not apply battery voltage for longer than 5 seconds. The coil could overheat.*

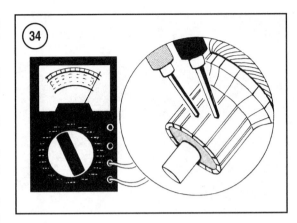

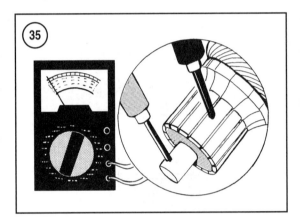

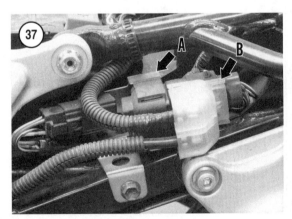

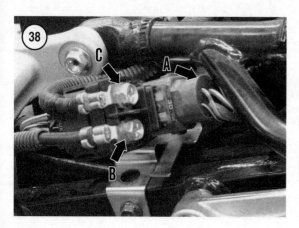

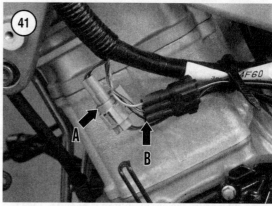

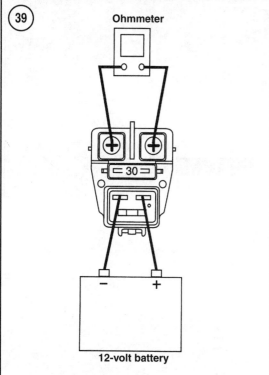

2. Connect an ohmmeter and a 12-volt battery to the starter relay terminals as shown in **Figure 39**. Check the continuity across the two load terminals.

   a. When the battery is connected, there should be continuity (zero ohms) across the two load terminals.

   b. When the battery is disconnected, there should be no continuity (infinity) across the load terminals.

3. Disconnect the battery from the starter relay.

4. Connect an ohmmeter to the starter relay terminals as shown in **Figure 40**, and measure the resistance. The resistance should be within the range specified in **Table 1**.

**Input Voltage Test**

1. Remove the tail piece as described in Chapter Fifteen.

2. Remove the starter relay from its mounting tangs (A, **Figure 37**), and pull the cover (B) from the relay.

3. Disconnect the 4-pin primary connector (A, **Figure 38**) from the relay.

4. Connect a voltmeter's positive test probe to the yellow/green terminal in the primary connector. Connect the negative test probe to the connector's black/yellow terminal.

5. Turn on the ignition switch, press the starter button and measure the voltage. It should equal battery voltage.

**SIDESTAND SWITCH**

**Removal/Installation**

1. Disconnect the negative battery cable.

2. Raise and support the fuel tank as described in Chapter Eight.

3. Remove the left fairing side panel (Chapter Fifteen).

4. Disconnect the 2-pin sidestand switch connector (A, **Figure 41**).

5. Remove the sidestand switch bolt (A, **Figure 42**) and lower the switch (B) from the sidestand bracket. Note how the switch wiring is routed through the motorcycle.

6. Installation is the reverse of removal. Note the following:

   a. Apply Suzuki Thread Lock 1342, or its equivalent, to the mounting bolt and tighten it securely.

   b. Route the switch wire along its original route. Secure it in place with the clamps or holders noted during removal.

   c. Make sure the switch plunger engages the stop (C, **Figure 42**) when the sidestand is raised.

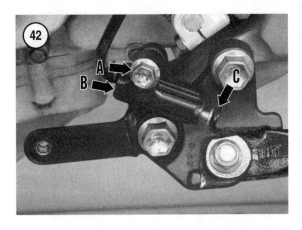

### Sidestand Switch Diode Test

A multicircuit tester (Suzuki part No. 09900-25008), or its equivalent, is needed to perform this test.

1. Perform Steps 2-4 of the sidestand switch removal.

2. Set the test knob on the tester to diode.

3. Connect the positive test probe to the green terminal in the switch side of the connector. Connect the negative test probe to the black/white terminal.

4. Move the sidestand to the up position and read the voltage on the meter.

5. Move the sidestand to the down position and read the voltage on the meter.

6. If the voltage is outside the range specified in **Table 1**, replace the sidestand switch.

7. If the diode test cannot be performed, test the continuity of the sidestand switch by performing the following:

   a. Connect an ohmmeter to the terminals in the switch side of the connector terminals as described in Step 3.

   b. Move the sidestand to the up position. The meter should indicate continuity.

   c. Move the sidestand to the down position. The meter should indicate no continuity.

   d. If the switch fails either of these tests, it is faulty and must be replaced. ,

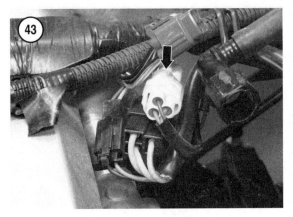

### GEAR POSITION (GP) SENSOR

#### Removal/Installation

1. Remove the clutch as described in Chapter Six.

2. Follow the gear position sensor wire, and disconnect the 3-pin gear position sensor connector (**Figure 43**).

3. Note how the wire is routed and secured to the crankcase. Remove the clamps (A, **Figure 44**) securing the wire to the crankcase. Release the wire's grommet (B, **Figure 44**) from the crankcase.

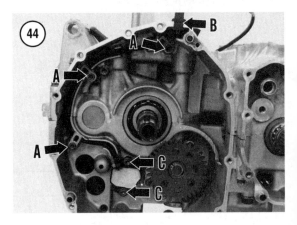

4. Remove the gear position sensor bolts (C, **Figure 44**).

5. Remove the gear position sensor and its O-ring from the crankcase.

6A. On 1999 models, remove the locating pin (A, **Figure 45**) and spring from the shift drum.

*NOTE*
*Two locating pins are used on 2000-on models.*

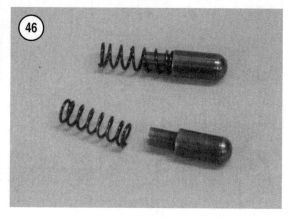

2. Disconnect the 3-pin gear position sensor connector (**Figure 43**).

3. Connect an ohmmeter to the blue and black/white terminals in the switch side of the connector.

4. Shift the transmission into neutral and read the ohmmeter. It should indicate continuity.

5. Shift the transmission into a gear and read the meter. It should indicate no continuity

### Voltage Test

1. Raise and support the fuel tank (Chapter Eight).

2. Use a 0.5-mm back probe pin to back probe the pink terminal in the harness side of the gear position sensor connector (**Figure 43**).

3. Connect the voltmeter positive test probe to a back probe pin in the pink terminal. Connect the negative test probe to a good ground.

4. Raise the sidestand and turn the ignition switch on.

5. Successively shift the transmission into each gear, first through sixth, and read the voltage. It should equal or exceed the specified gear position sensor voltage (**Table 1**) in every gear except neutral.

### TURN SIGNAL/SIDESTAND RELAY

### Removal/Installation

The turn signal/sidestand relay consists of the turn signal relay, sidestand relay and the diode. It sits on the left intake duct (B, **Figure 18**).

1. Disconnect the negative battery cable.

2. Remove the left upper panel as described in Chapter Fifteen.

3. Pull straight up and remove the relay (B, **Figure 18**) from its mount.

4. Installation is the reverse of removal. Firmly press the relay into its mount so the relay terminals engage their mates.

### Sidestand Relay Test

1. Remove the turn signal/sidestand relay as described in this section.

2. Use an ohmmeter to check the continuity between terminals D and E on the relay (**Figure 47**). There should be no continuity.

3. Check the continuity of the relay while applying 12 volts by performing the following:

    a. Connect the negative side of the battery to the C terminal in the relay. Connect the positive battery terminal to the D terminal.

6B. On 2000-on models, remove the locating pins (A and B, **Figure 45**) and springs from the shift drum.

7. Installation is the reverse of removal. Note the following:

    a. Lubricate a new O-ring with Suzuki Super Grease A, and install it onto the gear position sensor.

    b. Seat a spring onto each locating pin (**Figure 46**), and install the locating pin(s) into the shift drum (A and B, **Figure 45**). On 1999 models, install the single pin and spring into the hole along the drum's outer circumference (A, **Figure 45**).

    c. Apply Suzuki Thread Lock 1342 to the threads of the gear position sensor bolts (C, **Figure 44**), and tighten the bolts securely. Do not overtighten the bolts. The plastic housing could crack.

    d. Make sure the flat side of the wire clamp faces the wire and that each clamp rests against its stop on the crankcase.

### Continuity Test

1. Raise and support the fuel tank (Chapter Eight).

b. Use an ohmmeter to check the continuity between terminals D and E on the relay. There should be continuity.

4. Replace the turn signal/sidestand relay if it fails either portion of this test.

### Diode Test

1. Remove the turn signal/sidestand relay (this section).

2. Set a multicircuit tester (Suzuki part No. 09900-25008 or its equivalent) to diode test.

3. Refer to **Figure 48** and connect the tester probes to the indicated terminals in the diode (**Figure 47**).

4. Replace the turn signal/sidestand relay if any voltage is outside the specified range.

### Turn Signal Relay Test

If a turn signal light does not turn on, first inspect the bulbs. If the bulbs work correctly, check the turn signal switch as described in this chapter and check all electrical connections within the turn signal circuit.

If all of these items are working, replace the turn signal/sidestand relay.

## LIGHTING SYSTEM

The lighting system consists of a headlight, taillight/brake light, license plate light and turn signals.

Always use the correct bulb as indicated in **Table 2**.

Because the battery provides the power for the lighting system, always check the battery condition when the lights do not operate correctly. If the battery is fully charged, check the fuse for the affected circuit. Replace the fuse as necessary. If the battery and fuse are working properly, inspect the switch for the specific light as described in this chapter.

### Headlight Bulb Replacement

> *WARNING*
> *If a headlight bulb has just burned out or has just been turned off, it is **hot**! Do not touch the bulb until it cools.*

> *CAUTION*
> *All models are equipped with quartz-halogen headlight bulbs. Do not touch the bulb glass. Traces of oil from your hands or fingers drastically reduce the service life of the bulb. Clean any oil or other chemicals from the bulb with a cloth moistened in alcohol or lacquer thinner.*

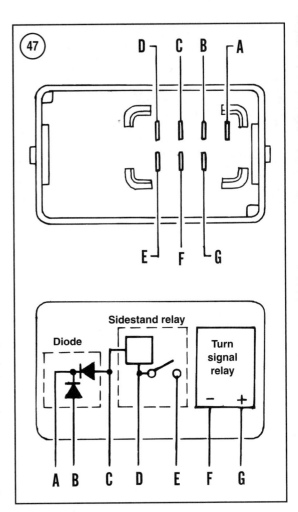

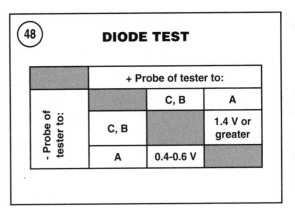

The following photographs are shown with the front fairing removed for photographic clarity. Bulbs can be replaced with the fairing on the motorcycle.

Refer to **Figure 49**.

### *Low beam*

1. Remove the left and right upper panels from the front fairing (Chapter Fifteen).

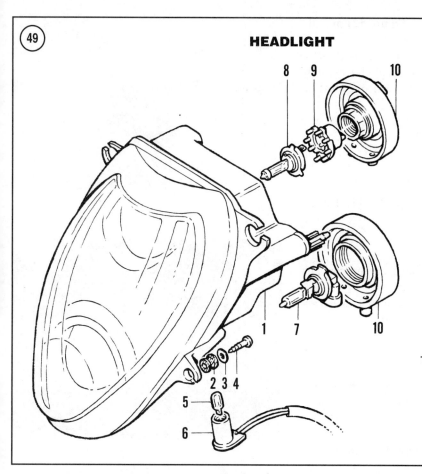

HEADLIGHT

1. Headlight assembly
2. Damper
3. Washer
4. Screw
5. Position lamp bulb
   (all models except
   U.S., California,
   Canada and Australia)
6. Position lamp socket
   (all models except
   U.S., California,
   Canada and Australia)
7. High beam bulb
8. Low beam bulb
9. Adapter
10. Boot

9

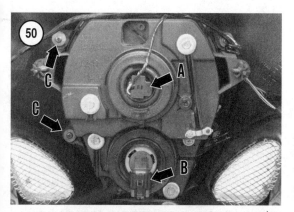

2. Disconnect the electrical connector (A, **Figure 50**) by pulling it straight out from the back of the headlight assembly.

3. Pull the tab (**Figure 51**) and remove the rubber dust cover. Check the rubber cover for tears or deterioration and replace it if necessary.

4. Unhook the light bulb retaining clip (A, **Figure 52**) and pivot it out of the way.

5. Remove and discard the blown bulb (**Figure 53**).

6. Install the new bulb so its tang (B, **Figure 52**) engages the notch in the headlight housing.

7. Hook the retaining clip (A, **Figure 52**) over the bulb to hold it in place.

8. Install the rubber cover (**Figure 51**) so the *TOP* on the cover sits at the top of the headlight assembly. Make sure the cover is correctly seated against the lens assembly and bulb.

9. Correctly align the electrical plug terminals with the bulb and connect it to the bulb. Push the connector (A, **Figure 50**) until it bottoms on the bulb and the rubber cover.

10. Check headlight operation.

11. Adjust the headlight as described in this chapter.

### *High beam*

1. Remove the center panel from under the front fairing (Chapter Fifteen).

2. Reach up into the fairing, release the lock tab and disconnect the connector (B, **Figure 50**) from the bulb.

3. Rotate the bulb (A, **Figure 54**) counterclockwise (rider's point of view) until its tabs align with the slots in the housing. Remove the bulb (**Figure 55**).

4. Align the tabs of the new bulb with those in the housing, insert the bulb, and turn it clockwise to lock it in place.

5. Install the connector (B, **Figure 54**) onto the bulb.

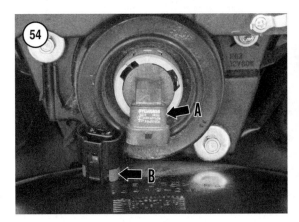

### Headlight Housing
### Removal/Installation

1. Remove the front fairing (Chapter Fifteen).

2. Disconnect the connectors (A and B, **Figure 50**) from each bulb. Note screws securing wire holder.

3. Remove the headlight assembly screws (C, **Figure 50**) and remove the assembly from the front fairing.

4. Installation is the reverse of removal. Install the wire holder onto the screws noted during removal.

### Headlight Adjustment

Proper headlight adjustment is critical to both the rider and to on-coming drivers. Always check the headlight beam adjustments whenever the load on the motorcycle is changed.

1. Each headlight bulb has a horizontal (A, **Figure 56**) and vertical adjuster (B). Turning a horizontal adjuster clockwise or counterclockwise moves a beam left or right. Turning a vertical adjuster raises or lowers a beam.

2. When adjusting either headlight bulb, first adjust the bulb horizontally and then vertically.

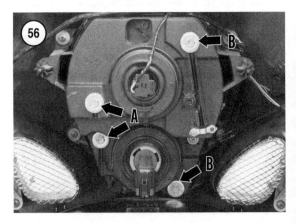

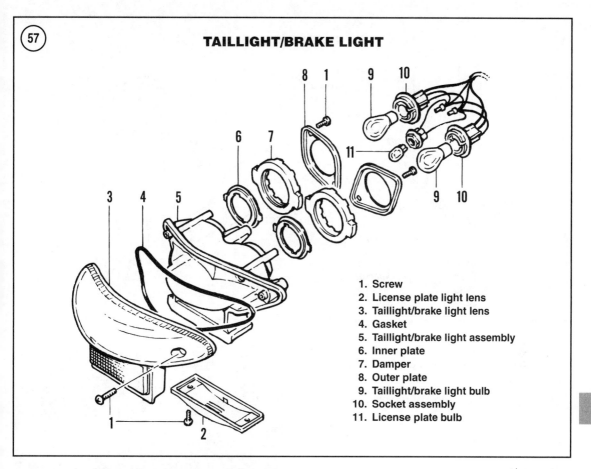

**TAILLIGHT/BRAKE LIGHT**

1. Screw
2. License plate light lens
3. Taillight/brake light lens
4. Gasket
5. Taillight/brake light assembly
6. Inner plate
7. Damper
8. Outer plate
9. Taillight/brake light bulb
10. Socket assembly
11. License plate bulb

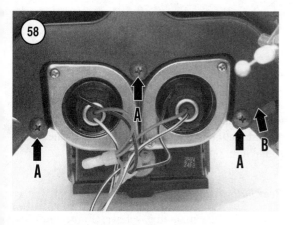

**Position Bulb Replacement
(All Models Except U.S., California,
Canada and Australia)**

1. Remove the front fairing center panel as described in Chapter Fifteen.

2. Reach into the front fairing and rotate the position bulb socket assembly counterclockwise. Remove the bulb/socket assembly from the base of the headlight unit.

3. Pull the bulb from the socket and install a new bulb.

4. Insert the socket into the base of the headlight unit, rotate it clockwise and lock it in place.

5. Install the center panel into the front fairing (Chapter Fifteen).

**Taillight/Brake Light**

Refer to **Figure 57**.

*Bulb replacement*

1. Remove the mounting screws and lower the lens from the taillight assembly.

2. Push the bulb into the socket, and then turn the bulb and remove it. Discard the blown bulb.

3. Align the bulb pins with the bulb socket grooves. Push the bulb into the socket, and then turn and release it. Check that the bulb is locked in the bulb socket.

4. Repeat for the other bulb if necessary.

5. Check taillight and brake light operation.

6. Install the lens. Make sure its gasket is in place.

*Housing removal/installation*

1. Remove the tail piece (Chapter Fifteen).

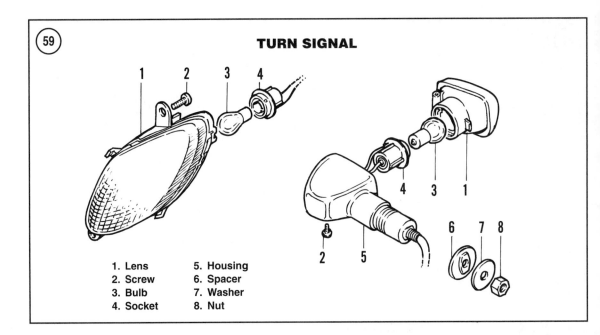

**TURN SIGNAL**

1. Lens
2. Screw
3. Bulb
4. Socket
5. Housing
6. Spacer
7. Washer
8. Nut

2. Remove the mounting screws (A, **Figure 58**). Lower the housing from the bracket (B, **Figure 58**) in the tail piece.

3. Installation is the reverse of removal.

**License Plate Light**

Refer to **Figure 57**.

*Bulb replacement*

1. Remove the mounting screws, and pull the cover from the housing.

2. Pull the bulb straight out of the socket.

3. Installation is the reverse of removal. Firmly press the bulb into the socket.

*Housing removal/installation*

The license plate housing is part of the tail-light/brake light assembly.

**Turn Signal**

Refer to **Figure 59**.

*Front bulb replacement*

1. Remove the left or right upper panel from the front fairing (Chapter Fifteen).

2. Turn the socket (A, **Figure 60**) counterclockwise, and pull the socket from the turn signal housing.

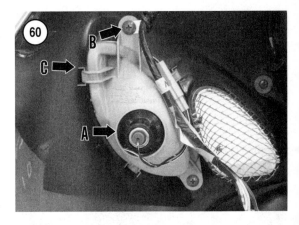

3. Press the bulb (**Figure 61**) into the socket, and then turn and remove it.

4. Installation is the reverse of removal. Check turn signal light operation.

*Rear bulb replacement*

1. Remove the mounting screws (**Figure 62**) and pull the lens from the housing.

2. Turn the socket counterclockwise, and remove the socket from the lens (**Figure 63**)

3. Push the bulb into the socket, turn the bulb and re-move it from the lens. Discard the blown bulb.

4. Installation is the reverse of removal. Check turn signal operation.

*Front housing removal/installation*

1. Remove the left or right upper panel from the front fairing (Chapter Fifteen).

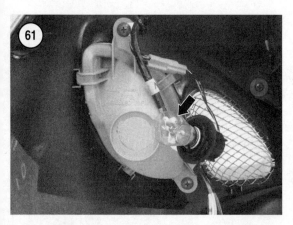

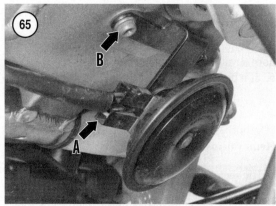

2. Turn the socket (A, **Figure 60**) counterclockwise, and pull the socket from the turn signal housing.

3. Release the wiring from the cable clamp on the upper housing screw (B, **Figure 60**).

4. Remove each housing screw (B, **Figure 60**) and pull the housing from the front fairing. Note that each tab on the housing engages a mounting boss (C, **Figure 60**) in the fairing.

5. Installation is the reverse of removal.

### *Rear housing removal/installation*

1. Remove the tail piece (Chapter Fifteen).

2. Disconnect the relevant 2-pin turn signal connector (A or B, **Figure 64**). Note how the wiring is routed through the motorcycle.

3. Remove the mounting nut, washer and spacer from inside the rear fender.

4. Pull the turn signal housing from the fender and remove it.

5. Installation is the reverse of removal. Route the wiring along the same path noted during removal.

## HORN

### Removal/Installation

1. Remove the fairing side panel from the left side (Chapter Fifteen).

2. Disconnect the 2-pin connector (A, **Figure 65**) from the horn.

3. Remove the bolts (B, **Figure 65**) and lower the horn and bracket from the frame.

4. Installation is the reverse of removal.

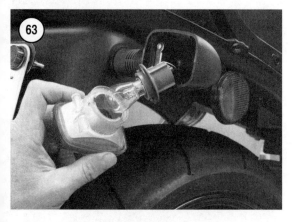

### Testing

1. Disconnect the electrical lead from the negative battery terminal.

2. Remove the left fairing side panel (Chapter Fifteen).

3. Disconnect the 2-pin connector (B, **Figure 65**) from the horn.

4. Use jumpers to connect a 12-volt battery to the horn terminals. The horn should sound.

5. If it does not, replace the horn.

## METER ASSEMBLY

### Removal/Installation

The meter assembly is a single integrated unit. It includes a liquid crystal display (LCD), fuel gauge, tachometer, speedometer, engine coolant temperature gauge and various light emitting diodes (LEDs). The LCD individual gauges and LEDs cannot be replaced. If any component in the assembly fails, replace the meter assembly.

1. Remove the front fairing as described in Chapter Fifteen.

2. Disconnect the meter connector (A, **Figure 66**) from the meter assembly.

3. Remove the mounting bolts (A, **Figure 67**).

4. Disengage the meter posts (B, **Figure 66**) from the dampers on the fairing bracket and remove the meter assembly.

5. Installation is the reverse of removal. Make sure the meter posts (B, **Figure 66**) engage the damper in the fairing bracket.

### Resetting

When the ignition switch is turned on, the needle on each gauge swings to its maximum setting and then returns to zero. This is part of the self-checking operation. If a needle does not return to zero, reset the gauges by performing the following:

1. Press and hold the meter's function button (B, **Figure 67**).

2. Turn the ignition switch on.

3. Three to five seconds after turning on the ignition switch, release the function button, and then immediately press it twice.

4. Each needle should return to zero. Complete the process within 10 seconds.

5. If a needle does not return to zero, replace the meter assembly.

### Inspection

If either the speedometer, odometer or trip meter fails to operate properly, inspect the wiring and connectors in the speedometer circuit and test the speed sensor (this chapter). If the wiring and speed sensor are working properly, replace the meter assembly.

## SPEED SENSOR

### Removal/Installation

1. Remove the left fairing side panel (Chapter Fifteen).

2. Follow the speed sensor lead, locate the 3-pin speed sensor connector (B, **Figure 41**) and disconnect the connector.

3. Remove the speed sensor bolt (**Figure 68**), and pull the sensor from the engine sprocket cover.

4. Installation is the reverse or removal.

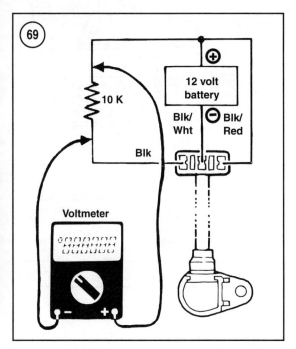

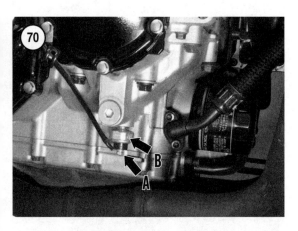

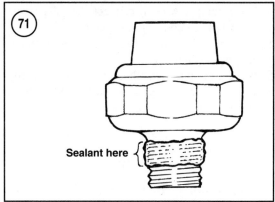

reading should change from 0 to 12 volts or from 12 to 0 volts. If it does not, replace the sensor.

## OIL PRESSURE SWITCH

### Removal/Installation

1. Disconnect the negative battery cable.
2. Remove the left fairing side panel (Chapter Fifteen).
3. Disconnect the electrical wire from the terminal (A, **Figure 70**) on the oil pressure switch (B).
4. Unscrew and remove the oil pressure switch from the crankcase.
5. Installation is the reverse of these steps. Note the following:
   a. Apply a light coat of Suzuki 1207B sealant, or its equivalent, to the switch threads where shown in **Figure 71**.
   b. Tighten the oil pressure switch to 14 N•m (10 ft.-lb.).

### Test

As soon as the ignition switch is turned on, the oil pressure indicator should turn on (**Figure 72**). As soon as the engine is started, it should go out. If the oil pressure is less than the normal operating pressure, the symbol flickers and the indicator LED turns on and stays on.

If the warning light is not operating correctly or does not come on when the ignition switch is *on* with the engine not running, perform the following test:

1. Check the engine oil level as described in Chapter Three. Add oil if necessary.
2. Remove the fairing side panel from the left side (Chapter Fifteen).
3. Disconnect the electrical wire from the terminal (A, **Figure 70**) on the oil pressure switch.

a. Route the cable along the path noted during removal.
b. Tighten the speed sensor bolt to 4.5 N•m (40 in.-lb.).

### Test

1. Remove the speed sensor (this chapter).
2. Connect the negative battery terminal to the black/white terminal in the sensor side of the connector (B, **Figure 41**). Connect the positive battery terminal to the sensor's black/red terminal.
3. Connect a 10 k ohm resistor to the black/red and black terminals on the sensor side of the connector.
4. Connect the voltmeter across the resistor as shown in **Figure 69**.
5. Touch the pick-up surface of the sensor with a screwdriver and watch the voltmeter. The voltage

4. Use a jumper wire to connect the oil pressure switch wire to a good engine ground.

5. Turn the ignition switch on. The oil pressure indicator light should turn on.

6. If it does not turn on, check the wiring and connectors between the oil pressure switch and the meter assembly. If they are good, replace the meter assembly.

## SWITCHES

### Continuity Test

Switches can be tested for continuity with an ohmmeter or a test light (refer to Chapter One). For continuity diagrams for various switches, refer to on the wiring diagrams at the back of this manual.

To test a particular switch:

1. Turn to the relevant wiring diagram, and locate the continuity diagram for the switch being tested.

2. Disconnect the switch connector, and check continuity at the terminals on the switch side of the connector. If a connector plugs directly into the switch (such as into the front brake light switch), check the continuity at the terminals on the switch.

3. Set the switch to each of its operating positions, connect ohmmeter test leads to the indicated terminals, and compare the results with the appropriate switch continuity diagram.

4. For example, **Figure 73** shows a continuity diagram for a typical push button switch. The horizontal line indicates which terminals should show continuity when the switch is operated.

### Precautions

When testing a switch, note the following:

1. First check the fuse for the related circuit as described in *Fuse* in this chapter.

2. Check the battery as described in *Battery* (this chapter). Charge the battery if required.

3. Disconnect the negative battery cable if the switch connectors are not disconnected from the circuit.

> *CAUTION*
> *Do not try to start the engine with the battery disconnected.*

4. When separating two connectors, pull the connector housings and not the wires.

5. After locating a defective circuit, check the connectors to make sure they are clean and properly connected. Check all wires going into a connector housing. Make sure each wire is properly positioned and that the wire end is not loose.

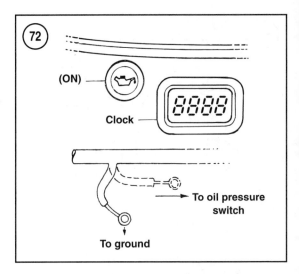

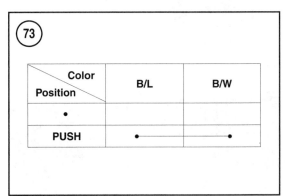

| Position \ Color | B/L | B/W |
|---|---|---|
| • | | |
| PUSH | •———— | ————• |

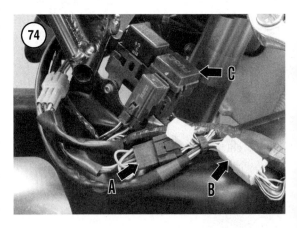

6. When reconnecting electrical connector halves, push them together until they click or snap into place.

7. If the switch or button does not perform properly, replace it.

### Right Handlebar Switch Removal/Installation

1. The right handlebar switch includes the following switches:

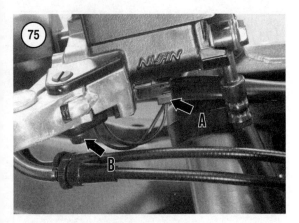

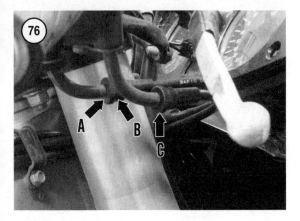

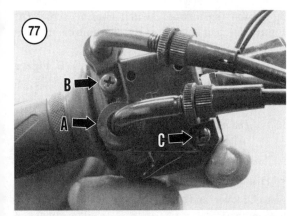

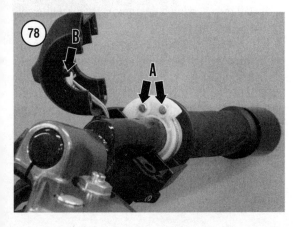

a. Engine stop switch.

b. Starter button.

c. Front brake light switch (electrical connectors only—the switch is separate).

d. Headlight switch (all models except U.S., California, Canada and Australia).

2. If the right handlebar switch is being replaced, perform the following:

a. Disconnect the negative battery cable.

b. Remove the right fairing side panel and the left upper panel (Chapter Fifteen).

c. Locate the 9-pin right handlebar switch connector (A, **Figure 74**). Disconnect the right handlebar switch connector.

d. Remove any cable ties securing the switch wiring harness to the frame. Note how the wires are routed through the frame. New wires must be routed along the same path.

e. Disconnect the connectors (A, **Figure 75**) from the front brake light switch.

> *NOTE*
> *The switches located within the right handlebar switch housing are not available separately. If any switch is damaged, replace the right handlebar switch. The front brake light switch is a separate unit and can be replaced independently.*

3. At the throttle grip, loosen the cable locknut (A, **Figure 76**) on the return cable, and turn the adjuster (B) all the way toward the switch assembly to allow maximum slack. Repeat this on the pull cable (C, **Figure 76**).

4. Unthread the return cable clamp nut (A, **Figure 77**), and lower it from the switch housing.

5. Remove the front switch housing screw (B, **Figure 77**), and lower the pull cable clamp from the switch housing.

6. Remove the rear switch housing screw (C, **Figure 77**), and separate the housing halves (**Figure 78**).

7. Disconnect each cable end (A, **Figure 78**) from the throttle drum, and feed the cables through the lower housing half.

8. Install by reversing these removal steps while noting the following:

a. Route the pull cable through the front port in the lower switch half and the return cable through the rear port.

b. Apply grease to the cable ends, and connect the throttle cable ends (A, **Figure 78**) to the throttle drum.

c. Lower the upper switch half over the throttle drum so the indexing pin (B, **Figure 78**) engages the hole in the handlebar, and install the

switch housing screws (B and C, **Figure 77**).
Secure the pull cable clamp under the forward
screw (B, **Figure 77**).

   d. Route the electrical cable along the path noted
during removal. Make sure the electrical connectors are free of corrosion and are tight.

   e Check the operation of each switch mounted in
the right handlebar switch housing.

   f. Operate the throttle grip and make sure the
throttle linkage operates smoothly. If any binding or sluggish operation is noted, carefully
check throttle cables. They must be correctly
attached to the throttle drum and throttle linkage, and they must properly routed with no
tight bends in the cables.

   g. Adjust the throttle cable free play (Chapter
Three).

**Left Handlebar Switch
Removal/Installation**

1. The left handlebar switch housing is equipped
with the following switches:

   a. Headlight dimmer switch.

   b. Turn signal switch.

   c. Horn button.

   d. Clutch switch (electrical connectors only—the
switch is separate).

   e. Passing button (all models except U.S., California, Canada and Australia).

2. If the left handlebar switch is being replaced, perform the following:

   a. Disconnect the electrical lead from the battery
negative terminal.

   b. Remove the fairing side panel and the upper
panel from the left side (Chapter Fifteen).

   c. Disconnect the 9-pin left handlebar switch connector (B, **Figure 74**).

   d. Remove any cable ties securing the switch wiring harness in place. Note how the wires are
routed through the frame. New wires must be
routed along the same path.

   e. Disconnect the connectors from the clutch
switch (**Figure 79**).

*NOTE*
*The switches located within the left
handlebar switch housing are not
available separately. If one switch is
damaged, replace the left switch housing assembly. The clutch switch is a
separate unit and can be replaced independently.*

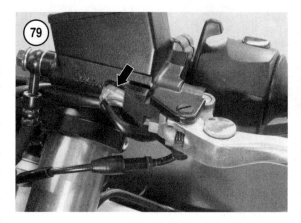

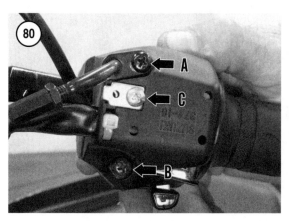

3. Loosen the forward switch housing screw (A,
**Figure 80**), and lower the fast idle cable clamp from
the housing.

4. Remove the rear switch housing screw (B, **Figure
80**) and separate the housing halves.

*NOTE*
*The middle screw (C, **Figure 80**) in the
switch housing is a friction adjuster for
the fast idle lever.*

5. Disconnect the cable end (**Figure 81**) from the
fast idle lever, and feed the cable through the lower
housing half.

6. Install by reversing these removal steps while noting the following:

   a. Apply grease to the cable end, position the
lower switch half onto the handlebar, and connect the cable end (**Figure 81**) to the fast idle
lever.

   b. Make sure its pin in the upper switch half engages the hole in the handlebar.

   c. Install the switch housing screws (A and B,
**Figure 80**). Secure the cable clamp under the
front switch housing screw (A, **Figure 80**).

   d. Check the operation of each switch mounted in
the left handlebar switch housing.

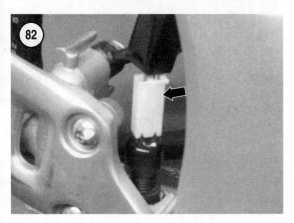

9

e. Adjust the fast idle speed as necessary (Chapter Three).

## Front Brake Switch Removal/Installation

1. Disconnect the electrical connectors (A, **Figure 75**) from the front brake switch.
2. Remove the mounting screw (B, **Figure 75**), and lower the switch from the brake lever assembly.
3. Installation is the reverse of removal.

## Rear Brake Switch Removal/Installation

The rear brake switch sits on the inside of the brake pedal/footpeg assembly. The switch can be removed with the assembly on the motorcycle, but removing the brake pedal/footpeg assembly is recommended.

1. Roll back the rubber boot and disconnect the electrical connector (**Figure 82**) from the rear brake switch.
2. Remove the footpeg bracket bolts (**Figure 83**), and rotate the brake pedal/footpeg assembly. Support the assembly so the brake lines are not excessively stressed.
3. Disconnect the switch spring (A, **Figure 84**) from the boss on the brake pedal.
4. Hold the adjusting nut (B, **Figure 84**). Loosen the switch and remove it.
5. Installation is the reverse of removal. Tighten the footpeg bracket bolts (**Figure 83**) to 26 N•m (19 ft.-lb.).
6. Adjust the rear brake switch as described in Chapter Three.

## Clutch Switch Removal/Installation

1. Disconnect the electrical connectors from the clutch switch (**Figure 79**) on the clutch lever assembly.
2. Remove the mounting screw (**Figure 85**), and lower the switch from the lever assembly.
3. Installation is the reverse of removal.

## FUSES

When troubleshooting any electrical problem, first check for a blown fuse. A blown fuse has a break in the element (**Figure 86**). Before replacing a blown fuse, however, determine the reason for the failure. This may be caused by worn-through insulation or a disconnected wire that is shorted to ground. Check by testing the circuit the fuse protects.

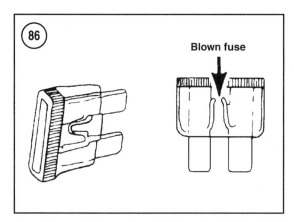

Blown fuse

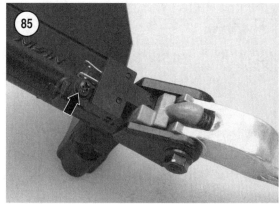

## Main Fuse Replacement

All models are equipped with a single 30-amp main fuse.

1. Remove the tail piece (Chapter Fifteen).
2. Remove the starter relay cover.
3. Pull the fuse (**Figure 87**) from the starter relay. Visually inspect the fuse.
4. Install a new fuse and push it into place until it bottoms.

## Circuit Fuse Replacement

Individual circuit fuses are located in the fuse box (C, **Figure 74**), which sits on the left intake duct. The fuse box contains two spare fuses (10A and 15A). Replace the spare fuse as soon as possible (if used).

1. Remove the left upper panel from the front fairing (Chapter Fifteen).
2. Open the fuse panel top cover.
3. Use needlenose pliers to remove the suspect fuse.

4. Install a replacement fuse of the same amperage.

## WIRING DIAGRAMS

Wiring diagrams for all models are located at the end of this manual.

### Table 1 ELECTRICAL SYSTEM SPECIFICATIONS*

| | |
|---|---|
| **Battery** | |
| Type | YT12A-BS Maintenance free (sealed) |
| Capacity | 12 volt 36 kC (10 amp hour)/10 HR |
| Maximum current draw | Less than 3 mA |
| **Alternator** | |
| Type | Three-phase AC |
| No-load voltage (when engine is cold) | 65 volts or more (AC) @ 5000 rpm |
| Regulated voltage (charging voltage) | 13.5-15.0 volts @ 5000 rpm |
| Maximum output | Approx 400 W @ 5000 rpm |
| Stator resistance | 0.2-0.4 ohms |
| **Ignition System** | |
| Type | Electronic ignition (transistorized) |
| Firing order | 1-2-4-3 |
| **Ignition timing** | |
| 1999 models | 4° BTDC @ 1150 rpm |
| 2000 models | |
| Cylinders Nos. 1 and 4 | 11° BTDC @ 1150 rpm |

(continued)

## Table 1 ELECTRICAL SYSTEM SPECIFICATIONS* (continued)

| | |
|---|---|
| **Ignition timing** | |
|   2000 models (continued) | |
|     Cylinders Nos. 2 and 3 | 3° BTDC @ 1150 rpm |
|   2001-on models | |
|     U.S., California and Canada models | 4° BTDC @ 1200 rpm |
|     All models except U.S., California and Canada | |
|       Cylinders Nos. 1 and 4 | 11° BTDC @ 1150 rpm |
|       Cylinders Nos. 2 and 3 | 3° BTDC @ 1150 rpm |
| **Crankshaft position sensor** | |
|   Resistance | 180-280 ohms |
|   Peak voltage (when cranking) | 3 volts or more |
| **Ignition coil resistance** | |
|   Primary | |
|     1999-2001 models | 0.8-1.2 ohms |
|     2002-on models | 1.0-1.6 ohms |
|   Secondary | |
|     1999-2001 models | 8-15k ohms |
|     2002-on models | 10-16.5k ohms |
| **Ignition coil primary peak voltage** | 80 volts or more when cranking |
| **Starter relay resistance** | 3-5 ohms |
| **Spark plug** | |
|   Type | NGK: CR9E, Denso: U27ESR-N |
|   Gap | 0.7-0.8 mm (0.028-0.032 in.) |
| **Gear position sensor voltage** | 0.6 volts or more |
| **Sidestand switch voltage** | |
|   Sidestand up (on) | 0.4-0.6 volts |
|   Sidestand down (off) | 1.4-1.5 volts |

*k × 1000.

**9**

## Table 2 BULB AND FUSE SPECIFICATIONS

| Item | Watt (quantity) |
|---|---|
| **Headlight** | |
|   High beam | 60/55 W |
|   Low bearm | 55 W |
| **Position/parking light** | 5 W |
| **Tail/brake light** | 21/5 W (2) |
| **Turn signal** | 21 W (4) |
| **License plate light** | 5 W |
| **Meter assembly light** | LED |
| **Tachometer light** | LED |
| **Speedometer light** | LED |
| **Fuel meter light** | LED |
| **Engine coolant temperature meter light** | LED |
| **Turn signal indicator light** | LED |
| **High beam indicator light** | LED |
| **Neutral indicator light** | LED |
| **Fuel indicator light** | LED |
| **Oil pressure indicator light** | LED |
| **Fuel injector indicator light** | LED |
| **Engine coolant temperature indicator light** | LED |
| **Headlight fuse** | |
|   High | 15 amp |
|   Low | 15 amp |
| **Signal fuse** | 15 amp |
| **Ignition fuse** | 15 amp |
| **Fuel fuse** | 10 amp |
| **Fan fuse** | 10 amp |
| **Main fuse** | 30 amp |

Table 3 ELECTRICAL SYSTEM TORQUE SPECIFICATIONS

| Item | N•m | in.-lb. | ft.-lb. |
|------|-----|---------|---------|
| Crankshaft position sensor mounting bolt | 5.5 | 49 | – |
| Flywheel bolt | 120 | – | 89 |
| Footpeg bracket bolts | 26 | – | 19 |
| Oil pressure switch | 14 | – | 10 |
| Spark plug | 11 | 97 | – |
| Speed sensor bolt | 4.5 | 40 | – |
| Stator bolt | 10 | 89 | – |

# CHAPTER TEN

# COOLING SYSTEM

This chapter describes repair and replacement procedures for the cooling system components. During cooling system service, compare any measurements to the specification in the tables at the end of this chapter. During assembly, tighten fasteners as specified. Refer to Chapter Three for routine cooling system maintenance.

*WARNING*
*Do not remove the radiator cap when the engine is hot. The coolant is hot and under pressure. Scalding could result if the coolant comes in contact with skin. To prevent injury, let the engine cool before removing any cooling system component.*

*WARNING*
*Engine coolant is toxic. Do not flush coolant down a drain or pour it on the ground. Place spent coolant into a suitable container and dispose of it properly. Do not store coolant where it is accessible to children or pets.*

## HOSES AND CLAMPS

Hoses deteriorate with age and should be replaced periodically or when they show signs of cracking or

leaking. The spray of hot coolant from a cracked hose can injure a rider or passenger. Loss of coolant can also lead to engine overheating, which can cause excessive damage.

When any component of the cooling system is removed, inspect its hose(s). Replace them as necessary.

The small diameter coolant hoses are very stiff and sometimes difficult to install onto their fittings. Soak the ends in hot water to make them pliable. Do not apply any type of lubricant to the inner surfaces of the hoses. They could slip off when the engine is running even with hose clamps securing them in place.

1. Make sure the cooling system is cool before removing any coolant hose.

2. Replace the hoses with original equipment replacement hoses. These hoses are designed so they fit correctly.

3. Loosen the clamps on the hose being replaced. Slide the clamps back from the component fittings.

*CAUTION*
*Do not pry or twist too hard when removing a stubborn hose from the radiator. The aluminum radiator inlet and outlet fittings are easily damaged.*

4. Twist the hose to release it from the fitting. If the hose has been on for some time, it probably is diffi-

cult to break loose. If so, carefully insert a pick tool or small screwdriver under the hose and pry the hose from the fitting.

5. Examine the fittings for cracks or other damage. Repair or replace the fitting as necessary. If the fitting is in good condition, use sandpaper and clean off any hose residue. Wipe the fitting clean with a cloth.

6. Inspect the hose clamps for rust and corrosion. Replace the clamps if necessary. Hose clamps are as important as the hoses. If they do not hold the hoses tightly in place, coolant leaks from the system. For best results, always use the screw-adjusting-type hose clamp. This type of clamp has superior holding ability and can be easily released with a screwdriver.

7. With the hose correctly installed onto each fitting, position the clamp 12.78 mm (1/2 in.) away from the end of the hose. Position the hose clamp over the fitting, and tighten the clamp.

## COOLING SYSTEM INSPECTION

1. Start the engine and run it until it reaches operating temperature. While the engine is running, a pressure surge should be felt when the water pump outlet hose (**Figure 1**) is squeezed.

2. If steam is observed at the muffler outlet, the head gasket might be damaged. If enough coolant leaks into a cylinder(s), hydrolock could prevent engine cranking. Coolant may also be present in the engine oil. If the oil visible in the oil inspection window is foamy or milky-looking, coolant is leaking into the engine. If so, correct the problem before returning the motorcycle to service.

3. Check the radiator for clogged or damaged fins. If more than 15 percent of the radiator fin area is damaged, repair or replace the radiator.

4. Check all coolant hoses for cracks or damage. Replace any questionable hose.

5. Make sure all hose clamps are tight but not so tight that they cut the hoses. Refer to *Hoses and Clamps* earlier in this chapter.

6. Pressure test the cooling system as described in Chapter Three.

## COOLANT RESERVOIR

### Removal/Installation

1. Securely support the motorcycle on a level surface.

2. Remove the left fairing side panel (Chapter Fifteen).

3. Disconnect the overflow hose (A, **Figure 2**) from the reservoir.

4. Remove the reservoir mounting bolts. Watch for the bracket behind the forward bolt (B, **Figure 2**).

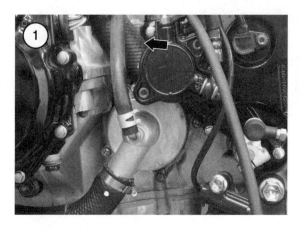

5. Pull the coolant reservoir way from the frame.

6. Disconnect the reservoir inlet hose (C, **Figure 2**) from the fitting at the base of the reservoir and place a finger over the hose fitting. Remove the reservoir.

7. Remove the filler cap, and drain any residual coolant from the reservoir. Dispose of the coolant properly.

8. If necessary, clean the inside of the reservoir with a liquid detergent. Thoroughly rinse the reservoir with clean water. Remove all detergent residue from the reservoir.

9. Install by reversing these removal steps. Install the bracket behind the forward reservoir bolt (B, **Figure 2**). Tighten the reservoir bolts securely.

## RADIATOR

*WARNING*
*When the engine is warm or hot, the fan may start even with the ignition switch turned off. Never work around the fan or touch the fan until the engine and coolant are completely cool.*

### Removal/Installation

Refer to **Figure 3**.

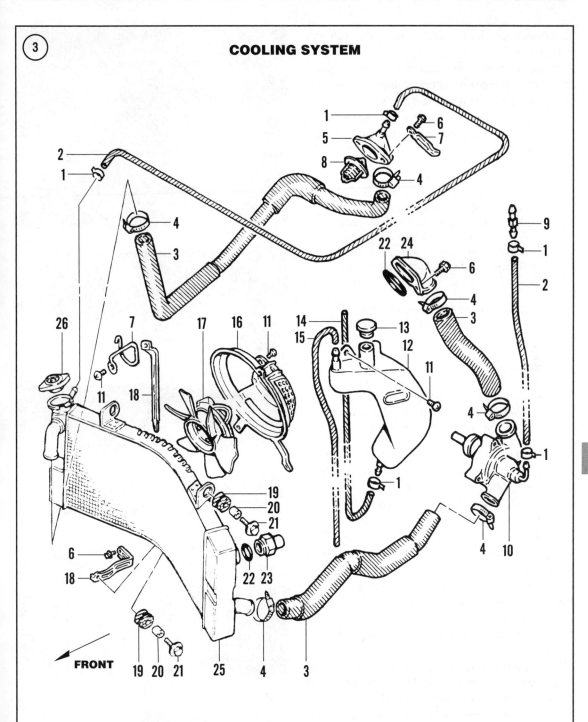

**COOLING SYSTEM**

3

FRONT

| | | |
|---|---|---|
| 1. Clamp | 10. Water pump | 19. Damper |
| 2. Bypass hose | 11. Screw | 20. Collar |
| 3. Coolant hose | 12. Reservior | 21. Radiator bolt |
| 4. Clamp | 13. Reservior | 22. O-ring |
| 5. Thermostat |     filler cap | 23. Thermoswitch |
|     housing | 14. Inlet hose | 24. Water jacket |
| 6. Bolt | 15. Overflow hose |     fitting |
| 7. Holder | 16. Shroud | 25. Radiator |
| 8. Thermostat | 17. Fan motor | 26. Radiator cap |
| 9. Fitting | 18. Bracket | |

10

1. Remove the fairing side panel from each side (Chapter Fifteen).

2. Raise and support the fuel tank (Chapter Eight). Disconnect the negative battery cable.

3. Drain the coolant (Chapter Three).

4. Disconnect the 2-pin radiator fan connector (A, **Figure 4**) and the 2-pin connector (B) from the thermo switch.

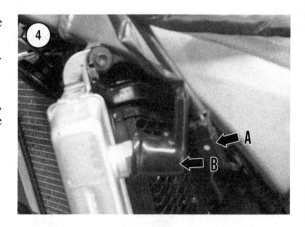

> *NOTE*
> *Even though the cooling system has been drained, some residual coolant remains in the radiator and hoses. Place a drain pan under each hose as it is disconnected from its fitting. Also have shop rags handy to wipe up any spilled coolant.*

5. Disconnect the water pump hose (**Figure 5**) from the radiator fitting. Use a rag to plug the end of the hose.

> *WARNING*
> *Coolant is very slippery, especially if spilled on concrete or a similar surface. Do not walk on spilled coolant. Wipe it off the floor immediately. Also clean any coolant off the soles of shoes.*

6. Disconnect the coolant reservoir hose (A, **Figure 6**) and the thermostat housing bypass hose (B) from their fittings on the radiator filler neck.

7. Release the hose clamp, and disconnect the thermostat housing hose (C, **Figure 6**) from the radiator fitting.

8. Remove the upper oil cooler mounting bolts (**Figure 7**) that secure the oil cooler to the radiator. Watch for the collar and damper installed with each mount.

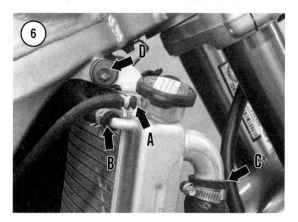

9. Remove the upper radiator-mounting bolt (D, **Figure 6**) from each side of the radiator. Watch for the collar in radiator damper.

10. Remove the lower radiator mounting bolt (**Figure 8**) and collar.

11. Carefully remove the radiator from the frame. To avoid damaging either the fender or radiator, do not strike the front fender during removal.

12. Inspect the radiator as described in this section.

13. Install by reversing these removal steps while noting the following:

    a. Replace all radiator hoses if they are deteriorated or are damaged in any way.

    b. Make sure the damper and collar are in place on each radiator and oil cooler mount.

    c. Make sure the radiator fan and thermoswitch electrical connections are tight and free of corrosion.

    d. Refill and bleed the cooling system as described in Chapter Three.

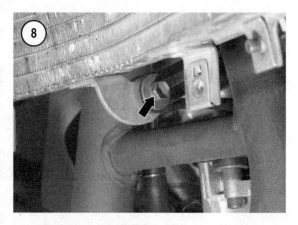

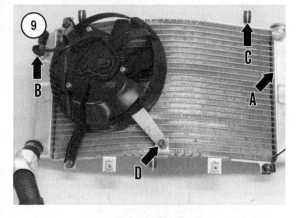

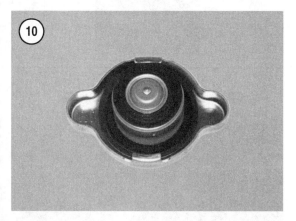

*CAUTION*
*Do not press too hard or the cooling fins and tubes may be damaged, thereby causing a leak.*

4. Carefully straighten out any bent cooling fins with a putty knife or a similar broad tipped tool.

5. Check for cracks or leaks (usually a moss-green colored residue) at all hose fittings and both side tank seams (A, **Figure 9**).

6. Inspect all mounts and brackets for cracks or damage.

7. Check for leaks at the thermoswitch (B, **Figure 9**). Make sure the switch is securely installed in the radiator.

8. Inspect the rubber damper (C, **Figure 9**) in each radiator mount. Replace any damaged or deteriorating damper.

9. To prevent radiator oxidation, touch up any areas where paint is worn off with a light coat of spray paint.

10. Inspect the seals on the radiator cap (**Figure 10**). Pressure test the cap (Chapter Three).

## THERMOSWITCH

### Removal/Installation

1. Remove the fairing side panel from the left side (Chapter Fifteen).

2. Drain the coolant (Chapter Three).

3. Disconnect the 2-pin electrical connector from the thermoswitch (B, **Figure 4**) on the left side of the radiator.

4. Loosen and remove the thermoswitch (B, **Figure 9**) from the radiator. Discard the O-ring installed behind the thermoswitch.

5. Installation is the reverse of removal.
   a. Install a new O-ring onto the thermoswitch.
   b. Tighten the thermoswitch to 17 N•m (12.5 ft.-lb.).

### Inspection

1. Remove the radiator fan assembly as described in this chapter. This allows access to the back of the radiator for inspection.

2. If compressed air is available, blow out dirt and bugs with short bursts of air directed at the backside of the radiator core.

3. Flush off the exterior of the radiator with a garden hose on low pressure. Spray both the front and back to remove all debris. Carefully use a whiskbroom or stiff paintbrush to remove any stubborn dirt from the cooling fins.

### Resistance Test

1. Remove the thermoswitch as described in this section.

2. Fill a beaker or pan with oil, and place it on a stove or hot plate.

*NOTE*
*The thermometer and the sensor must not touch the container sides or bottom. If either does, test readings will are inaccurate.*

3. Place a thermometer in the pan of oil.

**10**

4. Mount the thermoswitch so the threaded portion of the body is submerged as shown in **Figure 11**.

5. Attach an ohmmeter to the sensor terminals as shown. Check the continuity as follows:

   a. Gradually heat the oil to the off-on temperature indicated in **Table 2**, and check the continuity. The sensor should have continuity.

   b. Turn off the heat, and let the oil cool to the on-off temperature in **Table 2**. The switch should not have continuity at this temperature.

6. Replace the thermoswitch if it fails any portion of this test.

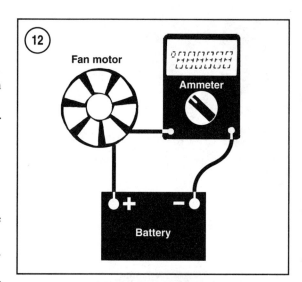

### RADIATOR FAN

**Removal/Installation**

Refer to **Figure 3**.

1. Remove the radiator as described in this chapter.

2. Place a blanket or large towels on the workbench to protect the radiator.

3. Remove the radiator fan mounting bolts (D, **Figure 9**), and lift the fan assembly from the radiator.

4. Install by reversing the removal steps.

**Test**

1. Remove the fairing side panel from the left side (Chapter Fifteen).

2. Disconnect the 2-pin radiator fan connector (A, **Figure 4**).

3. Use jumpers to connect a 12-volt battery directly to the connector. Connect the positive radiator fan terminal to the blue terminal in the fan side of the connector; connect the battery negative terminal to the connector's black terminal (fan side).

4. The fan should turn when power is directly applied to the fan.

5. Connect an ammeter in line between the fan and the battery as shown in **Figure 12**. Measure the load current. It should not exceed the specification in **Table 2**.

6. Replace the fan if it does not operate (Step 4) or if load current is excessive (Step 5).

### RADIATOR FAN RELAY

**Removal/Installation**

1. Remove the left upper panel from the front fairing (Chapter Fifteen).

2. Pull the radiator fan relay (**Figure 13**) straight up, and remove it from its mounting tang.

3. Disconnect the 4-pin connector from the relay.

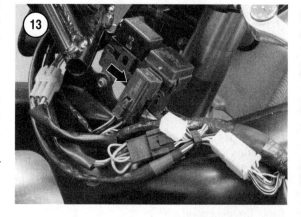

4. Installation is the reverse of removal. Make sure the relay's damper securely engages the mounting tang.

**Test**

1. Remove the radiator fan relay (**Figure 13**) as described in this section.

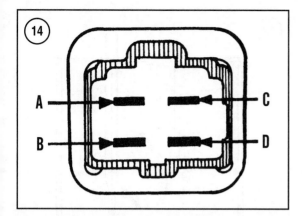

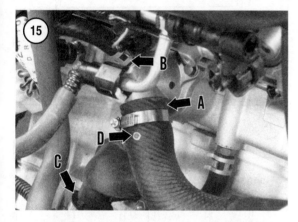

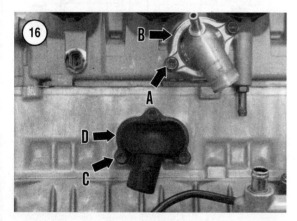

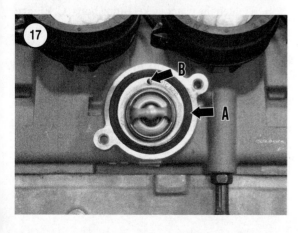

2. Check the continuity between the A and B terminals on the relay (**Figure 14**). The relay should not have continuity.

3. Use jumpers to connect the positive terminal of a 12-volt battery to the C terminal on the relay (**Figure 14**). Connect the negative battery terminal to the D relay terminal.

4. Check the continuity between the A and B terminals on the relay. The relay should have continuity while voltage is applied.

5. Replace the relay if it fails either portion of this test.

## ENGINE COOLANT TEMPERATURE (ECT) SENSOR

The ECT sensor is part of the fuel injection system. Refer to Chapter Eight.

## THERMOSTAT

### Removal/Inspection/Installation

The thermostat (**Figure 3**) sits inside a housing on the back of the cylinder head.

1. Drain the cooling system as described in Chapter Three.

2. Remove the fuel tank, air filter housing and throttle bodies (Chapter Eight).

3. Release the hose clamps, and disconnect the radiator hose (A, **Figure 15**) and bypass hose (B) from the thermostat housing.

4. Remove the thermostat housing bolts (A, **Figure 16**), and then lower the housing (B) from the cylinder head.

5. Remove the thermostat (A, **Figure 17**).

6. If necessary, test the thermostat as described in this section.

7. Inspect the thermostat for damage and make sure the spring is not sagging or broken. Make sure the rubber seal is in good condition with no deterioration or other damage. Replace the thermostat and seal if necessary.

8. Clean any debris or coolant residue from the thermostat housing. Make sure the ports are clear.

9. Installation is the reverse of removal. Note the following:

    a. Apply Suzuki Super Grease A, or its equivalent, to the rubber seal on the thermostat.

    b. Seat the thermostat so its air bleed hole (B, **Figure 17**) faces the top of the cylinder head.

    c. Tighten the thermostat housing bolts (A, **Figure 16**) to 10 N•m (89 in.-lb.).

    d. Position the radiator hose so its alignment dot (B, **Figure 15**) faces rearward.

**10**

e. Refill and bleed the cooling system (Chapter Three).

## Test

Test the thermostat to ensure proper operation. Replace the thermostat if it remains open at normal room temperature or stays closed after the specified test temperature has been reached.

*NOTE*
*The thermometer and the thermostat must not touch the container sides or bottom. If either does, the test readings are inaccurate.*

1. Suspend the thermostat and thermometer in a pan of water (**Figure 18**).

*NOTE*
*Valve operation may be sluggish and can take 3-5 minutes for the valve to operate properly and to open completely. Replace the thermostat if the valve fails to open. A thermostat cannot be serviced. Make sure to replace it with one of the same temperature rating.*

2. Gradually heat and gently stir the water until it reaches the valve opening temperature in **Table 1**. At this temperature the thermostat valve should open.
3. Continue heating the water until its temperature equals the valve lift temperature specified in **Table 1**.
4. Measure the valve lift (**Figure 19**). It should equal or exceed the specification in **Table 1**.
5. Replace the thermostat if it fails either portion of this test.

## WATER JACKET FITTING

### Removal/Installation

Refer to **Figure 3**.
1. Drain the cooling system as described in Chapter Three.
2. Remove the fuel tank, air filter housing and throttle bodies (Chapter Eight).
3. Release the hose clamp and disconnect the water pump output hose (C, **Figure 15**) from the water jacket fitting.
4. Remove the water jacket fitting bolts (C, **Figure 16**), and pull the water jacket fitting (D) from the cylinder block. Remove and discard the O-ring.
5. Installation is the reverse of removal.
   a. Install a new O-ring.

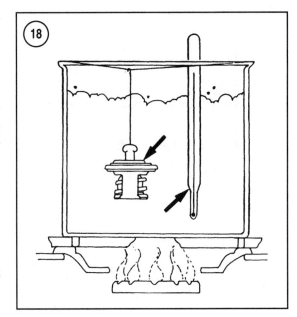

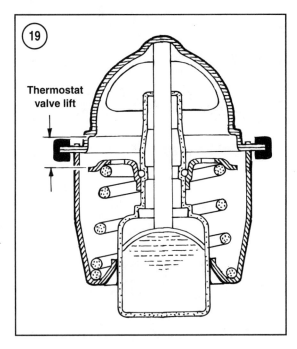

b. Tighten the water jacket fitting bolts (C, **Figure 16**) to 10 N•m (89 in.-lb.).

## WATER PUMP

### Removal/Installation

1. Remove the fairing side panel from the left side (Chapter Fifteen).
2. Remove the coolant reservoir (this chapter).
3. Remove the engine sprocket cover (Chapter Seven).
4. Inspect the area between the water pump and crankcase (A, **Figure 20**) for oil or coolant leaks. If

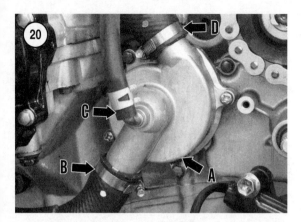

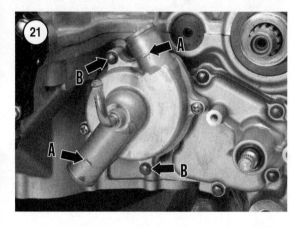

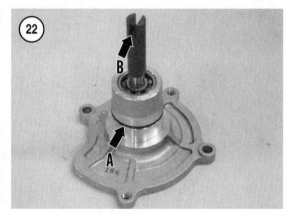

8. If necessary, disassemble and inspect the water pump as described in this section.

9. Install the water pump by reversing these removal steps. Note the following:

    a. Install a new O-ring (A, **Figure 22**) onto the water pump. Lubricate the O-ring with Suzuki Super Grease A, or its equivalent.

    b. Align the slot in the water pump shaft (B, **Figure 22**) with the raised tab on the oil pump shaft, and then install the water pump into the crankcase. The water pump shaft must engage the oil pump shaft. Reposition the water pump shaft as necessary, and seat the water pump in the crankcase. Tighten the water pump mounting bolts (B, **Figure 21**) to 10 N•m (89 in.-lb.).

    c. Install the pump input hose (B, **Figure 20**) and output hose (D) so their indexing dots align with the indexing marks (A, **Figure 21**) on the pump fittings.

    d. Make sure all hose clamp screws are tight.

    e. Refill and bleed the cooling system as described in Chapter Three.

    f. Start the engine and check for leaks before installing the fairing side panel.

**Disassembly**

Refer to **Figure 23**.

1. Remove the cover screws (**Figure 24**), and separate the pump cover from the housing. Discard the cover O-ring (A, **Figure 25**).

2. Thoroughly clean the pump housing (**Figure 26**) and cover (**Figure 25**) in solvent to remove all coolant residue.

3. Turn the impeller (A, **Figure 26**), and check the bearing for noise, roughness or excessive play. If any of these are noted, replace the bearing and oil seal as described in this section.

4. Remove the impeller bolt (B, **Figure 26**) from the shaft.

5. Lift the lockwasher (A, **Figure 27**), gasket (B) and impeller (C) off the shaft and out of the pump housing.

6. Pull the shaft (B, **Figure 22**) from the pump housing.

7. Inspect the water pump as described in this section.

**Assembly**

1. Apply Suzuki Super Grease A to the pump shaft (**Figure 28**), and install the shaft (B, **Figure 22**) into the housing.

engine oil leaks are found, inspect the water pump oil seal and O-ring. If coolant leaks are noted, inspect the mechanical seal and seal washer.

5. Drain the coolant and engine oil. (Chapter Three).

6. Disconnect the input hose (B, **Figure 20**), bypass hose (C) and output hose (D) from their respective fittings. Note how the indexing dots on the input and output hoses align with the indexing marks (A, **Figure 21**) on their fittings.

7. Remove the water pump mounting bolts (B, **Figure 21**), and pull the pump from the crankcase. Discard the water pump O-ring (A, **Figure 22**).

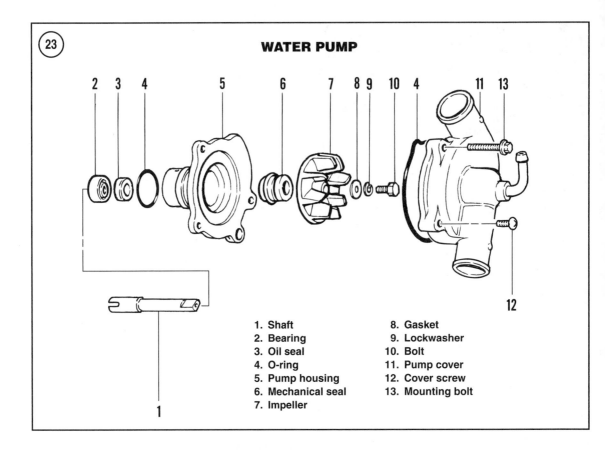

**WATER PUMP**

1. Shaft
2. Bearing
3. Oil seal
4. O-ring
5. Pump housing
6. Mechanical seal
7. Impeller
8. Gasket
9. Lockwasher
10. Bolt
11. Pump cover
12. Cover screw
13. Mounting bolt

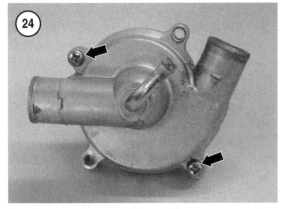

2. Install impeller (C, **Figure 27**) so its flats engage those on the shaft.

3. Install the gasket (A, **Figure 27**) and a new lockwasher (B). The metal side of the gasket (A, **Figure 29**) and the concave side of the lockwasher (B) must face the impeller.

4. Install the impeller bolt (B, **Figure 26**). Apply Suzuki Thread Lock 1342 to the bolt threads, and tighten the impeller bolt (**Figure 30**) to 8 N•m (71 in.-lb.).

5. Lubricate a new O-ring with coolant, and fit the O-ring into the groove in the pump cover (A, **Figure 25**).

6. Position the pump cover onto the pump housing, and install the cover screws (**Figure 24**). Tighten the water pump cover screws to 6 N•m (53 in.-lb.).

**Inspection**

1. Visually inspect the mechanical seal (A, **Figure 31**) and the pump housing (B) for corrosion, damage or signs of leaking. Pay attention to the area where the mechanical seal seats against the housing. If necessary, replace the mechanical seal as described later in this section.

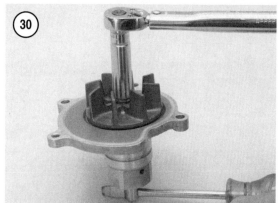

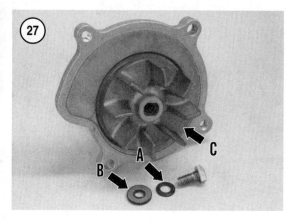

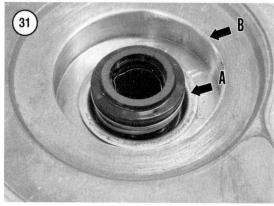

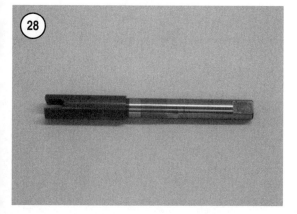

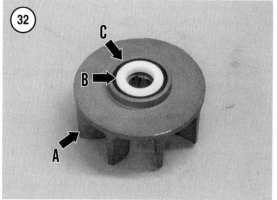

10

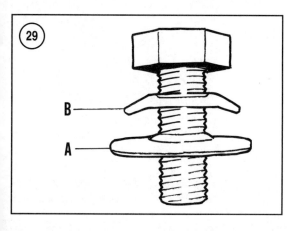

2. Visually inspect the pump shaft (**Figure 28**) for scoring or other signs of damage.

3. Check the impeller blades (A, **Figure 32**) for corrosion or damage. If corrosion is minor, clean the blades. Replace the impeller if corrosion is excessive or if the blades are cracked or broken.

4. Manually rotate the bearing (**Figure 33**). Replace the bearing if it is noisy or has excessive play.

5. Inspect the impeller seal (B, **Figure 32**) and rubber seal (C) for signs of damage or leaking. Replace the impeller seal and rubber seal by performing the following:

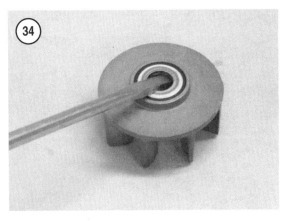

a. Pry the impeller seal (**Figure 34**) and then the rubber seal from the impeller.

b. Lubricate a new rubber seal with Suzuki Super Grease A, or its equivalent, and install it.

c. Fit a new impeller seal into place so its marked side faces into the impeller (**Figure 35**).

d. Drive the seal into place with a driver or socket that matches the impeller seal's outside diameter.

6. Inspect the water pump cover (B, **Figure 25**) for corrosion and damage. Remove any corrosion from the cover. Make sure the inlet, outlet and bypass fittings are clear.

7. Replace any worn or damaged part. Use the Suzuki bearing remover to replace a bearing or mechanical seal. If this special tool is unavailable, take the pump to a Suzuki dealership for service.

## Mechanical Seal, Oil Seal and Bearing Replacement

A bearing set remover (Suzuki part No. 09921-20220) is needed to remove the bearing and mechanical seal from the water pump. Do not remove the mechanical seal without this tool. The pump housing can be damaged. If the bearing or mechanical seal re-

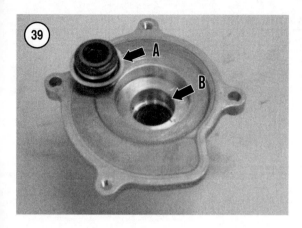

quires replacement and the tool is unavailable, take the pump to a dealership for service.

1. Remove the mechanical seal (A, **Figure 31**) from the pump housing. Follow the tool manufacturer's instructions.

2. Pry the oil seal (**Figure 36**) from the pump housing.

3. Remove the bearing (**Figure 33**) from the pump housing.

4. Clean and dry the housing bore.

5. Apply engine oil to the outer surface of the bearing, and set it squarely in the housing bore (**Figure 37**). The side of the bearing with the manufacturer's marks must face out.

6. Select a bearing driver or socket that matches the outside diameter of the bearing. Drive the bearing into the housing until it bottoms.

7. Pack the lips of a new oil seal with Suzuki Super Grease A. Set the oil seal into the housing bore so the side with the manufacturer's marks faces out. Select a bearing driver or socket that matches the outside diameter of the oil seal. Drive the seal into the housing until it bottoms. Refer to **Figure 38**.

8. Apply Suzuki Bond 1207B, or an equivalent sealant, to the seating surface of a new mechanical seal (A, **Figure 39**). Set the mechanical seal squarely into the housing bore (B, **Figure 39**).

9. Select a bearing driver or socket that matches the outside diameter of the seal seat, and drive the seal into the bore until it bottoms (A, **Figure 31**).

10

### Table 1 COOLING SYSTEM SPECIFICATIONS

| Item | Specification |
| --- | --- |
| Coolant | |
|   Type | Antifreeze/coolant compatible with aluminum radiator |
|   Ratio | Mixed with distilled water @ 50:50 ratio |
| Capacity | |
|   Engine | Approx. 2700 ml (2.9 U.S. qt. ) |
|   Reservoir | Approx. 250 ml (0.3 U.S. qt. ) |
| Radiator cap opening pressure | 95-125 kPa (13.5-17.8 psi) |
| System test pressure | 120 kPa (17 psi) |
| Thermostat | |
|   Valve opening temperature | Approx. 82° C (180° F) |
|   Valve lift/temperature | Over 8.0 mm at 95° C (over 0.31 in. at 203° F) |

### Table 2 COOLING SYSTEM ELECTRICAL SPECIFICATIONS

| Item | Specification |
| --- | --- |
| Thermoswitch operating temperature | |
|   Off-on | Approximately 105° C (221° F) |
|   On-off | Approximately 100° C (212° F) |
| Radiator fan load current (maximum) | 5 amps |

## Table 3 COOLING SYSTEM TORQUE SPECIFICATIONS

| Item | N•m | in.-lb. | ft.-lb. |
|------|-----|---------|---------|
| Coolant bypass fitting | 14 | – | 10 |
| Engine coolant temperature gauge sensor | 18 | – | 13 |
| Impeller bolt | 8 | 71 | – |
| Thermoswitch | 17 | – | 12.5 |
| Thermostat housing bolt | 10 | 89 | – |
| Water jacket fitting bolt | 10 | 89 | – |
| Water pump cover screw | 6 | 53 | – |
| Water pump mounting bolt | 10 | 89 | – |

# CHAPTER ELEVEN

# WHEELS, TIRES AND DRIVE CHAIN

This chapter covers the front and rear wheels, tires and drive chain.

When servicing components described in this chapter, compare any measurements to the specification in **Table 1** at the end of this chapter. Replace worn or damaged components. During assembly, tighten fasteners to the specified torque.

## MOTORCYCLE STAND

Many procedures in this chapter require that the motorcycle be supported with a wheel off the ground. A motorcycle front end stand (**Figure 1**) or swing arm stand does this safely and effectively. Before purchasing or using a stand, check the manufacturer's instructions to make sure the stand works on the motorcycle. Perform the required modification(s) on the stand or motorcycle before lifting the motorcycle. When using a motorcycle stand, have an assistant standing by.

An adjustable centerstand can also be used to support the motorcycle with a wheel off the ground. Again, check the manufacturer's instructions before lifting the motorcycle with an adjustable centerstand. It is also necessary to be able to tie down one end of the motorcycle.

Regardless of the method used to lift the motorcycle, make sure it is properly supported before walking away.

## BRAKE ROTOR PROTECTION

Protect the rotor when servicing a wheel. Never set a wheel down on the brake rotor. It may be bent or scratched. When a wheel must be placed on its side, support the wheel on wooden blocks (**Figure 2**). Position the blocks along the outer circumference of the wheel so the rotor lies between the blocks and does not rest on them or contact the ground.

## FRONT WHEEL

### Removal

1. Securely support the motorcycle on level ground. Remove both fairing side panels from the motorcycle.
2. Shift the transmission into gear to prevent the motorcycle from rolling in either direction.

*NOTE*
*Insert a piece of vinyl tube or wood between the pads of each caliper once the*

*caliper is removed. This way, the pistons are not forced out of the cylinder if the brake lever is inadvertently squeezed. If this does happen, the caliper may have to be disassembled to reseat the pistons and the system will has to be bled. By using the wood, bleeding the brake is not necessary when installing the wheel.*

3. Remove each front brake caliper (Chapter Fourteen). Use a bungee cord to suspend the calipers from the motorcycle.

4. Remove the front fender (Chapter Fifteen).

5. Loosen both clamp bolts on the right fork leg (A, **Figure 3**).

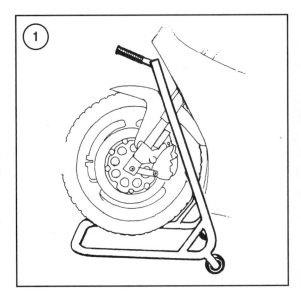

*NOTE*
*On 1999-2001 models, use a socket or wrench to loosen the front axle. On 2002-on models, use a 24-mm Allen socket on the front axle (B, **Figure 3**). If a 24-mm Allen socket is unavailable, fashion a tool (**Figure 4**) from a bolt and two nuts that measure 24 mm across opposite flats. This tool also works on the swing arm pivot shaft on 2003-on models.*

6. Unscrew the axle (B, **Figure 3**) from the spacer nut on the left fork leg, but do not remove the axle at this time.

7. On the left fork leg, loosen the clamp bolts (A, **Figure 5**) and remove spacer nut (B).

*CAUTION*
*If using a jack, place a piece of wood on the jack pad to protect the oil pan.*

8. Place a suitable size jack or wooden blocks under the oil pan to support the motorcycle securely with the wheel off the ground. Lift the motorcycle.

9. Pull the axle (B, **Figure 3**) from the wheel and fork legs.

10. Lower the wheel, and roll it from between the front fork legs.

*CAUTION*
*Do not set the wheel down on the brake disc. It may get scratched or warped. Set the tire sidewalls on two wooden blocks.*

11. Inspect the wheel as described in this chapter.

### Installation

1. Make sure the bearing surfaces of each fork leg, the spacer nut and axle are free from burrs and nicks.

2. Insert the spacer nut (B, **Figure 5**) into the left fork leg.

3. Tighten the clamp bolts on the left fork leg (A, **Figure 5**) to 23 N•m (17 ft.-lb.).

4. Correctly position the wheel so the directional arrow (**Figure 6**) points in the direction of forward wheel rotation.

5. Apply a light coat of grease to the front axle.

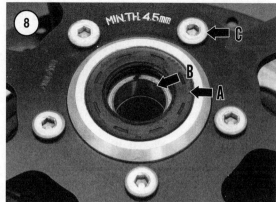

6. Position the wheel between the fork legs, lift the wheel and insert the front axle through the right fork leg, the wheel hub and into the spacer nut.

7. Install the axle (B, **Figure 3**) into the spacer nut. Tighten the front axle to 100 N•m (74 ft.-lb.).

8. Install both brake calipers (Chapter Fourteen).

9. Remove the motorcycle support so both wheels rest on the ground.

10. Shift the transmission into neutral.

11. Apply the front brake, push down hard on the handlebars and pump the fork four or five times to seat the front axle.

12. Tighten the clamp bolts on the right fork leg (A, **Figure 3**) to 23 N•m (17 ft.-lb.).

13. Roll the motorcycle back and forth several times. Apply the front brake as many times as necessary to make sure all brake pads seat against the brake disc correctly.

11

**WHEEL INSPECTION**

During inspection, compare all measurements to the specification in **Table 1**. Replace any part that is damaged, out of specification or worn to the service limit.

1. Remove the wheel as described in this chapter.

2. On a rear wheel, remove the collar (A, **Figure 7**) from each side.

3. Inspect the seal(s) (A, **Figure 8**, typical) for excessive wear, hardness, cracks or other damage. If necessary, replace the seal(s) as described in this chapter.

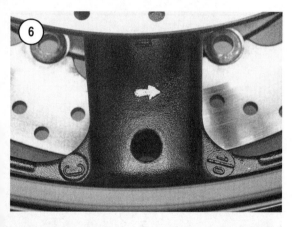

4. Inspect the bearings (B, **Figure 8**) as described in this chapter.

5. Remove any corrosion from the axle (**Figure 9**) or collar (**Figure 10**) with a piece of fine emery cloth.

6. Check axle runout with a dial gauge and V-blocks (**Figure 11**). Replace an axle that exceeds its specified runout limit (**Table 1**).

7. Install the wheel on a truing stand. Check wheel runout by performing the following:

    a. Measure the radial (up and down) runout of the wheel rim with a dial indicator as shown in **Figure 12**.

    b. Measure the axial (side to side) runout of the wheel rim with a dial indicator as shown in **Figure 12**.

8. If the wheel runout is out of specification (**Table 1**), inspect the wheel bearings as described in this chapter. Note the following:

    a. If the wheel bearings are in good condition, the wheel must be replaced.

    b. If either wheel bearing is worn, disassemble the hub and replace both bearings as a set.

9. Check the tightness of the brake disc bolts (C, **Figure 8**). If a bolt is loose, remove and reinstall the bolt. Apply Suzuki Thread Lock Super 1360, or its equivalent, to the threads of the brake disc bolts. Torque the brake disc bolts on a front wheel to 23 N•m (17 ft.-lb.); on a rear wheel to 35 N•m (26 ft.-lb.).

10. Visually inspect the brake discs. Measure the brake disc runout as described in Chapter Fourteen. If brake disc runout is excessive, measure wheel runout. If wheel runout is within specification, replace the brake disc as described in Chapter Fourteen.

11. Check the tightness of the rear sprocket nuts (B, **Figure 7**). If a nut is loose, tighten it 60 N•m (44 ft.-lb.).

12. Inspect the wheel for dents, bending or cracks. Check the rim and rim sealing surface (cast wheels) for scratches that are deeper than 0.5 mm (0.02 in.). If any of these conditions are present, replace the wheel.

13. Because the caliper(s) are off the disc(s) at this time, check the brake pads for wear. Refer to Chapter Fourteen.

## WHEEL BEARING INSPECTION

1. Pry the seal(s) (**Figure 13**, typical) from the hub or rear coupling.

> *CAUTION*
> *Do not remove the wheel bearings for inspection purposes. Wheel bearings are damaged during removal. Remove the wheel bearings only if they are to be replaced.*

2. Turn each bearing (B, **Figure 8**) by hand. The bearings must turn smoothly with no noise.

3. Inspect the play of the inner race of each wheel bearing. Check for excessive axial play or radial play

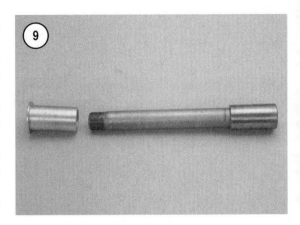

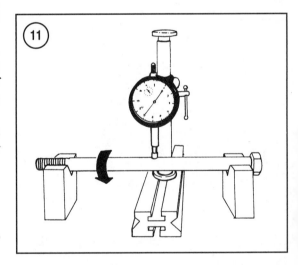

(**Figure 14**). Replace the bearing if it has an excessive amount of free play.

4. On sealed bearings, check the outer seal for buckling or other damage that would allow debris to enter the bearing.

5. On non-sealed bearings, check the balls for evidence of wear, pitting or excessive heat (bluish tint). Replace the bearings if necessary. Always replace the bearings as a complete set. When buying new bear-

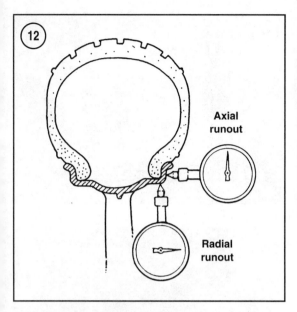

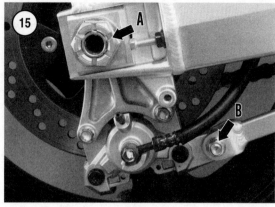

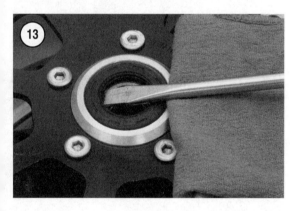

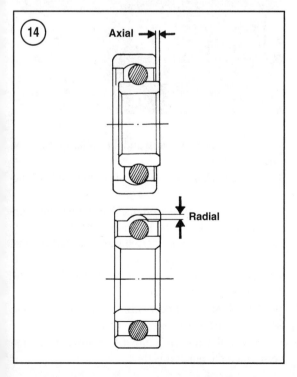

ings, take the old bearings along to ensure a perfect match.

6. Check the bearing fit in the hub or coupling by trying to move the bearing laterally in the bore. The bearing should fit tightly. Loose bearings allow the wheel to wobble. If a bearing is loose, the bearing bore in the hub or coupling is probably worn or damaged.

7. Replace questionable bearings. Ensure a perfect match by comparing the old bearing to the new one.

### REAR WHEEL

**Removal**

The rear wheel can be removed with the brake caliper installed. Simply lower the brake caliper bracket with the caliper installed.

1. Securely support the motorcycle on a level surface. Remove the fairing side panel from each side.

2. On U.S., California and Canada models, remove the cotter pin from the rear axle nut (A, **Figure 15**). Discard the cotter pin. A new one must be installed during assembly.

3. Have an assistant apply the rear brake, and then loosen the axle nut (A, **Figure 15**).

4. Block the front wheel to prevent the motorcycle from rolling in either direction while the bike is raised.

*CAUTION*
*If using a jack, place a piece of wood on the jack pad to protect the oil pan.*

5. Place a suitable size jack or wooden blocks under the oil pan to support the motorcycle securely with the rear wheel off the ground. Lift the motorcycle.

6. Loosen the rear torque arm nut (B, **Figure 15**).

7. Loosen the chain adjuster locknut (A, **Figure 16**) and the chain adjuster (B) on each side of the swing arm to allow maximum slack in the drive chain.

11

8. Remove the rear axle nut (A, **Figure 15**). On all models except U.S., California and Canada, remove the washer.

9. Pull the rear axle (C, **Figure 16**) from the left side of the motorcycle. The adjuster blocks come off when the rear axle is withdrawn. The adjuster blocks are not interchangeable. Mark them with an R (right) and L (left) so they can be reinstalled on the correct side.

10. Lower the caliper/bracket assembly from the brake disc.

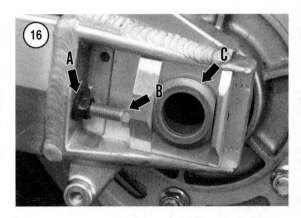

*NOTE*
*Insert a piece of vinyl tubing or wood into the caliper in place of the brake disc. This way, the pistons are not forced out of the cylinders if the brake pedal is inadvertently pressed. If this does happen, the caliper must be disassembled to reseat the pistons, and the system has to be bled. By using the wood, bleeding the brake is not necessary when installing the wheel.*

11. Push the wheel forward, and remove the drive chain from the rear sprocket.

12. Pull the wheel rearward, and remove the wheel from the swing arm.

13. Suspend the caliper bracket from the frame with a bungee cord or piece of wire to relieve any strain from the hose.

14. Remove the collar from the left and right sides of the wheel.

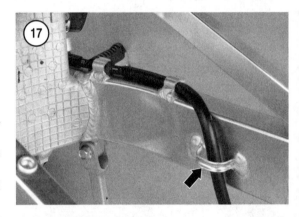

*CAUTION*
*Do not set the wheel down on the brake disk. It may get scratched or warped. Set the sidewalls on two wooden blocks.*

15. Inspect the wheel as described in this chapter.

## Installation

1. Clean all dirt and burrs from the axle-contact surfaces in the swing arm.

2. Apply a light coat of grease to the axle, bearings, collars (**Figure 10**) and seals.

3. Install the left and right collars (A, **Figure 7**) into each side of the rear hub. The shoulder on each collar should face the bearing.

4. Check that the rear brake hose is routed through the holder on the inside of the swing arm (**Figure 17**).

5. Position the wheel into place and roll it forward. Install the drive chain onto the rear sprocket.

6. Move the wheel toward the left side.

7. Raise the rear brake caliper and fit it onto the brake disc. Make sure the caliper bracket (**Figure 18**) sits between the swing arm and the collar in the right side of the hub.

8. Seat each chain adjuster in the correct side of the swing arm.

9. Raise the rear wheel up and into alignment with the swing arm. From the left side of the motorcycle, insert the rear axle through swing arm, rear wheel, the caliper bracket and out through the right side of the swing arm. Push the axle all the way to the right until it bottoms in the chain adjuster.

10. On all models except U.S., California and Canada, install the washer on the rear axle.

11. Install the rear axle nut (A, **Figure 15**). Finger-tighten the nut at this time.

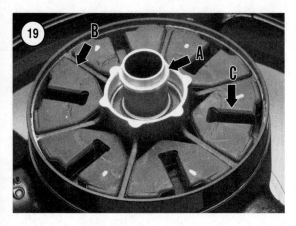

12. Adjust the drive chain as described in Chapter Three.

13. Tighten the rear torque arm nut (B, **Figure 15**) to 35 N•m (26 ft.-lb.).

14. Torque the axle nut to 100 N•m (74 ft.-lb.), and tighten each chain adjuster locknut securely.

15. On U.S., California and Canada models, install a new cotter pin onto the rear axle nut and bend both ends over completely.

16. If removed, install the rear brake caliper (Chapter Fifteen).

17. Lower the motorcycle and remove the jack or wooden block(s) from under the oil pan. Remove the blocks from the front wheel.

18. Roll the motorcycle back and forth several times. Apply the rear brake as many times as necessary to make sure the brake pads are seated against the brake disc correctly.

19. Place the motorcycle on the sidestand.

## REAR COUPLING AND REAR SPROCKET

### Removal/Installation

1. Remove the rear wheel as described in this chapter.

2. If still in place, remove the collar (A, **Figure 7**) from the left side.

3. If the rear sprocket is going to be removed, break loose the rear sprocket nuts (B, **Figure 7**) at this time.

4. Pull straight up and remove the rear coupling assembly (C, **Figure 7**) from the rear hub.

> *NOTE*
> *If the rear coupling assembly is difficult to remove, tap on the backside of the sprocket (from the opposite side of the wheel through the wheel spokes) with the wooden handle of a hammer.*

5. Remove the inner retainer (A, **Figure 19**) from the rear coupling assembly.

6. If necessary, remove the rear sprocket nuts (B, **Figure 7**) and separate the rear sprocket from the rear coupling.

7. Remove the dampers (B, **Figure 19**) from the rear hub.

8. Install by reversing these removal steps while noting the following:

    a. Install each damper so its knob (**Figure 20**) locks into the hole (A, **Figure 21**) in the hub.

    b. Align the rear coupling bosses (A, **Figure 22**) with the cutouts in the rubber dampers (C, **Figure 19**), and press the rear coupling onto the hub.

**11**

c. If removed, install the rear sprocket so the side with the I.D. stamp (D, **Figure 7**) faces out away from the rear coupling.

d. Apply Suzuki Thread Lock Super 1360 to the stud threads, and tighten the rear sprocket nuts (B, **Figure 7**) to 60 N•m (44 ft.-lb.). Recheck the sprocket nuts after the first few rides or until they seat to the sprocket.

## Inspection

1. Inspect the rubber dampers (**Figure 20**) for signs of damage or deterioration. If damaged, replace the dampers as a set.

2. Inspect the raised webs (B, **Figure 21**) in the rear hub. Check for cracks or wear. If any damage is visible, replace the rear wheel.

3. Inspect the rear coupling assembly (**Figure 22**) for cracks or damage and replace if necessary.

4. Inspect the rear sprocket teeth. If the teeth are worn (**Figure 23**), replace the rear sprocket as described in this section.

> *CAUTION*
> *If the rear sprocket requires replacement, also replace the engine sprocket and the drive chain. Never install a new drive chain over worn sprockets or a worn drive chain over new sprockets. The old part wears out the new part prematurely.*

5. If the rear sprocket requires replacement, also inspect the drive chain (Chapter Three) and engine sprocket (Chapter Seven). They also may be worn and need replacing.

6. Inspect the seal for excessive wear, hardness, cracks or other damage. If necessary, replace the seal as described in the front or rear hub sections in this chapter.

7. Inspect the bearings as described in this chapter.

## FRONT HUB

### Disassembly

Refer to **Figure 24**.

1. Remove the front wheel as described in this chapter.

2. Carefully pry out each seal (**Figure 13**). Place a shop cloth under the tool to protect the hub. Discard all removed seals. They cannot be reinstalled.

3. If necessary, remove the brake disc bolts (C, **Figure 8**) and remove the disc.

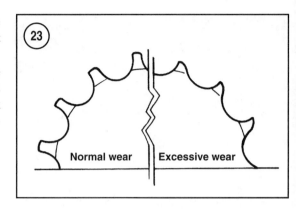

**23**

Normal wear | Excessive wear

4. Before proceeding further, inspect the wheel bearings (B, **Figure 8**) as described in this chapter. If they must be replaced, perform Step 5A or Step 5B.

5A. If the special tools are not used, perform the following:

a. To remove the right and left bearings and distance collar, insert a soft aluminum or brass drift into one side of the hub (**Figure 25**).

b. Push the distance collar to one side and place the drift on the inner race of the lower bearing.

c. Tap the bearing out of the hub with a hammer, working around the perimeter of the inner race. Remove the bearing and distance collar.

d. Repeat for the bearing on the other side.

> *WARNING*
> *Wear safety glasses while using the wheel bearing remover set.*

5B. To remove the bearings with a wheel bearing remover set, perform the following:

a. Select the correct size remover head tool and insert it into the bearing (**Figure 26**).

b. Turn the wheel over and insert the remover shaft into the backside of the adapter. Tap the shaft and force it into the slit in the adapter (**Figure 26**). This forces the adapter against the bearing inner race.

c. Tap on the end of the shaft with a hammer and drive the bearing out of the hub (**Figure 27**). Remove the bearing and the distance collar.

d. Repeat for the bearing on the other side.

6. Clean the inside and the outside of the hub with solvent. Dry with compressed air.

### Assembly

> *CAUTION*
> *Always install **new** bearings. The old bearings are damaged during removal and must not be reused. Replace bearings as a set. If any one bearing in a*

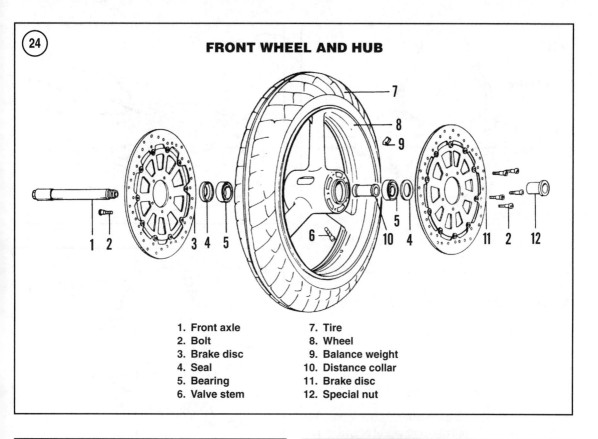

**FRONT WHEEL AND HUB**

1. Front axle
2. Bolt
3. Brake disc
4. Seal
5. Bearing
6. Valve stem
7. Tire
8. Wheel
9. Balance weight
10. Distance collar
11. Brake disc
12. Special nut

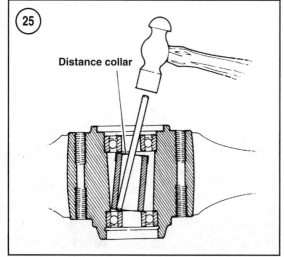

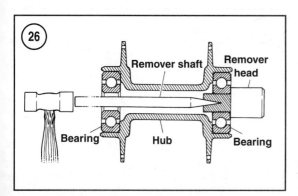

*wheel is worn, replace all the bearings in that wheel. On the front wheel, replace both wheel bearings. On the rear wheel replace both wheel bearings as well as the rear coupling bearing.*

1. On non-sealed bearings, pack the bearings with Suzuki Super Grease A, or its equivalent. To pack the bearings, spread some grease in the palm of your hand and scrape the open side of the bearing across the grease until the bearing is completely packed full of grease. Spin the bearing a few times to determine if there are any open areas. Repack if necessary.

2. Blow any debris out of the hub.

**11**

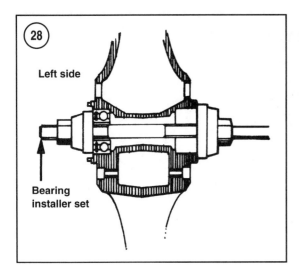

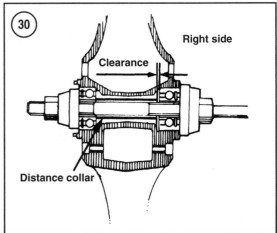

3. Apply a light coat of grease to the bearing seat in the hub.

> *CAUTION*
> *Install non-sealed bearings with the single sealed side facing outward. Make sure the bearings are completely seated.*

4A. If using a bearing installer (Suzuki part No. 09941-34513) to install the front wheel bearings, perform the following:

> *NOTE*
> *When replacing the bearings in the front hub, install the left bearing first and then the right bearing.*

a. Set the left bearing into the hub with the sealed side facing out, and assemble the bearing installer as shown in **Figure 28**.

b. Tighten the bearing installer (**Figure 29**) and pull the left bearing into the hub until it is completely seated. Remove the bearing installer.

c. Turn the wheel over (right side up) on the workbench, and install the distance collar.

d. Set the right bearing into the hub with the sealed side facing out, and assemble the bearing installer as shown in **Figure 30**.

e. Tighten the bearing installer and pull the right bearing into the hub until there is a *slight* clearance between the inner race and the distance collar. Do not press the parts completely together.

f. Remove the bearing installer.

4B. If special tools are not available, perform the following:

> *NOTE*
> *When replacing the bearings in the front hub, install the left bearing first and then the right bearing.*

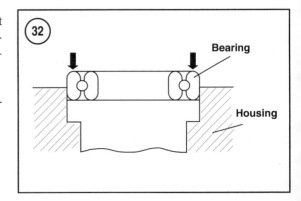

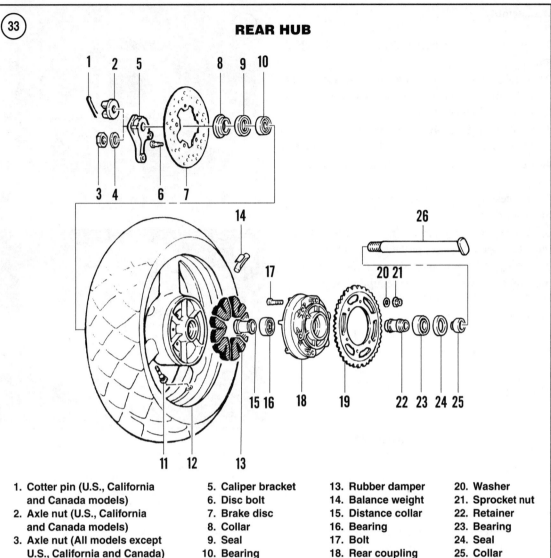

**REAR HUB**

1. Cotter pin (U.S., California
   and Canada models)
2. Axle nut (U.S., California
   and Canada models)
3. Axle nut (All models except
   U.S., California and Canada)
4. Washer (All models except
   U.S., California and Canada)
5. Caliper bracket
6. Disc bolt
7. Brake disc
8. Collar
9. Seal
10. Bearing
11. Valve stem
12. Wheel
13. Rubber damper
14. Balance weight
15. Distance collar
16. Bearing
17. Bolt
18. Rear coupling
19. Rear sprocket
20. Washer
21. Sprocket nut
22. Retainer
23. Bearing
24. Seal
25. Collar
26. Rear axle

11

a. Set the left bearing into place in the hub so its sealed side faces out.

b. Using a bearing driver or socket that matches the diameter of the outer bearing race, tap the first bearing squarely into place in the hub (**Figure 31**). Tap on the outer race only (**Figure 32**). Do not tap on the inner race or the bearing might be damaged. Make sure the bearing is completely seated in the hub.

c. Turn the wheel over on the workbench and install the distance collar.

d. Use the same tool set-up, and drive the right bearing into the hub until there is a *slight* clearance between the inner race and the distance collar.

5. If the brake disc was removed, perform the following:

a. Apply a small amount Suzuki Thread Lock Super 1360 to the brake disc bolt threads before installation.

b. Install the brake disc. Tighten the brake disc bolts (C, **Figure 8**) to 23 N•m (17 ft.-lb.).

6. Pack the lips of the new seals with Suzuki Super Grease A, or its equivalent, and install the seals (A, **Figure 8**). Drive each seal into the hub with a bearing driver or socket that matches the outside diameter of the seal (**Figure 31**).

**REAR HUB**

Refer to **Figure 33**.

## Disassembly

1. Remove the rear wheel as described in this chapter.

2. If still in place, remove the collar (A, **Figure 34**) from the brake disc side of the hub and from the rear coupling (A, **Figure 35**).

3. Pry the seal (B, **Figure 34**) from the brake disc side of the hub and from the rear coupling (B, **Figure 35**).

4. Remove the rear coupling from the hub as described in this chapter.

5. If necessary, remove the brake disc bolts and remove the disc.

6. Before proceeding further, inspect the wheel bearings (C, **Figure 21**) as described in this chapter.

7. If the bearing must be replaced, remove the bearings from the rear hub and rear coupling by performing Step 5A or Step 5B of *Front Hub, Disassembly* in this chapter.

8. Clean the inside and the outside of the hub with solvent. Dry with compressed air.

## Assembly

> *CAUTION*
> *Always install **new** bearings. The bearings are damaged during removal and must not be reused.*

1. On nonsealed bearings, pack the bearings with Suzuki Super Grease A or its equivalent. To pack the bearings, spread some grease in the palm of your hand and scrape the open side of the bearing across the grease until the bearing is completely packed full of grease. Spin the bearing a few times to determine if there are any open areas. Repack if necessary.

2. Blow any debris out of the hub.

3. Apply a light coat of grease to the bearing seat in the hub.

> *CAUTION*
> *Install partially sealed bearings with the single sealed side facing outward. Make sure the bearings are completely seated.*

4A. If using a bearing installer (Suzuki part No. 09941-34513) to install the rear wheel bearings, perform the following:

> *NOTE*
> *When replacing the bearings in the rear hub, install the right bearing first and then the left bearing.*

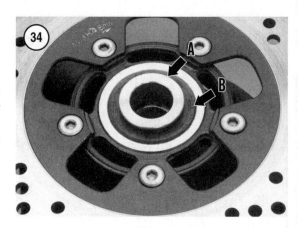

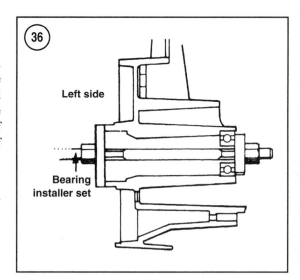

a. Set the right bearing into the hub with its sealed side facing out, and assemble the bearing installer as shown in **Figure 36**.

b. Tighten the bearing installer (**Figure 29**) and pull the right bearing into the hub until it is completely seated. Remove the bearing installer.

c. Turn the wheel over (left side up) on the workbench and install the distance collar.

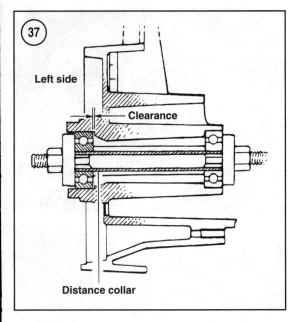

**Left side**

Clearance

Distance collar

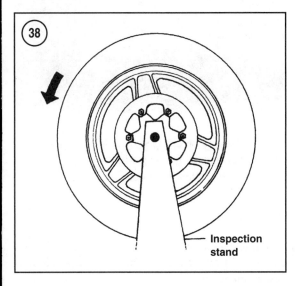

Inspection stand

the inner race or the bearing might be damaged. Make sure that the bearing is completely seated.

c. Turn the wheel over on the workbench and install the distance collar.

d. Use the same tool set-up and drive the left (C, **Figure 21**) bearing into the hub until there is a slight clearance between the inner race and the distance collar. Do not press them completely together.

5. Install a new bearing into the rear coupling. Use the bearing installer (Suzuki part No. 09941-34513) to pull the bearing into the coupling or repeat Step 4B.

6. If the brake disc was removed, perform the following:

a. Apply a small amount Suzuki Thread Lock Super 1360 to the threads of the brake disc bolts.

b. Tighten the brake disc bolts to 35 N•m (26 ft.-lb.).

7. Pack the lips of a new seal with Suzuki Super Grease A. Drive the seal (B, **Figure 34**) in the brake disc side of the hub.

8. Install the collar (A, **Figure 34**) into the hub. The collar's shoulder must face the bearing.

9. Install the rear coupling into the rear wheel as described in this chapter. Repeat Step 7 and Step 8 to install the oil seal (B, **Figure 35**) and collar (A) into the coupling.

**11**

### WHEEL BALANCE

Before balancing the wheel, make sure the wheel bearings are in good condition and properly lubricated. Also check the brakes for drag. The wheel must rotate freely.

When balancing the wheels, do so with the brake disc(s) and the rear coupling attached. These components rotate with the wheel and affect the balance.

1. Remove the front or rear wheel as described in this chapter.

2. Mount the wheel on an inspection stand (**Figure 38**) so the wheel can rotate freely.

3. Spin the wheel , and let it coast to a stop. Mark the tire at the lowest point with chalk or light colored crayon.

4. Spin the wheel several more times. If the wheel keeps coming to rest at the same point, it is out of balance.

5. Attach a test weight (**Figure 39**) to the upper (or light) side of the wheel, and repeat Step 4.

6. Experiment with different weights until the wheel comes to rest at a different position each time it is spun.

d. Set the left bearing into the hub with the sealed side facing out, and assemble the bearing installer as shown in **Figure 37**.

e. Tighten the bearing installer and pull the left bearing into the hub until there is a *slight* clearance between the inner race and the distance collar. Do not press them completely together.

f. Remove the bearing installer.

4B. If the special tools are not used, perform the following:

a. Set the right bearing onto the hub with its sealed side facing out.

b. Using a bearing driver or socket that matches the diameter of the outer bearing race, tap the bearing squarely into place in the hub. Tap on the outer race only (**Figure 32**). Do not tap on

7. Remove the test weights, thoroughly clean the rim surface, and install the correct size weight(s) onto the rim. Make sure they are secured in place so they do not fly off when riding.

## TIRES

> *WARNING*
> *The original equipment wheels are designed for tubeless tires. Do not install a tube inside a tubeless tire. Excessive heat may build up in the tire and cause the tube to burst.*

> *CAUTION*
> *The wheels can be damaged during tire removal. Work carefully to avoid damaging the tire beads, inner liner of the tire or the wheel rim (sealing surfaces). Insert rim protectors between the tire irons and rim to protect the rim.*

> *CAUTION*
> *Tires are more difficult to replace when the rubber is hard and cold. If the weather is hot, place the wheels and new tires in the sun or in a closed automobile. The heat helps soften the rubber, easing removal and installation. If the weather is cold, place the tires and wheels inside a warm building.*

> *CAUTION*
> *It is easier to replace tires when the wheel is mounted on a raised platform. A metal drum with the drum edge covered by a length of garden or heater hose (split lengthwise) works well. Whatever method is used, support the brake disc (front wheel) to prevent damage.*

Tire performance is greatly affected by tire pressure. Inspect the pressure frequently. Refer to **Table 1** for original equipment tire specifications. If using another tire brand, follow its recommendation.

Follow a break-in period for new tires. New tires have significantly less adhesion ability until scrubbed in. Do not subject a new tire to hard corning, hard acceleration or hard braking for the first 160 km (100 miles).

## Changing

Due to the size of the tire and tight bead/rim seal, changing tires can be difficult. Incorrect installation can damage both the tire and/or wheel. It is recom-

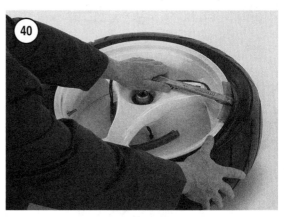

mended the tires be changed by a dealership with tire equipment designed for alloy wheels.

Refer to the following procedure as a guideline.

### Removal

1. If reusing the tire, mark the valve stem location on the tire so it can be installed in the same position for easier balancing.

2. Remove the valve core to deflate the tire.

3. Use a bead breaker and break the bead all the way around the tire. Do not try to force the bead with tire irons. Make sure both beads are clear of the rim beads.

4. Lubricate the tire beads with soapy water on the side to be removed first.

5. Using rim protectors, insert a tire iron under the bead (**Figure 40**). Force the bead on the opposite side of the tire into the center of the rim and pry the bead over the rim with the tire iron.

6. Insert the second tire iron next to the first to hold the bead over the rim. Then work around the tire with the first tool prying the bead over the rim (**Figure 41**). Work slowly by taking small bites with the tire irons. Taking large bites or using excessive force can damage the tire bead or rim.

7. If the tire is tight and difficult to pry over the rim, use a third tire iron and a rim protector. Use one hand and arm to hold the first two tire irons, and then use the other hand to operate the third tire iron when prying the tire over the rim.

8. Turn the wheel over. Insert a tire iron between the second bead and the same side of the rim that the first bead was pried over (**Figure 42**). Force the bead on the opposite side from the tool into the center of the rim. Pry the second bead off the rim, working around the wheel with the two rim protectors and tire irons.

9. Remove the valve stem and discard it. Remove all rubber residue from the valve stem hole and inspect the hole for cracks and other damage.

10. Remove old balance weights from the rim surface.

## Inspection

> *WARNING*
> *Carefully consider whether a tire should be replaced. If there is any doubt about the condition of the existing tire, replace it. Do not take a chance on a tire failure at any speed. If there is any doubt as to wheel/tire condition, take them to a dealership for a thorough inspection.*

1. Carefully clean the rim bead with a brush. Do not use excessive force or damage to the rim sealing surface will occur. Inspect the sealing surface for any cracks, corrosion or other damage.

2. If any one of the following is observed, replace the tire:

    a. A large puncture or split in the tread area.

    b. A bulge, puncture or split on the sidewall.

    c. Any type of ply separation.

    d. Tread separation or excessive abnormal wear pattern.

    e. Tread depth of less than the minimum in **Table 1** for original equipment tires. Aftermarket tire tread depth minimum may vary.

    f. Damage to either sealing bead.

    g. The cord is cut in any place.

    h. Flat spots in the tread from skidding.

    i. Any abnormality in the inner liner

## Installation

> *WARNING*
> *After installing new tires, follow the tire manufacturer's instructions for break-in.*

1. Install a new valve stem.

2A. If installing the original tire, carefully inspect it for any damage.

2B. If installing a new tire, remove all stickers from the tire tread.

3. Lubricate both beads of the tire with soapy water.

4. Make sure the correct tire, either front or rear, is installed on the correct wheel and that the direction arrow on the tire faces in the same direction as the wheel direction arrow. The sensor wheel, mounted on the left side of the front wheel, can be used to identify wheel rotation.

5. If remounting the old tire, align the mark made in Step 1 of *Removal* with the valve stem. If installing a new tire, align the balance mark on the bead (indicating the lightest point of the tire) with the valve stem.

6. Place the backside of the tire into the center of the rim. The lower bead should go into the center of the rim and the upper bead outside. Use both hands to push the backside of the tire into the rim (**Figure 43**) as far as possible. Use tire irons when it becomes difficult to install the tire by hand.

7. Press the upper bead into the rim opposite the valve. Pry the bead into the rim on both sides of the initial point with a tire iron, working around the rim to the valve stem (**Figure 44**). If the tire wants to pull up on one side, either use another tire iron or your knee to hold the tire in place. The last few inches are usually the most difficult to install. If possible, continue to push the tire into the rim by hand. Relubricate

**11**

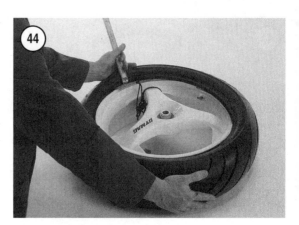

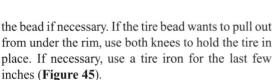

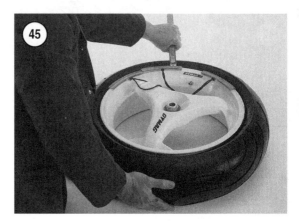

the bead if necessary. If the tire bead wants to pull out from under the rim, use both knees to hold the tire in place. If necessary, use a tire iron for the last few inches (**Figure 45**).

8. Check the bead on both sides of the tire for an even fit around the rim. Make sure the balance mark aligns with the valve stem.

9. Lubricate both sides of the tire with soapy water.

> *WARNING*
> *Always wear eye protection when seating the tire beads onto the rim. Never exceed 56 psi (4.0 k/cm² ) inflation pressure. The tire could burst, causing injury. Never stand directly over the tire while inflating it.*

10. Inflate the tire until the beads seat into place. A loud pop should be heard as each bead seats against its side of the rim.

11. After inflating the tire, check to see that the beads are fully seated and the tire rim lines are the same distance from the rim all the way around the tire (**Figure 46**). If one or both beads do not seat, deflate the tire, relubricate the rim and beads with soapy water and reinflate the tire.

12. Inflate the tire to the specified pressure (**Table 1**). Screw on the valve stem cap.

13. Balance the wheel as described in this section.

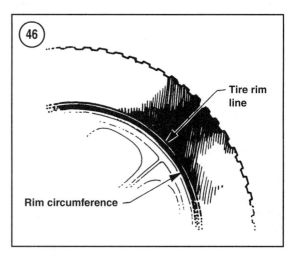

Tire rim line

Rim circumference

### Repairs

Only use tire plugs as an *emergency* repair. Refer to the manufacturer's instructions to install, and note the vehicle weight and speed restrictions. After performing an emergency tire repair with a plug, consider the repair temporary and replace the tire at the earliest opportunity.

Refer all tire repairs to a dealership or other qualified motorcycle technician.

## DRIVE CHAIN

### Inspection

Refer to *Drive Chain* in Chapter Three for inspection procedures.

### Replacement

All models are originally equipped with an O-ring chain that uses a staked master link (**Figure 47**). On

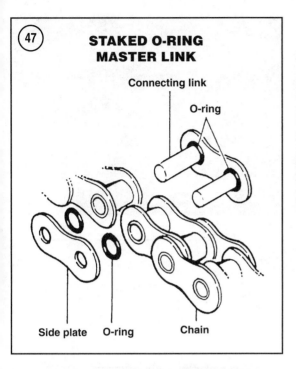

**STAKED O-RING MASTER LINK**

Connecting link

O-ring

Side plate     O-ring          Chain

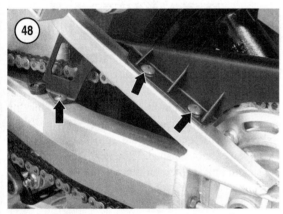

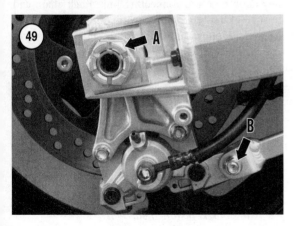

tool (Suzuki part No. 09922-22711). If using an aftermarket tool, follow its operating instructions. Use the following steps to supplement the instructions provided with that chain tool.

Refer to **Table 1** for drive chain specifications. Refer to *Drive Chain* in Chapter Three for routine drive chain inspection and lubrication procedures.

1. Securely support the motorcycle on a level surface.

2. Block the front wheel so the motorcycle does not roll in either direction while the rear wheel is off ground.

3. Remove the engine sprocket cover (Chapter Seven).

4. Remove the screws (**Figure 48**), and lift the chain guard from the swing arm.

5. On U.S., California and Canada models, remove the cotter pin from the axle nut (A, **Figure 49**).

6. Have an assistant apply the rear brake, and then loosen the axle nut (A, **Figure 49**).

7. Block the front wheel to prevent the motorcycle from rolling in either direction while the motorcycle is on a jack or wooden blocks.

*CAUTION*
*If using a jack, place a piece of wood on the jack pad to protect the oil pan.*

8A. If using a jack, perform the following:
    a. Remove both fairing side panels (Chapter Sixteen).
    b. If necessary, place a suitable size jack or wooden blocks under the oil pan to support the motorcycle securely with the rear wheel off the ground. Lift the motorcycle.

8B. Raise the rear of the motorcycle with a safety stand.

9. Loosen the rear torque arm nut (B, **Figure 49**).

10. Loosen the chain adjuster locknut (A, **Figure 50**) and the chain adjuster (B) on each side of the swing arm to allow maximum slack in the drive chain.

11. Assemble the chain tool, following the manufacturer's instructions.

these models, the chain can be replaced with the swing arm mounted on the motorcycle.

The following procedure describes the removal and installation of a drive chain with a drive chain

11

12. Rotate the wheel and located crimped pins on the master link. Break the chain at this point.

13. Install the chain tool across the link (**Figure 51**) to be removed. Operate the tool and push the connecting link out of the side plate to break the chain. Remove the side plate, connecting link and O-rings (**Figure 47**).

> *WARNING*
> *Never reuse the connecting link, side plate and O-rings. They could break and cause the chain to separate. Reusing a master link may cause the chain to come apart and lock the rear wheel, causing a serious accident.*

14. Remove the drive chain.

15. If installing a new drive chain, count the links of the new chain, and if necessary, cut the chain to length as described in *Cutting a Drive Chain to Length* in this section. Refer to **Table 1** for the original equipment chain size and link length.

> *NOTE*
> *Always install the drive chain through the swing arm before connecting and staking the master link.*

16. Install the drive chain through the swing arm and around the engine sprocket with both link ends located at the top of the rear sprocket.

17. Refer to **Figure 47**, and assemble the new connecting link by performing the following:

   a. Install a *new* O-ring on each connecting link pin. Apply the lubricant supplied with the new master link kit.

   b. Insert the connecting link through the inside of the chain and connect both chain ends together.

   c. Lubricate the remaining two *new* O-rings with additional lubricant, and install them onto the connecting link pins.

   d. Install the side plate with its identification mark facing out (away from the chain), and crimp it into place with needlenose pliers.

   e. Use the appropriate size plate holder to press the plate onto the pins until the link width equals the specification in **Table 1**. Link width is the distance between the outside edges of the two chain plates (A, **Figure 52**).

18. Install the flair rivet pin into the chain tool following the manufacturer's instructions. Assemble the chain tool onto the master link and carefully stake each pin in the connecting link until the outside diameter of each pin (B, **Figure 52**) equals the specification in **Table 1**.

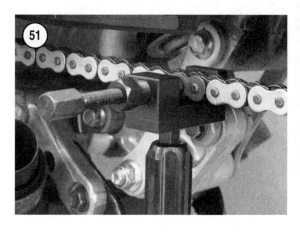

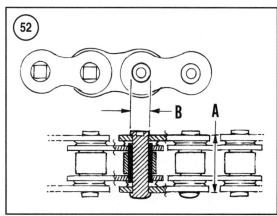

19. Remove the chain tool and inspect the link for any cracks or other damage (**Figure 53**). Check the staked area for cracks. Make sure the master link O-rings were not crushed. If there are any cracks on the staked link surfaces or other damage, remove the link and install a new one.

20. If there are no cracks, pivot the chain ends where they hook onto the connecting link. Each chain end must pivot freely. Compare by pivoting other links of the chain. If one or both drive chain ends cannot pivot on the connecting link, the chain is too tight. Remove and install a *new* connecting link assembly.

> *WARNING*
> *An incorrectly installed connecting link may cause the chain to come apart and lock the rear wheel, causing an accident. If a proper chain tool is not available, take the motorcycle to a dealership. Do not ride the motorcycle unless absolutely certain the connecting link is installed correctly.*

21. Rotate the rear wheel and chain to make sure the chain is traveling over both sprockets without any binding.

22. Reinstall the chain guard onto the swing arm.

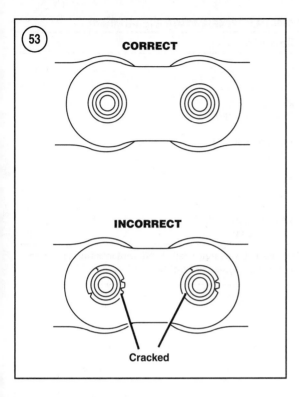

53

**CORRECT**

**INCORRECT**

Cracked

23. Adjust the drive chain and tighten the rear axle nut as described in Chapter Three.

### Cutting a Drive Chain to Length

**Table 1** lists the correct number of chain links required for original equipment gearing. If the replacement drive chain is too long, cut it to length as follows:

1. Stretch the new chain on a workbench.

2. If installing a new chain over original equipment gearing, refer to **Table 1** for the correct number of links for the new chain. If sprocket sizes were changed, install the new chain over both sprockets with the rear wheel moved forward to determine the correct number of links to remove. Make a chalk mark on the two chain pins to be cut. Count the chain links one more time or check the chain length before cutting.

> *WARNING*
> *Using a grinder as described in Step 3 causes flying particles. Wear eye protection.*

3. Grind the head of two pins flush with the face of the side plate with an angle grinder or suitable grinding tool.

4. Press the side plate out of the chain with a chain breaker. Support the chain carefully while doing this. If the pins are still tight, grind more material from the end of the pins and then try again.

5. Remove the side plate and push out the connecting link.

6. Install the new drive chain as described in this section.

**11**

### Table 1 WHEELS, TIRES AND DRIVE CHAIN SPECIFICATIONS

| Item | Specification |
|---|---|
| **Axle runout limit** | |
| Front | 0.25 mm (0.010 in.) |
| Rear | 0.25 mm (0.010 in.) |
| **Drive chain** | |
| 21-pin length | 319.4 mm (12.6 in.) |
| Chain free play | 20-30 mm (0.8-1.2 in.) |
| Links | 112 links |
| Link width | 21.85-22.15 mm (0.860-0.872 in.) |
| Pin outside diameter | 5.45-5.85 mm (0.215-0.230 in.) |
| Type | RK GB50GSV Z3 |
| **Tire** | |
| Type | Tubeless |
| Size | |
| Front | 120/70 ZR17 (58W) |
| Rear | 190/50 ZR17 (73W) |
| **Inflation pressure (cold)*** | |
| Front | |
| Solo | 290 kPa (42 psi) |
| Rider and passenger | 290 kPa (42 psi) |
| | **(continued)** |

**Table 1 WHEELS, TIRES AND DRIVE CHAIN SPECIFICATIONS (continued)**

| Item | Specification |
|---|---|
| Tire | |
| Inflation pressure (cold)* (continued) | |
| Rear | |
| Solo | 290 kPa (42 psi) |
| Rider and passenger | 290 kPa (42 psi) |
| Tread minimum depth | |
| Front | 1.6 mm (0.06 in.) |
| Rear | 2.0 mm (0.08 in.) |
| Wheel runout limit | |
| Axial | 2.0 mm (0.08 in.) |
| Radial | 2.0 mm (0.08 in.) |
| Wheel size | |
| Front | 17 × MT 3.50 |
| Rear | 17 × MT 6.00 |

*Tire inflation pressure is for original equipment tires. Aftermarket tires may require different inflation pressure. The use of tires other than those specified by the manufacturer may cause instability.

**Table 2 WHEELS, TIRES AND DRIVE CHAIN TORQUE SPECIFICATIONS**

| Item | N•m | in.-lb. | ft.-lb. |
|---|---|---|---|
| Brake disc bolt | | | |
| Front | 23 | – | 17 |
| Rear | 35 | – | 26 |
| Engine sprocket nut | 145 | – | 107 |
| Fork leg clamp bolt | 23 | – | 17 |
| Front axle | 100 | – | 74 |
| Rear axle nut | 100 | – | 74 |
| Rear sprocket nut | 60 | – | 44 |
| Torque arm nut | | | |
| Front | 28 | – | 21 |
| Rear | 35 | – | 26 |

# CHAPTER TWELVE

# FRONT SUSPENSION AND STEERING

This chapter covers the front fork and steering components. Wheel removal and hub service are addressed in Chapter Eleven. When servicing the components described in this chapter, compare any measurements to the specifications in **Table 1** at the end of this chapter. During assembly, tighten fasteners to the torque specified in **Table 2**.

## HANDLEBARS

Each handlebar mounts to the handlebar holder on the top of the upper fork bridge. One handlebar can be removed independently of the other. Remove, service and reinstall one handlebar assembly, and then service the other assembly.

### Removal/Installation

1A. When servicing the right handlebar, perform the following:
    a. Remove the brake master cylinder as described in Chapter Fourteen. Secure the master cylinder assembly to the frame. Keep the front brake master cylinder and reservoir in an upright position to prevent air from entering the system.
    b. Remove the right handlebar switch (Chapter Nine).
    c. Remove the throttle grip as described in *Handlebar Grip Replacement* in this chapter.

1B. When servicing the left handlebar, perform the following:
    a. Remove the clutch master cylinder as described in Chapter Six. Secure the master cylinder assembly to the frame. Keep the clutch master cylinder and reservoir in an upright position to prevent air from entering into the system.
    b. Remove the left handlebar switch (Chapter Nine).
    c. Remove the left handlebar grip as described in *Handlebar Grip Replacement* in this chapter.

2. Pull the trim cap from each handlebar clamp bolt.

3. Loosen the handlebar clamp bolts (A and B, **Figure 1**), and slide the handlebar from the holder.

4. Installation is the reverse of removal. Note the following:
    a. Install the handlebar so the cutout in the handlebar aligns with the outside hole (A, **Figure 1**) in the handlebar holder.
    b. Tighten the handlebar clamp bolts to 10 N•m (89 in.-lb.).
    c. If necessary, bleed the brake and clutch systems. Add fluid to either reservoir as needed.
    d. Adjust the throttle operation as described in Chapter Three.

e. Check the operation of all functions in both handlebar switch assemblies.

## Inspection

Check the entire handlebar for cracks or damage. Replace a bent or damaged handlebar immediately. If the motorcycle has been involved in a crash, thoroughly examine both handlebars, handlebar holder, fork bridges, steering stem and front fork for any signs of damage or misalignment. Correct any problem immediately.

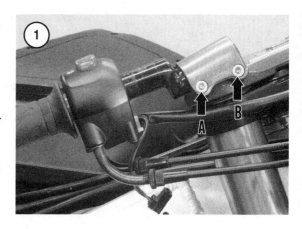

## HANDLEBAR GRIP REPLACEMENT

1. Remove the screw (A, **Figure 2**) and weight (B) from the end of the handlebar.

2A. For throttle grip replacement, perform the following:

    a. Remove the right handlebar switch (Chapter Nine).

    b. Remove the throttle grip screw, and slide the throttle grip from the handlebar.

    c. Slide the new throttle grip onto the handlebar. Tighten the throttle grip screw.

    d. Install the right handlebar switch (Chapter Nine).

2B. For left grip replacement, perform the following:

    a. Slide a thin screwdriver between the left grip and handlebar. Spray electrical contact cleaner into the opening under the grip.

    b. Pull the screwdriver out, and quickly twist the grip to break its bond with the handlebar. Slide the grip off the handlebar.

    c. Clean all rubber or sealant residue from the handlebar.

    d. Install the new grip following the manufacturer's directions. Apply an adhesive, such as ThreeBond Griplock, between the grip and handlebar. Follow the adhesive manufacturer's instructions for drying time before operating the motorcycle.

## HANDLEBAR HOLDER

### Removal

1. Remove the fuel tank as described in Chapter Eight.

2. Remove the front fairing and both intake ducts (Chapter Fifteen).

3. Study the cable and hose routing at the front of the motorcycle. Make a drawing of the routing. The hoses must all be rerouted along their original paths during assembly.

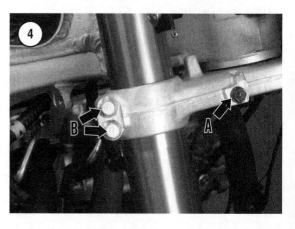

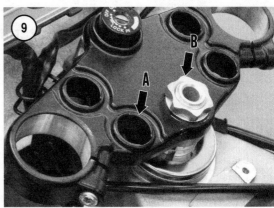

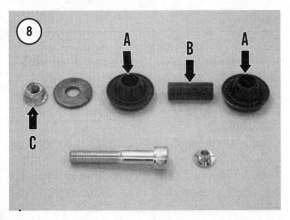

4. Release each wiring harness from the clamp (**Figure 3**) on the upper fork bridge.

5. Release the wiring harness and clutch hydraulic cable from the clamp on the left side of the frame.

6. Remove the nut (A, **Figure 4**), and release the brake hose from the clamp on the lower fork bridge.

7. Remove the cable holder bolt (**Figure 5**), and lower the cable holder from the right side of the frame. Note how the throttle and fast idle cables are routed. They must be rerouted through this holder the same way during assembly.

8A. If the handlebar holder is being replaced, remove each handlebar (this chapter).

8B. If the handlebar holder is being removed for steering head or front fork service, remove the brake master cylinder (Chapter Fourteen) and the clutch master cylinder (Chapter Six).

9. Remove the trim cap from each handlebar holder bolt (A, **Figure 6**).

10. Remove each handlebar holder nut and washer from the handlebar holder bolts.

11. Remove the handlebar holder bolts (A, **Figure 6**).

12. Lift the handlebar holder (B, **Figure 6**) from the upper fork bridge.

13. Each handlebar holder mount (**Figure 7**) consists of two dampers (A, **Figure 8**) and a collar (B). Pull the upper damper from the upper fork bridge, and lower the remaining damper and collar from the upper fork bridge. Repeat for each remaining handlebar holder mount.

**Installation**

1. Assemble the handlebar holder mounts (**Figure 7**) by performing the following:

    a. Press a collar (B, **Figure 8**) into a damper (A).

    b. From under the upper fork bridge, feed the collar/damper through a hole (A, **Figure 9**) in the upper fork bridge.

12

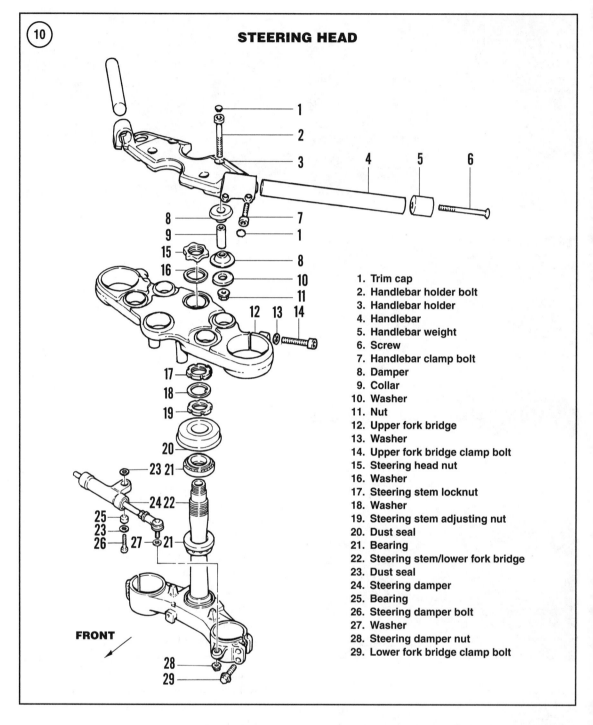

**STEERING HEAD**

10

1. Trim cap
2. Handlebar holder bolt
3. Handlebar holder
4. Handlebar
5. Handlebar weight
6. Screw
7. Handlebar clamp bolt
8. Damper
9. Collar
10. Washer
11. Nut
12. Upper fork bridge
13. Washer
14. Upper fork bridge clamp bolt
15. Steering head nut
16. Washer
17. Steering stem locknut
18. Washer
19. Steering stem adjusting nut
20. Dust seal
21. Bearing
22. Steering stem/lower fork bridge
23. Dust seal
24. Steering damper
25. Bearing
26. Steering damper bolt
27. Washer
28. Steering damper nut
29. Lower fork bridge clamp bolt

FRONT

c. Press another damper through the top of the fork bridge until the damper engages the collar (**Figure 7**).

d. Repeat for each remaining handlebar holder mount.

2. Set the handlebar holder (B, **Figure 6**) onto the upper fork bridge.

3. Lower a handlebar holder bolt (A, **Figure 6**) through each mount.

4. From under the upper fork bridge, fit the washer and handlebar holder nut (C, **Figure 8**) onto the bolt. Finger-tighten the nut.

5. Repeat Step 4 for each remaining handlebar holder bolt.

6. Tighten the handlebar holder nuts to 35 N•m (26 ft.-lb.).

7. Install the trim caps into the handlebar holder bolts.

8. Complete installation by reversing Steps 1-8 of the removal procedure. Note the following:

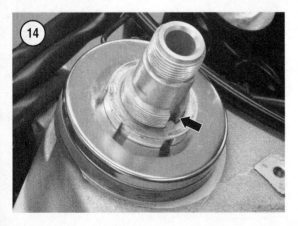

a. Tighten the handlebar clamp bolts (A and B, **Figure 1**) to 10 N•m (89 in.-lb.).

b. Tighten the throttle cable holder bolt (**Figure 5**) to 4 N•m (35 in.-lb.).

### STEERING HEAD AND STEM

The steering stem nut wrench (Suzuki part No. 09940-14911) and nut wrench socket (Suzuki part No. 09940-14960), or equivalent tools, are needed to service the steering head.

### Removal

Refer to **Figure 10**.

1. Remove the fuel tank as described in Chapter Eight.

2. Remove the front fender, both fairing side panels and the front fairing (Chapter Fifteen).

3. Remove the front wheel (Chapter Eleven).

4. Remove the handlebar holder (this chapter).

5. Disconnect the 6-pin ignition switch connector (**Figure 11**) from its harness mate.

6. Remove the steering damper and each fork leg as described in this chapter.

7. Remove the steering head nut (B, **Figure 9**) and its washer.

8. Remove the upper fork bridge (**Figure 12**) from the steering stem.

9. Loosen the steering stem locknut (**Figure 13**).

10. Remove the locknut, and remove the lockwasher (**Figure 14**). Note that the tab on the lockwasher engages the cutout in the rear of the steering stem.

> *NOTE*
> *Support the steering stem weight while removing the adjusting nut, or the assembly will drop out of the steering head.*

11. Loosen the steering stem adjusting nut. Hold onto the steering stem and remove the adjusting nut (A, **Figure 15**).

12. Gently lower the steering stem assembly from the frame. Do not worry about loose steel balls. Both bearings are caged ball bearings with no loose parts.

13. Remove the dust cap (B, **Figure 15**) and dust seal (**Figure 16**) from the top of the steering head.

14. Carefully remove the upper bearing inner race (A, **Figure 17**) and the upper bearing (B).

15. Remove the lower bearing (A, **Figure 18**) from the steering stem.

> *CAUTION*
> *Do not remove the lower bearing inner race and seal (B, **Figure 18**) from the steering stem unless the race is going to be replaced. The race is pressed onto the steering stem and is damaged during removal.*

16. Inspect the steering stem as described in this section.

### Installation

1. Make sure the bearing outer races (**Figure 19**) are clean and properly seated in the steering head.

2. Apply an even, complete coat of Suzuki Super Grease A, or its equivalent, to the outer races. Also pack both bearings with grease.

3. Install the lower bearing (A, **Figure 18**) onto the steering stem.

> *NOTE*
> *The fork receptacles in the steering stem are offset and must face toward the front of the motorcycle. This is necessary for proper alignment with the fork receptacles in the upper fork bridge.*

4. Position the steering stem with the fork receptacles facing forward. Carefully slide the steering stem (A, **Figure 20**) up into the frame.

5. Install the upper bearing (B, **Figure 20**) into the top of the steering head, and then install the inner race (A, **Figure 17**).

6. Install the dust seal (**Figure 16**) so its lip faces down into the steering head.

7. Seat the dust cap (B, **Figure 15**) onto the steering head.

8. Install the adjusting nut (A, **Figure 15**) onto the steering stem, and then perform the following:

    a. Tighten the steering stem adjusting nut to 45 N•m (33 ft.-lb.).

    b. Turn the steering stem from side to side (**Figure 21**) five to six times to help seat the bearings.

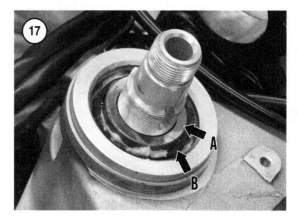

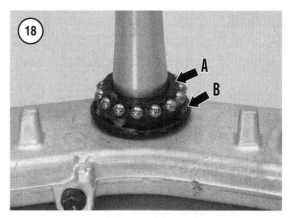

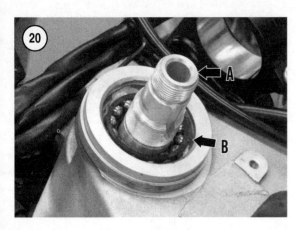

*NOTE*
*In substep c, the amount adjustment varies for each motorcycle. After loosening the adjusting nut one-quarter to one-half turn, there must be no bearing preload detected in the steering stem.*

   c. Loosen the adjusting nut one-quarter to one-half turn.

9. Check the steering head bearing adjustment by performing the following:

   a. Check the bearing preload by turning the steering stem from side to side five to six times (**Figure 21**). It should turn smoothly without drag or binding. There should be no preload. If necessary, loosen the adjuster nut in one-eighth-turn increments and recheck the preload.

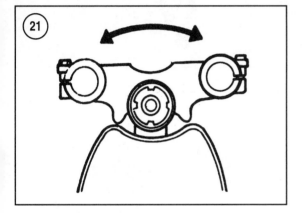

   b. Check for bearing free play by grasping one fork clamp area on the lower fork bridge. Try to rock the side of the lower fork bridge up and down. There should be little or no bearing free play, which means little or no rocking in the steering head. If any play is felt, tighten the adjusting nut one-eighth of a turn. Recheck the play.

   c. Repeatedly check the bearing free play and preload, and then make any necessary adjustments. The steering head bearings are properly adjusted when there is little or no free play and absolutely no preload.

10. Install the lockwasher so its tab engages the slot in the steering stem (**Figure 14**).

11. Install the steering stem locknut (**Figure 13**). Hold the adjusting nut with a ring nut wrench, and tighten the locknut to 80 N•m (59 ft.-lb.) (**Figure 22**).

12. Lower the upper fork bridge (**Figure 12**) onto the steering stem.

13. Install the washer and the steering head nut (**Figure 9**). Snug the nut.

14. Slide each fork leg assembly through the lower and upper fork bridges.

15. Tighten the lower fork bridge clamp bolts (B, **Figure 4**) on each side so they hold each fork leg in place.

16. Tighten the steering head nut (**Figure 23**) to 90 N•m (66 ft.-lb.).

17. Loosen the lower fork bridge clamp bolts (B, **Figure 4**), and remove each fork leg.

18. Install the handlebar holder (this chapter).

19. Install each fork leg (later in this chapter).

20. Check the movement of the front fork and steering stem assembly. The steering stem must turn freely from side to side.

21. Grasp the fork leg and move them fore and aft. There should be no free play.

**12**

22. Install the steering damper as described in this chapter.

23. Connect the 6-pin ignition switch connector (**Figure 11**) to its harness mate.

24. Install the wheel (Chapter Eleven) and fuel tank (Chapter Eight).

25. Install the front fender, front fairing and both fairing side panels (Chapter Fifteen).

### Inspection

1. Clean the upper and lower bearings. Make sure the degreaser is compatible with the bearing cage. Thoroughly dry the bearings with compressed air. Make sure all solvent is removed from each bearing.

2. Wipe the old grease from each inner race. Clean each race with a rag soaked in solvent, and thoroughly dry the races.

3. Wipe the old grease from the outer races (**Figure 19**) in the steering head, and then clean the outer races with a rag soaked in solvent. Thoroughly dry the races with a lint-free cloth.

4. Check the races for pitting, galling and corrosion. If any race is worn or damaged, replace the race(s) and bearing as an assembly as described in this chapter.

5. Inspect the seal (B, **Figure 18**) on the lower fork bridge.

6. Check the welds around the steering head for cracks and fractures. If any damage is found, have the frame repaired at a competent frame or welding shop.

7. Check the balls for pitting, scratches or discoloration indicating wear or corrosion. Replace the bearing if any balls are less than perfect.

8. If the bearings are in good condition, pack them thoroughly with Suzuki Super Grease A or an equivalent good-quality, water-proof bearing grease. Pack both sides of the cage so grease surrounds each ball.

9. Thoroughly clean all mounting parts in solvent. Dry them completely.

10. Inspect the steering head nut, washer, steering stem adjusting nut and locknut for wear or damage. Pay attention to the threads. If necessary, clean them with an appropriate size metric tap or replace the nut(s). If the threads are damaged, inspect the appropriate steering stem threads for damage. If necessary, clean the threads with an appropriate size metric die.

11. Inspect the steering stem nut washer for damage, and replace if necessary. If damaged, check the underside of the steering stem nut for damage, and replace as necessary.

12. Inspect the steering stem and the lower fork bridge for cracks or other damage. Make sure the fork bridge clamping areas are free of burrs and the bolt holes are in good condition.

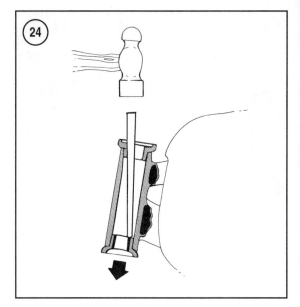

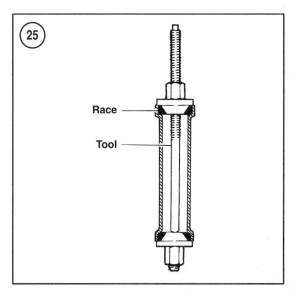

13. Inspect the upper fork bridge for cracks or other damage. Check both the upper and lower surface of the fork bridge. Make sure the fork bridge clamping areas are free of burrs and the bolt holes are in good condition.

14. Replace any worn or damaged component. If any bearing or race is worn or damaged, replace both bearing sets completely.

## STEERING HEAD BEARING RACE

### Replacement

A bearing/race installer set (Suzuki part Nos. 09941-34513 and 09913-70210, or their equivalents) is needed to perform this procedure.

(26)

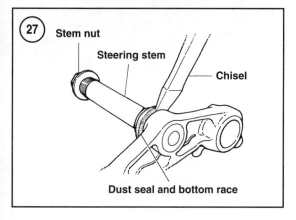

(27) **Stem nut**

**Steering stem**

**Chisel**

**Dust seal and bottom race**

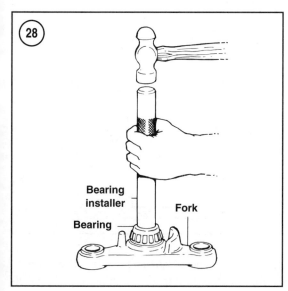

(28)

**Bearing installer**

**Fork**

**Bearing**

1. Remove the steering stem as described in this chapter.

2. Insert an aluminum drift into the steering head, and carefully tap the lower race from the head (**Figure 24**). Repeat for the upper race.

3. Chill the new bearing races in a freezer for a few hours to shrink the outer diameter of the race as much as possible.

4. Clean the race seats in the steering head. Check for cracks or other damage.

5. Insert the new race into the steering head with the tapered side facing out, and square the race with the bore.

*CAUTION*
*When installing the bearing outer races, do not let the tool shaft contact the face of the bearing race. It could be damaged.*

6. Assemble the tool through the bearing race according to the manufacturer's instructions. Refer to **Figure 25**.

7. Hold the installer shaft and slowly turn the upper nut until the tool and outer race are square with the steering head bore (**Figure 26**).

8. Turn the upper nut, and slowly press the race into the bore until the race bottoms (**Figure 19**).

9. Turn the special tool over and repeat this procedure for the lower bearing race.

### STEERING STEM BEARING RACE

### Replacement

Do not remove the steering stem lower bearing inner race and seal (B, **Figure 18**) unless they are replaced with new parts. The race can be difficult to remove. If the race cannot be removed as described in this procedure, take the steering stem to a dealership.

Never reinstall a race that has been removed. It is no longer true and damages the rest of the bearing assembly if reused.

1. Install the steering stem nut onto the top of the steering stem to protect the threads.

2. Use a chisel to loosen the lower race from the shoulder at the base of the steering stem (**Figure 27**). Slide the race and seal off the steering stem. Discard them.

3. Clean the steering stem with solvent and dry it thoroughly.

4. Position the new seal with the flange side facing up.

5. Slide the seal and the inner race onto the steering stem until the race stops on the raised shoulder.

6. Align the race with the machined shoulder on the steering stem. Slide a steering bearing installer (Suzuki part No. 09925-18010), or a piece of pipe, (**Figure 28**) over the steering stem until it seats against the inner circumference of the race. Drive the race onto the steering stem until it bottoms.

**12**

## STEERING DAMPER

### Removal/Inspection/Installation

Refer to **Figure 10**.

1. Securely support the motorcycle on a level surface with the front wheel off the floor.

2. Remove the center panel as described in Chapter Fifteen.

3. Remove the cotter pin from the steering damper stud, and remove steering damper nut (A, **Figure 29**) and its washer. Discard the cotter pin.

4. Remove the steering damper bolt (B, **Figure 29**) and its dust seal.

5. Disengage the steering damper stud from the mount on the lower fork bridge, and remove the damper. Watch for the dust seal that sits between the damper bearing and the mount on the steering head.

6. Inspect the steering damper body, bearing and seals for signs of leaks (**Figure 30**).

7. Move the steering damper rod into and out of the body. It should move smoothly.

8. Replace the steering damper if any defect is found.

9. Installation is the reverse of removal. Note the following:

   a. Lubricate the damper bearing and the concave side of each dust seal with Suzuki Super Grease A, or its equivalent.

   b. Install a dust seal on each side of the bearing so the concave sides face the bearing. Refer to **Figure 31**.

   c. Tighten the steering damper nut (A, **Figure 29**) and steering damper bolt (B) to 23 N•m (17 ft.-lb.).

   d. Install a new cotter pin through the steering damper stud.

## FRONT FORK

### Front Fork Service

To simplify fork service and prevent the mixing of parts, remove, service and install the fork legs individually.

### Removal

> *NOTE*
> *For fork assembly removal only, do not perform Step 4. This step is only necessary if the fork is going to be disassembled for service.*

Refer to **Figure 32**.

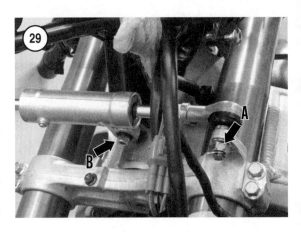

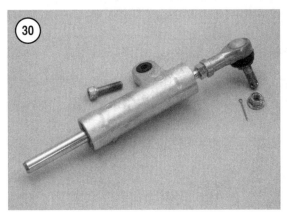

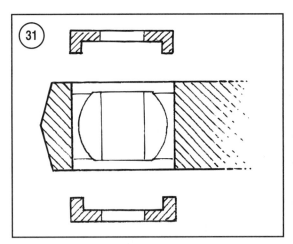

1. Securely support the motorcycle on a level surface.

2. Remove the front fender, both fairing side panels and the front fairing (Chapter Fifteen).

3. Remove the front wheel as described in Chapter Eleven.

4. If servicing the fork leg, perform the following:

   a. Remove the handlebar holder (this chapter).

   b. Place a drain pan under the fork tube to catch fork oil that may drain out.

   c. Slightly loosen (just break it loose) the damper rod Allen bolt (**Figure 33**) at the base of the

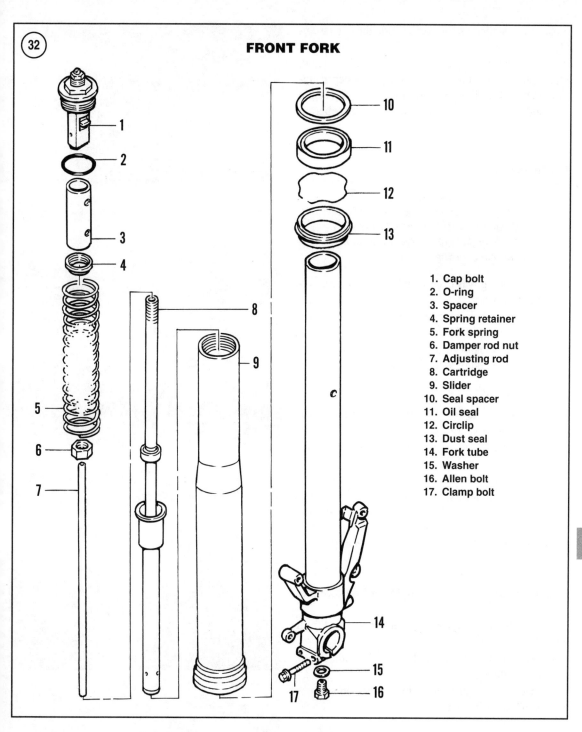

**FRONT FORK**

1. Cap bolt
2. O-ring
3. Spacer
4. Spring retainer
5. Fork spring
6. Damper rod nut
7. Adjusting rod
8. Cartridge
9. Slider
10. Seal spacer
11. Oil seal
12. Circlip
13. Dust seal
14. Fork tube
15. Washer
16. Allen bolt
17. Clamp bolt

12

slider. If the bolt is loosened too much, fork oil starts to drain out of the fork tube.

d. Turn the rebound damper adjuster (A, **Figure 34**) counterclockwise to its softest setting.

e. Loosen the upper fork bridge clamp bolt (B, **Figure 34**).

f. Loosen the fork cap bolt (C, **Figure 34**).

5. If not loosened in Step 4, loosen the upper fork bridge clamp bolt (B, **Figure 34**).

6. Loosen the lower fork bridge clamp bolts (**Figure 35**).

7. Carefully lower the fork assembly out of the upper and lower fork bridges. If necessary, rotate the fork leg slightly while pulling it down. Take the fork assembly to the workbench for service. If the fork is not going to be serviced, wrap it in a bath towel or blanket to protect the surface from damage.

8. If both fork assemblies have been removed, mark them with an *R* (right side) and *L* (left side). Each

must be reinstalled on the correct side during assembly.

9. If the Allen and cap bolts were loosened in Step 4, place the fork assembly in a drain pan. Keep it upright to avoid spilling fork oil through the top of the fork slider. Disassemble the fork leg as described in this section.

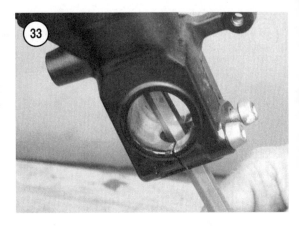

### Installation

> *NOTE*
> *If both fork assemblies are removed, install each fork assembly onto the correct side of the motorcycle. Refer to the marks made during removal.*

1. If the fork leg was disassembled for service, perform the following:

    a. Slide the fork leg assembly through the lower and upper fork bridges.

    b. Tighten the lower fork bridge clamp bolts (**Figure 35**) enough to hold the fork leg.

    c. Tighten the fork cap bolt (**Figure 36**) to 23 N•m (17 ft.-lb.).

    d. Loosen the lower fork bridge clamp bolts, and lower the fork leg.

    e. If necessary, repeat substeps a-d for the other fork leg.

    f. Install the handlebar holder (this chapter).

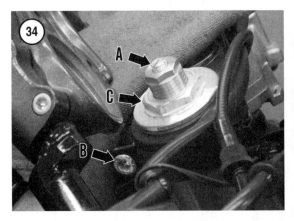

2. Slide the fork leg assembly through the lower and upper fork bridges until the slider rests against the bottom of the handlebar holder. Refer to **Figure 37**.

3. Tighten the upper fork bridge clamp bolt (B, **Figure 34**) and the lower fork bridge clamp bolts (**Figure 35**) to 23 N•m (17 ft.-lb.).

4. If necessary, repeat Step 2 and Step 3 for the other fork leg.

5. Install the front fender (Chapter Fifteen) and front wheel (Chapter Eleven).

6. Install the front fairing and the fairing side panels (Chapter Fifteen).

7. If necessary, adjust the front suspension settings as described in Chapter Three.

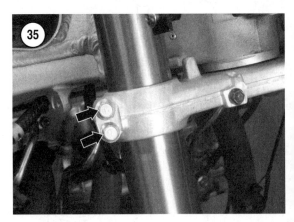

### Disassembly

Refer to **Figure 32**.

1. The following Suzuki tools, or their equivalents, are required to disassemble the fork leg:

    a. Front fork spacer holder (part No. 09940-94930).

    b. Stopper plate (part No. 09940-94922).

    c. Front fork assembling tool (part No. 09940-30221).

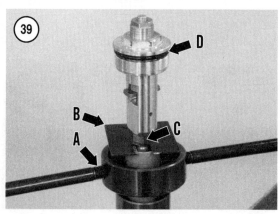

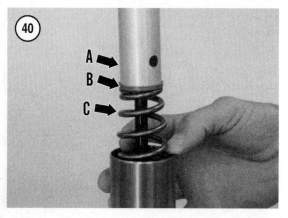

    d. Inner rod holder (part No. 09940-50120).

    e. Fork oil level gauge (part No. 09943-74111).

2. If the Allen bolt was not loosened during the fork removal sequence, perform the following:

    a. Secure the fork slider horizontally in a vise with soft jaws.

    b. Have an assistant compress the fork tube into the slider. This places additional pressure on the cartridge to keep it from rotating while loosening the Allen bolt.

    c. Use an Allen socket and impact wrench to loosen the Allen bolt (**Figure 33**) on the bottom of the slider. Do not remove the Allen bolt and gasket from the slider at this time. The fork is still full of fork oil.

*WARNING*
*The cap bolt is under spring pressure. Exercise caution when unthreading the cap bolt.*

3. Secure the fork vertically in a vise with soft jaws. Completely unscrew the fork cap bolt (**Figure 38**) from the fork slider.

4. Install the front fork spacer holder (A, **Figure 39**) following the manufacturer's instructions.

5. Use the spacer holder (A, **Figure 39**) to compress the fork spring. Insert the stopper plate (B, **Figure 39**) between the damper rod nut (C) and the spacer.

6. Hold the damper rod nut and turn the cap bolt (D, **Figure 39**) off the damper rod.

7. Remove the stopper plate (B, **Figure 39**) and the spacer holder (A).

8. Remove the adjusting rod from the cartridge damper rod.

9. Remove the spacer (A, **Figure 40**), spring retainer (B) and fork spring (C).

10. Remove the fork leg from the vise. Invert the fork leg and pour the oil from the end of the fork slider. Pump the damper rod in and out to expel oil from the cartridge. Dispose of the fork oil properly.

11. Remove the Allen bolt (**Figure 41**) and its gasket from the end of the fork tube. If the Allen bolt has not been loosened, hold the cartridge with the front fork assembling tool (**Figure 42**) and remove the Allen bolt.

12. Remove the cartridge assembly from the top of the fork slider.

*NOTE*
*The bushings in this fork assembly remain in the fork slider. They cannot be replaced.*

13. Secure the fork slider horizontally into a vise with soft jaws. Pull the fork tube from the fork slider.

14. Pry the dust seal (**Figure 43**) from the slider.

**12**

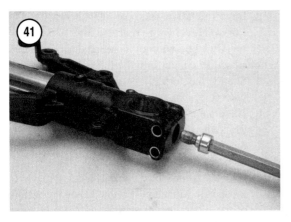

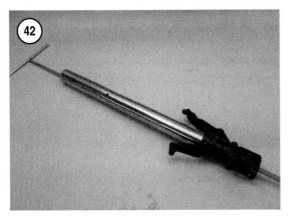

15. Remove the circlip (**Figure 44**) from its groove in the slider.

16. Pry the oil seal (A, **Figure 45**) from the slider, and remove the seal spacer (B). Discard the oil seal.

17. Inspect the components as described in this section.

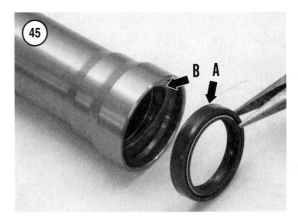

### Assembly

1. Lubricate the bushings (A, **Figure 46**) in the fork slider with Suzuki L01 fork oil.

2. Install the spacer (B, **Figure 45**) into the slider.

3. Pack the lips of a new seal with Suzuki Super Grease A. Set the seal into the slider so it is square in the bore (**Figure 47**). The side with the manufacturer's marks must face out.

4. Using a driver that matches the outside diameter of the oil seal (**Figure 48**), drive the oil seal into the slider until the circlip groove (**Figure 49**) is visible above the top of the oil seal.

5. Install the circlip into the slider so it sits securely in the circlip groove (**Figure 44**).

6. Lubricate the dust seal with Suzuki Super Grease A, and seat it in the slider (**Figure 43**).

7. Insert the cartridge into the top of the fork tube until the cartridge bottoms in the tube.

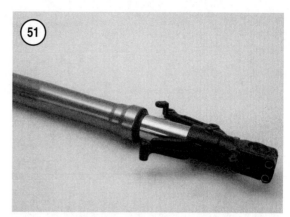

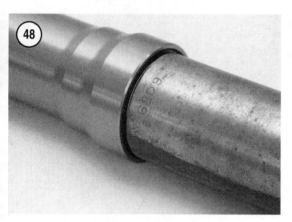

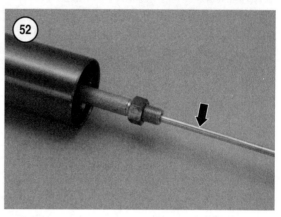

8. Install a new gasket onto the Allen bolt and apply Suzuki Thread Lock 1342, or its equivalent, to the bolt threads.

9. Insert the Allen bolt into the fork tube (**Figure 41**), and turn it into the cartridge. Hold the cartridge with the front fork assembling tool (**Figure 42**), and tighten the front fork Allen bolt to 40 N•m (30 ft.-lb.).

10. Carefully insert the fork tube (A, **Figure 50**) into the slider (B) until the leg bottoms. Refer to **Figure 51**.

11. Install the adjusting rod (**Figure 52**) into the damper rod.

12. Fill the fork with oil, set the oil level and complete fork assembly as described in *Fork Oil Adjustment* in this section.

**12**

## Inspection

> *CAUTION*
> *Do not clean the cartridge (A, **Figure 53**) in solvent. It is difficult to remove all the solvent from the cartridge, and this solvent contaminates the fork oil. Instead, wipe the cartridge with a clean cloth, and set it aside for inspection and assembly.*

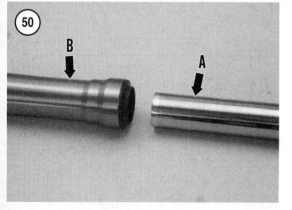

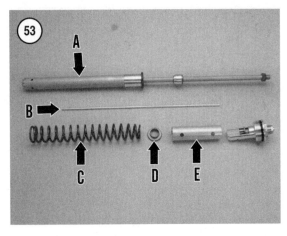

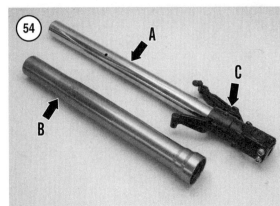

1. Thoroughly clean all parts, except the cartridge, in solvent and dry them. Check the fork slider for wear or scratches.

2. Check the cartridge assembly (A, **Figure 53**) for straightness and damage. Manually move the damper rod in and out of the cartridge. It should move smoothly.

3. Roll the adjusting rod (B, **Figure 53**) along a surface plate or a piece of glass. Replace the rod if it is not straight.

4. Check the threads and nut at the end of the cartridge damper rod for damage. Clean the threads with an appropriate size metric tap and/or die if necessary.

5. Make sure the oil holes in the cartridge assembly are clear. Clean them if necessary.

6. Check the fork tube (A, **Figure 54**) for straightness. If bent or excessively scratched, it should be replaced.

7. Inspect the threads in the top of the fork slider (B, **Figure 54**) for wear or damage. Clean the threads with the appropriate size metric tap if necessary.

8. Check the slider for dents or exterior damage that may cause the fork tube to stick. Replace the slider if necessary.

9. Inspect the mounting boss (C, **Figure 54**) on the fork tube for cracks or other damage. If damaged, replace the fork tube.

10. Inspect the bushings (A, **Figure 46**) in the fork slider. If either is scratched or scored, replace the fork slider. The bushings cannot be replaced.

11. Inspect the inner surfaces in the slider for damage or burrs. Pay attention to circlip groove (B, **Figure 46**) and sealing surfaces. Clean the slider if necessary.

12. Inspect the cap bolt (**Figure 55**) for signs of damage. The cap bolt cannot be serviced. If any damaged is noted, replace it. Inspect the cap bolt O-ring. Replace it as necessary.

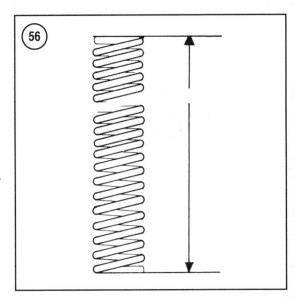

13. Visually inspect the fork spring (C, **Figure 53**), spring retainer (D) and spacer (E) for cracks or other signs or wear.

14. Measure the uncompressed free length of the fork spring as shown in **Figure 56**. Replace the spring if it has sagged to less than the service limit specified in **Table 1**.

15. Replace any worn or damaged parts.

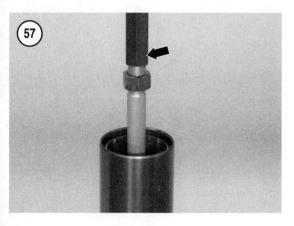

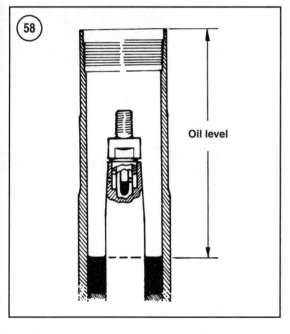

Oil level

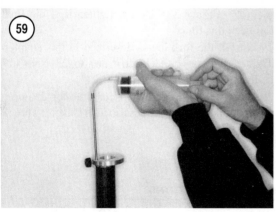

**Fork Oil Adjustment**

1. Secure the fork leg vertically in a vise with soft jaws.

2. Push the fork slider down onto fork tube until the slider bottoms.

3. Turn the inner rod holder (**Figure 57**) onto the cartridge damper rod. Compress the cartridge damper rod until it bottoms.

4. Refer to **Table 1** and add the recommended amount of fork oil to the fork leg.

*NOTE*
*During the bleeding procedure, the fork oil level must remain above the top of the cartridge assembly. If the oil level drops below this level, air may enter the cartridge, nullifying the bleeding procedure.*

5. Bleed the air from the cartridge by performing the following.

    a. Keep the fork assembly in a vertical position during bleeding.

    b. Use the inner rod holder to slowly move the damper rod up and down using full travel strokes (**Figure 57**).

    c. Repeat this more than 10 times or until the fork oil is free of bubbles.

    d. If necessary, add additional fork oil until the oil is almost level with the top of the compressed fork slider.

    e. Hold the fork tube, and slowly move the slider up and down several stokes until bubbles no longer emerge from the oil.

    f. Keep the fork assembly in this vertical position for 5-10 minutes to allow any additional trapped air to escape. Tap the side of the fork leg to expel any bubbles adhering to the side of the fork leg.

6. Set the fork oil level by performing the following:

    a. Hold the fork assembly vertical and fully compress the fork slider.

    b. The oil level is the distance from the top of the compressed fork slider to the upper edge of the oil (**Figure 58**).

    c. Use an accurate ruler and the Suzuki oil level gauge or its equivalent (**Figure 59**) to set the oil level to the value in **Table 1**.

    d. Allow the oil to settle completely, and then recheck the oil level. Adjust the oil level if necessary.

7. Remove the inner rod holder (**Figure 57**) from the damper rod.

8. Turn the damper rod nut until the distance from the top of the damper rod to the top of the nut equals 11 mm (0.43 in.). Refer to **Figure 60**.

9. Install the fork spring so the end with the smaller coils is up (**Figure 61**).

10. Install the spring retainer (B, **Figure 40**) and the spacer (A).

**12**

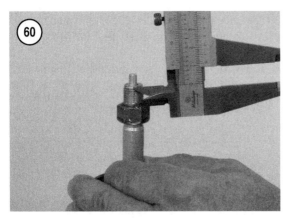

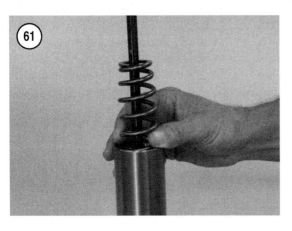

11. Install the front fork spacer holder (A, **Figure 39**) following the manufacturer's instructions.

12. Use the spacer holder to compress the fork spring, and insert the stopper plate (B, **Figure 39**) between damper rod nut (C) and the spacer.

13. Lubricate the cap bolt O-ring with fork oil. Turn the cap bolt (D, **Figure 39**) onto the damper rod, and manually tighten the cap bolt against the damper rod nut.

14. Hold the cap bolt, and tighten damper rod nut (C, **Figure 39**) to 29 N•m (21 ft.-lb.).

15. Use the spacer holder to compress the spring, and remove the stopper plate (B, **Figure 39**).

16. Slowly release the spacer holder so the spacer slides up and engages the tabs on the cap bolt (**Figure 62**).

17. Remove the spacer holder. Make sure the spacer still engages with the cap bolt (**Figure 63**).

18. Pull the fork slider up against the cap bolt, and turn the cap bolt into the slider. Tighten the cap bolt securely (**Figure 38**). Do not tighten it to the final torque at this time.

19. Install the fork leg as described in this chapter. Tighten the cap bolt (**Figure 36**) to 23 N•m (17 ft.-lb.).

20. Adjust the spring preload, compression damping and rebound damping as described in Chapter Three.

**Table 1 FRONT SUSPENSION SPECIFICATIONS**

| Item | Specification | Service limit |
|---|---|---|
| Fork spring free length | 245.1 mm (9.65 in.) | 240 mm (9.45 in.) |
| Front fork adjustments | | |
|    Spring preload | Fifth groove from top | – |
|    Rebound damping | 3 clicks out | – |
|    Compression damping | 9 clicks out | – |
| | (continued) | |

**Table 1 FRONT SUSPENSION SPECIFICATIONS (continued)**

| Item | Specification | Service limit |
|------|---------------|---------------|
| Front fork oil | | |
| Capacity per leg | 480 ml (16.2 U.S. oz.) | |
| Level | 98 mm (3.86 in.) | – |
| Viscosity | Suzuki L01 fork oil or equivalent | – |
| Front fork stroke | 120 mm (4.72 in.) | – |
| Steering tension | 200-500 grams (7.05-17.64 oz.) | – |

**Table 2 FRONT SUSPENSION AND STEERING TORQUE SPECIFICATIONS**

| Item | N•m | in.-lb. | ft.-lb. |
|------|-----|---------|---------|
| Damper rod nut | 29 | – | 21 |
| Fork bridge clamp bolts | 23 | – | 17 |
| Front axle | 100 | – | 74 |
| Front axle clamp bolt | 23 | – | 17 |
| Front fork Allen bolt | 40 | – | 30 |
| Front fork cap bolt | 23 | – | 17 |
| Handlebar clamp bolt | 10 | 89 | – |
| Handlebar holder nut | 35 | – | 26 |
| Steering damper bolt | 23 | – | 17 |
| Steering damper nut | 23 | – | 17 |
| Steering head nut | 90 | – | 66 |
| Steering stem adjusting nut (initial torque) | 45 | – | 33 |
| Steering stem locknut | 80 | – | 59 |
| Throttle cable holder bolt | 4 | 35 | – |

12

# CHAPTER THIRTEEN

# REAR SUSPENSION

This chapter covers service and repair of the rear suspension components. Rear wheel removal and rear hub service appear Chapter Eleven.

When inspecting components in this chapter, compare measurements to the specifications in **Table 1**. Replace parts that are worn, damaged or out of specification. During assembly, tighten fasteners to the specified torque.

## SHOCK ABSORBER

### Removal/Installation

Refer to **Figure 1**.

1. Remove the rider's seat and each fairing side panel as described in Chapter Fifteen.

2. Remove the fuel tank (Chapter Eight)

3. Securely support the motorcycle on a level surface with the rear wheel off the ground.

4. Remove the rear wheel (Chapter Eleven).

5. Remove the nut (A, **Figure 2**) from the lower shock absorber bolt. Pull the lower shock absorber bolt (A, **Figure 3**) from the left side.

6. Remove the nut (A, **Figure 4**) from the upper shock absorber bolt, and pull the bolt (B) from the mount.

7. Lift the shock absorber from the suspension lever, and pull the shock out from the top of the frame.

8. Inspect the shock absorber as described in this section.

9. Installation is the reverse of removal. Note the following:

   a. Apply a light coat of Suzuki Super Grease A, or its equivalent, to the bolts and to the shock absorber upper and lower mounts.

   b. Fit the shock absorber into place so its compression damping adjuster (C, **Figure 4**) faces the left side.

   c. Install and finger-tighten the mounting hardware.

   d. Tighten each shock absorber mounting nut to 50 N•m (37 ft.-lb.).

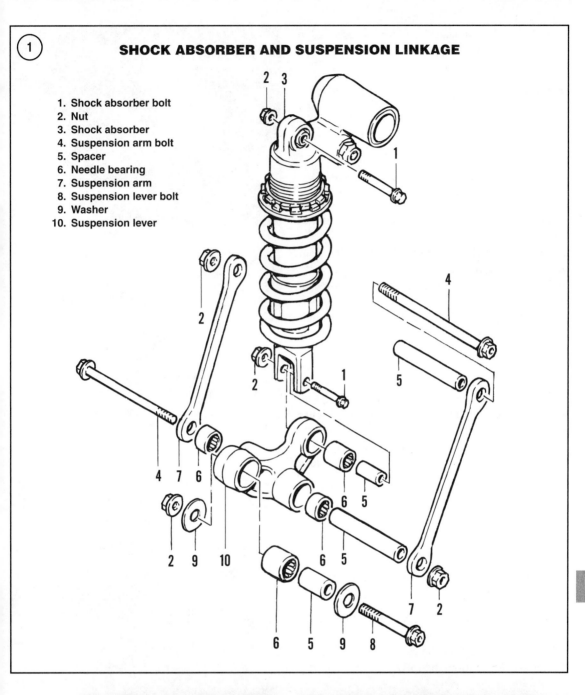

**(1)**

## SHOCK ABSORBER AND SUSPENSION LINKAGE

1. Shock absorber bolt
2. Nut
3. Shock absorber
4. Suspension arm bolt
5. Spacer
6. Needle bearing
7. Suspension arm
8. Suspension lever bolt
9. Washer
10. Suspension lever

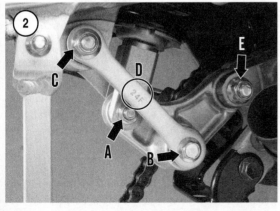

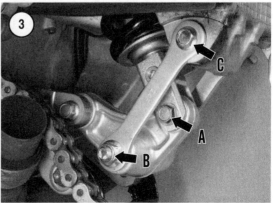

**13**

e. Adjust the rear shock absorber as described in Chapter Three.

## Inspection

*WARNING*
*The shock absorber contains highly compressed nitrogen gas. Do not tamper with or open the housing. Do not place it near an open flame or other extreme heat source. Do not weld near the shock.*

1. Inspect the shock absorber housing (A, **Figure 5**) for dents, damage or oil leaks.
2. Check the spring (B, **Figure 5**) and spring seats for cracks or other damage.
3. Inspect the rubber stopper (A, **Figure 6**) for wear or deterioration.
4. Inspect the upper (A, **Figure 7**) and lower mounts (B, **Figure 6**) for wear or damage. Pay attention to the damper in the upper mount.
5. Check the reservoir (B, **Figure 7**) for dents, damage or signs of leaks.
6. Rotate the compression damping adjuster (C, **Figure 7**) and the rebound damping adjuster (C, **Figure 6**) from one stop to another. Each adjuster should rotate freely and engage the detent at each stop.
7. If any part is worn or damaged, replace the shock absorber.

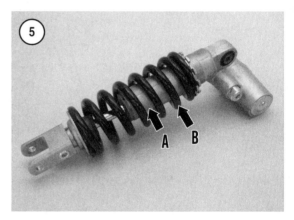

## Disposal

*WARNING*
*The nitrogen must be released from the gas reservoir before the shock absorber is discarded.*

1. Remove the cover (D, **Figure 7**) from the gas reservoir.
2. Remove the cap from the valve.
3. Release the gas from the valve.

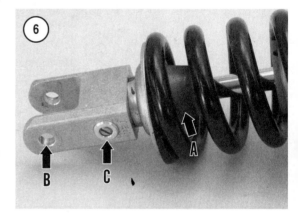

## SUSPENSION LINKAGE

### Removal

Refer to **Figure 1**.
1. Remove the fairing side panel from each side described in Chapter Fifteen.
2. Securely support the motorcycle on a level surface.
3. Support the rear wheel so it does not drop when the suspension linkage is removed.
4. Remove the nut (B, **Figure 3**) from the lower suspension arm bolt. Pull the lower suspension arm bolt (B, **Figure 2**) from the right side.

*CAUTION*
*The suspension arms are symmetrical and can be installed on either side. After prolonged use, however, each develops a unique wear pattern and should be reinstalled on its original side. Before removing the suspension arms, mark them with an L (left) or R (right) so they can be reinstalled on the original sides.*

5. Remove the nut (C, **Figure 2**) from the upper suspension arm bolt. Lower the right suspension arm

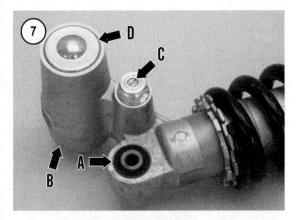

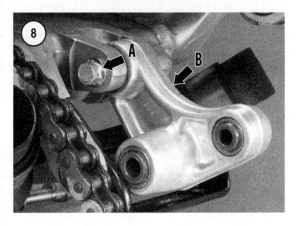

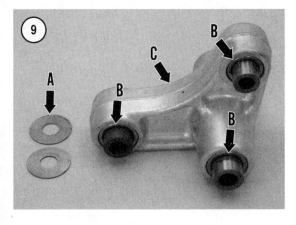

from the linkage. Note that each arm is installed with its identification mark (D, **Figure 2**) facing out.

6. Pull the upper suspension arm bolt (C, **Figure 3**) from the left side, and lower the left suspension arm from the motorcycle.

7. Remove the nut (A, **Figure 2**) from the lower shock absorber bolt.

8. Pull the lower shock absorber bolt (A, **Figure 3**) from the left side, and lower the suspension lever from the shock mount.

9. Remove the nut (E, **Figure 2**) from the suspension lever bolt.

10. Remove the suspension lever bolt (A, **Figure 8**) from the left side, and lower the suspension lever (B) from its frame mount. Watch for the washer (A, **Figure 9**) that sits between each side of the suspension lever and the frame mount.

## Installation

1. Apply a light coat of Suzuki Super Grease A, or its equivalent, to the bolts, suspension lever washers and the lever's frame mount.

2. Place a washer (A, **Figure 9**) onto each side of the suspension lever's forward pivot, and slide the lever (B, **Figure 8**) into its frame mount.

3. Insert the suspension lever bolt (A, **Figure 8**) from the left side. Loosely install the nut (E, **Figure 2**) onto the bolt.

4. Raise the suspension lever so its rear pivot sits between the arms of the lower shock mount.

5. Insert the shock absorber mounting bolt (A, **Figure 3**) from the left side. Loosely install the nut (A, **Figure 2**) onto the bolt.

6. Set the left suspension arm into position so its identification mark faces out. Align its upper hole with the mount in the swing arm, and install the suspension arm bolt (C, **Figure 3**).

7. On the right side, fit the right suspension arm onto the upper bolt so its identification mark faces out (D, **Figure 2**), and loosely install the nut (C).

8. Pivot each suspension arm forward until their lower mounts align with the center pivot on the suspension lever.

9. Install the lower suspension arm bolt (B, **Figure 2**) from the right side, and loosely install the nut (B, **Figure 3**).

10. Tighten the mounting hardware to the indicated specification. Tighten the fasteners in the following order:

   a. Tighten the suspension lever nut (E, **Figure 2**) to 78 N•m (58 ft.-lb.).

   b. Tighten the lower shock absorber nut (A, **Figure 2**) 50 N•m (37 ft.-lb.).

   c. Torque the upper (C, **Figure 2**) and lower (B, **Figure 3**) suspension arm nuts to 78 N•m (58 ft-.lb.).

11. Install the fairing side panels (Chapter Fifteen).

## Inspection

1. Remove each spacer (B, **Figure 9**) from its pivot in the suspension lever. Note that the lever uses three different sized spacers (**Figure 10**). Each must be reinstalled in the correct location during assembly.

13

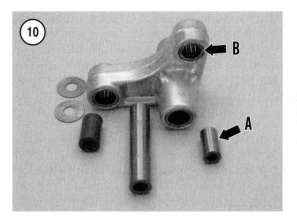

2. Inspect each spacer (A, **Figure 10**, typical) for wear and damage.

3. Inspect each suspension lever bearing as follows:

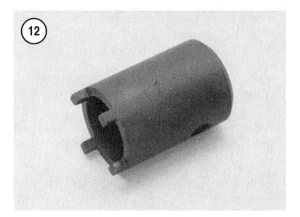

    a. Use a clean, lint-free rag and wipe off surface grease from each needle bearing (B, **Figure 10**, typical).

    b. Manually turn each bearing. It should turn smoothly without excessive play or noise.

    c. Check the rollers for evidence of wear, pitting or rust

    d. Reinstall each spacer (B, **Figure 9**) into its bearing(s) and slowly rotate each spacer. The spacers must turn smoothly without excessive play or noise.

    e. Replace any worn or damaged bearings as described in *Suspension Lever Needle Bearing Replacement* in this chapter.

4. Inspect the suspension lever (C, **Figure 9**) for cracks or damage.

5. Inspect the suspension arms (**Figure 11**) for bending, cracks or damage. Replace as necessary.

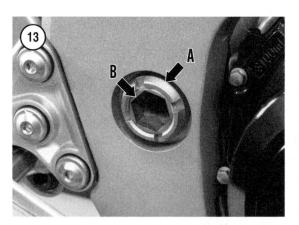

6. Clean the bolts and nuts in solvent. Check the bolts for straightness. A bent bolt restricts movement of the linkage.

7. Replace any part that is worn or damaged.

8. Lubricate the bearings and spacers with Suzuki Super Grease A, or its equivalent. Insert each spacer into its original pivot in the suspension lever.

## SWING ARM

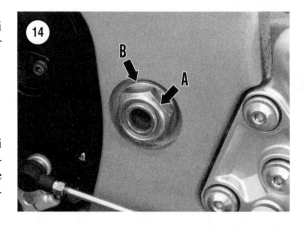

The swing arm pivot thrust adjuster socket (Suzuki part No. 09940-14970 or equivalent) is needed to remove and install the swing arm. Do not service the swing arm without this tool (**Figure 12**) or its equivalent.

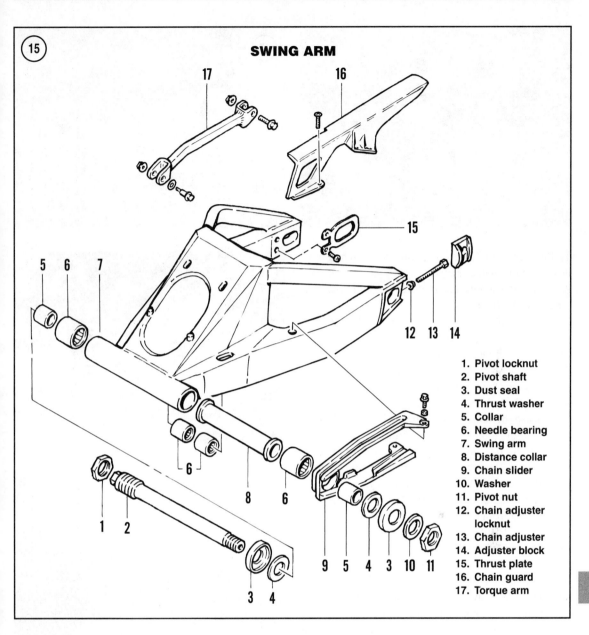

**SWING ARM**

1. Pivot locknut
2. Pivot shaft
3. Dust seal
4. Thrust washer
5. Collar
6. Needle bearing
7. Swing arm
8. Distance collar
9. Chain slider
10. Washer
11. Pivot nut
12. Chain adjuster locknut
13. Chain adjuster
14. Adjuster block
15. Thrust plate
16. Chain guard
17. Torque arm

**13**

## Preliminary Inspection

The condition of the swing arm bearings affects the handling of the motorcycle. Worn bearings cause wheel hop, pulling to one side under acceleration and pulling to the other side during braking. Check the condition of the swing arm bearings by performing the following inspection:

1. Remove the rear wheel as described in Chapter Eleven.

2. Remove the nut (C, **Figure 2**) and suspension arm bolt (C, **Figure 3**) from the swing arm mount. Lower the suspension arms away from the swing arm.

3. On the right side, make sure the swing arm pivot locknut (A, **Figure 13**) is tight.

4. On the left side, make sure the pivot nut (A, **Figure 14**) is tight.

5. The swing arm is now free to move under its own weight.

6. Grasp both ends of the swing arm. Try to move it from side to side in a horizontal arc. If more than a slight amount of movement is felt, the swing arm bearings are worn and must be replaced.

7. Grasp both ends of the swing arm and move it up and down. The swing arm should move smoothly with no binding or abnormal bearing noise. If binding or noise is noted, the bearings are worn. Replace them.

## Removal

Refer to **Figure 15**.

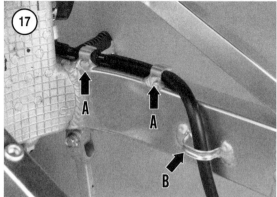

1. Remove the fairing side panel from each side as described in Chapter Fifteen.

2. Securely support the motorcycle with the rear wheel off the floor.

3. Drain the fluid from the rear brake, and disconnect the brake hose (**Figure 16**) from the rear brake caliper. Insert the loose end of the brake hose into a plastic bag.

4. Remove the rear brake caliper (Chapter Fourteen).

5. Break the chain and remove the rear wheel (Chapter Eleven).

6. Release the brake hose from the holders (A, **Figure 17**) at the top of the swing arm.

7. Carefully pull the rear brake hose from the guide (B, **Figure 17**) on the inboard side of the swing arm. Suspend the hose so it is out of the way.

8. Remove the screws (**Figure 18**), and remove the chain guard from the swing arm.

9. Use a hydraulic jack or wooden blocks to support the swing arm.

10. If still installed, remove the nut (C, **Figure 2**) and upper suspension arm bolt (C, **Figure 3**). Lower the suspension arms away from the swing arm.

11. Remove the shock absorber (this chapter).

12. On the right side, use the swing arm pivot thrust adjuster socket, and remove the pivot locknut (A, **Figure 13**).

*NOTE*
*A 27-mm hex socket is needed to hold the swing arm pivot shaft on 1999-2002 models. A 24-mm Allen head is needed on 2003-on models. If a 24-mm Allen socket is unavailable, make a pivot shaft holder (**Figure 19**) from a bolt and two nuts that measure 24-mm across opposite flats. This tool also works on the front axle on 2002-on models. A 36-mm socket is needed to turn the pivot nut on all models.*

13. Hold the pivot shaft (B, **Figure 13**), and loosen the pivot nut (A, **Figure 14**) on the left side. Remove

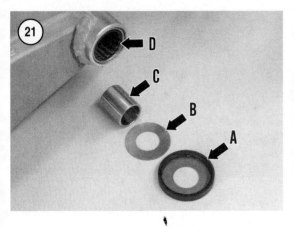

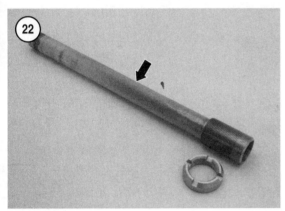

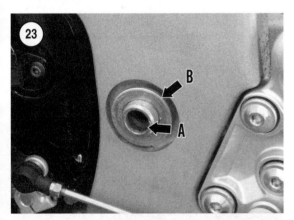

the pivot nut and washer (B, **Figure 14**) from the pivot shaft.

14. Loosen the pivot shaft (**Figure 20**), and remove it from the right side.

15. Lower the swing arm from the frame. Watch for the dust seal (A, **Figure 21**) on each side of the swing arm pivot.

16. If the swing arm bearings are not being serviced, place a strip of duct tape across each dust seal. This protects the bearing assemblies and prevents the loss of any small parts.

17. Inspect the swing arm and lubricate all bearings as described in this chapter.

### Installation

1. Lubricate the swing arm and suspension linkage bearings, the pivot shaft (**Figure 22**) and collars with Suzuki Super Grease A, or its equivalent, before installation.

2. Make sure a dust seal (A, **Figure 21**) and its thrust washer (B) are in place each side of the swing arm pivot.

3. Raise the swing arm, and fit it between the frame pivots.

4. Insert the swing arm pivot shaft (**Figure 20**) through the pivot boss in the right side of the frame, through the swing arms and out through the pivot boss in the left side. Refer to A, **Figure 23**.

5. Install the pivot shaft into the pivot boss, and tighten the pivot shaft (**Figure 24**) to 15 N•m (11 ft.-lb.).

6. On the left side, install the washer (B, **Figure 23**) onto the end of the pivot shaft, and loosely install the pivot nut (A, **Figure 14**).

7. Set the thrust clearance by tightening the swing arm pivot fasteners in the order described below. Tighten each fastener to the specified torque.

   a. Hold the pivot shaft, and tighten the pivot nut (**Figure 25**) to 100 N•m (74 ft.-lb.).

13

b. Install the pivot shaft locknut (A, **Figure 13**) onto the pivot shaft (B).

c. Use the pivot thrust adjuster socket to tighten the pivot shaft locknut (**Figure 26**) to 90 N•m (66 ft.-lb.).

8. Move the swing arm up and down, and check for smooth movement or excessive play. If the swing arm is tight or loose, the fasteners were either tightened in the wrong sequence or to an incorrect torque specification. Repeat Steps 5-7.

9. Install the shock absorber as described in this chapter.

10. Align each suspension arm with the pivot boss under the swing arm. Install the upper suspension arm bolt (C, **Figure 3**) from the left side and install the nut (C, **Figure 2**). Tighten the suspension arm nut to 78 N•m (58 in.-lb.).

11. Route the rear brake hose across the swing arm and through the guide (B, **Figure 17**) on the inboard side of the swing arm.

12. Secure the brake hose in the holders (A, **Figure 17**).

13. Install the chain guard (**Figure 18**) onto the swing arm.

14. Install the rear wheel and drive chain (Chapter Eleven). Adjust the chain as described in Chapter Three.

15. Install the rear brake caliper, add brake fluid, and bleed the rear caliper (Chapter Fourteen).

16. Install both fairing side panels (Chapter Fifteen).

**Disassembly**

Refer to **Figure 15**.

1. Remove the swing arm assembly as described in this section.

2. Remove the mounting bolts and remove the chain slider from the swing arm.

3. If still in place, remove the dust seal (A, **Figure 21**) and thrust washer (B) from each side of the swing arm pivot.

4. Remove the collar (C, **Figure 21**) from the needle bearing (D) in each side of the swing arm pivot.

5. Remove the collar (**Figure 27**) from the suspension pivot on the bottom of the swing arm.

6. Remove the front torque arm nut (**Figure 28**) and bolt, and then pull the torque arm from the swing arm.

7. Inspect the swing arm as described in this section.

**Assembly**

1. Lubricate the needle bearings (D, **Figure 21**) and collars (C) with Suzuki Super Grease A, or its equivalent.

2. Install the collar (**Figure 27**) into the suspension arm pivot boss on the swing arm. Make sure the ends of the collar are flush with the end of each needle bearing.

3. Install the collar (C, **Figure 21**) into the needle bearing (D) on each side of the swing arm pivot.

4. Install a thrust washer (B, **Figure 21**) into each dust seal (A). Press a dust seal onto each end of the swing arm pivot until the seal is completely seated.

5. Install the swing arm assembly as described in this section.

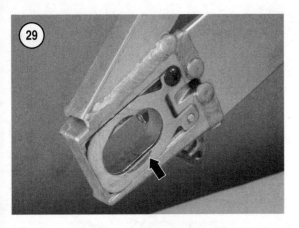

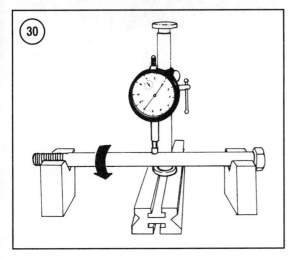

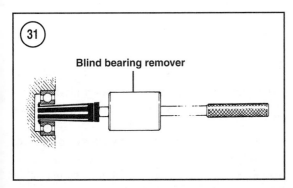

**Blind bearing remover**

6. Install the brake torque arm onto the swing arm. Tighten the front torque arm nut (**Figure 28**) to 28 N•m (21 ft.-lb.).

### Inspection

1. Wash the bolts and collars in solvent, and thoroughly dry them.

2. Inspect the collars (C, **Figure 21** and **Figure 27**) for wear, scratches or score marks.

3. Check the bolts for straightness. A bent bolt restricts swing arm movement.

4. Inspect the needle bearings (D, **Figure 21**) in the swing arm pivot and the suspension arm pivot as follows:

   a. Use a clean, lint-free rag and wipe off surface grease from the pivot area needle bearings.

   b. Turn each needle bearing with a finger. The bearing should turn smoothly without excessive play or noise. Check the rollers for evidence of wear, pitting or rust

   c. Reinstall each collar into its bearing, and slowly rotate the collar. Each must turn smoothly without excessive play or noise.

   d. Remove the collars.

5. Replace any worn or damaged needle bearing(s) as described in this chapter.

6. Inspect the thrust plate (**Figure 29**) on each side of the swing arm.

7. Check all welds on the swing arm for cracks or fractures.

8. Inspect the drive chain adjuster and locknut for wear or damage.

9. Check the pivot shaft for straightness with V-blocks and a dial indicator (**Figure 30**). Replace the pivot shaft if its runout equals or exceeds the service limit specified in **Table 1**.

10. Inspect the drive chain slider for wear or damage, and replace as necessary.

11. If necessary, replace any damaged part(s).

## SUSPENSION BEARING REPLACEMENT

### Swing Arm Needle Bearing

Do not remove the needle bearings unless they must be replaced. The needle bearings are damaged during removal.

A blind bearing puller is needed to remove the needle bearings. They can be installed with a homemade tool.

*NOTE*
*Replace the collar when replacing the swing arm needle bearings. These parts should always be replaced as a set.*

1. If still installed, remove the dust seals (A, **Figure 21**), thrust washers (B) and collar (C) from the swing arm pivot.

2. Note the position of the bearing (D, **Figure 21**) relative to the edge of the swing arm pivot. If necessary, measure the distance from the outside surface of the pivot to the outside surface of the bearing.

3. Insert the blind bearing puller through the needle bearing, and expand it behind the bearing (**Figure 31**).

13

4. Using sharp strokes of the slide hammer, withdraw the needle bearing from the pivot boss.

5. Remove the bearing puller and the bearing.

6. Withdraw the distance collar located between the bearings in the pivot bore.

7. Thoroughly clean out the inside of the pivot bore with solvent, and dry it with compressed air.

8. Apply a light coat of Suzuki Super Grease A to the exterior of the new bearings and to the inner circumference of the pivot bore.

> *CAUTION*
> *Install one needle bearing at a time. Make sure the bearing enters the pivot boss squarely, or the bearing and the pivot boss may be damaged.*

9. Position the bearing with the manufacturer's marks facing out.

10. Locate and square the new bearing in the pivot bore. Assemble the homemade tool (**Figure 32**) through the pivot bore so the large washer presses against the bearing (**Figure 33**).

11.. Hold the nut adjacent to the bearing being installed. Tighten the nut on the opposite end of the tool, and slowly pull the bearing into the pivot bore (**Figure 34**). Set the bearing to the position noted in Step 2.

12. Disassemble the tool.

13. Install the distance collar into the swing arm pivot.

14. Repeat Steps 9-12 and install the other bearing.

15. Make sure the bearings are properly seated. Turn each bearing by hand. It should turn smoothly.

16. Lubricate the new bearings with Suzuki Super Grease A.

17. Use the same tool to replace the suspension arm pivot bearings in the bottom swing arm.

### Suspension Lever Bearing

A bearing remover/race installer set (Suzuki part No. 09921-20240 and part No. 09941-34513, or equivalent tools) are needed to replace the suspension lever bearings.

Do not remove the needle bearings unless they must be replaced. Needle bearings are damaged during removal.

> *NOTE*
> *If the needle bearings are replaced, replace the pivot collars at the same time. These parts should always be replaced as a set.*

1. If still installed, remove the collars (A, **Figure 35**).

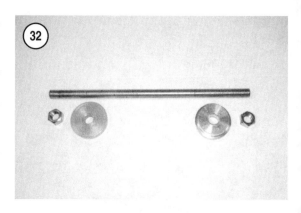

> *CAUTION*
> *Three different size bearings are used in the suspension lever. Mark a bearing front, center and rear as they are removed. Compare the old bearing to the new ones during bearing installation. The two bearings in the center pivot (C, **Figure 35**) are identical.*

2. Note the position of a bearing (B, **Figure 35**) relative to the edge of the suspension lever pivot. If necessary, measure the distance from the outside surface of the pivot to the outside surface of the bearing.

3A. Remove each bearing with the bearing remover set. Follow the tool's instructions.

3B. Remove the bearing with a blind bearing puller by performing the following:

   a. Insert a blind bearing puller through one needle bearing, and expand it behind the bearing (**Figure 31**).

   b. Using sharp strokes of the slide hammer, withdraw the needle bearing from the front pivot hole.

   c. Remove the tool and the bearing.

   d. Repeat substeps a-c for the remaining bearings.

4. Thoroughly clean out the inside of the pivot bores with solvent. Dry them with compressed air.

5. Apply a light coat of Suzuki Super Grease A to the exterior of the new bearings and to the inner circumference of the pivot bores.

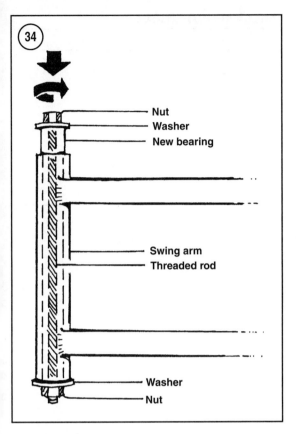

Nut
Washer
New bearing

Swing arm
Threaded rod

Washer
Nut

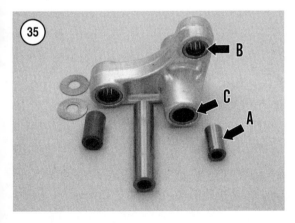

*CAUTION*
*Three different size bearings are used in the suspension lever. Install a bearing in the proper pivot (front, center or rear) in the suspension lever. The two bearings in the center pivot (C, Figure 35) are identical.*

*CAUTION*
*Install one needle bearing at a time. Make sure the bearing is square to the pivot bore.*

6A. To install the bearings without a press, perform the following:

   a. Locate and square the new bearing in the appropriate pivot bore.

   b. Install the bearing with a driver or socket that matches the diameter of the bearing outer diameter. Drive the bearing into the bore until it sits in the location noted in Step 2.

   c. Check that the bearing is properly seated. Turn each bearing by hand. The bearing should turn smoothly.

   d. Repeat for the remaining bearings.

6B. To install the bearings with a press, perform the following:

   a. Support the suspension lever in a press.

   b. Locate and square the new bearing in the pivot bore.

   c. Press the bearing into the bore until it is in the location noted in Step 2.

   d. Repeat for the remaining bearings.

7. Pack the needle's of the new bearing with Suzuki Super Grease A.

8. Install the new collar (A, **Figure 35**) into each location.

**13**

**Table 1 REAR SUSPENSION SPECIFICATIONS**

| Item | Specification |
|------|---------------|
| Rear wheel travel | 140 mm (5.51 in.) |
| Shock absorber | |
|   Spring preload (spring set length) | |
|     Standard setting | 183 mm (7.2 in.) |
|     Rebound damping | 11 clicks out |
|     Compression damping | 8 clicks out |
| Swing arm pivot-shaft runout | 0.3 mm (0.01 in.) |

**Table 2 REAR SUSPENSION TORQUE SPECIFICATIONS**

| Item | N•m | in.-lb. | ft.-lb. |
|------|-----|---------|---------|
| Rear axle nut | 100 | – | 74 |
| Shock absorber mounting nut | 50 | – | 37 |
| Suspension arm bolt/nut | 78 | – | 58 |
| Suspension lever bolt/nut | 78 | – | 58 |
| Swing arm | | | |
|   Pivot nut | 100 | – | 74 |
|   Pivot shaft locknut | 90 | – | 66 |
|   Pivot shaft | 15 | – | 11 |
| Torque arm nut | | | |
|   Front | 28 | – | 21 |
|   Rear | 35 | – | 26 |

# CHAPTER FOURTEEN

# BRAKES

This chapter describes repair and replacement procedures for the brake system components.

When servicing a brake system component, compare measurements to the specification at the end of this chapter. Replace any part that is worn, damaged or out of specification. During assembly, tighten fasteners to the specified torque.

## BRAKE SERVICE

*WARNING*
*Do not ride the motorcycle until the front and rear brakes, as well as the brake light, are working properly.*

*WARNING*
*Do not use silicone-based (DOT 5) brake fluid on the motorcycles covered in this manual. Silicone-based fluid can damage the brake components, leading to brake system failure.*

*WARNING*
*Never reuse brake fluid. Contaminated brake fluid can cause brake failure. Dispose of used brake fluid properly.*

*WARNING*
*When working on the brake system, do **not** inhale brake dust. It may contain asbestos, which can cause lung injury and cancer. Wear a face mask that meets OSHA requirements for trapping asbestos particles. Wash hands and forearms thoroughly after completing the work. **Never** use compressed air to clean any part of the brake system.*

The work area and all tools must be absolutely clean during brake service. Caliper and master cylinder components can be damaged by debris that enters the brake system. Do not use sharp tools inside the master cylinders and calipers, or on the pistons.

Note the following when servicing the brake system.

1. Disc brake components rarely require disassembly. Do not disassemble them unless necessary.

2. When adding brake fluid, only use DOT 4 brake fluid from a sealed container. Other types of brake fluid may vaporize and cause brake failure.

3. Always use the same brand of brake fluid. One manufacturer's brake fluid may not be compatible with another's.

4. Brake fluid absorbs moisture from the air, which greatly reduces its ability to perform correctly. Pur-

14

chase brake fluid in small containers, and properly discard any small leftover quantities.

5. Use only DOT 4 brake fluid or brake parts cleaner to wash parts. Never use petroleum-based solvents on internal brake system components. This causes the seals to swell and distort. Replace the seals as necessary.

6. When a brake banjo bolt or brake line nut is loosened, the system is opened and must be bled to remove air. If the brakes feel spongy, this usually means air has entered the system. For safe operation, refer to *Brake Bleeding* in this chapter.

7. After disconnecting a hose from a brake component, insert the hose end into a plastic bag. Use a rubber band to close and seal the bag around the hose so brake fluid does not dribble onto the motorcycle. To prevent brake fluid damage, note the following:

   a. Protect the motorcycle with a plastic cover. Even a few drops of brake fluid can damage painted, plated or plastic surfaces.

   b. Keep a bucket of soap and water close to the motorcycle while working on the brake system. If brake fluid spills on any surface, immediately wash the area with soap and water and then rinse thoroughly.

   c. To control the flow of brake fluid when refilling the reservoirs, punch a small hole into the seal of a new container. Put this hole next to the edge of the pour spout.

8. Always install a new sealing washer against each side of a hose fitting anytime the banjo bolt or hose has been removed.

## BRAKE BLEEDING

### Bleeding Tips

Bleeding removes air from the hydraulic system. Air in the brakes increases brake-lever or brake-pedal travel, and it makes the brakes feel soft or spongy. Under extreme circumstances, it can cause complete loss of brake pressure.

Refer to *Brake Service* in this chapter.

1. Clean the bleed valve and area around the valve before beginning. Make sure the opening in the valve is clear.

2. Use a box end wrench to open and close the bleed valve. This prevents damage to the valve, especially one that is rusted in place.

3. Replace a bleed valve with damaged threads or a rounded hex head. A damaged valve is difficult to remove, and it cannot be properly tightened.

4. Use a clear catch hose (**Figure 1**) so the fluid can be seen as it leaves the bleed valve. Air bubbles in the

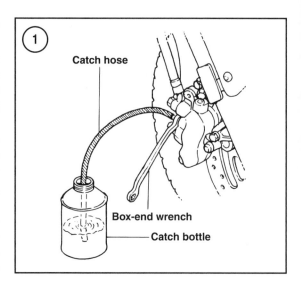

Catch hose

Box-end wrench

Catch bottle

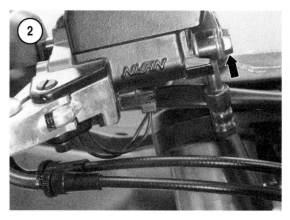

catch hose indicate air may be trapped in the brake system.

5. Open the bleed valve just enough to allow fluid to pass through the valve and into the catch bottle. If a bleed valve is too loose, air can be drawn back into the system around the valve threads.

6. If air is entering around the bleed valve threads, apply silicone brake grease around the valve where it emerges from the caliper. The grease should seal the valve and prevent the entry of air. Wipe away the grease once the brakes have been bled.

7. If the front brakes are difficult to bleed, remove the master cylinder assembly. Tilt the assembly so the brake-hose banjo bolt (**Figure 2**) sits below the fluid port in the master cylinder reservoir. Hold the master cylinder assembly in this position, and pump the brake lever several times. Any trapped air bubbles rise into the reservoir. Reinstall the master cylinder assembly and continue bleeding.

8. Gently tapping the banjo bolts at the calipers, master cylinders and any other hose connections in the brake line also helps dislodge trapped air bubbles.

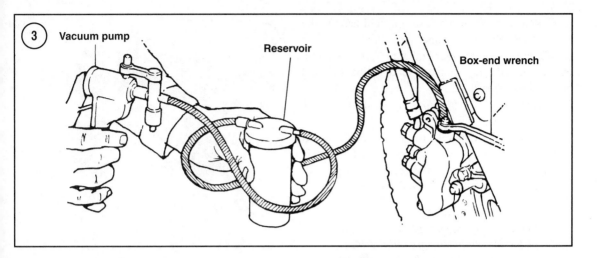

3 Vacuum pump

Reservoir

Box-end wrench

### Bleeding Procedure

1. Check all banjo bolts in the system. They must be tight before bleeding the brakes.

2. Remove the dust cap from the caliper bleed valve, and fit a box-end wrench onto the valve.

*NOTE*
*When bleeding the front brakes, turn the handlebars to level the front master cylinder.*

3. Clean all debris from the top of the master cylinder reservoir, and remove the top cover, diaphragm plate (front brake) and the diaphragm from the reservoir.

4. Add brake fluid to the reservoir until the fluid level reaches the reservoir upper limit. Loosely install the diaphragm and the cover. Leave them in place during this procedure to keep dirt out of the system and so brake fluid cannot spurt out of the reservoir.

5A. When manually bleeding the brakes, perform the following:

a. Connect a length of clear tubing to the bleed valve (**Figure 1**, typical). Place the other end of the tube into a clean container. Fill the container with enough fresh brake fluid to keep the end submerged. The tube should be long enough so that it loops higher than the bleed valve. This helps prevent air from being drawn back into the caliper during bleeding.

*NOTE*
*As brake fluid enters the system, the level in the master cylinder reservoir drops. Add brake fluid as necessary to keep the fluid level 10 mm (3/8 in.) below the reservoir top so air is not drawn into the system.*

b. Pump the brake lever or brake pedal a few times. Then firmly depress it until it stops, and hold it in this position.

c. Open the bleed valve with the wrench. Let the brake lever or pedal move to the limit of its travel, and then close the bleed valve. Do not release the brake lever or pedal while the bleed valve is open.

d. Repeat substep b and substep c until the brake fluid flowing from the hose is clear and free of air bubbles.

5B. When vacuum bleeding, perform the following:

a. Assemble the vacuum tool following the manufacturer's instructions.

b. Connect the pump reservoir catch hose to the bleed valve on the brake caliper (**Figure 3**).

*NOTE*
*When using a vacuum pump, keep an eye on the brake fluid level in the master cylinder reservoir. It drops quite rapidly. This is particularly true for the rear reservoir, which does not hold as much brake fluid as the front. Stop often and check the brake fluid level. Maintain the level at 10 mm (3/8 in.) from the top of the reservoir so air is not drawn into the system.*

c. Operate the vacuum pump to create vacuum in the hose.

d. Use a wrench to open the bleed valve. The vacuum pump should pull fluid from the system. Close the bleed valve before the brake fluid stops flowing from the system (low vacuum pressure) or before the master cylinder reservoir runs empty. Add fluid to the master cylinder reservoir as necessary.

e. Operate the brake lever or brake pedal a few times, and release it.

14

f. Repeat substeps c-e until the fluid leaving the bleed valve is clear and free of air bubbles.

6. When bleeding the rear brake, perform Step 5 on each bleed valve, one on the inboard caliper half and one on the outboard half.

7. Refer to Step 7 in *Bleeding Tips* if the system is difficult to bleed.

8. Test the feel of the brake lever or pedal. It should feel firm and offer the same resistance each time it is operated. If the lever or pedal feels soft, air is still trapped in the system. Continue bleeding.

*NOTE*
*The setting on the front brake lever adjuster affects bleeding. Initially bleed the front brakes with the adjuster turned to the No. 6 setting. Once the brakes feel solid, check the feel with the adjuster in several different settings. If the lever feels soft at any setting or if the lever hits the handlebar, air is still trapped in the system. Continue bleeding.*

9. When bleeding is complete, disconnect the hose from the bleed valve. Tighten the caliper bleed valve to 7.5 N•m (66 in.-lb.).

10. When bleeding the front brakes, repeat Steps 1-10 on the opposite front caliper.

11. Add brake fluid to the master cylinder reservoir as needed to keep the fluid level adjusted correctly.

12. Install the diaphragm, diaphragm plate (front brake) and top cap. Make sure the cap is secured in place.

13. Test ride the motorcycle slowly at first to make sure the brakes are operating properly.

## BRAKE FLUID DRAINING

Before disconnecting a front or rear brake hose, drain the brake fluid. Draining the fluid reduces the amount of fluid that can spill out when system components are removed.

This section describes two methods for draining the brake system: manual and vacuum. An empty bottle, a length of clear hose and a wrench are required for manual draining. A hand-operated vacuum pump with a reservoir is required for vacuum draining.

1. Remove the dust cap from the bleed valve. Remove all dirt from the valve and its outlet port.

2A. When manually draining the brakes, perform the following:

a. Connect a length of clear hose to the bleed valve on the caliper. Insert the other end into a container (**Figure 1**, typical).

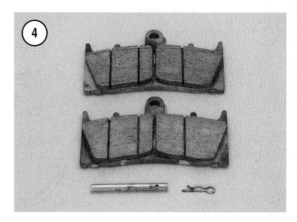

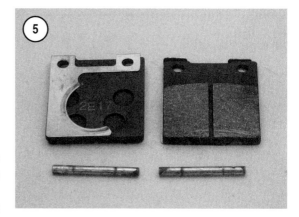

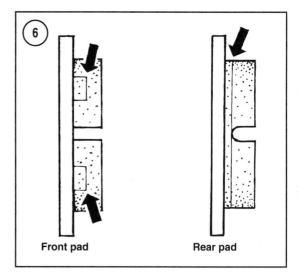

Front pad                                    Rear pad

b. Apply the front brake lever or the rear brake pedal until it stops. Hold the lever or pedal in this position.

c. Open the bleed valve with a wrench, and let the lever or pedal move to the limit of its travel. Close the bleed valve.

d. Release the lever or pedal, and repeat substep c and substep d until brake fluid stops flowing from the bleed valve.

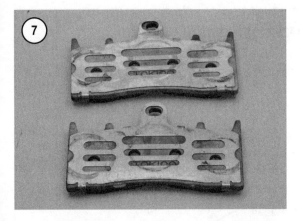

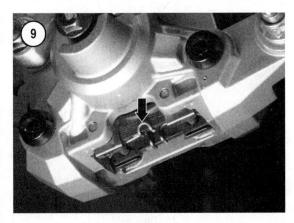

2B. When vacuum draining the fluid, perform the following:

a. Connect the pump reservoir catch hose to the bleed valve on the brake caliper (**Figure 3**).

b. Operate the vacuum pump to create a vacuum in the hose.

c. Use a wrench to open the bleed valve. The vacuum pump should pull fluid from the system.

d. When fluid has stopped flowing through the hose, close the bleed valve.

e. Repeat substeps b-d until brake fluid no longer flows from the bleed valve.

3. If draining the front brake system, repeat this procedure on the opposite caliper.

4. Discard the brake fluid properly.

### BRAKE PAD INSPECTION

Brake pad wear depends upon riding habits and conditions. Frequently check the brake pads for wear.

To maintain even brake pressure on the disc, always replace all pads in a caliper at the same time. When replacing the front brake pads, replace all pads in *both front calipers* at the same time.

The brake hose does not need to be disconnected from the caliper during brake pad replacement. If the hose is removed, the brakes have to be bled. Disconnect the hose only when servicing the brake caliper.

1. Remove the brake pads as described in this chapter. **Figure 4** shows the front brake pads from one caliper. For rear brake pads, refer to **Figure 5**.

2. Inspect the brake pads by performing the following.

a. Inspect the friction material for surface dirt and grease or oil contamination. Remove light surface contamination with sandpaper. If any contamination has penetrated the surface, replace the brake pads.

b. Inspect the brake pads for excessive or uneven wear and any damage. Replace the brake pads if either pad is worn to the bottom of the wear groove (**Figure 6**).

*NOTE*
*All pads in a caliper should show approximately the same amount of wear. If the pads are wearing unevenly, the caliper may not be operating correctly.*

c. Inspect the metal shim on the back of front (**Figure 7**) or rear (**Figure 5**) pads for corrosion and damage.

3. Inspect the brake disc as described in this chapter.

4. Check the friction surface of the new pads for any debris or manufacturing residue. If necessary, clean the pads with brake parts cleaner followed by fine sandpaper.

5. Check the pad springs for wear, damage or fatigue. Examine the spring in a front caliper, (**Figure 8**) or rear caliper (**Figure 9**). Replace the pad springs if any shows sign of damage or excessive wear.

6. Thoroughly clean any corrosion or road dirt from the pad spring(s) and pad pin(s).

7. Service the brake disc as follows:

a. Use brake cleaner and a fine grade emery cloth to remove all brake pad residue and any rust from the brake disc. Clean both sides of the disc.

**14**

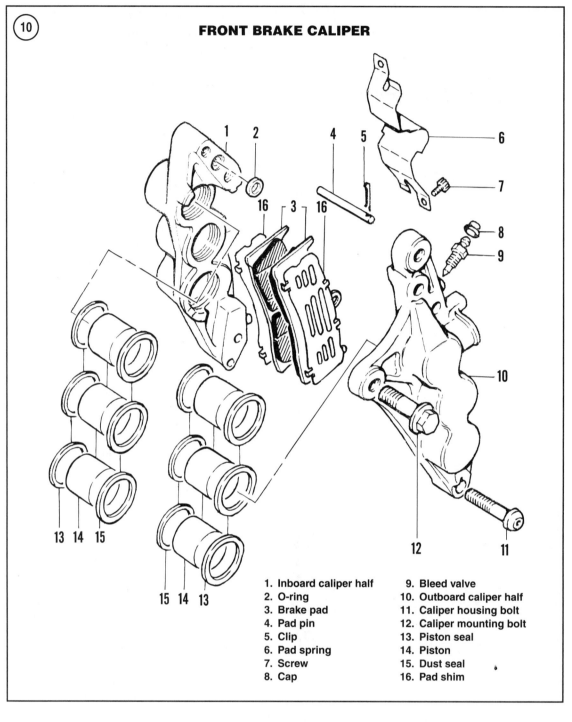

**FRONT BRAKE CALIPER**

1. Inboard caliper half
2. O-ring
3. Brake pad
4. Pad pin
5. Clip
6. Pad spring
7. Screw
8. Cap
9. Bleed valve
10. Outboard caliper half
11. Caliper housing bolt
12. Caliper mounting bolt
13. Piston seal
14. Piston
15. Dust seal
16. Pad shim

b. Check the brake disc for wear as described in this chapter.

## FRONT BRAKE CALIPER

Refer to *Brake Service* in this chapter. Refer to **Figure 10**.

## Brake Pad Removal/Installation

1. Securely support the motorcycle on a level surface.

2. To prevent the front brake lever from being applied, secure a block of wood or another spacer between the brake lever and the throttle grip so the brake lever cannot be inadvertently squeezed.

3. Remove the pad spring screws (A, **Figure 11**), and lift the pad spring (B) from the caliper.

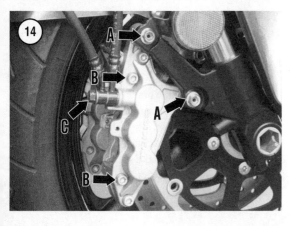

4. Pull the clip (A, **Figure 12**) from the pad pin, and slide out the pad pin (B). Note that the clip sits between the outboard brake pad and the caliper body.

5. Remove the inboard (A, **Figure 13**) and outboard (B) pads.

6. Inspect the brake pads as described in this chapter.

*WARNING*
*When purchasing new pads, check with the dealership to make sure the friction compound of the new pads is compatible with the disc material.*

7. During new pad installation, the fluid level in the master cylinder will rise as the caliper pistons are repositioned. When installing new brake pads, perform the following:

   a. Clean all debris from the top of the master cylinder.

   b. Remove the top cover, diaphragm plate and diaphragm from the reservoir.

   c. Use a syringe to remove approximately half of the brake fluid from the reservoir.

   d. Remove the caliper mounting bolts (A, **Figure 14**), and remove the caliper.

   e. Temporarily reinstall the old brake pads into the caliper. Seat each pad against its set of pistons fully.

*NOTE*
*The pistons should move freely. If they do not, remove and inspect the caliper as described in this section.*

   f. Insert a large flat blade screwdriver or tire iron between the old brake pads. Push the pistons back into the caliper bores. This creates room for the new brake pads. Constantly check the reservoir level and make sure the fluid does not overflow. Draw out excess fluid as necessary with a syringe.

   g. Remove the old brake pads, and install the caliper onto the inboard side of the bracket on the fork leg. Tighten the front caliper mounting bolts (A, **Figure 14**) to 39 N•m (29 ft.-lb.).

8. Fit the pad shim (**Figure 7**) onto the back of each new brake pad. Install the new outboard pad (**Figure 15**) first and then the inboard pad (A, **Figure 13**) into the caliper. Position each brake pad so its friction material faces the brake disc. Carefully push it into the caliper until it bottoms.

9. Insert the pad pin (**Figure 16**) through the caliper and through both brake pads. Install the clip (**Figure 17**) so it sits between the outboard pad shim and the caliper (A, **Figure 12**).

14

10. Set the pad spring (B, **Figure 11**) into place on the caliper. Secure the spring in place with the pad spring screws (A, **Figure 11**).

*CAUTION*
*Always replace all pads in both front brake calipers as a set.*

11. If installing new brake pads, repeat Steps 1-11 for the opposite caliper.

12. Remove the spacer from the front brake lever.

13. Pump the front brake lever to reposition the brake pads against the brake disc.

14. Refill the master cylinder reservoir, if necessary, to maintain the correct fluid level. Install the diaphragm, diaphragm plate and top cover. Tighten the cover screws securely.

### Caliper Removal/Installation

1A. If removing the caliper for disassembly, perform the following:

    a. Remove the brake pads as described in this section.

    b. Slightly loosen each caliper housing bolt (B, **Figure 14**).

    c. Remove the caliper mounting bolts (A, **Figure 14**), and lift the caliper from the brake disc. Note that the caliper sits on the inboard side of the bracket on the front fork.

    d. Insert a piece of wood between the pistons (A, **Figure 18**). Operate the brake lever and drive the pistons partially from their cylinders.

*NOTE*
*The caliper hose, as well as the crossover hose attach to the right caliper. Consequently, the banjo bolt on the right caliper is longer than the banjo bolt on the left caliper. Do not mix the bolts.*

    e. Remove the banjo bolt (B, **Figure 18**) and sealing washers attaching the brake hose(s) to the caliper assembly. Remove two sealing washers from the left caliper, three from the right.

    f. Place the loose end of the brake hose(s) in a plastic bag to prevent residual brake fluid from leaking out.

1B. If the caliper is not being disassembled, remove the caliper mounting bolts (A, **Figure 14**), and lift the caliper from the brake disc. Note that the caliper sits on the inboard side of the bracket on the front fork.

2. If necessary, disassemble and service the caliper assembly as described in this section.

3. Install by reversing the removal steps while noting the following:

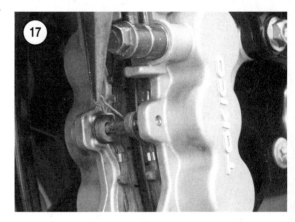

    a. Carefully lower the caliper assembly onto the disc. If the caliper was not serviced, exercise caution so the leading edges of the brake pads are not damaged.

    b. Position the caliper so its mount sits against the inboard side of the bracket on the front fork leg. Secure the brake caliper to the front fork with the caliper mounting bolts (A, **Figure 14**). Torque the front caliper mounting bolts to 39 N•m (29 ft.-lb.). Make sure the reflector sits behind the upper caliper mounting bolt.

    c. Install the brake hose(s) onto the caliper. Install a new sealing washer on each side of the brake

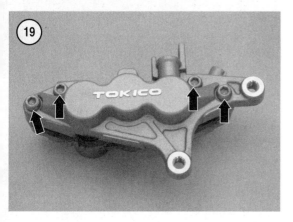

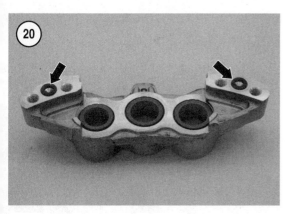

g. Install the brake pads, and bleed the brakes as described in this chapter.

**Caliper Disassembly**

1. Remove the brake pads and caliper as described in this chapter.
2. Remove the caliper housing bolts (**Figure 19**) loosened during the removal procedure.
3. Separate the caliper body halves. Remove and discard the O-rings (**Figure 20**). New O-rings must be installed during assembly.

*NOTE*
*If the pistons were partially forced out of the caliper body during removal, Steps 4-7 may not be necessary. If the pistons or caliper bores are corroded or dirty, a small amount of compressed air may be necessary to completely remove the pistons from their bores.*

4. Tighten the bleed valve.

*WARNING*
*In the next step, the piston may shoot out of the caliper with considerable force. Keep your hands out of the way. Wear shop gloves and safety goggles when using compressed air to remove the pistons.*

5. Place the caliper body face down on a rubber mat. The mat helps seal the fluid passages. Press the caliper firmly into the mat, and apply the air pressure in short bursts to the hydraulic passageway on the caliper body. Repeat this process for the other caliper body half.
6. If only one or two pistons come out of the caliper body, perform the following:
    a. Push the piston(s) back into the caliper body, and set the caliper body face down on the mat.
    b. Place a flat piece of plastic or a wooden shim under the freed piston(s).
    c. Press the caliper firmly into the mat, and apply air to the passage as described in Step 5. The shim prevents the freed piston(s) from coming out too far so the other piston(s) can be driven from their respective bores.
    d. Remove each piston by hand (**Figure 21**) from its bore.
7. Repeat the Steps 4-6 for the other caliper half.

*CAUTION*
*In the following step, do not use a sharp tool to remove the dust and piston seals*

hose fitting(s) and install the banjo bolt (C, **Figure 14**). Use two sealing washers on the left caliper, three on the right.
d. Position each brake hose so its neck sits against the outboard side of the stop post. On the right caliper, the crossover hose (C, **Figure 18**) must sit behind the master cylinder hose as shown.
e. Torque the brake hose banjo bolt (C, **Figure 14**) to 23 N•m (17 ft.-lb.).
f. If the caliper was disassembled for service, torque the front caliper housing bolts (B, **Figure 14**) to 21 N•m (15.5 ft.-lb.).

**14**

*from the caliper cylinders. Do not dam-
age the cylinder surface.*

8. Use a piece of wood or plastic scraper and carefully push the dust seal (A, **Figure 22**) and the piston
seal (B) in toward the center of the cylinder and out of
their grooves. Remove the dust and piston seals from
each cylinder in each caliper half, and discard all
seals.

9. If necessary, turn out and remove the bleed valve.

10. Inspect the caliper assembly as described in this
section.

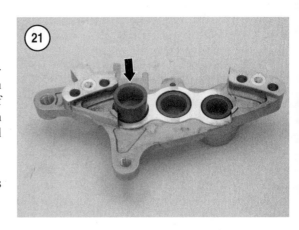

### Caliper Assembly

1. Soak the new dust seals and piston seals in DOT 4
brake fluid.

2. Coat the cylinder bores and pistons with DOT 4
brake fluid.

3. Carefully install a new piston seal (**Figure 23**)
into the lower groove in each cylinder. Make sure
each seal is properly seated in its respective groove.

4. Carefully install a new dust seal (**Figure 24**) into
the upper groove in each cylinder. Make sure all seals
are properly seated in their respective grooves.

5. Repeat Step 3 and Step 4 for the other caliper body
half.

6. Position the pistons (**Figure 21**) with the open
ends facing out, and install the pistons into the caliper
cylinders. Push the pistons into the cylinders until
they bottom.

7. Repeat Step 6 for the other caliper body half.
Make sure all pistons are installed correctly.

8. Coat the *new* O-rings in DOT 4 brake fluid, and
seat the O-rings into depression in the inboard caliper
half (**Figure 20**).

9. Assemble the caliper halves. Make sure the
O-rings remain properly seated.

10. Install the caliper housing bolts (**Figure 19**).
Evenly tighten the bolts securely. The housing bolts
are tightened to specification after the caliper is
mounted on the front fork.

11. If removed, install the caliper bleed valve assembly. Tighten it to 7.5 N•m (66 in.-lb.), and install the
cap.

12. Install the caliper and brake pads as described in
this chapter.

13. Bleed the brakes as described in this chapter.

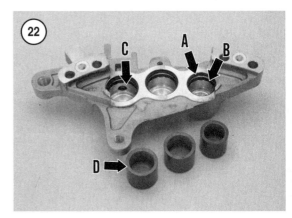

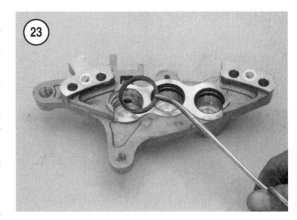

### Caliper Inspection

1. Clean both caliper body halves and all pistons in
DOT 4 brake fluid. Thoroughly dry the parts.

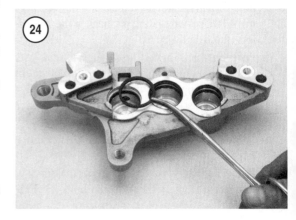

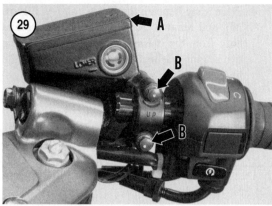

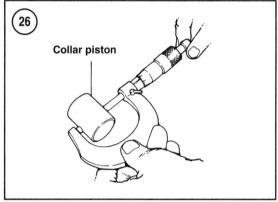

Collar piston

2. Apply compressed air to the fluid passageways in the base of the cylinder bores. Clean out the passages, if necessary, with fresh brake fluid.

3. Apply compressed air to the fluid passageways that connect each caliper half. Clean them with an aerosol brake parts cleaner if necessary.

4. Inspect the dust seal groove and the piston seal groove in all cylinders for damage. If any groove is damaged or corroded, replace the caliper assembly.

5. Inspect the cylinder walls (C, **Figure 22**) and pistons (D) for scratches, scoring or other damage.

6. Measure the cylinder bores with a bore gauge (**Figure 25**) or vernier caliper. Refer to the specifications in **Table 1**.

7. Measure the outside diameter of the pistons with a micrometer (**Figure 26**) or vernier caliper.

8. Inspect the threads in the banjo bolt (**Figure 27**) and the bleed valve (**Figure 28**). If either part is worn or damaged, clean it with a metric thread die or replace it.

9. Apply compressed air to opening(s) in the banjo bolt and bleed valve. Make sure they are clear.

10. Inspect both caliper bodies for damage. Inspect the threads of the caliper housing bolt holes, banjo bolt hole and the bleed valve hole. Clean any thread with an appropriate size metric tap or replace the caliper assembly.

14

### FRONT BRAKE MASTER CYLINDER

Refer to *Brake Service* in this chapter.

#### Removal

1. If servicing the master cylinder, perform the following:

   a. Drain the brake fluid from the front brakes as described in this chapter.

   b. Clean the top of the master cylinder.

   c. Remove the top cover (A, **Figure 29**), diaphragm plate and diaphragm from the master cylinder reservoir.

d. Place a rag beneath the banjo bolt (A, **Figure 30**), and remove the bolt. Separate the brake hose from the master cylinder. Watch for the two sealing washers, one from each side of the brake hose fitting.

e. Place the loose end of the brake hose into a plastic bag to prevent brake fluid from leaking onto the motorcycle. Seal the bag with a rubber band, and tie the loose end of the hose up to the handlebar.

2. Disconnect the electrical connectors (B, **Figure 30**) from the brake switch.

3. Remove the master cylinder clamp bolts (B, **Figure 29**), and lower the master cylinder from the handlebar.

4. If servicing the master cylinder, drain any residual brake fluid from the master cylinder and reservoir. Note the position of the protector in the reservoir.

## Installation

1. Set the front master cylinder onto the right handlebar so its clamp mating surface aligns with the indexing dot.

2. Mount the clamp with the UP mark facing up, and install the master cylinder clamp bolts (B, **Figure 29**). Tighten the upper mounting bolt first, then the lower bolt leaving a gap at the bottom. Tighten the front master cylinder clamp bolts to 10 N•m (89 in.-lb.).

3. Connect the electrical connectors (B, **Figure 30**) to the brake light switch.

4. Fit the brake hose onto the master cylinder so the hose neck seats against the front side of the stop post. Install a new sealing washer onto each side of the hose fitting, and tighten the brake hose banjo bolt (A, **Figure 30**) to 23 N•m (17 ft.-lb.).

5. Refill the master cylinder reservoir, and bleed the front brakes as described in this chapter.

## Disassembly

1. Remove the master cylinder (**Figure 31**) as described in this section.

2. Turn out the mounting screw (A, **Figure 32**), and lift the front brake light switch from the reservoir.

3. Remove the nut (B, **Figure 32**) from the brake lever pivot bolt.

4. Remove the brake lever pivot bolt (A, **Figure 33**), and slide the lever from the master cylinder bracket.

5. Roll the rubber boot (**Figure 34**) from the piston in cylinder bore.

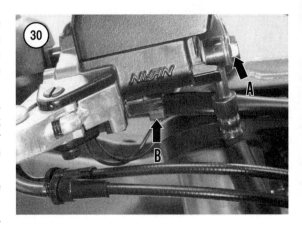

6. Press the piston into the cylinder bore, and use snap ring pliers to remove the internal snap ring (**Figure 35**).

7. Remove the piston (A, **Figure 36**) and the spring assembly (B) from the cylinder bore.

8. Remove the protector from the bottom of the reservoir. Note the position of the protector in the reservoir. It must be reinstalled with this same orientation.

## Assembly

Refer to **Figure 31**.

1. Soak new cups in DOT 4 brake fluid for at least 15 minutes to make them pliable. Coat the inside of the cylinder bore with brake fluid before assembly.

2. Install the new primary cup (A, **Figure 37**) onto the tapered end of the spring (B). Roll the new secondary cup (C, **Figure 37**) onto the piston (D).

*CAUTION*
*When installing the piston assembly, do not allow the cups to turn inside out. They will become damaged and allow brake fluid to leak within the cylinder bore.*

3. Install the spring/primary cup assembly (B, **Figure 36**) into the master cylinder bore with the primary cup facing out toward the brake lever.

4. Lubricate the master piston (B, **Figure 36**) with fresh brake fluid, and install the assembly into the cylinder bore. The large, flat end of the master piston must face the primary cup as shown in **Figure 36**.

5. Press the piston into the bore, and secure it in place with a snap ring (**Figure 35**). The snap ring (**Figure 38**) must be seated fully in the groove inside the cylinder bore.

6. Lubricate the boot with fresh brake fluid. Carefully roll the boot over the piston so the boot seals the master cylinder bore. Refer to **Figure 34**.

7. Install the brake lever assembly as follows:

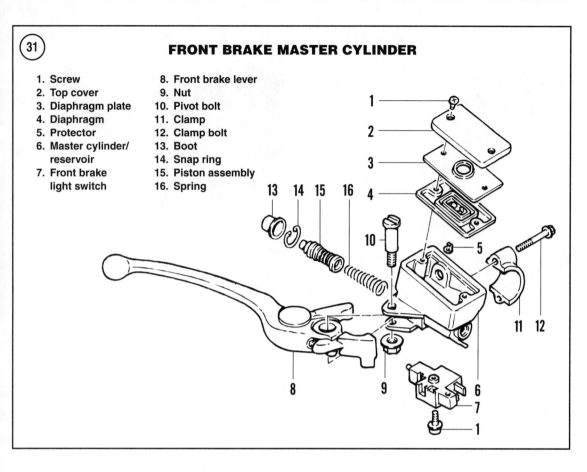

**FRONT BRAKE MASTER CYLINDER**

1. Screw
2. Top cover
3. Diaphragm plate
4. Diaphragm
5. Protector
6. Master cylinder/ reservoir
7. Front brake light switch
8. Front brake lever
9. Nut
10. Pivot bolt
11. Clamp
12. Clamp bolt
13. Boot
14. Snap ring
15. Piston assembly
16. Spring

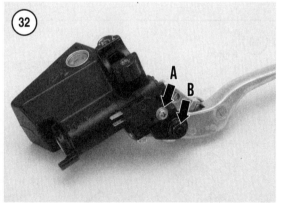

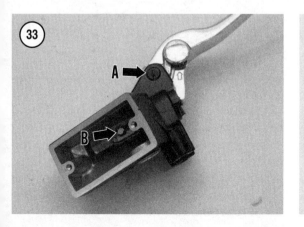

14

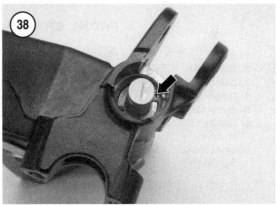

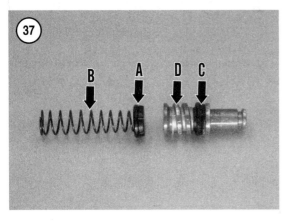

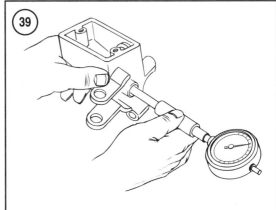

a. Lubricate the pivot bolt with waterproof grease.

b. Fit the brake lever/adjuster assembly into place in the lever boss, and install the pivot bolt (A, **Figure 33**).

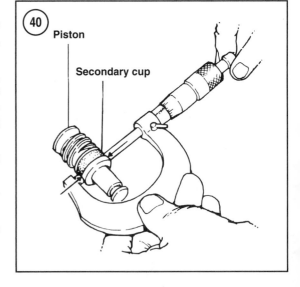

c. Turn the nut (B, **Figure 32**) onto the pivot bolt, and tighten the nut securely. Check that the brake lever moves freely. If there is any binding or roughness, remove the pivot bolt and brake lever. Inspect the parts.

8. Install the front brake switch, and tighten the screw (A, **Figure 32**) securely.

9. Seat the protector in port on the bottom of the reservoir as noted during removal.

10. Install the master cylinder as described in this section.

### Inspection

Compare measurements to the specifications in **Table 1**. Replace any part that is worn, damaged or out of specification.

1. Clean all parts in DOT 4 brake fluid. Inspect the cylinder bore surface and piston contact surfaces for signs of wear, corrosion or damage. If less than per-

fect, replace the master cylinder assembly. Do not hone the master cylinder bore.

2. Inspect the primary cup (A, **Figure 37**) and secondary cup (C) for signs of wear and damage. If less than perfect, replace the piston assembly.

3. Measure the cylinder bore with a bore gauge (**Figure 39**) or vernier caliper.

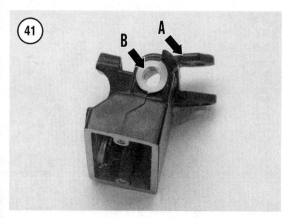

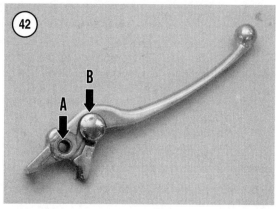

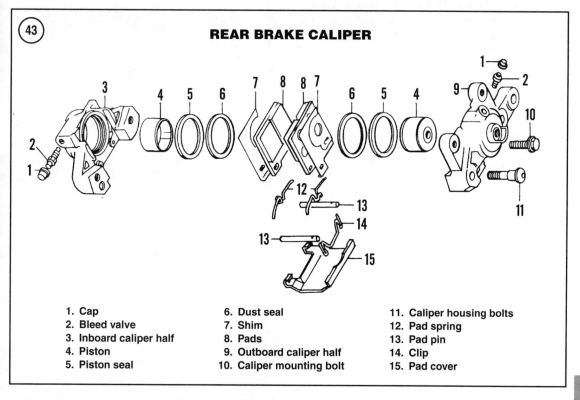

**REAR BRAKE CALIPER**

| 1. Cap | 6. Dust seal | 11. Caliper housing bolts |
|---|---|---|
| 2. Bleed valve | 7. Shim | 12. Pad spring |
| 3. Inboard caliper half | 8. Pads | 13. Pad pin |
| 4. Piston | 9. Outboard caliper half | 14. Clip |
| 5. Piston seal | 10. Caliper mounting bolt | 15. Pad cover |

14

4. Inspect the spring contact surface of the piston (D, **Figure 37**) for signs of wear and damage. If less than perfect, replace the piston assembly.

5. Check the other end of the piston for wear caused by the hand lever. If worn, replace the piston assembly.

6. Measure the outside diameter of the piston with a micrometer (**Figure 40**).

7. Check the lugs on the brake lever boss (A, **Figure 41**) for cracks or elongation.

8. Inspect the threads in the brake hose port (B, **Figure 41**). Clean the threads with an appropriate size metric thread tap or replace the master cylinder assembly.

9. Make sure the port (B, **Figure 33**) in the bottom of the reservoir is clear. During assembly, install the protector over the port.

10. Inspect the pivot hole (A, **Figure 42**) in the brake lever for cracks or elongation.

11. Inspect the adjuster (B, **Figure 42**) on the lever. If worn or damaged, replace the hand lever as an assembly.

12. Check the top cover, diaphragm and diaphragm plate for damage and deterioration. Replace as necessary.

**REAR BRAKE CALIPER**

Refer to *Brake Service* in this chapter. Refer to **Figure 43**.

## Brake Pad Replacement

*CAUTION*
*Check the pads more frequently as the pad thickness approaches the wear limit line (Figure 6). On some pads, the limit line is close to the metal backing plate. If pad wear happens to be uneven, the backing plate could come in contact with the disc and cause damage.*

1. Securely support the motorcycle on a level surface.

2. To prevent the rear brake pedal from being applied, tie the end of the pedal up to the frame. That way if the brake pedal is inadvertently pressed, the pistons are not forced out of the cylinders.

3. Squeeze the sides of the pad cover, and remove the cover from the caliper.

4. Pull the clip (**Figure 44**) from the hole in each pad pin, and remove the clip.

5. Remove the forward pad pin (A, **Figure 45**), and remove the pad spring (B) from each brake pad. If necessary, press the tang (**Figure 46**) of each pad spring to release tension on the pad pin (A, **Figure 45**).

6. Remove the rear pad pin (A, **Figure 47**) and lower the inboard pad (B) and then the outboard pad (**Figure 48**) from the caliper.

7. Clean the pad recess and the end of both pistons with a soft brush. Do not use solvent, a wire brush or any hard tool that could damage the cylinders or pistons.

8. Carefully remove any rust or corrosion from the brake disc.

9. Thoroughly clean any corrosion or road dirt from the pad springs, pad pins and clip.

10. Check the friction surface of the new pads for debris. If necessary, clean the pads with an aerosol brake cleaner.

11. During new pad installation, the fluid level in the master cylinder rises as the caliper pistons are repositioned. If installing new brake pads, perform the following:

   a. Remove the tail piece (Chapter Fifteen).

   b. Clean all debris from of the top of the master cylinder.

   c. Remove the top cover and diaphragm from the reservoir.

   d. Use a syringe to remove approximately half of the brake fluid from the reservoir.

   e. Remove the caliper mounting bolts (A, **Figure 49**), and remove the caliper.

   f. Temporarily install the old brake pads into the caliper. Seat each pad against its set of pistons.

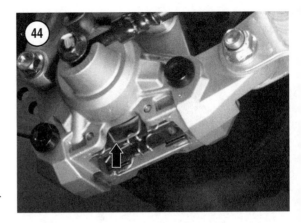

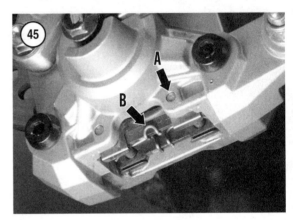

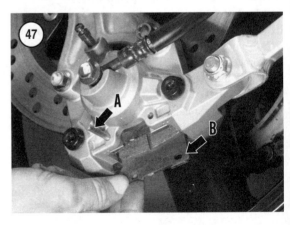

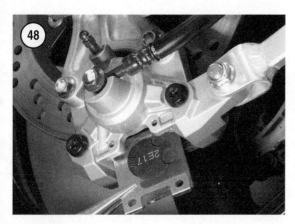

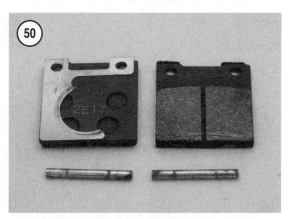

*NOTE*
*The pistons should move freely. If they do not, remove and service the caliper as described in this section.*

g. Insert a large flat blade screwdriver or tire iron between the brake pads. Push the pistons back into the caliper bores. This creates room for the new brake pads. Constantly check the reservoir and make sure the fluid does not overflow. Draw out excess fluid as necessary.

h. Remove the old brake pads, and install the caliper onto the inboard side of the bracket. Tighten the rear caliper mounting bolts (A, **Figure 49**) to 26 N•m (19 ft-lbs.).

12. Install the shims (**Figure 50**) onto the new brake pads so the closed end of the shim faces the rear of the motorcycle.

13. Install the outboard brake pad (**Figure 48**) and the inboard pad (B, **Figure 47**) into the caliper.

14. Position the rear pad pin (A, **Figure 47**) so its clip hole faces down, and then insert the rear pad pin through the caliper and through both pads.

15. Install the outboard pad spring so its rear tang sits above the rear pin. The pin's loop must engage the pad (**Figure 51**).

16. Press the forward tang of the pad spring up into the caliper (**Figure 46**), and install the forward pad pin (A) so it passes through the outboard brake pad and under the spring tang. Make sure the clip hole in the pad pin faces down.

17. Repeat Step 15 and Step 16, and install the inboard pad spring.

18. Push the pins into the caliper until they bottom.

19. Slide the pin clip fingers (**Figure 52**) through the hole in both pins, and push the clip into the caliper until the clip locks onto the pins (**Figure 44**).

20. Install the pad cover and make sure it is locked in place.

21. Untie the rear brake pedal.

14

22. Pump the rear brake pedal to reposition the brake pads against the brake disc.

23. Refill the master cylinder reservoir, if necessary, to maintain the correct fluid level as indicated on the side of the reservoir. Install the diaphragm and the top cover. Install the screws and tighten them securely.

## Caliper Removal/Installation

1. If the caliper assembly is going to be disassembled for service, perform the following:

> *NOTE*
> *By performing substep b, compressed air may not be necessary for piston removal during caliper disassembly.*

a. Remove the brake pads as described in this section.

> *CAUTION*
> *Do not allow the pistons to travel out far enough to contact the brake disc. If this happens the pistons may scratch or gouge the disc during caliper removal.*

b. Apply the brake pedal to push the pistons part way out of caliper assembly for ease of removal during caliper service.

c. Loosen each caliper housing bolt (B, **Figure 49**).

d. Place a drain pan under the rear caliper and remove the banjo bolt and sealing washers (C, **Figure 49**).

e. Place the loose end of the brake hose into a plastic bag to prevent brake fluid from leaking. Secure the bag with a rubber band, and suspend the hose from the motorcycle.

2. Remove the torque arm nut (D, **Figure 49**) and bolt, and separate the torque arm from the caliper.

3. Remove each caliper mounting bolt (A, **Figure 49**), and lower the caliper from the caliper bracket and brake disc.

4. If necessary, disassemble and service the caliper assembly as described in this section.

5. Install by reversing these removal steps while noting the following:

a. Fit the caliper assembly onto the disc so the caliper rests against the inboard side of the caliper bracket. If the brake pads are in the caliper, be careful so the leading edge of the brake pads are not damaged.

b. Install the rear caliper mounting bolts (A, **Figure 49**), and tighten them to 26 N•m (19 ft.-lb.).

c. Secure the torque arm to the rear caliper. Tighten the rear torque arm nut (D, **Figure 49**) to 35 N•m (26 ft.-lb.).

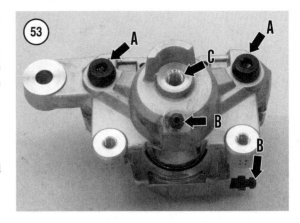

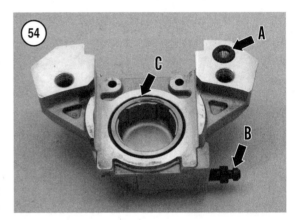

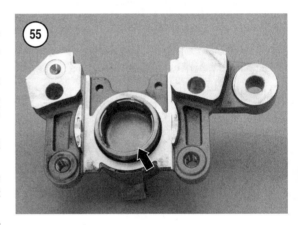

d. Install a new sealing washer to each side of the brake hose fitting and install the banjo bolt. Tighten the brake hose banjo bolt (C, **Figure 49**) to 23 N•m (17 ft.-lb.).

e. Torque the rear caliper housing bolts (B, **Figure 49**) to 30 N•m (22 ft.-lb.).

f. Bleed the rear brake as described in this chapter.

## Caliper Disassembly

1. Remove the brake pads and rear caliper as described in this chapter.

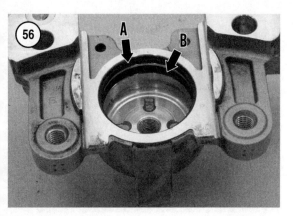

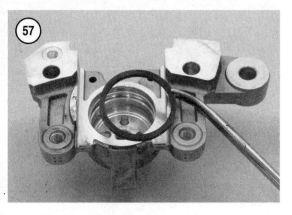

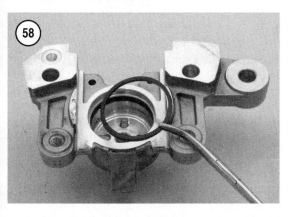

2. Remove the two caliper housing bolts (A, **Figure 53**) loosened during the removal procedure.

3. Separate the caliper body halves. Remove and discard the O-ring (A, **Figure 54**). A new O-ring must be installed every time the caliper is disassembled.

*NOTE*
*If the pistons were partially forced out of the caliper body during removal, Step 4 and Step 5 may not be necessary. If the pistons or caliper bores are corroded or dirty, a small amount of compressed air may be necessary to completely remove the pistons from the caliper body bores.*

4. Place a piece of soft wood or folded shop cloth over the end of the piston and the caliper body. Turn this assembly over with the piston facing down onto the workbench top.

*WARNING*
*In the next step, the piston may shoot out of the caliper body with considerable force. Keep your hands out of the way. Wear shop gloves and safety goggles when using compressed air to remove the pistons.*

5. Apply the air pressure in short bursts to the hydraulic fluid passageway and force the piston out of the caliper bore.

6. Remove the piston (**Figure 55**) from the bore. Repeat for the other caliper body half.

*CAUTION*
*In the following step, do not use a sharp tool to remove the dust and piston seals from the caliper cylinders. Do not damage the cylinder surface.*

7. Use a piece of wood or plastic scraper and carefully push the dust seal (A, **Figure 56**) and the piston seal (B) in toward the caliper cylinder and out of their grooves. Remove the dust and piston seals from the other caliper half. Discard all seals.

8. If necessary, remove the bleed valve (B, **Figure 54**) from each caliper half.

9. Inspect the caliper assembly as described in this section.

**Caliper Assembly**

1. Soak the new dust and piston seals in DOT 4 brake fluid.

2. Coat the piston bores and pistons with DOT 4 brake fluid.

3. Carefully install the new piston seal (**Figure 57**) into the lower groove in a cylinder.

4. Carefully install the new dust seal (**Figure 58**) into the upper groove in the cylinder. Make sure all seals are properly seated in their respective grooves.

5. Repeat Step 3 and Step 4 for the other caliper half.

6. Position the piston (**Figure 55**) with the open end facing out, and install the piston into the caliper cylinder. Push the piston into the cylinder until it bottoms (C, **Figure 54**).

7. Repeat Step 6 for the other caliper half. Make sure both pistons are installed correctly in their original bores.

**14**

8. Coat the new O-ring with DOT 4 brake fluid, and install the O-ring (A, **Figure 54**) into its recess.

9. Assemble the caliper halves. Make sure the O-ring (A, **Figure 54**) remains seated in its recess.

10. Install the two caliper housing bolts (A, **Figure 53**) and tighten them securely. They are tightened to specification after the caliper is installed on the caliper bracket.

11. If removed, install a bleed valve (B, **Figure 53**) into each caliper half. Tighten the bleed valve to 7.5 N•m (66 in.-lb.).

12. Install the caliper and brake pads as described in this section.

13. Bleed the rear brake as described in this chapter.

### Caliper Inspection

1. Clean both caliper halves and pistons in fresh DOT 4 brake fluid. Dry the parts thoroughly.

2. Make sure the fluid passageways in the base of the cylinder bores are clean. Apply compressed air to the openings to make sure they are clear.

3. Apply compressed air to the fluid passageways in the caliper halves.

4. Inspect the piston and dust seal grooves (A, **Figure 59**) in each caliper half for damage. If damaged or corroded, replace the caliper assembly.

5. Inspect the cylinder walls (B, **Figure 59**) and pistons (A, **Figure 60**) for scratches, scoring or other damage.

6. Inspect the threads of the banjo bolt hole (C, **Figure 53**), caliper mounting bolt holes (C, **Figure 59**) and the housing bolt holes (B, **Figure 60**). Dress the threads with a metric tap as necessary.

7. Inspect the bleed valve threaded hole in each caliper half. If worn or damaged, dress the threads with a metric tap or replace the caliper assembly.

8. Inspect the bleed valve and banjo bolt. Apply compressed air to the opening(s) and make sure they are clear.

9. Inspect both caliper bodies for damage. Replace the caliper assembly.

10. Measure the cylinder bores with a bore gauge or vernier caliper (**Figure 25**). Measure the outside diameter of the pistons with a micrometer or vernier caliper (**Figure 26**). Replace any part that is out of specification (**Table 1**).

### REAR BRAKE MASTER CYLINDER

Refer to *Brake Service* in this chapter. Refer to **Figure 61**.

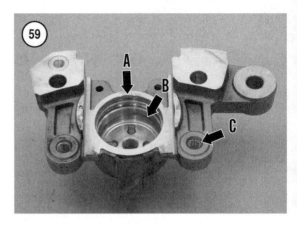

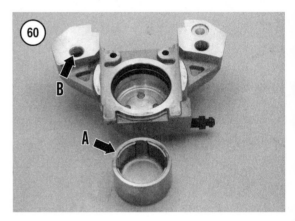

### Removal

1. Securely support the motorcycle on a level surface.

2. Remove the tail piece as described in Chapter Fifteen.

3. Drain the brake fluid from the rear brake as described in this chapter.

4. Release the clamp (A, **Figure 62**) and disconnect the reservoir hose from the fitting on the master cylinder. Use a rubber band to secure the hose inside a plastic bag.

5. Note how the brake hose initially runs forward from the master cylinder, turns 180° and runs rearward along the swing arm (B, **Figure 62**). It must be repositioned with this same orientation during installation.

6. Remove the banjo bolt (C, **Figure 62**), and disconnect the brake hose from the fitting on the master cylinder. Secure the brake hose inside a plastic bag.

7. Remove the cotter pin (A, **Figure 63**) and washer from the inboard end of the clevis pin.

8. Pull the clevis pin (B, **Figure 63**), and disconnect the pushrod clevis (C) from the brake pedal.

9. Remove the master cylinder mounting bolts (A, **Figure 64**), and then remove the master cylinder from behind the footpeg bracket.

**REAR MASTER CYLINDER AND BRAKE HOSE**

1. Screw
2. Top cover
3. Diaphragm
4. Reservoir
5. Bolt
6. Clamp
7. Reservoir hose
8. Screw
9. Hose fitting
10. O-ring
11. Mounting bolt
12. Master cylinder body
13. Sealing washer
14. Brake hose
15. Banjo bolt
16. Piston assembly
17. Pushrod
18. Snap ring
19. Boot
20. Nut
21. Cotter pin
22. Washer
23. Clevis
24. Clevis pin

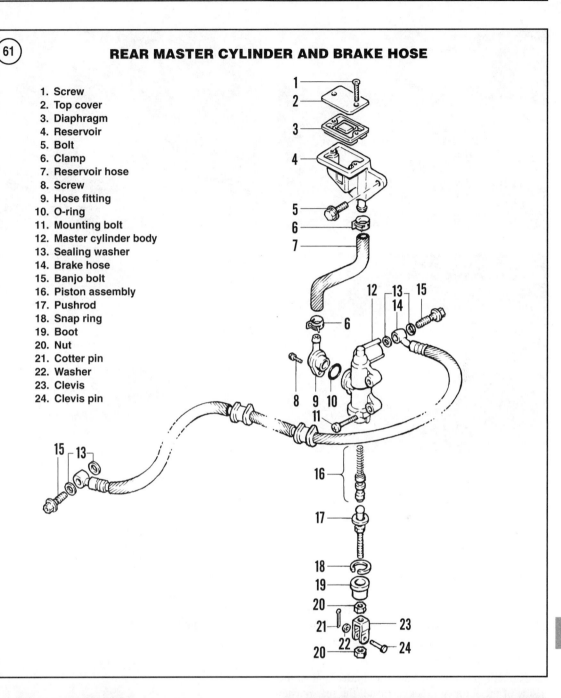

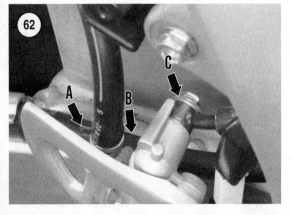

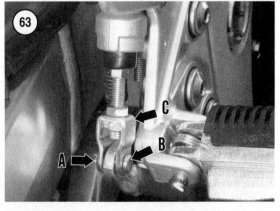

14

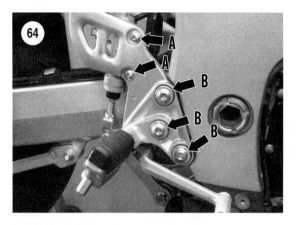

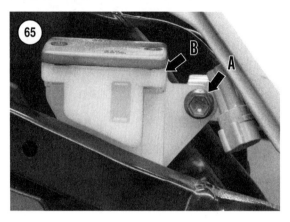

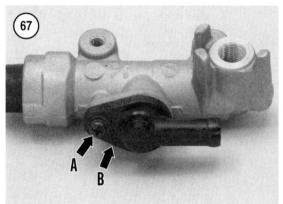

10. If necessary, remove the reservoir bolt (A, **Figure 65**), and fluid reservoir (B) from the motorcycle. Note how the reservoir hose is routed through the motorcycle.

### Installation

1. If removed, fit the fluid reservoir (B, **Figure 65**) into place so the reservoir hose follows the path noted during removal. Insert and securely tighten the reservoir bolt (A, **Figure 65**).

2. Correctly position the master cylinder against the inside of the footpeg bracket. Install the rear master cylinder mounting bolts (A, **Figure 64**), and tighten to 10 N•m (89 in.-lb.).

3. Position the pushrod clevis (C, **Figure 63**) so it aligns with the mount on the brake pedal. Install the clevis pin (B, **Figure 63**) through both parts. Slide the washer over the inboard end of the clevis pin, and install a *new* cotter pin (A, **Figure 63**).

> *NOTE*
> ***Figure 66*** *shows the inside of the footpeg bracket for photographic clarity. The bracket does not need to be removed during master cylinder service.*

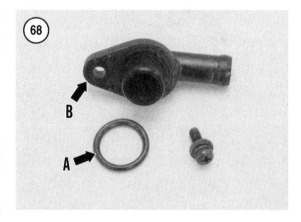

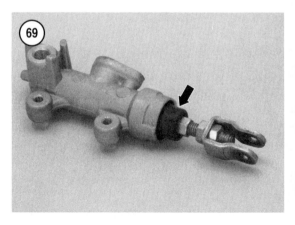

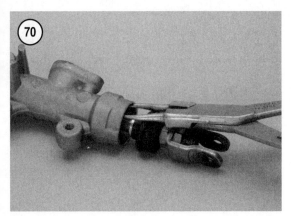

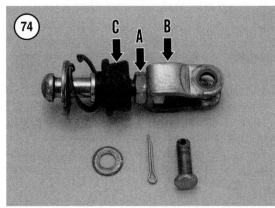

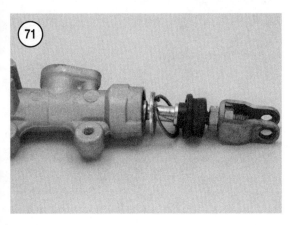

4. Correctly position the brake hose fitting onto the port so the fitting post (A, **Figure 66**) engages the cutout in the master cylinder. The brake hose must initially run forward from the master cylinder and then turn 180° and run rearward along the swing arm as noted during removal.

5. Install a new sealing washer onto each side of the brake hose fitting, and turn in the banjo bolt (C, **Figure 62**). Tighten the brake hose banjo bolt to 23 N•m (17 ft.-lb.).

6. Connect the reservoir hose to the fitting on the master cylinder. Secure the hose in place with the clamp (A, **Figure 62**).

7. Add brake fluid to the reservoir, and bleed the rear brake as described in this chapter.

8. Install the tail piece as described in Chapter Fifteen.

### Disassembly

1. Remove the rear master cylinder as described in this section.

2. Remove the screw (A, **Figure 67**), and pull the reservoir hose fitting (B) from its port on the master cylinder. Remove and discard the O-ring (A, **Figure 68**) from the port.

3. Roll the rubber boot (**Figure 69**) from the pushrod.

4. Use snap ring pliers to remove the pushrod snap ring (**Figure 70**) from the master cylinder body.

5. Pull the pushrod assembly (**Figure 71**) and the piston assembly (**Figure 72**) from the master cylinder.

6. Remove the top cover (A, **Figure 73**) and diaphragm (B) from the fluid reservoir. Pour out any residual brake fluid and discard it.

7. If necessary, loosen the clevis locknut (A, **Figure 74**), and turn the clevis (B) and lower nut from the pushrod.

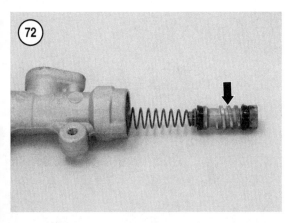

**14**

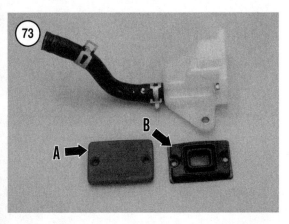

## Assembly

1. If removed, turn the clevis (B, **Figure 74**) and lower nut onto the pushrod.
2. Soak the new cups in DOT 4 brake fluid for at least 15 minutes to make them pliable. Install the new cups onto the new piston assembly.
3. Coat the inside of the cylinder bore with DOT 4 brake fluid before the assembly of parts.
4. Install the tapered end of the spring (A, **Figure 75**) onto the piston (B).

> *CAUTION*
> *When installing the piston assembly, do not allow the cups (C, **Figure 75**) to turn inside out. This damages the cups and allows brake fluid leaks within the cylinder bore.*

5. Insert the piston assembly (**Figure 72**) into the cylinder bore.
6. Install the pushrod assembly (**Figure 71**) so the pushrod engages the end of the piston, and press the pushrod assembly into the cylinder until it bottoms.
7. Hold the pushrod assembly in this position, and install the snap ring (**Figure 70**). Make sure the snap ring is correctly seated in its groove.
8. Roll the rubber boot (**Figure 69**) into the body so it is completely seated in the cylinder
9. Install a new O-ring (A, **Figure 68**) into the hose port in the master cylinder body. Apply a light coat of brake fluid to the O-ring.
10. Install the reservoir hose fitting (B, **Figure 67**) onto the master cylinder. Secure the fitting in place with the mounting screw (A, **Figure 67**).
11. Install the master cylinder as described in this section.
12. Adjust the brake pedal height as described in Chapter Three.
13. Tighten the rear brake master-cylinder-rod locknut (A, **Figure 74**) to 18 N•m (13 ft.-lb.).

## Inspection

During inspection, compare any measurements to the specifications in **Table 1**. Replace any part that is out of specification, worn or damaged.
1. Clean all parts in DOT 4 brake fluid.
2. Inspect the cylinder bore surface (**Figure 76**). If it is less than perfect, replace the master cylinder assembly. The body cannot be replaced separately.
3. Make sure the fluid passageway (**Figure 77**) in the master cylinder body is clear. Clean it if necessary.
4. Measure the cylinder bore with a bore gauge (**Figure 78**) or vernier caliper.

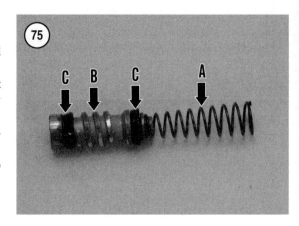

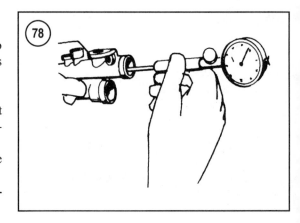

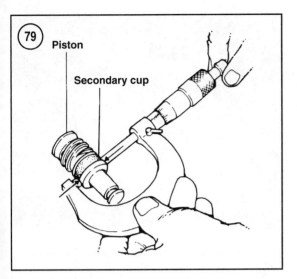

8. Check the end of the piston for wear caused by the pushrod.

9. Inspect the piston pushrod assembly (**Figure 74**) for wear or damage. Make sure the rubber boot (C, **Figure 74**) is in good condition. Replace the boot if necessary.

10. Inspect the threads of the banjo bolt hole (A, **Figure 80**) and the mounting bolt holes (B) in the master cylinder. If worn or damaged, dress the threads with a metric tap. Replace the master cylinder if necessary.

11. Check the reservoir hose fitting (B, **Figure 68**) for damage.

12. Inspect the reservoir, top cover and diaphragm for wear or damage.

13. Inspect the brake hose and reservoir hose for wear or deterioration.

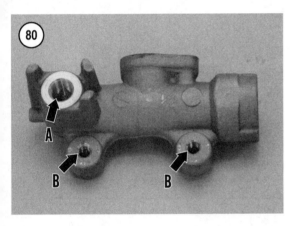

## BRAKE PEDAL/FOOTPEG ASSEMBLY

### Removal/Lubrication/Installation

1. Securely support the motorcycle on a level surface.

2. Remove the cotter pin (A, **Figure 63**) and washer from the inboard end of the clevis pin (B). Withdraw the clevis pin from the pushrod clevis (C, **Figure 63**), and separate the clevis from the brake pedal.

3. Remove the master cylinder mounting bolts (A, **Figure 64**), and remove the master cylinder from the footpeg bracket.

4. Use a wire or bungee cord to suspend the master cylinder from the frame so the brake hoses are not strained.

*NOTE*
*Two washers are used with each footpeg bracket bolt: an inboard and an outboard washer. The inboard washer sits between the footpeg bracket and the frame.*

5. Remove each footpeg bracket bolt (B, **Figure 64**) and the washers.

6. Turn the footpeg bracket, and disconnect the electrical connector (B, **Figure 66**) from the rear brake light switch (C). Watch for the bushing (A, **Figure 81**) in each hole of the bracket.

7. Remove the brake pedal by performing the following:

   a. Unhook the rear brake light switch spring (B, **Figure 81**) and brake pedal spring (C) from the brake pedal post.

   b. Remove the snap ring (D, **Figure 81**), and slide the brake pedal from the pivot on the footpeg

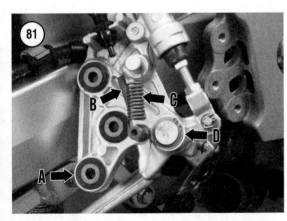

5. Measure the outside diameter of the piston with a micrometer (**Figure 79**).

6. Check the entire master cylinder body for wear or damage. If damaged in any way, replace the master cylinder assembly.

7. Inspect the piston cups (C, **Figure 75**) for signs of wear and damage. If less than perfect, replace the piston assembly. The cups cannot be replaced separately.

**14**

bracket. Watch for the washer between the brake pedal and the footpeg bracket.

8. Inspect the brake pedal and footpeg bracket for cracks or damage and replace if necessary.

9. Clean the footpeg bolts with solvent, and inspect them for wear or damage.

10. Install the pedal and footpeg bracket by reversing these removal steps while noting the following:

    a. Lubricate the brake pedal pivot and spring with Suzuki Super Grease A or an equivalent grease.

    b. Make sure a bushing (A, **Figure 81**) is in place in each bracket mount.

    c. Install an inboard and an outboard washer onto each footpeg bracket bolt. The inboard washer must sit between the bracket and the frame. Tighten each front footpeg bracket bolt (B, **Figure 64**) to 26 N•m (19 ft.-lb.).

    d. Tighten the rear master cylinder mounting bolts (A, **Figure 64**) to 10 N•m (89 in.-lb.).

    e. Use a new cotter pin (A, **Figure 63**) when connecting the pushrod clevis to the brake pedal.

    f. Adjust the rear brake pedal height as described in Chapter Three.

## BRAKE DISC

The brake disc(s) can be removed from a wheel hub once the wheel is removed.

### Inspection

Small nicks and marks on the disc are not important, but deep radial scratches reduce braking effectiveness and increase brake pad wear. If these grooves are evident and the brake pads are wearing rapidly, replace the disc.

The specifications for brake disc thickness are listed in **Table 1**. The minimum (MIN) thickness is also stamped on the disc face (A, **Figure 82**). If the specification stamped on the disc differs from the table, use the specification on the disc.

Do not machine a disc down to compensate for warp. If a disc is warped, the brake pads may be dragging on the disc due to a faulty caliper and causing the disc to overheat. Overheating can also be caused by unequal pad pressure on the sides of the disc. If a disc is overheating, troubleshoot the brakes as described in Chapter Two.

> *NOTE*
> *The brake disc can be measured with the wheel mounted on the motorcycle.*

1. Measure the thickness of the disc at several locations around the disc with a vernier caliper or a mi-

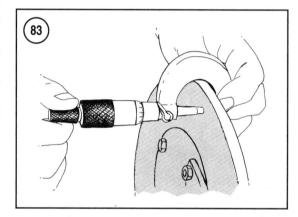

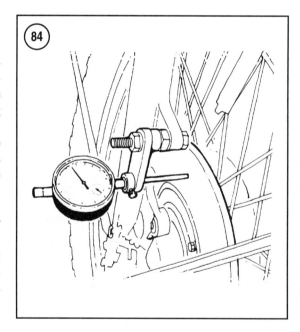

crometer (**Figure 83**) to obtain an average. Replace the disc if the thickness in any area is less than the service limit in **Table 1** or stamped on the disc.

2. Make sure the disc mounting bolts (B, **Figure 82**) are tight prior to performing the following steps.

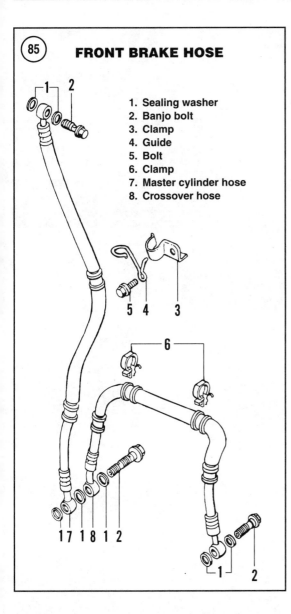

**FRONT BRAKE HOSE**

1. Sealing washer
2. Banjo bolt
3. Clamp
4. Guide
5. Bolt
6. Clamp
7. Master cylinder hose
8. Crossover hose

*warped. Set the wheel on two wooden blocks high enough for the disc to clear the ground.*

1. Remove the front or rear wheel as described in Chapter Eleven.

2. Insert a piece of wood or vinyl tube between the pads. If the brake lever or pedal is inadvertently applied, the pistons will not be forced out of the cylinders.

3. Remove the brake disc bolts (B, **Figure 82**), and remove the disc from the hub.

4. Install by reversing these removal steps while noting the following:

    a. Position the disc so its direction arrow points in the direction of forward wheel rotation.

    b. Apply Suzuki Thread Lock Super 1360, or its equivalent, to the threads of the disc bolts.

    c. Tighten the front disc brake bolts to 23 N•m (17 ft.-lb.) and the rear disc bolts to 35 N•m (26 ft.-lb.).

3. Slowly rotate the wheel and measure the disc runout with a dial indicator (**Figure 84**). If runout is excessive, check for loose brake disc bolts, inspect the wheel bearings and examine the surface of the brake disc. If these are in good condition, replace the brake disc.

4. Clean any rust or corrosion from the disc, and wipe it clean with a rag soaked in lacquer thinner or brake parts cleaner. Never use an oil-based solvent that may leave an oil residue on the disc.

5. Inspect the floating disc fasteners located between the outer and the inner rings of the discs. If any of them are damaged, replace the disc.

**Removal/Installation**

*CAUTION*
*Do not set the wheel down on the disc surface. The disc could be scratched or*

**BRAKE HOSE REPLACEMENT**

Refer to *Brake Service* in this chapter.

**Front Brake Hoses**

Refer to **Figure 85**.

1. Remove the front fairing (Chapter Fifteen).

2. Drain the fluid from the front brakes (this chapter).

3. Remove the bolt (**Figure 86**) securing the brake hose holder to the lower fork bridge, and release the brake hose from the holder.

4. Release the brake hose from the holder (A, **Figure 87**) on the right side of the fender.

5. Squeeze the arms on each rear holder (B, **Figure 87**) together, and pull the holder from the rear of the fender.

6. On the right side, perform the following:

14

a. Remove the banjo bolt (A, **Figure 88**) and sealing washers, and disconnect the crossover hose (B) and master cylinder hose (C) from the right caliper. Be prepared to catch brake fluid that dribbles from the hose fittings.

b. Secure the end of the each brake hose in a plastic bag so brake fluid does not dribble onto the motorcycle.

c. Discard the sealing washers.

7. On the left side, remove the banjo bolt (A, **Figure 89**) and sealing washers. Disconnect the crossover hose (B, **Figure 89**) from the left caliper. Secure the hose end in a plastic bag, and remove the crossover hose. Discard the sealing washers.

8. Remove the banjo bolt (A, **Figure 90**) and sealing washers, and disconnect the hose from the master ylinder. Secure the end of the hose in plastic bag. Discard the sealing washer.

9. Carefully remove master cylinder hose down and out from behind the throttle cables on the right side.

10. Install new hoses in the reverse order of removal while noting the following:

a. Route each hose along the original path as noted during removal.

b. Position the brake hoses so their necks sit against the outboard side of the stop post on the each caliper. Refer to **Figure 88** and **Figure 89**. On the master cylinder, rest the hose neck (B, **Figure 90**) against the rear side of the stop post.

c. Install new sealing washers on each side of the hose fittings. Use three sealing washers when securing the crossover hose (B, **Figure 88**) and master cylinder hose (C) to the right brake caliper.

d. Tighten the brake hose banjo bolts to the 23 N•m (17 ft.-lb.).

e. Refill the master cylinder reservoir and bleed the front brakes as described in this chapter.

**Rear Brake Hose**

Refer to **Figure 61**.

*NOTE*
*Refer to rear master cylinder removal/installation procedure when replacing a reservoir hose.*

1. Drain the brake fluid (this chapter).

2. Remove the rear wheel (Chapter Eleven).

3. Remove the banjo bolt (**Figure 91**), disconnect the brake hose from the rear caliper, and insert the hose end into a plastic bag. Remove and discard the sealing washer installed on each side of the hose fitting.

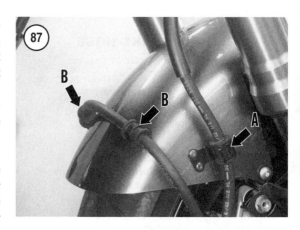

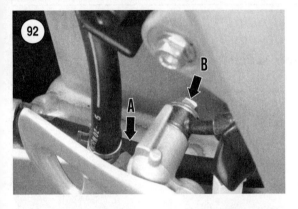

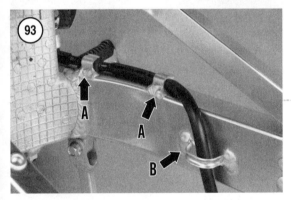

*NOTE*
*The rear brake hose initially runs forward from the rear master cylinder. It then turns rearward (A, **Figure 92**), and runs along the swing arm. The new hose must also follow this path.*

4. Remove the banjo bolt (B, **Figure 92**), disconnect the brake hose from the rear master cylinder, and secure the hose end in a plastic bag. Remove and discard the sealing washer installed on each side of the hose fitting.

5. Release the brake hose from the holders (A, **Figure 93**) on the swing arm, and pull the hose from the guide (B).

6. Installation is the reverse of removal. Note the following:

   a. Route the brake hose (A, **Figure 92**) along the original path as noted during removal.

*NOTE*
***Figure 66** shows the inside of the footpeg bracket for photographic clarity. The bracket does not need to be removed during brake hose replacement.*

   b. Fit the brake hose onto the master cylinder so that the hose post (A, **Figure 66**) engages the cutout in the mater cylinder.

   c. Install new sealing washers on each side of the brake hose fittings.

   d. Torque the brake hose banjo bolts to 23 N•m (17 ft.-lb.).

   e. Secure the brake hose under the holders (A, **Figure 93**) on the swing arm, and route the hose through the guide.

   f. Refill the master cylinder reservoir and bleed the rear brake as described in this chapter.

**14**

**Table 1 BRAKE SPECIFICATIONS**

| Item | Standard mm (in.) | Service limit mm (in.) |
|---|---|---|
| Brake disc runout (front and rear) | – | 0.30 (0.16) |
| Brake disc thickness | | |
|   Front | 4.8-5.2 (0.189-0.205) | 4.5 (0.177) |
|   Rear | 4.8-5.2 (0.189-0.205) | 4.5 (0.177) |
| Brake fluid | DOT 4 | – |
| Brake pedal height | 55-65 (2.2-2.6) | – |
| Front brake caliper | | |
|   Cylinder bore | | – |
|     Leading | 24.000-24.076 (0.9449-0.9479) | – |
|     Trailing | 27.000-27.076 (1.0630-1.0660) | – |
|   Piston diameter | | |
|     Leading | 23.925-23.975 (0.9419-0.9439) | – |
| | (continued) | |

### Table 1 BRAKE SPECIFICATIONS (continued)

| Item | Standard mm (in.) | Service limit mm (in.) |
|---|---|---|
| Front brake caliper | | |
| Piston diameter (continued) | | |
| Trailing | 26.920-26.970 (1.0598-1.0618) | – |
| Front master cylinder | | |
| Cylinder bore | 15.870-15.913 (0.6248-0.6265) | – |
| Piston outside diameter | 15.827-15.854 (0.6231-0.6242) | – |
| Rear brake caliper | | |
| Cylinder bore | 38.180-38.256 (1.5031-1.5061) | – |
| Piston diameter | 38.098-38.148 (1.4999-1.5019) | |
| Rear master cylinder | | |
| Cylinder bore | 12.700-12.743 (0.5000-0.5017) | – |
| Piston outside diameter | 12.657-12.684 (0.4983-0.4994) | – |

### Table 2 BRAKE TORQUE SPECIFICATIONS

| Item | N•m | in.-lb. | ft.-lb. |
|---|---|---|---|
| Brake disc bolt | | | |
| Front | 23 | – | 17 |
| Rear | 35 | – | 26 |
| Brake hose banjo bolt | 23 | – | 17 |
| Caliper bleed valve | 7.5 | 66 | – |
| Front caliper mounting bolt | 39 | – | 29 |
| Front caliper housing bolt | 21 | – | 15.5 |
| Front footpeg bracket bolt | 26 | – | 19 |
| Front master cylinder clamp bolt | 10 | 89 | – |
| Rear caliper mounting bolt | 26 | – | 19 |
| Rear caliper housing bolt | 30 | – | 22 |
| Rear master cylinder mounting bolt | 10 | 89 | – |
| Rear master-cylinder-rod locknut | 18 | – | 13 |
| Torque arm nut | | | |
| Front | 28 | – | 21 |
| Rear | 35 | – | 26 |

# CHAPTER FIFTEEN

# BODY AND FRAME

This chapter contains removal and installation procedures for the seats, mirrors, fairing panels and sidestand.

As soon as a panel is removed from the motorcycle, reinstall all mounting hardware onto the removed panel. This ensures the panels are reinstalled with all the needed fasteners.

After removing a panel, wrap it in a towel or blanket. Store a panel in a safe place where it cannot be damaged.

## BODY PANEL FASTENERS

Several types of fasteners are used to attach the various body panels to each other and to the frame. Note the type of fastener used before removing a panel. An improperly released fastener can damage a body panel.

### Trim Clip

Quick release trim clips are used at various locations on different body panels. Installing a worn trim clip through the mounting holes can be difficult. The plastic trim clips degenerate with heat, age and use. The ends may break off or become distorted so they cannot close down sufficiently to allow insertion into the holes. Replace damaged trim clips as necessary.

To remove a trim clip, push the center pin into the head with a Phillips screwdriver (A, **Figure 1**). This releases the inner lock so the trim clip can be withdrawn from the body panel (B, **Figure 1**).

To install a trim clip, push the center pin outward so it protrudes from the head. Insert the clip through the mounts (C, **Figure 1**), and push the pin into the clip (D, **Figure 1**) to lock the clip in place.

### Quick Fastener Screw

The quarter-turn quick fastener screws (DZUS fasteners) are used mainly to secure one body panel to one another. Use a Phillips screwdriver and turn the fastener one-quarter turn counterclockwise to release it from the adjacent body panel. The screw usually stays with the outer body panel as it is held in place with a plastic washer. This screw can be reused many times. To reinstall, push fastener in and turn clockwise one-quarter turn.

### Flat Head Clip

To remove a flat head clip, insert a screwdriver under the head, and pry the head out of the clip (A, **Figure 2**).

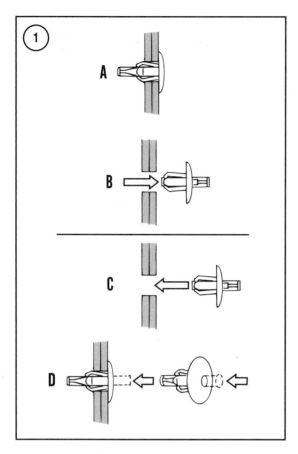

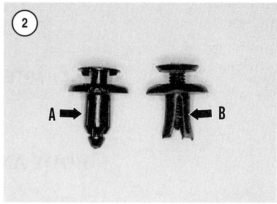

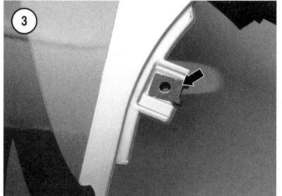

This releases the pawls in the clip. Remove the flat head clip from the panel.

Install a flat head clip with its head protruding from the clip. Insert the clip through the panels. Press the head into the clip to open the pawls and lock the clip in place.

A worn flat head clip (B, **Figure 2**) can be difficult to install through body panels. These are relatively inexpensive and should be replaced as necessary.

### Special Nut

A special nut (Tinnerman clip) is a U-shaped metal clip (**Figure 3**) that is pushed onto the edge of a body panel. It usually remains secured to the body panel during removal. If this special nut falls off, lightly crimp it together and push it back into place on the panel.

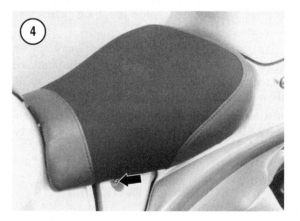

## SEAT

### Removal/Installation

1. Securely support the motorcycle on a level surface.
2. Remove the seat bolt (**Figure 4**) from each side of the motorcycle.

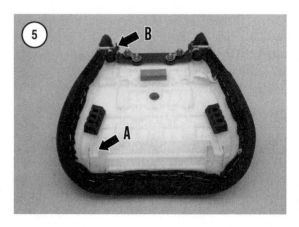

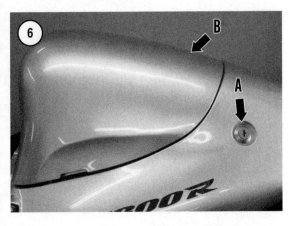

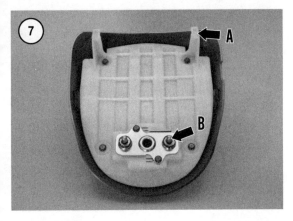

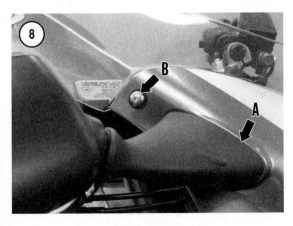

(A, **Figure 5**) and bolt bosses (B) are not damaged. Replace the seat if any damage is discovered.

5. To install the front seat, perform the following:

   a. Slide the seat rearward until the seat hooks (A, **Figure 5**) engage the seat retainer on the frame.

   b. Lower the seat onto the frame, and install each seat bolt (**Figure 4**). Check that the seat is firmly bolted into place.

### PASSENGER SEAT/TAIL COVER

**Removal/Installation**

Either a passenger seat or a tail cover fits onto the rear of the tail piece. The following procedure describes the removal and installation of a tail cover. The procedure is identical for a passenger seat.

1. Insert the ignition key into the lock (A, **Figure 6**) on the left side of the tail piece.

2. Turn the key clockwise and lift the rear of the tail cover (B, **Figure 6**).

3. Pull the tail cover rearward, and remove it.

> *WARNING*
> *Do not repair a damaged seat hook or bolt boss. These are molded into the seat base and must be solid with no fractures or cracks in order to safely secure the seat/tail cover. A repaired hook may lead to a seat working loose during a ride.*

4. Inspect the seat hook (A, **Figure 7**) and locking posts (B) on the underside of the tail cover. Replace the tail cover if a hook or lock post is damaged.

5. To install the tail cover, perform the following:

   a. Slide the tail cover forward until the seat hooks engage their retainers.

   b. Push the rear of tail cover down until it locks in place.

   c. Check that the tail cover is firmly secured in place.

**15**

### MIRROR

**Removal/Installation**

1. Roll back the boot (A, **Figure 8**) from its mount on the fairing.

2. Remove each mirror bolt (**Figure 9**), and lower the mirror from the fairing bracket mounts (A, **Figure 10**).

3. Installation is the reverse of removal. Pay attention to the following:

   a. The fairing bracket mirror mounts (A, **Figure 10**) must engage the holes in the fairing ears.

3. Lift the front of the seat, and pull it forward until the seat hooks disengage from the frame.

> *WARNING*
> *Do not repair a damaged seat hook or bolt boss. These are molded into the seat base and must be solid with no fractures or cracks to safely secure the seat. A repaired hook or boss may lead to a seat working loose during a ride.*

4. Inspect the plastic base on the underside of the seat for cracks or damage. Make sure the seat hooks

b. The rubber damper must be in place on the mirror (**Figure 11**).

## FRONT FAIRING

### Removal/Installation

Refer to **Figure 12**.

1. Securely support the motorcycle on a level surface.
2. Remove the upper panel from the left and right sides (this chapter).
3. Disconnect the 6-pin fairing subharness connector (A, **Figure 13**).

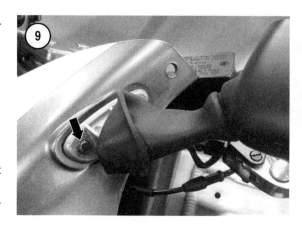

*NOTE*
*The front fairing can be removed with the windshield installed. However, the fairing is more flexible and easier to remove if the windshield is off.*

4. Remove the windshield screw (B, **Figure 8**) and washer from the fairing ear on each side.
5. Remove the rubber nut (**Figure 14**) from each mount, and slide the windshield from the front fairing.
6. Remove the mirror (this chapter) from each side.
7. Remove the trim clip securing the center panel to the inner panel on each fairing side panel.
8. Remove the screws (A, **Figure 15**) securing the front fairing to the fairing side panel on each side of the motorcycle.
9. Spread the fairing ears (B, **Figure 10**) so the fairing clears the mirror mounts (A) on the fairing bracket.

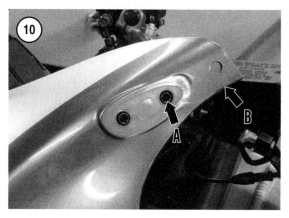

10. Pull the fairing forward, disengage the fairing locating posts (A, **Figure 16**) from the meter assembly grommets (A, **Figure 17**), and disengage each air scoop (B, **Figure 16**) from its intake duct (B, **Figure 17**). Remove the fairing to the bench.
11. Installation is the reverse of removal. Pay attention to the following:

a. The fairing locating posts (A, **Figure 16**) must engage the meter assembly grommets (A, **Figure 17**).
b. Each air scoop (B, **Figure 16**) must mate securely with its intake duct (B, **Figure 17**).
c. The mirror mounts (A, **Figure 10**) must completely engage the holes in the fairing ears.

## UPPER PANEL

### Removal/Installation

Refer to **Figure 12**.

1. Securely support the motorcycle on a level surface.

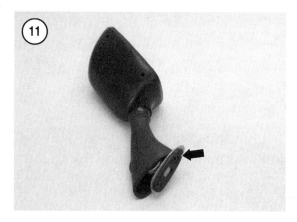

2. Remove the trim clip (A, **Figure 18**) and bolt (B) from the left upper panel.

3. Remove the bolt (**Figure 19**) securing the left and right upper panels in place. Note how the arms of the left and right panels mate with one another.

4. Remove the left upper panel (C, **Figure 18**) from the front fairing. Refer to **Figure 20**.

5. Repeat Step 2, and remove the right upper panel from the front fairing.

6. Installation is the reverse of removal. Make sure the arms on the left and right upper panel mate as shown in **Figure 19**.

12

## FRONT FAIRING

1. Windshield
2. Upper panel
3. Fairing bracket
4. Intake duct
5. Front fairing
6. Center panel

1

2

4

3

5

4

6

15

13

14

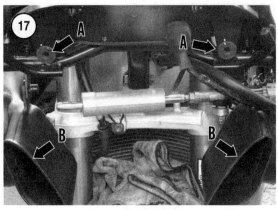

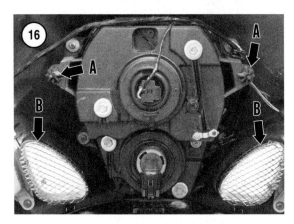

## CENTER PANEL

### Removal/Installation

The center panel mounts inside the front edge of the front fairing. Refer to **Figure 12**.

1. Remove the fasteners that secure the center cover to the front fairing and to the inner panel on each fairing side panel.

2. Move the center cover rearward until it clears the fairing, and lower it from the front fairing.

3. Installation is the reverse of removal. Make sure the center cover sits above the lip of the front fairing and inside the inner panel.

## INTAKE DUCT

### Removal/Installation

Refer to **Figure 12**.

1. Remove the front fairing (this chapter).

2. When removing the right intake duct, perform the following:

    a. Pull the radiator fan relay (B, **Figure 13**) straight up, and remove it from its mounting tang.

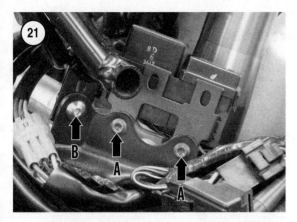

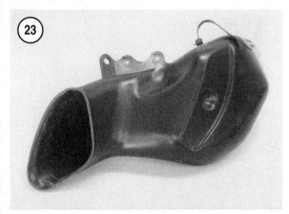

b. Release the wire from the cable holder (C, **Figure 13**) on the right intake duct. Note which wires are secured in this holder.

c. Remove the mounting bolts (A, **Figure 21**), and lift the fuse panel bracket from the intake duct.

d. Secure the bracket and fan relay out of the way.

3. Remove the intake duct screw (B, **Figure 21**) from the fairing bracket.

4. Pull the duct forward and out of the intake port on the frame (**Figure 22**).

5. Inspect each intake duct (**Figure 23**) for cracks or other damage.

6. Installation is the reverse of removal. Make sure each duct fully engages its frame port (**Figure 22**).

## FAIRING BRACKET

### Removal/Installation

1. Remove the front fairing as described in this chapter.

2. Remove the nut (A, **Figure 24**) from the upper fairing bracket bolt, and then remove the bolt.

*NOTE*
*The lower fairing bracket bolt threads into a weld nut.*

3. Remove the lower fairing bracket bolt (B, **Figure 24**).

4. Remove the fairing bracket from the steering head.

5. Installation is the reverse of removal. Tighten the fairing bracket fasteners to 23 N•m (17 ft.-lb.).

## FAIRING SIDE PANEL

### Removal/Installation

Refer to **Figure 25**.

The inner panel (A, **Figure 26**) and the top cover (B) mount to the inside of each fairing side panel. These parts come out with the side panel.

1. Securely support the motorcycle on a level surface.

2. Remove the rear lower panel (this chapter).

3. Remove the trim clip that secures the center panel to the inner panel (A, **Figure 26**) on each side fairing.

4A. On 1999 models, remove the lower screws (A, **Figure 27**) from one fairing side panel.

*NOTE*
*A metal brace (**Figure 28**) was added to the side panels on 2000-on models. An additional screw (B, **Figure 27**) se-*

**15**

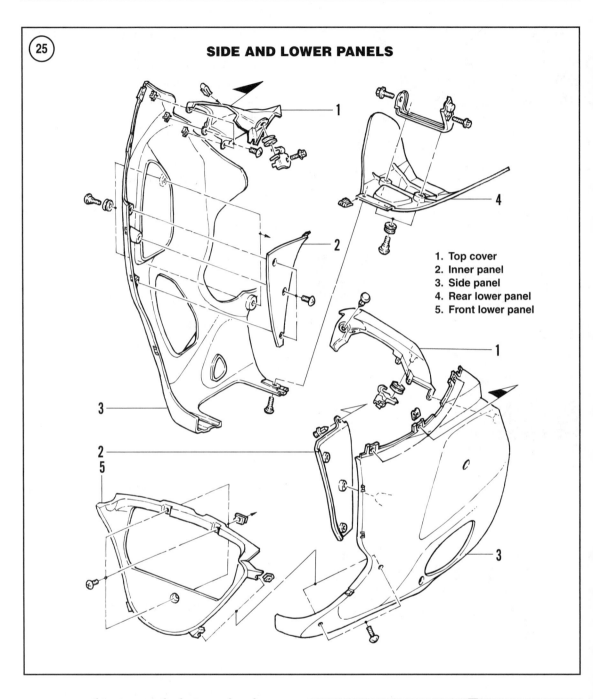

**SIDE AND LOWER PANELS**

25

1
2
4

1. Top cover
2. Inner panel
3. Side panel
4. Rear lower panel
5. Front lower panel

1
3
2
5
3

*cures this strap to the bottom of each side panel.*

4B. On 2000-on models, remove the lower screws (A and B, **Figure 27**) from one fairing side panel.

5. Remove the upper screws (A and B, **Figure 15**) from the fairing side panel.

6. The top cover includes a post (C, **Figure 26**) that mates with a grommet on the frame (**Figure 29**). Lift the rear of the top cover and disengage this post from the grommet.

7. Lower the fairing side panel, and remove it from the motorcycle.

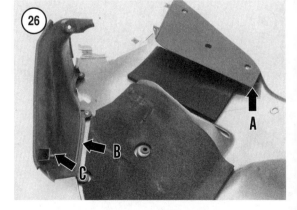

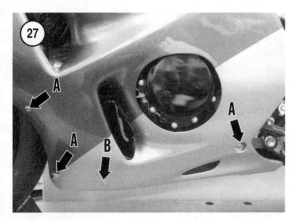

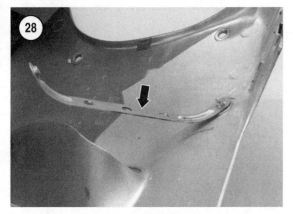

8. Repeat Steps 4-7 and remove the fairing side panel from the other side. Do not remove the brace screw (B, **Figure 27**) from this side. Remove the second panel with the brace attached.

9. If necessary, remove the inner panel (A, **Figure 26**) or the top cover (B) from the side panel.

10. Installation is the reverse of removal.

   a. Slide the side panel forward so the holes in the side panel align with those in the frame and front fairing (if installed).

   b. Press the post on the top cover down into the grommet in the frame (**Figure 30**).

### FRONT LOWER PANEL

**Removal/Installation**

1. Remove the fairing side panel from each side (this chapter).

2. Remove the mounting screws (A, **Figure 31**). Remove the front lower panel (B, **Figure 31**) from the motorcycle.

3. Installation is the reverse of removal.

### REAR LOWER PANEL

**Removal/Installation**

1. Securely support the motorcycle on a level surface.

2. Remove the lower panel screws (**Figure 32**), and remove the panel. Note how the front lip (**Figure 33**) of the rear lower panel sits on the two fairing side panels.

3. Installation is the reverse of removal.

### TAIL PIECE

**Removal/Installation**

Refer to **Figure 34**.

15

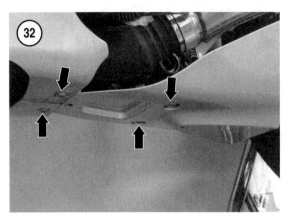

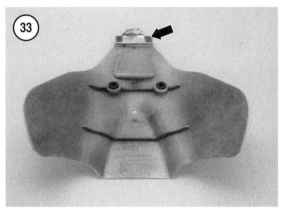

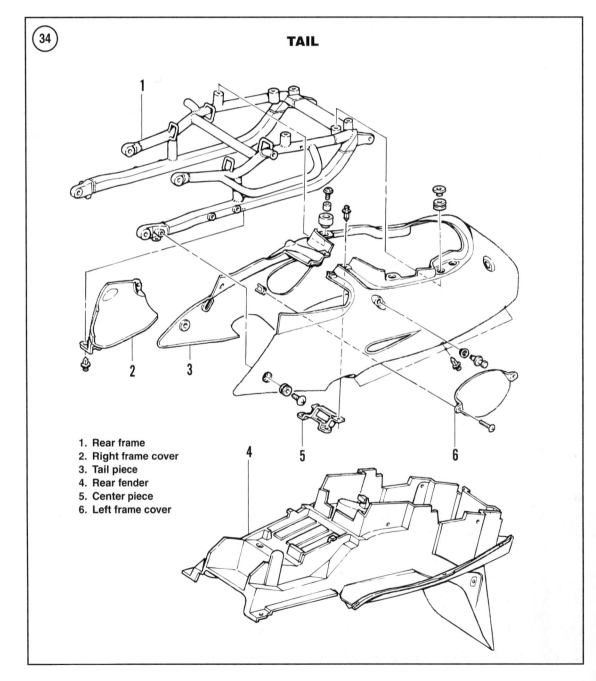

TAIL

1. Rear frame
2. Right frame cover
3. Tail piece
4. Rear fender
5. Center piece
6. Left frame cover

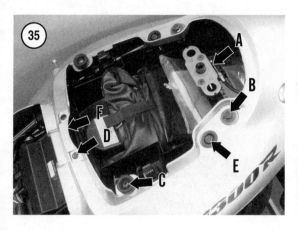

1. Securely support the motorcycle on a level surface.

2. Remove the rider's and the passenger seats (this chapter).

3. Disconnect the cable end (A, **Figure 35**) from the passenger seat lock.

4. Remove the mounting bolts (B, **Figure 35**), mounting screws (C) and trim clips (D) from the top of the tail piece. Watch for the bushing installed on each mounting bolt (**Figure 36**).

5. On models with a passenger grab rail, remove the mounting bolts (E, **Figure 35**) and remove the grab rail.

6. Remove the Allen bolt (A, **Figure 37**) and mounting screw (B) from each side of the tail piece.

7. Remove the trim clips (**Figure 38**) that secure each side of the tail piece to the rear fender.

8. Spread the arms of the tail piece, and lift the front of the piece rearward. Watch for the center piece (F, **Figure 35**) that joins the two sides of the tail piece.

9. Disconnect the 3-pin taillight connector (**Figure 39**), and remove the tail piece.

10. Installation is the reverse of removal.

   a. Make sure the center piece (F, **Figure 35**) is secured to each side of the tail piece.

   b. Include a bushing (**Figure 36**) with each mounting bolt (B, **Figure 35**).

   c. Make sure a damper is in place in the bolt and screw mounts (B, C and E, **Figure 35**) in the tail piece.

**15**

### FRONT FENDER

**Removal/Installation**

1. Securely support the motorcycle on a level surface.

2. Release the brake hose (A, **Figure 40**) from the holder on the right side of the fender.

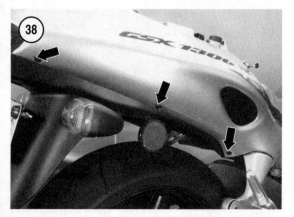

3. Squeeze the arms on each rear hose holder (B, **Figure 40**) together, and pull the holder from the rear of the fender.

4. Remove each fender screw (**Figure 41**) and its washer from both sides of the fender.

5. Carefully remove the fender from between the fork legs.

6. Installation is the reverse of removal.

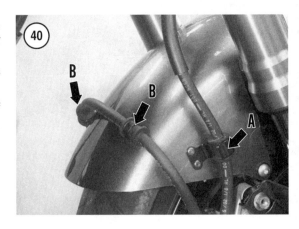

## SIDESTAND

### Removal/Installation

1. Remove the fairing side panel from the left side.

2. Remove the sidestand switch bolt (A, **Figure 42**), and remove the switch from the sidestand bracket.

3. Turn out the sidestand bracket bolts, (B, **Figure 42**), and lower the sidestand from the frame.

4. Check the sidestand for damage and make sure the nut (C, **Figure 42**) is tight on the pivot bolt.

5. Inspect the springs and mounting posts for cracks or damage.

6. Apply Suzuki Super Grease A, or its equivalent, to the spring mounting posts and to the pivot on the sidestand.

7. Installation is the reverse of removal. Pay attention to the following:

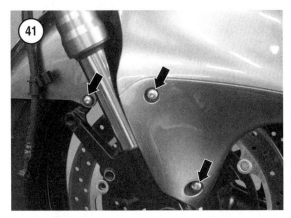

   a. Apply Suzuki Thread Lock 1342 to the threads of the sidestand bracket bolts (B, **Figure 42**), and tighten them to 95 N•m (70 ft.-lb.).

   b. Apply Suzuki Thread Lock 1342 to the threads of the sidestand switch bolt (A, **Figure 42**). Tighten the bolt securely. Make sure the switch plunger (D, **Figure 42**) engages the stop on the sidestand.

8. Move the sidestand up and down to check for freedom of movement.

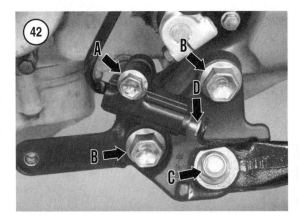

## FOOTPEG ASSEMBLY

### Front Left Side

#### *Removal/installation*

1. Securely support the motorcycle on a level surface.

2. Remove the shift pedal (Chapter Seven).

> *NOTE*
> *Two washers are used on each footpeg bracket bolt: an inboard and an outboard washer. The inboard washer sits between the footpeg bracket and the frame.*

3. Remove each footpeg bracket bolt (**Figure 43**) and the washers.

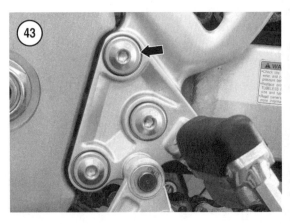

4. Lower the footpeg bracket from the motorcycle. Watch for a bushing in each bracket mounting hole.

5. Clean the footpeg bolts with solvent, and then inspect them for wear or damage. Replace if necessary.

6. Install the footpeg bracket by reversing these removal steps while noting the following:

   a. Make sure a bushing is in each bracket mounting hole.

   b. Install an inboard and outboard washer on each footpeg bracket bolt. The inboard washer must sit between the bracket and the frame. Torque each front footpeg bracket bolt (**Figure 43**) to 26 N•m (19 ft.-lb.).

### Front Right Side

Follow the procedure in *Brake Pedal/Footpeg Assembly* (Chapter Fourteen).

### Rear Set

1. Remove the tail piece (this chapter).

2. Remove each footpeg bracket bolt, and lower the footpeg bracket from the frame.

3. Installation is the reverse of removal. Torque each rear footpeg bracket bolt to 35 N•m (26 ft.-lb.).

**Table 1 BODY AND FRAME TORQUE SPECIFICATIONS**

| Item | N•m | in.-lb. | ft.-lb. |
| --- | --- | --- | --- |
| Fairing bracket fasteners | 23 | – | 17 |
| Footpeg bracket bolt | | | |
|   Front | 26 | – | 19 |
|   Rear | 35 | – | 26 |
| Sidestand bracket bolt | 95 | – | 70 |

# INDEX

16

**16**

16

# 1999 U.S., CALIFORNIA AND CANADA

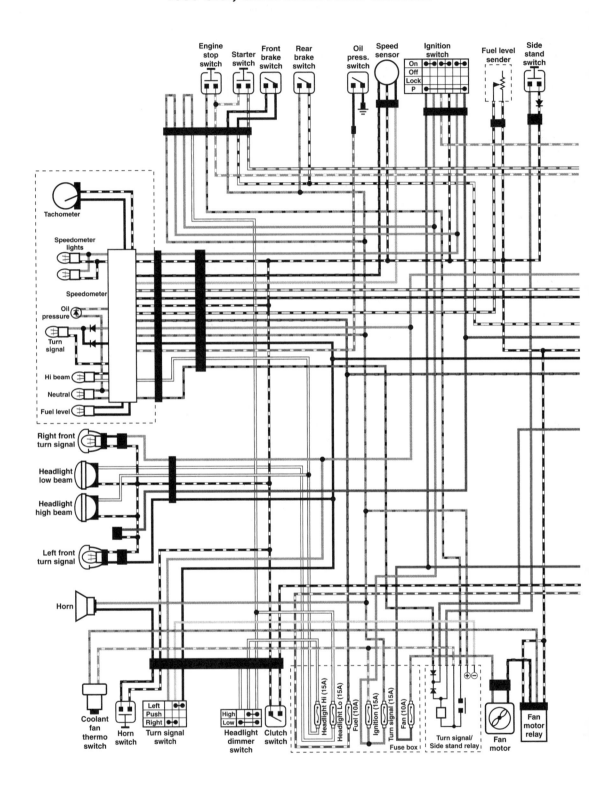

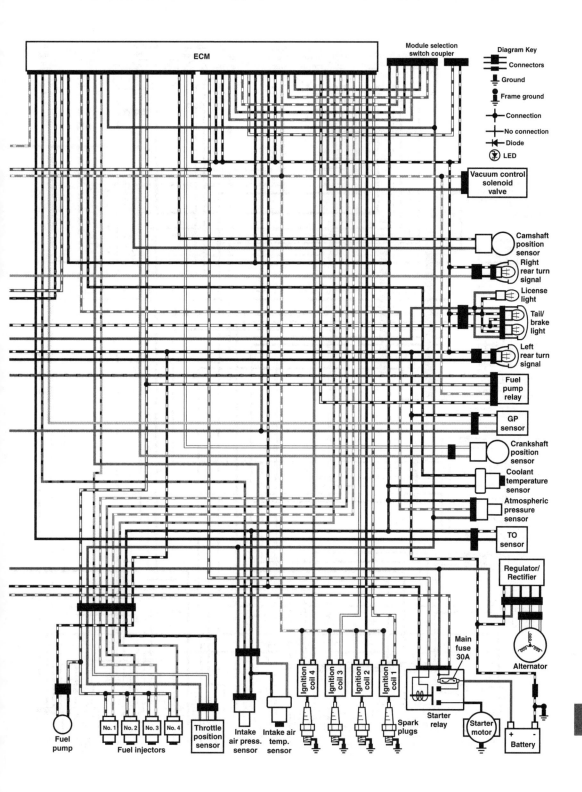

# 1999 ALL MODELS EXCEPT U.S., CALIFORNIA AND CANADA

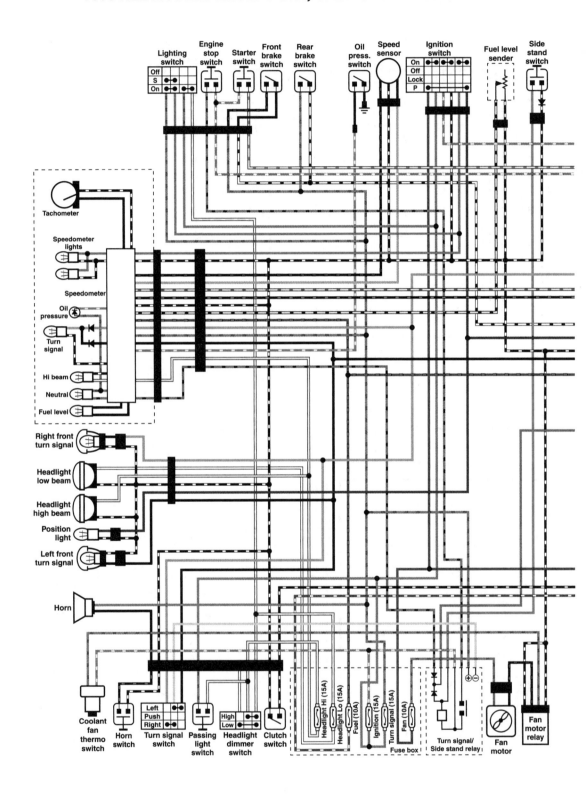

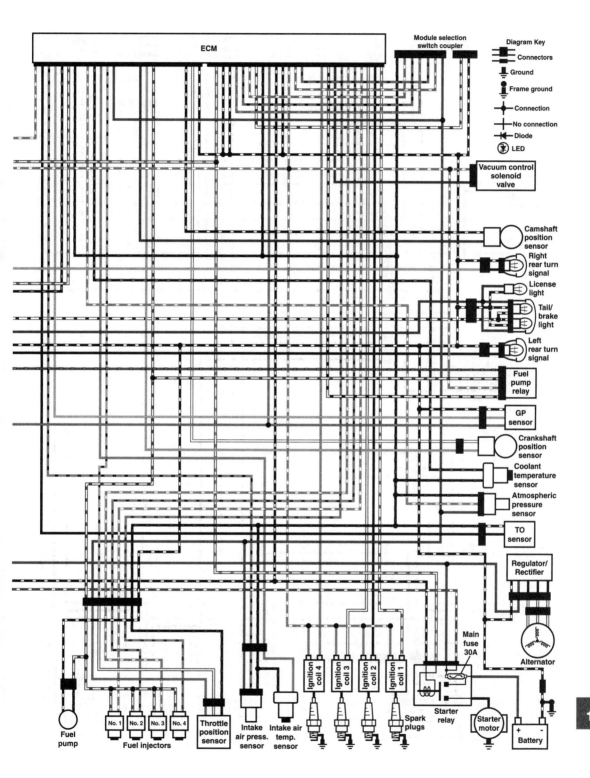

## 2000 U.S., CALIFORNIA AND CANADA

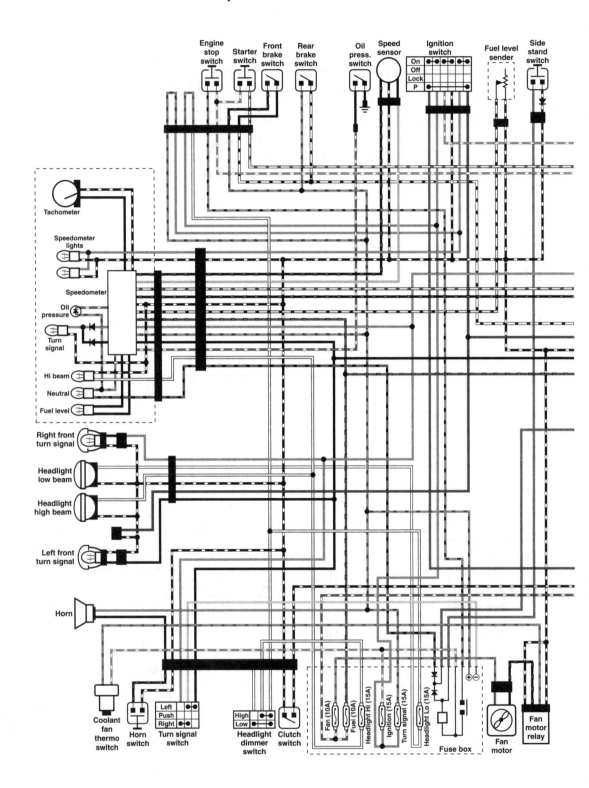

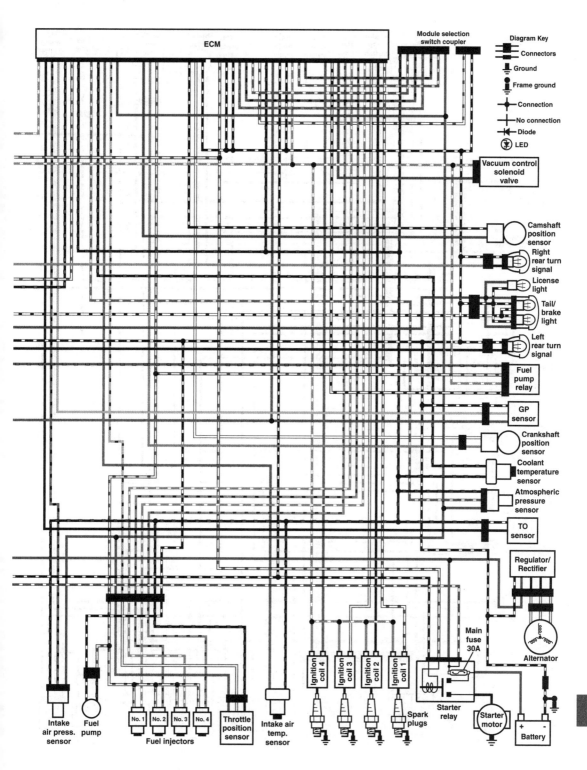

## 2000 ALL MODELS EXCEPT U.S., CALIFORNIA AND CANADA

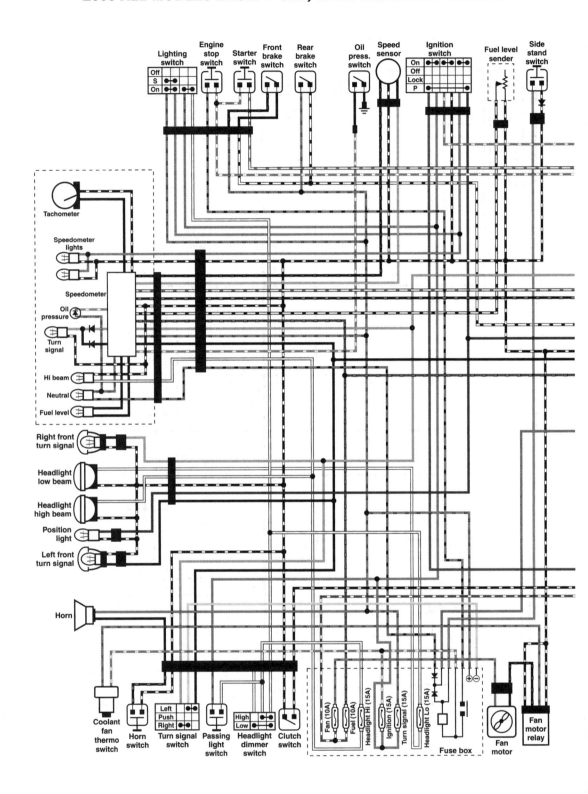

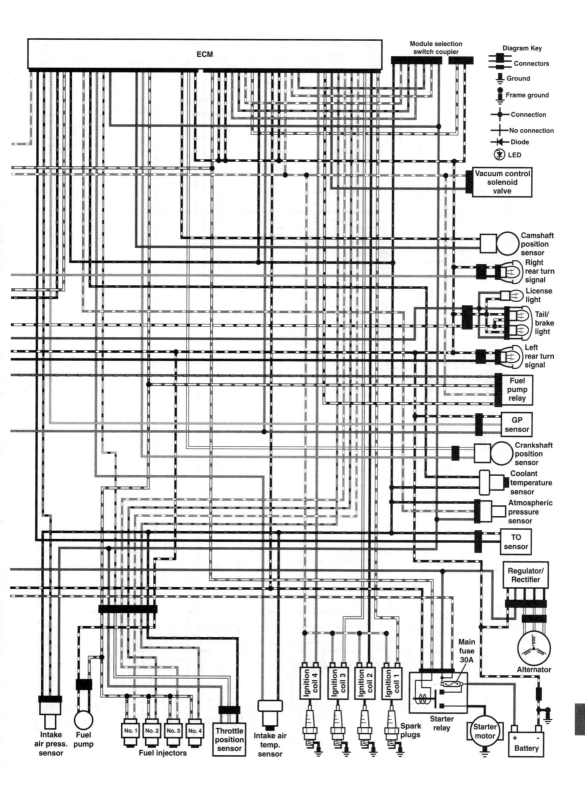

## 2001-2002 U.S., CALIFORNIA AND CANADA

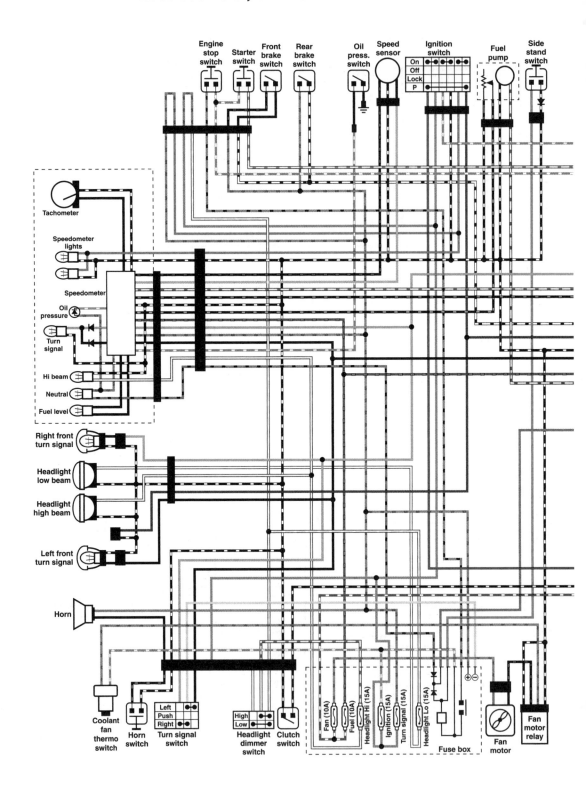

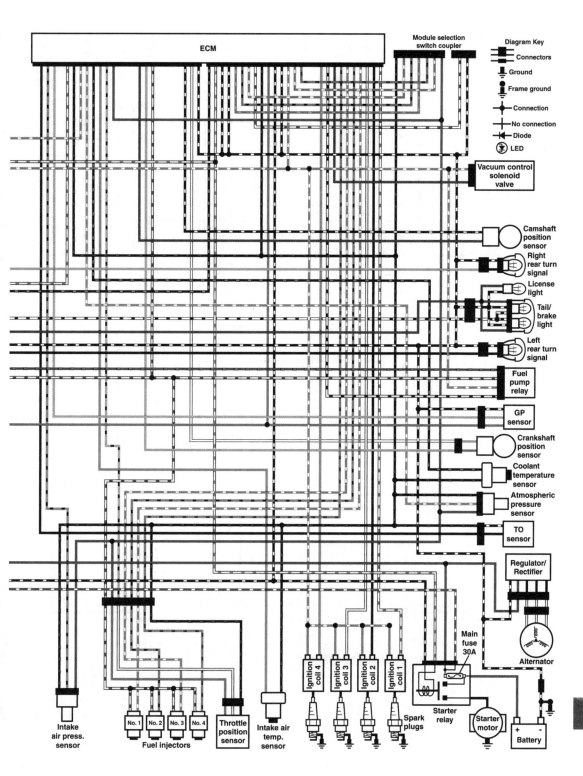

## 2001-2002 ALL MODELS EXCEPT U.S., CALIFORNIA AND CANADA

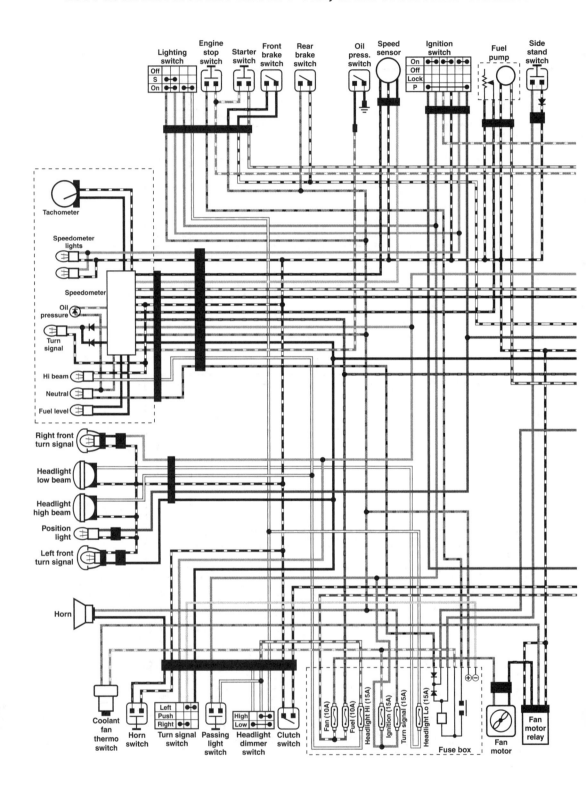

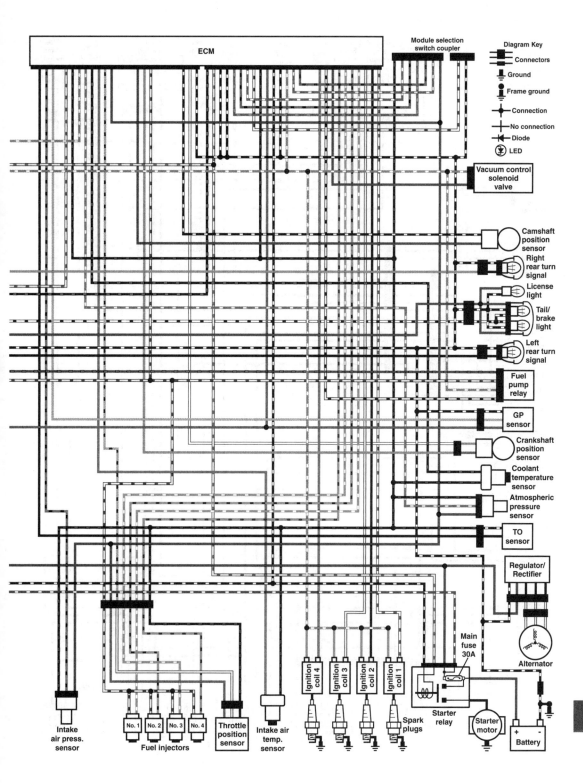

17

## 2003 U.S., CALIFORNIA AND CANADA

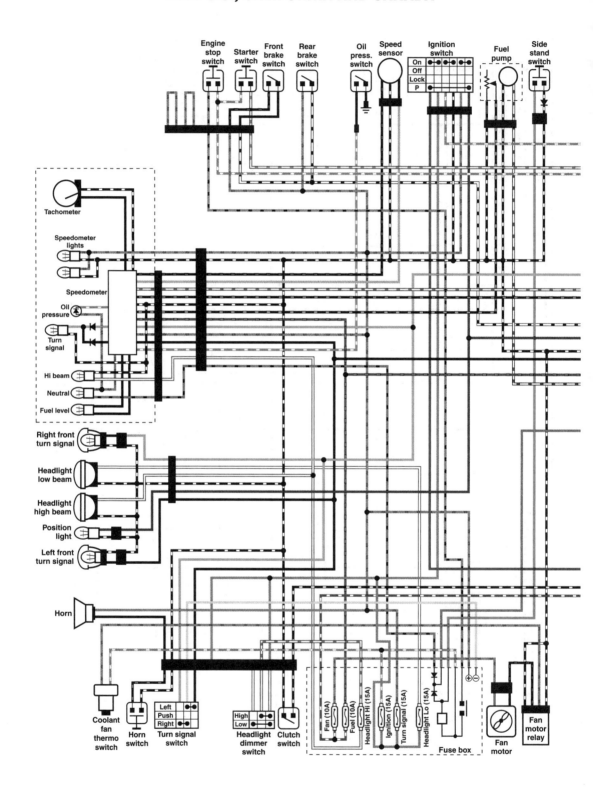

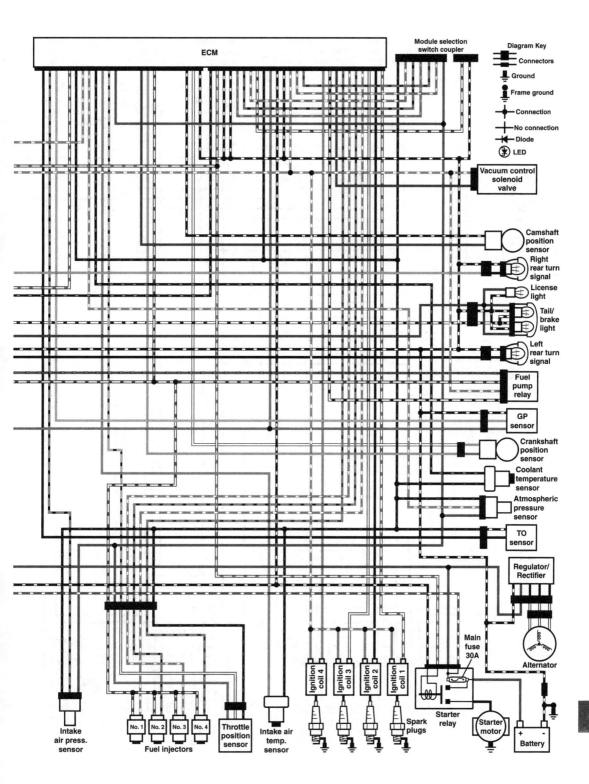

17

## 2003-2004 ALL MODELS EXCEPT U.S., CALIFORNIA AND CANADA

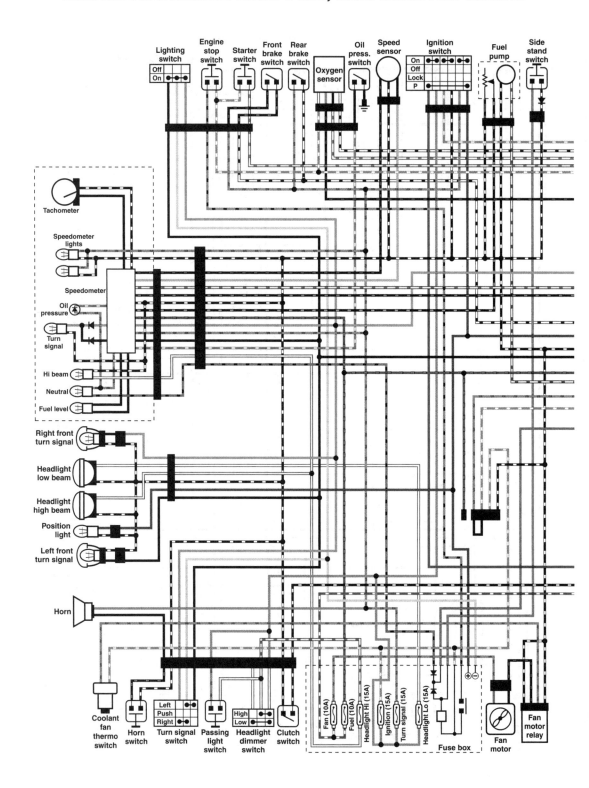

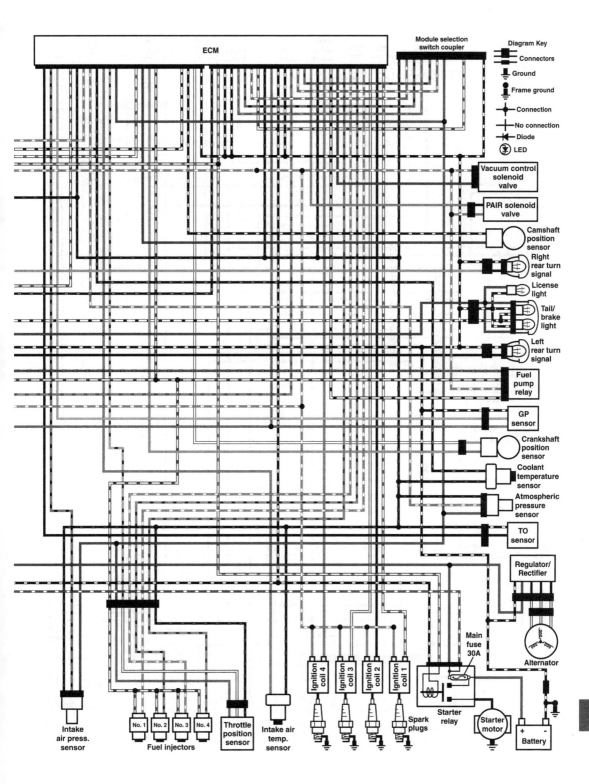

## 2004 U.S., CALIFORNIA AND CANADA

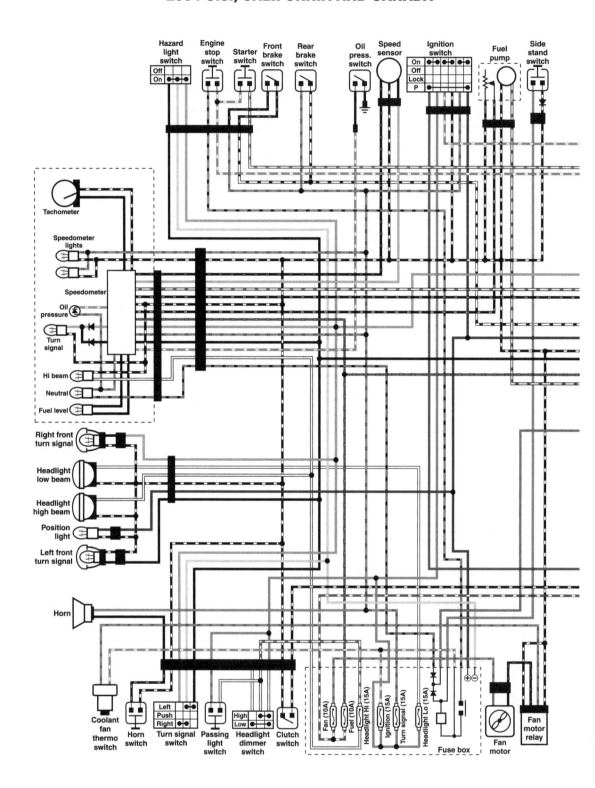

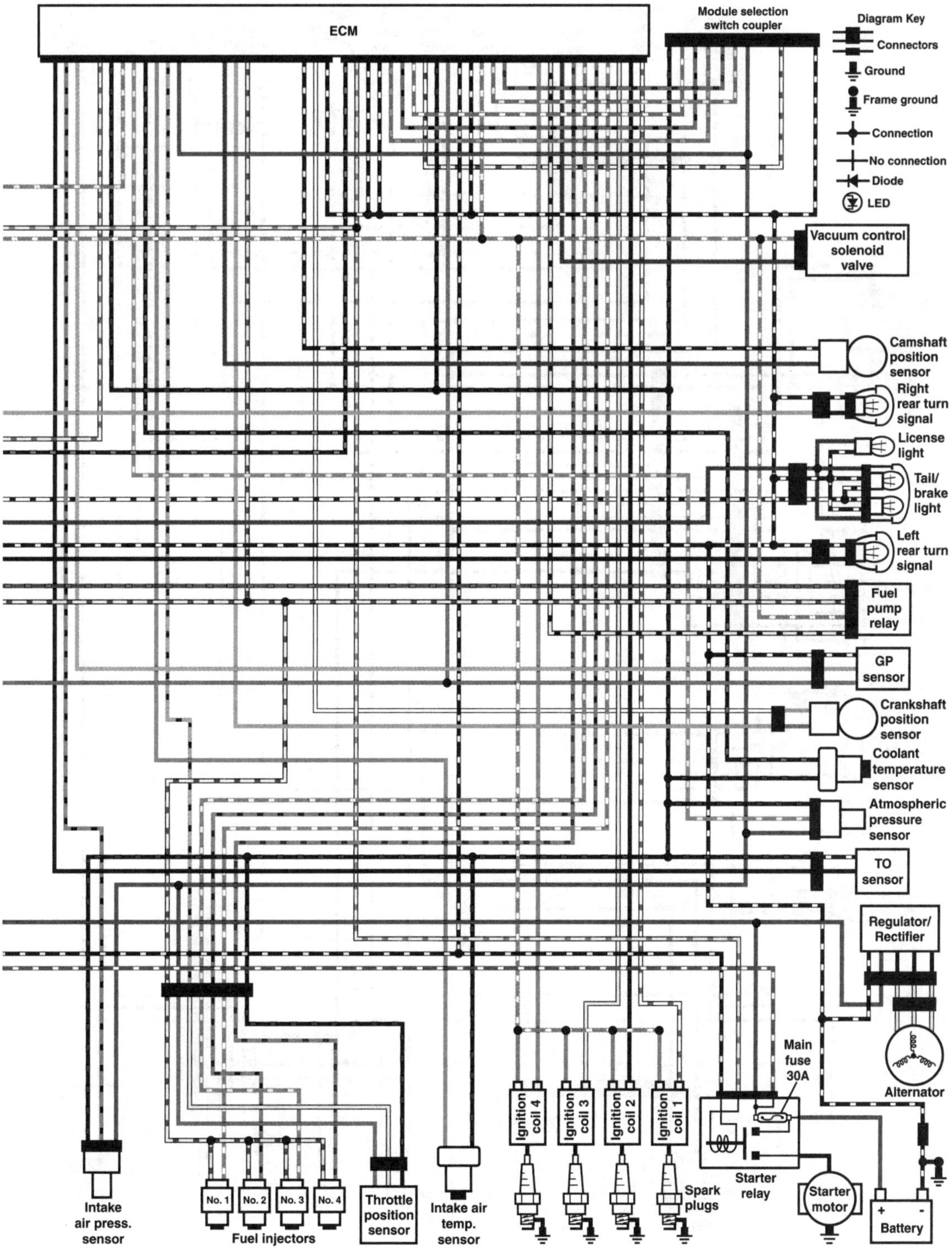

ECM

Module selection switch coupler

Diagram Key
- Connectors
- Ground
- Frame ground
- Connection
- No connection
- Diode
- LED

Vacuum control solenoid valve

Camshaft position sensor

Right rear turn signal

License light

Tail/brake light

Left rear turn signal

Fuel pump relay

GP sensor

Crankshaft position sensor

Coolant temperature sensor

Atmospheric pressure sensor

TO sensor

Regulator/Rectifier

Alternator

Main fuse 30A

Starter relay

Starter motor

Battery

Ignition coil 4

Ignition coil 3

Ignition coil 2

Ignition coil 1

Spark plugs

Intake air press. sensor

Fuel injectors

No. 1  No. 2  No. 3  No. 4

Throttle position sensor

Intake air temp. sensor

17

## 2005-ON U.S., CALIFORNIA AND CANADA

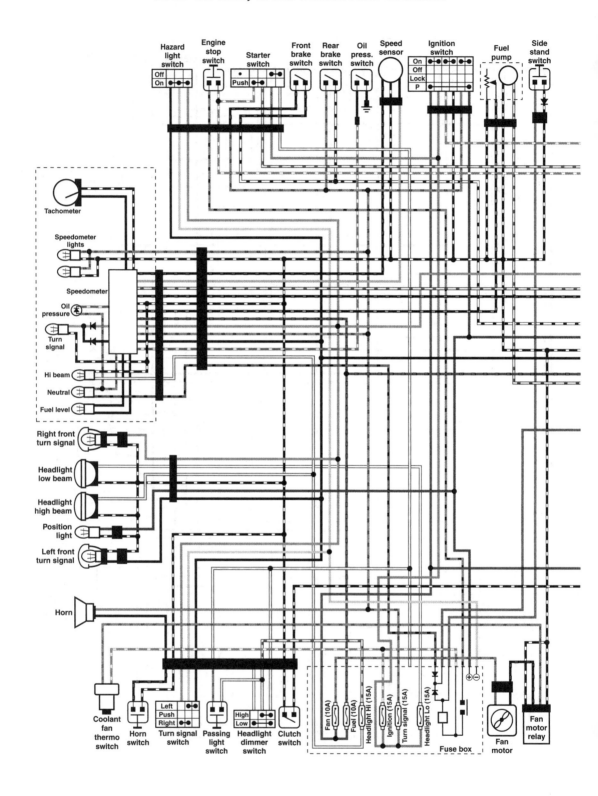

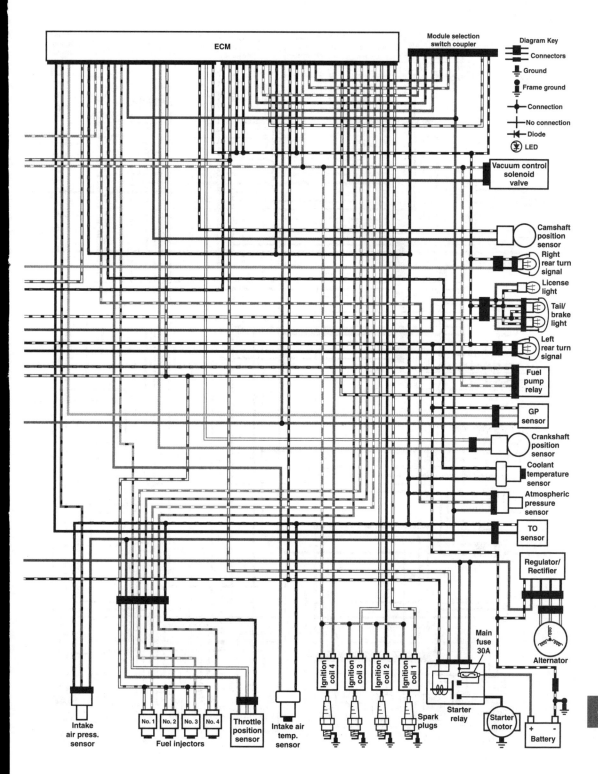

## 2005-ON UK AND EUROPE

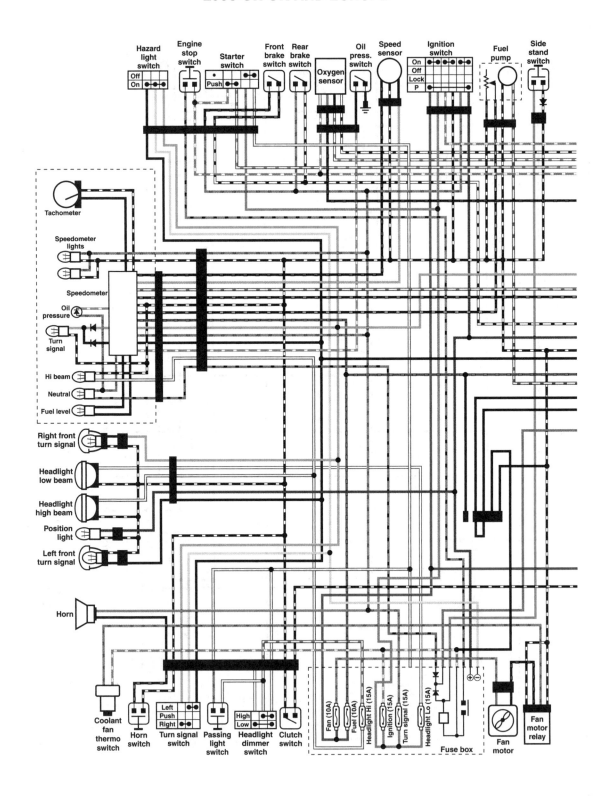

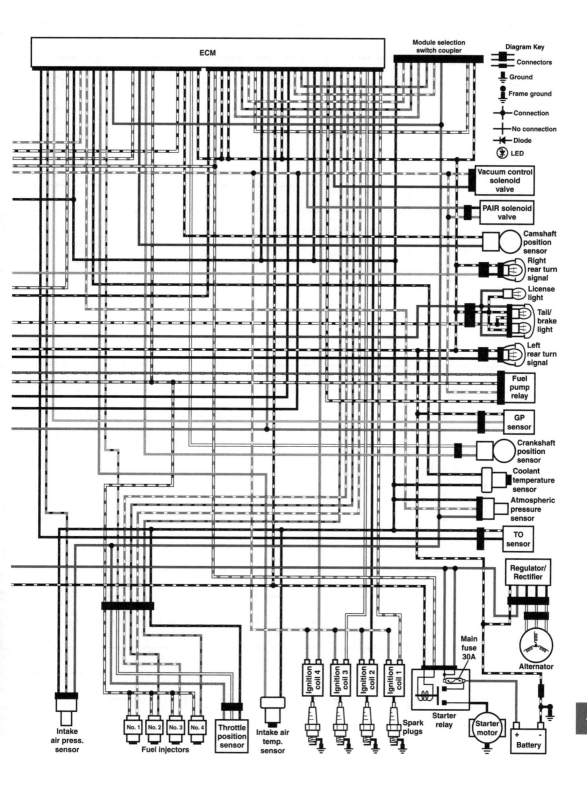

# MAINTENANCE LOG

| Date | Miles | Type of Service |
|------|-------|-----------------|
|      |       |                 |
|      |       |                 |
|      |       |                 |
|      |       |                 |
|      |       |                 |
|      |       |                 |
|      |       |                 |
|      |       |                 |
|      |       |                 |
|      |       |                 |
|      |       |                 |
|      |       |                 |
|      |       |                 |
|      |       |                 |
|      |       |                 |
|      |       |                 |
|      |       |                 |
|      |       |                 |
|      |       |                 |
|      |       |                 |
|      |       |                 |
|      |       |                 |
|      |       |                 |
|      |       |                 |
|      |       |                 |
|      |       |                 |
|      |       |                 |
|      |       |                 |
|      |       |                 |